Also by Martin J. Sherwin

*American Prometheus: The Triumph and Tragedy of
J. Robert Oppenheimer* (with Kai Bird)

A World Destroyed: Hiroshima and Its Legacies

*Jonathan Schell: The Fate of the Earth, The Abolition, The Unconquerable
World* Martin J. Sherwin, editor (The Library of America)

GAMBLING
WITH ARMAGEDDON

GAMBLING
WITH
ARMAGEDDON

NUCLEAR ROULETTE FROM HIROSHIMA TO
THE CUBAN MISSILE CRISIS, 1945–1962

MARTIN J. SHERWIN

Alfred A. Knopf   New York   2020

THIS IS A BORZOI BOOK PUBLISHED BY ALFRED A. KNOPF

www.aaknopf.com

Library of Congress Cataloging-in-Publication Data
Names: Sherwin, Martin J., author.
Title: Gambling with Armageddon : Nuclear Roulette from Hiroshima to the
    Cuban Missile Crisis, 1945–1962 / by Martin J. Sherwin.
Other titles: Nuclear roulette from Hiroshima to the Cuban Missile crisis,
    1945–1962
Description: First edition. | New York : Alfred A. Knopf, 2020. | "A Borzoi Book." |
    Includes bibliographical references and index.
Identifiers: LCCN 2019057322 (print) | LCCN 2019057323 (ebook) |
    ISBN 9780307266880 (hardcover) | ISBN 9780525659310 (ebook)
Subjects: LCSH: Cuban Missile Crisis, 1962. | Nuclear crisis control—United
    States—History—20th century. | Arms race—History—20th century. | World
    politics—1945–1955. | World politics—1955–1965. | Nuclear warfare—United
    States—History. | Kennedy, John F. (John Fitzgerald), 1917–1963.
Classification: LCC E841 .S468 2020 (print) | LCC E841 (ebook) |
    DDC 972.9106/4—dc23
LC record available at https://lccn.loc.gov/2019057322
LC ebook record available at https://lccn.loc.gov/2019057323

Front-of-jacket images (detail): (Atomic bomb)Rue des Archives / Granger;
(John F. Kennedy) Bettmann/ Getty Images; (U.S. Navy off of Cuba) allstein bild
Granger; (Nikita Khrushchev) Bettmann / Getty Images; (Hiroshima) Alamy /
CSU Archives / Everett Collection.
Spine-of-jacket image: (Fidel Castro) Keystone Press / Alamy.
Jacket design by Jenny Carrow

Manufactured in the United States of America
First Edition

Andrea Barbara Sherwin

1965–2010

Sparks of sweet memories light the darkness

Man has mounted science, and is now run away with. I firmly believe that before many centuries more, science will be the master of men. The engines he will have invented will be beyond his strength to control. Someday science may have the existence of mankind in its power, and the human race commit suicide, by blowing up the world.

—HENRY ADAMS, 1862

I can go in my office and pick up a telephone, and in 25 minutes, millions of people will be dead.

—PRESIDENT RICHARD M. NIXON, 1974

Contents

Prologue

In October 1962 I was a junior officer in the U.S. Navy attached to Patrol Squadron 31, an antisubmarine warfare (ASW) training unit based at North Island Naval Air Station. This was California, but from the prime San Diego real estate we inhabited, we looked across to "Florida," the elegant Hotel del Coronado, where Marilyn Monroe, Tony Curtis, and Jack Lemmon had ushered in the sixties with the film *Some Like It Hot*.

1

DESPITE MY modest rank—I was the squadron's air intelligence officer—my responsibilities made me the custodian of our top-secret documents: our deployment orders in the event of war. Those orders were periodically updated, and when they were, a senior staff officer from Fleet Headquarters, always accompanied by an armed marine, arrived with a sealed envelope. A ritual followed: I signed for the new envelope, and he signed for the envelope that I removed from my top-secret safe, a miniature vault embedded in my large office safe. Except on these occasions, this inner sanctum was never unlocked. I had no expectation of ever learning what was in those envelopes (clippings from the *New York Times*, we joked), since they would be opened only in the event of a national emergency.

On a date in mid-October that I cannot recall, I was informed by telephone that a new envelope would arrive at an appointed time. This was soon after I received the disappointing news that an around-the-world flight I was scheduled to co-navigate for an admiral was canceled. Within days all leaves were revoked. According to rumors at our local hangout, the Mexican Village, the cause was rising tensions in Berlin.

Although we were on the West Coast, a sense of being engaged in an international crisis permeated my squadron's ranks. Extra munitions, and weapons we had never before stored, were delivered to our hangars. Friends at El Toro, the Marine Corps Air Station north of San Diego, told me that marines in full battle gear were being flown east aboard military air transports. Something important was happening, and we were going to be part of it.

On Monday, October 22, before President Kennedy informed the world that he had ordered Cuba blockaded, I was directed to retrieve the top-secret plans from my safe and deliver them—with the obligatory armed marine escort—to my commanding officer. Our squadron's senior staff—the captain, the executive officer, and the operations officer—had assembled in the captain's office to review the war plans. My recollection is that we would deploy to an airfield in Baja California, Mexico. The rationale was to disperse military aircraft beyond the reach of Soviet missiles. Some junior officers—all of us bachelors—joked that the beaches of Baja "would be a delightful place to die."

I did not know until I researched this book how close to death we had come.

2

A WORLD away from Coronado, California, another junior officer, stationed at a strategic rocket facility nine hundred miles east of Moscow, opened an envelope not very different from the one I had delivered to my squadron's senior officers.

Valery Yarynich, who was exactly my age, had a different reaction to what he read. A junior officer and communications specialist, stationed at division headquarters in Kirov, his unit was the central command center for five intercontinental missile battalions. After President Kennedy's October 22 speech demanding that the Soviet Union remove its missiles from Cuba, Yarynich was deployed to a missile base in Siberia to help supervise command and control communications.

"At the peak of the confrontation," he told the American journalist David Hoffman, he received a message containing the code-word "BRONTOZAVR." That was the combat-alert go code—the dreaded signal to open the top-secret communications envelopes and transition the R-7 liquid-fueled intercontinental ballistic missiles to war readiness. "I cannot forget," Yarynich recalled, "the mixture of nervousness, surprise and pain on the faces of each operator, without exception—officers, enlisted men, women telephone operators."

The unthinkable moment had arrived: Nuclear war was a mere press of a button away.

It was the most devastating war in world history. The estimated number of North American deaths was upwards of 200 million. Double, perhaps even quadruple that number of Soviet, Eastern European, and Chinese citizens perished, and no one had any reliable data on how many Western Europeans, Africans, Asians, South Pacific Islanders, and others the radioactive fallout killed as it circumnavigated the globe. Cuba became a wasteland, and there were few structures left standing in Moscow and Washington, DC.

It was an unthinkable war, but not an unimagined one. In 1957 the Australian writer Nevil Shute described its denouement in his eerily tranquil apocalyptic novel *On the Beach*. Adapted for the screen by John Paxton and directed by Stanley Kramer, in 1959 *On the Beach* premiered simultaneously in major U.S. cities and Moscow, to reports of viewers sobbing as Gregory Peck, Ava Gardner, Fred Astaire, and Anthony Perkins stoically prepared in Australia, where the movie is set, for the arrival of deadly radioactive clouds carrying the fallout from the nuclear war recently fought in the Northern Hemisphere. They were the last survivors of the human race, going quietly into endless night.

3

BUT THE Cuban missile crisis did not replicate *On the Beach*, leaving thoughts of a Cuban missile war to pass into history. While participants in (and historians of) the crisis never tire of recalling its details and dangers, the majority of the generation that lived through it, and subsequent generations, never became emotionally engaged with its potential consequences. It was neither Vietnam nor Watergate—nor Dallas, Texas, on November 22, 1963.

It was just the most devastating event in world history . . . that *somehow* didn't happen.

That *somehow* is the subject of this book.

GAMBLING
WITH ARMAGEDDON

1

A Reflection on Luck in History

It could have been a sheet of invisible ice, a partially covered banana peel, or a crack in the sidewalk. Hundreds of people had walked over or around or through it without incident, but his shoe touched it in just the wrong way. His right leg slid forward, his arms flailed, his body arched back, and he crashed to the ground. The sound of his skull cracking was heard for half a block, even on that busy New York City street.

He was dead because of bad luck.

Had he not slipped, he would have arrived at the Thirty-Fourth Street train station at 4:59 p.m. and shortly thereafter detonated the homemade bomb he was carrying in his briefcase. Everyone who forced their way onto the crowded cars of the northbound number 3 train eleven minutes later was extraordinarily lucky. They were lucky because their would-be assassin had been unlucky. They would never learn that they were alive because he had died. They would go about their affairs unaware that his bad luck had bequeathed them the luckiest day of their lives.

Metaphorical patches of black ice and slippery fruit peels have altered the course of history in much the same way as genetic mutations have transformed species. But unlike biologists, historians tend to overlook those deviations caused by inexplicable luck, both good and bad: They are too hard to discern, even harder to contextualize, and—most problematic—they resist rational explanation.

Such oversights notwithstanding, good luck and bad are immutable parts of the human experience. They are often the fulcrums around which major events pivot. In no area of historical research is this truer than in the study of nuclear weapons in general, and the Cuban missile crisis in particular.

In a review of *Thirteen Days*, Robert Kennedy's posthumously published memoir of the Cuban missile crisis, former secretary of state Dean Acheson asserted that war was avoided due to "plain dumb luck."

When I began my research for this book I was certain he was wrong. Now that I am finished I know he was right.

2

World War III Was About to Begin

Saturday, October 27

In foreign affairs brains, preparation, judgment, and power
are of utmost importance, but luck is essential.
—DEAN ACHESON, 1969

Five days after I retrieved my squadron's deployment orders, World
War III was about to begin. It was 5:00 p.m. Eastern Daylight Time
(EDT); the date was October 27; the place was the Caribbean Sea,
latitude 26° north, longitude 68° west.

It was not going to be started by Fidel Castro, Nikita Khrushchev,
or John Kennedy. The instigator was a thirty-four-year-old Soviet
submarine captain who had just given the order to arm a nuclear torpedo aimed at a fleet of U.S. Navy vessels.

The story of how he was goaded into giving that order, and how
his gamble with Armageddon was prevented, alters the accepted
explanation of how the Cuban missile crisis was resolved. Crisis
management was in the mix, but the indispensable ingredient was
luck. *Very good luck.*

1

FIVE O'CLOCK EDT in Washington, D.C., is midnight in Moscow.
It has been almost six days (five days and twenty-two hours, to be
exact) since President Kennedy announced his decision to blockade
Cuba. This is only the initial step, he said, to force the Soviet Union
to remove the nuclear missiles it had secretly shipped to the island
over the past several months: "These actions may only be the beginning," he warned. "We will not prematurely or unnecessarily risk the

costs of worldwide nuclear war in which even the fruits of victory would be ashes in our mouth, but neither will we shrink from that risk at any time it must be faced."

Three days and several hours ago the U.S. Navy deployed an armada of sixty-three ships—three aircraft carriers, two cruisers, twenty destroyers, reinforced by two surface patrol units, an anti-submarine warfare (ASW) unit, and a logistic support unit—on a "quarantine" line stretching along an arc five hundred miles north of Havana from Cape May between 27° and 30° north, 75° west, and 20° north 65° west. Thus far two freighters have been stopped without incident; but, carrying no military contraband, their crews did not resist.

It has become increasingly apparent to all the principals—Khrushchev, Kennedy, and Castro—that the military activities of each passing day exponentially increase the danger of a hostile incident escalating out of control. Along with potential clashes on the blockade line, U.S. reconnaissance flights over Cuba were fired on this afternoon. Without the president's knowledge, the commander of the Strategic Air Command (SAC), Gen. Thomas S. Power, elevated his forces to defense condition 2 (DEFCON 2), a mere step away from war (DEFCON 1). In Europe SAC was authorized to load nuclear weapons onto aircraft assigned to initiate first strikes against the Soviet Union.

Tens of thousands of U.S. soldiers and marines are conspicuously assembling in Florida and elsewhere in preparation for an invasion of Cuba.

On the island of Okinawa, an erroneous message has been sent to a U.S. missile command center ordering it to launch its missiles against targets in China and the Soviet Union.

In addition to the ships on the quarantine line, a strike force consisting of the carriers *Randolph*, *Independence*, and *Enterprise* and their escorts, is within range of Cuba.

The three contending leaders are acutely aware, and worried (at least Khrushchev and Kennedy are), that at any moment events could slip from their control.

2

CASTRO IS enraged beyond worry. Well informed about the U.S. military preparations, he is certain that an attack is "almost imminent within the next 24 to 72 hours." In response to Kennedy's address he ordered general mobilization, and today he has commanded his anti-aircraft batteries to shoot down U.S. aircraft overflying his island; several low-flying U.S.A.F. reconnaissance jets have had close calls.

Earlier this Saturday afternoon (October 27) a Soviet commander, whom Castro badgered into action, fired a surface-to-air missile (SAM/SA-2) at a U.S.A.F. U2. It found its target and killed the pilot, Maj. Rudolph Anderson, who was trapped in his destroyed plane. Khrushchev had authorized the general in charge of Soviet forces in Cuba "to repulse the enemy . . . with all the power of the Soviet forces," but he had not expected this authority to be used short of an invasion. The missile had been fired without Moscow's permission, but neither President Kennedy nor any of his advisers know that. The chairman of the Joint Chiefs of Staff urges the president to authorize an attack on the SAM site. "They fired the first shot," one of Kennedy's advisers declares.

Certain now that he can do little to prevent an assault, Castro has become grimly fatalistic. Determined to confront the inevitable head-on, regardless of the consequences, he has dictated a letter to Khrushchev urging him to launch Soviet missiles against the United States *should U.S. forces invade* his island. If "the imperialists invade Cuba with the goal of occupying it . . . the Soviet Union must never allow the circumstances in which the imperialists could launch the first nuclear strike against it."

Living so intensely at the center of the crisis, Castro has abandoned hope of a peaceful resolution. Embracing Armageddon as an act of retributive justice, he has become an inadvertent major player in the resolution of the crisis.

3

KHRUSHCHEV, STILL in his Kremlin office at one in the morning, is desperate to avoid Armageddon (or anything approaching it). He had recklessly gambled that nuclear missiles could be installed in Cuba undetected. But he has lost that bet, and now he is frantic to escape the consequences of the dangerous crisis he has created. He wants the confrontation resolved peacefully, but he has no intention of giving up the missiles without getting something in return. The unauthorized destruction of the U2, and Castro's call for a first strike, are terrifying: They suggest to the Soviet leader that he has lost control over events in Cuba.

He is close to exhaustion, nearly overcome by contradictory emotions that have roiled him for days. He is six thousand miles from Havana, but only thirty-two minutes from an intercontinental Minuteman missile launched from the United States. He is frightened of skidding sideways into a nuclear war. Yet he remains furious about the blockade of Cuba, which he considers an illegal, outrageous act of war.

The so-called quarantine is a blockade: It is "outright banditry. . . . The folly of degenerate imperialism . . . [and an] act of aggression that pushes mankind toward the abyss of a world nuclear-missile war," he angrily wrote to Kennedy on October 24. He appeared determined to dare the Americans to attack a Soviet vessel.

But today, two days later (Friday, October 26), both the mounting tension and the circumstances have changed his tone. As U.S. ASW forces close in on Soviet submarines, he writes a heartfelt personal letter to President Kennedy.

It is an extraordinary communication, perhaps the most revealing statement of Soviet rationality during the entirety of the Cold War. In it Khrushchev abandons the facade of his indifference to nuclear war and pleads for a peaceful resolution. He warns: "Mr. President, we and you ought not now to pull on the ends of the rope in which you have tied the knot of war, because the more the two of us pull, the tighter that knot will be tied. And a moment may come when that knot will be tied so tight that even he who tied it will not have the strength to untie it, and then it will be necessary to cut that knot. And what that would mean is not for me to explain to you, because you yourself understand perfectly of what terrible forces our countries dispose."

That is the most-quoted section of Khrushchev's letter. But the next two sentences, often ignored, make the point that he wishes to negotiate a peaceful end to the crisis: "Consequently, if there is no intention to tighten that knot, and thereby to doom the world to the catastrophe of thermonuclear war, then let us not only relax the forces pulling on the ends of the rope, let us take measures to untie that knot. We are ready for this."

The letter is a clear pivot toward accepting a settlement, though its significance is not recognized by the president's exhausted advisers. Secretary of Defense Robert S. McNamara complains that it's full of rhetoric but devoid of logic. "A very McNamara attitude," Kennedy's national security adviser, McGeorge Bundy quipped decades later.

Nevertheless, despite this obvious move toward denouement, the most dangerous moments of the Cuban missile crisis are yet to come.

4

PRESIDENT KENNEDY too is dealing with powerful conflicting emotions. Pacing the floor of the Oval Office, he is talking to his brother, the attorney general, wondering if he is being too cautious, too aggressive, too flexible, too rigid, or simply too worried. Having recently read Barbara Tuchman's history of the origins of World War I, *The Guns of August,* he is acutely aware that a war can begin simply because no one knows how to stop it. "Pierre," he says to his press secretary, Pierre Salinger, "Do you realize that if I make a mistake in this crisis 200 million people are going to get killed?"

He is infuriated with his military chiefs for their cavalier attitude toward war, and he is losing patience with his advisers, who are still offering contradictory recommendations. Like Khrushchev, Kennedy wants a peaceful resolution, but he too has a bottom line: The Soviets must remove their missiles from Cuba.

Kennedy and Khrushchev are enemies—ideological and military adversaries—who have blundered into a confrontation that neither wanted nor anticipated. Each is aware that an accident, or even a misinterpretation, can instantly ignite a nuclear exchange. Yet each feels obliged to continue to press his goals *despite* recognizing that nothing he can achieve is worth the consequences of a nuclear war.

Their positions are reinforced by their alliance obligations, the domestic pressures all leaders confront regardless of the nature of their governments, and concerns for their personal political survival: "You would have been impeached [had you not taken these actions]," Bobby assured his brother during a wrenching moment of doubt. The president agreed.

"One of the ironic things is that Mr. Khrushchev and I occupy approximately the same political positions inside our governments," Kennedy later reflected. "He would like to prevent a nuclear war but he is under severe pressure from his hardline crowd, which interprets every move in that direction as appeasement. I've got similar problems. . . . The hardliners in the United States and the Soviet Union feed on one another."

Kennedy wants the missiles removed without paying any visible price for their departure. His strategy, McNamara later explained, is to "squeeze the Soviets" until they ship their missiles back to the Soviet Union. But he has to be careful: If he squeezes too hard he might force a violent response.

Khrushchev is determined to extract face-saving concessions as the price for retrieving his missiles, but the challenge he faces is to devise an offer that is both acceptable to his Presidium comrades and difficult for the president to refuse. The great unknown is how firmly each can insist on his position without driving the other to an act of military violence.

What they share—and what histories of the Cuban missile crisis have generally agreed that they shared—is the conviction that the fate of the world is in their hands.

They are mistaken.

5

ON THIS Saturday evening, October 27, 1962, the fate of the world is not in the hands of any head of state. It has slipped from their grasp, inadvertently and furtively, to that of three young Soviet navy officers: Capt. 2nd Rank Valentin Grigorievich Savitsky, Brigade Chief of Staff Capt. Vasily Alexandrovich Arkhipov, and political officer Ivan Semyonovich Maslennikov. Trapped in a floundering Project 641 Soviet submarine, one of them will be driven before sunset to a decision that, if executed, is certain to trigger the nuclear war that Khrushchev and Kennedy are striving to prevent.

3

"We Will Die, but We Will Sink Them All"

Each of you has in your hands the potential to start the next
world war . . . and so Comrades, do try to keep us out of war.
—ADM. L. F. RYBALKO TO THE FOUR SUBMARINE CAPTAINS

The immediate cause of World War III is the military
preparation of it.
—C. WRIGHT MILLS

Captain Savitsky's submarine is an integral part of Khrushchev's
strategy for "increas[ing] the pressure." It is designated B-59. To
NATO forces, a Soviet Project 641 class boat (a submarine is properly referred to as a boat) is an F-class, a "Foxtrot," a name no more
descriptive of either its purpose or its origins than its Soviet moniker.
It was built to sink ships, primarily ships of the U.S. Navy. Its lineage
extends back to a diesel-electric submarine designed for that task—
the advanced-type XXI U-boats the Germans constructed near the
end of World War II.

1

B-59 IS one of four Foxtrots—B-4, B-36, B-59, and B-130—
comprising the Sixty-Ninth Torpedo Submarine Brigade. They are
the advance contingent of Operation Kama, the Soviet navy's hastily
drawn plan to participate in Premier Khrushchev's scheme to arm
Cuba with nuclear missiles. Determined not to be left out, the Soviet
Admiralty has hatched a project to station seven ballistic missile submarines in the Cuban port of Mariel. But with all nuclear boats in

drydocks and temporarily out of commission, the Foxtrots are the fallback submarines of choice.

Preparations for their voyage has been rushed, chaotic, and extraordinarily stressful for officers and crew. As the Admiralty cobbles together half-baked plans, daily changes are the norm. Adjustments include the number of submarines that will be deployed, the nature of their mission, their orders, cargo swaps, and even the introduction of a new weapons system. "Each of the staff's departments demanded that all its new directives be followed," Ryurik Ketov, commander of B-4, recalled. The alterations, contradictions, and additions nearly overwhelmed the submarines' captains.

Initially the boats were to travel openly, but that was countermanded, and a secret passage was imposed. At some point each submarine's armaments were supplemented with a torpedo mounted with a nuclear warhead ("special weapon"), unique for Foxtrot crews and a source of considerable tension for their commanders. "All of these orders were a source of anxiety," Ketov reported. "While it is one thing to move ships openly . . . it is quite another when one's boat is for unknown reasons loaded with atomic weapons and sent with vague objectives seemingly neither for a simple transfer, nor for active duty in Cuba. After all," Ketov continued, "*before the mission became covert, even the officers' families were kept informed and prepared for relocation to Cuba.*"

That officers and their families had been told they were going to Cuba is both surprising and significant. The destination was top secret from the plan's inception. For purposes of deception the mission was code-named Anadyr, for a well-known river in northeastern Siberia, and, to further disguise the destination, the troops were issued cold-weather gear. Ketov's revelation (never before remarked on in Western missile crisis literature) confirms the failure of coordination between the navy and other services. The problem appears to have stemmed from an absence of experience with joint operations. "Operation Anadyr," explained Gen. Viktor Yesin, "was unique. It was the first operation after World War II in which all of the military forces of the Soviet Union, including the Strategic Rocket Troops, took part."

It is no exaggeration to suggest that there were two Soviet missile crises: The first involved Soviet ground, air, and rocket forces sent to Cuba; the second—and far more dangerous one—involved the Soviet navy's submarines. It was their confrontation with U.S. ASW forces in the Sargasso Sea that came close to subverting Kennedy's and Khrushchev's efforts to reach a diplomatic settlement.

2

AT 0400 hours on the night of October 1, 1962, the quartet of Foxtrots slipped at thirty-minute intervals from their berths on the Kola Peninsula into the North Sea "after a so-called oral briefing." Upset that the "unclear and contradictory information" that they had received in slipshod briefings and poorly written orders were confusing, the captains had met on their own to "develop a tactical scheme." Their assigned mission was "to strengthen the defense of the island of Cuba." But exactly how they were to accomplish that goal was unspecified: "We went in blindly not knowing what was in store for us," Ketov remembered.

It was a journey to a tropical paradise through a North Sea hell.

Twelve days later, on October 13, they entered Hades. The Atlantic erupted with a storm so severe that the submarines were in constant danger of being destroyed. "I have never in my whole career in the Navy seen anything like it in the Pacific or the Atlantic, or anywhere at all," Nikolai Shumkov, B-130's commander, remembered. "It was terrible. . . . The manifolds on the diesel engines were all busting open. We had to take one of the diesel engines off-line constantly to be able to fix it . . . sailors were thrown against bulkheads as they tried to work."

His colleague Alekei Dubivko, commander of B-36, reported an equally terrifying experience: "All of our outboard hatches had leaks. Our mechanic told me: 'Commander, it is dangerous to go down deeper than 230 feet.'"

3

ON OCTOBER 24 the four Foxtrots, variously disabled from their ordeal, reached their assigned quadrants in the U.S. Navy's quarantine area. What exactly was happening up there? Had a war begun? What actions were appropriate? The submarine commanders, out of radio contact with Moscow for days, could only guess. Uninformed about the details of the crisis, they were at a decided disadvantage in dealing with the U.S. Navy's ASW forces.

B-59 was detected almost immediately, and the ASW squadron's ships, aircraft, and helicopters attempted to force it to surface. In 1962, surfacing a Soviet submarine was normally a daunting challenge. Under most circumstances a Foxtrot was capable of evading its pursuers. But there are circumstances, such as those B-59 was now confronting, when a submarine's need to stay in a particular area, combined with its technological limitations, put it at a severe disadvantage.

4

FIRST ASSEMBLED in the Leningrad shipyard late in the 1950s, Foxtrot submarines are diesel-electric attack boats capable of undertaking long-range patrols of twenty thousand nautical miles, lasting up to ninety days. Measuring three hundred feet from bow to stern, they typically carried a crew of seventy-eight officers and men who had learned to live in severely overcrowded quarters. Even by this standard, B-59 was congested, having deployed with an added complement of communications and other specialists. Within the narrow hull a tangled matrix of pipes, bunks, torpedo tubes, valves, wires, engines, battery compartments, rooms, tables, and much else leaves but few square feet of open deck on which to walk. Even today, picking one's way through a Foxtrot submarine, it is hard to imagine how half that number of men could live under water for an extended period.

In 1962 the U.S. Navy's ASW forces considered the Foxtrot a challenging adversary: It was fast, and for a conventionally powered submarine its engines were relatively quiet (and therefore hard for sonar equipment to detect). The best of the Soviet navy's nonnuclear submarines, the Foxtrot was less expensive to build and more reliable—that is, it had a better safety record—than the Soviet nuclear submarines the Admiralty had assigned to Anadyr. But at the time of the crisis, every nuclear boat was in drydock undergoing modifications in response to a series of accidents.

That coincidence would have near-fatal consequences.

The maneuvering capabilities of Project 641 boats are far in advance of other submarines in its class, and its weapons systems are formidable. It carries up to thirty-six mines, a collection of antisubmarine weapons, and twenty-two two-ton torpedoes, each packing 880 pounds of explosive. It can also fire nuclear-tipped torpedoes with warhead yields of fifteen kilotons, a force equal to the atomic bomb that destroyed Hiroshima. In October 1962, *unknown to the U.S. Navy,* each of the four submarines carried such a weapon.

When a *nuclear* weapon is on board (this was the first deployment in which Project 641 submarines carried nuclear torpedoes), a special weapons officer assumes responsibility for its security. He sleeps, eats, and passes his time near it. He controls access to the forward torpedo room and sets strict rules: Only authorized personnel can enter, and all who do must surrender weapons, tools, matches, lighters, or anything else that could conceivably damage the weapon. He is also responsible for arming the weapon if it is going to be used.

Life aboard Project 641 boats is governed by repetitive routines and responsibilities that keep the crew engaged during long voyages. Discipline is rigid, but food is normally plentiful and good, although this deployment is anything but normal.

The sleeping and toilet facilities are, to say the least, suboptimal.

Sleeping is based on "hot bunking" (normal aboard all ships at that time), with the fifty-six enlisted men sharing twenty-seven small bunks built into the aft torpedo compartment. All members of the crew, officers and enlisted men, share three toilets and two showers; freshwater rationing limits their use to one shower per crew member per week. Not surprisingly, the air quality is often putrid.

But the submariners are trained to endure these conditions, and in truth, except during emergencies or operations that require excessive periods of submersion—as now—there is nothing about life aboard a Project 641 submarine that the crew is not prepared to handle. Claustrophobia is never a problem, according to one submarine captain. Personnel have the choice to either "get over it or shut up."

5

B-59's PRIMARY limitation is its conventional propulsion system, and that has put it in extreme danger. Unlike nuclear-powered submarines, Foxtrots cannot remain underwater. They have to surface periodically or run at periscope depth to recharge their batteries. Yet for days it has been impossible for B-59 to rise close enough to the surface to restore its nearly depleted batteries, because it is being tracked by U.S. Navy ASW ships and aircraft. The aircraft carrier *Randolph* (CV-15) and destroyers *Bache* (DD-470), *Beale* (DD-471), *Cony* (DD-508), *Eaton* (DD-510), and *Murray* (DD-576) have been pursuing it for two days, trying to force it to rise. At one point the hydroacoustic specialist aboard B-59 reported "14 surface units" hunting in its vicinity.

At 4:59 EDT, October 27, the crew of the *Beale* made positive contact with B-59 and began dropping practice (relatively low-yield explosive) depth charges. The intention was to signal the captain of the Soviet submarine to surface his boat.

Thirty minutes later, at 5:29, the USS *Blandy*, which had arrived on station several days earlier with the USS *Essex* carrier group, was almost on top of B-59. Capt. Edward Kelley, the *Blandy*'s skipper, decided to employ an unorthodox (and unauthorized) tactic: He ordered the crew to throw hand grenades (rather than the lower-impact practice depth charges) encased in rolls of toilet paper tubes in the vicinity of B-59. "It felt like you were sitting in a metal barrel which somebody is constantly blasting with a sledgehammer," Senior Lt. Vadim Orlov, the communications officer on B-59, recalled. "The situation was quite . . . shocking for the crew"—and for Captain Savitsky.

6

B-59's CREW is dealing with more than just terrifying explosions. Internally conditions are horrific.

The warm Caribbean waters have turned the boat's interior into a veritable sauna. The coolest section is a stifling 113 degrees Fahrenheit, and the temperature in the engine room has reached an unbearable *142–149 degrees*. Designed to operate in the North Atlantic, the

Foxtrot submarines have no air-conditioning; the engines' heat and the pervasive body odor have turned the humid air rancid. The carbon dioxide level is dangerous, and the sub's maneuvering capability has been compromised.

To make matters worse, the desalinization equipment has malfunctioned, leaving fresh water in short supply. Most of the crew are covered with rashes and ulcers. The dreadful conditions have left many looking "like they had just been freed from Auschwitz or Buchenwald."

A crewmember recorded that "people [are] dropping like dominoes." "Today three sailors fainted from overheating again," another writes. "We are sailing with a risk of dropping down to six thousand meters. This is how much [ocean] we have under [our boat]. The regeneration of air works poorly, the carbon dioxide content is rising, and the electric power reserves are dropping. Those who are free from their shifts, are sitting immobile, staring at one spot. . . . Temperature in the sections is above 50 [122 Fahrenheit]. In the diesel [engine room]—61 degrees [142 Fahrenheit]."

B-36 is experiencing similar difficulties. "People were fainting at their battle stations," Captain Dubivko recalled. "Up to 14 cases a day because the temperature in the sub was 150 degrees Fahrenheit, except for the end compartments which were slightly cooler, no more than 100 to 115 degrees Fahrenheit where the men went for a breather."

7

THREE DAYS earlier, on October 24, the advisers President Kennedy assembled on October 16 (later designated the Executive Committee of the National Security Council—ExComm) directed the State Department to send a telegram to the U.S. Embassy in Moscow. It instructed U.S. ambassador Foy Kohler to inform the Soviet government that "Quarantine Forces will drop four or five harmless explosive sound signals [in the vicinity of Soviet submarines] which may be accompanied by the international code signal 'IDKCA' meaning 'rise to the surface. . . . Submerged submarines, on hearing this signal, should surface on an easterly course. Signals and procedures employed are harmless."

Sending this message was a sensible crisis-management precaution, a responsible warning meant to avoid a misunderstanding at sea that could lead to a catastrophe. But Secretary of Defense McNamara, who suggested this initiative, and the other members of ExComm, who endorsed it, never thought to check with a submariner about the likely efficacy of such a message. Nor did they ask themselves how they could be certain that the Soviet submarine captains received the message.

They did not.

The Soviet government officially rejected it, and the Soviet admiral in charge of the submarine brigade, the first deputy head of the Soviet navy, Vitaly Fokin, refused to notify the submarine captains about the procedure that U.S. Navy ASW forces intended to follow if they encountered his boats.

No one familiar with the culture and code of conduct of submariners will be surprised at the Soviet reaction, as irresponsible as it may appear. There is simply no circumstance in which a submarine commander—Soviet or American—would voluntarily surface his boat in response to an enemy's request, signaled by explosive charges, sonar, or any other means.

Being forced to the surface is more than an embarrassment: It is a mark of incompetence, defeat, humiliation—and in this case would also have been an act of direct insubordination. The Soviet submarine commanders were ordered not to allow their boats to be exposed to U.S. Navy forces: "The responsibility for not letting ourselves be detected [was] enormous," Captain Ketov confirmed.

A Cold War cat-and-mouse game—U.S. ASW forces trying to surface Soviet submarines, Soviet submarines evading U.S. ASW forces—had been ongoing for more than a decade. But on October 27 the contest had turned deadly: The captain of B-59, Valentin Savitsky, was beginning to think that he was under attack.

"Of course, once one had . . . experience[d] first-hand what it was like on the receiving end of the depth charges it was possible to somehow go about one's business with a good understanding of the situation," Ketov wrote, recalling his own experiences. "However, when this . . . is imposed for the first time on someone with no practical knowledge of it, it is a different matter altogether."

Two days earlier Captain Savitsky (who had never been on the receiving end of U.S. Navy ASW tactics) surmised from a radio intercept that the situation "in the world above" might lead to the imminent outbreak of hostilities. He had received orders "to open a continuous communication channel with Moscow," which, Ketov explained, "could only be understood at the time as presaging a fundamental change in mission. . . . Even the beginning of combat operations against the US Navy."

Was war beginning? Had it begun? It was difficult to confirm anything. "Moscow was totally jammed. There was nothing. . . . Emptiness. It was like Moscow doesn't exist," Ketov related. "We knew things were coming to a head, that trouble was brewing," Captain Dubivko added. A sonar operator on B-36 [mis?]identified the sound of a torpedo attacking the submarine, but it had submerged fast enough to avoid being struck.

8

WHAT NO one in the United States government knows—not the Joint Chiefs, the Central Intelligence Agency (CIA), the Defense Intelligence Agency (DIA), or U.S. Navy Intelligence—is that one of the twenty-two torpedoes aboard B-59 (and aboard each of the other three Foxtrots of the Sixty-Ninth Brigade) is armed with a fifteen-kiloton nuclear warhead. Its range is nineteen kilometers, about twelve miles. If fired, it could easily sink a carrier and several other ships in the ASW fleet.

"We were on the brink of war because during the continuous communications sessions we received orders to have [nuclear] weapons at standby," Captain Shumkov remembers. "To stand by for firing weapons, or to be ready to fire weapons. That meant that the next order to follow would be to fire weapons."

The persistence of the explosions around B-59 has put Captain Savitsky (nicknamed the "Sweater") and his crew in a fearful state. The putrid air, the insufferable heat, and the terrifying pounding of explosive charges have led Savitsky to conclude that he is under attack. The U.S. Navy is trying to destroy his submarine.

"Maybe the war has already started up there, while we are doing somersaults here," he screams. In a rising fury he directs the special weapons officer "to assemble it [the nuclear torpedo] to battle readiness. . . . *We're gonna blast them now! We will die, but we will sink them all—we will not become the shame of the fleet.*"

9

AT THIS point readers might want to pause to ponder the role played by chance, in history as in each of our lives. Little is foreordained, and history is *not* a collection of inevitable events. The destinies of nations, just like the lives of individuals, are moved inexorably forward through crossroad after crossroad, by decisions and by chance, with the influence of each in constant flux: On one occasion "the road not taken" may have been dangerously mined, but on another it was the safe route.

Luck, extraordinary luck, good luck, or even "plain dumb luck" at that moment took command of events aboard B-59. The image that leaps to mind is an exaggerated childhood fantasy: Superman swooping out of the sky to miraculously block B-59's torpedo.

If he was being attacked, Savitsky was actually *obliged* to fire his nuclear weapon. In a presail special weapons briefing to the four submarine commanders, the chief of staff of the Northern Fleet, Vice Adm. A. I. Rassokha, made it clear that the nuclear torpedoes were the submariner's *first* line of defense. "I suggest to you, commanders," he said without ambiguity, "that you use the nuclear weapons *first*, and then you will figure out what to do after that."

The four captains had made a pact: "We made it between us, absolutely clear. . . . If one of my friends would deploy [fire] nuclear weapons," Ketov revealed years later, "I would deploy them too."

Using a familiar colloquialism, the deputy commander in chief of the Soviet navy, Admiral Fokin, reinforced Vice Admiral Rassokha's recommendation: "If they slap you on the left cheek, do not let them slap you on the right one," he told the captains, referring to the nuclear torpedoes.

Savitsky was being slapped, again and again. "He was in a bad condition," Capt. 3rd Rank Anatoly Andreyev, a B-59 crewmember, noted at the time: "The commander's nerves are shot to hell, he's yelling at everyone and torturing himself. . . . He is already becoming paranoid, scared of his own shadow. He's hard to deal with. I feel sorry for him and at the same time angry with him for his rash actions."

Savitsky's directions to the special weapons officer were the response of a man confronting destiny. He and his crew could passively accept being killed by the U.S. Navy, or they could die putting up an honorable resistance. "Shaming the fleet" was unthinkable.

4

Capt. Vasily Alexandrovich Arkhipov

Mere chance . . . and the prudence of the brigade's Chief
of Staff Vasily Arkhipov—who happened to be on board—
prevented the [nuclear] combat operations.
—CAPT. RYURIK A. KETOV

When a flotilla—either surface ships or submarines—sets sail on an
important mission it is customary in virtually every navy for senior
members of the fleet staff—the officers responsible for planning
and overseeing the operation—to sail aboard one of the vessels. If
the flotilla is composed of several types of ships—carriers, cruisers, destroyers—the entire staff is likely to occupy the principal one,
usually the carrier. However, the limited space aboard Project 641
submarines made a unified staff deployment impossible. Senior staff
members were therefore distributed—arbitrarily—among the four
boats. The brigade commander, Capt. Vitaly Agafonov, boarded B-4,
while his brigade chief of staff, Capt. Vasily Alexandrovich Arkhipov, embarked on B-59, Savitsky's submarine.

1

ARKHIPOV WAS thirty-six years old in October 1962. Handsome,
married, well educated, modest and thoughtful, he was an archetypal
product of the Soviet system. Born into a peasant family that until
1932 had barely scraped out a living farming in a small village outside
Moscow, he and his family were forced to move several times in his
young life until his father—who must have had more than a rudi-
mentary education—found steady work as a bookkeeper at a mine.

Vasily Alexandrovich was smart and ambitious, but with limited options at home and war on the horizon, a military career was an easy choice. At sixteen he applied to and was accepted into the elite Leningrad Naval Special School. The atmosphere of the academy and Leningrad pleased him, but in 1941 Nazi forces laid siege to the city, and along with his entire class, Vasily was transferred to the Kirov Caspian Higher Naval School, in Baku. The capital of the Azerbaijan Soviet Socialist Republic, the city has a broad harbor that opens into the Caspian Sea. It is also located in an oil-rich area that the Nazis sought to capture soon after Vasily arrived. But the Soviet counteroffensive of November 1942 permanently halted the Wehrmacht's advance, and Vasily and his classmates were saved from another forced relocation.

On August 8, 1945, the Soviet Union declared war on Japan, and Arkhipov, who had spent the war years studying and training, received orders to report on board a minesweeper that patrolled the Sea of Japan. It was a short, uneventful tour, followed by a new set of orders that sent him back to Baku for advanced training. Recognized as capable and talented, he was invited to join the Communist Party. Accepting the invitation put him on a fast track for promotion.

Submarine school was next, and over the course of the following decade he advanced steadily. In July 1961, at the age of thirty-five, he was assigned the prestigious position of deputy commander (executive officer) of the first Project 658–class nuclear-powered ballistic-missile submarine, K-19.

It was a fateful appointment.

2

DESIGNED AND hastily built in a frantic effort to catch up to the U.S. Navy's rapidly expanding nuclear submarine fleet, K-19 was victimized by a rushed construction schedule and a series of imprudent decisions. To say it was accident-prone is to indulge in understatement.

In 1959, before the boat was even commissioned, a fire killed three workmen who were assembling its ballast tanks. A short time later six female workers, who were gluing rubber lining into a poorly ventilated water cistern, died from inhaling the glue's fumes. The following year a faulty control rod seriously damaged the reactor. During sea trials a water leak in the same reactor forced an emergency surfacing. Later that same year the galley's waste system clogged and flooded one of the submarine's compartments. A few months later the main circuit pump failed when its coolant system sprang a serious leak. Early in 1961 a sailor was killed when a hatch slammed shut on him while he was loading one of the submarine's R-13 SLBMs (submarine-launched ballistic missiles).

K-19's crew began to refer to their boat as "Hiroshima."

But all these accidents, mishaps, and setbacks paled compared with the disaster that befell K-19 shortly after Arkhipov took up his new duties.

On July 4, 1961, while the submarine was participating in exercises off the southern coast of Greenland, both its long-range radio system (its only communications link to Moscow) and its reactor coolant system failed. A leak caused the water pressure to plummet in the stern reactor, rendering the coolant pumps useless. Control rods were inserted but failed to stabilize the reactor. The rising temperature almost melted the fuel rods. The hasty construction of K-19 had led to many oversights, including the lack of a backup cooling system. The nuclear-armed boat was in danger of emulating its sobriquet.

There is no record of Arkhipov's role during the frantic hours that followed, but we know that he supported Capt. N. V. Zateyev's controversial decision to sacrifice a group of sailors rather than abandon ship. With no backup coolant system in place, someone cleverly thought to create one by welding a water-supplying pipe into an airvent valve that would deliver water (coolant) to the reactor. It was a desperate, smart, dangerous gamble.

The area in which the welding had to be done was saturated with lethal levels of radioactivity. Even radiation protection gear could not shield the men for more than ten to fifteen minutes. But by rotating three teams of two and three volunteers each, the substitute coolant pipes were welded into place and, miraculously, K-19 was saved.

But not the brave sailors who had volunteered for the assignment. Of the 139 crewmembers, 22 died of radiation poisoning—eight in a matter of days, the rest in the next two years. "That was the first time I felt: 'Yes, this is radiation,'" Zateyev said. None of them knew that the protective garments they had been issued were in reality chemical protection suits that were useless against radioactivity; no proper radiation protection gear had been supplied to K-19.

Fifteen months later Arkhipov was aboard B-59.

3

IT WAS a lucky deployment. Several versions of how Arkhipov prevented a nuclear war have come to light. While differing in specific details, they make the same point: Were it not for Arkhipov's intervention, a torpedo with a fifteen-kiloton nuclear warhead would likely have been fired at the U.S. Navy's fleet.

Captain Ketov, the commander of B-4 and Savitsky's close friend, has provided the most detailed description of the dramatic events that took place in those critical minutes aboard B-59.

Savitsky "had spent all day trying to escape the ASW forces but, having run down the battery, was forced to surface to recharge. . . . While surfacing," Ketov recounts, B-59 "came under machine-gun fire from [U.S. ASW S-2] Tracker aircraft. The fire rounds landed either to the sides of the submarine's hull or near the bow. All these provocative actions carried out by surface ships in immediate proximity, and ASW aircraft flying some 10–15 meters [less than 30–50 feet] above the boat, had a detrimental impact on the commander, prompting him to take extreme measures . . . the use of 'special weapons.'"

I have no trouble believing Ketov's account, having been a member of an ASW squadron flight crew, albeit a P2V rather than an S-2 Tracker squadron. Firing live ammunition at a Soviet submarine—or any other unnecessary hostile action against any Soviet vessel—was strictly prohibited. Secretary McNamara had made that clear to the chief of naval operations (CNO), Adm. George Anderson, during a bitter exchange in the navy's Pentagon Command Center four nights earlier (October 23). But perhaps the crew of the Tracker had "not gotten the word." Or perhaps the combustible mix of adrenaline, testosterone, and frustration led the Tracker crew to demonstrate clearly to that "Commie sub" just who had won the cat-and-mouse game. Whatever the reason for firing live ammunition in the vicinity of the submarine, and provocatively "buzzing" it, those young U.S. Navy aviators came close to precipitating a war, perhaps even a nuclear war.

"*Mere chance,*" Ketov continues, "prevented Savitsky from resorting to the use of 'special weapons' at this time. A delay in diving time *and the prudence of the brigade's Chief of Staff Vasily Arkhipov* [on board as another matter of chance] prevented the combat operations which the B-59 could have initiated."

The after-action report prepared in December 1962 adds vivid details to Ketov's description of the reception B-59 received when it surfaced: "Airplanes and helicopters from the aircraft carrier *Randolph* flew over the submarine 12 times at the altitude of 20–100 meters [65–328 feet]. With every overflight they fired their aviation cannons (there was a total of about 300 shots). . . .

"The destroyers maneuvered around the submarine at a distance of 20–50 meters demonstratively aiming their guns at the submarine, dropped depth bombs and hydro-acoustic buoys when they crossed the course of the submarine, lifted flag signals and shouted in the loudspeaker demanding that the [submarine] stop. Similar actions were undertaken also in regard to submarine B-130."

Another account, this one by Vadim Orlov, at the time a twenty-five-year-old intelligence officer, does not mention a strafing incident by a Tracker aircraft. Orlov was the head of the special radio intercept team that had been inserted aboard B-59, and it is certain that he was belowdecks at the time: "The Americans hit us with something stronger than the grenades," Orlov recalled. "We thought—that's it—the end. After this attack the totally exhausted Savitsky, who in addition to everything was not able to establish connection with the General Staff, got furious. He summoned the officer who was assigned to the nuclear torpedo, and ordered him to assemble it to battle readiness."

"But we did not fire the nuclear torpedo," Orlov continues. Savitsky "was able to rein in his wrath after consulting with Second

Captain Vasily Alexandrovich Arkhipov and his deputy political officer Ivan Semyonovich Maslennikov. Following their recommendations, he made the decision to come to the surface."

In 1997 Arkhipov provided his own version of what happened when B-59 was forced to surface. Surrounded by an aircraft carrier, nine destroyers, four P2Vs, three Tracker airplanes, and coast guard forces, the officers on the conning tower were overwhelmed. "Overflights by planes just 20–30 meters above the submarine's conning tower, use of powerful searchlights that blinded Savitsky, fire from automatic cannons (over 300 shells), dropping depth charges, cutting in front of submarines by destroyers at dangerously [small] distance, targeting guns at the submarine, yelling from loudspeakers to stop engines, etc."

Convinced that he was under attack, Savitsky ordered an "urgent dive" and "arm torpedo in the front section [the nuclear torpedo]." But when he tried to descend he was [luckily] blocked by the signaling officer who had somehow in his excitement become stuck near the top of the conning tower ladder. During that short delay Arkhipov realized that the planes were firing "past and along the boat." It was not an attack. "Cancel dive, they are signaling," he countered.

In an interview with the historian Svetlana Savranskaya in 2002, Orlov "emphasized the crucial role played by the brigade chief of staff Vasily Arkhipov in talking Captain Savitsky out of any rash actions." And, as confirmation, in March 2004 Arkhipov's widow, Olga Grigoryevna, a physics teacher in Baku, reported that her husband had told her the story of how Captain Savitsky almost fired a nuclear torpedo at an American destroyer.

She also believed that his experience aboard K-19 had played a role in his intervention. "He'd seen with his own eyes what radiation did to people," she told an interviewer. "This tragedy [K-19] was the reason he would say no to nuclear war."

———

Capt. Vasily Arkhipov's success persuading Captain Savitsky to rescind his decision to ready the nuclear torpedo to fire was a seminal act on a grand scale. It called upon maturity and good judgment in the most difficult of circumstances. He saved not only himself and Savitsky's crew, but also the lives of thousands of U.S. sailors and millions of innocent civilians who would have been killed in the nuclear exchanges that certainly would have followed from the destruction B-59's nuclear torpedo would have wreaked upon those U.S. Navy vessels.

4

THE PLIGHT of B-59, the contrasting reactions of Captains Savitsky and Arkhipov, the unauthorized use of grenades by U.S. Navy ships and machine-gun fire by navy aircraft, combined with the Soviet and American communications failures, form an astonishing tale with an obvious moral: Unanticipated events can happen no matter how carefully actions are planned. Avoiding their terrible consequences is often as much a matter of luck as it is of careful management.

Luck, both good and bad, comes in many guises. It can be as simple as a hidden patch of slippery ice or a carelessly discarded article that diverts the pedestrian's path around the ice. Or it can be the random distribution of personnel aboard four submarines. Whatever prior experiences endowed Captain Arkhipov with the maturity and courage to dissuade Captain Savitsky will remain hidden, perhaps forever.

The extraordinary (and surely disconcerting) conclusion has to be that on October 27, 1962, a nuclear war was averted not because President Kennedy and Premier Khrushchev were doing their best to avoid war (they were), but because Capt. Vasily Arkhipov had been randomly assigned to submarine B-59.

5

The Long Cuban Missile Crisis, 1945–1962

A New Framework

For every action there is an equal and opposite reaction.
—ISAAC NEWTON, THIRD LAW OF MOTION

Every action produces counter action, hence they [Western powers] resist fiercely.
—NIKITA KHRUSHCHEV, 1961

In a century filled with horrific wars, the Cuban missile crisis came close to producing the most horrifying war of all—"the final failure," in President Kennedy's words. How and why the United States and the Soviet Union nudged each other to the edge of the nuclear abyss, and how they avoided a suicidal plunge, is the paramount story of our age. In lives gambled and saved, it was history's luckiest nonevent.

It was "insane," Kennedy remarked, "that two men, sitting on the opposite sides of the world, should be able to decide to bring an end to civilization." But these many years later that "insane" possibility still exists and governs the way nuclear weapons states function. A new history of the decisions that led to the Cuban missile crisis, and a close analysis of the decisions that produced its peaceful resolution, thus remain compelling and relevant.

1

ALTHOUGH GENERALLY understood as a confrontation between the Soviet Union, the United States, and Cuba, the missile crisis was in fact far broader in its origins, scope, and consequences than its Russian name (the "Caribbean Crisis"), its Cuban name (the "October

Crisis"), or its American name suggests. It was a global event—an integral part of the wider Cold War, and a consequence of the nuclear arms race that began with the atomic bombing of Hiroshima.

That savage beginning of the nuclear age gave rise to new concepts of diplomacy, security, and war. But decisions about how the atomic weapon would be integrated into international relations fell to the leaders of the U.S. and Soviet governments.

In the seventeen years between the atomic bombing of Hiroshima and October 1962, Truman and Stalin, Eisenhower, Kennedy, and Khrushchev, made choices that led the Soviet premier to sneak his missiles into Cuba, and the president to demand their removal, even at the risk of war.

Those seventeen years were the most intense period of military and diplomatic adaptation to a new weapon in modern history. Imagining and experimenting with ways to make nuclear arms serve national objectives were the period's defining characteristics. Distinguished by prodigious theorizing and experimenting, first the United States and then the USSR struggled to come to grips with the purposes and consequences of their arsenals.

Were they really useful for war? Was it necessary to have more weapons than the other, or just enough? How many was enough? How should they be deployed? How should they be targeted? Were they primarily a deterrent, or war-fighting weapons? Could they support diplomacy? If so, how? Would they make war obsolete, or just more horrible?

Into this opportunity gap rushed military and civilian strategists ("defense intellectuals") with an abundance of arcane doctrines, many of which were unfettered insanity as the historical record reveals. Theories of nuclear weapons and nuclear war—preemptive wars and limited wars—proliferated, as did schemes for reinforcing diplomacy with threats, tests, and deployments.

Guided by those theories, both superpowers came to rely in the mid-1950s on their nuclear weapons and delivery systems to contain the foreign policy ambitions of the other. As Cold War historian Melvyn Leffler determined, nuclear superiority encouraged risk taking, and much of the nuclear arms race concentrated on limiting the ability of the other to take risks. The ultimate irony of the Cuban missile crisis was that Khrushchev took the most dangerous risk of the Cold War in order to limit the risks the United States could take.

2

AN IRON law of chronology—the chronological framework a historian chooses—determines how a historical event is perceived, understood, and explained. The narrowest—and most frequent—framing of the Cuban missile crisis is restricted to the thirteen days between October 16, 1962—the day President Kennedy was notified that the Soviets had secretly deployed offensive missiles to Cuba—and October 28, the day Premier Khrushchev agreed to remove them.

In the familiar American telling, Soviet aggression was the cause of the crisis, Castro was irrelevant, and the United States was the uncontested victor. This is the version of the crisis that Robert Kennedy described in his memoir, *Thirteen Days,* published posthumously in 1969. It is a centerpiece of the Camelot legend.

In 1997 the historians Aleksandr Fursenko and Timothy Naftali offered a broader and deeper view. In their pathbreaking history, *One Hell of a Gamble: Khrushchev, Castro, and Kennedy,* they locate the "seeds" of the missile crisis "in the story of the Cuban revolution." Without doubt Castro's success, and his alliance with the Soviet Union, created the circumstances that led to the confrontation with the United States. But neither Castro nor Communism can explain *why Khrushchev chose strategic nuclear armed missiles* to defend the Cuban revolution. Seemingly an impetuous choice, it was, in fact, dictated by the role that nuclear weapons played in the preceding seventeen years of Cold War geopolitical competition.

The atomic bombings of Hiroshima and Nagasaki, President Dwight D. Eisenhower's deployments of nuclear missiles to Europe and Asia, Secretary of State John Foster Dulles's brinkmanship, President Kennedy's nuclear weapons buildup—as well as Khrushchev's own use of "nuclear diplomacy"—led Khrushchev to view those missiles as the deterrent du jour. The United States, he rationalized, had "surrounded us with military bases and kept us at gunpoint [with nuclear missiles]." If he sent similar weapons to Cuba "we would have a balance of fear [and nuclear strike capability], as the West phrased it," and Cuba would be safe.

3

THE FAILURE after nearly sixty years to "historicize" an event as significant as the Cuban missile crisis—that is, to explain it within its
larger historical context—is highly unusual, although, in retrospect,
it's easy to see why the roots of the crisis have been overlooked in
histories of the event.

Its resolution captured the admiration of the American public,
and secured the handsome young president's reputation as a tough
and effective leader. His steely nerves, the Camelot version explained,
faced down the Soviets at the brink of nuclear Armageddon. There
seemed no compelling reason to look further into its history.

The president and his close advisers reinforced this heroic narrative through leaks to friendly journalists, who promoted the administration's performance as a model of nuclear-age "crisis management."

President Kennedy's assassination in November 1963 precluded
challenges to this triumphalist narrative. There can be little doubt
that during the 1964 election campaign his Republican opponent
would have attacked both his pledge not to invade Cuba, and pursued
the (accurate) suspicion that he had offered to remove U.S. missiles
from Turkey in exchange for the withdrawal of the Soviet missiles
in Cuba. Had that scenario played out, the prevailing view of the
Cuban missile crisis as a flawless Kennedy triumph could not have
been sustained.

Finally, recordings of Kennedy's advisers, taped secretly by the
president, were declassified in time to divert researchers from expanding history's view of those thirteen days. Providing detailed documentation of the Cold War's most serious existential policy debates,
the recordings of ExComm meetings reveal how each of the president's advisers tried to influence his decisions. Understandably, the
historian Sheldon Stern observed, historians could not resist writing
about the crisis from the perspective of "a fly on the wall."

4

THOSE CABINET Room and Oval Office recordings also captured
the words of the president. Combined with memorandums and
notes, the tapes make it possible to follow Kennedy's torturous deci-

sion making as the crisis unfolded. "I think we ought to, beginning right now, be preparing . . . to take out these missiles," the president declared at the first ExComm meeting.

But within two days he emerged as the primary advocate for blockading Cuba.

How the president freed himself from the conventional Cold War attitudes his advisers advocated—why he changed his mind and resisted initiating a military strike—is the central question of the Cuban missile crisis and the ultimate subject of this book. After all, had he authorized the bombings and invasions urged by the Joint Chiefs of Staff and most members of ExComm, the crisis would have developed quite differently.

The United States had a superior global nuclear arsenal, and a conventional military advantage in the Caribbean, but suffered a severe intelligence deficit. In addition to the Soviet Union's medium- and intermediate-range missiles in Cuba, the CIA estimated that 11,000 conventionally armed Soviet troops were on the island when, in fact, there were 42,000 Soviets armed with tactical nuclear weapons.

Could Khrushchev have resisted responding with a military strike if thousands of Soviet soldiers were killed in the massive bombing raids the Joint Chiefs recommended? Could Kennedy have accepted thousands of Americans massacred by Soviet tactical nuclear weapons as they stormed the beaches of Cuba?

These critical questions never had to be answered because serendipity intervened—in the form of a providentially arranged lunch between the president and his UN ambassador, Adlai Stevenson, at the White House on October 16, the first day of the crisis.

"An attack would very likely result in Soviet reprisals—Turkey, Berlin, etc.," Stevenson warned. The missiles had to be removed, he agreed, but "it should be clear as a pikestaff that the U.S. was, is and will be ready to negotiate the elimination of bases and anything else. . . . <u>Blackmail and intimidation never, negotiation and sanity always</u>," he concluded in the final underlined sentence of his memorandum that summarized his conversation with the president.

During the next forty-eight hours, after what proved to be a turning point in the president's thinking, Kennedy reconsidered the military options and began to track Stevenson's singular, insistent advocacy for "explor[ing] the possibilities of a peaceful solution." As difficult as their relationship was, Stevenson's suggestions of October 16 and 17 roused the president's prudent instincts, and he adopted many of his UN ambassador's ideas.

Stevenson's warning that West Berlin was an easy target for a Soviet reprisal was particularly influential. "Our problem is not merely Cuba but it is also Berlin," President Kennedy told the Joint Chiefs three days later. They were mutual hostages. America's NATO allies would not support an invasion of Cuba if it jeopardized West Berlin's survival.

5

ONCE THE Cuban missile crisis is integrated into the grand sweep of how nuclear weapons were used by the superpowers between 1945 and 1962, the ideas that incited it are clearly revealed.

We learn that before the bomb existed, policy makers recognized the threat to humanity that nuclear weapons would pose, and the concomitant advantages that a nation in sole possession of the bomb might acquire: "The world in its present state of moral advancement compared with its technical development would be eventually at the mercy of such a weapon," Secretary of War Henry L. Stimson warned Harry S. Truman, the new president, on April 25, 1945. "In other words, modern civilization might be completely destroyed."

But Truman's secretary of state perceived an immediate advantage in that terrifying possibility. A successful demonstration of the bomb's power, James Byrnes told the president in May 1945, "might well put us in a position to dictate our own terms at the end of the war."

Relying on the bomb to shape diplomacy and military policy in the postwar world was a wartime decision. "It was ever present in my mind," Byrnes recalled in an interview, "that it was important that we should have an end to the war before the Russians came in."

Stalin had no doubt that the atomic bombings of Hiroshima and Nagasaki were meant to signal just that. America intended to use its atomic monopoly to intimidate him, and he wasted no time getting his own atomic bomb. Regardless of the myriad other forces that would shape the Soviet-American relationship—economics, ideology, geography, national ambitions, alliances—it was clear from August 6, 1945, that nuclear weapons would command a central role.

Domestic considerations also influenced how nuclear weapons were seen, valued, and utilized during those formative seventeen years. Whether it was the unease Truman and Byrnes shared about a possible congressional investigation if atomic bombs were not used against Japan, or Eisenhower's assumption that a large nuclear arsenal would buy cheap security, or Kennedy's expansion of America's nuclear arsenal to validate his Cold War credentials, or Khrushchev's decision to emulate Eisenhower's massive retaliation initiative, the bomb was a major domestic influence on both sides of the Iron Curtain.

President Kennedy even intended to promote his enlarged nuclear arsenal during his 1964 reelection campaign. Significant attention has been paid to his June 1963 American University "peace" speech. But read his campaign rhetoric on November 22, 1963, in Fort Worth, Texas, just hours before he was assassinated:

> In the past 3 years we have increased the defense budget of the United States by over 20 percent; increased the program of acquisition for Polaris submarines from 24 to 41; increased our Minuteman missile purchase program by more than 75 percent; doubled the number of strategic bombers and missiles on alert; doubled the number of nuclear weapons available in the strategic alert forces; increased the tactical nuclear forces deployed in Western Europe by over 60 percent. . . . I hope those who want a stronger America and place it on some signs will also place those figures next to it.

Khrushchev, too, used nuclear weapons for domestic purposes. Committed to improving Soviet living standards, he adopted another Eisenhower policy: Nuclear weapons, he informed the Presidium in December 1959, reduced the need for large numbers of conventional forces. Since the Soviet Union was not planning to attack anyone, he wrote to his colleagues, a large conventional army was redundant: "I think that now it would be foolish to have atomic and hydrogen bombs and missiles and at the same time to maintain a large army." To bolster the Soviet economy, he proposed that the reductions be made unilaterally.

6

THE DISCOVERY of the Soviet missile deployment initially confronted President Kennedy with the choice between war or political failure; and his decision to blockade Cuba left Khrushchev with the same alternative. Their shared fear of political failure was moderated, however, by their mutual recognition that the use of nuclear weapons would be a catastrophe. As the crisis heated and slid toward war, they worked in blind alliance to prevent that "final failure."

Character and wisdom overcame firmly held Cold War doctrines and the rigid attitudes of hard-line advisers. To prevent nuclear war, both men had to violate principles to which they and their administrations were committed. They had to abandon promises they had made to allies, and to their military staffs. To end the crisis peacefully they had to adopt policies they had rejected a week earlier.

Kennedy was compelled to make a public pledge that the United States would not invade Cuba—a concession that addressed Khrushchev's rationale for putting missiles in Cuba—and he promised Khrushchev, in a secret agreement, that the United States would soon remove the Jupiter missiles that the Eisenhower administration had ordered deployed to Turkey—the very missiles that had so galled Khrushchev and, he claimed, given him the idea of stationing Soviet missiles on Cuban soil.

Khrushchev had to swallow even harder. He had to surrender his ambition of equalizing the "balance of fear" by creating a permanent strategic missile installation ninety miles from American territory. He had to admit that his scheme had failed even though he insisted that he had gotten the best of the bargain. Castro's revolution was secured, and the U.S. missiles in Turkey were removed. The "Caribbean Crisis represents a jewel of our foreign policy," he declared. It "achieved exceptional success for Cuba without a single shot."

But as the crisis played out, Khrushchev—by yielding first—lost the public relations contest. He had been caught in the act and had been forced to remove his missiles. Regardless of his successes, the perception of a humiliating retreat eclipsed the reality of political gains.

7

OTHER IRONIES associated with the resolution of the crisis abound. Had Khrushchev not announced on Sunday, October 28, that he would withdraw his missiles, Kennedy prepared to end the crisis peacefully on Monday. On Saturday evening, October 27, he authorized Secretary of State Dean Rusk to arrange for UN Secretary General U Thant to propose a missile swap—the U.S. missiles out of Turkey in exchange for the Soviet missiles out of Cuba—which he intended to accept.

Khrushchev's duplicity—in lying about his secret missile deployment—shattered the trust that back-channel personal communications between the two heads of state had been building. Yet, in the aftermath of the crisis, a more stable U.S.–Soviet relationship developed. As Anastas Mikoyan, Khrushchev's closest Presidium confidant, observed decades later, "The missile crisis was the result of our adventurism. . . . Paradoxically, it has helped us lower the risks of war. If there had been no Cuban missile crisis, we should perhaps have organized it."

The final irony was the most transformative. Contention over the existence of West Berlin diminished after the crisis. The Soviet commitment to Communist Cuba, and Kennedy's no-invasion pledge, transformed the Caribbean island into the strategic equivalent of West Berlin. Any Soviet attempt to expel U.S. forces from West Berlin ran the risk of putting Castro's government in jeopardy.

8

AN ADDITIONAL element of the crisis has not received the attention it deserves: technology. Not just the technology that gave birth to the nuclear age, but the vast array of technologies that, along with nuclear weapons, shaped the history of the Cold War. They made things possible, and because they were possible, they were attempted.

Ballistic missiles, surface-to-air antiaircraft missiles, tactical missiles, and the U2 aircraft were virtual partners to the decision makers in both creating and resolving the crisis.

By transforming the nuclear arms race from a competition for bigger and better bombs into a contest for longer-range missile-delivery systems (intercontinental ballistic missiles, or ICBMs), it's reasonable to conclude that Sputnik initiated the crisis. In response to the possibility that the Soviet Union had developed missiles that could reach the United States, President Eisenhower solicited NATO approval to deploy American Jupiter intermediate-range missiles (IRBMs) to Turkey and Italy. In turn, it was those very missiles that gave Khrushchev the idea of sending Soviet missiles to Cuba.

The crisis also changed both men. It changed their views of each other. It changed their relationships to their military establishments. It changed their political futures—strengthening Kennedy's and weakening Khrushchev's.

It also exposed the multiple poles of the so-called bipolar international system. The United Nations, for example, played a far greater role in the crisis than either the United States or the Soviet governments were willing to acknowledge. It provided a global forum that forced the superpowers to proceed more cautiously, and to explain their policies on a world stage. And offstage, UN Secretary General U Thant played a critical role as both mediator and moderator. It is sobering to contemplate that if the United Nations had not existed, the crisis might not have ended without violence.

The crisis also increased hostility between China and the Soviet Union, and readjusted the ties between the United States and its European allies. And it had a salutary effect on Kennedy's Latin American outreach, the Alliance for Progress. Secretary of State Dean Rusk's energetic effort to gain the support of the Organization of American States (OAS) for the "quarantine" gave the nations of South America a sense that a U.S. administration was taking them seriously, perhaps for the first time.

Fidel Castro's role in the crisis demonstrated how great-power diplomacy and strategy can be manipulated, undercut, and even controlled by small states with little power—whether clients or enemies. How

Castro chose to respond to the crisis had a major influence on decisions in Moscow and Washington, although no U.S. policy maker acknowledged that. By accepting the offer of Soviet missiles, Castro made the crisis possible. By goading a Soviet SAM [surface-to-air missile] crew on October 27 into destroying a U2, and by suggesting to Khrushchev that the Soviet Union launch a preemptive nuclear attack if the United States invaded Cuba, Castro hastened Khrushchev's October 28 rush to resolution. And, after the settlement, by refusing to allow UN inspectors into Cuba, Castro forced Kennedy to retract his insistence that UN observers monitor the withdrawal of Soviet missiles.

It is reasonable to conclude that while Kennedy and Khrushchev managed the course of the crisis, Castro manipulated its timing.

9

AMONG THE many ironies associated with the Cuban missile crisis is the revelation that neither Kennedy nor Khrushchev was aware of how tenuous their control was over events. During the tense six days that followed the president's October 22 speech, he estimated the chances of a nuclear war as between "one out of three and even."

But as frightening as those odds were, he had underestimated the danger. He was unaware that on the most dangerous day of the crisis, October 27, the commander of a Soviet submarine in the quarantine area ordered a nuclear torpedo readied to fire at U.S. warships. He did not know that a rogue U.S. officer in Okinawa's missile fields ordered an unauthorized launch against China and the Soviet Union. Nor did Kennedy know that just hours before his speech, Khrushchev and his closest advisers—consumed with fear of a U.S. attack—had "seriously considered using nuclear weapons on America." As the historian James Hershberg notes: "In the supercharged atmosphere of the missile crisis, with forces on high alert, any direct clash, whether intentional or accidental, was fraught with the danger of uncontrollable escalation."

What led to these existential moments? What prompted Khrushchev, who feared a war with the United States, to undertake a gamble that had such a high risk of precipitating a war? And what prompted John Kennedy, who did not want a war with the Soviet Union, to adopt a strategy that handed control over the decision for war or peace to the Soviet premier? "I call upon Chairman Khrushchev," he appealed, "to move the world back from the abyss of destruction."

And if Khrushchev had refused?

It seems irrational today. Yet in 1962, it made perfect sense to the national security custodians of both nations precisely because the evolution of U.S.–Soviet Cold War relations during the first seventeen years of the nuclear age had set the stage for just such a confrontation.

Under the patina of stability claimed for nuclear deterrence lurked the threat of a preemptive first strike by one side or the other. That risk led each nation's security guardians to adopt policies that moved them closer to the confrontation they were desperately trying to avoid—but nevertheless periodically considered.

President Eisenhower contemplated just such a mad idea. On September 8, 1953, in a memorandum to John Foster Dulles, he wrote that there were circumstances related to an intense arms competition when "we would be forced to consider whether or not our duty to future generations did not require us to *initiate* war at the most propitious moment that we could designate."

BOOK I

THE MAKING OF
THE NUCLEAR AGE,
1945–1962

Nuclear Decisions in the White House and the
Kremlin That Led to the Cuban Missile Crisis

PART ONE

Truman and Stalin:
The "Irresistible Glitter of Nuclear Weapons"

The glitter of nuclear weapons. It is irresistible if you come
to them as a scientist [or a president or premier]. . . . It is
something that gives people an illusion of illimitable power,
and it is, in some ways, responsible for all our troubles . . .
—FREEMAN DYSON, 1980

6

"This Is the Greatest Thing in History"

When a "bomb" is finally available, it might, perhaps, after
mature consideration, be used against the Japanese.
—FRANKLIN D. ROOSEVELT, SEPTEMBER 18, 1944

If we, as a professedly Christian nation, feel morally free to
use atomic energy in that way [Hiroshima and Nagasaki],
men elsewhere will accept that verdict. Atomic weapons will
be looked upon as a normal part of the arsenal of war and
the stage will be set for the sudden and final destruction of
mankind.
—JOHN FOSTER DULLES TO TRUMAN, AUGUST 10, 1945

World War II restored war's battered reputation. The Great War,
the one Americans fought in 1917 "to end all wars," purged American
culture of Teddy Roosevelt's war-builds-character mantra; isolationism dominated the postwar decades. But then came the Good War.
The circumstances of its beginning, and its triumphant conclusions,
in Europe and Asia, created a very different postwar atmosphere.

It had the perfect start: A surprise attack that unified the nation.
No declaration of war before that infamous Sunday morning,
December 7, 1941, when Japanese bombs rained down on our navy at
Pearl Harbor. Certain of our innocence, we joined together against
duplicitous enemies. So, in this war (*un*like all prior and subsequent
wars), there was little dissent. We were a divided nation on December 6, 1941; on December 8 we were united.

1

EVERYONE KNEW someone whose son, brother, daughter, sister, mother, or father was in the military. America lost many young men: 405,000 were killed in combat, and 671,000 returned home wounded. But that shared sorrow bound us tighter. On the home front the war effort was supported in large and small ways. Children collected newspapers and tin cans for recycling, wives volunteered for community service, rationing was accepted, and our fathers— those too old or physically unable to fight—were air raid wardens. When the sirens blared, we pulled the curtains, shut off the lights, and crawled under beds and pianos (probably a bad idea). But we were not bombed; we were not invaded; we did not starve. In the space of those three years and eight months—December 7, 1941 to August 14, 1945—we defeated the Nazis, the Japanese, and, for good measure, the Great Depression.

It had been a good war, *the Good War.* It was a war for justice. It was a war to eliminate the depravity that had enveloped Europe and Asia. Is it a surprise that we forgot how disillusioned our parents had felt in 1919? If the Soviets misbehaved (after being saved, we insisted, by our generosity), they would have to contend with the ire of "the Greatest Generation"—which, by the way, had a monopoly on a heretofore unimaginably powerful new weapon.

2

THE WAR'S final months were extremely difficult for President Harry S. Truman. "I feel like the moon, the stars and the planets have fallen on me," he said on April 12, 1945. He was so ill informed, so distant from Roosevelt's inner circle, that assuming the role of commander in chief seemed beyond his ability. But the war against Germany ended in less than a month, and three months later Japan surrendered under a nuclear cloud that he had unleashed.

In the seven and a half years that followed Japan's surrender, Truman confronted domestic and foreign policy issues that would have challenged the political skills of his predecessor. To deal with several of them, he leaned on the atomic bomb—a temptation that preset the Cold War's nuclear agenda.

The nuclear age was introduced to the world on August 6, 1945. Hiroshima, and then Nagasaki, made the atomic bomb synonymous with our victory, the symbol of our superiority, and a metaphor for our hegemonic postwar status. Our monopoly of the atomic bomb epitomized the superiority of American science, American industry, and the American military. Trumpeted as the crowning technological achievement of the war, it signaled the dominant role the United States would play in the postwar world.

Even before its debut, the bomb was recognized as more than just a powerful new weapon. It was the harbinger of a "new world," an unprecedented invention that would alter how governments thought about power and diplomacy, war and peace. "As long as we can out-produce the world, can control the seas, and can strike inland with the atomic bomb, we can assume certain risks otherwise unacceptable," Secretary of the Navy James Forrestal wrote in 1947.

3

THE ATOMIC bombings of Hiroshima and Nagasaki are the seminal events of post-1945 history. Simultaneously existing in the past, present, and future, they define a potential power that had previously been the purview only of deities: the end of life on earth. Secretary of War Henry L. Stimson, the cabinet officer President Roosevelt charged with overseeing the secret Manhattan Project, understood its significance. He had closely followed the new weapon's development, and had thought deeply about its implications. By April 12, 1945, the day President Roosevelt died, Stimson believed that the atomic bomb was the key to postwar relations with the Soviet Union.

"Within four months," he told President Truman on April 25, "we shall in all probability have completed the most terrible weapon ever known in human history." Disagreements with Stalin over Poland, reparations, and Lend-Lease had to be reconsidered in light of the atomic bomb. Some form of international control of this new force was essential for postwar peace, and for that Stalin's cooperation was necessary.

Stimson feared, he informed Truman, that a postwar nuclear arms race could lead to "modern civilization [being] completely destroyed." Such an unthinkable possibility demanded the American government's full attention. "Our leadership in the war and in the development of this weapon," he counseled, *"has placed a certain moral responsibility upon us which we cannot shirk without very serious responsibility for any disaster to civilization which it would further."*

In his memoir, Truman recalled Stimson's briefing. The secretary of war, he said, was "at least as much concerned with the role of the atomic bomb in the shaping of history as [with] its capacity to shorten the war."

Stimson's message to Truman was that he needed to focus on the most profound challenge of the impending nuclear age: "If the problem of the proper use of this weapon can be solved the peace of the world and our civilization can be saved."

But what did Stimson have in mind when he spoke of "the proper use of this weapon"? Was it the need for an especially careful assessment of the considerations that President Roosevelt expressed in September 1944 when he discussed the use of the atomic bomb with Churchill? "When a 'bomb' is finally available it might, perhaps, after mature consideration, be used against the Japanese," their precisely worded memorandum records.

Curiously, for all his perceptive thinking about the postwar implications of atomic weapons, there is little evidence that Stimson shared Roosevelt's prudence ("might, perhaps, after mature consideration") about the military use of the atomic bomb. Nowhere in his diary is there an indication that he questioned whether atomic weapons should be used during the war. The primary question was whether they would be ready on time, and the possible diplomatic advantages of using them.

This was not due to a lack of thought and attention. Stimson spent hours pondering the revolutionary impact of the atomic bomb. Its emergence on the world stage raised issues that "went right down to the bottom facts of human nature, morals and government," he confided in his diary a month before he discussed the bomb's significance with Truman.

It is surprising, therefore, that while recognizing the revolutionary implications of the bomb's development, Stimson did not question whether using it against Japan might produce unintended, undesirable consequences. He knew that his close adviser John McCloy believed that atomic bombing a Japanese city should be avoided. Yet he never suggested to Roosevelt or Truman that its military use might incur a moral liability—an issue he *did* raise with respect to the conventional bombing of urban centers—or that the chances of securing Soviet postwar cooperation might be diminished by such a demonstration.

Perhaps what his friend Supreme Court justice Felix Frankfurter once referred to as Stimson's habit of setting his mind "at one thing like the needle of an old Victrola caught in a groove" may help to explain how he overlooked exactly what he sought to avoid: the use of the atomic bomb in a manner that would drive a wedge of distrust between the two most powerful wartime allies.

His position as secretary of war, and his preoccupation with winning the war, certainly help to explain Stimson's thinking. From its inception he had integrated the Manhattan Project thoroughly into the war effort. Though initiated by scientists committed to winning a presumed race for the bomb against Germany, the atomic project was supported by policy makers as a weapon of war to be used against any enemy.

Expecting that a postwar monopoly of the atomic bomb would give the United States a powerful new military advantage, first Stimson and Roosevelt, then Stimson, Truman, and Secretary of State James F. Byrnes eagerly anticipated its diplomatic advantages.

As early as December 1944 Stimson and Roosevelt discussed using the "secret" of the atomic bomb as a means of obtaining a quid pro quo from the Soviet Union. With that objective in mind, and while it remained in a state of becoming, the bomb's potential influence on future diplomatic negotiations was limited only by each policy maker's imagination.

4

A CLOSE look at how Stimson defined the nature of the diplomatic problems between Moscow and Washington, and the opportunities he believed the bomb created to resolve those problems to America's advantage, further explains how he thought about the relationship between its use and its usefulness. "It [the atomic bomb] has this unique peculiarity," he mused the day before Roosevelt died. "Although every prophecy thus far has been fulfilled by the development and we can see that success is 99% assured, yet only by the first actual war trial of the weapon can the actual certainty be fixed."

The desire for assurance that the bomb would meet its most ambitious expectations increased as the Potsdam Conference—the final wartime gathering of the Allied leaders—drew nearer. "Over any . . . tangled wave of problems [with Stalin] the S-1 [atomic bomb] secret would be dominant and yet we will not know until after [the Potsdam Conference] whether this is a weapon in our hands or not," Stimson wrote on May 12. "It seems a terrible thing to gamble with such big stakes in diplomacy without having your master card in your hand."

It was a gamble that Stimson persuaded Truman not to take. Arguing that it was critical to know whether the United States had a workable atomic bomb before negotiating postwar agreements with Stalin, he urged Truman to postpone the conference (originally set to convene July 1) until July 15.

The test of the [plutonium] bomb was scheduled for July 16.[*]

5

IN THE three months between Roosevelt's death and the Potsdam Conference, Truman and his new secretary of state, James F. Byrnes, embraced the idea that a successful wartime use of the atomic bomb would endow American diplomacy with significant advantages. As disagreements with the Soviet Union over postwar issues mounted, the bomb's anticipated value soared. Byrnes came to the heady conclusion that it "might well put us in a position to dictate our own terms at the end of the war."

In order to understand how the bomb came to be seen and valued

---

[*] The intense attention to the success of the plutonium bomb test (July 16, 1945) suggests a focus on the postwar production of atomic bombs. The uranium-235 bomb was a simple design that Los Alamos scientists were confident would work. It was not tested before it was dropped on Hiroshima. Therefore whether or not the plutonium bomb test was successful, an atomic bomb was available for wartime use. However, the more complicated design for the plutonium bomb was more efficient, and if it worked it would enhance production of atomic bombs after the war as weapons-grade plutonium was more readily producible than U-235.

as the key to America's postwar diplomatic influence, it is necessary to explore the ideas that led from Stimson's "moral responsibility . . . which we cannot shirk," to Byrnes's hyperbolic ("dictate our own terms") expectations. There was no epiphany, but rather a steady accumulation of assumptions that attached themselves, like barnacles to a ship's bottom, to the Truman administration's Potsdam strategy.

The process began subtly during the Roosevelt administration. At a meeting on December 31, 1944, in which the president and Stimson discussed postwar relations with the Soviet Union and the expected U.S. atomic monopoly, they wondered whether the "secret" of the bomb might be used as a diplomatic carrot. Perhaps it could be offered as a bargaining chip to obtain a "quid pro quo from the Soviet Union," Stimson recorded in his diary. Months later, when Truman and his closest advisers turned to the bomb to help them find "some way of persuading Russia to play ball," it was not a new thought.

With the Red Army occupying Poland and half of Germany, America's conventional diplomatic advantages were diminishing daily. Though the expectations invested in the bomb invited phantasmagoric predictions, Truman and Byrnes comfortably adopted them, along with the idea that the bomb would somehow neutralize Soviet advantages: "The bomb as a merely probable weapon had seemed a weak reed on which to rely," Stimson explained in his memoirs, *"but the bomb as a colossal reality was very different."*

6

STIMSON ARRIVED at the Potsdam Conference with one purpose in mind: to personally inform the president that the bomb was "a colossal reality." He had arranged that the report describing the bomb's test be delivered to him. Unexpected torrential rain had delayed the debut of the nuclear age by almost six hours, but at 5:30 a.m. on July 16, 1945, a flash "brighter than a thousand suns" lit the Alamogordo desert in New Mexico.

The courier arrived with the report at Stimson's Potsdam residence five days later, on the morning of July 21. "It was an immensely powerful document," Stimson recorded, "clearly and well written with supporting documents of the highest importance." Prepared by Gen. Leslie Groves, who, under Stimson's authority, had overseen the Manhattan Project, it was an impressive description of the test's success:

"At 0530, on 16 July 1945, in a remote section of the Alamogordo Air Base, New Mexico, the first full scale test was made of the implosion type atomic fission bomb," Groves reported. The test was a complete success. "Based on the data which it has been possible to work up to date," Groves estimated the explosion's force "in excess of the equivalent of 15,000 to 20,000 tons of TNT," adding, "this is a conservative estimate."

Groves's report went on to describe a fireball brighter than several midday suns; a mushroom cloud that shot 41,000 feet into the substratosphere; an explosive force that shattered a window 125 miles away; a crater stretching 1,200 feet in diameter; a mangled forty-ton steel tower one-half mile from the explosion. To make his point even clearer, he wrote that even the Pentagon (whose construction he had directed) would not be a safe shelter from this weapon.

At 3:30 p.m., after carefully studying the report (Stimson did everything with great deliberation), the seventy-eight-year-old secretary of war was driven to "the Little White House," Truman's Potsdam residence. Uncharacteristically excited, he reviewed the details: "The President was tremendously pepped up by it and spoke to me of it again and again when I saw him. He said it gave him an entirely new feeling of confidence."

7

TRUMAN DID not waste time displaying his "new feeling of confidence." Returning at 5:00 p.m. to the Fifth Plenary Session, he took forceful command of the debate for the first time. "I shall state frankly what I think," he told Stalin. Churchill was astonished. "He stood up to the Russians in a most emphatic and decisive manner, telling them as to certain demands that they absolutely could not have and that the United States was entirely against them.

"Now I know what happened to Truman yesterday," the prime minister noted after being shown the message from Groves. "When he got to the meeting after having read this report he was a changed man. He told the Russians (and the British, Churchill could have added) just where they got on and off and generally bossed the whole meeting."

Averell Harriman, the United States ambassador to the Soviet Union, confirmed Churchill's assessment. In a conversation with Stimson, he remarked that "the news from US" appeared to have cheered up the American delegation despite the annoying escalation of Soviet demands.

That evening Truman reviewed the day's events with his secretary of war, and assured him that despite Soviet demands he was standing firm. "He was apparently relying greatly upon the information as to S-1 [Stimson's code-name for the atomic bomb]," Stimson recorded. In fact, it appeared that the "program for S-1 is tying in what we are doing in all fields."

The effect of Groves's report was not limited to the president and his secretary of war. Several days later Secretary of State Byrnes explained to Special Ambassador Joseph E. Davies how important he considered America's atomic monopoly. Byrnes "was having a hard time with reparations," Davies wrote in his diary, but the "details as to the success of the atomic bomb, which he had just received, gave him confidence that the Soviets would agree as to these difficulties."

8

THE NEWS of the successful test at Alamogordo fundamentally altered how Truman evaluated the diplomatic and military cards he and Stalin held. Stimson had referred to the atomic bomb in his diary as a royal straight flush, and Truman was now playing that hand. He had come to the Potsdam Conference intent on persuading Stalin to send Soviet forces into the war against Japan. But the news from Alamogordo changed his mind. The bomb, as Stimson would reflect when he wrote about its impact at Potsdam, was a game changer; it was "the Great Equalizer," and it appeared to make Soviet assistance unnecessary, and therefore unwelcome.

Find out whether "[Gen. George C.] Marshall felt that we needed the Russians in the war or whether we [now] could get along without them," he instructed Stimson. Marshall's answer was unambiguous. With the atomic bomb a reality, Soviet assistance was no longer needed. But he was quick to add that if Stalin intended to enter the war for his own purposes, he could not be stopped.

The timing of the end of the war was now the critical issue. Could it be terminated before the Soviets were ready to attack Japan, claim Japanese territory, and gain a share of its postwar occupation? It was a scenario that Truman and Byrnes were determined to avoid, and they believed the bomb made that possible. In his conference diary, Walter Brown, Byrnes's press secretary, recorded that "the Secretary [Byrnes] was still hoping for time, believing after atomic bomb Japan will surrender and Russia will not get in so much on the kill."

9

ON AUGUST 2 Truman left the Potsdam Conference in a buoyant mood. Returning to the ship on which he had crossed the Atlantic to meet his predecessor's fabled war partners, Winston Churchill and Joseph Stalin, he was in high spirits. Two weeks earlier, on July 14, when the USS *Augusta* had docked at Antwerp, he had disembarked still the insecure stand-in for the most revered American president since Abraham Lincoln. Now, by contrast, as he was piped aboard an hour ahead of Britain's King George VI, who would soon arrive to pay his respects, the gangplank felt firmer, more his own, and the job he had inherited 113 days earlier, under a cloud of fear and skepticism, no longer intimidated him.

The Potsdam conference was Truman's Normandy; he had landed on the European continent and defeated the skeptics, the critics, and his own fears. At this final gathering of the Big Three Allies of World War II, he had been one of them, even first among equals, and he had made it clear over the course of those critical two weeks that he had taken President Roosevelt's place, permanently and unapologetically.

The successful test of the atomic bomb had played the major role in boosting Truman's confidence, and he looked forward to the military and diplomatic advantages he expected from its use against Japan.

———

The decision to use atomic bombs against Japanese cities was Truman's, and it was the decision that defined his early presidency. The American public applauded. It was a decision for victory. It had "saved a million American lives," the president (and Stimson) later insisted, and the nation eagerly embraced that view. "This is the greatest thing in history," he told the sailors aboard the *Augusta* on August 6 when he learned that Hiroshima had been destroyed.

Stalin's reaction was different.

7

"The Secret of the Atomic Bomb Might Be Hard to Keep"

Japan was about to surrender anyway, and the secret of the
atomic bomb might be hard to keep.
—STALIN TO AMBASSADOR HARRIMAN, AUGUST 8, 1945

Stalin returned from the Potsdam Conference anxious and angry.
"That noisy little shopkeeper" (his reference to Truman) had been
irritating and confrontational. The hardening of the American positions on a broad range of issues irked the Soviet leader, just as Soviet
demands for reparations from Germany had exasperated the Americans. The result was little progress at Potsdam on either postwar
political settlements or the economic assistance that the war-ravaged
Soviet Union so desperately needed.

Even more worrisome to Stalin was his impression that Truman
was preparing to challenge Soviet postwar ambitions, with force if
necessary. Three days after receiving General Groves's report, on July
24, the president had approached Stalin at the end of the afternoon
session to inform him about the existence of the atomic bomb. His
atomic energy advisory committee (Stimson's Interim Committee)
had urged the president to make such an approach, believing that
postwar cooperation with the Soviets would be damaged if Stalin
had no prior warning before the atomic bomb was used against Japan.

But the members of the Interim Committee had in mind a more
serious and complete presentation than the perfunctory conversation
that Truman initiated. Alone with Stalin and his interpreter, he said
he wanted to inform him that "We have a new weapon of unusual
destructive force." The remark was made in a manner so casual that
Stalin understood that further discussion was unwelcome.

1

MY COMPUTER'S dictionary defines a secret as "something that is kept *or meant to be kept* unknown or unseen by others." Secrets, this discerning definition suggests, are porous. They are "meant to be kept." But if the intended target discovers the secret, it also acquires the ability to manipulate its source. On July 24 Truman and his entourage fell into that trap.

The Manhattan Project was the United States government's most secret undertaking of World War II. It was not divulged to members of Congress, to the secretary of state, or even to Vice President Harry Truman. But it *was* monitored by the Soviet Union's security and military intelligence agencies, the NKVD and the GRU.

The first espionage reports about the atomic bomb program arrived in Moscow in 1941, before the Manhattan Project was organized. The information was provided by a highly placed British citizen, John Cairncross, who was spying for the Soviet Union. Stalin, always suspicious of misinformation plants, was skeptical. But caution, and the encouragement of a few "trusted" scientists (although, in truth, Stalin never trusted any scientist), led him to authorize an exploratory nuclear program. By the summer of 1945 it had produced little of significance, but it had succeeded in bringing together an experienced team of physicists, chemists, and engineers led by the nuclear physicist Igor Kurchatov.

2

IN HIS memoir Truman reports that on July 24 Stalin responded to his "new weapon" revelation with the comment: "I hope you make good use of it against the Japanese." But as the distinguished historian of Soviet nuclear history, David Holloway, discovered, all the nearest witnesses, including the interpreter, V. N. Pavlov, agree that Stalin merely nodded, and may or may not have said, "Thank you." Surprised by this dismissive reply, but relieved that he had not been asked for further details, Truman assumed that Stalin had missed the significance of what he had said.

But it was Truman who had misconstrued Stalin's cool response. Before leaving for Potsdam, Stalin had been briefed by the NKVD on the Manhattan Project's progress, and so he was more angered than surprised by Truman's vague revelation. "On returning to his Pots-dam villa," Marshal Georgy Zhukov recalled, Stalin told Vyacheslav M. Molotov what Truman had said. "They're raising the price," the Soviet foreign minister opined, to which Stalin replied: "Let them. We'll have to have a talk with [Igor] Kurchatov today about speeding up our work."

Having been well informed about the atomic bomb program long before Truman—he may even have learned about the success of the Alamogordo test before the president—his nonchalant response ini-tiated his strategy of "tenacity and steadfastness," a form of "reverse atomic diplomacy." To the end of his life, Stalin took every oppor-tunity to trivialize the significance of the United States' nuclear weapons.

Thirteen days later his suspicion that Truman intended to use the new weapon to intimidate him was confirmed.

3

NEWS OF the atomic bombing struck Stalin like a "thunderbolt," another leading historian of the Soviet Union, Vladislav Zubok, wrote. The fact that he should have expected it seems to have made little difference. It was not the bomb's development or even the news of its successful test that jolted him; it was the manner in which it was introduced: "on an essentially defeated enemy," in J. Robert Oppen-heimer's words. It was that fact that led Stalin to interpret Hiroshima as a calculated threat, "a gauntlet thrown down by Truman . . . that he had to respond to," Holloway concluded.

Whether the use of the atomic bomb was motivated in whole, in part, or not at all as a warning to Stalin, that is how he understood it. His first response was to advance the date of his army's entry into the war against Japan. As General Marshall had predicted, the Soviets would declare war on Japan if it served their purposes, and it clearly did. Stalin had planned to send his forces into Manchuria by August 11. But now any delay promised unwelcome consequences.

Weighing the cost of entering the war before Soviet forces were fully reinforced against what he knew about the weakened condition of the Japanese military, Stalin found the decision easy. He considered Japan defeated, and, moreover, he was confident that the Japanese army understood its hopeless situation.

4

FOR MORE than a month, Naotake Satō, Japan's ambassador to Moscow, had been trying to meet with Foreign Minister Molotov to propose territorial concessions to the Soviet Union in exchange for its assistance in arranging more favorable surrender terms than the United States was offering. "Unconditional surrender is the only obstacle to peace," Foreign Minister Shigenori Tōgō had wired Satō on July 13.

But Stalin had no interest in being a mediator; he intended to be a conqueror. He believed that Japan would have surrendered weeks earlier but for its government's deep antipathy to the American demand for "unconditional surrender." Fearful now that the atomic bombing might break Japan's will, he opted for war.

He acted quickly. Signing a new set of orders on the afternoon of August 7, he moved the date of his army's assault against Japanese forces in Manchuria to the early-morning hours of August 9.

5

"THE JAPANESE were at present looking for a pretext to replace the present government with one which would be qualified to undertake a surrender," Stalin told Ambassador Harriman on August 8. "The bomb might give them this pretext."

During that conversation in the Kremlin, which took place as Soviet troops were preparing to overrun Japan's Manchurian army, Stalin and Harriman frankly discussed the implications of the bombing of Hiroshima. Their exchange, reported in a dispatch by George F. Kennan, deputy chief of the U.S. Mission in Moscow, revealed how Soviets and Americans each viewed the significance of the new weapon. ("On the surface the conversation was quite straightforward," David Holloway observed. "But the subtext seems clear enough."):

> STALIN: "We have entered the war, in spite of your attempt to end it before we did so."

> HARRIMAN: "The atomic bomb will end the war; we have it, and
> it was very expensive to build; it will have a great impact on
> postwar international relations."
> STALIN: "Japan was about to surrender anyway, and the secret of
> the atomic bomb might be hard to keep."

Stalin may have found it difficult to repress a grin while making that pointed remark, given the atomic espionage his spies had gathered since 1941. But other points that he and Harriman exchanged are equally revealing, especially with reference to the central role that nuclear weapons would soon play in U.S.–Soviet relations.

First, it is certain that the Truman-Byrnes strategy of using the atomic bomb promptly—as Truman wrote in his personal diary, so "Japan will surrender and Russia will not get in so much on the kill"—was precisely how Stalin interpreted the atomic bombing of Hiroshima, and he said as much to Harriman. It was clear to him that this was not just another new weapon, but rather an entirely new factor in the U.S.–USSR relationship, all to the Soviet Union's disadvantage.

It also suggests that Harriman, an experienced diplomat, was instructed to make the point to Stalin that the bomb was indeed a game changer that favored the United States: "It will end the war. . . . We have it. . . . Very expensive to build. . . . It will have a great impact on postwar international relations," Kennan recorded Harriman saying to Stalin.

Each of those comments was a talking point intended to make it clear to Stalin—and to Molotov, who was also present—that America's atomic monopoly had reset the postwar balance of power in America's favor. Truman and Secretary of State Byrnes wanted Stalin to understand that "the greatest thing in history" had tilted the advantage toward the United States.

While nothing that Harriman said could have surprised Stalin, it surely disturbed him. "Stalin must have regretted now that more had not been done during the war to support the atomic project," Holloway surmised in his in-depth study, *Stalin and the Bomb*. Drawing a parallel between Stalin's refusal to prepare for Hitler's attack on the Soviet Union in 1941, and his failure to support more than a perfunctory Soviet atomic bomb project during the war, Holloway wrote: "Hiroshima was not as immediately threatening as the German attack, but its consequences for the Soviet Union were potentially dangerous."

6

"THE NEWS [of Hiroshima] had an acutely depressing effect on everybody," observed the Moscow correspondent for the British *Sunday Times* in an August article: "It was clearly realized that this was a New Fact in the world's power politics, that the bomb constituted a threat to Russia." Some even thought, Alexander Werth continued, "that Russia's desperately hard victory over Germany was now 'as good as wasted.'"

"Before the atom bomb was used . . . I was sure we could keep the peace with Russia," General Eisenhower (who was in Moscow) told a journalist. "Now, I don't know. . . . People are frightened and disturbed all over."

Andrei Sakharov's reaction to the news of Hiroshima reflected the general attitude of Soviet scientists. On August 7, when the physicist read Truman's Hiroshima announcement at a newspaper stand in Moscow, he was "so stunned that my legs practically gave way," he wrote in his memoirs. "There could be no doubt that my fate and the fate of many others, perhaps of the entire world, had changed overnight. Something new and awesome had entered our lives."

7

WHATEVER THE motivations for the second atomic bombing—on Nagasaki, August 9—it reinforced the message Stalin read into the Hiroshima attack, and added another. The United States was prepared to use its atomic weapons under any circumstances, even for revenge and punishment. There appeared to be no barriers, and so there was now no reason to believe that cities in the Soviet Union were off limits. "They are killing the Japanese and intimidating us," Stalin told his foreign minister.

In a matter of days Stalin began to transform a cautious scientific atomic energy research program into a frantic enterprise—designated Problem No. 1—committed to overtaking the American achievement. He told Kurchatov on August 18 to "provide us with atomic weapons in the shortest possible time. You know that Hiroshima has shaken the whole world. The balance has been destroyed. Provide the bomb—it will remove a great danger from us."

He soon put Lavrenty Beria—the efficient, ruthless, sadistic NKVD chief—in command of what quickly became a Soviet version of the Manhattan Project. Meeting with Kurchatov, the physicist who directed the Soviet atomic bomb program, Stalin told him to "carry out the work quickly, and in the crude basic manner." He did not want originality, the historian Sergey Radchenko explained, he wanted nuclear parity as fast as possible in order to avoid "Washington's blackmail."

From Stalin's point of view there was an important distinction between the Manhattan Project and the Soviet effort: Kurchatov was not engaged in a presumed race against an enemy for an atomic bomb; he was in a race for an atomic bomb against time, against the moment when the Soviet Union's erstwhile ally might consider unleashing atomic weapons on Moscow.

Espionage was the key to speed. "Take measures to organize acquisition of documentary materials on the atomic bomb! The technical process, drawings, calculations," read a secret message dated August 22 from military intelligence in Moscow to the head of a GRU spy ring in Canada.

The following day the consul at the Soviet Embassy in Tokyo was dispatched to Hiroshima to report on the extent of the damage. Within a week German scientists, captured months earlier by Soviet forces, were sent to institutes on the Black Sea to begin work on isotope separation. At about the same time a special commission was sent to Central Asia to investigate whether uranium-mining operations could be accelerated.

One of Beria's earliest initiatives was to organize slave-labor battalions to begin construction of the many facilities needed to produce a replica of the Manhattan Project. Stalin was kept apprised of everything, and all of the top Soviet leadership—Stalin, Beria, Molotov, Mikoyan, and Georgy Malenkov—read the Hiroshima-site reports sent to Moscow. They confirmed everyone's worst fears.

Regardless of the crippling cost and the sacrifices it would exact, Stalin designated the atomic bomb project his highest priority.

8

HIROSHIMA MAY also have affected Stalin's attempt to participate in the occupation of Japan. The Soviet assault into Manchuria had been successful, unexpectedly easy in fact: Japan's vaunted Kwantung Army had retreated before Soviet attacks and surrendered within ten days, on August 19. By September 2, when the formal surrender documents were signed aboard the USS *Missouri* in Tokyo Bay, Soviet forces had occupied northern China as far south as the Liaotung Peninsula, northern Korea, southern Sakhalin, and most of the Kurile Islands. But Stalin also wanted to occupy Hokkaido, Japan's northern island, and had proposed the idea to the Politburo [renamed the Presidium in 1952] as early as June. The success of the Manchurian operation had made this possible, and on August 16 he wrote to Truman explaining his intentions and his motives. The Japanese had occupied the Soviet Far East in 1918–22, and he wanted Truman to understand that it was a matter of pride for Soviet forces to accept the surrender of the Japanese army on the northern half of Hokkaido.

Truman refused, promptly and unambiguously: Japanese forces on the main islands would surrender only to the Americans.

Three days later a serious Soviet–U.S. clash was set in motion. On August 19, angered by Truman's rejection, Stalin sent orders to the Soviet Far Eastern Front forces to occupy northern Hokkaido as well as southern Sakhalin, and the southern Kurile Islands. Detailed plans for the invasion of Hokkaido followed.

But on August 22 Stalin had second thoughts and countermanded his orders: "To avoid the creation of conflicts and misunderstanding with respect to the allies, it is categorically forbidden," he wrote his Far East commander, "to send any ships or planes at all in the direction of the island of Hokkaido."

Stalin may have taken this action because he desperately needed postwar economic assistance from the United States. Or it may have been because he was increasingly troubled by what appeared, after the destruction of Nagasaki, to be an almost casual American attitude toward the use of the new weapon.

It is most probable that he took all his needs and concerns into account, and it is also probable that he was responding to what Harriman had been instructed to make clear:

The atomic bomb "will have a great impact on postwar international relations."

8

"Our Momentary Superiority"

The question then is how long we can afford to enjoy our momentary [atomic] superiority in the hope of achieving our immediate . . . objectives.
—HENRY L. STIMSON TO PRESIDENT TRUMAN, SEPTEMBER 12, 1945

Before the first nuclear device was tested on July 16, 1945, Manhattan Project scientists initiated a debate over the bomb's expected impact. Would its use compel an end to war, or would it precipitate an arms race that could destroy civilization? Would attacking a Japanese city promote the international control of atomic energy, or would it shatter cooperation with the Soviet Union? Would such an attack bring an end to the war against Japan? Would it curtail Stalin's plans for expansion in Europe and Asia? The answers the president accepted to those questions in 1945 influenced how nuclear weapons would be valued and used over the next seventeen years.

1

HARRY TRUMAN was fatefully dropped into the middle of that pre-Hiroshima debate, intellectually and emotionally unprepared to engage its details and consequences. As a result he often deferred to his more-experienced, better-informed, and often hawkish secretary of state, James F. Byrnes. Convinced that dropping atomic bombs on Japanese cities would constrain Stalin's territorial ambitions, Byrnes guided the new president into history as the progenitor of nuclear war.

By the end of August 1945, the clarity of war—the clear focus on achieving victory—transitioned to the fog of peace. In Washington and Moscow, London and Paris, Tokyo and Berlin, governments scrambled to figure out their next steps. Byrnes and Truman expected to intimidate Stalin with the atomic bombings of Hiroshima and Nagasaki. Stalin was determined to disappoint them. In London, Clement Attlee, who had replaced Churchill as prime minister in July, was searching for ways to keep Britain a major international power. In Paris, Charles de Gaulle was working to salvage whatever *grandeur* he could from the stigma of Vichy and the heroism of the Communist-dominated *Résistance*. Gen. Douglas MacArthur and Emperor Hirohito were beginning to form an occupation alliance in Tokyo, and in both East and West Germany, new leaders were searching for legitimacy.

2

IN THE five weeks between Japan's surrender on August 14 and the last cabinet meeting that Secretary of War Stimson attended on September 21, the debate that fixed the role of nuclear weapons in postwar diplomacy was resolved. Byrnes and Stimson were the protagonists, and Truman was the referee. Initially agreeing with Stimson that it was necessary to cooperate with Stalin on atomic energy issues, the president concluded the debate by supporting Byrnes. Though well known to historians of the Cold War, the debate's significance has been underappreciated, given its consequences.

Byrnes was an imposing presence in 1945. He had served in government since 1911, first as a congressman from South Carolina and later as a senator. In historian George Mowry's view, he was "the most influential Southern member of Congress between John Calhoun and Lyndon Johnson." In 1941 Roosevelt appointed Byrnes to the Supreme Court, but asked him to resign and head the Office of Economic Stabilization and the Office of War Mobilization after Pearl Harbor. Referred to as the "assistant president," he had expected to be chosen as Roosevelt's running mate in 1944, but the nod went to Truman. It is hardly surprising that the new president leaned heavily on Byrnes during the war's trying last months.

From the beginning of his tenure as the new president's foreign policy adviser, Byrnes believed that America's atomic monopoly would constrain Stalin's ambitions. He made that clear in a late-August conversation with Stimson's assistant, John McCloy, who reported to his boss that Byrnes "was quite radically opposed to any approach to Stalin whatever [about cooperating on the international control of atomic energy]." He wished, McCloy concluded, "to have the implied threat of the bomb in his pocket during the [foreign ministers'] conference" he was to attend in London on September 4.

Never one to duck an issue—and at this point in his seventy-eighth year, Stimson considered nothing more consequential than the atomic bomb's influence on Soviet-American relations—he requested an early interview with the president.

3

AT THREE o'clock on September 12 Stimson entered the Oval Office, took a seat across from Truman, and, in his intense, methodical manner, began a line-by-line review of the memorandum he had written for the occasion.

Beginning with an explanation of why his current view that cooperation with the Soviet Union on atomic energy was so different from the position he had taken at the Potsdam Conference, he read: "In handing you today my memorandum about our relations with Russia in respect to the atomic bomb, I am not unmindful of the fact that when in Potsdam I talked with you about the question whether we could be safe in sharing the atomic bomb with Russia while she was still a police state . . ."

He had concluded, he said, that it was not only safe but necessary to cooperate with the Soviet Union on atomic energy matters. Any attempt to use the bomb "as a direct lever to produce the [hoped-for democratic] change[s]" was certain to have the opposite effect: "I believe that this long process of change [toward democracy] in Russia is more likely to be expedited by the closer relationship in the matter of the atomic bomb which I suggest and the trust and confidence that

I believe would be inspired by the method of approach which I have outlined."

Stimson's memorandum argued for a policy adjustment. Echoing President Roosevelt's primary postwar goal—continuing a cooperative relationship with the Soviet Union—he urged the president to eschew Byrnes's strategy of atomic confrontation—having "the implied threat of the atomic bomb in his pocket"—and reinstate the late president's strategy of empathy. Using the bomb as a diplomatic stick, he believed, was certain to toughen Stalin's resistance to United States initiatives and, more seriously, "inspire them to . . . an all-out effort to [build their own atomic bombs]."

Hiroshima ensured that U.S.–Soviet relations were "virtually dominated by the problem of the atomic bomb," Stimson insisted, explaining that "relations may be perhaps irretrievably embittered by the way in which we approach the solution of the bomb with Russia. For if we fail to approach them now and merely continue to negotiate with them, having this weapon rather ostentatiously on our hip, their suspicions and their distrust of our purposes and motives will increase."

The consequences were obvious, at least to Stimson: "If the solution is achieved in that spirit, it is much less likely that we will ever get the kind of covenant we may desperately need in the future."

The bomb was a discovery without precedent. It was not merely a more lethal weapon, but "a first step in a new control by man over the forces of nature too revolutionary and dangerous to fit into the old concepts," Stimson said.

It was a threat to civilization for which the United States bore a very special responsibility. "If we feel, as I assume we must," he emphasized, "that civilization demands that someday we shall arrive at a satisfactory international arrangement respecting the control of this new force, the question then is how long we can afford to enjoy our momentary superiority in the hope of achieving our immediate peace council objectives."

4

THAT WAS the crux of the matter: taking advantage of "momentary superiority" versus seeking an international arrangement that would eliminate the bomb's threat to civilization. Would the administration design its atomic energy policies to achieve its short-range goals, as Byrnes wished, or would it strive for initiatives that might produce a future devoid of nuclear weapons?

"Whether Russia gets control of the necessary secrets of production in a minimum of say four years or a maximum of twenty years," Stimson maintained, "is not nearly as important to the world and civilization as to make sure that when they do get it they are willing and cooperative partners among the peace-loving nations of the world."

Arguing that the key to a collaborative agreement with the Soviet Union was to engage in direct negotiations, he declared that Stalin should be treated as the critical wartime partner he had been. "The Soviets would be more apt to respond sincerely to a direct and forthright approach than would be the case if the approach were made as a part of a general international scheme, or if the approach were made after a succession of express or implied threats."

In closing, Stimson returned to a point that he had made on April 25 when he first briefed Truman about the Manhattan Project: "Our leadership in the war and in the development of this weapon," he had emphasized, "has placed a certain moral responsibility upon us which we cannot shirk without very serious responsibility for any disaster to civilization which it would further."

The moment for exercising that "moral responsibility" was now, and how it would play out hinged on "our method of approach to the Russians."

Stimson left the Oval Office convinced that he had been successful. The president said "that he was in full accord with each statement that I made and that his view on the whole thing was in accord with me. He thought that we must take Russia into our confidence."

But the historical record suggests otherwise. It is more likely that Truman was being solicitous of his venerable (and fatigued) secretary of war, who was scheduled to retire in just nine days after five distinguished, stressful years overseeing the United States' victorious military forces.

5

SEPTEMBER 21 was Stimson's last day as secretary of war, and he considered it one of the most important of his tenure. The president had invited him to present his views on the atomic bomb's relationship to the future of U.S.–Soviet relations to the entire cabinet, and he was eager to take up the challenge. Speaking extemporaneously, he reiterated his two main points: "(1) that we should approach Russia at once with an opportunity to share on a proper quid pro quo the bomb; and (2) that this approach to Russia should be to her directly and not through the UNO [United Nations Organization], or any similar conference of a number of lesser states."

He had persuaded his audience, he believed: "There was a general discussion around the table at which the two or three who had started off with an emphatic secrecy proposal ultimately rather yielded to my views."

While it appeared that way to Stimson, when historians unearthed the reactions of Secretary of the Navy James Forrestal, Secretary of the Treasury Fred Vinson, and Secretary of Agriculture Clinton Anderson, it became clear that they (and others)—like Truman before them—were being respectful to their departing colleague. There was little support among the members of Truman's cabinet for neutralizing America's atomic advantage.

Stimson's call for moral responsibility and his warning against "enjoy[ing] our momentary superiority" failed to garner support. Even with Byrnes in London at the foreign ministers meeting, his view held sway. If an atomic monopoly assured superiority, the majority of Truman's advisers favored monopoly.

It is difficult to avoid the conclusion that President Truman and his cabinet were convinced that the atomic bomb was the key to containing Stalin's territorial ambitions. But Stalin was not cowed, and the confrontation between the erstwhile Allies evolved into a Cold War stalemate. The bomb had not yet altered the conduct of international relations, but it provided Truman and his administration the confidence that they could aggressively pursue their postwar ambitions.

6

IN THE remaining six years of Truman's tenure the deteriorating U.S.–Soviet relationship methodically integrated nuclear weapons into American military and foreign policy, a process that cast the character of Cold War diplomacy. The threat of atomic warfare became increasingly present in U.S. dealings with the Soviet Union and, within less than a decade, in the Soviet Union's dealings with the United States.

The process was gradual. Driven by the basic elements of the Stimson-Byrnes debate, it persisted until June 25, 1950, when the Korean War removed what little ambiguity remained. There were two opposing views. The first was the desire to prevent a nuclear arms race through negotiations for some form of international control of atomic energy. The second was the belief that it was necessary to rely on a superior American nuclear arsenal to counter Soviet aggression.

The wartime director of the Los Alamos nuclear weapons laboratory, the physicist J. Robert Oppenheimer, was the primary intellectual spokesman for international control negotiations. The intellectual leader of the atomic-arms-for-security faction was Paul Nitze, who in 1949 succeeded George F. Kennan (the author of "Containment" and an Oppenheimer ally) as the director of the State Department's Policy Planning Staff.

Oppenheimer was both the "father of the atomic bomb" and the sire of the original plan for the international control of atomic energy, the misnamed Acheson-Lilienthal Report. Developed over six weeks of intensive discussion in the winter of 1946, the report proposed (among other ideas) an inspection regime and an international atomic development authority to control the nuclear supply chain from uranium mining to the operation of all nuclear facilities capable of producing weapons.

The first and most comprehensive arms control initiative, it was transformed—with President Truman's consent—by Bernard Baruch, his ambassador to the UN Atomic Energy Commission. Baruch designed a treaty that guaranteed the U.S. atomic monopoly until the United States was satisfied that all elements of the agreement were fulfilled. As Oppenheimer and Acheson predicted, the Soviets rejected the proposal, assuring a nuclear arms race.

It occurred sooner than expected. On August 29, 1949—four years and twenty-three days after a B-29 (the *Enola Gay*) released an atomic bomb over Hiroshima—the Soviet Union successfully tested a nuclear weapon. The radioactive fallout that revealed the secret Soviet test ignited a furious debate in the United States. Was the appropriate response a crash program to build fusion (hydrogen) bombs, weapons with unlimited explosive power?

It was necessary to achieve "a quantum leap" ahead of the USSR, a major supporter of the "superbomb" argued, and President Truman agreed. Meeting on January 31, 1950, with the secretaries of state and defense, and the chairman of the Atomic Energy Commission (AEC), he set aside the moral objections of the AEC's General Advisory Committee—"its use carries much further than the atomic bomb itself the policy of exterminating civilian populations"—and approved the hydrogen bomb initiative during a meeting he cut short to seven minutes. The decision was necessary, he insisted, *"if only for bargaining purposes with the Russians,"* even if he had no intention of authorizing the weapon's military use.

Truman's rationale was as momentous as his decision to support the hydrogen bomb program. Accumulating weapons for "bargaining purposes" established an escalation logic that had no military limit. Arguments that a particular number of nuclear weapons were a sufficient deterrent held little sway compared with the diplomatic bargaining value of more and better weapons. The AEC promptly became, its chairman later wrote, "nothing more than a major contractor" for the Pentagon.

Within months Paul Nitze added a strategic rationale to Truman's diplomatic strategy. Convinced that the U.S. military was unprepared to deal with a nuclear-armed Soviet adversary, he organized the creation of the seminal strategic doctrine of the Cold War: "United States Objectives and Programs for National Security." NSC 68 (National Security Council 68) asserted that the Soviet Union was "animated by a new fanatic faith" and intended "to impose its absolute authority over the rest of the world." It was necessary, Nitze's document argued, to begin a massive buildup of both conventional and nuclear arms.

By the end of the year (1950) the buildup was under way, and atomic weapons were an integral part of U.S. military strategy. The U.S. arsenal contained almost three hundred various types of atomic weapons to be "utilize[d] promptly and effectively." In the event of war, the Strategic Air Command (SAC) was prepared to deliver devastating nuclear strikes against the Soviet Union. SAC's commander, Gen. Curtis LeMay, promoted a plan to deliver "the entire stockpile of atomic bombs in a single massive attack," one hundred and thirty-three nuclear weapons on seventy Soviet cities.

George Kennan considered the decision to rely on nuclear weapons a national disaster: "I fear that the atomic bomb, with its vague and highly dangerous promise of 'decisive' results," he wrote in an eighty-page memorandum, "will impede understanding of the things that are important to a clear policy and will carry us toward the misuse and dissipation of our national strength."

Even before NSC 68, President Truman had not been shy about flaunting nuclear weapons during crises if he thought doing so would persuade the Soviet Union to retreat. He had hinted at "atomic diplomacy" in March 1946 when Stalin delayed withdrawing his troops from northern Iran. In 1948, during the Berlin blockade, he deployed B-29 bombers (allegedly nuclear capable but actually not) to England. And during the Korean War, the president once again sent B-29s— this time to Guam—to signal U.S. resolve.

Asked at a press conference in November 1950, after the Chinese had crossed the Yalu River on November 25 in support of the retreating North Koreans, whether U.S. resistance "will include the atomic bomb," Truman replied: "That includes every weapon that we have."

But despite approving the stockpiles and strategic plans, Truman resisted the military's importuning to loosen presidential authority over nuclear weapons development and—from the air force point of view—severely limited the nuclear arsenal's expansion. Furthermore, he declined to release control of nuclear weapons to the military, remarking: "I don't think we ought to use this thing unless we have to. . . . You have got to understand that this is not a military weapon. It is used to wipe out women, children and unarmed people."

Truman's public remarks reflected his ambivalent attitude toward nuclear weapons, which he confirmed in private counsel. He had used them in war and was committed to maintaining nuclear superiority over the Soviet Union, but he resisted the temptation to exploit their potential fully. He generally emphasized how much nuclear weapons threatened humanity, rather than how well they supported U.S. military and diplomatic policies. "It is a terrible weapon, and it should not be used on innocent men, women, and children," he quickly added to his remarks at his November 30 Korean War press conference. And, five months later, in April 1951, after Gen. Douglas MacArthur brazenly called for the use of nuclear weapons against Chinese targets, Truman fired him.

In his farewell address the president made a point of warning Congress (as Stimson had warned him in April 1945) against "being hurried forward, in our mastery of the atom . . . toward yet unforeseeable peaks of destructive power [when mankind could] destroy the very structure of a civilization . . . such a war is not a possible policy for rational men."

PART TWO

Eisenhower, Khrushchev, Castro, and the "Weapon of Mass Destruction"

The weapon of mass destruction is a sterile and hopeless weapon which may for a time serve as an answer of sorts to itself and as an uncertain sort of shield against utter cataclysm, but which cannot in any way serve the purposes of a constructive and hopeful foreign policy.
—GEORGE F. KENNAN, 1958

9

"We Face a Battle to Extinction"

Russia is definitely out to communize the world. . . .
we face a battle to extinction between the two systems.
—DWIGHT D. EISENHOWER DIARY, 1946

On January 20, 1953, Dwight David Eisenhower was sworn into office as the thirty-fourth president of the United States. He had been the supreme commander of Allied forces in Europe during World War II and, most recently, had served simultaneously as president of Columbia University (on leave) and supreme commander of NATO. He had campaigned as a Republican against Korea, Communism, and corruption, with the campaign slogan "K1C2." Promising to end the war in Korea, to keep America safe from Communism, to end corruption in government, and to secure national prosperity, he had trounced his Democratic opponent, the former governor of Illinois, Adlai Stevenson.

Eisenhower entered the White House determined to avoid the blunders he attributed to his predecessor. Truman had "lost China," mismanaged the Korean War, and been unable to dislodge Communist governments in Eastern Europe because he had failed to go on the offense. His foreign policy had been reactive, and while some of his responses to Communist advances—the Marshall Plan and the Berlin airlift, for example—had been successful, he had more often than not left the initiative to the Soviets and their Communist allies.

Combating the influence of Communism at home and abroad was the campaign's theme. "If we had been less trusting. If we had been less soft and weak, there would probably have been no war in Korea!" Ike told a campaign audience. His running mate, Richard

Nixon (anticipating the alliterations of his future vice president Spiro Agnew), accused Stevenson of earning a "Ph.D. from Dean Acheson's cowardly college of Communist containment."

President Eisenhower intended to reverse Truman's errors by initiating a foreign policy sea change. His first priority was to develop an aggressive, coherent anti-Communist program. The military strategies he oversaw during World War II would return to center stage, with nuclear weapons playing the preeminent role. He had believed in overwhelming force in war, and as president he wanted compelling power in peace. The clearest path to acquiring that power was to promote the primacy of America's nuclear arsenal. "It was not until Eisenhower's presidency," the historian Andrew Erdmann concluded, "that American nuclear strategy and foreign policy were truly integrated at a high policy level."

1

IN 1953 Eisenhower was confident in his abilities, and his luck. Raised in Abilene, Kansas, in a large religious family with meager resources, he had led an all-American life. A natural athlete with ingratiating social skills, this son of a railroad mechanic grew into a small-town hero. He boxed, played football and baseball, hunted and fished, and succeeded in school. Two years after graduating from Abilene High School he was accepted into West Point. There he played football and poker and graduated in the middle of the storied class of 1915, "the class the stars fell on." He claimed baseball as his favorite outdoor sport, but indoors it was poker, which he learned to play strategically as a very young boy. "At West Point and during his career between the wars, Ike augmented his salary by playing poker," Matthew Holland noted in *Eisenhower Between the Wars*. He was a "regular winner."

Successful poker players like Eisenhower are meticulous strategists who also believe that they are smart *and* lucky, a personality trait that encourages high-stakes gambles. On June 6, 1944, Eisenhower took the greatest gamble of World War II: After careful planning he sanctioned the invasion of Normandy despite the threat of treacherous weather. With that decision he risked the lives of tens of thousands of men, his career, and perhaps the fate of the Allied war effort—and he won.

He emerged from the war a modern George Washington: a revered general, beloved and trusted.

Despite his lack of academic qualifications or any knowledge of civilian higher education, in 1948 the trustees of Columbia University appointed him their thirteenth president. It was a job ill-suited to his temperament and experience, but that didn't matter. The provost, the deans, and an array of academic administrators made things happen the way they needed to happen, whether Ike was present or not—and he often was not present.

In December 1950 he took a leave of absence from the university—retaining his position as president—to become the first supreme commander of the North Atlantic Treaty Organization (NATO). Retiring two years later from active duty (again) to seek the Republican presidential nomination, he continued as president of Columbia throughout his campaign. It was his only civilian job prior to his election, and the experience stayed with him. He had learned that in civilian life, as in the military, delegating responsibilities could get the job done.

Americans felt lucky to have Ike as their leader. In place of the hapless Harry Truman, who had steered the country into an Asian quagmire, and whose approval ratings in 1952 were 22 percent—the lowest of any president's to date—the nation now had a *real* leader, a war hero, a man of decision. They expected Ike to cow the Chinese Communists and end the agonizing stalemate in Korea.

Eisenhower's World War II experience had taught him to pursue an offensive strategy, with overwhelming military superiority, that would keep the enemy in doubt. Truman's "passivity" had to be replaced with a confrontational policy that injected insecurity into Soviet calculations. Forcing the Kremlin's leaders to worry about how the United States might respond to aggression would instill uncertainty, and uncertainty would induce caution.

In close collaboration with his secretary of state, John Foster Dulles, and John Foster's younger brother, Allen Dulles, the director of the Central Intelligence Agency (CIA), Eisenhower prepared a radical dual-track foreign policy. John Foster was the public face of track one, the administration's political policies. Allen, at the CIA, managed the second track, covert operations.

2

EISENHOWER HAD genuine misgivings about nuclear weapons. He had opposed the atomic bombings of Hiroshima and Nagasaki "on the basis of my belief," he wrote in his 1948 World War II memoir, "that Japan was already defeated . . . and secondly because I thought that our country should avoid shocking world opinion by the use of a weapon whose employment was, I thought, no longer mandatory as a measure to save American lives." It was a critique he repeated fifteen years later: "I was against it [the atomic bombings] on two counts. First, the Japanese were ready to surrender, and it wasn't necessary to hit them with that awful thing. Second, I hated to see our country be the first to use such a weapon."

But that mistaken decision had occurred in 1945, when Ike was a general who had won his war. Now, seven years later, he was the newly elected president of the United States facing a determined enemy, a corrosive conflict, and a mounting national debt. It was a Normandy moment. To deal with it, Eisenhower bet on a "silver bullet," the recently developed hydrogen bomb: a weapon of heretofore unimagined force that, when triggered, emulates the sun's fusion reaction.

His administration's "New Look," announced by Secretary of State Dulles in a speech to the Council on Foreign Relations (CFR), proclaimed that nuclear weapons were America's first line of defense. With that gamble, he transformed the structure and nature of international relations, perhaps forever.

It was, as Ike intended, a radical shift from Truman's nuclear weapons policies.

3

EISENHOWER RECOGNIZED that nuclear war was irrational, but as he succeeded Truman, he seized on nuclear weapons as the most cost-effective and efficient means of reinforcing American objectives. Tactical (smaller) atomic weapons, he suggested, could enhance U.S. diplomacy by creating a "nuclear tripwire" that shifted the responsibility of initiating a full-scale nuclear war to the Soviets. Would this policy shift inject uncertainty and caution into Soviet decision making? It was a gamble.

Ike, like General MacArthur, was also willing to gamble that the use of atomic weapons in Korea would be advantageous, although he did not publicize the idea. Like President Truman, in public speeches President Eisenhower discussed the dangers that nuclear weapons posed rather than their strategic advantages. But those advantages were real, and unlike his predecessor, in the privacy of White House conferences, he was often the foremost champion of actually using nuclear arms.

When discussing nuclear issues, the president (publicly) and the former general (privately) advocated diametrically different views.

On March 31, 1953, at a special meeting of the National Security Council, Eisenhower assessed the pros and cons of using nuclear weapons in Korea. "The President," the minutes of the meeting record, "raised the question of the use of atomic weapons in the Korean War. Admittedly, he said, there were not many good tactical targets, but he felt it would be worth the cost if, through use of atomic weapons, we could (1) achieve a substantial victory over the Communist forces and (2) get to a line at the waist of Korea [presumably the thirty-eighth parallel]."

The problem was political. America's citizens and allies feared atomic war. "Nevertheless," the minutes of the meeting continue, "the President and Secretary Dulles were in complete agreement that somehow or other the taboo which surrounds the use of atomic weapons would have to be destroyed."

Five weeks later, at another NSC meeting dealing with Korea—shortly after his famous "Chance for Peace," speech, in which he declared: "Every gun that is made, every warship launched . . . signifies, in the final sense, a theft from those who hunger and are not fed . . . Under the cloud of threatening [nuclear] war, it is humanity hanging from a cross of iron"—Eisenhower confirmed his determination to normalize atomic weapons.

Responding to a report from Gen. Omar Bradley, chairman of the Joint Chiefs of Staff, of Chinese Communist activity at several North Korean air bases, the President inquired whether these airfields might not prove a target which would test the effectiveness of the atomic bomb. Bradley doubted their "usefulness," to which Eisenhower responded that "he had reached the point of being convinced that *we have got to consider the atomic bomb as simply another weapon in our arsenal.*"

That had *not* been Truman's policy. He had assigned atomic weapons to a supporting role—a strategy, Eisenhower believed, that handicapped their potential military and diplomatic value. The key to success, in the former general's view, was to move America's nuclear arsenal to the fore. The U.S. nuclear monopoly had ended in August 1949, but it could still exploit its quantitative lead.

Eisenhower's initiative—promotionally dubbed the New Look— was formally promulgated in the top-secret National Security Council document, 162/2, which he signed on October 30, 1953. Designed "to meet the Soviet threat . . . [and] to avoid seriously weakening the U.S. economy," it decreed a new role for nuclear weapons.

Developed over many months by select committees that the president closely monitored, it called for "the effective use of U.S. strategic air power against the USSR" and the establishment of overseas bases as "essential to the conduct of the military operations on the Eurasian continent in case of general war." It mandated "a strong military posture, with emphasis on the capability of inflicting massive retaliatory damage by offensive [nuclear] striking power."

His New Look, Eisenhower insisted, was a "reaffirmation and clarification" of the strategy for the defense of Western Europe that he had developed as NATO's commander (December 1950—May 1952). But the "clarification" emphasized a radical shift to reliance on nuclear weapons, a departure that clearly distinguished it from earlier strategies.

"Eisenhower personally intervened in the final discussions of 1953 to insure [*sic*] that [the Strategic Air Command's nuclear bombers] should be recognized not as '*a* major deterrent' to Soviet aggression, but as '*the* major deterrent,'" McGeorge Bundy wrote in his history of the first fifty years of the nuclear arms race.

The military's strategic mission was delivered, almost in its entirety, to the SAC, tasked to quickly annihilate Soviet forces, industrial areas, cities, and their populations. We should "put all our resources into our SAC capability and into hydrogen bombs," the

president told the NSC as late as 1957. It was his "opinion that . . .
our main reliance, though not our sole reliance, should be on nuclear
weapons."

At the core of NSC 162/2 was the revolutionary strategic
posture—a significant extension of NSC 68—that the United States
"will consider nuclear weapons as available for use as other munitions."

4

SPEECH, ESPECIALLY when it represents the president's views, matters. And so it is hard to exaggerate the impact on the conduct of the
Cold War—or on world history—of this radical shift in how U.S.
nuclear weapons policy was promoted. It removed all ambiguity about
the role of America's weaponized atom in the next four decades of
Soviet-American relations. It tethered traditional diplomacy to politically charged quantitative and qualitative comparisons of American
and Soviet stockpiles. And it convinced the Soviet leadership that it
could only negotiate with the United States as an equal when it could
match American nuclear threats with nuclear threats of its own.

Massive retaliation was in the first instance a military strategy,
but it also was a public relations initiative directed at domestic and
foreign audiences. On the one hand it was meant to reassure the
American public. But its primary purpose was to frighten the new
Soviet leaders and stymie their ambitions. Its principal result, however, was to establish a blueprint for Nikita Khrushchev to create his
own "nuclear brinkmanship."

Returning in July 1955 from the Geneva Summit Conference,
where he discussed the consequences of thermonuclear war with
Western leaders, Khrushchev was convinced that his intimation of
massive retaliation had assured Soviet security. "Our enemies probably feared us [now] as much as we feared them," he concluded from
his conversations with Eisenhower and Britain's prime minister,
Anthony Eden: "They now knew [because of our nuclear weapons]
that they had to deal with us honestly and fairly, that they had to
respect our borders and our rights, and they couldn't get what they
wanted by force or by blackmail."

———

Without ever mentioning nuclear weapons—but leaving no doubt that he was referring to them—on January 12, 1954, Dulles unveiled the administration's new doctrine. It was the most notable speech of his career, but it had been largely written by Eisenhower, "and all of it had been approved by him." The United States, Dulles explained to his Council on Foreign Relations audience, would thereafter protect its allies and oppose any Soviet aggression with a "deterrent of massive retaliatory power." This application of overwhelming force, "at a time and place of our own choosing," would provide "maximum protection at a bearable cost."

Thenceforth nuclear weapons were no longer an element of American military power; they were its *primary* instrument. The policy, Dulles explained, was a response to a diabolical Soviet master plan to "bankrupt" the American economy. The Kremlin's intention was to create crises that forced the United States to deploy vast numbers of expensive conventional forces to Europe and Asia.

It was a brilliantly constructed public relations rationale; a perfect political fit for a fiscally conservative president and an anxious, cost-conscious public. Promising a simple way to keep Communism at bay while (allegedly) saving taxpayer dollars, it made the case for nuclear weapons without arcane discussions of strategy. "They [the Soviet government]" were planning to "nibble us to death all over the world in little wars," Vice President Richard Nixon told the *New York Times* two months later. The United States therefore "would rely in the future primarily on our massive mobile retaliatory [nuclear] power."

In the shadow of the Great Depression, World War II, and the Korean War, the public was persuaded that their general-president understood how to keep them both safe and solvent.

5

DULLES'S SPEECH—the public expression of NSC 162/2—was a transformative declaration heard around the world, but nowhere more clearly than in Moscow. Formulated in the spring and summer of 1953 during the seven months that followed Stalin's death on March 5, Eisenhower's New Look was created just as the old Soviet order disappeared. Stalin had died of a stroke less than two months after Ike's inauguration, and the Kremlin's senior leadership was scrambling to form a successor government.

There were no plans for transition and no precedent for succession. There was confusion, infighting, and, especially after Dulles's "Massive Retaliation" speech, a serious concern that the United States intended to take advantage of the political turmoil. "In the months following Stalin's death," Khrushchev remembered, "we believed that America would invade the Soviet Union and we would go to war."

In fact, Stalin's death offered the best opportunity since 1945 to explore the possibility of easing tensions, but the president and Dulles "pretty much rejected détente," the distinguished Cold War historian Melvyn Leffler concluded. No member of the administration, or any member of the three study groups writing NSC 162/2, was assigned to consider how Soviet-American relations might be improved.

Despite Stalin's death, the administration's view was unwavering: "There is no evidence that the Soviet leadership is prepared to modify its basic attitudes and accept any permanent settlement with the United States," the National Security Council's policy makers asserted, without expending a serious effort to explore that assumption.

Why was such an obvious opportunity ignored? One possible explanation is that the President and his secretary of state had developed a nuclear idée fixe. Persuaded that their plans for an aggressive nuclear doctrine would stymie Soviet ambitions, they did not seek a détente with the Kremlin's new leaders. Such an initiative was a distraction that would have required a new set of assumptions that had no representation within the administration.

Stalin's death was not seen as an opportunity to relax tensions; rather it was welcomed as a fortuitous event that reinforced expectations that the New Look would produce the desired results. "The risk of Soviet aggression will be minimized by maintaining a strong security posture," they wrote, "based on massive atomic capability."

Eisenhower and Dulles's nuclear obsession was reinforced by another shared view: That "damnable philosophy," Communism, was immutable.

In the administration's lexicon, Soviet Communism was Stalinism, and Stalinism was Communism; it was irrelevant whether Stalin was alive or dead. "Russia is definitely out to communize the world . . . [and] we face a battle to extinction between the two systems," Eisenhower had written in his diary in 1946. "This is a war of light against darkness, freedom against slavery, Godliness against atheism."

The threat of Communism had to be eliminated. American morality had to prevail. "If you are imposing a moral program in this world," Eisenhower said, "you have to stand behind it with strength." For Ike the crusader, nuclear weapons provided that strength.

The "battle" might even require eliminating the Soviet menace. An arms race could lead to a garrison state, Ike wrote to John Foster Dulles. It might force the United States "to consider whether or not our duty to future generations did not *require* us to initiate war at the most propitious moment we could designate."

In the ensuing years Eisenhower had found no reason to change his view, but unlike his less-disciplined friend, Gen. George Patton, he was skilled at keeping his controversial political opinions from the public. Occasionally, however, he allowed them to slip out in confidential exchanges. "To accept the Communist doctrine and try to live with it," he told Greece's Queen Frederika in 1958, would cost "too big a price to be alive." He would "rather be atomized than communized," he claimed in a conversation with the British ambassador.

Stalin's death could not alter the struggle to the death between the United States and the Soviet Union . . . but the New Look could. When Dulles announced that doctrine the United States possessed about twelve hundred nuclear weapons. Eight years later, in 1961, when Eisenhower warned in his farewell address to the nation "against the acquisition of unwarranted influence . . . by the military-industrial complex," he knew whereof he spoke. He had encouraged, approved, and overseen a colossal expansion of the Pentagon's control over nuclear weapons, and a nuclear arsenal that now exceeded twenty thousand weapons. It was an "insane accumulation," noted the journalist-historian James Carroll, that "cast the [nuclear] arsenal in its iron mountain of permanence."

10

"An Extraordinary Departure"

What made Khrushchev remarkable was that he chose to
change. His strategy of peaceful coexistence with
the West . . . was an extraordinary departure and a real risk.
—LLEWELLYN THOMPSON, U.S. AMBASSADOR TO USSR,
1957–1962

On the other side of the Iron Curtain, beginning in February 1956,
Khrushchev set about reforming the Soviet Union. In the last days
of the Twentieth Congress of the Communist Party, he announced a
new look of his own that transformed the domestic and international
behavior of the Soviet government.

1

IN 1956, having outmaneuvered his competitors—Georgy Malenkov, Vyacheslav Molotov, and Lavrenty Beria—for the leadership of
the Party, Khrushchev set about promoting a series of domestic and
international reforms. To achieve his goal, he concluded that it was
necessary to destroy Stalinism and Stalin's legacy.

It was a revealing decision; a big idea that would solve an intrac-
table problem (not unlike his decision to secretly ship ballistic missiles to Cuba). It required courage, imagination, and planning.
Khrushchev was long on the first two but, characteristically (as with
his missiles-to-Cuba ploy), he skimped on planning. Aware that a
full-throated denunciation of Stalin would infuriate many senior
Presidium members, he nevertheless composed a four-hour, 26,000-
word speech designed to thoroughly revise Stalin's reputation.

Speaking at a secret session limited to selected delegates, he declared—in the two most important and dramatic speeches in Soviet Cold War history—an end to Stalinist-era policies.

Khrushchev's most dramatic (and dangerous) presentation—"The Cult of Personality and Its Consequences"—condemned Stalin's arbitrary rule and his murderous purges. "It was the bravest and most reckless thing he ever did," his biographer William Taubman wrote. "The Soviet regime never fully recovered, and neither did he." It led to demands for reform throughout Eastern Europe—in Poland and Hungary especially—and to an attempt by committed Stalinists to replace him.

In addition to his assault on Stalin's legacy (soon referred to as Stalin's "Second Funeral"), Khrushchev condemned Stalin's doctrine of inevitable war as an irrational idea in the nuclear age. "The willfulness of Stalin showed itself not only in decisions concerning the internal life of the country," Khrushchev declared, "but also in the international relations of the Soviet Union." The destructive power of nuclear weapons—especially the hydrogen bomb—made war with the West unthinkable. he proclaimed. The struggle against capitalism would continue, but in an atmosphere of peaceful coexistence.

Khrushchev's Twentieth Party Congress speeches were his political declaration of independence. But even more significant (for our purposes), his speech declaring "peaceful coexistence" was also a signal that the Soviet Union's leader recognized—and was willing to declare—that war in the nuclear age was a suicidal venture.

"What made Khrushchev remarkable was that he chose to change," the U.S. ambassador to the Soviet Union, Llewellyn Thompson, observed. "His strategy of 'peaceful coexistence' with the West . . . was an extraordinary departure fraught with risk." The fact that it was presented in secret to a select Soviet audience confirmed its authenticity. It was not propaganda but rather a declaration of intent.

"Khrushchev wanted the Soviet Union to be taken seriously as a global superpower, and he wanted to be recognized as a leader of historical significance," notes the historian of Soviet culture, Rósa Magnúsdóttir: "He played the role of the peacemaker, ready to reconcile with the United States and to serve as a proverbial middleman between the socialist and anti-Soviet bloc." Along with his reactive nuclear bluster, he "emphasized soft power . . . and personal exchanges with Western countries."

No initiative by any head of government, before or since, had been as radical, as noteworthy, and as underappreciated by an American administration for its transformative significance. Passed to the CIA by Israeli intelligence, which had procured a copy of Khrushchev's speeches in April, they were initially dismissed by DCI director Allen Dulles with the speculation that Khrushchev was probably drunk, and had delivered them extemporaneously and spontaneously.

A remarkably ignorant judgment, it revealed the shallowness of Dulles's curiosity, his disdain for analytical intelligence, and the rigidity of his views about the Soviet Union.

2

FOLLOWING THE publication of his peaceful coexistence declaration, Khrushchev felt pressured to demonstrate that he had not pandered to the West. His most consequential effort to make that clear occurred two weeks after the Soviet invasion of Hungary, on November 18, 1956, at the Polish Embassy in Moscow: "If you don't like us, don't accept our invitations, and don't invite us to come to see you. Whether you like it or not, history is on our side. *We will bury you,*" he told a dozen NATO ambassadors, who promptly walked out.

It was a harsh undiplomatic pronouncement that had serious unintended consequences. Widely reported, it was repeatedly denounced and used to "prove" Khrushchev's hostile intentions. When he visited the United States in 1959, it dogged many of his stops. Two years later a more secure Khrushchev displayed a different attitude. In an attempt to melt increasingly icy relations, he approved a cultural initiative—an international Tchaikovsky Piano Competition—to be held in Moscow in April 1958.

Given the Soviet Union's prodigious musical talents, their triumph was expected. But a lanky twenty-three-year-old Texan named Van Cliburn overwhelmed the judges and the audience with his stunning renditions of Tchaikovsky's First Piano Concerto and Rachmaninoff's Third Piano Concerto. He brought the Soviet audience to its feet applauding for eight long minutes. But was it possible to present the gold medal to an American?

"Is he the best?" Khrushchev responded when Dmitri Shostakovich, the chairman of the competition, telephoned him.

"Yes."

"Then give him the prize," Khrushchev replied, and arrived at the award ceremony to embrace America's Cold War–pianist hero.

The only musician to be showered with ticker tape in a New York parade, Van Cliburn was celebrated by *Time* as "The Texan Who Conquered Russia."

3

As THESE seemingly minor events suggest, the American-Soviet Cold War combined hostility with compromise, a mélange of contradictory policies driven by geopolitics and diplomacy, ideology and paranoia. It existed on two levels—a Cold War of the map (the geopolitical struggle for allies, land, and markets) and a Cold War of the mind (the ideological conflict between capitalism and Communism)—and the threat of nuclear war intensified both.

While each nation's nuclear arsenal posed an existential threat to the other, their governments remained in constant communication and negotiation. While segments of each nation's citizens were sympathetic to the other, the intense ideological differences—and the angst that their expanding nuclear arsenals produced—created irrational reactions from otherwise rational actors. "General war is unthinkable," President Eisenhower wrote several weeks after Sputnik, "yet you rightly say that we must be ready to make an exception to this when our priceless values are directly threatened."

Convinced that nuclear weapons were the best way to protect those values, Eisenhower rejected all proffered alternatives. When Gen. Matthew Ridgway—army chief of staff, creator of the Eighty-Second Airborne Division during World War II, and leader of the counteroffensive against the Chinese intervention in the Korean War—objected to the New Look, Eisenhower fired him. His replacement, Gen. Maxwell Taylor, wartime commander of the 101st Airborne Division, was forced to swear his allegiance to the policy: "Loyalty in spirit as well as in letter is necessary," he was told.

But Taylor's disdain for massive retaliation—"another expression for the principle of first strike," George Kennan had famously declared—led him to renege. The next war was likely to be limited, he insisted, and a policy of flexible response made more sense than a commitment to creating a potential nuclear holocaust.

On this point Eisenhower was "inflexible," his biographer Geoffrey Perret concluded, quoting the president as saying: "Anything of Korean proportions would be one for the use of atomics." If war breaks out, the president told Taylor, during one of their debates over the role of the Strategic Air Command, the war plans call for winning it with air power. The army's role will be "keeping order inside the United States. The Army will be the stabilizing thing after the big war, the force that pulls the nation together again."

4

It was not an idle comment. Relying on "atomics" was Eisenhower's strategy. During his first presidential term massive retaliation was his announced response to a Soviet incursion into Western Europe. And during his second term, tactical nuclear weapons became the *un*announced reaction to the possibility of a North Korean assault against the South.

Maintaining the security of South Korea—the Republic of Korea (ROK)—was a serious commitment, but by 1956 Eisenhower considered it too expensive. Replacing fifty thousand American troops with tactical nuclear weapons would be a double saving. The nuclear weapons proposed for the ROK were "free." The atomic cannons and Honest John atomic rockets were obsolete, unsuitable for NATO forces. South Korea, notes an analysis in the *Asia-Pacific Journal*, was the "only place in the world where the U.S. could secretly deploy soon to be scrapped nuclear weapons that could target the Soviet Union."

A clever plan stymied by a legal impediment.

Introducing any new type of weapon onto the Korean Peninsula was illegal. Section 13(d) of the Korean Armistice Agreement forbade "the introduction into Korea [North and South] of reinforcing military equipment, except for the replacement on the basis of piece-for-piece (of equipment destroyed, damaged or worn out) of the same effectiveness and the same type."

A Neutral Nations Supervisory Commission (NNSC)—the eyes and ears of the "non-introduction" clause—was an additional obstacle. Composed of military representatives from Sweden and Switzerland as well as Poland and Czechoslovakia, the commission made it impossible to deploy tactical nuclear weapons without their being noticed.

Following recommendations from the Joint Chiefs of Staff (JCS), the Eisenhower administration insisted (without evidence) that North Korea violated 13(d) in 1956, and demanded the NNSC's suspension. When Sweden and Switzerland bowed to American pressure, the South expelled the sixteen Czech and Polish inspectors. The JCS proposed three options: (1) suspend the armistice agreement; (2) interpret paragraph 13(d) more flexibly; (3) charge that the North had acquired nuclear weapons.

The result was a significant debate, seldom mentioned despite its importance to the future history of the Korean Peninsula, and to what it revealed about President Eisenhower's attitude toward treaty commitments that restricted his ability to deploy nuclear weapons. It was the only time that Secretary of State Dulles argued—based on legal and political considerations—against the president's preference for deploying nuclear weapons.

Dulles considered the Pentagon's suggestions misguided. Such a blatant violation of the armistice agreement was sure to cause serious criticism from allies as well as enemies, and it was farfetched to believe that the Soviet Union would deliver nuclear weapons to the Chinese or North Koreans.

Gridlock! Until January 14, 1957, when Eisenhower ordered the NSC Planning Board to evaluate "the kinds of nuclear-capable weapons to be introduced [into South Korea] and the question of storage of nuclear warheads in Korea."

Remarkably, despite the president's instructions, Dulles continued to object for several months. In April, for example, he argued at another NSC meeting that the political disadvantages of illegally nuclearizing the Korean Peninsula outweighed any military advantage.

But less than a month later, on May 14, he acquiesced and announced that the United States was considering the introduction of "more modern, more effective" weapons into the ROK. Discerning

reporters understood that "modern" and "effective" meant "atomics."
The deployment of the nuclear cannons and Honest Johns began in
January 1958, and a year later the air force "permanently stationed a
squadron of nuclear-tipped Matador cruise missiles—aimed at China
and Russia as well as North Korea."

The president's orders were that the deployment could be neither
confirmed nor denied.

11

"There Is Not Communists . . . but Cubanists"

The president of the United States didn't even invite me for a
cup of coffee, because I wasn't worthy of a cup of coffee with
the president of the United States.
—FIDEL CASTRO

The thing we should never do in dealing with revolutionary
countries, in which the world abounds, is to push them
behind an iron curtain raised by ourselves. On the contrary,
even when they have been seduced and subverted and are
drawn across the line, the right thing to do is to keep the way
open for their return.
—WALTER LIPPMANN, JULY 1959

Less than four months after driving Cuba's long-reigning dictator,
Fulgencio Batista, into exile on January 1, 1959, Fidel Castro visited
the United States "on a mission of friendship." He had been the prime
minister of Cuba since February 16, but chose to come as a private citizen. Shunning an official invitation was vintage Castro. He intended
to explain his revolution's purpose and goals directly to the American
people, and he did not want his movements limited by the constraints
of an official visit.

1

GEORGE W. HEALEY JR., the president of the American Society of
Newspaper Editors, facilitated the visit by inviting Castro to address
its annual meeting on April 17: "This man has made news and we

should see and hear him so that we can understand him better, and perhaps have him understand us better," Healey responded to his critics.

The trip was an eleven-day publicity tour designed to win the hearts and minds of the American people. "Smiles, lots of smiles," Castro was told by the Madison Avenue public relations agent hired for the occasion, and from April 15 to April 25 he grinned for the cameras, answered questions calmly and courteously, discussed U.S.–Cuban relations with congressmen, senators, Vice President Richard Nixon, and journalists. He spoke at Harvard, Princeton, and Columbia Universities, visited Yankee Stadium, ate hot dogs, laid a wreath at the Lincoln Memorial, and campaigned like a skilled North American politician.

The timing of his arrival was fortuitous. Spring and a budding social-justice movement mingled in the dormitories and lecture halls of college campuses. Just four years earlier Rosa Parks had refused to move to the back of a Montgomery, Alabama, bus; two years later the Reverend Ralph Abernathy organized the Southern Christian Leadership Conference; and by April 1959 the outline of Martin Luther King's dream was taking shape.

The civil rights movement was stirring, and progressive Americans, from Berkeley, California, to New York City, were as impatient for decolonization abroad as they were for racial equality at home. The charismatic, thirty-two-year-old bearded revolutionary, in olive-green fatigues, appeared to be the harbinger of a new order, and not only to students. "Castro symbolizes hope to millions of Cubans," Hubert Humphrey told his Senate colleagues, insisting that it behooved the United States to assure him of its cooperation.

"I am a man responsive to public opinion," Castro declared—in English—to an enthusiastic crowd of fifteen hundred who had gathered at Washington's National Airport to welcome him with repeated roars of "Viva Castro!" That his plane was (typically) two hours late only stirred their enthusiasm. Healey was there too, along with several senior Department of State representatives, and a substantial security force augmented in response to a flurry of death threats.

It was a perfect setting for Castro to send a message to both the American people and his adversaries. The greetings concluded, he plunged into the cheering throng to shake hands and distribute bear hugs, making it clear that he had contempt for those who thought they could intimidate him.

He was an instant media star.

He was also a deft politician. Lunching the following day at the Statler Hotel with Acting Secretary of State Christian A. Herter, he toasted President Eisenhower and all Americans, and praised the long history of "friendly" relations between Cuba and the United States. He saw no reason, he declared, why relations between the United States and Cuba should not be "the best."

Over lunch he had an animated conversation with Senator Alexander Wiley, the ranking Republican member of the Senate Foreign Relations Committee. Afterward, in response to a reporter's critical question, he extended an open invitation to U.S. journalists to visit Cuba and freely report what they saw.

Castro's only incaution occurred when he was informed that United States wire services had reported that a hostile crowd met him at the airport. Fiercely protective of his image, he protested: "That's not true. There were only about 33 pickets. . . . I was given a wonderful reception." Had he known that many of the pickets had been paid to protest, there is no doubt that his complaint would have been more colorful.

2

FARTHER DOWN Pennsylvania Avenue, Castro's reception was cooler. President Eisenhower had departed for the Augusta National Golf Club to avoid meeting him. Earlier, he had considered denying Castro a visa, but had been persuaded that such a move would backfire. Committed to stability and order, Eisenhower was hostile to any Third World politician who advocated social and economic reforms. He had reluctantly accepted Batista's demise because his cruelty, corruption, and dictatorial rule had become liabilities. Yet, even past the point of certainty that Batista would be routed, the administration continued to provide him with military support. Castro neither forgot nor forgave that.

Nevertheless, in January 1959, when Fidel had driven triumphantly through the streets of Havana, there was cause for the American public to welcome Cuba's new leader. His reputation, promoted over the past two years by journalists who interviewed him in his rebel encampments—most especially Herbert Matthews of the *New York Times*—was of a progressive revolutionary seeking justice and a better life for his countrymen. Hints of Marxist sympathies were few, and even those that appeared to be valid seemed timid in context.

In the past three months, however, the revolutionary government's actions had reignited earlier discussions in Washington about the political provenance of Castro's policies. The public trials and executions of almost five hundred of Batista's henchmen by mid-April, criticisms of private property, and slogans such as "Revolution first, elections later," tarnished the democratic image that the July 26 Movement had garnered in news accounts from its encampments in Cuba's Sierra Maestra mountains.

McCarthyism at home was subdued by 1959, but its central question: "Are you now, or have you ever been, a Communist?" remained the litmus test the Eisenhower administration applied to Third World leaders.

3

WAS FIDEL a Communist? By April that was a hotly debated question in the press, in Congress, and in the White House. Castro had come to the United States to allay those fears, and at every opportunity he denied having any Communist connections. On Capitol Hill, he told senators on April 16 that Communism did not have a chance in Cuba if he could feed his people. The following day, mingling with a crowd several blocks from the Cuban Embassy on 16th Street NW, he declared, "There is not Communists, not capitalists but Cubanists." Then, as if advocating a Marshall Plan for Cuba, Fidel explained his bottom line to the assembly of admirers: "If we are happy and we have food and money to spend, it could not be Communists in Cuba. But we have to have money to buy machinery and to build new industries in Cuba."

It was a clear statement that economic support could lead to Cuban-American cooperation, but no one in the administration was paying attention.

Vice President Richard M. Nixon was the administration's chief investigator of Castro's political proclivities. He was not charged with discovering the new Cuban leader's views about how his country and the United States could promote a positive relationship. The question was simply whether Castro was with us or against us.

On Sunday afternoon, April 19, at the vice president's invitation, Fidel settled into a chair in Nixon's small Capitol Hill office, for what turned out to be a historic three-hour conversation.

Nixon was preachy rather than curious, and focused on making it clear to Castro how the United States expected his government to behave. Castro explained why he had supported certain actions, but appears not to have had the opportunity to explain what arrangements might be mutually acceptable for building an agreeable Cuban-American relationship.

The conversation began with encouragement from Nixon, and ended with a rhetorical question: Was Castro "incredibly naive about Communism or under Communist discipline," Nixon asked in his summary memorandum of their talk. Although his "guess [was] the former," Castro's determination to free his country from the control of free-enterprise capitalists had raised the vice president's suspicions.

"I thought you might like to see a copy of the confidential memorandum of my conversation with Castro," "Dick" wrote to Democratic senator Mike Mansfield, the majority whip. Additional copies went to President Eisenhower, Allen Dulles, Christian Herter, and the gravely ill John Foster Dulles.

The memorandum offers insights into the attitudes of both men. In particular it highlights Nixon's views on political leadership, proper economic policies, the challenge of Communism, and the Eisenhower administration's concerns about Castro, although Fidel's intentions are filtered by Nixon's views. Too revealing and interesting to summarize, the memorandum is lightly abridged with subject headings added for clarity.

Nixon titled his memorandum "Rough draft of a summary of conversation between the vice-president and Fidel Castro," and organized his recollections into discrete topics.

CASTRO CONCERNED TO MAKE A GOOD IMPRESSION:
When Castro arrived for the conference he seemed somewhat
nervous and tense. He apparently felt that he had not done as
well on "Meet the Press" as he had hoped. . . . I reassured him
at the beginning of the conversation that "Meet the Press" was
one of the most difficult programs a public official could go on
and that he had done extremely well—particularly having in
mind the fact that he had the courage to go on in English rather
than to speak through a translator. . . .

ELECTIONS IN CUBA: I suggested at the outset that while I
understood that some reasonable time might elapse before it
would be feasible to have elections it would nevertheless be
much better from his viewpoint if he were not to state so categorically that it would be as long as four years before elections
would be held. . . . He went into considerable detail as he had
in public with regard to the reasons for not holding elections,
emphasizing particularly that "the people did not want elections
because the elections in the past had produced bad government."

EXECUTIONS: He used the same argument that he was simply
reflecting the will of the people in justifying the executions of
war criminals and his overruling the acquittal of Batista's aviators. In fact, he seemed to be obsessed with the idea that it was
his responsibility to carry out the will of the people whatever it
might appear to be at a particular time.

CASTRO'S REASON FOR VISITING USA: It was also apparent
that as far as his visit to the United States was concerned that
his primary interest was "not to get a change in the sugar quota
or to get a government loan but to win support for his policies
from American public opinion."

NIXON'S ARGUMENTS REGARDING DEMOCRATIC INI-
TIATIVES: It was this almost slavish subservience to prevailing majority opinion—the voice of the mob—rather than his
naive attitude toward Communism and his obvious lack of

understanding of even the most elementary economic principles which concerned me most in evaluating what kind of leader he might eventually turn out to be. That is the reason why I spent as much time as I could trying to emphasize that he had the great gift of leadership, but that it was the responsibility of a leader not always to follow public opinion but to help to direct it in the proper channels. . . .

I used the same argument with regard to freedom of the press, the right to a fair trial before an impartial court, judge and jury, and on other issues which came up during the course of the conversation. In every instance he justified his departure from democratic principles on the ground that he was following the will of the people. . . .

CASTRO IS "INCREDIBLY NAIVE" ABOUT COMMUNISM: I frankly doubt that I made too much impression upon him but he did listen and appeared to be somewhat receptive. . . . As I have already indicated he was incredibly naive with regard to the Communist threat and appeared to have no fear whatever that the Communists might eventually come to power in Cuba. He said that during the course of the revolution there had been occasions when the Communists overplayed their hand and "my people put them in their place." He implied that this would be the situation in the future in the event that the Communists tried to come to power.

CASTRO'S PRIMARY CONCERN IS ECONOMIC PROGRESS: It was apparent that while he paid lip service to such institutions as freedom of speech, press and religion that his primary concern was with developing programs for economic progress. He said over and over that a man who worked in the sugar cane fields for three months a year and starved the rest of the year wanted a job, something to eat, a house and some clothing and didn't care a whit about whether he had freedom along with it. . . .

USA ARMS TO LATIN AMERICA ARE USED FOR SUPPRES-SION: He indicated that it was very foolish for the United States to furnish arms to Cuba or any other Caribbean country. He said "anybody knows that our countries are not going to be able to play any part in the defense of this hemisphere in the event a world war breaks out. The arms governments get in this hemisphere are only used to suppress people as Batista used his arms to fight the revolution. It would be far better if the money that you give to Latin American countries for arms be provided for capital investment." I will have to admit that as far as his basic argument was concerned here I found little that I could disagree with!

CASTRO PREFERS GOVERNMENT FUNDS TO PRIVATE CAPITAL FOR ECONOMIC DEVELOPMENT: We had a rather extended discussion of how Cuba could get the investment capital it needed for economic progress. He insisted that what Cuba primarily needed and what he wanted was not private capital but government capital. He gave me some rather confused arguments as to why plants that were licensed and/or owned and operated by the government would serve the best interests of Cuba better than privately owned enterprises.

I told him quite bluntly that his best hope as far as the U.S. was concerned was not in getting more government capital but in attracting private capital. . . .

AGRARIAN REFORM: He explained his agrarian reform program in considerable detail justifying it primarily on the ground that Cuba needed more people who were able to buy the goods produced within the country and that it would make no sense to produce more in factories unless the amount of money in the hands of consumers was increased.

CASTRO SENSITIVE TO CRITICISM FROM USA PRESS: He rather bitterly assailed the United States press for what he called their unfair reporting of the revolution after he came to power. . . . I would not be surprised if his sensitivity with regard to criticism might eventually lead him to take some rather drastic steps toward curtailing freedom of the press in the future.

CASTRO SEES AMERICANS AS FEARFUL OF EVERYTHING: He also spoke rather frankly about what he felt was a very disturbing attitude on the part of the American press and the American people generally. His argument went along this line: "Yours is a great country—the richest, the greatest, the most powerful in the world. Your people, therefore, should be proud and confident and happy. But every place I go you seem to be afraid—afraid of Communism, afraid that if Cuba has land reform it will grow a little rice and the market for your rice will be reduced—afraid that if Latin America becomes more industrialized American factories will not be able to sell as much abroad as they have previously.

You in America should not be talking so much about your fear of what the Communists may do in Cuba or in some other country in Latin America, Asia or Africa—you should be talking more about your own strength and the reasons why your system is superior to Communism or any other kind of dictatorship."

CASTRO INSISTS THAT HE IS NOT A COMMUNIST: . . . Significantly enough he did not raise any questions about the sugar quota nor did he engage in any specific discussions with regard to economic assistance. His primary concern seemed to be to convince me that he was sincere, that he was not a Communist and that his policies had the support of the great majority of the Cuban people.

CASTRO IS "EITHER INCREDIBLY NAIVE OR UNDER COMMUNIST DISCIPLINE": My own appraisal of him as a man is somewhat mixed. The one fact we can be sure of is that he has those indefinable qualities which make him a leader of men. Whatever we may think of him he is going to be a great factor in the development of Cuba and very possibly in Latin American affairs generally. He seems to be sincere, he is either incredibly naive about Communism or under Communist discipline—my guess is the former. . . . But because he has the power to lead to which I have referred we have no choice but at least to try to orient him in the right direction.

4

THE DISCOVERY by the historian Jeffrey Safford of Nixon's "Castro memorandum" in Senator Mike Mansfield's papers resolved a mystery: Why had Nixon quoted selectively from the document in his book *Six Crises,* and his memoir, but refused to publish the full text? The most likely answer is the five final words of his conclusion: "He [Castro] seems to be sincere, he is either incredibly naive about Communism or under Communist discipline—*my guess is the former.*"

It is easy to understand Nixon's retrospective discomfort with his "guess," but consider the possibility that in April 1959, Nixon had read Castro correctly. Khrushchev certainly thought so. As he reports in his memoirs, *Khrushchev Remembers,* at the time of Castro's visit to the United States, Cuba had not only refused to recognize the USSR, but "Castro was pursuing a very cautious policy toward us." No one in Moscow believed that Castro was a Communist. But there was reason to hope that U.S. hostility to his reforms, and the encouragement of trusted associates who were Communists (Castro's brother Raúl and Ernesto "Che" Guevara, among others), would make him one.

Castro's version of his meeting with Nixon supports Khrushchev's view and suggests that the vice president's "guess" was correct. Castro told a meeting of Americans and Russians, who had gathered in Havana in 1992 to review the history of the Cuban missile crisis: "When I visited in April I explained [to Nixon] the social and economic situation in Cuba, the poverty, the inequality, the hundreds of thousands of unemployed, the landless peasants, the measures that we had to adopt to solve the situation." At that time "our program was not a socialist program," he confessed. "It was the [1953] Moncada program. It was an advanced social program, but it was not a socialist program. It was not a communist program."

5

CASTRO CAME to the United States with a clear vision of a cooperative relationship, but he had only the vaguest notion of how to implement it. His trip was exploratory, a naive attempt to gain the support of the American people for his program of economic reform.

It was preceded by some very good press, most remarkably an

interview broadcast on January 11 to an audience of more than twelve million television viewers. Several days earlier, Ed Sullivan, the host of a popular Sunday-night CBS variety show, had flown to Cuba for a 2:00 a.m. interview with Castro. Impressed by his personality and ambitions, Sullivan aired six minutes of the interview and then remarked: "This is a very fine young man, and a smart young man. With the help of God, and our prayers, and the help of the American government, he'll come up with the sort of democracy down there that America should have."

But neither the American president nor God's emissaries shared Sullivan's opinion of Castro. New York's archbishop, Cardinal Francis Spellman, called Sullivan to explain that the Church had a decidedly different view of Cuba's new leader, and a few months later Eisenhower made it clear that he agreed.

"The president of the United States didn't even invite me for a cup of coffee, because I wasn't worthy of a cup of coffee with the president of the United States," Castro remarked to his 1992 Havana Conference guests. Soon after, he continued, "American economic pressures of all types began [and] they became stronger and stronger."

6

As Castro talked his way around the East Coast of the United States he was guided by two commitments. The first was his intention to free Cuba from the yoke of U.S. economic domination, and the second was to eliminate Cuban poverty. Convinced that these goals were intertwined, he nevertheless did not believe that a Communist government was the answer. Moscow was six thousand miles from Havana. Far better to restructure his country's relationship with the United States than bet the survival of his revolution on support from a distant nation that had never been an active player in the Western Hemisphere. A reform program harnessed to a charm tour seemed the best strategy in April 1959, and he had come to the United States to win hearts and minds, just as Nixon believed he had.

Nixon was probably correct too about Castro's naïveté, which was expansive rather than limited to Communism and economics. He was seriously naive about American politics. He believed that the American people would recognize the injustices he sought to correct, and would compel their government to support the programs he was putting in place. He had led a successful revolution in Cuba; why shouldn't he succeed in revolutionizing American-Cuban relations?

During the early days of his trip he believed that he was succeeding. One of his most remarkable efforts was an impromptu request to appear before the Senate Foreign Relations Committee. After receiving word that Castro would like to talk with committee members, Senator William Fulbright, the committee's chair, assembled an informal gathering. Senator Wiley (who had spoken with Castro during the luncheon hosted by Acting Secretary of State Herter) was blunt: "What is your connection with Communism, if any?"

"None," Castro countered.

Did he plan to confiscate the Guantánamo Naval Base?

"No" . . . and so on.

Senator John Sparkman reported that Castro "made a very good impression." He also made a convert: Rep. James G. Fulton switched, he said, from being "neutral and suspicious" to being Castro's "amigo nuevo [new friend]."

"We think that he acquitted himself well," the *Washington Post and Times-Herald* editorialized.

He also defanged Christian Herter, who reported to Eisenhower that Castro was "a most interesting individual, very much like a child in many ways, quite immature regarding the problem of government, and puzzled and confused by some of the practical difficulties now facing him."

A child-leader on a mission to influence the American people and their government! Castro asserted at every opportunity that he was not a Marxist, and the headlines make it clear that his message was understood:

"Red Label Is Rejected By Castro,"

"Castro Rules Out Role As Neutral; Opposes Reds,"

"Castro Tells Princeton [students] Freedom Can Be Held,"

"Castro Promises Cuba Will Honor Agreements,"

"Cubans Most Democratic in West—Castro,"

"Castro's Eloquence Impressive in UN."

And the crowds were impressive too: "10,000 Hear Castro at Harvard,

"20,000 Hail Castro at N.Y. Station."

What was the point of this Yankee campaign, if not to assure Americans that the leader of Cuba's new government was not a Communist?

At least not in April 1959.

7

NOR, ACCORDING to intelligence sources, even by the end of the year. A comprehensive Special National Intelligence Estimate, "The Situation in the Caribbean Through 1959," concluded that while Castro himself was not a Communist, and "the Communists probably do not now control Castro," they nevertheless "are in a position to exert influence in his regime." And, in November, when the conservative deputy director of the CIA, Gen. Charles P. Cabell, testified before a Senate subcommittee investigating "Communist Threat to the US through the Caribbean," he stated emphatically that "our information shows that the Cuban Communists do not consider him [Fidel Castro] a Communist Party member or even a pro-Communist."

But Castro did convert or, more accurately, was converted, in a rapid two-step process: rejection and embrace. Castro's reforms proved anathema to Eisenhower, who approved sanctions intended to force him from power. "The Americans had cut off the Cubans' supply of oil, and the Cubans were obliged to turn to us for help," Khrushchev explained in his memoir.

"Castro's scenario at this time [1959] did not contemplate the massive help in the form of economic aid and weapons that he later received from the Soviet Union," Philip W. Bonsal, the U.S. ambassador in Havana, later wrote. He "became oriented towards dependence on the Soviet Union only when the United States, by its actions in the spring and summer of 1960, gave the Russians no choice other than to come to Castro's rescue."

Aleksandr Alekseyev, the Soviet Union's "man in Havana," a KGB agent who befriended Castro (and became Moscow's ambassador to Cuba), validated Bonsal's view: "In the end the Americans made what in my view are unpardonable steps when they tried to force the Cubans to turn off the revolutionary path. If there hadn't been . . . what shall we call it . . . such pressure from the American leaders, maybe the Cuban revolution wouldn't have been so radicalized."

8

IT WAS not immediately obvious to the Soviets that they would be able to take advantage of Cuba's distress. "It was urgent that we organize an oil delivery to Cuba on a massive scale," Khrushchev remembered. "But that was easier said than done." Tankers were in short supply, Soviet shipping was stretched, and the effort might have failed had Italy not agreed to sell the Soviets the additional ships they needed to keep Cuba humming.

Diplomats, military hardware, technical assistance, and an array of generous trade arrangements followed, providing Castro with an alternative that set Cuban–U.S. relations on a rapid course toward hostility.

"The thing we should never do in dealing with revolutionary countries, in which the world abounds," wrote Walter Lippmann, the dean of American journalists, whose column, "Today and Tomorrow" was required reading in Washington, "is to push them behind an iron curtain raised by ourselves. On the contrary, even when they have been seduced and subverted and are drawn across the line, the right thing to do is to keep the way open for their return."

Eisenhower had a different view. They would be allowed to "return" only when they had anti-Communist governments.

12

"General Disarmament Is the Most Important"

Khrushchev's Visit to the USA

It turned out that everything was the opposite [of what we had feared]. That's how uninformed we were. We didn't know things [about the USA] that were probably known to the whole world.
—NIKITA S. KHRUSHCHEV

The question of general disarmament is the most important one facing the world today.
—EISENHOWER-KHRUSHCHEV COMMUNIQUÉ, CAMP DAVID, SEPTEMBER 25, 1959

On September 15, 1959, four months after Fidel Castro ended his whirlwind U.S. tour, Nikita Khrushchev arrived in the United States. The president, who had avoided Castro by rushing off to the Augusta National Golf Club, was on hand to welcome his Communist guest. The Soviet Union's rapidly expanding nuclear arsenal, and Khrushchev's demand that the United States abandon West Berlin, had prompted the invitation. Worried about escalating tensions, Eisenhower had taken the bold step of welcoming his dangerously armed adversary to the Cold War's first U.S.–Soviet tourism-summit; its unstated purpose was to begin preparations for an arms control initiative.

1

EISENHOWER HAD been president for more than six years in 1959, when he began to consider inviting Khrushchev to the United States.

Increasingly worried about the deteriorating state of U.S.–USSR relations, he did not want his legacy to be a nation on the brink of nuclear war. He had promoted the expansion of America's nuclear weapons in search of cheap security, but the Soviet Union had followed his lead. The result was both unprecedented insecurity and an extremely costly nuclear arms race.

There were too many areas of disagreement between the United States and the Soviet Union, and he had too few months left in office to systematically develop strategies for lowering tensions. Conflicts in Southeast Asia, potential hostilities in the Taiwan Straits, Eastern Europe, West Berlin, and the escalating weapons race dominated public discussions of foreign affairs. A dramatic initiative, such as inviting Khrushchev to visit the United States, appealed to his gambler's instinct. It was not Normandy, but it would certainly be a surprise, and it might even prove a game changer. He considered it an "ace in the hole."

The decline in relations between the U.S.A. and USSR during the past several years was also of concern to Llewellyn Thompson, the Department of State Sovietologist and current ambassador to the Soviet Union. In a March 4 telegram Thompson had urged high-level meetings "now," before relations deteriorated further.

"I must confess that at first I didn't believe it," Khrushchev wrote in his memoirs, recalling his reaction to the invitation only weeks after his contentious "Kitchen Debate" with Vice President Richard Nixon. "It was all so unexpected. We were not prepared at all for something like that."

2

DESCENDING ON a red carpet from his Tupolev 114 passenger jet to the tarmac of Andrews Air Force Base, Khrushchev was in high spirits. His flight to the United States—nonstop from Moscow to Washington, D.C.—was a triumph. "How proud we were to travel on such a plane," he recalled. "The United States didn't have such a [long-range] passenger plane until sometime after that."

Nor, inexplicably, did the United States have a ramp at Andrews high enough to reach the exit doors of this airborne behemoth. "So we descended from the plane in a not especially elegant manner. . . .

Good for our boys!" Khrushchev chuckled. "They've built a giant passenger plane. . . . And the other guys have nothing like it."

Greeted by a crowd that appeared more curious than enthusiastic, and a military band playing the Soviet national anthem, Khrushchev politely announced that he had come to the United States "with open heart and good intentions. The Soviet people want to live in friendship with the American people." Eisenhower's remarks were equally amicable, and—the welcoming speeches completed—the president, the premier, and Mrs. Khrushchev climbed into the backseat of a limousine to lead the motorcade to the capital.

Khrushchev smiled and waved to the gawking, hushed onlookers (estimated at 200,000) as the military bands lining the road filled the void of silence. "They seemed to look at us as some kind of strange creatures," Khrushchev recalled, "as if to say. . . . Why have they come here anyhow?" Thousands were protesters waving black flags. "It seemed more like a funeral procession than a parade," according to one participant. Khrushchev's daughter, Rada Khrushcheva, in a following car, remembered the ride as resembling "the silence of the tomb." It was as if Khrushchev and his entourage were "from the moon," she recalled. "Later I realized that that was the way Americans thought of us."

Given the strained relations between the USA and the USSR, Khrushchev's November 1956 "We will bury you" speech still rankled. Eisenhower's invitation to the chairman of the Communist Party of the USSR was as much of a surprise to the American public as it was to Khrushchev. "Our relations then were so strained that an invitation for a friendship visit by the head of the Soviet government and first secretary of the CPSU Central Committee seemed simply unbelievable," Khrushchev recalled, echoing many Americans.

3

KHRUSHCHEV'S VISIT was a sensational occasion with wide-ranging significance. With the exception of attending the wartime conferences in Tehran, Iran, and Potsdam, Germany, Stalin had not traveled beyond Soviet-controlled areas. For many in the Soviet Union's inner circle (most of whom came of political age under Stalin) traveling to the United States seemed unbecoming for a Soviet leader.

Khrushchev was taking a big risk, but gambling was also at the core of his personality.

As the first Soviet leader to set foot on United States soil, Khrushchev breached powerful diplomatic, psychological, and political barriers that had constrained initiatives to improve relations between the former wartime allies. The trip contributed to his understanding (and even appreciation) of the United States, and remained a consistent influence on his thinking. "A Soviet Union [and leader] that interacted with the rest of the world," Llewellyn Thompson observed, "was far less dangerous than one lost in its own isolation."

The visit transcended foreign policy by improving the American public's comfort level with the Soviet leader and the Soviet public's view of the United States. The two weeks that Khrushchev spent spanning the continent—Washington, D.C., New York City, Los Angeles, San Francisco, Des Moines, and Pittsburgh—effectively discredited the objections of anti-Communists to his visit. It was a people-to-people program at the highest political level, and a lesson on the value of personal diplomacy.

It is even fair to say that by putting to rest the paranoia promoted by the most virulent anti-Communists, Khrushchev's visit hammered the final nail into McCarthyism's coffin.

"Because of our importance in the world, it is vital that we understand each other better," Eisenhower declared at the welcoming state dinner. Friendship was a necessity, the Soviet architect of "peaceful coexistence" responded, "because our two countries are much too strong and we cannot quarrel with each other."

This was a theme—containing the danger of nuclear weapons— that Khrushchev repeated throughout his stay, and it was among the first topics he raised when he met with Eisenhower and his advisers at the White House.

The trip was off to a polite, serious start that would increase in complexity over the course of twelve more days.

4

KHRUSHCHEV'S TU 114 landed at Andrews AFB laden with baggage—most of it in the heads of the Soviet visitors. They were not arriving in just another capitalist country; they were descending into the center of the anti-Communist universe. They were entering the Soviet Union's reality check: the "country," Khrushchev believed, "whose power had decisive significance." The United States had more wealth, more military power, more anti-Soviet venom than all the nations of Western Europe combined: "In our imaginations and our conception of what the outside world was like, the United States held a special place," Khrushchev admitted. "After all, this was our country's most powerful opponent, the leader of the capitalist countries, and the one that set the tone for the entire anti-Soviet crowd in the outside world."

That "tone" included an economic blockade of the Soviet Union. An export ban included agricultural and industrial products that were important to the still-war-damaged Soviet economy, and import restrictions that embargoed Soviet boutique items, such as Russian vodka, caviar, and even Russian crabs, targeted with the "absurd" argument, Khrushchev angrily noted, that they were harvested by "slave labor."

The USA was the colossus, and the Soviet's leaders approached it with a huge inferiority complex that heightened their wariness of any possible slight.

"To the day of his death," Khrushchev recalled, Stalin "kept drilling it into our heads that we, his comrades-in-arms of the Politburo, were really unfit . . . that with our very first personal contact we would not know how to represent our homeland in an honorable way . . . the imperialists would simply crush us." They will "wring your necks like chickens," Stalin mocked.

Khrushchev's visit to the United States thus became a personal test as important to him as the Potsdam Conference had been to Truman. Would he prove Stalin right? Would the president of the United States make him look foolish? Was he prepared to deal as an equal with this wealthy, powerful archrival on its home ground? Outwardly he was representing his country, but internally he was engaged in a gut-wrenching challenge that animated his entire visit. He had to be certain that he was treated with respect, as his host's equal. Any apparent insult—and there were several—would be challenged.

5

KHRUSHCHEV'S EXPERIENCES in the United States revealed how he responded to personal challenges, and how his personality underpinned his foreign policy initiatives. As he planned for his arrival, he was angry, excited, and wary.

He was angry because the Eisenhower administration had ignored all his efforts to improve relations with the West. As his American biographer, William Taubman, noted, from the beginning of his tenure Khrushchev had "set out to ease Cold War tensions." He had welcomed Western influence into the Soviet Union, promoted "peaceful co-existence," decreased the size of the Soviet military, accepted Western disarmament positions, removed Soviet troops from Finland and Austria, encouraged reform in Eastern Europe, and lobbied for a four-power (USA, France, Britain, USSR) summit, "or at least an informal invitation to the United States."

"We have refused these overtures, or made their acceptance subject to conditions he as a Communist considers impossible," Ambassador Thompson reported to the State Department in March 1959: "We are in the process of rearming Germany and strengthening our bases surrounding Soviet territory [including placing Jupiter missiles in Turkey and Italy]. Our proposals for settling the German problem would in his opinion end in dissolution of the Communist bloc and threaten the regime in the Soviet Union itself. He has offered a European settlement based on the status quo while we engage in economic competition. This we have also rejected and he has therefore determined to nail it down without our consent."

"What do Eisenhower and Dulles want?" Khrushchev had raged a year earlier. "Apparently they want to meet and talk over the liquidation of the socialist system in the Soviet Union." Hitler had tried that, he pointedly added.

6

THE INVITATION seemed a stunning reversal, however. Was it a signal of peace? That was a possibility, now that John Foster Dulles had died. Khrushchev had no doubt that Dulles had manipulated the president and promoted the administration's aggressive anti-Soviet policies. Dealing directly with Eisenhower would be different, he expected. "I really like [Eisenhower]," he had told an American visitor in 1958. "At the Geneva conference [July 1955] he took me to the bar after every meeting and we had a drink together." He was eager to "sit down and have another talk with him."

As they planned the trip, Khrushchev and the Presidium were both excited and wary. Every day of their stay, and every anticipated event, from the moment they stepped onto American soil, was carefully considered: "We were somewhat concerned about what the welcoming ceremony would be, whether some form of discrimination might occur," he remembered. "They [the Americans] could pointedly omit doing something that was normally done for a visiting head of government, and in this way they would be dealing us a kind of moral blow."

"On what level were we being invited?" Was the invitation for the head of government or the chief of state? Would the delegation be greeted with full presidential honors? If not, they warned the ambassador to the United States, Mikhail Menshikov, the Americans should understand that Eisenhower would receive similar treatment when he visited Moscow.

Should Nina Petrovna, Khrushchev's wife, accompany him? How about Foreign Minister Andrei Gromyko? Should his wife be included? "Ordinary people abroad take a better attitude toward men who come as guests with their wives [and] other family members," Anastas Mikoyan, the well-traveled member of the Presidium, assured Khrushchev. But should they include a scientist? A writer? Should they go by ship? By plane? If they flew, could they be certain to arrive on time? "If we were late that would be damaging to our prestige," Khrushchev fretted. (How different from Castro's attitude!)

The questions seemed endless, and the worries inflated. "Of course," Khrushchev recognized in retrospect, "our demands were exaggerated," but "we wanted to emphasize these demands in order to rule out any possible discrimination, because we knew that such a desire did exist on their part."

A profound ignorance of the United States reinforced their insecurity. "We had an extremely poor knowledge of the United States then," Khrushchev confessed. The Soviet leadership was "up to [its] ears in domestic problems," and with respect to foreign affairs, "We were mainly concerned with questions of war and peace."

No aspect of the trip better illustrates their lack of intelligence about America than their reaction to a proposed Eisenhower-Khrushchev meeting at Camp David. "What exactly was this Camp David?" Khrushchev asked. Astonishingly, he was unable to get a clear answer; no one seemed to know. Was it a "quarantine facility?"—a place the president met with people he "didn't trust"? "Why not meet in Washington?" It seemed to be "a kind of discriminatory action."

Camp David, he finally learned, was the president's country retreat in Maryland—built during World War II for President Franklin Roosevelt. It was his dacha, so to speak, and it was an honor to be invited there. "It turned out that everything was the opposite [of what we had feared]," and so "we then accepted the invitation with pleasure, and of course we didn't tell anyone about our doubts."

"That's how uninformed we were. We didn't know things that were probably known to the whole world."

"Today," Khrushchev confessed, as he composed his memoir, "all of this is not only funny to me; I feel a little bit ashamed." But since the Bolshevik Revolution, "the capitalists [had] always tried to wound our pride and humiliate us. . . . That's why I reacted in such a touchy way."

And in a larger sense, that same sense of inferiority, that certainty that "the capitalists" were bent on mortifying—and destroying—the Soviet Union in every sphere and in every way, underpinned virtually all of Khrushchev's diplomacy, including his nuclear weapons policies.

7

THE SOVIETS, as it turned out, did not have a monopoly on visitation anxiety; Americans, many of them the educated elite, showed themselves to be comparably provincial. While a slim majority of the public favored the invitation to Khrushchev (according to Gallup polls), many conservative strategists and pundits were furious that the president had invited a Communist "trojan horse" into their midst. Henry

Kissinger considered the initiative an act of foolish idealism. Showing Khrushchev what America was really like was a waste of time, he opined. The Cold War was not the product of misunderstanding, but rather the result of Soviet determination to expand its influence and destroy Western democracies. David Lawrence, the editor of *U.S. News & World Report,* considered the Soviet leader "just another Hitler" and ranted in an editorial against the president's invitation.

William F. Buckley Jr., the urbane editor of the *National Review,* abandoned his sophisticated facade and editorialized that the Hudson River should be filled with red dye to create a "figurative river of blood." More than a diplomatic faux pas was at stake, these critics insisted; Khrushchev's appearance could deal a devastating blow to anti-Communist solidarity. It would weaken the resolve of the American public to stand up to the Soviet Union, confuse our allies, and devastate the morale of those "held captive" to Communism. "The dumb resignation being shown to the invitation," was a clear sign of a failure of will, the *Wall Street Journal* declared: The administration was following the path of "sentimental irrationality," having lost its bearings since the death of its ideological navigator, John Foster Dulles.

The leadership of the Catholic Church strenuously objected to Khrushchev's visit. Cardinal Richard Cushing of Boston reacted to the invitation with a stinging denunciation. Cardinal Spellman of New York labeled Khrushchev a "menace." "Today's announcement [of an invitation to Khrushchev] leaves a deep wound," Cardinal John O'Hara of Philadelphia telegrammed the president. In the nation's capital Archbishop Patrick O'Boyle ordered priests to ignore Khrushchev, urging Washington Catholics to pray for the "enslaved millions." Throughout the country "mourning masses" were held in Polish, Hungarian, and other Eastern European Catholic churches. In New York City a Hungarian Catholic congregation draped its church's facade in black.

Eastern Orthodox churches held impromptu memorial services hours before Khrushchev arrived. In Los Angeles, Russian congregations formed the Committee of the United Russian Anti-Communist Organizations. Some Protestant leaders raised similar cries of alarm. Comparing Khrushchev to "an international Dillinger," Dr. Clyde Kennedy, president of the Council of Christian Churches, called the visit "morally wrong." The Reverend Carl McIntire, president of the International Council of Christian Churches, and a familiar voice on some six hundred radio stations, organized a mass prayer rally around the Washington Monument.

The most politically sophisticated reaction to the visit among religious leaders came from the Jewish community. Primarily concerned with the suppression of Jewish life in Communist countries, its leaders saw Khrushchev's visit as an opportunity to publicize the Soviet Union's mistreatment of Jews. The American Jewish Committee (AJC) took the lead in this effort, publishing *The Plight of the Jews in Eastern Europe*. With the support of fifteen senators and the State Department, the AJC sought a meeting with Khrushchev. Although their efforts produced meager immediate results, they were an early indication of how Jewish groups would work to keep the treatment of Soviet Jews on the bipartisan agenda.

Veterans' organizations made their contribution to the chorus of contempt. The Veterans of Foreign Wars passed a measure boycotting the visit and asked its chapters "not to display Russian flags." Surprisingly, the American Legion was more flexible, and amenable to the administration's appeals. Holding its convention a few weeks before Khrushchev's visit, it accepted Vice President Nixon's assurances that President Eisenhower would take a "tough line with Khrushchev." After considerable debate, the delegates voted to support the visit, but definitely not any further meetings.

The pervasive extent of the anti-Communist consensus in the United States—and the residue of McCarthyism—was underlined in the reaction of organized labor. The AFL-CIO executive committee voted 22 to 3 to boycott Khrushchev during his visit. He would be refused an audience with union leaders, site visitations with the rank and file, and a platform at the AFL-CIO convention in San Francisco.

8

ADVOCATES OF cultural diplomacy can point to Khrushchev's visit to the United States as evidence that American popular culture was attractive even to those who claimed that it was a source of corruption and profligacy. Having extended to Khrushchev the courtesy of designing his own tour of the United States, the Eisenhower administration was asked to arrange two special choices. Hoover Dam? The Grand Canyon? *Nyet.* The first secretary of the Communist Party of the Soviet Union wished to visit Hollywood and Disneyland.

There is a hint of irony in Khrushchev's itinerary choices. Hollywood and Disneyland, the founts of America's fantasy world, did not exactly reflect the serious concerns on his mind in September 1959. The escalating nuclear arms race was at the top of his list—as it was on Eisenhower's—but he did not know that his 1,060 nuclear weapons compared so unfavorably with the more than 15,000 that the United States had available in Europe, Asia, and North America. Eisenhower too was unsure about the size of the gap. The U2 reconnaissance flights over the Soviet Union (initiated in 1956) had made it clear that the U.S. arsenal was substantially larger than the USSR's, but exactly how much larger was unknown. The nuclear arms race was refracted through convex and concave mirrors. Hollywood and Disneyland may well have been metaphorically appropriate for the somber issues to be discussed.

9

NOT ALL Americans opposed the visit of the Communist leader who had threatened to bury them. The liberal Catholic journal *Commonweal* cheered the departure from the "Dulles line" and welcomed the easing of tensions. *America,* another Catholic publication, urged a dignified reception: "Please, no gimmicks to win his endorsement of soap, breakfast food, or cola drinks," it editorialized. The *Wall Street Journal,* perhaps a bit self-consciously, wanted Khrushchev confronted with "American vigor and strength, not weakness and decadence." Almost a thousand letters of support arrived at the White House and State Department, including many invitations to visit homes. Mrs. Phyllis Mooney invited the premier for coffee and a homemade apple pie that "makes strong men weak."

Khrushchev, however, was determined to maintain an image of strength whether confronted with man-melting apple pie or anti-Communist hostility.

Hollywood provided the hostility. Visiting Twentieth Century–Fox Studios on September 19, accompanied by his official tour guide, Henry Cabot Lodge Jr., U.S. ambassador to the UN, Khrushchev began well enough. On the soundstage of the movie *Can-Can*, he met an excited Shirley MacLaine, who greeted him in her best fractured Russian. He enjoyed the cast's special performance and, according to reports, was delighted to lunch with Frank Sinatra. Marilyn Monroe, Gary Cooper, Elizabeth Taylor, and other notable Hollywood personalities paid their respects. But, that evening, when the president of Fox, Spyros Skouras, introduced him to a Los Angeles Town Hall audience with a snarky remark about his "We will bury you" speech, Khrushchev rose to the challenge.

Hostile rhetoric was not going to make him "a little shaky in the knees," he retorted, and then made it clear that nuclear weapons remained in the forefront of his mind. "If you want to go on with the arms race, very well," he told Skouras. "We accept that challenge. As for the output of rockets—well, they are on the assembly line. This is a most serious question. It is one of life or death, ladies and gentlemen. One of war and peace."

There was more rhetorical warspeak than peacespeak as Hollywood's obsessive anti-Communism continued to goad Khrushchev to rancor. Skouras's remark was followed by a similar dig—"You shall not bury us"—by LA's mayor, Norris Poulson. Then the Disney Company rubbed salt into Khrushchev's wounded pride by claiming that "security concerns" precluded his visit to Disneyland. "I would very much like to go and see Disneyland. But then, we cannot guarantee your security, they say. Do you have rocket launching pads there? . . . What is it? Is there an epidemic of cholera there or something? Or have gangsters taken hold of the place that can destroy me?"

Departing Los Angeles the next morning, Ambassador Lodge was high on anxiety and short on diplomacy. He had "tried to talk [the] Mayor out of this speech," he assured his indignant guest. "We have no control over local politicians," Lodge explained to an incredulous first secretary of the Communist Party, who believed that Washington and corporate tycoons controlled everything.

After another contentious evening—a private dinner in San Francisco hosted by Walter Reuther, the head of the United Auto Workers, that ended in an argument about the sycophantic role of unions in the Communist East—the tour's atmosphere improved. Khrushchev met with Harry Bridges, the left-leaning leader of the longshoremen's union, who pronounced him "a good man." The two playfully traded hats, and Khrushchev donned his longshoreman's signature white cap for the remainder of the day.

On September 23 Khrushchev and his entourage flew to Des Moines, Iowa. A convivial meeting with Governor Herschel Loveless and Mayor Charles Iles was followed by a drive to the town of Coon Rapids, where he visited the farm of Roswell Garst. They had met in 1955 when Garst toured the Soviet Union lecturing on the use of hybrid seed corn and modern fertilizers to produce high-yield crops. Promoting "peace through corn" (without any sense of irony), Garst sold thousands of tons of his hybrid seeds and spent hours with Khrushchev discussing his innovative farming techniques. Helping the Soviet Union improve its farming methods, Garst told reporters on the eve of Khrushchev's visit, was in "our own selfish interests." It would be dangerous for the world to have a Russia that was both hungry and had the H-bomb.

The mood in Iowa was "the most relaxed of the entire visit to America," Khrushchev reported.

His reception in Pittsburgh—his last stop before returning to Washington—continued to sooth the irritation created by California anti-Communism. Receiving a symbolic key to the city, Khrushchev assured Mayor Thomas Gallagher that "I will only open those doors that you will allow me to open."

10

KHRUSHCHEV'S LAST two days in America, September 25 and 26, were spent with President Eisenhower at Camp David. This summit entre-nous was the climax of the trip, and numerous meetings, both private and fully staffed, were planned. Disarmament, Berlin, and trade were the major items on the agenda. While nothing concrete was agreed upon, an illusion of cooperation emerged. Eisenhower even admitted to his national security adviser that the West Berlin situation was "abnormal," as Khrushchev had contended. He had "[broken] the ice" with Eisenhower, Khrushchev wrote in his memoirs.

A "Spirit of Camp David" was attached to the gathering. It suggested that the next summit would melt some of the Cold War's most solidly frozen issues. The result, Eisenhower believed, was that future conversations would be conducted in a "more reasonable fashion."

To further promote the atmosphere of impending collaboration, the president accepted Khrushchev's invitation to visit the Soviet Union. In the end (as in the beginning) the two leaders agreed that the nuclear issue trumped all else: "The question of general disarmament is the most important one facing the world today."

The next morning, in high spirits, Khrushchev boarded his Tupolev 114. He had dived into the belly of the capitalist colossus and emerged unscathed and proud. He had brooked no insults, responded powerfully to every slight, and had met the president of the United States on equal terms. His initial anxieties about whether he and his delegation would be treated with respect were forgotten. He had proved Stalin wrong: He had "represented his homeland in an honorable way." Both diplomatically and emotionally he was prepared to continue his Camp David conversations with Eisenhower in May, in Paris. "If only the President could serve another term," he told Ambassador Thompson at a New Year's Eve party, "he was sure our problems could be solved."

11

In a 1992 interview, Khrushchev's son-in-law, the journalist Alexei Adzhubei, summarized his father-in-law's American visit, in which he had participated: "This was his finest hour, the best time of his life. He never had such a good time after that. . . . He tried to be restrained, and it seemed like nothing surprised him in America, but of course he was stunned by everything . . . he was fascinated by America."

Apparently Soviet citizens shared those feelings. When Khrushchev's plane landed in Moscow, Adzhubei went on to recall, "It was the first time in our history when . . . hundreds of thousands of people came out on the streets to greet him of their own free will, not on orders." As historian Rósa Magnúsdóttir notes, Khrushchev's visit "may have had more lasting significance [for the Soviet public] than changes in Soviet-American relations at the official level."

But there were many who did not greet Khrushchev as a returning hero. Adzhubei explained: "He felt some pressure from some of his Party comrades [who] thought he put too much value in friendship with the Americans. And he felt this in his bones, because the tradition of confrontation, the struggle between Communism and Imperialism, was being violated. . . ."

13

"We Cannot Let the Present Government There Go On"

It would be desirable, if possible, for US to break relations
with Cuba, in concert with other countries some time before
January 20th.
—PRESIDENT DWIGHT D. EISENHOWER

The United States electoral system is fraught with anachronisms, among them the long transition before the president-elect takes office. At the end of the eighteenth century, given a large country connected by the speed of horse, there were practical reasons to schedule four months between Thomas Jefferson's election in November and his inauguration on March 4, 1801. It is astonishing, however, that it took 136 more years before the Twentieth Amendment to the Constitution compressed that long lame-duck session into a shorter—but still longer than necessary—two and a half months; sufficient time for a lame-duck administration to impose commitments on its successor.

1

IN THE seventy-three days between Richard Nixon's defeat on November 8, 1960, and John Kennedy's inauguration on January 20, 1961, everyone in the Eisenhower administration associated with JMATE—the CIA's plan for the invasion of Cuba—pushed it toward operational readiness, and none more actively than the president. He was determined to see Castro ousted, and he did not trust Kennedy to do the job on his own initiative. During the campaign Ike said he would "do almost anything to avoid turning the country over to 'the young genius,'" one of his derisive epithets for JFK. But he (and Nixon) had not done enough, and now he was furious. His blood pressure "soared to dangerous levels" at the news of Kennedy's victory, and he developed "a terrible case of flatulence." It was "the repudiation of everything I've done for eight years," he told his staff.

There was still time, however, to make it more difficult for the new president to repudiate the plan to oust Castro.

Eisenhower's attitude toward covert operations was firm and unemotional. As Richard Bissell, the CIA's deputy director for plans, whom Dulles had personally selected to oversee the operation, remembered, the president "did not seem troubled by moral doubts about the propriety of clandestine operations." Neither the CIA's participation in the overthrow of Mohammad Mosaddeq in August 1953, Iran's legitimately elected prime minister, nor the ousting in June 1954 of Guatemala's democratically elected president, Jacobo Árbenz, had elicited any "squeamishness" or concerns about their "rightness or wrongness" from the president. Dealing with Castro was no different.

Eisenhower demanded progress training the "Cuban freedom fighters" in Guatemala, the continuation of sabotage, and if necessary even preparations for assassination. He indicated to Dulles that he wanted the operation "expedited," and he intended to reinforce his successor's commitment to Castro's overthrow by breaking diplomatic relations with Cuba before he left office.

He made this clear at a White House meeting on December 28. Discussing the readiness of the various aspects of JMATE with the State Department's Livingston Merchant, the president said, "It would be desirable, if possible, for US to break relations with Cuba, in concert with other countries some time before January 20th."

Gen. Andrew Goodpaster, Eisenhower's staff secretary, recorded a different phrasing, but made the same point: "He [Eisenhower] was inclined to think that it might be time to recognize the anti-Castro front as the Cuban Government. He added that he would like to see a definite move taken in this matter before January 20th, and said that the State Department should be thinking of some definite action that could be brought about before that time."

As Ike's luck would have it, Castro relieved the State Department of the need to create a "definite action." On January 2, 1961, he obliged the president with a pretext by demanding that the U.S.

Embassy in Havana ("a nest of provocateurs and spies") reduce its staff from eighty-seven to eleven. "This calculated action on the part of the Castro Government is only the latest of a long series of harassments, baseless accusations, and vilification. There is a limit to what the United States in self-respect can endure," Eisenhower directed his press secretary, James Hagerty, to announce the following day. "That limit has now been reached . . . the Government of the United States is hereby formally terminating diplomatic and consular relations with the Government of Cuba."

The last legal barrier to an invasion had been removed.

2

EISENHOWER'S DECISION responded to the importuning of his closest constituency, a powerful group of business leaders. Two weeks earlier they had invited Director of Central Intelligence (DCI) Allen Dulles to a meeting in New York with the intent of sending a clear message to the White House: "Get off of dead center and take some direct action against Castro." Organized by Henry Holland, a major fund-raiser for a coalition of anti-Castro Cuban organizations, the attendees included Standard Oil's vice president for Latin America, the chairmen of the Cuban-American Sugar Company and the Freeport Sulphur Company, the presidents of the American Sugar Domino Refining Company and the American and Foreign Power Company, and representatives from Texaco, International Telephone and Telegraph, and other corporations with Cuban business interests—all fearful that Castro intended to (and would) nationalize their properties.

The coalition had a proactive agenda that Dulles explained the next day, December 21, to the so-called Special Group, the secret administration committee of interagency representatives charged with eliminating Castro and his government. Sabotaging the sugar crop, interrupting the electric power supply, and embargoing food, drugs, and spare parts for critical machinery were among their milder suggestions.

Having the U.S. Navy blow up a ship in Cuba's Levisa Bay was another proposal. In addition, the cabal informed Dulles, it intended to produce a series of policy papers "designed to help US policy planners" in a post-Castro Cuba whose government "should not be left-oriented."

The president's national security adviser, Gordon Gray, took careful notes, but urged the Special Group (which had been meeting "with increasing frequency since mid-November") "not [to] authorize any action until he had cleared the matter with his 'associate'" (obviously the president).

At the conclusion of the January 3 White House meeting, at which the decision to sever diplomatic relations was confirmed, someone raised the question of when to brief the new administration on the details of JMATE. The minutes record that "no definite schedule was agreed upon but the concensus [*sic!*] of the meeting was that appropriate briefings should be considered for the near future."

The inauguration was in seventeen days.

3

JOHN KENNEDY had campaigned for the presidency to the right of Richard Nixon. The Eisenhower administration, he repeatedly asserted, had failed to check Communist advances. It had left European allies uncertain about America's commitment to their defense. Its huge nuclear weapons buildup had ignored a "missile gap" that favored the Soviets. The president's imprudent fiscal policies had weakened national security by cutting U.S. conventional forces to a perilous level.

Worst of all, the administration had permitted Communism to thrive just "eight jet minutes from the coast of Florida." But "we have not finished with Mr. Castro," he promised a Jacksonville audience. "This is a struggle for freedom in Latin America that will go on for the next ten years."

These failures were both dangerous and revealing: "If you can't stand up to Castro," Kennedy chided Nixon, "how can you expect to stand up to Khrushchev?" What the government of the United States should do, candidate Kennedy's campaign staff announced prior to his final (foreign policy) televised debate with Nixon, was to unleash Cuban "fighters for freedom."

Long before that October 21 debate, training Cuban freedom fighters is exactly what President Eisenhower had authorized and promoted, although Kennedy did not have detailed information about the program. Allen Dulles had informed him in July, "in general terms," about developing CIA guerrilla actions against Castro, but as the historian Peter Wyden concluded in his *The Bay of Pigs*: "Kennedy probably did not learn of major military plans against Cuba until he was briefed by Dulles and Bissell in Palm Beach [on November 18, 1960] after his election."

It is not known what Kennedy thought at that moment about his own campaign's perspicacity, but we do know that he would come to regret his anti-Castro campaign rhetoric.

In his 1965 memoir, *Waging Peace*, Eisenhower insisted that no invasion plans were passed on to the incoming administration, only that there were "units of Cuban refugees busily training and preparing for a return to their native land. Specific plans for a military invasion [did not exist]."

In an extended September 10, 1965, interview with the Long Island newspaper *Newsday*, the former president repeated that "no tactical or operational plan [was] even discussed" before or during the transition to the Kennedy administration. He had made no commitments that might bind the new president's dealings with the Castro problem, Ike insisted. "At no time did I put before anybody anything that could be called a plan [to invade Cuba]. . . . [There was] no commitment by me or by anyone in my administration." The *Newsday* interviewer reported further that Eisenhower "doubts that Kennedy felt 'he was frozen to any position by me.'"

New York Times journalist Max Frankel reported a very different handoff. "On meeting his successor, Eisenhower told Kennedy he must not allow the Castro government to survive. When Kennedy asked whether he should support the Cuban exiles then being trained . . . in Guatemala, Ike replied, 'to the utmost.'"

Frankel, whose book on the Cuban missile crisis does not provide reference notes, was referring to a White House meeting on January 19, 1961, the day before Kennedy's inauguration. President Eisenhower had invited the president-elect, and a select group of his top aides and advisers, to a transition meeting. Clark Clifford, a Kennedy confidant whose experience as President Truman's special counsel earned him an invitation and a role in the new administration's changeover, took detailed notes. When the issue of Cuba came up, "Eisenhower, with Kennedy on his left, made it clear that the project was going very well and that it was the new administration's 'responsibility' to do 'whatever is necessary' to bring it to a successful conclusion." Eisenhower added: "We cannot let the present government there go on."

Five days later, on the twenty-fourth, as the new administration began to settle in, Clifford sent Kennedy a memorandum. He reminded the president that his predecessor had said: "It was the policy of this government to help the exiles 'to the utmost' and that this effort should *be* 'continued and accelerated.'"

Eisenhower's assertions that there was no invasion plan bear an uncanny resemblance to Bill Clinton's 1998 disquisition to a grand jury on the "meaning of 'is.'" In Ike's case it was the meaning of "a plan." As the CIA historian Jack Pfeiffer explained: "The definition of a military plan [in Eisenhower's mind] seems to have focused on [the requirement for] an actual site for the landing." Lacking this detail, the former general insisted that there had been no invasion plan. But, Pfeiffer continued, Eisenhower "conveniently ignored the major change that was made in the concept in November of 1960. What was to have been an infiltration . . . became an amphibious *invasion plan* calling for a major enlargement of the exile Brigade and air operations."

There is further evidence that Eisenhower went to great lengths to cover up his contributions to the Bay of Pigs invasion. He not only dissembled in public statements, but it appears that he manipulated the oral history interviews conducted by historians for his presidential library. A careful reading of those interviews made it clear—at least to Pfeiffer—that the Bay of Pigs was "apparently banned as a topic in oral history interviews conducted with Eisenhower, and various of his senior subordinates who were close to the operation."

The topic had been airbrushed from the Eisenhower administration's history.

4

THE NEW administration's claims that Kennedy had been reluctant to support his predecessor's invasion plan rival Eisenhower's own evasions about his role in organizing, planning, and promoting the operation. Initially, at least, the new president was as committed as his predecessor to ridding Cuba of Castro, but he was also as determined as Eisenhower to achieve that goal without a trace of U.S. government involvement. Eisenhower had ordered that "our hand should not show in anything that is done," and Kennedy agreed. It was the "plausible deniability" caveat that led, step by step, to the "perfect failure."

The irony of the Kennedy administration's hostile relationship with Castro is that the president understood, and even sympathized with, the Cuban Revolution. During his Senate career he had often made the point that colonialism created oppression, and that Third World countries deserved to be freed from the economic shackles that countries like France had imposed on nations like Algeria.

A significant facet of the early Cold War was a furious competition for the allegiance of Third World nations, but the consequences of imperialism in Latin America were as despised as were the consequences of imperialism in Africa and Asia, except that there United States business interests were the toxic irritant. In Cuba, for example, American corporations owned half of the sugar-producing land, and almost all cattle ranches, mines, oil refineries, and utilities.

Kennedy intended to meet the challenge of Latin American hostility to American imperialism by emulating Franklin Roosevelt's "Good Neighbor" policy. And he considered it important enough to flag it in his inaugural address.

"To our sister republics south of our border," the president "offer[ed] a special pledge—to convert our good words into good deeds—in a new Alliance for Progress—to assist free men and free governments in casting off the chains of poverty." The plan—the largest aid program to the developing world—envisioned twenty billion dollars in loans and assistance to Latin American nations to promote democracy and undertake meaningful social reforms. It was a mini–Marshall Plan, motivated by the same assumption as the original: Communism thrives on poverty and despair; the best antidote to Communism was improved living standards.

But Kennedy knew Latin American governments would not support the Alliance—or indeed any other United States initiative—if the U.S. military invaded Cuba. JMATE had to be covert.

Clark Clifford's notes of the White House transition meeting indicate that no one in Kennedy's entourage had raised questions suggesting "any reluctance or hesitation" about Eisenhower's invasion plan. Even if just as a matter of courtesy or political caution, it was nevertheless true that Castro, Cuba, and Brigade 2506 were near the top of the pile of policy baggage that awaited the new occupant of the Oval Office.

Kennedy moved swiftly and secretly. A week into his presidency he did something that Eisenhower had avoided: He ordered the JCS to review the CIA's invasion plans—but secretly. The process could not be "staffed," the Chiefs were told, and everything related to their review had to be kept within the confines of their offices. They were forbidden to discuss anything about JMATE with subordinates. And the president made it clear that they were being asked to "advise"; they were not to become "involved." "Plausible deniability" and the future of the Alliance for Progress hovered over the entire process.

5

THE JCS analysts found the CIA plan slipshod, incomplete, and unprofessional. Gen. David Shoup, the marine corps commandant, remarked sarcastically, "If this kind of an operation can be done with this kind of force, with this much training and knowledge about it, then we [the marines] are wasting our time in our divisions; we ought to go on leave three months out of four."

But the document that was delivered to the White House on February 3, "Military Evaluation of the CIA Paramilitary Plan— Cuba," gave a different impression. The chances of success were "favorable," it noted, although it made the point that "ultimate success will depend upon political factors, i.e., a sizable popular uprising or substantial follow-up [U.S.] forces." "Follow-up" was a sop: The Chiefs knew that both Eisenhower and Kennedy had pointedly ruled out military intervention. The former—"a popular uprising"— was an irrepressible, persistent CIA fantasy that drove the program over a cliff. It might have served as a red flag for the president were it not for the fact that Allen Dulles and Richard Bissell assured both the JCS analysts and the president that "the chance of uprisings was 'increasing.'"

So were the president's concerns about the operation's "noisiness." After a briefing by Bissell, Kennedy was overheard to say: "Dick, remember I reserve the right to cancel this right to the end."

PART THREE

Kennedy, Khrushchev, Castro, and the Bay of Pigs

Let all our neighbors know that we shall join with them to
oppose aggression or subversion anywhere in the Americas.
And let every other power know that this Hemisphere intends
to remain the master of its own house.
—JOHN F. KENNEDY INAUGURAL ADDRESS

14

"Eisenhower Is Going to Escape"

Only when our arms are sufficient beyond doubt can we be
certain beyond doubt that they will never be employed.
—JOHN F. KENNEDY INAUGURAL ADDRESS

Khrushchev learned the news first. It was noon in Moscow when at
4:00 a.m. EST on November 9, 1960, an exhausted John Kennedy
retired to his bedroom at the family's compound in Hyannis Port,
Massachusetts, "not completely confident that he had won." But during the five hours he slept, the cliffhanger election was resolved by a
mere 0.1 percent of the popular vote, 112,827 more for Kennedy than
for the Republican candidate, Richard Nixon. The president-elect's
Electoral College margin was the closest since 1916, 303 to 219. Not
exactly a mandate, but victory nevertheless.

Khrushchev was pleased. He "beamed with satisfaction" at the
news. He had kept his good opinion of the candidate to himself,
and delayed a spy swap (U2 pilot Francis Gary Powers for KGB Col.
Rudolf Abel) until well after the election. He believed Kennedy was
more reasonable than the virulently anti-Communist Richard Nixon,
whom he detested.

1

KHRUSHCHEV'S LETTER of congratulations was among the first the
president-elect read, and one of the two he was most attentive to in
replying. It hinted at a summit and called for a return to the cooperative relationship that had characterized the presidency of Franklin D. Roosevelt. "The destinies of world peace depend largely on

the state of Soviet-American relations," Khrushchev wrote, assuring the president-elect that he was ready to develop "the most friendly relations." He then listed his top priorities: The Soviet government was ready "to solve such a pressing problem as disarmament, [and] to settle the German issue through the earliest conclusion of a peace treaty."

Depending on one's view of the Soviet Union and its leader, an American reader in 1960 could interpret the message as either solicitous and hopeful, or as "peace propaganda." Khrushchev was reaching out, which meant that his note was both. Though Kennedy chose to read it through a skeptical Cold War lens, he took pains to craft a generous reply.

Having taken the trouble to consult his friend Charles "Chip" Bohlen, one of the State Department's two leading Soviet experts, he was surprised by Bohlen's suggestion of a curt one-line answer. Kennedy chose to ignore this advice, and drafted a "friendly and hopeful" response: "I am most appreciative of your courtesy in sending me a message of congratulations. The achievement of a just and lasting peace will remain a fundamental goal of this nation and a major task of its President. I am most pleased to have your good wishes at this time."

It was an early sign of the independent judgment he would exhibit as president.

There is much to be learned from this seemingly inconsequential incident about John Kennedy's attitude toward the Soviet Union and Khrushchev, and his understanding of the nature of Cold War diplomacy. However much he distrusted the Soviet premier, he was eager to develop a working relationship with him. The Cold War was a competition, and Kennedy was eager to engage his opponent. "Civility is not a sign of weakness," he remarked in drafting his reply, and he remained steadfastly committed to that principle. Even through October 1962, despite Khrushchev's lying during the prelude to the Cuban missile crisis, Kennedy adhered to diplomatic civility and compromise. It was one reason the crisis was peacefully resolved.

2

"IN OCTOBER 1957, the Soviet Union had launched simultaneously
the first space capsule to orbit the earth and a new Cold War offensive to master the earth," wrote Theodore "Ted" Sorensen, summarizing the world as seen from Hyannis Port. Since 1951 Sorensen had
been Kennedy's speechwriter and confidant. He had drafted portions
of Kennedy's book *Profiles in Courage*—which won the 1956 Pulitzer
Prize—and most of Kennedy's speeches.

A native of Lincoln, Nebraska, he was a Unitarian, a conscien-
tious objector, and a lawyer whose life experiences, religious beliefs,
and general outlook contrasted with—but never clashed with—
Kennedy's. Their relationship was symbiotic: Sorensen's loyalty,
work ethic, and felicitous writing style suited Kennedy's intellect,
personality, and public persona. Kennedy's intellect, personality, and
ambitions—for himself and for his country—appealed to Sorensen's
deepest instincts. They developed a seamless working relationship
and a genuine friendship. By 1960 no observer of their partnership
would question Sorensen's ability to reflect accurately John Kennedy's
thoughts about diplomacy, public policy, or world affairs.

"In the three years that followed [Sputnik], the freedom of West
Berlin had been threatened by a Soviet ultimatum, backed by boasts
of medium-range ballistic missiles targeted on Western Europe,"
Sorensen wrote in *Kennedy*, summarizing the president's international
perspective on the eve of his election. South Vietnam was under siege
by "a campaign of guerrilla tactics and terror planned and supplied
by the Communist regime in Hanoi," and Laotian independence was
facing similar assaults. "The Soviets had invested several billions
of dollars in military and economic aid in the developing nations,
including arms for Indonesia, the Aswan Dam for Egypt, steel mills
for India and more arms for the Algerian rebels. The Russian and
Chinese Communists had competed for a Central African base in
Ghana, in Guinea, in Mali and particularly in the chaotic Congo."
But perhaps the most threatening situation was the one closest to
American shores. Fidel Castro was playing host to a growing number
of Soviet and Warsaw Pact forces in Cuba, and he was organizing "a
campaign to subvert Latin America."

Eisenhower "is going to escape, and all the pigeons are coming home on the next President," Kennedy had grimly remarked during the campaign, referring to the proliferation of Communist activities around the globe. The United States was not prepared to confront this offensive: "American military might was too thinly stretched and too weakly financed." In the president-elect's view the U.S. missile programs—the backbone of defense policy—had started late and had produced only limited success. Our ability to compete successfully against the Soviets and Chinese was hampered by "under-financed" foreign aid programs that did little to win the hearts and minds of poverty-stricken populations. Kennedy also considered the United Nations "in disarray," and democracy everywhere on the defensive, as evidenced by recent anti-American riots in Japan and Venezuela.

The Eisenhower administration had made no effort, the aspiring New Frontiersmen concluded, to connect with "the new forces of economic development and social justice" in Latin America, or even with "the new forces of economic unity and growth" in Western Europe: "Other nations were uncertain what we meant when we talked—or whether we meant it when we talked—about the equality of man or about our desire for disarmament or about our commitment to defend freedom." The country was rudderless, and in order to set a bold new course it was necessary to undertake a complete makeover of U.S. foreign and military policy.

On the eve of his election, John Kennedy's view of his predecessor and his foreign policy was as disdainful of Eisenhower as Ike had been of Truman and his policies. "He'd often discuss how President Eisenhower's main points were his smile and how people just thought he was a benevolent man," Priscilla Wear—a Kennedy administrative assistant—recalled. "But I don't really think that he felt President Eisenhower was capable."

3

DURING MOST of American history the pressures generated by domestic politics, economic ambitions, and security considerations had contributed in varying degrees to shaping the nation's foreign policy objectives. But with the outbreak of the Cold War, the relationship between foreign and domestic politics was compressed. Soviet policies so inflamed popular anti-Communism, and anti-

Communism became so enmeshed in the nation's political discourse that combating Communism came to constitute the quintessence of U.S. foreign policy. Rhetoric about cooperating with the Kremlin to lower the risk of war was well received by the public, but actually entering into an accommodating arrangement with the Soviets was a high-risk political commitment.

In 1960 the Cold War was still evolving, and both superpowers entertained fantasies of global hegemony, a goal that encouraged increasing their nuclear arsenals. For a decade and a half the Strategic Air Command (SAC) and its supporters had lobbied to subordinate every significant aspect of United States foreign policy to the quest for nuclear superiority. To counter Soviet initiatives, they argued, more nuclear weapons were necessary.

Troubled by the consequences of the escalating arms race, on March 16, 1958, Eisenhower's special assistant for national security affairs, Gen. Robert Cutler, wrote to his boss that military requirements called for "all the nuclear weapons that could be produced and as rapidly as possible." The result was an increase in the number of targets, rather than increased security. A point of horrendous danger had been reached, he reported. In a recent war game *7 million kilotons* of nuclear explosives had been detonated. Anticipating the concept of nuclear winter by decades, Cutler worried that "the effect of any such exchange is quite incalculable. No one knows what the concentrated explosion of 7,000,000 KTs involving nuclear material would do [to] the weather, to crop cycles, to human reproduction, to the population of all areas of the world. . . . It is possible that life on the planet might be extinguished."

4

JOHN KENNEDY had never seen General Cutler's memo, but he too believed that the Eisenhower administration's massive retaliation doctrine was dangerous. And also a failure. Nuclear weapons were a deterrent against a nuclear attack, but of little use against a limited incursion. It made no sense—and it was hardly credible—to threaten to begin a nuclear war in response to a conventional assault. The Korean War had made that clear. Everyone in the new administration agreed that the defense strategy of the United States needed a serious overhaul. Flexible response would replace massive retaliation, but the nuclear arms race would continue unabated.

If Khrushchev had paid closer attention to Kennedy's campaign speeches, he might not have been sanguine about U.S.–Soviet cooperation, at least the sort of cooperation he had in mind. His top priorities were a final settlement of the division of Germany, the elimination of West Berlin, and a nuclear arms agreement that would contain the arms race. His collective-farming initiatives had been a disaster, and his efforts to provide more consumer items had been impeded by his military's incessant demands for more weapons, delivery systems, and manpower. An arms control treaty would help to free resources that he could redirect to his domestic programs.

Regardless of how dangerous Kennedy believed nuclear weapons had become—and how much he wished to work out an arms control treaty with Khrushchev—he was not about to accept the political repercussions of challenging America's reliance on its nuclear arsenal. He had embraced nuclear superiority during his campaign, and he continued to promote the value of nuclear weapons. His strategy for escaping the consequences of Eisenhower's massive retaliation policy (which relied almost completely on the Strategic Air Command) was to surround the SAC's vast nuclear arsenal with conventional forces, and to minimize its deterrent role by increasing the navy's ballistic missile submarine force.

In Kennedy's mind he was sidelining Eisenhower's nuclear strategy, but in Khrushchev's view the president was expanding it.

5

KENNEDY AND Khrushchev had a lot to learn about each other, and about the new complexities of post–Eisenhower/Dulles diplomacy. Both leaders were ambitious, inclined to use all means available to seek transformative initiatives, but without a clear sense of the limits that nuclear weapons had imposed on diplomacy. It was another period of adjustment. Only fifteen years since 1945 and the dawn of the nuclear age. Only eleven years since 1949 and the first successful Soviet atomic bomb test, the formation of NATO, and the Communist conquest of the Chinese mainland. Only seven years since Stalin's death in 1953, and the end of fighting on the Korean Peninsula. Only five years since 1955, and the formation of the Warsaw Pact.

And it was only three years since October 1957, when Sputnik took to the heavens—beeping "a message beyond men's ordinary fantasies"—and shattered America's confidence in its technological superiority. "It appears that their Germans [scientists] are better than our Germans," the comedian Bob Hope quipped. But it was no laughing matter: Americans were frightened. On January 20, 1961, when President Kennedy urged his fellow citizens: "Ask not what your country can do for you, but what you can do for your country," he knew that his country's men and women expected him to do something very specific for them: Restore their lost sense of security.

6

JOHN KENNEDY inherited a foreign policy in flux. Every aspect of U.S. Cold War strategy, including alliance diplomacy, was unstable. France was on the brink of quitting NATO and acquiring an independent nuclear arsenal (*force de frappe*), and there was even talk of Chancellor Konrad Adenauer distancing West Germany from the influence of the United States by acquiring independent nuclear weapons. The administration's paroxysm of alliance insecurity was most prominently focused on its European allies, but there was much to worry about in Latin America and Asia. Just two weeks before Kennedy's inauguration on January 20, 1961, Khrushchev had announced his support for "Wars of National Liberation," in a speech that the new administration took as a direct challenge. A strategy for reinforcing established relationships and building new ones was high on the new president's foreign policy agenda.

The president-elect's selection of cabinet members reflected his disquiet about the state of international relations. His razor-thin margin of victory, his aggressive anti-Communist campaign rhetoric, his natural political caution, and perhaps even a touch of personal insecurity led him to "run with the wind" in selecting the members of his cabinet. Arthur Schlesinger Jr., soon to become White House special assistant, was disappointed by the conservative bent of Kennedy's choices. His "undue capitulation to the Establishment in the foreign and defense field(s)," suggested "a dreadful sense of his own relative inexperience," Schlesinger wrote to a friend. Speculating further, he concluded that he has "placed foreign and defense policy too much in the hands of insiders."

The most prominent foreign policy insider was DCI Allen Dulles who, along with FBI director J. Edgar Hoover, was among the president-elect's first reappointments. As Schlesinger suspected, Kennedy retained the Republican Dulles to solidify his bipartisan Cold War credentials. "It may be," a later DCI speculated, "that the young former senator from Massachusetts, who followed World War II's largest legend to the White House, just could not displace the Cold War's first [CIA] legend."

7

By 1960 Allen Welsh Dulles was more than a CIA legend; he was the architect, director, and guiding spirit of a well-funded alternative government that operated on behalf of the president (and occasionally on its own), beyond the reach of Congress, the courts, or public opinion. For the past eight years, what his brother, the secretary of state, could not accomplish through diplomacy, Allen sought to arrange through covert operations. If John Foster was born with a silver spoon in his mouth, his younger brother was delivered with the addition of a silver bullet in his hand. Espionage was his forte and his passion. No member of the administration seemed to enjoy his job more.

Born in 1893 in Watertown, New York, into a prominent political family (his grandfather John W. Foster was President Benjamin Harrison's secretary of state, and his uncle Robert Lansing held the same position in Woodrow Wilson's administration), Allen easily gravitated to the corridors of power in Washington and Wall Street after graduating from Princeton.

By the time he was recruited into the Office of Strategic Services (OSS) at the outbreak of World War II, Allen Dulles had served in U.S. embassies in Istanbul, Vienna, Bern, and Paris (as a member of the American delegation to the 1919 Paris Peace Conference), headed the State Department's Near East Division, coauthored two books criticizing isolationism, worked at the storied law firm of Sullivan & Cromwell, directed the Council on Foreign Relations, and served as its secretary for a decade (1933–1944).

In June 1942, encouraged to establish a comprehensive intelligence service by the British, President Franklin D. Roosevelt issued a military order creating the OSS, as an agency of the Joint Chiefs of Staff (JCS). He appointed attorney William Donovan its head, and "Wild Bill," as he had been known to his friends since high school, set the can-do bar high: Whatever it takes, get the job done.

Under General Donovan's direction, the OSS operated during the war in both the European and Asian theaters—infiltrating operatives behind enemy lines, organizing and training resistance fighters, assassinating enemy agents, and collecting intelligence. It was the brainy warriors' service—the incubator for the CIA—heavily populated by intellectuals, professionals, and scions of distinguished WASP families. Allen Dulles oversaw its station in Bern, Switzerland, where he established connections with German émigrés and anti-Nazi intelligence officers. He was in contact with the plotters of the July 20, 1944, attempt to assassinate Hitler, discovered German plans for the development of the V-1 and V-2 rockets, was involved in secret negotiations in March 1945 that led to the surrender of German forces in northern Italy, and, when the war ended, assisted "useful" (i.e., anti-Communist) Nazis to escape Allied prosecution through the infamous "ratlines" to South America.

To the chagrin of its senior officers—Allen prominent among them—the OSS was disbanded in October 1945. But deteriorating relations with the Soviet Union led President Truman and Congress to include a new intelligence organization, the Central Intelligence Agency, in the 1947 National Security Act. In 1950 Dulles was appointed the agency's deputy director of plans—the overseer of covert operations, his métier—and the rest is history.

It was a history that in many ways—both direct and indirect—led to the Cuban missile crisis.

8

IN AUGUST 1953, six months after President Eisenhower elevated Dulles to DCI, the new director carried out his first regime-change assignment. Mohammad Mosaddeq, the elected prime minister of Iran, had nationalized the assets of the Anglo-Iranian Oil Company, a British enterprise that had refused to cooperate with the Iranian government's demand for access to its books. Agents from MI6, Britain's CIA equivalent, suggested a joint operation to overthrow Mossadeq, and President Eisenhower endorsed the idea.

"Before going into the operation," the historian Stephen Ambrose wrote in his acclaimed biography of Eisenhower, "AJAX [the operation's code-name] had to have the approval of the President. Eisenhower participated in none of the meetings that set up AJAX; he received only oral reports on the plan; and he did not discuss it with his Cabinet or the NSC." Establishing a pattern he would hold to throughout his presidency—and after—he kept his distance and left no documents behind that could implicate him in any illegal coup. "But in the privacy of the Oval Office, over cocktails, he was kept informed by Foster Dulles, and he maintained a tight control over the activities of the CIA."

On August 19, 1953, the plotters, directed by CIA agent Kermit Roosevelt Jr.—a veritable doppelgänger of his "Rough Rider" grandfather, Teddy—unleashed the forces he had organized to topple the Iranian government. CIA funds had been generously distributed to journalists to accuse Mosaddeq of harboring Communist sympathies, thugs had been hired to riot in the streets, and the military's officer corps had been successfully bribed and suborned. Mosaddeq was arrested, the Shah (who had been forced to flee Iran days earlier) was returned to power, and United States oil companies received access to 40 percent of Iran's oil fields. It was a "splendid" coup.

It was also a perfect template for dealing with other "troublesome" Third World governments.

Jacobo Árbenz, the president of Guatemala, became the leader of one of those governments shortly after his election in 1950. Following through on his economic and social reform campaign promises, he threatened the landholdings of the United Fruit Company (UFC). While at Sullivan & Cromwell, John Foster had represented United Fruit, Allen had served on its board of directors, and Ed Whitman, UFC's senior public relations executive, was the husband of Eisenhower's private secretary.

In August 1953, with the Iranian coup having demonstrated the ease with which recalcitrant leaders could be replaced by more coop-erative ones, President Eisenhower authorized a $2.7 million bud-get for "psychological warfare and political action," "subversion," and "assassination," all cobbled together as Operation PBSUCCESS. Less than a year later, on June 18, 1954, 480 CIA-trained fighters landed in Guatemala. To the agency's distress, they were pinned down until CIA planes bombed Guatemala City. On June 27, when broadcasts threatening a U.S. invasion kept the Guatemalan army in its barracks, President Árbenz fled the country.

9

AT AN NSC meeting on the afternoon of March 17, 1960, Presi-dent Eisenhower decided that Fidel Castro should join Mosaddeq and Árbenz as yet another CIA Cold War trophy. He had come to this decision deliberately and predictably, but also reluctantly, har-boring the hope for almost a year that he could avoid actions that might antagonize the UN and the Organization of American States (OAS). Perhaps, he thought, one of the anti-Communist leaders in the Western Hemisphere could be cajoled into finding a way to rid Cuba of Communism.

"A Castro victory might not be in the best interests of the United States," Allen Dulles had informed him shortly before Fidel's forces marched into Havana on New Year's Day, 1959. That was news to Eisenhower, who recalled in his memoirs that this was the first time the DCI had told him that "Communists and other extreme radi-cals appear to have penetrated the Castro movement [and] if Castro takes over, they will probably participate in the government." He had dismissed earlier similar reports, he wrote, "because they originated with people who favored Batista."

Allen Dulles, he should have known, was among them.

CIA suspicions of Castro's Communist proclivities had been actively discussed for almost a year within the agency, the Penta-gon, and the State Department. Agents close to Batista acquired, and eagerly reported, both accurate and exaggerated information about Communist members of Castro's July 26 Movement. Fidel's brother Raúl and his lieutenant Ernesto "Che" Guevara were known Com-munists, and there were others, although no one had any credible information that Fidel shared their allegiance. But that was irrelevant. It was enough to conclude that a Castro government might include Communists.

A search was launched for a leader who was both anti-Batista and anti-Castro. But that was another fool's errand, and its failure precipitated a flurry of alternative suggestions ranging from military intervention, to persuading Batista to establish a friendly CIA-controlled junta, to a proposal that the U.S. government reverse course and embrace Fidel as an ally. Alfred Cox, the agency's chief of the Paramilitary Division (which included the psychological staff) suggested that "a practical way to protect United States interests would be to make secret contact with Castro, assure him of United States sympathy with some of his objectives, and to offer him support."

On New Year's Eve, after Castro's forces seized the city of Santa Clara, Batista and his family flew to the Dominican Republic. When the news reached Washington, a group of CIA, State, Pentagon, and White House officials discussed what action the United States should take "including direct intervention by U.S. Marines." But no option promised a good result.

Castro entered Havana a week later to a reception reminiscent of the liberation of Paris. Batista had alienated the last of his allies, and Fidel was "the idol of the masses," the CIA's chief of station reported to Washington.

Over the course of the following year—Eisenhower's last as president—relations between the Cuban and the United States governments descended like an aircraft on an inapt glide path. Whether or not a correction might have prevented the crash—Alfred Cox's sympathetic approach to Castro, for example—will be argued forever. But several things are clear: There were Communists in the Cuban government. Castro was determined to liberate his country's economy from American domination, and he took steps toward that end. President Eisenhower and his DCI were unwilling to tolerate his intentions. They had successfully (and easily) eliminated other reformers, and they saw no reason to believe that Castro was less vulnerable than Mosaddeq or Árbenz.

10

A "PROGRAM" to deal with Castro was necessary, Eisenhower told his DCI in the early months of 1960, and within weeks of that conversation the CIA had drafted a four-point "Program of Covert Action Against the Castro Regime." It called for creating a Cuban government in exile, a "powerful propaganda offensive," a "covert intelligence and action organization" inside Cuba, and "a paramilitary force for future guerrilla action" outside. "Because the policy makers [i.e., the president and his staff] feared censure by the United Nations and/or the Organization of American States," the CIA's *Official History of the Bay of Pigs Operation* explains, "the myth of 'plausible deniability' was the caveat that determined the CIA would be the principal implementing arm for the anti-Castro effort."

But definitely not a rogue arm, "acting out of control and independently," as Peter Wyden claims it did thirteen months later. Eliminating Castro and his government was an operation that President Eisenhower supported, and one—it is now clear from the available evidence—that he was determined to impose upon his successor.

It was a two-stage process. Stage one directed Allen Dulles to organize a guerrilla operation. "The president said that he knows of no better plan for dealing with this [Cuban] situation," Gen. Andrew Goodpaster wrote in his summary of the March 17, 1960, meeting of the National Security Council. "The President told Mr. Dulles he thought he should go ahead with the plan and the operations." But, he warned, *"Our hand should not show in anything that is done."*

"You may recall that not so very long after I became your Special Assistant," national security adviser Gordon Gray wrote to the president, "in a meeting you had with Allen Dulles and me you gave instructions that activities of the so-called 'Special Group' should not be recorded in any place except in the files of the Director of the Central Intelligence Agency. You did not wish that there be other copies."

Stage two was triggered by John Kennedy's election. "On 29 November 1960 the level of involvement of the US Government escalated sharply with the sudden resurgence of interest on the part of President Dwight David Eisenhower," the CIA's historian recorded. "Suddenly the President emerged as one of the principal decision makers in the period prior to the take-over by the Kennedy administration."

Richard Bissell, the CIA officer in charge of the operation, reported that after the election "the President [Eisenhower] made it clear he wanted all done that could be done with all possible urgency and nothing less on the part of any department." He even "led a discussion as to how best to organize the total US effort against the target."

In the fall of 1960, prior to the election, camps had been established in Guatemala to train several hundred guerrilla fighters. Their mission was to infiltrate Cuba, disrupt the economy by sabotaging critical resources, and in every way possible destroy the credibility of Castro's government in the hope that the citizenry would turn against him.

However, by Inauguration Day, January 20, 1961, fourteen hundred ardent anti-Castro Cubans were being trained and armed to invade their homeland. The original guerrilla infiltration operation, the plan before the November 8 election, had been scrapped. The new plan, a full-fledged invasion, would be delivered to former navy lieutenant John Fitzgerald Kennedy as an action program approved by the five-star general-president, who had organized and commanded the invasion of Normandy.

15

"AES Wholly Disapproves of the Project"

And I say to you now, Mr. President, that the prospects for
this plan [JMATE] are even better than our prospects were
in Guatemala.

—ALLEN DULLES TO PRESIDENT KENNEDY

Adlai Stevenson often awoke early to catch a plane to Washington,
D.C. He would typically schedule a full day of meetings at the State
Department, and, if the president was available, he would visit the
White House. There was always too much to do in New York City,
but if he didn't get to the capital frequently, he risked being left out
of the policy loop. America's ambassador to the United Nations was a
busy, harassed man. Representing his country in the world's premier
diplomatic arena was exhilarating, but doing it as a member of the
Kennedy administration was often disheartening.

1

THE PRESIDENT had never warmed to his erstwhile political rival,
and his brother Bobby was outright hostile. He was the family's hater,
and Adlai was a favorite prey. The wellspring of Bobby's enmity was
Stevenson's political history: As the Democratic Party's presidential
candidate in 1956, Adlai had resisted Jack's vice-presidential aspira-
tions. Four years later he had been cool, if not thoroughly opposed,
to seeing Jack Kennedy as the party's nominee. "I don't think he'd
be a good president," he told a friend. "I cannot in [good] conscience
throw my support to someone I do not think is up to it." Furious,

Jack told Adlai: "Look, I have the votes for the nomination and if you don't give me your support, I'll have to shit all over you. I don't want to do that but I can, and I will if I have to."

The brothers also believed that Stevenson had hoped to snag the nomination in the last minutes of the 1960 Democratic Convention. "We want Stevenson," his supporters thundered in a final effort to secure him a third presidential bid. Bobby's resentment ran deep.

Personality differences reinforced political hostilities. The macho Kennedy brothers considered Stevenson prissy. They judged his caution a sign of cowardice, his intellectual bent a form of confusion, and they even held his sexual orientation in doubt—a view that FBI director J. Edgar Hoover promoted. Irresolution was Adlai's style. "He never quite accomplishes anything," Bobby charged. When offered the position of ambassador to the United Nations, Stevenson—who aspired to be secretary of state—infuriated the president-elect by replying that he would "consider it."

To strain the relationship further, Stevenson had the annoying habit of turning conversations into lectures. Relations between the men deteriorated to the point that Jackie Kennedy (who liked Adlai) complained to Franklin Roosevelt Jr.: "Jack can't bear to be in the same room with him." Bobby confirmed his sister-in-law's observation: Adlai "used to drive [Jack] out of his mind . . . what a pain in the ass he was."

Stevenson had been selected for the UN position to provide political cover. He was the leader of the liberal wing of the Democratic Party, and his appointment was a tactical move to protect the administration's left flank. If he resigned in anger (and in conversations with friends Stevenson periodically did mention doing so), his supporters, who held Kennedy's liberalism suspect, would exact political retribution. So, despite his antipathy to Adlai, the president had to cork his brother's venom and pander to his ambassador. It was a complicated relationship.

Despite what Kennedy thought of Stevenson, he had entrusted him with a notable assignment. The global propaganda war with Communism was a critical dimension of the administration's Cold War strategy, and Kennedy was committed to publicly rallying allies and persuading neutrals. Eisenhower had been incompetent in this arena, in Kennedy's view, and he was determined to demonstrate this by example.

Kennedy was heavily invested in the military elements of the Cold War struggle, but he believed they could not be isolated from the global popularity contest between capitalism and Communism, Communism and democracy. International flare-ups were hotly debated in the UN, the Cold War's most important public arena. The U.S. position had to be well represented, but Kennedy worried that in a crisis Stevenson might not be up to the task.

2

STEVENSON, IN TURN, was given ample reason to wonder about Kennedy's competence. The first occasion occurred in April 1961, barely three months after the inauguration. The episode was the Bay of Pigs. Contrary to the administration's postinvasion spin, the new president hoped to take credit for sweeping Castro out of the Caribbean. We "were hysterical about Castro. . . . ," recalled McNamara. "Had the invasion succeeded without direct United States military intervention," Ted Sorensen said, "it would have been hailed as a great move. . . . So, in that sense, [the] great mistake was in failing to do it successfully."

The CIA's organizers had a similar view: "I think Kennedy is surrounded by a group of men with a much livelier awareness than the Republicans of the extreme crisis that we are living in," Richard Bissell—who had briefed the president-elect on the Eisenhower administration's invasion plans—wrote to a friend. "What I really mean is that the Democrats will be far less inhibited in trying to do something about it."

It was an accurate reflection of Kennedy's Cold War rhetoric, and of his stated enthusiasm for ridding the hemisphere of Castro and Communism. But it ignored the concern he shared with Eisenhower that "our hand should not show in anything that is done."

The more closely the president examined the CIA's plans prior to the invasion, the more improbable it appeared to him that plausible deniability could be assured: It was "too noisy." After discussing the Joint Chiefs' advice with his national security adviser, McGeorge

Bundy, Kennedy concluded that the Chiefs' suggestions were even "noisier" than the CIA's. As concerns replaced the early confidence that CIA assurances had created, a sense of anxious resignation took hold: "I think about it as little as possible," Kennedy replied with ill-concealed irony to Arthur Schlesinger when asked about "this damned invasion."

A typical wry Kennedy comment, his remark indicated the opposite of what he was saying. The invasion had become a gnawing matter—so many flaws coexisting with so much pressure to move forward. The planners countered each doubt with yet-stronger reassurances. CIA director Allen Dulles went so far as to tell Kennedy: "Mr. President, I know you're doubtful about this, but I stood at this very desk and said to President Eisenhower about a similar operation in Guatemala, 'I believe it will work.' And I say to you now, Mr. President, that the prospects for this plan are even better than our prospects were in Guatemala."

It was a preposterous statement, a lie rather than an assessment, but it did what Dulles intended: It kept the invasion on track.

3

SECOND-GUESSING SET in among the small circle of advisers privy to the operation, and cautious adjustments were made to reinforce plausible deniability. The most significant was the shift of the landing site from Trinidad, an area near Havana and the Sierra del Escambray mountains, to Playa Girón (the Bay of Pigs). At one point Kennedy called Bissell and told him that he must make José Miró Cardona, the head of the Cuban Revolutionary Council—the anti-Castro Cuban organization coordinating the Bay of Pigs invaders—"understand that either he accepts the idea of *no US military intervention* on his behalf and agrees to proceed on this basis or else the whole expedition would be immediately called off."

The message was duly delivered, but neither Cardona nor Bissell considered it irreversible.

The closer D-day approached, the more problematic the operation appeared. Not only had Castro flooded the Miami area with spies who kept him fully informed, but on April 6 the *New York Times* headlined: "Invasion Reported Near," and a CBS story followed. The next day the *Times* ran another story reporting that anti-Castro units were being trained at bases in Guatemala.

"Castro doesn't need agents here," Kennedy angrily remarked. "All he has to do is read our papers."

4

BUT THE president's anger at the *Times* was misplaced. Public information about the CIA operation had been available in American newspapers for months, and the *New York Times* was not the original source. Its April 6 story, which has received so much attention from historians, was both late and irrelevant to Castro's intelligence collecting about the CIA operation.

JMATE's cover had been blown months earlier, in October 1960. A Guatemalan newspaper had revealed that the CIA had purchased a $1 million local property to train Cuban exiles; the report was even confirmed by Guatemala's president in a television interview.

"Cuba Says Guatemala, U.S. Plot an Invasion," the *New York Daily News* reported during the week of October 8, seven months prior to the *New York Times* story. On the nineteenth the *Miami Herald* headlined: "Cuba Reports U.S. Aiding Anti-Castro Forces." The proliferation of information about the CIA's anti-Castro activities moved the FBI to open an "Overthrow Castro" file. It was mostly a collection of newspaper clippings . . . which the bureau classified secret.

The invasion of Cuba became an open secret that, incredibly, both the Eisenhower and Kennedy administrations chose to ignore. "In November I knew about the training ground in Guatemala," Senator Bourke Hickenlooper, a member of the Foreign Relations Committee, told his colleagues. "I was in Guatemala and, apparently, everybody in Guatemala knew about it. . . . It was supposed to be very covert, except that everybody in Central America knew."

In November, just days after Kennedy's election, *The Nation* magazine ran an editorial: "Are We Training Cuban Guerrillas?" and on January 10 the *Times*—at last—reported it in a front-page story that prompted Eisenhower to call a meeting with senior CIA, Defense, and State Department operatives to consider the consequences. According to a secret memorandum of their discussion: "The President decided that we should make no statement and continue to refuse to comment."

A State Department spokesman professed to know "absolutely nothing about" Cubans being trained in Guatemala.

Castro, on the other hand, knew almost everything.

5

THE OPERATION should have been altered or scrapped, but the presumption of damaging political consequences—plus more reassurances that the invaders would succeed—precluded cancellation. Eisenhower had maneuvered to ensure that Kennedy would have to follow through with his plan to oust Castro, and candidate Kennedy had promoted the idea. Now, as president, he could see no acceptable alternative. If disbanded, the anti-Castro brigade was certain to spread the word "through the country" that Kennedy had chickened out. The "disposal problem" was a political conundrum.

He had been too critical of the Eisenhower-Nixon administration's failure to expel Castro to cancel a plan, hatched on Eisenhower's watch, to do exactly what candidate Kennedy had insisted should have been done. The many persuasive arguments that Kennedy heard to abandon the enterprise were eclipsed by that political reality.

A National Security Council "Memorandum of Discussion [with the President] on Cuba," dated March 11, 1961, offers a clear view of Kennedy's ambivalence five weeks prior to the invasion: "The President expects to authorize U.S. support for an appropriate number of patriotic Cubans to return to their homeland," McGeorge Bundy wrote to the State Department, the CIA, and Arthur Schlesinger Jr., who was involved in the operation. "He believes that the best possible plan, from the points of view of combined military, political and psychological considerations, has not yet been presented, and new proposals are to be concerted promptly."

Senator William Fulbright, chairman of the Senate Foreign Relations Committee, read about the Guatemalan training camps with growing concern; everything about the impending operation seemed wrong. As a senator, Kennedy had been a member of the Foreign Relations Committee, and he respected Fulbright's intelligence and judgment. Fulbright was his first choice for secretary of state, but the Arkansan's record on civil rights reflected his constituency's Southern attitudes, and that had made his appointment impossible.

But Fulbright's views on Cuba were welcome, and in mid-March the president invited the senator to fly to Florida with him on Air Force One. It was the perfect opportunity. Working with his aide Pat Holt, Fulbright drafted a lengthy memorandum that critiqued the operation. It noted that the "secret" training program was well known throughout Latin America, that U.S. involvement could not be hidden, that an invasion would contravene several U.S. treaties and laws (which he specified) and, perhaps most damaging, that the enterprise "is of a piece with the hypocrisy and cynicism for which the United States is constantly denouncing the Soviet Union in the United Nations and elsewhere. The point will not be lost on the rest of the world."

The memorandum also anticipated the result. Fulbright predicted that the invaders would face stiff resistance that might require direct U.S. military support to achieve success, and if such support were offered, "we would have undone the work of thirty years in trying to live down earlier interventions. We would also have to assume the responsibility for public order in Cuba, and this would be an endless can of worms."

As Air Force One reached its cruising altitude, the president read Fulbright's memorandum and launched into a conversation that had nothing to do with Cuba. There was no turning back. But as events played out, it would become obvious that he agreed with Fulbright's analysis.

6

ADLAI STEVENSON had been neither consulted nor informed about the operation. When the invasion plans were finally brought to his attention on April 8, incompletely and dishonestly ("our briefing was probably unduly vague," Arthur Schlesinger Jr., the briefer, confessed), he was appalled and angry. "AES [Stevenson] made it clear that he wholly disapproves of the project," Schlesinger reported to the president. "[He] objects to the fact that he was given no opportunity to comment on it, and believes it will cause infinite trouble."

Preinvasion action began seven days later, on April 15. At dawn eight B-26 bombers attacked three Cuban airfields. Painted by the CIA with Cuban Air Force [FAR] markings, the bombers were flown by former Batista air force pilots. The planes had taken off from Nicaragua, but the CIA's account to the media identified the attackers as "a group of Cuban pilots deserting Premier Castro." To reinforce this report, a ninth B-26 was discharged on a "smoking-gun" mission. It too was freshly painted with the FAR insignia, and the cowling—the metal cover over the engine—had been removed, riddled with bullets, and replaced before it took off. After flying close enough to Cuba to appear to have been part of the attacking aircraft contingent, it turned north, shut down the "damaged" engine, and made a dramatic "emergency" single-engine landing at Miami International Airport.

"Three Cuba Air Bases Bombed as Pilots Revolt, Fly to U.S.," read the headline in the *Los Angeles Times*. "Castro Pilots Revolt; Blasts Kill 7," echoed the *Chicago Daily Tribune*. "A heroic blow for Cuban freedom was struck this morning by certain members of the Cuban Air Force," Cardona exulted.

The theatrical story of defection and air assault, supported by the evidence of the bullet-pierced B-26, persuaded most Americans, Ambassador Stevenson included. When Cuba's foreign minister, Raúl Roa Garcia, denounced the attacks at the UN, declaring the bombardment and the cover story a despicable CIA plot, Stevenson rose in righteous indignation to defend his country.

The planes "were Castro's own air force planes and, according to the pilots, they took off from Castro's own air force fields," he countered. Roa's charges were outrageous: Displaying a UPI wire photograph of the B-26's bullet-pierced cowling, Stevenson declared that "there would not under any conditions be an intervention in Cuba by United States armed forces."

Kennedy too was adamant: "I have emphasized before that this was a struggle of Cuban patriots against a Cuban dictator. While we could not be expected to hide our sympathies, we made it repeatedly clear that the armed forces of this country would not intervene in any way."

7

ADLAI STEVENSON had believed every word he had spoken at the UN on Sunday, April 16, which made his humiliation on Monday so hurtful.

Within twenty-four hours the CIA cover story had unraveled like the witless weekend fraternity prank it resembled. The Cubans had located shell fragments and auxiliary fuel canisters that could be traced to the United States through markings, and, in the mysterious process that so often links irony with incompetence, a genuine Cuban air force defector landed his plane in Miami: Its markings, reporters quickly noticed, were rather different from the CIA's imitation.

April 17, the day that news arrived that members of Brigade 2506 had landed early that morning on Playa Girón, may well have been the worst of Adlai Stevenson's life. He had been lied to by his government, ignored by his president, and was now branded a liar by the representatives of the international community with whom he dealt daily. A friend who saw him that evening was "shocked by his appearance. . . . I was sure that either he was desperately ill or that something frightful had happened."

He was not alone in his misery. Every member of the White House inner circle was sent to his damage-control station. The B-26 fiasco and Stevenson's humiliation at the UN precipitously altered the administration's priorities. "Plausible deniability" and the fate of the Alliance for Progress catapulted to the fore. Fulbright's warnings resonated. Rusk and Bundy could not square the president's insistence that there be no appearance of direct U.S. involvement in the operation with the pleadings of CIA officers for air strikes in support of the besieged invaders.

The president had to make the decision. Having retreated to his vacation home in Glen Ora, Virginia, to reinforce the impression that the U.S. government was not involved in the invasion, Kennedy was appalled by the combat reports. The CIA's promises that a spontaneous uprising of anti-Castro Cubans would support the invaders was a fantasy, and so were their assurances that the invading force would quickly overwhelm Castro's militia. When Secretary of State Dean Rusk called and recommended cancellation of the second wave of air strikes, Kennedy readily agreed.

No U.S. military support would be forthcoming. Kennedy understood, as the CIA planners and President Eisenhower had not, that even anti-Communist Latin Americans "hate US intervention more than they hate communism."

The invasion, however, was under way.

8

"WE WERE already mobilized when the air strike hit our air bases," Castro later recalled. "We had already dispersed our planes, and we were able to respond immediately. There is an enormous difference between a mobilized force—a mobilized people—and a people that is taken by surprise."

Surprise overwhelmed the CIA and the hapless invaders. Lacking air cover, they were quickly pinned down by the deployed Cuban militia; all escape routes from the landing beach were blocked. To make matters worse, a plane from Castro's air force destroyed the supply ship on which *all* the invasion force's ammunition had been loaded (another astonishing display of incompetent planning). With that the 2506's chances of success, or escape, disappeared.

Not a single CIA officer involved in planning the operation, most especially DCI Allen Dulles and his deputy director of plans, Richard Bissell, had believed that an American president, faced with such a debacle, would refuse to unleash whatever military support was necessary to achieve success. If the CIA's rebel army could not overthrow Castro, the CIA's planners were confident that the U.S. military would support his ouster. Despite all the president's warnings to the contrary ("We are not sending U.S. forces in. That is categorical"), they believed they had created a foolproof plan.

With air cover and numerous armed defectors purportedly assured, all the Brigade 2506 invaders would have to do, they were cheerfully told, "was to go straight into Havana." And if that scenario didn't work out as planned, the brigade's CIA handlers were confident that they would still march into Havana—behind the marines.

The entire operation was designed to "entrap" the president, Thomas L. Hughes, assistant secretary of state for intelligence and research, told the author.

In the end, however, it was the CIA along with the hapless invaders who were trapped. Within forty-eight hours Castro's forces had defeated, killed, or captured most of the invasion force. Perhaps that's not a surprise for, as it was later learned, the CIA's "formidable force" was both inadequately trained and irresponsibly assembled. "Many of the men had just arrived in Guatemala and never wielded a weapon," the historian Howard Jones discovered. "Only 135 of them were soldiers, and 240 were students. The remainder were doctors, lawyers, businessmen, peasants, and fishermen—some as young as sixteen, one as old as sixty-one."

9

BARELY THREE months into his presidency, Jack Kennedy had overseen an unprecedented foreign policy fiasco. "It was a catastrophe that the world's number-one power could do a thing like this," West Germany's military intelligence chief remarked. "Our feeling of trust in the American leadership diminished to a very low level."

The experience was devastating. "Jack had been on the phone" with his father most of the day, Rose Kennedy wrote in her April 19 diary entry. "Jackie said [Jack] was so upset all day & had practically been in tears. . . . Jackie seemed so sympathetic & said she had stayed with him until he had lain down as she had never seen him so depressed except once at the time of his operation." Ted Sorensen described him on the nineteenth as "anguished and fatigued" and "in the most emotional, self-critical state I had ever seen him."

The president's misery was pervasive. "The largest contribution I made in eight years at the White House," Walt Rostow recalled, "was my role in helping to mop up the Bay of Pigs failure. . . . All my friends and colleagues were having nervous breakdowns. They were in terrible shape; literally, they could not function."

Two days later, on Friday, April 21, Kennedy pulled himself

together and famously told a news conference: "There's an old saying that victory has a hundred fathers and defeat is an orphan. . . . I am the responsible officer of the government."

That was the right thing to do, his father assured him. "People like leaders who take responsibility . . . this is going to turn out to be one of the best things that ever happened to you."

Perhaps it would be, eighteen months later, when the healthy skepticism he absorbed about expert advice helped him navigate a peaceful path through the Cuban missile crisis. But for now, he told Sorensen, he felt blindsided. "You always assume that the military and intelligence people have some secret skill not available to ordinary mortals."

10

ALLEN DULLES had never thought of himself as an ordinary mortal. He was a Master Spy. He had helped destroy Hitler, contain Stalin, and eliminate left-leaning governments at Eisenhower's behest. His CIA was a Cold War praetorian guard that he led with aplomb and bravado. But his brazen self-assurance, and his willingness to bend the truth, finally destroyed him. Substituting expectations for facts and arrogance for analysis, he (and his deputy Richard Bissell) had underestimated Castro and misread the president.

"Allen Dulles was a frivolous man," Arthur Schlesinger Jr. observed. "He was most intelligent and a man of great charm, unlike his brother. But he was frivolous in the sense that he would make these decisions that involved people's lives and never really would think them through."

"I doubt my Presidency could survive another catastrophe like this," Kennedy concluded, recognizing that the Bay of Pigs disaster was now the defining event of his administration. There was no further room for failure and, to assure that, he consciously changed his decision-making style.

"I think that after the Bay of Pigs, he conducted national security operations in a different way," Sorensen observed. "He was more skeptical of the recommendations which came to him from the experts. He challenged their assumptions, their premises, even their facts. He made certain that everyone went on a written record of exactly where

they stood so that they would be thoughtful in their recommendations. He inquired not only as to the results of their recommendations but the consequences which we could expect from those results,
counter-consequences from those consequences, and so on. So that in
every way, after the Bay of Pigs he approached this kind of situation
in a more precise and knowledgeable fashion and kept the control of
the decision-making more tightly within his own hands."

11

STEVENSON'S EARLIER warning to Arthur Schlesinger—that the
CIA operation "will cause infinite trouble"—did not improve his
standing with the president. It appears that there was only one thing
Jack Kennedy and his brother disliked even more than an adviser
who gave bad advice: an adviser who had given good advice that the
president had rejected.

Stevenson did not understand this aspect of the Kennedy personality any better than he understood their suspicions of his motives.
His next initiative, to analyze the lessons that should be drawn from
the debacle, was even less appreciated than his accurate prediction.

The memorandum he sent about a week later was perfectly
designed to rankle John Kennedy. It condemned imperialism, lauded
foreign aid as an alternative to military intervention, explained why
Marxism was attractive to emerging governments, and made the case
that the Bay of Pigs invasion, and anything like it in the future, was
bound to put the United States in a bad light. "We are not going to
be destroyed in our beds even if Castro does continue to mismanage
Cuba for another decade," he wrote, ignoring Kennedy's view that
Castro could destroy the president at the polls. "Of one thing we may
be sure—the 19th Century system of gunboat diplomacy or landing
the Marines is highly unpopular."

None of this was news to Kennedy. It was what he believed, but
it was an analysis disconnected from American politics. The political environment, as Kennedy understood it, called for a clear commitment to anti-Communism. Idealism worked only so long as it
was carefully calculated to reinforce that fundamental fact. Stevenson
rejected that reality.

But he could not be ignored. An essential political asset for the president's reelection in 1964, Stevenson required stroking. He had been lied to by the White House, and then humiliated by his impassioned defense of the administration. His forecast that the CIA's predictions were absurd had not escaped the president's notice. As much as he disliked his ambassador, Kennedy understood that his point of view had value. Henceforth, it would be prudent to keep Stevenson informed about Cuba policies and, if only for political reasons, to acknowledge his counsel.

16

"Cuba Might Become a
Sino-Soviet Bloc Missile Base"

If people are not ready to die to get rid of communism, we
will never get rid of it in many cases.
—ALLEN DULLES, DIRECTOR OF CENTRAL INTELLIGENCE

If they [the USSR] should ever build a missile base or a
submarine base [in Cuba], we will be able to find that kind of
thing out promptly and with certainty.
—RICHARD BISSELL, CIA DIRECTOR OF PLANS

Less than two weeks after the invasion, the Senate Foreign Relations
Committee (SFRC) began hearings into the nation's worst foreign
policy setback since the Korean War. The Bay of Pigs invasion was
both a "perfect [military] failure" and an unmitigated political disaster. It diminished public confidence in President Kennedy's judgment
and created a rift between the administration and the most influential foreign policy committee on Capitol Hill. "I just see nothing
in our experience [of interventions] that would cause me to believe
that if [the Bay of Pigs invasion] had succeeded you would have been
much better off than you are now," Senator William Fulbright, chairman of the SFRC, admonished Secretary of State Dean Rusk.

The administration had ignored Congress in the run-up to the
invasion, and the members of Fulbright's committee were angry.
"We could have been of great assistance to the administration,"
Senator Wayne Morse, chairman of the Subcommittee on American
Republics Affairs, complained. "We have to reestablish an understanding with this administration. We should have been briefed a
long time ago," added Senator Hickenlooper. "The reluctance of the

State Department and CIA to advise with this committee condemns them," Senator George Aiken asserted.

1

IN A series of executive sessions (whose records remained closed to the public for twenty-three years), the members of the SFRC interrogated the secretary of state, the director of Central Intelligence, and the chairman of the Joint Chiefs of Staff about the origins, planning, and execution of the operation in an effort "to understand how the decision-making processes had failed so miserably."

Those hearings, which historians of the Cuban missile crisis generally have ignored, reveal a surprise: In one of the great ironies of the Cold War, the secretary of state anticipated Khrushchev's "harebrained" initiative of sending missiles to Cuba more than a year before the idea occurred to Khrushchev. To bolster his testimony, Secretary Rusk stated that among the motivations for the Bay of Pigs invasion was the possibility (nowhere to be found in the preinvasion discussions) that Cuba could become "a Sino-Soviet missile base."

At 10:05 on Monday morning, May 1, Rusk appeared before Senator Morse's subcommittee with all members of the Foreign Relations Committee present. "It is most unfortunate," Morse admonished in his opening remarks, "that the Foreign Relations Committee of the Senate and, particularly, [this] subcommittee did not have the benefit and opportunity of consulting with the State Department and the White House in advance of the decision that was made to support the exiles in the attempted invasion of Cuba."

Rusk, who had been consumed during the past week by the deteriorating situation in Laos, was eager to mount a respectable defense for the invasion. He had not prepared a formal statement, but spoke at length from notes about the decision-making process, the legal issues, the Communist threat to the hemisphere, the expectations for the invasion that failed to materialize, and related issues. But his most intriguing presentation was his ex post facto rationalization—which contemporary documents do not support—that a primary purpose of the invasion was to deny the Soviet Union the opportunity to deploy nuclear missiles to Cuba.

In straining to conjure justifications for the Bay of Pigs, Rusk fabricated a scenario that Khrushchev transformed into reality a year later. There "was also the prospect which had to be taken into account," Rusk informed a suspicious committee, "that Cuba might become a Sino-Soviet bloc missile base." That would not only directly threaten the United States, he continued, but whatever attempts were made to eliminate the threat would involve "a difficult bargaining position which might affect the stands of NATO and the defenses in other parts of the world with respect to the Soviet Union."

Cuba, the secretary lectured the committee, was not an isolated problem. It was linked to the "powerful offensive which the Sino-Soviet bloc is now making right around the world." To reinforce this point, he concluded with an apocalyptic peroration: It was necessary "to relate [the Bay of Pigs] episode to the broader struggle in which we are involved, but this is a part of *a war to the death* which we in our generation and for the next decades are going to be involved with."

Senator Fulbright was skeptical. "Do you really believe that [Cuba]," he asked sardonically, "even if it is covered with tanks and planes, would be a real serious military threat to the security of the United States in itself?"

"I think jet fighter bombers and missiles in Cuba," Rusk responded, "could impose a degree of blackmail upon the United States . . . that would be extremely serious for us."

"You do?" Fulbright retorted. "I wish you would explore that. I do not quite follow that."

The great danger, Rusk explained, was the *possibility of Soviet missiles in Cuba*. The Soviet Union had a limited number of intercontinental missiles with which to target the United States. But if they moved some of their many medium- and intermediate-range missiles to Cuba that would raise "an additional security threat [and] would inject an additional complicating policy problem into our dealings with our security problems in other parts of the world."

Of course, Rusk admitted, "This is somewhat speculative, Mr. Chairman, to try to look into the future, but in Cuba there will be opportunity . . . to inflict grievous danger on this country. . . . If there was any possibility that the [anti-Castro] Cubans could [remove the potential danger] themselves, this was something that we felt ought to be seriously considered."

"Did you have any objective evidence," Senator Frank Church asked, "to indicate that the type and character of the arms supplied to Castro were of a nature to constitute an offensive threat to the United States?"

"There was not objective evidence," Rusk admitted, but hastened to add that "this is one of the factors that necessarily were taken into account."

No one in the room took Rusk's Soviet missile deployment scenario seriously enough to ask him follow-up questions.

2

THE FOLLOWING afternoon was the CIA's turn to explain away its "Boy Scout operation," that "any 6-year-old kid would have known . . . was going to be a failure," in Senator Homer Capehart's withering characterization. Accompanied by Richard Bissell, the architect of the invasion, DCI Allen Dulles began his prepared testimony at 2:00 p.m. after notifying the committee that he would have to leave for an important National Security meeting at 3:45. In 105 minutes, he discussed the "grave threat" that Cuba posed, and the efforts the CIA had initiated to undermine the Castro regime. Insisting that the "operation was a Cuban one," he reviewed the military and economic assistance Castro's government received from the Communist bloc, the "careful planning" that went into the operation, the reasons it failed [Castro's "forces displayed a greater will to fight than we had expected"], and numerous other details. Not once, however, did he pick up on Rusk's point that the invasion was prompted by a concern that Soviet missiles might be sent to Cuba.

After Dulles departed, Bissell provided the committee with operational details.

In response to Senator Frank Carlson's query about whether the CIA could keep the Committee and the government "well informed" about the number of Soviet bloc personnel in Cuba, Bissell mentioned missiles. "If they should ever build a missile base or a submarine base, we will be able to find that kind of thing out promptly and with certainty."

Senator Church asked what contemporaries called the sixty-four-thousand-dollar question: "Was there, then, any evidence at all of nuclear weapons being shipped or missiles being shipped or missile launching pads? . . . Was there any evidence of these being actually established in Cuba?"

"No, sir," Bissell responded. "There was not."

Other questions and answers followed, but none touched on the possibility of nuclear missiles being delivered to Cuba. At 5:55 the committee adjourned—in the dark, when the hearing room's lights went out—leading Senator Fulbright to quip that he did "not know whether your people did it or the Russians did it."

Whoever did it had created a metaphor for the difficulty of getting an accurate accounting of the motivations and plans for the invasion. But the testimony of the past two days did demonstrate that in the aftermath of the Bay of Pigs, Khrushchev's later initiative should not have been such a surprise to the administration.

3

News of the hearings had spread through the Senate, leading several of its more curious members to ask Fulbright for a briefing. In response the chairman invited Rusk to return on the afternoon of May 3 to provide what details he was willing to share with a select group of recently elected senators. In a wide-ranging overview—more akin to a Diplomacy 101 lecture than a State Department briefing—the secretary discussed the Cold War, the new nationalism, the Sino-Soviet threat (his favorite topic), alliances around the globe, Laos, the Congo, foreign aid, and a host of other issues. One of those was the United Nations. It was the first issue he mentioned, and the one he discussed most passionately: "We came out of World War II with a strong determination . . . to make the United Nations work," and it was clear that he believed it did.

In dealing with the Sino-Soviet threat, Rusk insisted that "building a strong United Nations" was the highest priority. "It is not lost on the other nations of the world that the United Nations effort in the Congo, for example, is largely dependent upon the encouragement and support given to it by the United States." In the competition for the allegiance of the many newly independent countries, "most of them not allied with us," he considered a positive relationship between the United States and the UN important.

Anyone who listened to the secretary's discussion would not have been surprised that seventeen months later, after President Kennedy imposed a blockade on Cuba, Rusk would ardently support involving the UN in the effort to reach a peaceful resolution.

4

SIXTEEN DAYS later, on May 19, at 10:15, the chairman of the Joint Chiefs of Staff, Gen. Lyman Lemnitzer, began his testimony with the observation that "numerous press releases in recent weeks have implied that a major responsibility for the failure of the Cuban expeditionary force to establish themselves in their homeland rests with the Joint Chiefs of Staff." Denying any attempt at "recrimination," Lemnitzer nevertheless developed the theme, over more than three hours of testimony, that "the planning and operational direction of the Cuban expeditionary force was accomplished by the Central Intelligence Agency." The Pentagon was merely a peripheral player.

The senators were not convinced by the chairman's dodge, and their questions ranged from forced sympathy to outrage, with many falling into the puzzled category. It was difficult to understand precisely what the military's role was in the planning and operational phases, and queries focused on issues such as the Joint Chiefs' positive evaluations of the CIA's plans, paramilitary versus military operations, air support and lack thereof, the Cuban underground, the reasons for failure, the lack of adequate intelligence, ammunitions, weapons, supply ships, and numerous other operational matters.

Only one question related to missiles. Had Lemnitzer found any "evidence of an act of direct military aggression by Castro through Russia?" Senator Morse asked, adding that if there was such evidence it would surely "alter whatever plans we will have."

Lemnitzer agreed that missiles in Cuba would alter plans, and went on to remark that "in my appearances before the various committees, great concern was expressed about missile bases built in Cuba. My reply was that we have no specific information that they are under construction, but I am sure if we did detect such bases being constructed, that would put a new order of magnitude into the problem."

17

"It Will Be a Cold Winter"

They controlled, in a very real sense, the future of the world
between them, and it was logical that they should meet
instead of the President relying on what others told him about
Khrushchev.
—TED SORENSEN, 1964

The Bay of Pigs set Khrushchev's agenda, and his assessment of John
Kennedy. The American president was not only young and inexperienced; he was a gutless capitalist raised in a pampered environment.
He had not had the courage to send his military into Cuba, so he
would not have the backbone to resist Khrushchev's primary foreign
policy goal: forcing the Americans, British, and French to abandon
West Berlin. If Kennedy didn't acknowledge that a Western enclave
110 miles within East Germany was "abnormal" and a violation of
that country's sovereignty, Khrushchev would sign a separate peace
treaty with the German Democratic Republic (GDR). An independent East German state would have no obligation (as the Soviet
Union had) to recognize the 1945 agreement that guaranteed ground
and air access between West Germany and West Berlin.

When he met Kennedy in Vienna in June, he intended to settle
the Berlin anomaly.

1

KHRUSHCHEV'S MISUNDERSTANDING of Kennedy's character would
lead him through a series of defeats that ended with the humiliating removal of his missiles from Cuba. He measured the president's

refusal to support the anti-Castro invaders against his own decision to suppress the 1956 Hungarian uprising. But Kennedy's refusal to follow the CIA's recommendations to invade Cuba did not reveal weakness, as Khrushchev thought. On the contrary, it took extraordinary personal and political courage *not* to intervene.

In 1961, sending American troops to support the Bay of Pigs invaders was the Cold War default position. It was what Dulles, Bissell, and all the Joint Chiefs expected him to do, regardless of what he said. It was what Eisenhower and Nixon would have done. Politically, it was the safe move. Standing fast and absorbing the public humiliation of a badly planned fiasco was an act that revealed impressive fortitude.

John Kennedy may have been raised in an overly protected environment, but he lived in a body that tortured him daily, constantly threatened his life, and formed the pillars of his character.

Pain and the prospect of an early death shaped Kennedy into a fiercely determined personality, and a "great compartmentalizer." He accepted his ailments stoically, and took every opportunity to live to the fullest what scant life he thought he had left. He refused to allow physical torments to limit his physical activities on playing fields—or in bed.

His public image was upstanding and principled; his private behavior was neither. He was ambitious, charismatic, focused, curious, smart, devious, seriously ill, and ardently sexually driven. His personality—his character—was a complex construction of nature, nurture, and accident; luck really, both good and bad.

Born rich, handsome, and physically vulnerable, he had a medical history that amounts to "a story of lifelong suffering," thoroughly documented by his biographer Robert Dallek. He entered the world with defective adrenal glands that would lead to Addison's disease; his first brush with death occurred at age three, when scarlet fever almost killed him. Ten years later, fatigue, weight loss, and stomach ailments forced him to spend weeks at the Mayo Clinic. "God what a beating I'm taking. . . . Nobody able to figure what's wrong with me," he wrote a friend. Diagnosed with colitis, he was treated with corticosteroids that fostered osteoporosis and suppressed his immune system. Lower-back pain and recurrent infections constantly vexed him.

"Took a peak [*sic*] at my chart yesterday," he wrote a Choate classmate during one of his recurring hospitalizations, "and could see that they were mentally measuring me for a coffin. Eat drink & make Olive, as tomorrow or next week we attend my funeral."

Despite his maladies—which periodically sent him back to the Mayo Clinic and other hospitals—as a Harvard undergraduate he joined the swimming, sailing, and JV football teams, the latter leading to a spinal injury during a scrimmage. By graduation, it is probably fair to say, as Kennedy himself said earlier, he was "in rotten shape," and he probably was not any better in 1942 when, as a 4F, he tried to join the navy. He was physically unqualified but, with his ambassador-father's influence, his ailments were ignored, and Lieutenant Kennedy famously commanded a patrol-torpedo boat (PT-109) in the Solomon Islands.

On the night of August 1, 1943, the Japanese destroyer *Amagiri* cut it in half.

The swim to safety—towing an injured crewmember—took its toll on Kennedy's vulnerable back, and his determination to hide his injuries made things worse. "Jack feigned being well. . . . He did not let on to his crew or his commanding officer that he was ill or in pain," his executive officer attested.

His war experiences were transformative, another Kennedy biographer noted. He "emerged . . . with both his fatalism and his pragmatism sharpened to a fine edge: both to serve him well in the coming years."

In September 1947 Kennedy (by then a congressman from Massachusetts) collapsed during a visit to England. "That young American friend of yours," the admitting physician told Pamela Churchill, "he hasn't got a year to live." Returning by ship to the United States, attended by a nurse, Kennedy came close to confirming that diagnosis. Before he was carried off the ship on a stretcher, he received last rites.

He would spend his remaining days in pain.

Nor was the thought of death ever far from his mind. In 1948, when a storm made flying dangerous, Dallek recounts that Kennedy told his friend Ted Reardon: "It's okay for someone with my life expectancy [to fly]," but he wanted his sister Kathleen ("Kick") and Reardon to take a train. (Later that year Kick was killed in a plane crash in France.)

In the decade and a half that followed, pain and ambition vied to control John Kennedy's life. There was the exhausting campaign in 1952 for the Massachusetts Senate seat during which Kennedy suffered headaches, upper respiratory infections, stomachaches, urinary-tract discomfort, and constant back pain. But he campaigned tenaciously, and he won.

Later there was a back operation that almost killed him, numerous hospitalizations (nine, totaling forty-five days from May 1955 until October 1957, during his unsuccessful campaign to win the vice president's spot on the Democratic ticket). "The record of these two and a half years," Dallek notes, "reads like the ordeal of an old man, not one in his late thirties, in the prime of life."

Under the circumstances it was remarkable how much energy he had, and how thoroughly informed he was about policy details. "President Kennedy was the first president," Ambassador Averell Harriman insisted, "who [was] really his own Secretary of State. . . . [Franklin] Roosevelt selected the things he wanted to deal with. . . . But Pres. Kennedy dealt with every aspect of foreign policy . . . [and] knew about everything that was going on."

2

CURIOSITY, AS much as anything else, brought Kennedy and Khrushchev to Vienna. "They controlled, in a very real sense, the future of the world between them," Ted Sorensen wrote, "and it was logical that they should meet instead of the President relying on what others told him about Khrushchev."

The Soviet premier was equally curious about his new adversary. He had suggested a meeting in his November 9 congratulatory note to the president-elect, shrewdly mentioning his hope that "relations . . . would again follow the line along which they were developing in Franklin Roosevelt's time."

Kennedy had responded favorably in February, and while the Bay of Pigs threatened to intervene in April, neither American embarrassment nor Soviet "indignation" scuttled the event. Besides, the White House insisted, the summit in Vienna on June 3–4 "is *not* for the purpose of negotiating or reaching agreement on the major international problems that involve the interests of many countries."

It was an accurate prediction, but not as intended. No agreements would be reached at Vienna, where Khrushchev angrily raised two of the central issues that permeated the Cuban missile crisis: the Jupiter missiles that the Eisenhower administration had ordered deployed to Turkey and Italy (and that Kennedy supported), and the occupation of West Berlin by the Americans, British, and French. Ignoring Anastas Mikoyan's advice—"It's a new, young president so we should try to find understanding"—Khrushchev was determined to press Kennedy on both issues.

It was a colossal error. It destroyed the possibility of the détente that both he and Kennedy wanted, and it precipitated a confrontation in Berlin that embarrassed Khrushchev further. But he could not moderate his anxieties. The Germans had invaded his country twice in his lifetime, and he was determined to minimize their military power. A strong East Germany controlled by the Soviet Union was an effective barrier against future German aggression, but the existence of a Western enclave deep within the GDR threatened its security and its survival.

The security of the Soviet Union was primary, and on the afternoon of the first day of the conference, June 3, Khrushchev linked the Turkey missile deployment to Cuba. How was a country of six million people a threat to the United States? he asked Kennedy. You stated that you are "free to act," he scolded. "Then what should the USSR do?" The invasion of Cuba [the Bay of Pigs] had set a precedent, he said, and he asked what Kennedy would think if the USSR invaded Turkey in order to eliminate the threat that the deployment of American military equipment had created.

As Philip Nash, the leading historian of the Jupiter deployment, points out, Khrushchev was using his meeting with Kennedy to make two points that would soon inform his decisions. The first was his anger about the American missiles surrounding his country, and the second was his view that the situations in Turkey and Cuba were analogous.

The second day's conversations were further strained. World War II had ended sixteen years earlier, and the occupation of the Western sector of the city was now an anachronism, Khrushchev asserted. He had explained that to Eisenhower at Camp David, and he was more direct with Kennedy. It was important, he had written the president in May, that they address the "liquidation of a dangerous source of tension in the heart of Europe." The conclusion of a peace treaty would be a giant step toward improving U.S.–Soviet relations; the status quo was unacceptable.

Kennedy, however, intended to cling to the status quo: a divided Germany with the Federal Republic rearmed and a NATO participant. Any alternative acceptable to Khrushchev would cause difficulties with the British, French, and West Germans. He assured the premier that the United States would "live up to its commitments" to West Berlin "and its rights there." It was a matter of American security, not just a legal obligation. The United States was the alliance leader, and he could not back down on a commitment that had been sacrosanct since 1945. He had not become president, Kennedy said, "to preside over the isolation" of his country.

But in Khrushchev's view West Berlin was "a thorn," "an ulcer," that had to be eliminated. If Kennedy would not cooperate, "no force would prevent the USSR from signing a peace treaty." Any violation of GDR rights "would be regarded by the Soviet Union as open aggression with all the consequences that would ensue from this."

Prepared as he thought he was, Kennedy had not expected Khrushchev to be openly hostile, just as Khrushchev (believing that Kennedy could be pressured) had not expected the president to be resolute and defiant. They were at loggerheads, equally puzzled, and equally determined to maintain their positions.

Kennedy had come to Vienna, he said, "in the hope that the relations between their two countries could be improved," but Khrushchev's threats to sign a peace treaty by December augured a confrontation.

The United States was the one threatening war, Khrushchev responded, but "force would be met by force," and he presented Kennedy with an aide-mémoire that summarized his position.

"It will be a cold winter," the president concluded, and on that note the summit meeting of the two men who "controlled . . . the future of the world between them" was over.

3

CURIOUSLY, KENNEDY said of Vienna that Khrushchev "beat the hell out of me," and that it was "the worst thing in my life," an assessment that did not even approach the truth. Their conversations had been a standoff, not a Kennedy defeat. The president had stood firm against Khrushchev's threats, and had made it clear that he would not yield any allied rights related to West Berlin.

But in brushing aside the president's declarations that he was genuinely interested in better relations, and threatening a confrontation if Kennedy did not cooperate, Khrushchev left Kennedy angry, perplexed, deflated, and determined to resist. He had dashed the president's hope for a diplomatic triumph that could have repaired some of the festering political wounds inflicted by the Bay of Pigs. It was a disappointment that turned to anger and frustration, and it led to the political error of saying too much to journalists.

Rhetoric aside, Kennedy was analytical about Khrushchev's behavior, a reaction he would repeat during the Cuban missile crisis. His first challenge, he told the *New York Times* correspondent James "Scotty" Reston, was to understand "why he [Khrushchev] did it, and in such a hostile way. And second, to figure out what we can do about it."

The answer to the first question was the Bay of Pigs, he believed. Khrushchev thought that "anyone who was so young and inexperienced as to get into that mess could be taken. And anyone who got into it and didn't see it through had no guts. So, he just beat the hell out of me . . . I've got a real problem," the president concluded.

But it was a problem that he knew how to confront. He also told Reston that "he could never negotiate or deal with the Soviet leader as an equal until he [Kennedy] had shown strength and convinced the world of his steadfastness."

Firmness in response to Soviet challenges became the president's modus operandi.

Two personal assistants, Priscilla Wear and Jill Cowan (dubbed "Fiddle" and "Faddle" by the Secret Service), remembered the president's reaction to Vienna. "It really toughened him up; he realized that you had to be terribly tough with Khrushchev," Wear recalled. "He loved . . . the way Kenny O'Donnell [Kennedy's appointments secretary and special assistant], when he shook hands with Khrushchev, didn't smile," Cowan said. "He just stuck his hand straight out and grasped it. He said that's the way they played it; that's the way we ought to treat them and play it back. Everybody else had . . . tried to be charming with them."

4

Vienna refocused the administration's priorities: Berlin was an emergency. Its security immediately eclipsed all other issues. The role of the U.S. military in Europe had to be reviewed and reinforced. France and NATO, Laos and Vietnam, China and Taiwan, Egypt and Israel, the nuclear arms race—and Cuba—were now tethered to Kennedy's need to demonstrate to Khrushchev that he could not be intimidated.

Two consequential results of Vienna—at least for the history of the Cuban missile crisis—were the decision not to further consider the cancellation of the deployment of Jupiter missiles to Turkey, and confirmation that Khrushchev's highest priority was ejecting the United States and its allies from West Berlin.

President Kennedy also concluded that contingency plans for dealing with a confrontation over Berlin were "inadequate, incomplete, out-of-date, and inconsistent" with the available allied forces. It was too easy to imagine Khrushchev precipitating a war because he failed to appreciate the administration's unwavering commitment to the status quo.

The reassessment began immediately. The day after the Vienna conference, June 5, Kennedy flew to London to discuss contingency planning with Prime Minister Harold Macmillan and Foreign Secretary Alec Douglas-Home. They considered increasing military stockpiles for NATO forces, and agreed that preparations should be made for military probes in response to blockades, as well as an airlift to circumvent any effort to resist the probes.

Counterproposals to Khrushchev's position were discussed, but with the proviso, Kennedy insisted, that they contained no hint that the West might back down. "The prospects of an early diplomatic and, possibly, military confrontation with the Soviet Union," the Department of State's history of the Vienna conference concludes, "made it highly advisable for the Western Powers to re-examine their basic negotiating position on Berlin and Germany."

5

THE REEXAMINATION accelerated when the president returned to Washington. There were National Security Council sessions, and meetings with selected advisers that discussed "how [Khrushchev's] aide-memoire should be answered," and others on developing negotiating positions, and military responses to possible contingencies. The president consulted former secretary of state Dean Acheson, who, true to form, recommended a forceful response: Negotiations were "worse than a waste of time," he pronounced, and recommended a declaration of national emergency.

He was initially supported "by almost everyone," Sorensen remembered, including Secretary of Defense Robert McNamara. But, as soon as the president decided, "in a small private meeting," that he would ask Congress for the authority to call up troops without declaring a national emergency, McNamara—anticipating his acquiescence to the president during the Cuban missile crisis (and later to President Lyndon Johnson during the Vietnam War)—reversed his position. "In the formal National Security Council meeting, where the recommendation was presented and was somewhat strongly and acidly questioned by Mr. Acheson, Secretary McNamara was the best advocate of the view which he had only recently adopted himself."

Eschewing the Eisenhower option (leading with a nuclear threat), at the end of July Kennedy asked Congress for authority to call up military reserves and national guard divisions. The idea, according to Sorensen, was to make "an investment of men and honor so great . . . that the Communists would know we meant business."

Speeches and press conferences were a sure way for a president to convey policies, principles, and intentions to the Soviet leadership, and Kennedy was a master at this form of communication. When he spoke publicly he was informing Khrushchev that what he said was irrevocable, a public commitment to the American people.

Anticipating the principles that he would repeat in his Cuban missile crisis speech, he confirmed, on June 28, that he would protect West Berlin.

"The Soviet announcement that they intend to change unilaterally the existing arrangements for Berlin" is a grave threat to peace and security, he announced. Warning Khrushchev not to underestimate "the will and unity of democratic societies where vital interests are concerned," he made it clear that Berlin "involves the direct responsibilities and commitments of the United States, the United Kingdom and France. It involves the peace and the security of the Western World." No challenge to the rights and responsibilities of the allies for Berlin would be tolerated.

But the president also recognized that West Berlin was a problem for the Soviet Union. "Khrushchev is losing East Germany. He cannot let that happen," he told Walt Rostow, Bundy's deputy national security adviser. More than 4 million Germans had escaped to the West from the Soviet Zone of Occupation and then East Germany since 1945. In July 1961 over thirty thousand crossed the border. "If East Germany goes, so will Poland and all of Eastern Europe. He will have to do something to stop the flow of refugees," he said, and anticipated Khrushchev's solution. "Perhaps a wall. And we won't be able to prevent it. I can hold the Alliance together to defend West Berlin but I cannot act to keep East Berlin open."

To further convince Khrushchev that signing a peace treaty with the GDR could lead to war, the administration sent several private warnings to the Kremlin, and on July 25 Kennedy made another speech supporting West Berlin. Any attempt by either the Soviet Union or the GDR to block Western access to Berlin would be resisted, he warned: "The NATO shield was long ago extended to cover West Berlin—and we have given our word that an attack upon that city will be regarded as an attack upon us all."

West Berlin is both "an island of freedom . . . and a beacon of hope" he said, but more than anything else it is "the great testing place of Western courage and will, a focal point where our solemn commitments stretching back over the years since 1945, and Soviet ambition now meet in basic confrontation."

It was an uncompromising commitment, and in Khrushchev's view, "so far the worst spurt of intimidation," he told a group of Warsaw Pact leaders on August 4. He had responded, he reported, that "if they deploy one division in Germany, we will respond with two divisions, if they declare mobilization, we will do the same. . . . We are considering now . . . to deploy tanks defensively along the entire border."

He did not tell the delegates that he planned to build a wall.

6

ON THE morning of August 13, the residents of Berlin awoke to discover a barbed-wire barricade stretched along the border of their bifurcated city. It was the first stage of Khrushchev's plan to stem the hemorrhaging of East Germans to the West, and its preparation revealed uncharacteristic caution.

The president's warnings that West Berlin was sacrosanct had resonated in Moscow. Rather than the audacious initiative it appeared to be in 1961, Khrushchev's wall was a carefully calculated, cautious gamble. If the Americans threatened a confrontation, he planned to retreat. "As an extra precaution," his biographer William Taubman discovered, Khrushchev "decreed that the wall go up in stages; first, barbed wire, with concrete to follow [but] only if the West acquiesced."

It was a clever gambit: If allied soldiers trashed the barbed wire he could claim it was an impromptu East German action that he did not support. "Even so," Taubman continued, "the Soviets held their breaths on August 13, waiting to see how the Americans would react . . . When it became clear that the wire wouldn't be torn down, Sergei Khrushchev later wrote, 'Father sighed with relief. Things had turned out all right.'"

The president thought so too. He considered the wall a security guarantee for West Berlin. "Why would Khrushchev put up a Wall if he really intended to seize West Berlin?" Kennedy said to aides. "There wouldn't be any need of a Wall if he occupied the whole city. This is his way out of his predicament. It's not a very nice solution, but a Wall is a hell of a lot better than a war."

It was also a propaganda bonanza for the West, and the president wanted pictures of the wall spread far and wide. To assure the anxious people of West Berlin that the United States was committed to their city's survival, he sent sixteen hundred troops—whose progress he carefully monitored—and Vice President Lyndon Johnson to West Berlin.

It was a prudent response that received bipartisan backing at home. But ironically it almost led to another war. Eight months later Khrushchev mistakenly concluded that because the president had accepted the wall, he would accept Soviet missiles in Cuba.

7

In addition to engirdling West Berlin, Khrushchev ordered a gigantic nuclear test as another response to American determination to stand fast in West Berlin. It was an audacious, irresponsible action that was consistent with his understanding of how nuclear weapons should be employed in the service of diplomacy. The detonation—on October 30, 1961—was fifty-eight megatons (the so-called Tsar Bomb), far more powerful than any American weapon. It sent a warning that the Soviet nuclear arsenal was robust, and it provided some cover to his decision to abandon his threat to sign a peace treaty with East Germany by the end of the year.

When the bomb's designer, Andrei Sakharov, objected that the test was dangerous and unnecessary, Khrushchev responded angrily. "The number of tests, that's what matters most," he scolded Sakharov who was "poking his nose [into politics] where it doesn't belong." It was the scientists' job to "make your bombs and test them . . . We have to conduct our policies from a position of strength. . . . Our opponents don't understand any other language. We helped elect Kennedy last year. Then we met with him in Vienna, a meeting that could have been a turning point. But what does he say? 'Don't ask for too much . . . If I make too many concessions I'll be turned out of office.' . . . Why waste time talking to him?"

Khrushchev's nuclear arsenal was not equal to America's, but now he at least could claim: My test is bigger than yours.

BOOK II

THE
THIRTEEN DAYS,
OCTOBER 16–28, 1962

↑
| Kennedy vs. ExComm, the Joint Chiefs of Staff,
| Khrushchev, and Castro
↓

"The president bears the burden of responsibility. The advisers
may move on to new advice."
—PRESIDENT KENNEDY, DECEMBER 17, 1962

PART FOUR

Khrushchev's Missiles

My thinking went like this. If we installed the missiles secretly, and then the United States discovered the missiles after they were poised and ready to strike, the Americans would think twice before trying to liquidate our installations by military means. . . . The main thing was that the installation of our missiles in Cuba would, I thought, restrain the United States from precipitous military action against Castro's government.

—NIKITA S. KHRUSHCHEV

In the spring of 1962 Soviet relations with the United States seemed to move in a perpetual circle around the questions of Germany and arranging a ban on nuclear tests. *Germany and Berlin overshadowed everything.*

—SOVIET AMBASSADOR ANATOLY DOBRYNIN

18

"What If We Put Our Nuclear Missiles in Cuba?"

I believe [Khrushchev's] decision to bring the missiles
over to Cuba was to improve the correlation of forces.
—FIDEL CASTRO

The plan was bizarre, vintage Khrushchev, a wild, brilliant gamble
that promised a huge payoff for both his foreign and domestic policies. He had thought of it himself, and so he pushed it through the
Presidium—manipulating the doubters with alternating displays of
reason and combative confidence. He began by enlisting the support of an equally facile enthusiast, Marshal Rodion Yakovlevich
Malinovsky, his minister of defense. A military mind with questionable political sense, Malinovsky told a visiting Cuban delegation:
"There will be no big reaction from the U.S. side. And if there is a
problem, we will send the Baltic Fleet."

Despite such assurances, there were uncertainties. Would Castro
accept nuclear missiles? What if the missiles were discovered before
they were operational? How would Kennedy (whom Khrushchev still
considered a lightweight) react? Was a fallback plan necessary?

"Khrushchev possessed a rich imagination," Oleg Troyanovsky,
the premier's chief foreign policy adviser, recalled. "When some
idea took hold of him, he was inclined to see in its implementation an easy solution to a particular problem, a sort of cure-all. . . .
In such instances he could stretch even a sound idea to the point of
absurdity."

Positive thinking, bold ideas, and reckless action. No incident
more clearly reveals Khrushchev's mercurial character, ambitions,
worldview, limitations, and strengths than the Cuban missile crisis.

1

IN THE spring of 1962 Castro's survival was only one among many international problems Khrushchev confronted. Mao Zedong continued to challenge him for leadership of the Communist bloc. Kennedy proposed a nuclear test ban treaty that would freeze Soviet inferiority. The "German problem" (Khrushchev's fixation since 1958) remained unresolved despite the Berlin Wall and his threats to conclude a separate peace treaty with the German Democratic Republic.

In Khrushchev's view, intransigence and disrespect permeated U.S. policies, and that grated as much as the problems themselves. Something dramatic was necessary, and he had convinced himself that his plan to secretly deploy medium- and intermediate-range ballistic nuclear missiles to Cuba was the ideal solution. It would save Castro, reset the nuclear balance, leverage his efforts to force American, British, and French forces out of West Berlin, establish a significant military presence in the Western Hemisphere, and solidify his reputation as a bold and innovative leader.

2

FEW IDEAS have a single source, and every big idea has an identifiable moment when diffuse stimuli snap into a coherent thought. As Khrushchev recalled in his memoirs, he experienced such an epiphany in May 1962 during his visit to Bulgaria. It was a pro-forma trip that allowed the premier's mind to wander from the routine official obligations at hand to the nagging problems he had been pondering for months.

Cuba, Berlin, and America's superior nuclear arsenal crowded the upper layer of his list of challenges, all entwined in his mind by the exigencies of his international ambitions. But the threat of an American invasion of Cuba had forced the survival of its Communist government to the top. Before he left for Bulgaria he had approved two significant military aid shipments to Havana and had written to Castro offering continued support. "One thought kept hammering away at my brain," he wrote in his memoir. "What will happen if we lose Cuba?" Was there a way to provide real security for Castro in the face of Kennedy's determination to destroy his government?

It was not an idle thought. The Bay of Pigs invasion had led Cuba's defenders to believe that another invasion—this one by the armed forces of the United States—was inevitable. Castro's warnings of an attack were supported by Soviet intelligence. On March 17 a secret report noted that "the USA has completed preparations for an invasion of Cuba. A final decision by the Kennedy administration regarding the date of attack on Cuba is still to be made."

Was there an "answer [to] the American threat that would avoid war?" His recollections suggest that he thought the problem through logically. He could deploy Soviet ground forces to the island, but however many he sent could be overwhelmed by an American invasion. He could send ships and aircraft, but they would be equally vulnerable. There was no conventional response that could guarantee Cuba's security. How about tactical nuclear weapons? The Americans had many more. But there was an unconventional solution: strategic nuclear weapons, medium- (MRBM) and intermediate-range ballistic missiles (IRBM)—weapons similar to those that Eisenhower had ordered deployed to Europe and targeted against the Soviet Union. They would protect Cuba and—just as important, the historian Philip Zelikow argues—they would reinforce his efforts to resolve both the "German problem" and the unequal balance of his nuclear forces. They were a "cure-all" solution.

3

FROM HIS first briefing on nuclear weapons in September 1953, Khrushchev understood their savagery in general, and the special terror of the hydrogen bomb. "When I was appointed First Secretary of the Central Committee and learned all the facts of nuclear power I couldn't sleep for several days," he recalled. "Then I became convinced that we could never possibly use these weapons, and when I realized that I was able to sleep again."

And, perhaps, to dream about how those horrific weapons could support his most ambitious policies.

By 1962 Khrushchev was obsessed with nuclear weapons. They were a transformative force that defined national power. They were fearsome instruments of war (which he was determined to avoid: "Any fool can start a war," he often repeated), but as such they were splendid for reinforcing diplomacy. John Foster Dulles had made that clear from the beginning of the Eisenhower administration. What else were the doctrines of massive retaliation and brinkmanship but threats in the service of U.S. diplomatic objectives?

In October 1956, French, British, and Israeli armies invaded Egypt after its president, Gamal Abdel Nasser, nationalized the Suez Canal Company. Furious at this effort to overthrow his erstwhile ally, Khrushchev took a page from the American nuclear playbook. Over Premier Nikolai Bulganin's signature, Khrushchev ordered letters sent to the offending governments warning them that the Soviet Union could unleash nuclear attacks on their capitals if they did not withdraw their forces. "In what situation would Britain find itself," Bulganin wrote on Khrushchev's behest to Prime Minister Anthony Eden, "if she were attacked by stronger states, possessing all types of modern destructive weapons . . . for instance, rocket weapons"?

The French and Israeli governments were similarly put on notice.

Several weeks later the invading armies began to withdraw, and Khrushchev—like Chaucer's rooster, Chanticleer, who believed his crowing caused the sun to rise—became convinced that Soviet threats had precipitated the retreat.

It was another mistaken conclusion reached by combining specious assumptions with wishful thinking and inaccurate information. In fact, it was President Eisenhower's angry and pointed opposition to the invasion (about which he had not been informed) that ended the crisis.

"What does Anthony [Eden] think he's doing? Why is he doing this to me?" Ike shouted when told. Unwilling to accept such a brazen challenge to his leadership, he imposed harsh sanctions against Britain's currency before Bulganin's letters were delivered. Khrushchev's threats had contributed little if anything to ending the crisis. But his threats did have an important—and generally unrecognized—effect in Washington.

When Eisenhower learned of the letters, his mood was "somber," according to an aide who reported serious concern in the White House that Khrushchev's mercurial personality could lead to an irrational act, and even World War III.

Harking back to his World War II experiences, as he often did, the president feared that Khrushchev might be as furious as Hitler during his last days, remarking that a dictator in that frame of mind is extremely dangerous. "If the Soviets attack the French and the British directly, we would be in a war," he warned Allen Dulles.

The Soviets' Suez crisis bluff (and that is what it was) confirmed for John Foster Dulles and Eisenhower—and this is the important point—what Dulles had concluded months earlier: Khrushchev was "the most dangerous person to lead the Soviet Union since the October Revolution." Rather than "a coldly calculating person," he was emotional, and "obviously intoxicated much of the time." It was extremely dangerous to have a nuclear-armed adversary who "could be expected to commit irrational acts."

Khrushchev was not a heavy drinker, and was certainly not "intoxicated much of the time." John Foster, like his brother Allen, invested little serious study in understanding the Soviet leader, and his careless analysis had consequences. Suddenly Khrushchev's nuclear threats—now defined as the product of an erratic, irrational personality—became more credible than threats issued by Eisenhower or Dulles.

The ironic result was "brinkmanship blowback."

4

A YEAR later, on October 4, 1957, Khrushchev's brinkmanship credentials were enhanced. Sputnik, the first human-made satellite to orbit the earth, created anxiety, if not outright hysteria, in the United States. If the Soviets had rockets that could launch a satellite into orbit, then they had missiles that could send nuclear warheads smashing into North American cities. Suddenly the nuclear arms race was transformed: It was now a race for more efficient vehicles (than airplanes) for delivering nuclear weapons to their targets.

"Sputnik seemed to herald a technological Pearl Harbor, which was exactly what [physicist and hydrogen bomb advocate] Edward Teller, said it was," David Halberstam wrote in his history *The Fifties*.

A new arms race, a competition for long-range rockets, was on, and the USSR appeared to have a substantial lead. Perhaps to "rub it in," Khrushchev offered the United States the opportunity "to put instruments of ours aboard one of their [future] satellites," according to a memorandum of a meeting on the "Sputnik crisis," in which the president participated.

October 1957 was a heady moment for the Soviet Union's first secretary of the Central Committee of the Communist Party.

But Khrushchev failed to take advantage of his Sputnik moment, and by the time John Kennedy took over the presidency, the United States had leapfrogged the Soviet's long-range missile lead. On October 21, 1961, as the summer's Berlin crisis continued to smolder, the Kennedy administration announced that the Soviet Union's nuclear arsenal was no longer sufficient to present a credible nuclear threat—a declaration that embarrassed and enraged Khrushchev.

5

ROSWELL GILPATRIC, the deputy secretary of defense, made the presentation. Speaking at a Business Council conference at the Homestead Resort in Hot Springs, Virginia, he provided a broad outline of the nuclear balance of forces. His audience was a gathering of American business executives, but the speech was a direct warning to Moscow. Gilpatric was revealing, on behalf of the president, a heretofore closely guarded secret: "In short," he reported, "we have a second-strike capability which is at least as extensive as what the Soviets can deliver by striking first. Therefore, we are confident that the Soviets will not provoke a major nuclear conflict." The "hard facts" Secretary Gilpatric concluded, make it clear that the "United States [has] nuclear superiority."

For Khrushchev this was another example of American arrogance, and a frightening revelation. A little more than a year earlier, on June 29, 1960, the chairman of the KGB had warned him that "the Pentagon wants to launch a preventive war against the Soviet Union." But as long as the Americans believed that the Soviet Union could strike back, Khrushchev was confident that that would never happen.

On May 1, 1960, he again had been triumphant when his new surface-to-air missile, the S-75 Dvina, had downed Gary Powers's U2 over Sverdlovsk. But those illegal U2 overflights had exposed the inferiority of the Soviet Union's nuclear arsenal, and now he was humiliated and frightened.

Khrushchev also had become increasingly irritated about an aspect of U.S. nuclear policy that Gilpatric had *not* mentioned: In response to Sputnik, President Eisenhower had authorized intermediate-range nuclear missiles deployed to NATO allies: Thor missiles to Britain, and intermediate-range Jupiters to Italy and Turkey. The missiles in Turkey were a mere 130 miles from Soviet territory. "It really bothered him," his son, Sergei, recalled.

All these thoughts, or at least fragments of them, ran through Khrushchev's mind between the handshakes, speeches, banquets, and empty discussions he was having with Bulgarian Communist Party first secretary Todor Zhivkov and his Party officials. Communist Cuba was a prized possession in danger of being snatched back into the capitalist camp. Kennedy had as much as said so. In a January 1962 interview the president had granted Khrushchev's son-in-law, Alexei Adzhubei, the editor in chief of *Izvestia*, he had made a direct analogy between Hungary—which the Soviets had invaded in 1956—and Cuba.

"I was sure that a new attack [following the Bay of Pigs] was inevitable and that it was only a question of time," Khrushchev recalled thinking, and he worried about the consequences. "Losing revolutionary Cuba, the first Latin American country oppressed by the United States that chose a revolutionary road, would diminish the insurgent spirit of others [in Latin America]." And the converse was equally likely: "Saving Cuba for Socialism would be an example for other poor Latin American people."

The turning point for his decision, the Soviet historian Igor Belov discovered, came on May 17, in Bulgaria, when one of Khrushchev's entourage pointed to the Black Sea and told him that U.S. rockets in Turkey could reach any important industrial target in the USSR within ten minutes.

If Eisenhower and Kennedy could do that in defense of West Berlin, he could do the same in defense of Cuba. The analogy was perfect, Khrushchev thought, and the outcome he anticipated appealed to his affinity for drama.

Thinking about Cuba in these terms shifted it from the periphery of Soviet priorities to the center, and linked his leadership of the socialist world to Castro's survival.

Perhaps without recognizing it, he created a Soviet West Berlin in the Caribbean, a vulnerable symbol of his government's steadfastness; a commitment that had to be safeguarded to assure allies that the USSR was a reliable partner.

6

KHRUSHCHEV'S REASONING in 1962 tracked the Sputnik-inspired U.S. reevaluation of massive retaliation. With American cities now vulnerable to Soviet intercontinental missile [ICBM] attacks, was it likely that a president of the United States would respond with nuclear weapons to a Soviet incursion into Western Europe?

France's president, Charles de Gaulle, didn't think so, and other allied leaders appeared to share his doubts, a development that led John Foster Dulles to reconsider his signature nuclear strategy. The summary of a meeting on April 7, 1958, of Dulles and senior Defense Department officials reports Dulles "rais[ing] questions about the political and military relevance of massive retaliation. [He was] unsure that massive use of nuclear weapons is consistent with U.S. survival . . . and noted that European Allies are doubtful that the United States will come to their aid if an enlarged conflict could lead to U.S. destruction."

Eisenhower had adopted massive retaliation as a cost-effective deterrent to Soviet expansion, but after Sputnik he faced a *delivery-systems* race. The result was an escalated arms race and an increasingly bloated military budget. According to the Eisenhower biographer William Hitchcock: "Spending on the IRBM and ICBM programs together jumped from $161 million in 1955 to $515 million in 1956 and $1.3 billion in 1957."

Frightened by the administration's nuclear threats, Khrushchev had ordered the production of rockets and missiles in favor of bombers. "Our potential enemy—our most dangerous enemy—was so far away from us that we couldn't have reached him with our air force. Only by building up a nuclear missile force could we keep the enemy from unleashing war against us," he reasoned.

By 1953 the first Soviet ballistic missile was tested. The R-5 had a range of eight hundred miles and the capability of delivering a nuclear warhead. "In the hands of the Soviets," President Eisenhower wrote in November 1955, "a missile of about 1500 n[autical] mile range could be nearly as important offensively as would an intercontinental missile. . . . Therefore, it is important that the U.S. initiate a medium-range ballistic missile program to increase the probability that the U.S. is first to achieve a ballistic missile capability."

In March 1956 Eisenhower ordered an accelerated Manhattan Project approach to the challenge. The secretary of defense was to "establish two IRBM development programs." The air force would produce an intermediate-range ballistic missile designated Thor; the army would sponsor the Jupiter. When Sputnik's beeping sent chills down the spines of Washington's national security establishment, Thor and Jupiter were on hand to reassure NATO allies that the American nuclear umbrella was reliable.

A 1958 Pentagon study of the Soviet Union's expected response to stationing Thors and Jupiters in Europe rationalized that the Kremlin would recognize that "the underlying philosophy of NATO had prevailed." That "Soviet efforts to . . . weaken the cohesion of the alliance and to force withdrawal of U.S. military power, had at least temporarily failed or suffered a reversal." And that "the West [by deploying Thors and Jupiters within range of Soviet cities] was visibly demonstrating its cohesion and willing cooperation to present a unified front in opposition to Soviet objectives."

It was a statement that Khrushchev could have written with respect to the Soviet Union's willingness "to present a unified front [with Cuba] in opposition to [United States] objectives."

7

"WE NEEDED to discuss this [deploying missiles to Cuba] first with Fidel, but I came to the conclusion that if we organized everything secretly, even if the Americans found out about it, they would think twice before trying to liquidate Castro once the missiles were operational."

Khrushchev's calculations were a mirror image of the argument that Roswell Gilpatric had made in his October address. The missiles in Cuba would promote American caution toward Cuba, just as the Americans expected their own nuclear superiority to dampen Soviet adventurism. It was a strategy that President Eisenhower and John

Foster Dulles would have recognized: A Soviet version of brinkmanship, just ninety miles off the Florida coast.

At least one aspect of Khrushchev's calculations was realistic: He acknowledged that with a surprise attack on Cuba, the United States could destroy a huge proportion of his nuclear weapons before they could be launched. But he also knew that the United States could never be certain that it could destroy them all.

That, he reasoned, provided Cuba with the equivalent of Gilpatric's second strike. "Even if only one or two nuclear bombs reached New York City, there would be little of it left. If [his plan] worked out," Khrushchev concluded, "we would have a balance of fear, as the West phrased it," and Cuba would be safe.

When Khrushchev reflected on the balance of U.S. and Soviet nuclear forces, what impressed him most was the *imbalance of fear.* The proximity of U.S. nuclear missiles in Europe heightened Soviet fears of a nuclear strike far beyond what Americans experienced. "They [Americans] surrounded us with military bases and kept us at gunpoint," he recalled. But if his Cuban ploy succeeded, "the Americans would share the experience of being under the [nuclear] gun." He thought about being surrounded by American nuclear weapons a lot: "I was constantly thinking about it, especially while visiting Bulgaria."

8

KHRUSHCHEV'S VIEW of how the United States used nuclear weapons to intimidate his country led him to develop his own version of brinkmanship: the "meniscus" principle. "Let the enemy believe we are ready to strike at any provocation. Fill the nuclear glass to the brim . . . but don't pour the last drop to make the cup overflow. Be just like a meniscus, which, according to the laws of surface tension in liquid," he explained to his Presidium colleagues, "is generated in order that the liquid doesn't pour out past the rim."

Soviet policy, he concluded, is to "always have a [nuclear] wine glass with a meniscus. Because if we don't have a meniscus . . . we let the enemy live peacefully"—which allows it to behave in dangerous ways.

"An attack on Cuba is being prepared," he told the Presidium on

May 27, "and the only way to save Cuba is to put missiles there . . . , just as they put missiles in Turkey." Those missiles "scare us," he admitted, but now we are going "to give them back some of their own medicine."

"Every idiot can start a war, but it is impossible to win [a nuclear] war," and Kennedy, he believed, was too "intelligent" to behave like an idiot.

To protect Cuba, to even the balance of nuclear weapons and nuclear fear, and to reinforce his leverage to resolve the West Berlin problem, Khrushchev had no intention of letting the United States live peacefully. "The deployment of the missiles," his aide Fyodor Burlatsky later wrote in *Literaturnaya Gazeta*, was "political." Their purpose was to readjust "the relationship," and that meant equating the nuclear meniscus with nuclear brinkmanship.

19

"Without Our Help Cuba Will Be Destroyed"

Kennedy "would not set off a thermonuclear war if there
were our warheads there, just as they put their warheads on
missiles in Turkey."
—NIKITA KHRUSHCHEV

Convinced that his proposal would be simple to execute, Khrushchev encouraged his commanders to develop their plans quickly.
The Soviet Union would secretly ship a number of medium- and
intermediate-range nuclear missiles to Cuba and announce their
presence in November, after the U.S. midterm elections. In Khrushchev's mind it was little different from what the Americans had done
when they deployed their Jupiter missiles to Italy and Turkey. They
had neither warned nor consulted the Soviet Union, he rationalized
(conveniently ignoring that the U.S. deployment was public), and
therefore he saw no reason to warn or consult Washington.

1

THE MISSILES would be invisibly transported in the bowels of cargo
ships, off-loaded at night, camouflaged, moved to remote sites, and
installed. They were to be disguised as palm trees. That "is impossible to do," a senior military adviser in Cuba told Khrushchev. "There
was no place to hide a chicken, let alone a missile."

It was an idiotic idea, complained Gen. Anatoly Gribkov, the
officer responsible for planning the transfer of the missiles, troops,
and ancillary equipment to Cuba. Only someone "totally inexperienced in military matters" could have suggested it.

But neither Gribkov nor his staff imagined an alternative. So, diverting their eyes from this gaping defect, the planners proceeded. Their response bore a striking resemblance to the CIA's planning for the Bay of Pigs invasion.

The results, Khrushchev confidently informed the Presidium, would solve, in one brilliant stroke, two of the Soviet Union's major problems. First, the presence of these city-busting missiles within range of America's major urban centers would be the perfect deterrent to an invasion of Cuba. The Americans would not dare to undertake actions that might provoke a missile attack. Kennedy is "intelligent" he said, and "would not set off a thermonuclear war if there were our warheads there, just as they put their warheads on missiles in Turkey."

Second, the deployment of medium- and intermediate-range missiles ninety miles from U.S. territory would be a step toward shrinking the lead the United States held in strategic nuclear weapons. "This will be an offensive policy," Khrushchev assured the Presidium. Shrinking the balance of nuclear forces would counter America's nuclear threats and make it more difficult for the United States to resist Soviet initiatives.

Such a significant achievement would also provide Khrushchev with leverage to redirect rubles from the military sector to his distressed domestic economy. He had been trying for years to reduce the size of the army and navy, but American nuclear superiority had provided those resisting his policies with strong arguments.

Finally, but equally important to the Soviet chairman, his missile ploy would reinforce his stature as the global leader of the socialist world.

In 1956, following Khrushchev's speeches to the Twentieth Party Congress denouncing Stalin's crimes and his doctrine of inevitable war, Mao Zedong had attacked him as a revisionist. His call for "peaceful coexistence," Mao asserted, was a coward's doctrine that abandoned Communism's commitment to global revolution. "Some soft-hearted advocates of peace [Khrushchev]," an editorial in the Chinese Communist Party newspaper declared, "even naively believe that in order to relax tension at all costs the enemy must not be provoked."

Khrushchev was mindful that there were influential Maoists in the Cuban leadership.

The deployment of Soviet missiles to Cuba would have yet another important advantage, according to the minutes of several Presidium meetings. Khrushchev made it clear that he expected his Cuban missiles to provide him with a powerful new bargaining chip to deal with the problem that irked him most: West Berlin. This Western enclave, 110 miles within East German territory, was "the central issue dividing the U.S. and the USSR," Khrushchev lectured Pierre Salinger, President Kennedy's press secretary, during his May 1962 visit to Moscow. "Solving the Berlin problem [would] bring about a solution to all our problems."

2

THE IDEAS that led to the Cuban missile crisis—ideas that Khrushchev insisted he appropriated from Eisenhower's nuclear weapons policies—began to be translated into plans shortly after he returned from Bulgaria on May 20. His first steps were cautious. After discussing the deployment with his ambassador to Cuba, Aleksandr Alekseyev (who doubted that Castro would accept the missiles), he convened a full Politburo meeting on May 21 to explain his concerns about the Soviet-Cuban conundrum. He would not ask for a vote. He simply wanted his colleagues to appreciate the danger Cuba faced.

"Without our help Cuba will be destroyed," he told them. They "could not hope that the second [United States] attack [on Cuba] would be as badly organized as the first." His suggestion was to delay any decision for a few days. "I just shared with you my thoughts. You are not yet ready to make a decision. . . . I will also think about everything one more time," he accommodatingly concluded, "and in a week we will meet to talk about it."

Three days later Khrushchev again raised his proposal. The decision to move forward was foreordained, but Deputy Chairman Anastas Mikoyan, Khrushchev's closest confidant (and wisest counselor), was troubled by the idea. "We have to defend Cuba," he said, "but with this approach we risk provoking an attack on them and losing everything."

Having served as the Soviet Union's official emissary to Cuba in February 1960, Mikoyan had learned a great deal about Cuban–U.S. relations. While negotiating the oil-for-sugar agreement that had sealed the USSR-Cuba relationship, he had spent weeks in Castro's company listening to the *Comandante's* views on everything, including the United States' intentions. He understood the potential for serious trouble: There was "the danger of getting involved in war," he told his leader and his colleagues.

Khrushchev had anticipated that concern. He was against war, he said, but the Soviet Union could not function in a perpetual state of fear. If the United States believes that we are scared, he argued, they will begin to force us either to fight or "to start giving in." There was only one choice: Try to defeat the imperialists by whatever means are available short of war, but if war is imposed, then do whatever it takes to win it. "That was how [I] understood the situation," Khrushchev asserted. "This will be an offensive policy" that would realign "the correlation of forces."

The plan was discussed several more times, and, Khrushchev reported, he "offered not to speed up the decision on this question so that each of us got used to the plan and understood its consequences." But it seems clear from the record that he was working the room, with Defense Minister Malinovsky's support, pushing hard to create an atmosphere that would force the doubters into line.

Foreign Minister Andrei Gromyko was one of the doubters, albeit (like so many others) a silent one. Alone in his office with Alekseyev, "one on one," the ambassador recalled, "he suddenly said, 'I'm very much afraid that the military is going to put us in a very difficult position.'"

On May 24 an expanded meeting of the Presidium quickly made a unanimous decision to deploy R-12 and R-14 missiles to Cuba. A week or so later Khrushchev confirmed his plan with the Defense Council. The commander of the strategic missile forces, Marshal Sergey Biryuzov, was reported to be enthusiastic.

A delegation was sent to Cuba to gain Castro's consent.

3

IT CAME as a surprise to Khrushchev, and even more to Ambassador Alekseyev, that Castro accepted the missiles, but as a "contribution to the Socialist bloc." "Fidel, they are only for Cuba," Alekseyev explained, but to no avail. Castro saw his revolution as part of a global movement; he would accept the Soviet Union's missiles only as part of that struggle. It was a telling insight into the ideological zeal he would display five months hence.

In fact, from the Cuban perspective the crisis had begun already, as the historian Philip Brenner has argued. Under the circumstances, why not deploy the missiles openly? Castro asked. Cuba and the USSR had a security pact, and it was legitimate to authorize the Soviet Union to deploy weapons meant to enhance Havana's security. Such an approach would reinforce Cuban independence. But Khrushchev was adamant about secrecy, and Castro fell into line.

In choosing secrecy Khrushchev rationalized that he was following an American precedent. We "simply used the same means our enemy used towards us," he later wrote. "They [even] denied that they were having a reconnaissance [U2 flights] against us [and lied] when we brought one of them down." Even more galling had been President Eisenhower's declaration "that they had the right to openly lead a reconnaissance on the territory of our country if it was in their interests."

Well, Khrushchev thought, sending nuclear weapons to Cuba was a profound Soviet interest. "I believe [Khrushchev's] decision to bring the missiles over to Cuba was to improve the correlation of forces," Fidel Castro told the journalist Maria Shriver from the perspective of five decades. "I don't doubt that he wanted to protect Cuba, but I think his main priority was to improve the defense capabilities of the USSR. This was my critique then and still is today."

4

KHRUSHCHEV'S PLAN had begun simply enough. His forces would secretly ship missiles to Cuba that, if attacked, could devastate a few United States cities. Once they were in place and ready to fire, he would announce their presence. "The imperialist" behemoth then would not dare to invade his Cuban ally. But as the process of organizing evolved, the mission took on a life of its own.

Simplicity gave ground, one decision at a time, to complexity, and then confusion, as military planners added requirement upon requirement. It was not long before Khrushchev's simple idea resembled a giant matryoshka doll with components too numerous to count, inserted one within another.

To divert attention from its intended location, the enterprise was designated Anadyr. What better cover name for a secret plan to deliver missiles to a tropical island than a frozen river in the far north of Siberia? Combine the river's name with a wide distribution of heavy winter clothing to more than fifty thousand troops, and the essential elements—or at least the essential external elements—of the deception were in place.

The more immediate challenge was to keep the operation's location secret from almost all the participants, even senior officers scheduled to lead the deployment. "The main feature of the planning of Anadyr was to keep it within the walls of the General Staff," Gen. Alexey Butski explained and, like all closely guarded large operations, there was a price to pay for this security.

Anadyr began in May 1962 with the decision to ship to Cuba 24 R-12 (NATO-designated SS-4) MRBMs, each with a range of 1,100 miles, and 16 R-14 (SS-5) IRBMs, capable of traveling 2,500 miles. The missiles carried warheads ranging from two hundred kilotons of TNT to more than two megatons. This array of nuclear firepower would provide almost total coverage of the United States. "Now we can swat your ass," Khrushchev told Secretary of the Interior Stewart Udall without revealing his intention to use Cuba as his nuclear paddle.

The escalation began almost immediately. "We decided if we put missiles in Cuba, then we needed to protect them. So we also needed infantry . . . approximately several thousand." (The target number climbed to more than fifty thousand.) Of course those troops also had to be protected, especially against an air attack, and so antiaircraft batteries were added. Then "we decided that we needed artillery and tanks in case of a landing assault." Other significant weaponry that followed included Ilyushin IL-28 (nuclear-capable) bombers, MiG-21 fighters, an array of battlefield nuclear weapons that included about eighty short-range FKR-1 nuclear-capable cruise missiles (that could be fired at attacking U.S. Navy vessels), several dozen Luna tactical nuclear weapons (artillery to destroy assault troops), submarines armed with nuclear torpedoes, and surface-to-air missiles.

"Most of all we worried about being exposed from the air. The Americans were constantly flying over Cuba," Khrushchev fretted—a serious concern indeed, but one that was simply left to chance. Serious camouflage efforts were ignored.

In July, Khrushchev told the commander of Soviet forces in Cuba, Gen. Issa Pliyev, that the arsenal at his disposal was not for show. In the event of an American invasion, and if communications with Moscow became disrupted, Pliyev was "authorized to use" the tactical nuclear weapons [Lunas and cruise missiles] to repel the assault.

If deterrence failed, the Soviet's Cuban brigades were prepared for nuclear war.

5

KHRUSHCHEV HAD entrusted the plan's development to Defense Minister Malinovsky, who in turn organized a select group of General Staff planners. Secrecy was strict and pervasive—on the level of the U.S. wartime Manhattan Project—and it had similar consequences: People who could have anticipated problems were unaware that the enterprise existed, and others, who were in the know, abandoned their critical sensibilities in the rush to get on with their work.

Nuclear missiles, large and small, surface-to-surface, even surface-to-sea, were at the heart of the plan. The R-12 could bring Washington, D.C., and every city and SAC base to its south, within range of its 1-megaton warhead—the equivalent of sixty-six Hiroshima bombs. Thirty-six R-12s and their warheads were delivered to Cuba before the quarantine prevented further shipments.

It was a close call for the R-14 intermediate-range missiles. The blockade went into effect on October 24, threatening the ships carrying twenty-four R-14s and their support troops. The R-14s not only had twice the range (2,500 miles) of the R-12s, but their warheads were larger, up to 2.3 megatons. They could reach every state except Washington and the recently incorporated states of Alaska and Hawaii. Unwilling to risk the seizure of a ship carrying these missiles, Khrushchev ordered them to return to the Soviet Union. No intermediate-range missiles ever made it to Cuba.

However, the ships transporting the nuclear warheads for all the missiles had either arrived prior to the quarantine's initiation (the *Indigirka* on October 4), or had passed the quarantine line before it went into effect (the *Aleksandrovsk* arrived on October 25). They had unloaded a deadly and varied nuclear arsenal. In addition to the thirty-six 1-megaton warheads for the R-12s, there were twenty-four warheads for the R-14s, eighty 2-to-20-kiloton warheads for "winged rockets" (FKR cruise missiles), twelve 2-kiloton warheads for the Luna tactical artillery (for attacking assault troops), six warheads for the surface-to-sea missiles (for destroying offshore ships), and six 8-to-12-kiloton bombs for the IL-28 bombers that had been delivered in crates.

Neither the CIA, the DIA, navy intelligence, SAC intelligence, nor any U.S. government official was aware that the Soviets had succeeded in delivering 164 nuclear warheads to Cuba.

The plan called for deploying 51,000 combat-ready troops to Cuba between July and November. The first 42,000 arrived before the blockade prevented the final 8,000 members of the two R-14 missile regiments from reaching their destination. The CIA informed the president that there were 11,000 Soviet troops on the island and there was no report that they were armed with tactical nuclear weapons.

Soviet submarines were added to the deployment list, and nuclear-armed torpedoes were added to the submarines. No previous deployment of Foxtrot submarines had ever carried a "special weapon," and in retrospect their deployment makes little sense. Khrushchev had no intention of allowing a submarine commander to start a nuclear war with the United States. His objective was to sneak medium- and intermediate-range missiles into Cuba. What was the point of providing a submarine captain with the opportunity to begin World War III?

Whether or not Khrushchev knew exactly what armaments were aboard his submarines is unclear, but his admirals understood that Anadyr was about deploying nuclear weapons within range of the United States. The navy was not going to be left out of fully participating in this historic initiative, and at that moment 15-kiloton torpedoes were their nuclear chips.

The Soviets also deployed a formidable air defense system manned by two experienced divisions equipped with the deadly S-75 Dvina [designated SA-2 by NATO] antiaircraft system. These surface-to-air missiles could reach seventy thousand feet, and one of them had downed Gary Powers's U2 over Sverdlovsk on May 1, 1960.

The antiaircraft missile systems were backed up by forty MiG-21 and six MiG-15 fighter aircraft, six IL-28 nuclear-capable bombers, several dozen helicopters, twelve "Komar" gunboats, fourteen communication aircraft, tanks, artillery, and much else that could be used to confront an invasion.

In his memoir of the crisis, Col. Gen. Viktor Yesin, then a junior officer with the rocket forces, reported that on October 20 eight of the forty-two R-12 MRBMs were "brought to full military readiness . . . [including] the list of the targets, geodesic coordinates, types of nuclear explosions, their power and the main directions of launching." They could be prepared to fire in two and a half hours.

6

THE DAY before, on October 19, the JCS had met with the president and insisted that the only safe action was an immediate invasion. "I just don't see any other solution," Gen. Curtis LeMay, the air force chief of staff, declared, "except direct military intervention, right now." Chief of Naval Operations Adm. George Anderson supported LeMay: "I do not see that as long as the Soviet Union is supporting Cuba, that there is any solution to the Cuban problem except a military solution." Gen. Earle Wheeler, the chief of staff of the army, was equally certain that an invasion of Cuba was the soundest policy: "And so I say, from the military point of view, I feel that the *lowest risk* course of action is the full gamut of military action by us. That's it."

Had the United States invaded Cuba, that would, indeed, have been "it."

PART FIVE

October 16 (Tuesday),
Day One: Kennedy, Stevenson, and the ExComm;
Week One: Berlin and Blockade

Two roads diverged in a wood, and I,
I took the one less traveled by,
And that has made all the difference.
—ROBERT FROST, "THE ROAD NOT TAKEN"

"They're There"

After all, this is a political struggle as much as military.
—PRESIDENT KENNEDY, OCTOBER 16, 1962

McGeorge Bundy had slept fitfully the previous night, but he was not tired as he entered the White House elevator Tuesday morning, October 16, to ascend to the family quarters. He was angry, energized, and deep in thought. He had terrible news to convey, and he could not help but feel partly responsible for what he was about to reveal. As President Kennedy's national security adviser, he was more deeply involved than any other member of the administration—including the secretary of state—in formulating the country's policies toward the Soviet Union and Cuba. Somewhere along the line, it was now painfully clear, he had "dropped the ball." What he (and other members of the inner circle) had refused to believe over the past six weeks was true. Twelve hours earlier—at 9:00 p.m., October 15—Ray Cline, head of the CIA's directorate of intelligence, had called Bundy's home, interrupting a dinner party for Ambassador Charles "Chip" and Avis Bohlen, who were departing for Paris, with a cryptic, gut-wrenching message: "Those things we've been worrying about. . . . They're there."

"They" were Soviet surface-to-surface missiles.

"There" was Cuba.

1

SINCE SEPTEMBER 1, New York's Republican senator, Kenneth Keating, had been insisting in speeches, radio broadcasts, and interviews that he had solid information that the Soviet Union was shipping offensive missiles to Cuba, a charge the administration denied. But Keating was certain, he declared for the second time to his Senate colleagues on October 10, that the Soviets would soon "have the power to hurl rockets into the American heartland and as far as the Panama Canal Zone."

Accusing the administration of duplicity, he charged that "the Soviets know the fact [that there are offensive missiles in Cuba]. The Cubans know this fact. But in the view of the administration, our people are not entitled to know." James "Scotty" Reston, the *New York Times* Washington Bureau chief, raised the political stakes for the administration with a column: "On Cuba and Pearl Harbor— the American Nightmare:" "[E]ither . . . the Kennedy administration doesn't know what is going on in Cuba or, as Senator Keating strongly implies, . . . it is deceiving the American people."

The politics of national security always touched a sensitive administration nerve, but Keating's charges, presented so brazenly in the run-up to the 1962 midterm elections, had struck Bundy as political huckstering. Since August he had been advising the president to ignore them. "There is no evidence of any organized combat force in Cuba from any Soviet bloc country . . . [or] the presence of offensive ground-to-ground missiles; or of other significant offensive capability either in Cuban hands or under Soviet direction and guidance," the president announced at a September 13 news conference. "The major danger is the Soviet Union with missiles and warheads, not Cuba," he had remarked to an aide.

The Soviet Union must understand, Kennedy further informed the White House press corps (and thus Nikita Khrushchev), that "if at any time the Communist buildup in Cuba were to endanger or interfere with our security in any way . . . then this country will do whatever must be done to protect its own security and that of its allies."

The president had made these statements in September to strengthen his political position for the November elections, but their unintended consequence was to narrow his options in October. "In light of his public commitments . . . it was clear to the President throughout the crisis that every course of action must be measured by its effectiveness in removing the missiles," Bundy wrote years later.

The realities of domestic politics demanded no less. "An overwhelming majority of Americans and their representatives in Congress would expect and demand the action that Kennedy had promised," Bundy explained.

To reinforce the president's news conference statements, Bundy had taken to the airways to denounce Keating's charges. Appearing on *Issues and Answers*, ABC's popular weekly news show, he said that "there is no present evidence, and I think there is no present likelihood that the Cubans and the Cuban government and the Soviet government would in combination attempt to install a major offensive capability." Broadcast live on Sunday morning, October 14, his remarks were aired as air force major Richard Heyser piloted his U2 over Cuba, photographing the missile-launching sites that Bundy was now about to reveal to Kennedy.

2

BUNDY'S EMBARRASSMENT as he prepared to inform the president was deepened by his refusal during the past month to support the appeals of the new director of Central Intelligence, John McCone. He had been telling the president and his senior foreign policy advisers, including Bundy, that Keating was right. McCone had also urged frequent U2 reconnaissance flights over Cuba, which Bundy and Secretary of State Dean Rusk had opposed.

A Republican and former chairman of the Atomic Energy Commission during the last years of Eisenhower's presidency, McCone had been selected by Kennedy to replace Allen Dulles, after the legendary spymaster's aggressive promotion of the Bay of Pigs had led to his forced resignation. A staunch Catholic, an unyielding anti-Communist, a successful California businessman, and a recently remarried widower, McCone had been insisting for months that there was a Soviet military buildup in Cuba, especially noting the construction of numerous antiaircraft missile sites, which he said were being installed to protect offensive nuclear missiles.

No CIA analyst supported the DCI's "hunch," as he himself described his conclusion. The Soviets had never stationed nuclear weapons outside their territory, they said—incorrectly. In fact the Soviets had secretly deployed medium-range "Shyster" (SS-3) missiles to East Germany in 1958, but had withdrawn them a year later. The CIA's failure to circulate the report on this incident left analysts to assume that the policy of not deploying nuclear weapons beyond Soviet territory remained in place. Moreover, Marxist-Leninists behaved according to historical and predictable patterns, the CIA analysts insisted, and the items known to have been shipped to Cuba had been shipped elsewhere earlier.

It was an analysis that Bundy had presented to the *Issues and Answers* audience. "Everything that has been delivered in Cuba," he had explained, "falls within the categories of aid which the Soviet Union has provided, for example, to neutral states like Egypt, or Indonesia."

3

A GOOD analyst knows when to think outside the box, and when to allow imagination to challenge experience. "When you have a doctor's appointment," Leana Wen, MD, cautions patients, be sure to tell the doctor everything, not just your "chief complaint." The reason is simple: "Once the doctor focuses on just one possible scenario, he is less likely to look at the whole picture because other information can seem irrelevant."

This advice prompts a comparison of the diagnostic strategies employed by medical doctors and the analytical strategies of intelligence analysts. Both professions reach conclusions based on evidence, but if the doctor or the analyst organizes the information around a preconceived assumption, Dr. Wen warns us: "The chief complaint can actually be a distraction from the real story."

That's not a bad analogy for what happened to the CIA's analysts in the months that preceded the Cuban missile crisis.

"It was . . . [s]hocking," concluded President Truman's former secretary of defense Robert Lovett, "to find our Intelligence Services so deficient that it was possible to inject into an island some 90 miles off of our coast large weapons of this character without our having some word of it in a reliable and accurate form from ground level observers."

"American intelligence was good for nothing," Soviet general Anatoly Gribkov, the manager of Anadyr, mocked. "Thirty years later [in 1992], I was permitted to reveal everything at the Havana [Cuban–Russian–U.S. missile crisis review] conference, and they [the U.S. participants, including Robert McNamara and Theodore Sorensen] did not know anything. Fidel, the host of the conference, joked, 'You have got two penalties from the 10 yard line.'"

Beginning in July 1962, eighty-two ships under Soviet command or contract began to transport the troops, missiles, nuclear warheads, bombers, and other equipment (detailed in the preceding chapter) to Cuba. All the vessels made at least two round trips, eventually totaling 180 passages.

It was a Soviet coup: the largest secret deployment of nuclear weapons and their support personnel in history. And it was almost the most serious American intelligence blunder of the Cold War. One more week of clouds and rainstorms over Cuba, and enough Soviet missiles would have been operational to make any effort to remove them even more dangerous. Had that happened, U.S. political history, and perhaps even the history of the Cold War, would have been different.

How the CIA and Navy Intelligence analysts failed to recognize, let alone consider, that the Soviet Union was shipping offensive missiles to Cuba is a fascinating question.

The missiles and their minders were carried in the cargo holds of freighters photographed by U.S. Navy patrol planes. Missile sightings were reported to the CIA by Cuban contacts. Senator Keating insisted that the Soviets were placing surface-to-surface missiles in Cuba. And the director of the CIA, John McCone, told the president and several of his closest advisers that the placement of the Soviet antiaircraft missiles (SA-2s) suggested that they were located to protect surface-to-surface missiles.

Many historians of the CIA are not surprised. The Agency had failed to anticipate the Berlin blockade in June 1948, the first Soviet nuclear weapons test in August 1949, the beginning of the Korean War in June 1950, the Chinese entry into the war in November, the Suez crisis and the Soviet invasion of Hungary in 1956, the launch of Sputnik in October 1957, and the erection of the Berlin Wall in

August 1961, not to mention its assurances that Cubans would rise up against Castro when the Bay of Pigs invaders landed.

Hard as it may be for Americans to accept, there is considerable evidence that from its inception in 1947 through the end of Allen Dulles's tenure in 1961, the CIA's intelligence collection and prediction records were wanting.

One reason seems clear: Dulles privileged covert operations over analysis, and the many reports the CIA received from Cuban observers were discounted as exaggerations because they did not conform to expectations.

The discovery of the Soviet missiles by a U2 on October 14 was a late—and lucky—redemption.

4

THE CLOUD cover that for weeks had concealed Soviet activities in Cuba had finally lifted, and Maj. Richard D. Heyser could see the ground clearly, even from 72,500 feet. But only glancingly, because his attention returned to the airspeed indicator near the center of his instrument panel. Flying at an altitude where the air could barely support his plane—the "coffin corner" in U2 pilot jargon—the difference between safe maximum and minimum speeds was a mere seven miles per hour. If he exceeded top speed, his U2 could shatter. If he dropped below minimum speed, its engine could stall and his plane would plummet. It was the frailest aircraft, built to weigh as little as possible in order to fly as high as possible. To save weight there was no longitudinal spar (a strip of metal) to hold its wings in place; they were merely bolted to the plane's thin fuselage. No other aircraft required as much skill to keep aloft and together.

Heyser, sheathed in the latest pressurized flight suit to protect him from the high-altitude version of the bends, had departed Edwards Air Force Base in California shortly after midnight, October 14. He had flown across the southwestern United States, out over the Gulf of Mexico, and at 7:35 a.m. was heading due north over the western part of Cuba.

With the flick of a switch he felt the *thump-thump-thump* of his top-secret Hycon B and PerkinElmer 70mm tracking cameras swinging from horizons left and right. In the next six minutes they would create 928 amazingly sharp images. (He would learn that they recorded especially good ones of San Cristóbal.)

A good photo run requires a straight and level flight path—and nerves of steel when you are the likely target of a Soviet S-75 Dvina SA missile. In addition to keeping an eye on his airspeed and his camera's controls, Heyser watched intently for telltale wisps of smoke and upward-spiraling contrails.

Avoiding a missile attack at his altitude was tricky, to say the least. The standard procedure called for turning toward the missile and then, when it was too close to change course, veer sharply away in the hope that it flew by. It was a plausible tactic for a plane that could survive the strain of a violent turn, but altering the course of a U2 was a delicate process under any conditions: At sixty to seventy thousand feet, anything more than the gentlest turn would either tear off its wings or stall its engine.

As it turned out, Heyser was lucky. The Soviet air defense crews either had been taken by surprise, or had been instructed to hold their fire.

5

McCoy AFB, located ten miles south of Orlando, Florida, is a Strategic Air Command facility. Touching down on its runway on October 14 at 9:20 a.m., Heyser taxied his U2 to a hangar, where a crew removed its film canisters and directed him to a debriefing room. Still in his pressure suit, he described his flight to SAC's director of operations and the deputy chief of staff for intelligence. In the meantime his tracking film canisters were loaded onto a jet headed for SAC headquarters at Offutt AFB in Omaha, Nebraska. A second jet flew the primary film canisters to Andrews AFB outside Washington, D.C., from where a CIA agent drove them to the National Photographic Interpretation Center (NPIC). Analysis of Heyser's film began just three hours after he landed at McCoy.

Several weeks had passed since the last U2 mission over Cuba, so the photo interpreters (PIs) worked through the night to determine if Heyser's pictures held surprises. Scrutinizing the negative images to ensure maximum resolution, they examined each frame through their 3D glasses, comparing Heyser's images with photos of the same areas from earlier U2 flights. They could accurately measure the height and length of objects by calculating the angle of the sun from the time of day that the photos had been taken and then measuring the object's shadow.

About twenty-four hours into the process, the PIs were examining the images of San Cristóbal in Pinar del Río Province, an area directly southwest of Havana. A "Soviet style construction site" preparing what appeared to be a launch platform for a surface-to-surface medium-range ballistic missile caught their attention.

By early Monday evening on October 15 they had identified trailers, launchers, transport trucks, and a medium-range ballistic missile that matched the microfilmed photographs of an SS-4 provided by a Soviet spy, Oleg Penkovsky. Senior CIA officials were informed, and at 8:30 p.m., Bundy was called at his home.

6

KENNEDY INITIALLY took the news personally. "He can't do that to me," he seethed. Khrushchev had assured him in their private back-channel communications that he would not do anything to interfere with the November midterm elections, and he had publicly declared that he would never deploy offensive weapons to Cuba.

The president had been lied to, blindsided, and manipulated. He was in big trouble (a Republican landslide in a month? a Republican president in two years?), and it was in large part the result of his own initiatives.

Disdainful of the State Department's bureaucratic processes, and what he considered its unimaginative approach to relations with the Soviet Union, he had opened a private exchange of letters with Khrushchev, and had made the mistake of believing too much of what he was told. He had anointed his brother, the attorney general, to function as an alternative national security adviser and back-channel liaison. Bobby was to communicate freely with Georgi Bolshakov, a senior Soviet military intelligence (GRU) officer at the Soviet Embassy.

Prior to October 1962 Bobby and Georgi had met more than forty times—frequently at the attorney general's Virginia home—to discuss pressing Soviet-American issues. Bolshakov, the brothers believed, was a direct line to the Kremlin. It was a full-court press to "cajole, flatter and deter Khrushchev." But as was now painfully obvious, the wily Communist had outwitted Jack and Bobby. "Oh shit! Shit! Shit! Those sons of bitches Russians," Bobby raged when told the news.

He and his brother had been had, and he was furious.

After absorbing the full force of what Bundy reported, the president recovered his composure. He would keep to his schedule during the morning (as he would for the remainder of the week) to avoid raising suspicions about anything being amiss. In the meantime Bundy had less than three hours to organize a meeting of trusted advisers.

In addition to Bundy, the president listed fifteen others: his brother; Vice President Lyndon Johnson; Secretary of Defense Robert McNamara; Secretary of State Dean Rusk; Undersecretary of State George Ball; Secretary of the Treasury C. Douglas Dillon; Deputy Secretary of Defense Roswell Gilpatric; Deputy Undersecretary of State for Political Affairs U. Alexis Johnson; Assistant Secretary of State for Inter-American Affairs Edwin Martin; DCI John McCone; Assistant Secretary of Defense for International Security Affairs Paul Nitze; Special Counsel, and speechwriter Ted Sorensen; Chairman of the Joint Chiefs of Staff Gen. Maxwell Taylor; and Ambassador-at-Large Llewellyn Thompson, a highly regarded Soviet expert. (Another Soviet specialist, Chip Bohlen, then ambassador-designate to France, attended the first several sessions before leaving for his post in Paris.)

This is the group that became known as ExComm.

7

Few, if any, advisers to presidents have attained the celebrity accorded the men Bundy assembled in the Cabinet Room at 11:50 a.m. on October 16. Their careful consideration of the challenge, their firmness in the face of terrifying danger, and their wise counsel were critical to the peaceful resolution of the most dangerous event in world history—so runs the official narrative of their role in the resolution of the crisis.

Nothing could be further from the truth.

Given that nuclear war was avoided, and that the president publicly praised their assistance, it is no surprise that their individual and amalgamated reputations were gilded by journalists and historians. But documents that indicate otherwise began sprouting like unwelcome weeds in a manicured garden a quarter century after those triumphant "thirteen days."

Privately the president anticipated the emergence of those weeds. "Ken," he told his friend and ambassador to India, the economist John Kenneth Galbraith, "you will never know how much bad advice I had in those days."

Bad advice is often difficult to identify, especially when offered by people of influence and experience. In April 1961 John Kennedy understood that something was not quite right about what Allen Dulles and Richard Bissell proposed, but he did not know how to challenge them, nor could he offer an acceptable alternative. The result was the disastrous Bay of Pigs invasion, and a transformed president. As Ted Sorensen recalled, after the Bay of Pigs, Kennedy "conducted national security operations in a different way." He aggressively probed recommendations by challenging premises and "even facts." He was more skeptical of expert advice, and more confident that he could rely on his own assumptions and instincts.

Praising ExComm as the fount of the president's decisions distorts its role in the crisis. Its members did not make any of the critical decisions; all of them were made by the president. ExComm provided conventional ideas that Kennedy at first accepted, soon reconsidered, and after a number of indecisive meetings, rejected.

Domestic politics was never out of his mind, and here ExComm's role *was* critical. Composed of Eisenhower Republicans (Dillon and McCone), Kennedy Democrats, and professional diplomats, it served as a political sounding board, and its unanimous support was one of the president's primary objectives throughout the crisis.

It may not be off the mark to suggest (as the following chapters will demonstrate) that the challenge of bringing his advisers into line with his preferred responses to the Soviet missile deployment was as least as difficult as persuading Khrushchev to remove his missiles from Cuba. The Soviet leader, after all, did not want a war with the United States. On the other hand, most members of ExComm *did* want to bomb and invade Cuba.

21

"Actions Were Begun on October 3
to Prepare for Military Action Against Cuba"

The Joint Chiefs of Staff agreed that the recommended
sequence would be: get additional intelligence: make surprise
attacks on missiles, airfields, PT boats, SAMs and tanks:
concurrently reinforce Guantanamo: prepare to initiate an
invasion.
—SUMMARY OF JCS MEETING, OCTOBER 16, 1962

I have great respect for Mr. McNamara, but his insistence
that the United States never attempted to invade Cuba
ignores the facts.
—PIERRE SALINGER, 1989

The Joint Chiefs of Staff were nineteen hours ahead of the president, and six in front of the CIA's National Photographic Intelligence
Center (NPIC). When Strategic Air Command's photo interpreters
received the tracking copy of Major Heyser's U2 film, they scrolled
to the areas that refugee and agents' reports (gathered by the CIA
since June) had identified as centers of unusual activity. One such
area was a province southwest of Havana, Pinar del Río, where they
quickly found tell-tale signs of MRBMs in San Cristóbal. Their discovery passed promptly through SAC's chain of command, reaching
the Pentagon late in the morning of October 15. By 2:00 p.m.—
about seven hours before McGeorge Bundy was informed that Soviet
MRBMs were discovered in Cuba—the Joint Chiefs assembled for
their first Cuban missile crisis meeting.

1

"THE JOINT Chiefs of Staff saw Fidel Castro's regime as a cancer that must be removed, by whatever means proved necessary," according to Walter Poole, the official historian of the JCS. "They came to that conclusion in March 1960 and conveyed it repeatedly thereafter to their civilian superiors." They insisted that a Communist Cuba threatened the security of the Western Hemisphere, and they assured the commander in chief that it was possible to depose Castro "without precipitating a general war, and without serious effect on world opinion."

To all the military's senior leaders—Gen. Maxwell D. Taylor, JCS chairman; Gen. Earle G. Wheeler, army chief of staff; Gen. Curtis E. LeMay, air force chief of staff; Adm. George W. Anderson Jr., chief of naval operations (CNO); and Gen. David M. Shoup, marine corps commandant—the Soviet missiles were not only a threat but, as their recommendations made clear, an opportunity to eliminate the Communist cancer from the Western Hemisphere.

And they were ready. After the humiliation of the Bay of Pigs, Pentagon planners had developed contingency plans that assembled the full panoply of U.S. military might to oust Castro. Designated OPLANS (Operational Plans) 312-62, 314-61, and 316-61, these attack scenarios were a high priority, since senior military and administration officials anticipated that something Castro might do—or could be induced to do—would provide an opportunity to set an invasion in motion. "Solicitations were being made quietly as to any idea that could be offered to provoke Cuba into giving the United States an excuse to take appropriate action," Admiral Anderson remembered.

The most horrific proposals to gain an excuse were designated "Northwoods." Dated March 13, 1962, this sylvan-titled memo was the brainchild of current JCS chairman Gen. Lyman L. Lemnitzer. Subtitled: "Justification for US Military Intervention in Cuba," it was one of the reasons that President Kennedy refused to reappoint Lemnitzer to an additional term as chairman of the Joint Chiefs.

A rabid anti-Communist and right-wing ideologue, Lemnitzer was promoted by Eisenhower to the military's top job in 1960. He was one of Ike's favorite generals. A World War II staff officer who saw combat during the Korean War, "Lem" had a "bear-like" physique and "booming voice." Kennedy considered him ignorant and dangerous. "He thought Lemnitzer was a dope," Arthur Schlesinger Jr. recalled. "Lem was as dumb as a post," a senior NATO officer told the historian Philip Nash.

When the general enthusiastically briefed the president on how America's nuclear war plans would decimate the Soviet Union, Kennedy remarked to Dean Rusk: "And we call ourselves the human race." Not surprisingly Lemnitzer had an equally low opinion of his commander in chief. He said that Kennedy's refusal to send the U.S. military in support of the Bay of Pigs invaders was "absolutely reprehensible, almost criminal."

"Northwoods" proposed a list of "false flag" atrocities to be carried out by American operatives. Trained and controlled by the JCS, they and their actions would be blamed on fictitious Cuban government terrorists. The list proposed attacks against the Guantánamo Naval Base, including "over-the-fence" assaults, mortar attacks, and ammunition-dump blowups. Beyond Cuba, the memo proposed terror campaigns in Miami and Washington that involved exploding plastic bombs and assaults against Cuban refugees, all to be pinned on Castro's government.

The memo contained at least a dozen more schemes, but the most horrific—one that is difficult to imagine even being suggested—was to shoot down "a chartered civil airliner enroute [*sic*] from the United States to Jamaica, Guatemala, Panama or Venezuela. . . . The passengers could be a group of college students off on a holiday."

President Kennedy was appalled, and dismissed "Northwoods." But in August and September the Cubans and the Soviets appeared to be creating other justifications for the JCS to exploit. The significant increase of Soviet shipping to Cuba—double the monthly average in August and triple that in September—suggested that they were augmenting their military forces on the island. Intelligence reports identifying the arrival of Soviet technicians and military personnel, the construction of large launch complexes, and the extension of runways to accommodate high-performance aircraft "pointed unmistakably to the rapid development of Cuba into a Soviet base for offensive action against the United States," the Chiefs concluded.

In addition, on August 30 an unarmed U.S. patrol plane, flying twelve miles north of Cuba over international waters, was fired on by a Cuban ship. A week later a Soviet MiG-17 executed a simulated attack against two U.S. patrol aircraft within the Key West Air Defense Identification Zone. On September 17 a CIA analysis concluded that a suspected surface-to-air site at Banes, on the northeast coast of Cuba, was now believed to be a surface-to-surface launch complex. There was no follow-up.

On October 1 McNamara met with the Chiefs to discuss these provocations and the circumstances that would prompt a military assault against Cuba. His memo listed six contingencies that could provoke an invasion. They included evidence that Castro permitted offensive-weapons systems on Cuban territory; Cuban support for subversion in Latin America; and a decision by the president that activities in Cuba threatened U.S. national security.

Two days later (October 3), the JCS concluded that the criteria for attacking Cuba had been met. In addition to the observed shipments of military supplies, there was (unspecified) evidence that Cuban ships were delivering military equipment to Latin American rebels. "Obviously," according to a CNO *Report on the Naval Quarantine of Cuba, 1962*, "the first of these contingencies existed and certainly would prompt . . . President Kennedy to invoke the second."

"Accordingly," the report continued, *"actions were begun on October 3 to prepare for military action against Cuba."* The political objective included the elimination of the Soviet weapons and, "if necessary, the removal of the Castro regime to assure the permanent dislocation of these weapons."

It is possible, according to this CNO report (which was withdrawn from circulation and replaced by a document with a similar name), that had Khrushchev not sent his missiles to protect Castro, an invasion of the island could have occurred before the end of the month.

The preparation for the assault was conducted under the utmost clandestine conditions, which accounts for why so little is known about these plans. "It was absolutely essential that these preparations be carried out with strict secrecy," the CNO report explains. Instructions to the senior commanders carried the security designation "Top Secret, Exclusive." The Chiefs were not intent on hiding their intentions from Castro; they were very concerned about the Soviet Union. "Although the[ir] general appraisal was that . . . Khrushchev would not ignite a general war over U.S. action in Cuba, he might have been so inclined if aware of unusual preparedness without clear reason."

Between October 3 and 16—the day that Major Heyser's MRBM photographs were shown to President Kennedy—the Chiefs were preparing to implement their invasion plans. "All preparations prior to imposition of the 'naval quarantine' [as the blockade during the Cuban missile crisis was called]," the CNO report confirms, "were directed toward the execution of Commander in Chief, Atlantic's [CINCLANT] Operations Plan 312-62, followed by Plans 314-61 or 316-61."

The JCS October 3 decision to prepare for the invasion of Cuba gave the navy a head start on preparations for the quarantine. On October 3 CINCLANT readied his forces to blockade Cuba as part of the invasion scenario. Although those exact plans were not followed for the quarantine, the CNO report notes that "advance planning for its execution 20 days before had expedited greatly the implementation of the quarantine, since the composition of forces in both cases was essentially the same."

2

THE CHIEFS' initial discussion, according to the surviving abridged record of their October 15 meeting, focused on air strikes, airborne assaults, and amphibious landings as outlined in their most comprehensive operational plan, OPLAN 316-61. The first step, they agreed, was to transfer the Marine Corps Regimental Combat Team from Camp Pendleton in Southern California to the East Coast.

Shortly after the JCS took this decision, Secretary of Defense Robert S. McNamara joined the meeting. Uncertain that the photographic intelligence forwarded by SAC was accurate (it had yet to be confirmed by the NPIC), he urged caution. The president, he told the Chiefs, "wants no military action within the next three months, but he can't be sure as he does not control events."

On the other hand, McNamara continued, in the event that the missile sightings were confirmed, both domestic and foreign reactions would have to be considered. Moving the marines from Camp Pendleton would take eighteen to twenty days, and thus could not be accomplished secretly.

"We can't do what the British and French did over Suez [in 1956]," McNamara warned. We cannot "say we will take action [and] then do nothing while a long buildup is completed . . . [and] the enemy prepares and world pressure mounts." If an invasion of Cuba proved necessary, preparations for it would have to be organized covertly. Reserve air squadrons, McNamara gave as an example, could not be mobilized "until air strikes begin."

General Wheeler discussed the different logistical challenges posed by preparing air strikes versus preparing an invasion force. Here the meeting notes are redacted, leaving the details of the discussion unclear. But the point at issue was whether the Chiefs would recommend limiting air strikes to the missile sites and other military facilities, or recommend air strikes followed by invasion—the latter requiring far more preparation. "We should bring this problem to the President's attention as soon as possible," McNamara directed, and a thorough briefing for the commander in chief was agreed upon.

3

THE NEXT morning, Tuesday, October 16, almost two hours before President Kennedy met with the advisers Bundy had assembled, the Chiefs met again. There was no longer a question about the accuracy of the previous day's SAC photo intelligence. A representative from the Defense Intelligence Agency confirmed that three MRBM sites had been positively identified. The estimate of their ranges was seven hundred to eleven hundred miles, and it was possible that "an all-out effort could make them operational within 24 hours."

The implications were dire. "Once the missile sites become operational," noted the air force vice chief of staff, Gen. Seth McKee (substituting for General LeMay, who was out of the country), "Castro can threaten retaliation for any offensive move by the U.S. Delaying action until the missiles are set up could touch off nuclear war."

General Shoup shifted the focus from Castro to the Soviet Union. The deployment of these missiles was more likely a Soviet attempt "to pose a nuclear threat to the US without running a risk of nuclear retaliation against the Soviet Union." But regardless of whether the prime culprit lurked in Havana or Moscow, the JCS agreed that missiles in Cuba that could attack the United States were "so serious as to *require the US to take out the missiles by military effort.*"

To do the job right, Wheeler insisted, required both surprise air strikes and an invasion. Admiral Anderson seconded this one-two punch, adding that that was "the only way to eliminate the Communist regime from Cuba."

But was an invasion really necessary? "What threat is Cuba once missiles and aircraft are knocked out?" General Taylor asked, prompting General Shoup to suggest that it was worth considering an ultimatum to Moscow and Havana: "Remove the missiles or the US will destroy them."

In the end, however, the consensus was to fall back on OPLAN 316: "The recommended sequence," the meeting notes summarize, "would be: get additional intelligence; make surprise attacks on missiles, airfields, PT boats, SAMs and tanks; concurrently reinforce Guantanamo: prepare to initiate an invasion."

22

"Bomb the Missiles; Invade Cuba"

Tuesday, October 16, Washington
11:50 a.m. ExComm Meeting

I think we ought to, beginning right now, be preparing to
[destroy the missiles]. . . . We're certainly going to do number
one. . . . We're going to take out these missiles.
—PRESIDENT KENNEDY, OCTOBER 16, 1962

As Kennedy dressed to begin the first day of the most important crisis of his presidency, he confronted a full schedule of events. Before
attending his first Cuban missile crisis meeting he hosted a reception for Project Mercury astronaut Walter Schirra and his family;
met with a congressman, conferenced with Secretary of the Treasury
C. Douglas Dillon, Undersecretary of the Treasury Henry Fowler,
and political adviser for Israeli affairs Myer Feldman; chaired a meeting with his Panel on Mental Retardation and met with Chip Bohlen,
Soviet expert and his new U.S. ambassador to France, with whom he
no doubt shared the news of Soviet missiles in Cuba.

The afternoon was similarly crowded with meetings. A White
House luncheon in honor of the crown prince of Libya was his first
post-ExComm event. After lunch he addressed the National Foreign
Policy Conference for Editors, followed by another meeting with the
crown prince. Finally he was free at 6:30 to chair the second ExComm
meeting. But at 7:55 he departed to host a dinner with his wife, Jacqueline, that included the publisher of the *Washington Post,* Philip
Graham, and his wife, Katherine; Ambassador Bohlen; and Sir Isa-
iah Berlin, the distinguished philosopher and historian of ideas.

To keep the deliberations about the Soviet missiles secret, the
president would adhere to his busy schedule.

1

AT 11:50 a.m. the president and his handpicked advisers assembled in the Cabinet Room. Before moving to their chairs around the expansive walnut table, several peered at the photographic interpreters' displays. The president played for a few moments with his five-year-old daughter, Caroline, and then flipped the switch that activated the Tandberg tape-recording system he had ordered Secret Service agent Robert Bouck to install (secretly) several months earlier.

This first meeting established the parameters of the debate over how to respond to the discovery of the missiles. Accepting their presence as the Soviet equivalent to the deployment of Jupiter missiles to Turkey was dismissed as politically untenable: "Once they [the missiles] were there the political needs of the Kennedy administration urged it to take almost any risk to get them out," John Galbraith wrote. The missiles had to be removed, and everyone agreed that it was necessary to destroy them with air strikes, possibly followed by an invasion.

The president shared this view, but the meeting's recordings also reveal how differently he approached the challenge. While his advisers turned immediately to the military options, Kennedy repeatedly asked (during this and subsequent meetings) about Khrushchev's motive. His instinct to understand his adversary's thoughts reflected a different way of thinking, a curiosity that would soon welcome the alternatives to a military assault that Ambassador Adlai Stevenson would be the first to suggest.

Nevertheless the president left this first meeting determined to bomb the missile sites.

2

THE DISCUSSION began with a question: What exactly was "there"? And it continued with questions far more difficult to answer: Why had Khrushchev initiated such a provocative move? When would the missiles be ready to fire? Where were the nuclear warheads? How could the United States force Khrushchev to reverse course? The answers were fascinating, mostly wrong, and the solutions were uniformly belligerent.

The director of the National Photographic Intelligence Center, Arthur Lundahl, and his Soviet missile maven, Sydney Graybeal, began with a show-and-tell. What was clear to them mystified the assemblage, and it took almost an hour to clarify exactly what Major Heyser's photographs revealed. "How do you know that this is a medium-range ballistic missile?" the president asked. "How far advanced is this?" "[Is it] ready to be fired?" "How long before they [can be] fired?" "What does it have to be fired from?" and so on. To Robert Kennedy it looked "like someone was digging a basement."

The early commentaries were dominated by Secretary of Defense Robert McNamara and Secretary of State Dean Rusk.

Not surprisingly the secretary of defense immediately focused on the discovery's military implications. His first concern was whether nuclear warheads had been located. If not, then the full range of responses, including bombing the missile sites and invading Cuba, were possible. "It's inconceivable to me that the Soviets would deploy nuclear warheads on an unfenced piece of ground," he assured the president (incorrectly, as it turned out). "And hence [because no secure facility had been located] it seems extremely unlikely that they are now ready to fire, or may be ready to fire within a matter of hours, or even a day or two."

Rusk, who had testified to the Senate Foreign Relations Committee sixteen months earlier that a primary reason for the Bay of Pigs invasion was the administration's belief that "Cuba might become a Sino-Soviet bloc missile base," appeared struck with amnesia. "Mr. President," he began, "this is, of course, a very serious development. It's one that we, all of us, had not really believed the Soviets could carry this far."

Then, at considerable length (no doubt straining the president's patience), he detailed his view of the options: "One is the quick strike." He suggested calling up 150,000 reserves, reinforcing Guantánamo as well as the southeastern United States, and preparing "an overwhelming strike at any of [the Soviet military] installations, including the SAM sites."

Rusk's second option was a series of diplomatic initiatives, "if we had a few days from the military point of view."

He would encourage the Organization of American States (OAS) to condemn the Soviet buildup, and insist that an OAS team be allowed into Cuba to inspect the missile sites. He would then have the Canadian ambassador in Havana tell Fidel Castro that he was being victimized by the Soviet deployment, and that the "Soviets are preparing Cuba for destruction or betrayal." Other initiatives included consulting with our NATO allies, alerting the leaders of the anti-Castro organizations that could form an alternative Cuban government, and finally providing "General Eisenhower a full briefing before a public announcement is made."

"I think we'll be facing a situation that could well lead to general war," he concluded. "Now with that we have an obligation to do what has to be done, but to do it in a way that gives everybody a chance to pull away from it before it gets too hard."

The exchange that followed reflected a pattern that would be maintained during most ExComm discussions. Whether it was Bundy or McNamara, or others who followed Rusk, they would frequently ignore what the secretary of state had said. This seems surprising when reading the meetings' transcripts, as many of Rusk's points were perceptive and, in the course of the crisis, the president pursued several of his suggestions.

But a clearer understanding of the dynamics of those meetings emerges when one listens to the recordings. Whereas McNamara and Bundy state their views crisply, Rusk's interventions, spoken in his soft, deliberate Georgia accent, sound like an uninspired lecturer repeatedly circling a point.

McNamara spoke next, but he appeared to have little interest in "pull[ing] away." Without acknowledging any of the diplomatic initiatives that Rusk proposed, the secretary of defense immediately offered "some possible military alternatives."

Beginning with the premise that "any air strike will be planned to take place prior to the time [the missiles] become operational," he outlined the extent of an air assault. In addition to attacking the missile sites, and all possible nuclear-storage facilities, strikes would hit the airfields and the aircraft that may "be hidden by that time." While estimating that Cuban casualties would probably be in the

"low thousands," he ignored the thousands of Soviet military personnel who would be killed.

It is difficult not to conclude that the secretary of defense was too
overwrought to think clearly. If the Cubans had "hidden" their aircraft, how could they be targeted? And might not bombing nuclear-
storage sites ignite a nuclear conflagration? At the very least, such an
attack would spread deadly radiation far and wide. Could the Soviets
accept the slaughter of thousands of their troops from radioactive
fallout without a military response?

The strikes, he went on to explain, could be launched within a
matter of days, and if necessary "almost literally within a matter of
hours." In either case they would continue for several days, and would
be followed by an air and sea invasion within seven days "if the political environment made it desirable or necessary."

After discussing mobilization options, he asked the chairman of
the JCS to expand on his comments.

3

GENERAL TAYLOR'S main point was the importance of attacking
the missiles without warning: a surprise attack. Since it was not possible to know whether some of the missiles would be operational by
the time of the strike, surprise was the key to destroying them before
they could be launched. "We will never have the exact, perfect timing," he warned. "But we must do a good job the first time we go in
there, pushing 100 percent just as far, as closely, as we can with our
strike."

He then made the first reference to a naval blockade, although it
was as a follow-up rather than an alternative to the air strikes. After
destroying as many offensive weapons as possible, "We should prevent any more coming in, which means a naval blockade."

Rusk had a different view. It was not a question of whether we could
destroy any particular missile before launching. It was a question of
whether Khrushchev was ready to initiate a general nuclear war. "If
they shoot those missiles we are in a general nuclear war. . . . The
Soviet Union has got quite a different decision to make," he declared.

McNamara disagreed, based on the important point—one that he and the other members of ExComm would often ignore during the next thirteen days—that it would not be possible to know whether a missile was launched on orders from Moscow or Havana. He pointed out that "we don't know what kinds of communications the Soviets have with those sites. We don't know what kinds of control they have over the warheads" (or, he could have added, any of their other forces, such as submarines).

It's not clear how much attention the president had been paying, since he abruptly changed the subject. "What is the advantage?" he interrupted, shifting the discussion from response to motive. "Must be some major reason for the Russians to set this up. Must be that they're not satisfied with their ICBMs. What'd be the reason that they would—"

"To supplement their rather defective ICBM system," General Taylor responded before Kennedy could complete his thought. "That's one reason."

"Of course," the president continued, skipping back to Taylor's point about a blockade, "I don't see how we could prevent further ones from coming in by submarine. I mean, if we let them [the navy] blockade the thing, they come in by submarine." (No one bothered to explain to the president that given the length of the missiles—sixty-five feet—and the limited space on submarines, he need not worry about an underwater resupply network.)

The way to prevent that, McNamara replied, was to be clear that any additional missiles would be destroyed "the moment they come in."

Bundy turned the discussion to the scope of the air assault. Was it necessary, he asked McNamara, to attack Cuba's "whole air complex"? It was, McNamara affirmed, because the Cuban air force had MiG-21s. Whether or not they were armed with nuclear weapons, those planes could attack the southeastern United States with devastating results; they had to be eliminated.

Rusk, following the president's lead, returned the conversation to Khrushchev's motives. Referring to what DCI John McCone (who was in California at his stepson's funeral) had suggested a few weeks earlier, he said that Khrushchev "knows that we have a substantial nuclear superiority, but he also knows that we don't really live under fear of his nuclear weapons to the extent that he has to live under fear of ours." The Jupiter missiles in Turkey were a case in point.

Nuclear weapons in Turkey? They weren't exactly news to the president, but he was unclear about the details. "How many weapons do we have in Turkey?" he asked. "About fifteen," McNamara replied.

"Khrushchev may feel that it's important for us to learn about living under medium-range missiles," Rusk remarked, "and he's doing that to sort of balance that political, psychological flank." It was something of an abstract point, but Soviet documents and Khrushchev's memoirs support the secretary's (and McCone's) speculations.

4

RUSK THEN mentioned Berlin, a central consideration for the president. "Berlin is very much involved in this," he stated. Moscow had so often raised the Allied occupation of West Berlin as the chief irritant of the postwar settlement that Rusk wondered whether "Mr. Khrushchev is entirely rational about Berlin."

He then hypothesized a Khrushchev strategy that was rational to the point of cunning. Did he send his missiles to Cuba to set up a trade? Missiles out of Cuba, Allied troops out of West Berlin? Or was it his intention to "provoke us into a kind of action in Cuba" that would provide him with an excuse to "take action with respect to Berlin." In either case, Rusk declared, it was obvious that the Soviet government was acting on a gross misunderstanding of "the importance of Cuba to this country."

Berlin and Havana are 5,632 miles apart. But in October 1962 the president and the men advising him linked those cities as if they were neighbors. Almost every ExComm discussion that probed Khrushchev's motives concluded that his ultimate purpose was to use his missiles to force the Allies out of West Berlin, and no one believed this more strongly than the president.

It was a reasonable assumption. Since 1958 Khrushchev had been devising schemes for eliminating the irritating presence of hostile forces occupying a Western city 110 miles within Communist East Germany. When he met with President Eisenhower at Camp David, he kept returning to the necessity of resolving the Berlin anomaly. He hoped that he would not have to take drastic action; but, he threatened, if forced to, he would.

No issue irritated Khrushchev more than Western-occupied Berlin. Its postwar division into four Allied occupation zones—the American, British, and French zones in the west, and the Soviet zone in the east—created a tinderbox. It was the fulcrum of the Cold War in Europe, a minefield waiting to explode if one side or the other took a careless, aggressive step.

As relations deteriorated between the former wartime Allies, the United States, Britain, and France decided in 1948 to unify their zones and their currencies, in violation of their agreement with the Soviet Union. This prompted Stalin to renege on his obligation to permit land access to Berlin, but President Truman's massive Berlin Airlift prevailed. In May 1949 Stalin lifted his blockade. On September 30, 1949, the Federal Republic of Germany (FRG, West Germany) was created.

A second Berlin crisis, which began in 1958 but came to a head between July and October 1961, proved to be nearly as dangerous a U.S.–Soviet confrontation. A dispute over Western access to East Berlin brought Soviet and American tanks, each loaded with live ammunition, to their respective sides of Checkpoint Charlie. The alert levels of the U.S. garrison in West Berlin and the Strategic Air Command were raised. No one doubted that it had the potential to spin out of control.

5

TREASURY SECRETARY Douglas Dillon's primary concern was not to warn Khrushchev about America's plans. Rusk's suggestion that we inform our OAS and NATO allies, Dillon said, would get "us wide out in the open" to the Soviets' advantage: "I think that the chance of getting through this thing without a Russian reaction is greater under a quick strike." Bundy agreed, leading Kennedy to summarize the issues.

"Warning them, it seems to me, is warning everybody. . . . You can't sort of announce that in 4 days from now you're going to take them out. They may announce within 3 days that they're going to have warheads on them. If we come and attack, they're going to fire them. . . . Well, if they do that, then we're going to attack with nuclear weapons."

Then, turning to Taylor, the president asked how effective an attack on the missile sites would be.

"It'll never be 100 percent, Mr. President," was the disappointing answer. Deputy Secretary of Defense Roswell Gilpatric followed Taylor, recommending a full-scale assault. "If you're talking about a general air-attack program, you might as well think about whether we can eradicate the whole [Cuban] problem by an invasion just as simply, with as little chance of [negative public] reaction."

Taylor and Kennedy agreed.

Always sensitive to public opinion, the president asked how long the discovery of the Soviet missiles could be kept from Congress and the press? McNamara estimated a week. Rusk pointed out—sarcastically, one has to assume—that Senator Kenneth Keating had "already, in effect, announced it on the floor of the Senate." His estimate for the limits of secrecy was three to four days.

The president was collecting everyone's opinion, and Lyndon Johnson was asked to speak next: "You have any thoughts, Mr. Vice President?"

Johnson joined the conversation in support of an assault: "We have to take whatever action we must take to assure our security," and he went on from there to support air strikes and the invasion, if that was the judgment of the "responsible commanders." He dismissed Rusk's approach to the OAS and NATO "even though I realize it's a breach of faith, not to confer with them. We're not going to get much help out of them."

There were two or three different types of operations being discussed, the president remarked. The first was a strike on the three bases that had been identified. The second was McNamara's more thorough series of strikes on missiles, SAM sites, and Cuba's air bases. The third was all of the above with the addition of a blockade. And a fourth, he added, was the question of how much consultation, if any, should be done with our allies. "I don't know how much use consulting with the British has been," he wondered. "They'll just object. . . . Probably ought to tell them, though, the night before."

6

"WE HAVE the fifth one," Robert Kennedy interrupted, speaking for the first time. "The invasion . . . you're dropping bombs all over Cuba if you do the second . . . You're going to kill an awful lot of people and we're going to take an awful lot of heat. . . . It's almost incumbent upon the Russians . . . to send them in again" and perhaps to attack our missiles in Turkey or Iran (Iran? There were no U.S. missiles in Iran).

Responding to his brother's interjection, the president asked McNamara and Taylor: "How long does it take to get in a position where we can invade Cuba?" A month or two?

"No, sir. No, sir," McNamara responded. "It's a bare 7 days after the air strike, assuming the air strike starts the first of next week."

Taylor explained that there were two plans. The first would put ninety thousand troops into Cuba by air and sea within seven days after the first air strikes. The second would do the same in five days, if the military had more time to prepare for the invasion before air operations began.

Perhaps thinking back to CIA assurances that Cubans would rise up against their government when the invaders landed at the Bay of Pigs, the president asked if there was any information about what the "popular reaction" might be to air strikes and an invasion.

Taylor thought "great confusion and panic." Deputy CIA director Marshall Carter said it was hard to know how the Cubans would react. McNamara adopted the Allen Dulles–Bissell delusion that an air strike "might lead to an uprising." And Rusk, abandoning his earlier thoughts about diplomacy, added, "Do the whole job [air strikes and invasion]."

Robert Kennedy wanted the "whole job" initiated more promptly, and wondered why it was necessary to wait seven days. Taylor reminded everyone about the necessity for surprise. If you begin to position troops for an invasion before the air strikes began (in order to cut the start of the invasion to less than seven or five days) you lose the element of surprise. That was not a good trade-off. Then, astonishingly, McNamara again raised the fantasy of an uprising: "It's not probable, but it's conceivable that the air strike would trigger a nationwide uprising."

7

THE DISCUSSION was descending deeper into the details and politics of an invasion. The specific questions with which it had begun were being left behind, along with Rusk's early suggestions for diplomatic initiatives. (Were the missiles ready to fire? Had nuclear warheads been located? Should OAS and NATO allies be consulted? What were Khrushchev's motives?)

Robert Kennedy worried that waiting even five days to invade after air strikes was too long. World pressure against an invasion would build quickly, he warned, and the Soviets would be under pressure to retaliate. Wasn't there some way, he asked, to "get it [the invasion] started *so there wasn't any turning back?*"

Following his brother's thoughts, the president identified time as the unknown key variable. "Do we have two weeks?" he asked. "If we had two weeks, we could lay on all this and have it all [air assault and invasion] ready to go."

But neither Taylor, Bundy, McNamara, nor Carter could say when the missiles would become operational. "Even today," Taylor acknowledged, the missile site captured in the U2's photographs "might be operational."

The need for surprise was controlling, McNamara stated again. Even if they had two weeks, there was no possibility of shortening the time between the air strikes and the invasion. Aircraft, ships, armor, and troops had to be pre-positioned for an invasion, and that could not happen covertly. Pre-positioning could only begin simultaneously with the air strikes.

Bundy added a measure of diplomatic nuance to McNamara's presentation of a full-blown air assault. It would destroy the missiles, the SAM sites, and the eight airfields and aircraft that had retaliatory capability. "But, politically," Bundy asked, "if you're trying to get him [Khrushchev] to understand the limit and the non-limit and make it as easy for him as possible [to remove all offensive weapons], there's an enormous premium on having a small, as small and clear-cut, an action as possible, against the hazard of going after all the operational airfields becoming a kind of general war."

"*General!?*" the president exclaimed, startled by the thought.

8

THE DISCUSSION was again losing focus, as each discussant turned to the point that he considered most pressing. The president asked about the next step; the next twenty-four hours? Bundy suggested additional U2 reconnaissance, and talking with Senator Keating, an idea Kennedy squelched, but Bobby thought that ignoring Keating could become a political problem "afterwards."

Bundy returned to the size of the air strikes, and Dillon then raised an important question: "What, if anything, has to be done to be prepared for an eventuality of a Soviet reaction?"

Astonishingly, his intervention was ignored. The president had shifted to figuring out who "we really have to tell . . . I suppose, well, there's de Gaulle."

"Right," said Bundy. "You want de Gaulle. It's hard to say about [West German chancellor Konrad] Adenauer." SACEUR (Supreme Allied Commander Europe) and the commandant (of the American sector of Berlin) would also have to be informed.

Almost an hour had passed when the president began to conclude the meeting by proposing to meet again at 6:00 p.m. The first thing to be considered was timing. He had come to the realization that they did not have two weeks "while we're getting ready to roll. . . . Maybe we just have to just take them out.

"I think we ought to, beginning right now, be preparing to [take them out]," he said. "Because that's what we're going to do anyway. We're certainly going to do number one [attack the missile sites]. *We're going to take out these missiles.*"

Actions that he was leaving undecided for the moment included whether the air strikes would also target the SAM sites, the MiGs, the IL-28 bombers, and the air bases, which he referred to as number two. And, number three, whether the air strikes would be followed by an invasion. He finished by reaffirming that "we're going to do number one. . . . We ought to be making those preparations." (He did not mention a blockade.)

Bundy, who had earlier raised the political and diplomatic consequences of McNamara's assault scenarios, seemed surprised by the president's commitment to attacking the missiles. He wanted to know now "whether we have definitely decided against a political track." He thought that was a contingency "we ought to work out."

"We'll develop both tracks," Rusk said, and Kennedy confirmed that "we ought to do the OAS" (although he thought it "a waste of time," and he opposed informing NATO). The challenge was to prevent a leak, and he wanted everything kept secret. The only State Department personnel beyond those in ExComm to be informed were the Soviet specialists Chip Bohlen and Llewellyn Thompson. In the Defense Department "We've got to keep it as tight as possible."

McNamara, in his typical take-charge fashion, attempted to set the agenda for the next meeting. Everyone should return with prepared answers to three questions, he suggested. The first was whether to publicly announce that we are going to "act to take out any offensive weapons." The second was whether political action should precede any military action and, if so, what was the timing? He thought it should, with particular reference to Khrushchev. Finally, it was necessary to answer Kennedy's questions about the timing of the strikes.

As he often did, the president responded directly to the clarity of McNamara's analytical approach, and returned to the question of timing: "How many mornings from tomorrow morning would it take . . . to take out just these missile sites?" He then asked deputy CIA director Gen. Marshall Carter how long it would take to discover what offensive weapons were located around the rest of the island.

"Could take weeks, Mr. President," was the disappointing answer, which set off a discussion about U2 coverage, the problem of cloud cover, and the advantages and disadvantages of sending in low-level flights.

No decisions were taken and, after again summarizing the discussion, the president began to end the meeting, when Bobby suddenly asked: "How long would it take to take over the island?"

Taylor estimated that within five or six days "the main resistance ought to be overcome." After that, it would probably take another month "cleaning that up."

At this point several people began to leave, and the last recorded comment of note was the president wondering aloud "if CIA could give us . . . some idea about our reception there [Cuba]."

23

"I'll Tell My Big Brother on You"

Mongoose and the JCS
Tuesday, October 16, Washington

We would be prepared to immediately attack the Soviet Union in
the event that Cuba made *any* offensive move against this country.
—ROBERT MCNAMARA, OCTOBER 16

At 12:57 President Kennedy left the first ExComm meeting certain
about two decisions: The Soviet missiles had to be eliminated, and
he would select one of three military options to do the job. He would
continue to mull over the many questions he had raised, but not now.
In a few minutes he had to host a very different presidential activity:
a luncheon in honor of the crown prince of Libya. Determined to
adhere to his scheduled activities, it would take all of John Kennedy's powers of concentration to focus on the formalities of diplomacy
and the pretensions of political campaigning while planning military
actions that could escalate to a nuclear holocaust.

McNamara and Taylor followed the president out of the Cabinet
Room and headed to the Pentagon to brief the Joint Chiefs.

Rusk and Ball returned to their offices at the State Department
and prepared to consider next steps. They would be joined by Edwin
Martin, the assistant secretary for American republics affairs, and
Soviet experts Chip Bohlen and Llewellyn Thompson.

Robert Kennedy rushed to his Justice Department office where
the members of the Special Group Augmented (SGA) were waiting.

1

THE SPECIAL Group was an Eisenhower creation that the Kennedy administration inherited, and "augmented" by inserting the

attorney general at its head. Charged in March 1960 with overseeing CIA preparations for the invasion of Cuba, it was resuscitated and expanded in November 1961 to repair the political damage inflicted by the Bay of Pigs. Adm. George W. Anderson Jr. recalled that "as soon as I became a member of the Joint Chiefs of Staff, it was clear that there was a weekly meeting . . . as to what could be done to redress the [Bay of Pigs] situation."

Without a nod to irony, President Kennedy assigned his brother, the head of the Department of Justice, to direct a myriad of illegal activities that violated the Neutrality Acts for the purpose of ridding Cuba of Castro. But the law was considered flexible. "If the President says it's okay, and if the Attorney General says it's okay," a senior CIA offical told a skeptical colleague, "then it's okay." The sabotage and assassination program hatched by the Special Group Augmented was christened "Operation Mongoose."

The members of Mongoose included the CIA's director, John McCone (often represented by his deputy director for plans, Richard Helms); McGeorge Bundy, Alexis Johnson, representing State; McNamara and Roswell Gilpatric (his deputy); General Taylor, and the CIA's mercurial William Harvey—three martinis at every lunch and a loaded pistol visibly positioned on his desk.

Like the president and his predecessor, the attorney general (AG) was drawn to covert operations. They ran under the political radar, and the president could always deny that he had anything to do with them.

The meeting began at 2:30 with air force Gen. Edward Lansdale, the titular head of Mongoose operations; Richard Helms, the CIA's deputy director for plans; and several stand-ins representing the secretary of defense, the JCS, the State Department, and the United States Information Agency.

Bobby made it clear that he was speaking for the president as he castigated the group for its failure to accomplish anything significant during the past year. The responsibility for ridding Cuba of Castro brought out the toughest part of his character. "He was very difficult to deal with," the Special Group's secretary, Thomas Parrott, recalled. "He was arrogant; he knew it all. . . . He sat there, tie down, chewing gum, his feet up on the desk. His threats were transparent. "If you don't do it, I'll tell my big brother on you." After watching one of Bobby's Mongoose reprimand sessions, General Taylor remarked that "he could sack a town and enjoy it."

Bobby liked the aggressive orientation of the CIA's new enhanced sabotage program, and much of the meeting was devoted to reviewing its details. Intelligence collection had improved, he said, but there had been no successful acts of sabotage. When Helms asked for a clear explanation of Mongoose's ultimate objective, the AG replied that it was Castro, and (reflecting ExComm's discussion) that the president might come around to using U.S. forces to eliminate him. What is the percentage of Cubans, he asked, "whom we thought would fight for the regime if the country were invaded[?]," Helms recorded Bobby asking.

In the meantime, however, RFK wanted his Mongoose team to show results. Henceforth he would meet daily at 9:30 a.m. with the operational representatives.

In Bobby's mind Mongoose was a seamless part of the missile crisis.

2

AT 4:30 General Taylor, who would attend all ExComm meetings, briefed the Joint Chiefs. Serving as the communications link between the president's civilian and military advisers, his reports to the Chiefs would distill ExComm's discussions, providing at least one takeaway from those meetings. As a companion to the ExComm transcripts, Taylor's briefings highlight what he understood as the meetings' most important recommendations and conclusions. They were occasionally at odds with what the transcripts indicate and what the president thought.

Taylor announced the welcome news that the president had authorized "unlimited authority to use U2 reconnaissance." He also reported [incorrectly, according to the recorded ExComm conversations] that Secretary of State Dean Rusk "said he was not certain that the MRBMs were in Cuba." Also, that McNamara had faithfully stated, and supported, the JCS recommendations (air strikes and invade), but with the caveat that the missiles had to be attacked

(Above) A U.S. Navy helicopter hovering over a Soviet B-59 submarine whose captain ordered a nuclear torpedo readied to fire at U.S. Navy ships he believed were attacking him.

(Right) Crowded interior of a Foxtrot submarine.

Brigade Chief of Staff Vasily Arkhipov who persuaded B-59's captain not to fire the nuclear torpedo. He prevented a nuclear war.

The author, age twenty-five, was the air intelligence officer of his antisubmarine warfare training squadron during the Cuban missile crisis.

ROOSEVELT IS DEAD; TRUMAN TAKES OATH

WARM SPRINGS STROKE BRINGS END AT 3:35 P.M.

U. S. CHUTISTS REPORTED 20 MILES FROM BERLIN

CITY JOINS IN TRIBUTE

TRUMAN AT U.S. TILLER

Franklin Roosevelt had been president since 1933. His postwar goal was to continue good relations with the Soviet Union.

April 12, 1945, at 7:09 p.m. Senator Harry S. Truman is sworn in as president of the United States, with his wife, Bess, and daughter, Margaret, beside him.

Winston Churchill, Harry Truman, and Joseph Stalin at the Potsdam Conference. Truman delayed the conference to coincide with the scheduled test of the atomic bomb on July 16, 1945. Its success prompted him to take a harder line with Stalin.

Hiroshima after the first atomic bomb was dropped on August 6, 1945, completely destroying the city. Ninety-five percent of the estimated 200,000 casualties were civilians.

Secretary of War Henry Stimson (below left) opposed threatening the Soviet Union with the atomic bomb. Secretary of State James Byrnes (right) encouraged Truman to use "atomic diplomacy."

President Truman and Gen. Douglas MacArthur, commander of United Nations forces fighting in Korea, on Wake Island, October 15, 1950. MacArthur assured Truman that the Chinese would not intervene, but after they did he publicly recommended atomic bombing Chinese bases contrary to administration policy. Truman fired him on April 11, 1951.

Handsome, athletic, and likeable, Dwight Eisenhower graduated from West Point in 1915 and was promoted to General of the Army in 1944.

(Middle) Eisenhower speaking with troops before the Normandy invasion.

(Bottom) During his 1952 campaign for president, Eisenhower promised, if elected, to go to Korea to evaluate the situation. On November 29 he kept his promise.

On inauguration day, January 20, 1953, there were approximately 1,200 nuclear weapons in the U.S. arsenal. On January 17, 1961, when Eisenhower gave his farewell address, the U.S. nuclear arsenal contained more than 20,000 nuclear weapons.

Secretary of State John Foster Dulles (above right) with President Eisenhower promoted the administration's massive retaliation strategy while his brother, Allen Dulles CIA director (right), organized the overthrow of left-leaning third world governments.

The democratically elected prime minister of Iran, Mohammad Mosaddeq (left) was overthrown on August 19, 1953, in a coup, pictured below, organized by the CIA in cooperation with Britain's MI6 intelligence service.

Time magazine put President Jacobo Árbenz of Guatemala on its cover when he tried to limit the United Fruit Company's control of his country's economy—a cover later satirized. The Eisenhower administration's close ties with UFC led the president to authorize the CIA to organize his ouster in June 1954.

Vice President Richard Nixon shaking hands with Fidel Castro. President Eisenhower snubbed Castro by leaving Washington. Nixon "guessed" he was not a Communist after their nearly two-and-a-half hour meeting.

On April 15, 1959, Castro arrived in the United States. For eleven days he assured Nixon, senators, congressmen, and journalists that he was not a Communist. He campaigned like a seasoned politician. Right: at the Lincoln Memorial. Below: at the Bronx Zoo eating a hot dog.

On April 14, 1958 the judges at the first International Tchaikovsky Competition called Nikita Khrushchev (right) to ask if they could give first prize to an American, Van Cliburn (left). If he's the best, Khrushchev said, give it to him.

(Right) Nikita Khrushchev visited the United States from September 15 to 27, 1959, at Eisenhower's invitation. The visit was controversial.

(Below) Khrushchev's domestic agricultural problems motivated him to visit U.S. farms.

Meeting with Eisenhower at Camp David, Khrushchev emphasized nuclear disarmament, the abnormality of West Berlin, and trade.

before they were operational. He had explained the Chiefs' recommendations in some detail, he reported, and the general view of the "conferees [was] that our deterrent would keep Khrushchev from firing nuclear missiles [in response to U.S. military actions]," another rather skewed takeaway.

Taylor also divulged that the president had wondered aloud why Khrushchev had deployed missiles to Cuba, and he repeated Secretary Rusk's view that it was both to close the missile gap and "further his Berlin objectives." That conformed with the Chiefs' beliefs, and it passed without discussion.

"The question," Taylor concluded, "was whether to go for the missiles or go for missiles as well as blockade, to be followed by possible invasion." But that would tie up 250,000 U.S. troops, and would be "playing Khrushchev's game," he thought.

"What targets should be attacked?" (by air) was another question that was quickly resolved: "All significant military targets," in addition to the MRBMs, the MiGs, SAMs, patrol boats, and tank parks. A follow-up blockade was also recommended and, probably because work on the missiles might soon be completed, the eighteen-day buildup period for an invasion was "discarded."

At this point Secretary McNamara joined the meeting and expanded on Taylor's remarks. ExComm had considered three courses of action: The first was political moves, which he characterized as "useless" (a most interesting statement from the man who later insisted that he fully supported the president's efforts to avoid a war).

The second course of action combined open surveillance and a blockade against more weapons, "and if they use missiles we attack [the Soviet Union]—costly but might be worth the cost," (as the meeting notes record the secretary's assessment of World War III). The third option was significant military action that "might trigger a Soviet response."

There is no record of the discussion that followed, but it clearly drifted toward preparing for the Soviet response. The "JCS agreed," the notes state, "that the following *general war preparatory steps* were necessary: SAC on 1/8 airborne alert: disperse those SAC and NORAD aircraft carrying nuclear weapons; move Polaris subs from [the U.S. Navy submarine base] Holy Loch [Argyll, Scotland]; augment air defenses in the Southeast."

The JCS also disagreed with McNamara. Confident that Khrushchev would not start a nuclear war, they favored an attack even if the missiles were operational.

Finally, and perhaps reflecting the still-smarting frustrations over the Bay of Pigs, the Chiefs agreed that it was all or nothing. If the decision was limited to taking out the MRBMs, they would recommend against any action.

24

"Negotiation and Sanity, Always"

Tuesday, October 16, Washington, Afternoon

But the means adopted have such incalculable consequences
that I feel you should have made it clear that the existence
of nuclear missile bases anywhere is negotiable before we start
anything.
—ADLAI STEVENSON TO JFK, OCTOBER 17

On October 16 Adlai Stevenson boarded an early flight from New
York to Washington. He had a morning appointment at the State
Department, and also had arranged to see the president. Since his
Bay of Pigs humiliation, he was determined to remain in the foreign
policy loop, and President Kennedy felt obliged to accommodate.
Stevenson attended the luncheon for Libya's crown prince, and then,
at Kennedy's invitation, accompanied him to the family quarters on
the second floor of the White House.

1

WHEN KENNEDY showed his ambassador the U2 photographs,
Stevenson was as startled as the president had been hours earlier.
But he had a different reaction. "I suppose," the president explained
as Stevenson stared at the photos, "the alternatives are to go in by
air and wipe them out, or to take other steps to render the weapons
inoperable."

Not so, Stevenson replied. "Let's not go into an air strike until we
have explored the possibilities of a peaceful solution."

Adlai's appeal for diplomacy was the strongest reaction of its kind
to confront Kennedy since Bundy entered his bedroom at 9:00 a.m.,

and those seventeen words—reinforced by a supporting memorandum on Wednesday—urged an alternative response that the president had not considered.

Stevenson pointed out that while U.S. forces were superior in the Caribbean, any military action against Cuba could be countered by the Soviets in Berlin or Turkey, a reaction that was likely to escalate out of control. "To start or risk starting a nuclear war is bound to be divisive at best," he drily noted in his memo, "and the judgments of history (a serious concern to JFK) rarely coincide with the tempers of the moment."

Adlai said that he understood the president's dilemma. National security was preeminent and, if air strikes proved necessary, it was important to destroy the missiles before they were operational. "But the means adopted," he wrote in an underlined sentence, "have such incalculable consequences that I feel that you should have made it clear that the existence of nuclear missile bases anywhere is negotiable before we start anything."

The clarity of Stevenson's response on Tuesday, and the focus of his memorandum on Wednesday, October 17, was the vital role that world opinion would play once the crisis became public. Dealing every day with 109 UN ambassadors made him particularly alert to the role that credibility played in international affairs.

If a war, or even a serious confrontation, was going to result from U.S. actions, it was critical that Washington did not appear irresponsible. A diplomatic solution was worth trying. "As I have said," the ambassador reminded the president, "I think your personal emissaries should deliver your messages to C[astro] and K[hrushchev]."

It was important, Stevenson further counseled, not to lead with an announcement that an assault was imminent. It would be more effective to initiate the public disclosure of the missiles with an explanation of the facts, the gravity of the situation, and a notice that steps to correct it were under way. (The precise structure of Kennedy's "quarantine" speech a week later.)

If diplomatic steps failed to remove the missiles, military activity of some sort might follow. But so would "Soviet reprisals somewhere—Turkey, Berlin, etc." In that case: "It is important that we have as much of the world with us as possible."

The memorandum was a realistic analysis. It advocated negotiation as the best solution, and examined the important role of diplomacy if military force was necessary. "If war comes," Stevenson wrote, "our case must rest on stopping while there was still time the Soviet drive to world domination."

In formulating the U.S. response, he warned, it was necessary to understand that other nations would not view the Soviet missiles through Washington's lens.

"While the explanation of our action may be clear to us it won't be clear to many others." America's allies, he elaborated, had long lived under the threat of Soviet IRBMs and were unlikely to sympathize with an aversion to those same missiles in Cuba. United States missiles in Turkey and elsewhere would justify to others the Soviet Union's right to have a missile base in Cuba. And if we struck them, Stevenson continued, a Soviet attack against NATO bases would be seen as a legitimate retaliation.

The U.S. position, Stevenson affirmed, was that we would not negotiate "with a gun at our head." The missiles had to go, and if the Soviets wouldn't remove them, "we [would] have to do it ourselves." But he concluded with an unambiguous principle: "It should be clear as a pikestaff that the U.S. was, is and will be ready to negotiate the elimination of bases and anything else . . . blackmail and intimidation <u>never</u>, negotiation and sanity <u>always</u>."

2

A CAREFUL comparison of Stevenson's notes and memorandums with the president's shift away from the air strike option during the next forty-eight hours suggests that Adlai's strong and early advocacy of "explor[ing] the possibilities of a peaceful solution" provided Kennedy with a blueprint to do exactly that. In fact, Stevenson's suggestions of October 16 and 17 were congruent with nearly all the steps that the president followed in resolving the crisis.

Despite how closely Kennedy tracked Stevenson's suggestions, an objection to this interpretation is that John Kennedy harbored an intense dislike for his ambassador. His enmity toward Adlai even moved the president to encourage postcrisis reports that Stevenson had advocated "a Munich," suggesting that he was an American Neville Chamberlain. He was not cut from the same heroic cloth as the Kennedy brothers.

But Stevenson's persistent advocacy of diplomacy revealed an iron will and a stoic conviction that it was insane to ignore peaceful solutions. He doggedly stuck to his position throughout the crisis, despite the open hostility of most ExComm members. Defying their criticism, he maintained the clearest analysis of the dangers raised by the crisis and the range of diplomatic solutions available.

His performance moved Kennedy to confess grudgingly (perhaps in self-reflection) that he "admire[d]" his ambassador's "courage . . . in adhering to his position under fire." And Stevenson's forceful accounting of Soviet duplicity in the United Nations—during a televised debate with Soviet UN ambassador Valerian Zorin on October 25—was also unexpectedly tough. The Kennedy brothers publicly applauded it, but it made them uneasy about how Adlai might wield his new political image.

The thought that Stevenson had proposed a better way to deal with the Soviet missiles "annoyed" the president, and he said as much to Ted Sorensen. But like it or not (and Kennedy hated it), as he considered the likely consequences of military action during the first days of the crisis, Stevenson's proposals began to make more sense than the war whoops of the Joint Chiefs and ExComm majority.

The psychology is complicated: Despite the president's personal dislike of Stevenson-the-man, Stevenson's intellect spoke clearly, directly, and persuasively to the president's sensibilities. Their quiet conversation in the White House family quarters, and Stevenson's memo, planted the idea that there was a viable alternative to military actions. Kennedy would appropriate that view over the next two days, and harvest it as his own.

The president's support of the postcrisis condemnation of Stevenson's recommendations most likely reflected his angry recognition that this man he disdained, but whom he was forced by political necessity to employ and engage, had been responsible for pointing the way to his crowning foreign policy achievement. It was an infuriating thought, and he rejected it.

3

STEVENSON WAS not the president's sole correspondent on October 17. Treasury Secretary Douglas Dillon composed a very different memorandum for the commander in chief. An uncompromising call for a military solution, it had the ironic effect of reinforcing the president's interest in Stevenson's position. It was the first example of a pattern that would evolve as the week wore on. The ferocity of the hawks led Kennedy to search more thoroughly for ways of avoiding a fight.

The Soviet Union had deliberately challenged the United States, Dillon asserted, and how we reacted would "determine the future course of world events for many years to come." No less than "the survival of our nation demands the prompt elimination of the offensive weapons now in Cuba. This cannot be negotiable."

In light of how the crisis was resolved, it is important to examine Dillon's hyperbolic views (initially shared by the majority of ExComm) in an effort to understand the assumptions and ideas that prompted his extreme positions. His conviction that an immediate clash was preferable to compromise was grounded in the deep-seated anti-Communism that so many in positions of influence accepted in 1962. "We face a battle to extinction between the two systems," General Eisenhower had confided in his diary in *1946,* and Dillon believed the time for that battle had arrived.

The deployment of the missiles was a deliberate "public test" of our resolve, Dillon argued, and if we did not beat it back we would "lose all Latin America to Communism." Incorporating Eisenhower's "domino theory," he warned that the effect would be devastating even beyond the Western Hemisphere. Iran, Thailand, and Pakistan were likely to follow Latin America's nations to the dark side if the United States did not confront the Soviet challenge head-on.

To the concern that a surprise attack would create difficult public relations problems, Dillon responded that they could be ignored. "Accordingly," he wrote in response to a proposal raised during the second ExComm meeting, "I would reject the blockade course insofar as it is designed to lead to negotiations either in the UN or direct with Khrushchev."

To Dillon the only satisfactory solution was a military strike: "The survival of the entire free world fabric," was at stake, and neither public opinion nor any Soviet military response should be allowed to dampen the president's resolve.

4

STEVENSON HAD left his meeting with the president determined to promote a diplomatic solution. He would remain in Washington for that evening's ExComm meeting, and in the meantime he joined the afternoon gathering at the State Department. It was held in the conference room adjacent to the office of the undersecretary of state for economic affairs, George Ball.

Ball was a former law partner and a close friend who had helped manage Stevenson's presidential campaigns in 1952 and 1956, as well as a supporter of his bid for the 1960 nomination. He had a reputation for being clear-headed and perceptive and, despite his association with Stevenson, was well-enough regarded by Kennedy to have been tapped for ExComm.

Jumping ahead a year to an early debate over Vietnam highlights Ball's critical judgment. When Kennedy considered sending sixteen thousand military "advisers" to Vietnam, Ball offered lonely opposition. Reminding the president of France's disastrous experience in the region, he predicted that "within five years we'll have 300,000 men in the paddies and jungles and never find them again." Kennedy demurred: "George, you're just crazier than hell. That just isn't going to happen."

25

"Last Month I Should Have Said
That We Don't Care"

Tuesday, October 16, 6:30 p.m., ExComm Meeting

We certainly have been wrong about what he's [Khrushchev]
trying to do in Cuba. There isn't any doubt about that.
Not many of us thought that he was going to put MRBMs
in Cuba.
—PRESIDENT KENNEDY, OCTOBER 16, 1962

The ExComm members reassembled at 6:30 in the White House
Cabinet Room. The meeting began with an intelligence update.
General Carter reported that the photographic interpreters had identified sixteen to twenty-four solid-fuel missiles with a range of eleven
hundred miles. The president, with Bundy, McNamara, and Rusk
chiming in, pressed Carter as to whether he was certain of the type,
range, and identification of the missiles. Could there possibly be a
mistake? No mistake, the general assured them. They were definitely
MRBMs with a range that could send nuclear warheads into targets
across much of the East Coast of the United States.

1

RUSK BEGAN to summarize his afternoon meeting at State by presenting one of Stevenson's suggestions: "We are very much interested
in the possibility of a direct message to Castro, as well as Khrushchev . . . before an actual strike." But the president, more interested
in "the military thing," cut him off. He wanted to know if McNamara still favored "taking these [missiles] out."

It could be done with a twenty-four-hour notice, as early as Saturday (October 20) if the decision was made on Friday, the defense

secretary responded. But he added that the Joint Chiefs were opposed to such a limited strike. In their opinion attacking the missiles alone would leave the Cubans (and their Soviet allies) with too many military assets. Backing up McNamara, General Taylor reported that all the commanders, as well as the Chiefs, favored an assault against the full range of military targets, and if necessary, an invasion. "Take it [all] right out with one hard crack," he declared.

After further exchanges about a strike, McNamara presented three options. The first was to approach Castro, Khrushchev, and our allies, "which was likely to lead to no satisfactory result," he concluded, "and it [would almost stop] subsequent military action."

The second option introduced a new idea, "a blockade against offensive weapons entering Cuba." It would be supported by a permanent reconnaissance program, and he added: "We would be prepared to immediately *attack the Soviet Union* in the event that Cuba made any offensive move against this country."

"Attack who?" Bundy interrupted, not believing he had heard McNamara correctly.

"The Soviet Union," the secretary repeated. "In the event that Cuba made any offensive move against this country." However, he admitted, "It [this option two] has some major defects." (Indeed!)

Option three was "any of these variants of military action," and he went on to review them, repeating the Joint Chiefs' preference for the thorough destruction of Cuba's military capabilities. Even the limited option—striking only the missile sites—was not really limited, he explained, because it would involve several hundred sorties.

The comprehensive attack would involve seven hundred to one thousand sorties every day for five days, and an invasion would require up to 150,000 troops. "It seems to me almost certain," he warned, following the line of reasoning that Stevenson had presented to the president, "that any one of these forms of direct military action will lead to a Soviet military response of some type, some place in the world." But, departing from Stevenson, he concluded: "It may well be worth the price. Perhaps we should pay that."

McNamara then suggested that there were ways to deter Soviet retaliation: SAC could be put on a high alert, and "a very large-scale mobilization" could be authorized by declaring a national emergency. These moves would signal the Soviet government that we would respond to any military retaliation. Finally, there was the canard that would not go away: We should be prepared, he said, "for the possibility of a Cuban uprising."

All this was a bit much for Rusk, who uncharacteristically seized the floor and made the point that there wasn't "any such thing as a nonpolitical course of action." It was necessary to consider political preparations "in connection with any military action."

2

RUSK'S INTERVENTION made sense to Kennedy, and he began to review what had been said. But his thoughts kept running into one another. He was clearly tired, and perhaps impaired by the many medications he was taking to keep his various ailments under control. But despite a string of elided sentences, he managed to summarize the three basic points.

The first was that exposing the Soviet missile emplacements would garner significant political support. The second was that such a public exposure would "lose all the advantages of our strike." And the third was that a note to Khrushchev "might have some effect"— but on the other hand it might not.

None of this advanced strategic planning, but rather turned the president's attention to Khrushchev. "He's initiated the danger, really, hasn't he? He's the one that's playing at God, not us," he mused. And a few minutes later he confessed: "We certainly have been wrong about what he's trying to do in Cuba. There isn't any doubt about that. Not many of us thought that he was going to put MRBMs in Cuba."

Bundy then sprang the critical question: "What is the strategic impact on the position of the United States of MRBMs in Cuba? How gravely does this change the strategic balance?"

"I asked the Chiefs that this afternoon," McNamara answered. "And they said: 'Substantially.' My own personal view is: Not at all."

"You may say," the president interjected, supporting McNamara, that "it doesn't make any difference if you get blown up by an ICBM flying from the Soviet Union or one that was 90 miles away." But what if the missile deployment were only the first phase of the Soviet plan? "Then they just begin to build up those air bases there, and then put more and more. . . . Then they start getting ready to squeeze us in Berlin."

If the Soviets did succeed in militarizing Cuba, Bundy warned, attacking the island would lead to "general war," an observation that elicited a strange comment from President Kennedy: "That's why it shows the Bay of Pigs was really right. If we'd done it right. That was a choice between better and better, and worse and worse."

Whether anyone understood what the president meant by "better and better, and worse and worse" didn't seem to matter. His reference to the Bay of Pigs refocused the discussion.

"We have a war plan over there [at the Pentagon] for you," General Taylor announced. "[It] calls for a quarter of a million American soldiers, Marines, and airmen to take an island we launched 1,800 Cubans against, a year and a half ago."

That brought Robert Kennedy (who may well have understood what his brother had meant) into the discussion. He worried aloud that Castro could wield the Soviet missiles to obstruct U.S. initiatives. If there was a problem in Venezuela, for example, Castro could threaten to fire the missiles if the United States intervened.

"It makes them look like they're coequal with us," the president muttered.

"Last month I said we weren't going to [allow offensive weapons in Cuba]," he then recalled with both force and remorse. "Last month I should have said that we don't care. But when we said we are not going to, and then they go ahead and do it, and then we do nothing, then I would think that our risks increase."

That was the driving force behind all the deliberations. The president had drawn a red line at his September 13 press conference, and he was committed to standing by it.

"If at any time the Communist buildup in Cuba were to endanger or interfere with our security in any way," he had stated, "or [if Cuba were to] become an offensive military base of significant capacity for the Soviet Union, then this country will do whatever must be done to protect its own security and that of its allies."

In September that statement was meant to counter Republican senator Kenneth Keating's speeches claiming that the Soviets were sending missiles to Cuba. But now it was a Kennedy commitment that demanded the removal of the missiles.

"Well, so where are we now?" he asked, and began again to summarize the discussion. There was no point in communicating with Castro. But he thought that there was an advantage to "inform these governments in Latin America, as the Secretary [Rusk] suggests." Second, there were the NATO governments, "who have the right to some warnings." He would not tell them what he planned to do, but only what the Soviets had done, "let's say, 24 hours ahead of our doing something about it."

The reaction from most of the assembled advisers was immediate. Edwin Martin said the attack had to follow promptly after notification. Dillon could not see any advantage to announcing anything before striking. Robert Kennedy thought twenty-four hours was much too long. "I can't visualize doing it successfully that way," General Taylor asserted. "If you are going to strike you shouldn't make an announcement," McNamara added, and Bundy agreed.

George Ball spoke up for Stevenson in support of the president. Informing our allies might provide "an opportunity of a response which would preclude it [the strike]." While that was not likely, it was worth a try. There was also the option of a private message from the president to Macmillan and de Gaulle. It was an obligation, he insisted, although a warning of two hours or the night before might be sufficient. On the other hand: "If you notify [the Latin American governments] in advance, it may be all over."

As Kennedy pondered McNamara's three options, it became clear to him that the consequences lay in the details. The total assault the Chiefs supported began to reveal hidden hazards. Stevenson had warned about Soviet retaliation, and McNamara had too, and now it was the president's turn to consider how the Soviets might respond.

"I don't think we ought to abandon [the more limited option of] just knocking out these missile bases," he said. A broader assault "takes us into the city of Havana . . . and [a] much more hazardous [situation]." But he was not yet ready to eliminate that option. "We ought to be preparing now in the most covered [covert?] way to do one and two," he said, "with the freedom to make the choice about number one [attacking the missiles] depending on what information we have on it."

His summary appeared to satisfy everyone, and the conversation turned to preparations for one or another type of air assault. McNamara and Taylor explained that "mission folders have already been prepared on all the known targets," and the pilots would be ready to fly within twenty-four hours after the president ordered an attack. The problem, McNamara pointed out, was that the locations of many of the missiles, and all of the nuclear storage sites, were unknown.

At this point something set McNamara off in another direction. Discussing dropping thousands of bombs on Cuban civilians and Soviet military personnel expanded his thinking beyond his Pentagon responsibilities.

"I don't believe we have considered the consequences of any of these actions satisfactorily," he interjected, seemingly struck by the realization that they could be instigating a catastrophe. "I don't know quite what kind of a world we live in after we've struck Cuba, and we, we've started it."

3

THE EXCHANGES that followed offer insight into the contrasting moral, political, and military considerations the president would have to face.

"After we've launched fifty to a hundred sorties, what kind of a world do we live in?" McNamara repeated, asking: "How, how do we stop at that point?"

He didn't have an answer.

But it was the wrong question, General Taylor insisted. The Chiefs, he reminded the president, "feel so strongly about the dangers inherent in the limited strike, that they would prefer taking no military action rather than to take [that] strike." It would expose us to attacks that they could not prevent.

Doing his best to acknowledge Taylor's point, but at the same time reminding the general that other consequences had to be considered, Kennedy responded that once we began "to shoot up those airports" the operation expanded and "the dangers of the world-wide effects . . . to the United States are increased. That's the only argument for it [only attacking the missiles]. I quite agree that if [we were] just thinking about Cuba, the best thing to do is to be bold."

Ted Sorensen spoke up for the first time, pointing out that "there is a combination of the plans which might be considered. Namely the limited strike, and then the messages, or simultaneously the messages to Khrushchev and Castro, which would indicate to them that this was none other than simply fulfilling the statements we've made all along."

That was "a matter we've gotta think about tonight," the president decreed, adding (to laughter): "Let's not let the Chiefs knock us out on this one." Then, turning to Taylor, he pointed out that if the initial attack on Cuba was as thorough as the Chiefs preferred, "you really haven't got much of an argument against invading it."

To Kennedy's surprise, Taylor replied that he opposed an invasion: That could give the Soviets an excuse to move on West Berlin. McNamara agreed, and repeated how important it was "to think of the consequences here," which, in his mind (weirdly) included the certainty of an "uprising" (against Castro) in response to a massive bombing campaign.

Alexis Johnson, the State Department's deputy undersecretary for political affairs, pushed back on the inevitability of an uprising, and the question was bounced back and forth until Robert Kennedy asked: "Where are we six months from now?"

Half sentences and some ill-considered responses followed, until McNamara mentioned that after any limited attack a blockade would be necessary to prevent the Soviets from resupplying the island. "Then we're gonna have to sink Russian ships," Bobby said, and "Russian submarines," a possibility that led him straight to a doomsday scenario.

It was not RFK's most thoughtful intervention. Perhaps, he said, "we should just get into it and get it over with and . . . take our losses. . . . If he [Khrushchev] wants to get into a war over this."

Disturbed by Bobby's remark, McNamara suggested that "tonight we ought to put on paper the alternative plans and the probable, possible consequences . . . because . . . these actions have not been thought through clearly. The one that the Attorney General just mentioned is illustrative of that."

It was an appropriate suggestion that the president ignored. He had returned to his effort to understand why Khrushchev, whom he thought had behaved cautiously until now (citing Laos and Berlin as examples), had taken such a risk if "it doesn't increase very much their strategic strength. . . . Can any Russian expert tell us why?"

Ball and Bundy, hardly "Russian experts," nevertheless offered plausible answers, but Kennedy persisted: "Why does he put these in there, though? . . . It's just as if we suddenly began to put a major number of MRBMs in Turkey. Now that'd be goddamn dangerous, I would think."

"Well, we did, Mr. President," Bundy said, and Alexis Johnson added that we also had deployed MRBMs [actually IRBMs] to England "when we were short of ICBMs."

"Yeah, but that was during a different period," Kennedy responded, perhaps thinking that Khrushchev should not conflate the policies of the Eisenhower and Kennedy administrations.

Frustrated, Bobby continued to think out loud about confronting the inevitable: "Is there some other way we can get involved in this . . . Guantanamo Bay . . . or whether there's some ship that, you know, sink the *Maine* again or something."

While no one supported sinking another *Maine*, Taylor acknowledged that Guantánamo was vulnerable and had to be reinforced. Curiously, that prompted the president to revisit invading Cuba. "What about this invasion?" he asked Taylor. "If we were going to launch that . . . what do we have to be doing now so that ten days from now we're in a position to invade if that was immediate?"

"Military planning has been carried on for a considerable period of time," McNamara replied, and preparations that would not raise suspicions, including reconnaissance, were all in place. "The only thing we haven't done, really, is to consider fully these alternatives."

"Our principal problem," Bundy reflected, is to think, "What the world [will] be like if we do this, and what it will be like if we don't?"

Bundy's question made room for a variety of "incidental" issues that diverted attention from the missiles. The first intervention, seemingly out of the blue, came from Sorensen. He was concerned about the Bay of Pigs prisoners in Cuban jails. The administration had been negotiating with Castro through an intermediary (James Donovan) for their release in exchange for a large shipment of medical supplies and food. "This would be a good time to get the prisoners out," he suggested.

"You mean, take them out," Bundy said (and laughed). But Sorensen had meant "trade them out." Was it possible to do that now? the president asked. It was not, his brother replied.

The fact that Bobby was directing Mongoose, the top-secret operation to topple or assassinate Fidel, is probably what triggered Bundy's next comment: "We have a list of sabotage options. . . . I take it you are in favor of sabotage," he said to the president, and went on to list mining international or Cuban waters.

"Mining?" Kennedy repeated, and decreed "not now," and after a few more rounds of comments he prepared to leave.

He suggested that they meet the next morning at 11:00, that the participants prepare more concise analyses of the attack options and consider whether to approach Khrushchev through Soviet ambassador Anatoly Dobrynin. He was also concerned about his scheduled meeting on Thursday (October 18) with Andrei Gromyko, the Soviet foreign minister. He wanted an opinion on "whether we ought to . . . give him an ultimatum on this matter, or whether we just ought to go ahead without him."

But not knowing why Khrushchev had made this provocative move continued to bother the president, and he delayed his departure to return to the issue: "I can't understand their viewpoint, if they're aware of what we said at the press conferences. . . . I don't think there's any record of the Soviets ever making this direct a challenge, ever, really . . . since the [1948] blockade."

Several minutes later he reminded everyone that the Soviets had pressured the Chinese to back down during the 1958 Taiwan Straits crisis. They had also agreed to a cease-fire in Laos.

"I don't know enough about the Soviet Union," he said, "but if anybody can tell me any other time since the Berlin blockade where the Russians have given us so clear provocation, I don't know when it's been, because they've been awfully cautious really." And he wondered whether his mistake was in not warning Khrushchev last spring that he would not tolerate offensive weapons in Cuba.

The meeting had divided into separate conversations. The president's earlier indication that he was about to leave removed him as the focus of attention. But he had reversed course and remained in the room to wonder "why" Khrushchev had sent missiles to Cuba, rather than "what" to do about them. Whether it was because he was the president, or because his analytical mind simply approached problems differently, Kennedy needed to understand Khrushchev's thinking. It was an approach that connected automatically with the follow-up memorandum that Stevenson would send him the next day.

4

THE PRESIDENT left this second ExComm meeting having agreed with all his advisers that the Soviet missiles would be eliminated with military force (options one, two, or three). The meeting continued for about twenty minutes after his departure, with McNamara and Bundy dominating a discussion about the three military options and their consequences. "I think any military action does change the world," Bundy chimed in. "And I think not taking action changes the world. And I think these are the two worlds that we need to look at."

But no one "looked," and in short order Bundy went off on a bizarre tangent that reveals how compelling a military assault had become. He did not think his idea would normally be considered by the army and the Chiefs, he said, but he thought it might be the solution that ExComm had been searching for. He suggested "a quite large-scale [air] strike, followed by a [parachute] drop [of commandos], followed by a recovery of the people dropped."

The advantage of this, he explained, was to be certain that all the missiles had been destroyed. "There's always incompleteness in a military air operation," he warned, and the parachuted troops could destroy any missiles that had been missed. "You could drop a battalion of paratroopers and get [the missiles]," he explained. "Now what you do with a battalion, I grant you, is a hell of a problem."

A greater problem than anyone was prepared to consider. The meeting ended before anyone figured out how to extract the paratroopers.

PART SIX

October 17 (Wednesday)–October 22 (Monday): Kennedy Reconsiders and Promotes the Blockade

26

"Possible Courses of Action
and Unanswered Questions"

October 17, Wednesday

The main objective of taking Cuba away from Castro has
been lost. We have been overly consumed with the missile
problem.
—JOHN McCONE

In retrospect it's clear that October 17–18 were the pivotal days of
the missile crisis. On Wednesday several ExComm members reinforced Stevenson's views, and by Thursday night the president was
convinced that a blockade was the best option to force the missiles
out of Cuba.

Of course a blockade was a military action—an act of war under
international law that could (and almost did) lead to a conflict with
the Soviet Union. But it also was an action that invited negotiation,
and avoided the certainty of Soviet bloodletting. It was a signal to the
Soviet leader that Kennedy was willing to bargain, which is exactly
how Khrushchev interpreted it.

Blockading Cuba was not an original idea. It had been discussed
during the Bay of Pigs hearings, on several occasions by the Joint
Chiefs, and in Eisenhower administration policy papers that considered strategies for eliminating Castro and his government. What
was new on October 17 was the proposal that it *supplant* rather than
reinforce a military assault. That was a hard sell to the Chiefs and to
most ExComm members.

"I would reject the blockade course insofar as it is designed to lead
to negotiations either in the UN or direct with Khrushchev," Douglas

Dillon wrote to Kennedy, insisting that direct military action was the only effective way to deal with the Soviet missile deployment.

"It would be a pure disaster to try that [blockade without bombing or invasion]," Gen. Curtis LeMay declared two days later.

How and why John Kennedy backed away from the bombing and invasion options that were compelling during the first day of the crisis is a central question, and a cautionary lesson about how a president should weigh advice in making decisions for war.

1

EXCOMM ASSEMBLED for its third meeting at 8:30 a.m. Wednesday without the president, gathering at the State Department to avoid attracting the attention of White House reporters. It was preserved with minutes rather than recorded. George Ball led off with a forceful presentation of Stevenson's arguments against a military assault. Positing that Khrushchev had acted rashly, in response to an opportunity, he suggested devising a strategy that gave him an out. Bombing or invading Cuba could "throw the NATO allies in[to] disarray;" Britain and France might even create an independent Berlin policy, Ball feared. It made no sense to start a war before pursuing a diplomatic solution.

Llewellyn Thompson, recently ambassador to Moscow, had a different view of Khrushchev's motives. Having listened to many of the Soviet chairman's diatribes about the American occupation of West Berlin, he was sure that the missiles in Cuba were a calculated first step in Khrushchev's new Berlin offensive, "which is this gamble which he's shown for years he's reluctant to take," Thompson reasoned. "I think he's building up now and probing to see whether or not he could do it."

McCone generally agreed with Thompson and added (perceptively) that Khrushchev had three aims: (1) to furnish Cuba with significant retaliatory power if attacked; (2) to enhance the USSR's ability to attack the United States; (3) to establish a "hallmark" of accomplishment for Latin American nations.

But he also made the point, which supported Ball's suggestions, that bombing or invasion would kill Soviet military personnel and trigger retaliation and "substantial U.S. casualties." While the "situation [in Cuba] cannot be tolerated," McCone nevertheless argued for warning Khrushchev before acting, to avoid our being tarnished with a "Pearl Harbor indictment."

2

THE CHIEFS also met Wednesday morning. Their meeting began at 10:00 a.m. with Vice Adm. Herbert D. Riley, the director of the Joint Staff, reporting what McNamara had told him about the previous evening's ExComm meeting. He explained each of the options, concluding that virtually all of the discussion had been about the first option, strikes against the offending missiles, "after political preparations."

It was an unwelcome report. The Joint Staff had prepared operational plans for air strikes reflecting what the Chiefs considered all the acceptable contingencies, and restricting bombing to the missiles was not even on their list. "The JCS felt they should go on record as opposing strikes on MRBMs alone," the meeting notes record. "Otherwise, if things went wrong, they might get the blame."

At 11:20 General Taylor arrived from the ExComm meeting with news that State had proposed several political initiatives designed to "minimize damage to the alliance [NATO]," and to provide Khrushchev with an indication of U.S. resolve. A Kennedy-Khrushchev summit meeting was also suggested.

Taylor's sense of the latest ExComm meeting was that "there must be some political action before a showdown." The possibility of a blockade had been raised, he said, but it was supported only by those who believed "that striking missile sites alone is not enough." In response, the meeting notes record, the Chiefs concluded: "If we want to go to a blockade we must declare war."

This was the first mention of a declaration of war, and it sparked serious discussion. But whatever was said is lost to history. Was it a declaration of war against Cuba? Probably. But were the Chiefs also ready to declare war on the Soviet Union, if its ships ignored the blockade? The notes reveal no more than the declarative statement: "It was agreed that if we want to go to a blockade, we must declare war."

3

WHEN THE members of ExComm reassembled at 4:00 p.m. (once again without the president), they were joined by Dean Acheson, who was attending at President Kennedy's invitation. Acheson was a towering figure in the Democratic foreign policy community, and it was prudent to bring him into the decision-making process. As Truman's undersecretary of state and then secretary of state, he had been the architect of numerous Cold War strategies: the Truman Doctrine, the Marshall Plan, NATO, NSC 68, and the Korean War intervention, among other significant policies.

Pilloried by the Republicans for "losing China" and by Senator Joseph McCarthy for "protecting known Communists" in the State Department, Acheson had left office bitter, and convinced that there was no reasoning with Stalin. Khrushchev's accession had not changed his view that when dealing with the Soviet Union, it was necessary to take the offensive.

It was a critical meeting that, unfortunately, was not recorded, but it is clear from John McCone's summary memorandum that the discussions were wide-ranging. Were the Soviet missiles a serious threat? (McNamara and Gilpatric thought not.) Did they affect the nuclear strategic balance? (Taylor and McCone said they did.) Should diplomatic warnings precede an attack on the missiles? (McNamara and Taylor preferred not.) How would the Soviets respond? (Bohlen and Thompson predicted they would seize West Berlin.) The questions were difficult, and all the answers were contested, with a single exception: Everyone agreed that, in one way or another, the missiles had to be removed.

It was in this context that Ball again promoted the blockade alternative. Acheson forcefully demurred. He considered it a weak reaction to a provocative challenge. A direct attack on the offending missiles was the only effective response, he insisted, and warnings to Khrushchev and Castro would be counterproductive.

The "President should forget about the [November midterm] elections and should cancel all future campaign speeches," he said. When asked how the Soviets would react to their missiles being destroyed and their soldiers being killed, Acheson was certain that "the Soviets will react some place. We must expect this; take the consequences and manage the situations as they evolve." How? he was asked. We have to retaliate in kind, he replied. And then what? Then, Ted Sorensen recalls him saying, we have to hope that cooler heads will prevail.

According to Sorensen, Acheson's scenario gave the advocates of military force pause.

This was the last ExComm meeting that former ambassador to the Soviet Union Chip Bohlen attended before departing to his new post as U.S. ambassador to France, and he vigorously promoted his view. Like Thompson, he believed that there was always room to negotiate with Khrushchev if he did not hold all the cards. He opposed both an air strike without warning and an invasion, for many of the reasons Stevenson and Ball had mentioned. It would divide our allies, subject us to worldwide criticism, and undermine the possibility of a peaceful settlement. Countering Acheson, he advocated writing to both Khrushchev and Castro.

At several points McNamara repeated his view that the Soviet missiles did not alter the strategic balance, but they nevertheless could not be tolerated. They had to be eliminated before they became operational, and the political discussions recommended by Bohlen, Thompson, and Ball would delay an attack. Interestingly, Rusk moved away from his earlier emphasis on diplomacy and supported the idea of a surprise bombing attack on the missiles. He was confident that "world opinion would go along."

A detailed discussion of the advantages and disadvantages of the blockade option followed. Should it be total or partial? Was it advantageous to initiate a declaration of war? Would it lead to the collapse of Castro's government, a point that DCI McCone emphasized: "We have been overly consumed with the missile problem," he argued. "The main objective of taking Cuba away from Castro" has been lost.

4

WHEN THE meeting broke for dinner, Robert Kennedy and Sorensen drove to Andrews AFB to brief the president, who was returning from an afternoon of campaigning in Connecticut. Sorensen had composed a memorandum that summarized the day's discussions,

"Summary of Agreed Facts and Premises: Possible Courses of Action and Unanswered Questions."

The agreed facts were that Soviet missiles were in Cuba, that their warheads had not been located, that their presence could not be tolerated even if they did not alter the strategic balance. It was also agreed that in the event of military action, several NATO allies would be notified (but not consulted) immediately prior to its initiation. Selected Latin American nations would also be notified, and the president would not announce the attack until "after that action had been completed."

Sorensen then listed four "courses of action" labeled "tracks." Tracks A and C began with political and diplomatic initiatives, including letters to Khrushchev and Castro warning that if the missiles were not dismantled they would be destroyed. Additional proposals were to bring the Soviet Union's provocation before the United Nations, and to seek authorization for military action from the Organization of American States. Track B was "a military strike without prior warning," and Track D was a "full-scale invasion, to 'take Cuba away from Castro.'"

Track C was the new initiative. It began with "political actions, pressure and warning, followed by a total naval blockade, under the authority of the Rio Pact and either a Congressional Declaration of War on Cuba, or the Cuban Resolution of the 87th Congress affirming the Monroe Doctrine."

This section of the memorandum also described the number of sorties and other details associated with the bombing and invasion plans, including (probably as a courtesy) McGeorge Bundy's "commando raid" suggestion, introduced with the note: "Not yet considered."

The final section, "unanswered questions," summarized the enormity of the challenges the president would face in making his decision.

Which tracks would the Soviets react to most aggressively? Would Moscow be able to prevent its commanders from firing on the United States if they were attacked? Would Castro order his air force to attack the United States? Must a military strike occur before the missiles are operational? Would the Soviets respond by attacking U.S. missiles in Turkey or Italy? Or would they attack West Berlin?

How would the United States respond to such attacks? How would we respond if the Soviets defied our blockade? Should any members of Congress be consulted? Was it necessary to declare war? Should the president cancel his speaking schedule? Should NATO allies be briefed? What would be the fate of the eleven hundred Bay of Pigs prisoners in Cuban jails under each of the proposed scenarios? Would it be helpful (for propaganda purposes) to obtain Soviet denials privately (Gromyko) or publicly (UN)? How much more difficult would the military's task become with advance notices . . . if the missiles are concealed . . . or if they become operational? Was it necessary to call up reservists or declare a national emergency? Would we be successful in justifying a U.S. strike on Cuba to the world? And, finally, would the effect on our allies be worse if we did strike, or if we did not?

5

AFTER DISCUSSING the memo, and the general state of ExComm deliberations, the president left for the White House to begin sorting out his options. He had a lot to consider. How to eliminate the missiles had become more convoluted over the course of the day. He had retired last night (October 16) convinced that he had to choose between bombing the Soviet missile sites and invading Cuba, or both.

At 9:30 this morning (October 17), at a meeting with McCone, he indicated that he had not changed his mind. Nor did he have time in the hours before he left Washington to reconsider his options. He had expected greater clarity upon his return, but Sorensen's questions made it evident that yesterday's ExComm discussions were inadequate preparation for the decisions he had to make.

There was a lot to absorb before turning out the lights. In addition to thinking about Sorensen's questions, there was Stevenson's letter warning that dire consequences would result from leading with an attack on Cuba. And there was Dillon's hyperbolic memo arguing that there was no alternative to such an attack.

As the president pondered the conundrums he faced, ExComm reassembled and debated them until 11:45 p.m. The military options continued to dominate. Was a limited strike or a thorough bombardment the best military option? Should one or the other be launched without notice, or should they only follow a warning and ultimatum to Khrushchev and Castro? Was a blockade, coupled with ultimatums and preparations for further military action, an alternative? Thompson, Martin, and Gilpatric thought that it was, but only if coupled with a declaration of war. Taylor, McCone, and Rusk favored a surprise attack on the missiles. McNamara vacillated among all the military options.

The meeting ended pretty much where it had begun, without a consensus, or any particular recommendation for the president. McCone put the best possible interpretation into his memo for the file: The meeting had "served the purpose of airing the views of all parties responsible for giving advice to the President."

One suggestion was to begin the process of removing the missiles from Cuba with a blockade.

27

"What Action Lessens the Chance of a Nuclear Exchange?"

October 18, Thursday

I am persuaded that the disadvantages of an air strike are too great for us to undertake. I have, therefore, concluded that the blockade plan—while by no means wholly satisfactory—is the course we should follow.

—GEORGE BALL TO JFK, OCTOBER 18, 1962

On Thursday, October 18, during a full day of intense discussions, President Kennedy reversed course and began to track Stevenson's recommendations. His shift was the result of a deliberative process in which the preferences of his hawkish advisers led him to thoroughly reconsider the unpredictable consequences of a military strike that was certain to kill Russians.

This third day of ExComm deliberations began with the secretary of defense supporting the Joint Chiefs' preference for "nothing short of a full invasion" (provided there were no operational nuclear weapons in Cuba). It ended around midnight with the president, alone in the Oval Office, dictating a very different plan to a tape-recording system: "During the course of the day the opinions [of my advisers] had obviously switched," he said, "from the advantages of a first strike on the missile sites and on Cuban aviation, to a blockade."

What he did not say, but what emerges from studying what he had read the previous night and that morning, and from a close reading of (and listening to) the transcripts of this ExComm meeting, is that it was the president's opinion that had "obviously switched," and that he had coaxed his advisers into supporting a blockade in lieu of striking the missiles.

1

THE PRESIDENT awoke on this third day of the crisis (Thursday, October 18) to a collection of memorandums. The most compelling came from George Ball, who argued that the potential consequences of an air strike—anticipated as well as unanticipated—"are too great for us to undertake." Ball, channeling Stevenson, urged the president to choose the blockade option. Like McNamara and Kennedy, Ball believed that the Soviet missiles in Cuba did not alter the strategic balance.

The real "menace we face," he wrote, "is not the addition of new Soviet military capabilities so much as their moral and propaganda advantage." That, he said, had led the proponents of an air strike to see the Soviet deployment as a "test of will" requiring the United States to respond with decisive military force in order to maintain the confidence of our allies in our determination.

That argument was a colossal misunderstanding of the nature of American leadership, he insisted. A surprise attack on a small country would violate our traditions and our stated values "and condemn us as hypocrites" before the world. "We tried Japanese as war criminals because of the sneak attack on Pearl Harbor," he noted in a paragraph that surely caught the president's attention, and we condemned the Soviet intervention in Hungary in the strongest terms. A surprise attack against Cuba would "destroy our moral position and alienate our friends and allies."

In conclusion, he admitted, he found "the blockade plan unsatisfactory—primarily because it does not provide a way to prevent the Soviet missiles from becoming operational." This, however, was not a "conclusive argument," given that U.S. nuclear superiority was not affected. Then, appealing to Kennedy's Castro-phobia, Ball claimed that the blockade also had the potential (if it included banning petroleum, oil, and lubricants) to "bring the Cuban economy to a screeching halt." And if Khrushchev accepts the blockade, he expected the Cubans to "feel isolated and deserted and I think the days of the Castro regime will be numbered."

Another memo from Sorensen emphasized that time for a presidential decision was running out, and there was still no consensus. Headlined, "Two big questions [that] must be answered, and in conjunction with each other," it asked Kennedy to indicate which military action (including a blockade) he preferred, and what political action, if any ("in particular a letter of warning to Khrushchev"), should precede that action. It further encouraged the president to ask the JCS for their views on three issues: (1) an advance warning to Khrushchev; (2) the necessity of follow-up sorties to an initial "surgical" attack; and (3) the possibilities of a commando-type raid by parachute or helicopter.

2

THE CHIEFS' fifth crisis meeting started on October 18 at 9:30. It began with a briefing reporting the results of an October 15 U2 reconnaissance mission. Photographs of missile sites in four areas—Guanajay, San Julián, San Cristóbal, and Santa Cruz—were passed around, and "Mr. McLaughlin [briefer] said it will take six months to make the sites completely operational."

There is no indication of what followed this assessment, but if the notes are accurate it certainly should have been challenged, since several of the sites were earlier declared to be only days from operational status. However, the quotation was likely an error introduced into the notes either in 1976, when they were copied from the minutes, or in 1993, when those notes were typed. Six *days*, rather than "months," makes more sense given all the other known estimates, as well as the discussions that followed during the remainder of the meeting.

The new information (that the missiles would be operational in six days) unnerved General Taylor: "Now permanent missile sites show up. . . . This is really significant," he said, and reversed his opposition to an invasion. "I now feel air strikes are not enough, and occupation is the only answer."

The notes continue with Taylor's summary of five options that ExComm had considered at its meeting the previous evening. They differ from Sorensen's, a point worth highlighting to remind us that while the secret ExComm recordings indicate exactly what each participant said, they do not reveal what each participant heard and understood. Any lecturer who has answered questions from an audience will understand this distinction.

Option A, Taylor explained, would begin by notifying Western European and selected Latin American leaders on Tuesday (October 23) about the presence of Soviet missiles in Cuba, and the U.S. government's intention to remove them. The following day air attacks on the missile sites would be initiated, accompanied by a public statement and a message to Khrushchev. Taylor's presentation of this option concludes with the Dr. Strangelovian notation: "Then wait and see what happens." The secretary of state, Taylor reported, rejected this scenario.

Option B was more cautious than A: Khrushchev would be notified three days before the air attacks would begin. Secretary McNamara rejected this option.

Option C also alerted Khrushchev, but with the clear notice that we knew the location of the missiles, and we would prevent any others from entering Cuba. "Then would follow a declaration of war, complete blockade, air surveillance and readiness for additional actions." Taylor reported that "State is optimistic about this one."

Options D and E were similar: D would begin with some "limited political preliminaries" but would quickly transition to striking all the aforementioned targets except those connected with an invasion, which should be prepared for along with a blockade. Option E eliminated the "political preliminaries" and included both the air strikes and invasion.

There had been no support in ExComm for E—surprise attack—but Taylor believed that "there may be some stiffening when they see today's intelligence. I have changed my mind on invasion," he acknowledged, "and I think they will too."

The meeting wrapped up with another JCS consensus: The "minimum should be course E [the surprise attack] with complete blockade and air strikes on all significant targets except those that might be struck for an invasion."

General Taylor then left to attend the next ExComm meeting.

3

THE PRESIDENT entered the Cabinet Room at 11:00 a.m. aware that he faced a decision that could lead to "the final failure"—general nuclear war. He had read all the memorandums and had carefully considered Sorensen's questions. He had done his homework and was better prepared than he had been on Tuesday, as his pointed questions and general control of this ExComm session would demonstrate.

The meeting began with the new—unwelcome—intelligence that the JCS had received. Reviewing the U2 images, the director of the National Photographic Interpretation Center, Arthur Lundahl, reported that his photo interpreters had discovered two IRBM sites under construction.

With twice the range of MRBMs, and capable of carrying warheads with more than two times the yield, the IRBMs meant that every state in the lower forty-eight except Oregon and Washington was about to come within range of Soviet missiles. In addition, several cruise missile sites had been observed, along with an airfield at the western end of the island. Its seven-thousand-foot runway was presumably for the IL-28 bombers that were being uncrated and assembled.

The president studied the photographs, inquired about the extent of the photographic coverage of the island, and the number of observed missile sites and launchpads. Thinking ahead to the public relations challenges he would soon face, he asked if the missiles and launchpads could be identified by a layman if the photographs were released. Lundahl didn't think so; low-level photography would be necessary for that.

Dean Rusk spoke up as soon as the briefing ended. "Is it necessary to take action?" he asked, and then launched into a prepared statement that meandered through arguments both for and against various courses of action. References to *The Guns of August* (the bestselling history of the outbreak of World War I that Kennedy had urged everyone to read), what he called our "clear conscience" in World War II, the UN "blessing" for American actions in Korea, and British and French "isolation" over Suez, leading to—what? It was hard to say, even when he declared that Lundahl's briefing had moved him from favoring an air strike "to escalate general action, at least as far as Cuba is concerned, and possibly in other situations." His clearest recommendation was that the president rely on the Rio Pact, "our strongest legal basis for action." But a declaration of war, "which carries with it many legal privileges that are useful to have," was another option.

In conclusion (after the longest recorded soliloquy of the entire crisis), he read several paragraphs from a memorandum Chip Bohlen had written before he departed for Paris. Much like Stevenson and Ball, the former ambassador to Moscow argued that a diplomatic initiative was "an essential first step no matter what military course we determine on if the reply is unsatisfactory." He also discussed the pros and cons of a declaration of war, and concluded with the observation that "any belief in a limited quick action is an illusion and would lead us into a full war with Cuba . . . which would greatly increase the probability of general war."

Ignoring Rusk's remarks, McNamara addressed Kennedy. There were five attack alternatives, he explained, starting with bombing the missiles and escalating to "a full invasion," which he now recommended. Surprised, the president asked why he had changed his mind from air attacks to invasion.

The updated photography indicated more targets than air strikes could cover, the secretary explained, and Guantánamo could be vulnerable. Moreover, the IL-28 bombers could attack "our civilian population."

Robert Kennedy and General Taylor joined the expanding discussion of options I, II, and III until the president shifted the focus to timing. The "advantage of III [bombing the missiles, SAM sites, and airfields] is that you would hope to do it in a day." An invasion on the other hand, would be seven, eight, or nine days, "with all the consequences."

One of those consequences was the possibility of a Soviet missile launch against the United States. But such a launch, Kennedy thought, would not come from Cuba unless the Soviets were "going to be using them from everyplace."

Moscow might not be able to prevent such a launch of missiles if the island was attacked, McNamara responded. That was why the strikes he proposed were based on the assumption that there were no operational nuclear weapons in Cuba. If there were, then plans would have to be "modified substantially."

The secretary of defense then turned to the question of whether the Soviet missiles affected the military balance. Admitting that his views were not shared by the JCS, he insisted that the Soviet weapons did not seriously impact U.S. nuclear superiority. But even more to the point, he went on, that issue was irrelevant *"because it is not a military problem that we're facing. It's a political problem.* It's a problem of holding the alliance together. It's a problem of properly conditioning Khrushchev for our future moves . . . and the problem of dealing with our domestic public, all requires action that, in my opinion, the shift in military balance does not require."

It was a strong argument for a military response, but the president challenged its basic assumptions. With respect to holding the alliance together, Kennedy asked McNamara how our allies would view an attack on Cuba, and then answered his own question with a devastating critique: Most of them regarded Cuba as an American fixation; in fact, the president admitted, "They think we are slightly demented on this subject."

He then continued with as clear-eyed an analysis of the view from abroad as any administration member had ever made:

"So, there isn't any doubt that, whatever action we take against Cuba, no matter how good our films are, [this is] going to cause [problems] in Latin America, a lot of people would regard this [a military attack on Cuba] as a mad act by the United States, which is due to a loss of nerve. They will argue that taken at its worst, the presence of these missiles really doesn't change the [nuclear balance]. . . . With all the incentives to think the other way, viewing this as you do as an American, what's everybody else going to think who isn't under this gun?"

It was a stunning assessment from the man behind Operation Mongoose, a certifiably "demented" attempt to oust, or assassinate, a head of state. (The Kennedys "had been operating a god-damned Murder Incorporated in the Caribbean," Lyndon Johnson remarked years later.)

Given this statement and others that followed, it's hard to avoid the conclusion that the president's thoughts about how to deal with the missiles had turned a corner. He was now thinking as much about what might follow from an assault on Cuba as what could result from a failure to force the missiles out. He was in search of a Goldilocks solution, and at this point neither Rusk, McNamara, Taylor, Bobby, McCone, nor the Joint Chiefs were helping him find it.

Three interrelated issues had to be settled: Whether to bomb, invade, or blockade; whether to notify Khrushchev before a military strike; or whether (as Stevenson had suggested) to offer to trade American Jupiter missiles out of Turkey in exchange for Soviet missiles out of Cuba.

An ExComm vote at this point would have supported an invasion without notice, and no trades. But during the next hour the president persuaded his advisers to support his preferred choice.

Hanging over each of these decisions was the vulnerability of West Berlin to a Soviet assault.

4

PRESIDENT KENNEDY began his critique by deflecting Taylor's defense of an all-out invasion and raising Bohlen's insistence that it was essential to notify Khrushchev prior to any military action. Did the JCS think that twenty-four hours' notice before an invasion was possible? If so, how should it be done? By sending an emissary? A phone call? Or a Russian text, as Rusk suggested?

It was a brief exchange that made the point that diplomacy had to be considered. And it also offered the president a segue to suggest an idea that he brought into the meeting.

Would Khrushchev react differently, he asked, if he were given the opportunity to remove his missiles before the U.S. attacked them? "If we said to Khrushchev that 'we would have to take action against you. But if you begin to pull them out, we'll take ours out of Turkey.'"

There was no certainty that this strategy would work, Kennedy admitted, but he had subtly introduced Stevenson's idea of a trade into the conversation.

Ambassador Thompson quickly supported the president's implied criticism of striking before talking. Bombing missiles would "kill a lot of Russians," and among the risks would be a Soviet retaliation against those Jupiter missiles in Turkey and Italy. The alternative, and the ambassador's preference, was "this blockade plan" combined with a declaration of war. The Soviets were not likely to challenge a blockade against offensive military weapons, "if that's the way we pitched it before the world," Thompson asserted. Admittedly, it might lead to the same end, but this would do it in a way that minimizes the "danger of getting into the big war."

The president then reintroduced Berlin, America's Achilles' heel. Along with almost everyone else in the room, he believed that whatever Khrushchev was doing in the Caribbean was related to his long-standing effort to force the Allies out of Berlin. The Soviets, he worried, would blockade or seize the city in retaliation for anything we initiated, including a blockade.

Not a supporter of the blockade, McCone reinforced his preference for an invasion by asking if the president would like to hear how General Eisenhower had responded to the DCI's briefing the day before. The honest answer was no. Kennedy thought Eisenhower was out of touch with the world.

However, the president was scrupulous about informing his predecessor with the aim of keeping his criticisms of the administration to a minimum. He had even invited Eisenhower to a Camp David confessional after the Bay of Pigs. Admitting that he had altered some of the original plan and canceled the air strikes, he managed to retain Ike's silence. That same political strategy continued throughout the crisis.

McCone received a nod to give his report.

Eisenhower was as hawkish as the Joint Chiefs. Soviet bases in Cuba were intolerable, and an effort to remove them by bombing missiles, or even SAM sites, airfields, and other military targets (plans I, II, and III) was inadequate. Eisenhower believed, McCone stated, "that it should be an all-out military action." Still the general in outlook, he recommended going "right to the jugular." Attack Havana directly and take out the government.

The president's response was a revealing silence. He did not speak again until Rusk, Thompson, Taylor, Dillon, Bundy, and Ball had turned the conversation away from attack scenarios. When it returned to trying to figure out how to approach Khrushchev, and how such an approach might achieve something positive, the president again proposed the Stevenson rule: "Missile bases anywhere are negotiable." To give Khrushchev an exit option, Kennedy suggested giving "him some of our Turkey missiles."

This time the trade option gained traction. Bundy endorsed it, concluding that he did not "think we can keep that Turkish base." Rusk waffled, but recalled that the administration had approached the Turks the year before about dismantling the Jupiters. But McNamara, who was still tying himself into knots about the consequences of bombing versus invading, changed the subject to the hundreds of Soviet casualties that would result from the napalm and 750-pound bombs that would be used in an air attack. The price of eliminating the missiles, he predicted, would be high: "The very least it will be, will be to remove the missiles in Italy and Turkey." But he didn't believe that Khrushchev would settle for that.

The president seemed to agree: "The point is he's going to grab Berlin anyway." And Bundy made the surprising statement: "We pay that price."

Ball made an impassioned—and persuasive—argument against a "Pearl Harbor" assault, concluding: "This 24 hours [advance notice] to Khrushchev is really indispensable."

McNamara didn't think Khrushchev's reaction would necessarily be different with or without notice, but he conceded that ("as George suggested") it had the advantage of "causing less friction with the rest of the world." Even Dillon, who had been dead set against the idea of giving notice, accepted Ball's logic as long as it did not interfere with the military actions that would follow.

Berlin was the problem no matter what other choices were made, the president repeated. When Alexis Johnson suggested that a blockade would buy time, Kennedy responded: "He'll grab Berlin . . . [and then] we lost Berlin, because of these missiles . . . which do not bother [our NATO allies]."

Bundy, drifting into sarcasm (one has to assume), remarked: "If we could trade off Berlin and not have it our fault . . ." But what exactly do we mean when we say, "taking Berlin," McNamara asked. "That they take it with Soviet troops? That our troops get overrun? And then what do we do?"

"Go to general war," Taylor answered almost matter-of-factly (although he thought the Soviets would send in East German troops).

"You mean a nuclear exchange?" the president asked, incredulous. "You'd have to start at least with tactical nuclear weapons if he tried to attack Berlin," Rusk added.

"Let me ask you," Kennedy then interjected forcefully, refocusing the conversation. We have "two problems" dealing with the alliance. One is telling NATO governments that we require military action in response to the missiles. "There's no doubt that they will oppose that because they'll feel that their risks increase." On the other hand, if we fail to act, "then of course there will be a more gradual deterioration."

Concluding that some action was necessary to keep the alliance from disintegrating, the president then cut to the core of the issue. "Now, the question really is to what action we take which *lessens the chance of a nuclear exchange, which obviously is the final failure.*" The blockade left room for negotiation. It was the least violent of the options. Would a declaration of war have to accompany a blockade? he asked.

A chorus of simultaneous responses, most in the affirmative, made it impossible to identify the speakers. But the president again opposed the majority.

"I think we shouldn't assume that we have to declare war," he asserted. "Because it seems to me if you're going to do that . . . you have to invade." He asked everyone to "think." The first step would be a message to Khrushchev telling him that if the work on his missiles continues we will take them out. Simultaneously we launch the blockade. And we don't declare war because if we did, "our objective would be an invasion."

This was the turning point in the American decision-making process that structured the remainder of the crisis. The president had made up his mind—and made his view clear to his advisers—that it would be a dangerous mistake (as Stevenson had warned him) to begin with actions that killed Russians. But he wanted them convinced, not cowed.

28

"Flipping a Coin as to Whether You End Up with World War or Not"

October 18, Thursday

You want to make it . . . as easy as possible for [Khrushchev] to back down.

AMBASSADOR LLEWELLYN THOMPSON

The president had turned the corner, but most of the ExComm worried that he was headed down a blind alley. They considered a blockade without a declaration of war too timid to make Khrushchev back down. All agreed that the missiles had to go, but only Kennedy resisted both a declaration of war and actions that were certain to kill Russians.

As a plausible solution he had even put forward Stevenson's proposal to withdraw the Jupiter missiles in Turkey and Italy in exchange for the removal of the Soviet missiles from Cuba. But the first step had to be a clear message to Khrushchev that he faced the choice of either extracting his missiles without bloodshed, or seeing them destroyed. To avoid forcing a Soviet reaction, the president was willing to gamble that the blockade would prompt Khrushchev's compliance.

1

THE MEETING continued with just about everyone trying to modify the president's commitment to blockade without a declaration of war. The arguments varied. Ball worried that a blockade without such a declaration was illegal, and "a slow agony" that would be difficult for the public to accept. Thompson suggested a modified declaration of war against the missiles, but not the Cuban government. McCone believed that Khrushchev would order his ships "to go right through."

Bundy predicted an inevitable invasion. With everyone convinced that the Soviets were likely to retaliate against Berlin, Taylor made the case that "the credibility of our response in Berlin is enhanced by taking action in Cuba."

The chorus urging bombing and invasion led the president to backpedal, but as he did, he challenged his advisers with a hypothetical: "Let's say the situation was reversed." Suppose Khrushchev had threatened serious action if we put our missiles in Turkey. But we put them in anyway, and then he attacked them. "To me," the president added cryptically, "there's some advantages of that if it's all over [quickly]."

Exactly what he meant was not clear until several minutes later. It was an argument against an invasion. If Khrushchev had said that he was "going to knock out our missile sites, and went and did it one afternoon in Turkey, it would be different than if the Russian army started to invade Turkey." An invasion, he warned, multiplied the dangers: "Invasions are tough, hazardous," he said, and added that thousands of Americans would be killed.

(Military planners anticipated 18,000–19,000 casualties in ten days of combat, surely an underestimation. They were unaware that there were tactical nuclear weapons in Cuba. Moreover, the CIA estimated about 11,000 Soviet troops on the island when there were, as we have seen, actually some 42,000.)

Listening to the ExComm recording at this point highlights how freewheeling the discussions had become. The president had made it clear that beginning with an invasion was dangerous and irresponsible. He was against it. But none of his advisers were willing to rule out the idea, and conversations about how long it would take to prepare an invasion, including reinforcing Guantánamo (and removing dependents), continued.

Most of the analytical dialogue at this point was between the president and Ambassador Llewellyn Thompson. His association with Khrushchev during the past five years led Kennedy to pay close attention to his judgments about Soviet reactions to the various options. Most (but not all) of his assessments supported Kennedy's cautious approach.

Thompson warned that with a surprise bombing strike "you'd have killed a lot of Russians," and it was not possible to know what would follow. On the other hand, by giving Khrushchev notice prior to an attack he might threaten Turkey and Italy, "which would cause us considerable difficulty [with our allies]." The disadvantages the Soviets faced in the Caribbean would likely lead Khrushchev to choose military action in Berlin.

Thompson's preference was to blockade Cuba, and he believed the Russians would comply, especially if it was linked to a declaration of war. They were surprisingly legalistic, he said. The missiles, Khrushchev should be told, had to be "dismantled," and if not, "we would then take them out." But no one should be confident, he warned, that any of this would not lead to "the same thing," although the blockade did offer "much less danger [than bombing or invasion] of getting up into the big war."

"The big war" was the president's nightmare, and he continued to pepper Thompson with questions, especially related to Khrushchev "just grab[bing] Berlin." That was certainly a possibility, but in response to a strike, the ambassador thought it was more likely that he would "take out one of our bases in Turkey," and then say, "Now I want to talk."

He was also likely to claim that the missiles were for Cuba's defense and they were no different from the Jupiters in Turkey. "You want to make it . . . as easy as possible for him to back down," Thompson counseled, adding that Bobby's earlier criticism of the blockade as "a slow death" missed this point. It was important to open a dialogue about a "whole broad complex of questions [related to missile deployments], as Stevenson had argued. We've got to have it [the dialogue] eventually or else have war." Leading off with bombing, or bombing and invading, was "flipping a coin as to whether you end up with world war or not."

Turning directly to the question of whether or not to notify Khrushchev before an attack (a move that Thompson strongly endorsed), the president identified two purposes: the first was to "get his Russians [the Soviet troops guarding the missiles] out of there . . . or to back down if he wants to."

But Thompson saw it differently. The first advantage was to keep our allies "with us," especially if Berlin was attacked. The second reason was to give Khrushchev a chance to back down. And the third was to get him into a negotiation. Perhaps even an emergency summit conference.

In Thompson's view the key to extracting the missiles without a war had to include direct talks and clever bargains, which was exactly what Kennedy was now hoping for. But McCone and Dillon, the two veterans of the Eisenhower administration, were dead set against negotiating, arguing that Khrushchev would use it as a delaying tactic, talking while continuing to work on the missile emplacements. Military action was the only way to force Soviet compliance, they insisted.

McNamara, who had been uncharacteristically silent, diverted the conversation with the observation that there was still a lack of clear planning. There were only two serious alternatives, he had concluded: "a rapid introduction to military action . . . [and] a slow introduction to military action." The former notified Khrushchev shortly before striking, and the latter issued a political statement followed by a blockade. He confessed that he was not sure which course to follow, but he was certain that it was important to "plan for the earliest possible strike." The best way to clarify the alternatives, he suggested, was to organize two groups of Defense and State people who would develop their options and consider how the Soviets might respond.

It was a good suggestion, and no one objected.

The president was scheduled to meet with Soviet foreign minister Gromyko in a few hours, and the group discussed what Gromyko might say, and how the president should respond. Taylor expected that he would lie about the missiles. Rusk urged that the president reiterate his September 4 warning against offensive weapons. Robert Kennedy and Sorensen wanted Gromyko to be reminded that Khrushchev had promised not to do anything to disturb the status quo before the November midterm elections.

The president took it all in and agreed to meet with Rusk and Thompson a half hour before receiving Gromyko at 5:00 p.m. He informed the group that he had invited Robert Lovett, a former secretary of defense (among other posts) to the White House to "see whether he's got any thoughts" about how to handle the crisis. Later that night he would meet again with most of ExComm to nail down a final decision.

With that he departed.

Most of the ExComm members remained, and since the taping system continued to operate, several interesting clarifications about their individual positions were recorded. Taylor remained focused on mobilizing for a strike. Dillon continued to disparage the blockade because "the purpose of a war is to destroy your enemy." Martin thought the blockade might bring Castro down, to which Bobby Kennedy, still skeptical that it would work, replied: "Has a blockade ever brought anybody down?" Rusk, supporting Dillon, thought that at "minimum" the blockade had to be accompanied by a bombing strike against the missiles. Thompson, McNamara, and Bobby disagreed. A "unilateral blockade without a declaration of war [was] about the worst [option] of all," Alexis Johnson stated, urging that the support of the OAS was essential.

McNamara, returning to his earlier concern about the "price" of each option, now believed that the "minimum price [for getting the Soviet missiles out of Cuba] are missiles out of Turkey and Italy." Suddenly switching, he announced that he now preferred a blockade because it "reduces the very serious risk of large-scale military action."

2

AT 2:00 p.m., when the Chiefs reassembled, Taylor briefed them on what ExComm had discussed. His summary did not track well with a careful reading of the meeting's transcript. He minimized the president's clear preference for a blockade without a declaration of war, and downplayed his opposition to an invasion. It is most unlikely that this was a conscious distortion; that was not part of Taylor's character. Rather, it was probably the result of the overwhelming consensus of the meeting that a blockade without a declaration of war was not an adequate response to the challenge, and a reflection of Taylor's own views. If there is a psychological lesson to be learned from Taylor's presentation, it is that *we tend to hear most clearly what is already in our minds.*

Taylor explained to his colleagues that the secretary of state now believed that "action would have to be taken, and of a heavier kind than was contemplated yesterday" (although Rusk still thought Khrushchev should be informed in advance).

McNamara, too, Taylor said, had decided that the "new intelligence called for invasion" (although by the end of the meeting he had switched to supporting the blockade, a change that went unreported to the Chiefs).

The five plans that Taylor had reviewed during the morning meeting had been combined into three by the afternoon, he said. The first, a "maximum political effort," had been pushed off the table by the revelations of Soviet progress on their missile sites. The second combined a "military effort built around blockade then reconnaissance." And the third—the Chiefs' preference—was "no political discussion—air strike followed by invasion."

Taylor further reported that he had asked President Kennedy if the partial air strike could be eliminated, and although the minutes do not provide a direct answer, the next sentence reads: "We agreed to do Category III, IV, or V (extensive bombings or invasion)." At this point in the crisis, the consensus in the Pentagon was that the U.S. military would be the primary instrument for removing the Soviet missiles, and Taylor's briefing suggested (erroneously) that ExComm agreed.

All the back-and-forth, the options, and the discussions of the options, were too much for the impatient air force chief of staff: "Are we really [not] going to do anything except talk?" Gen. Curtis LeMay protested.

"Definitely," General Taylor assured him. "Probably there will be a political approach followed by warning, a blockade, hitting the missiles, and invasion—in that order. We will probably start in the early part of next week."

3

THE MEETING with Gromyko went as Kennedy expected—badly. It began with a difficult discussion about Berlin that reinforced the president's belief that Khrushchev would seize the city if the United States attacked Cuba. While Gromyko repeated Khrushchev's assurances that he would not raise difficult issues before the November election, he stated that the chairman was "compelled" to end the Western presence in Berlin; it was a "rotten tooth which must be pulled out."

Gromyko assured Kennedy that only defensive weapons were being shipped to Cuba, and the Soviets were training the Cubans to use them against an expected American invasion. Kennedy's response was clever, strategic, and planned. Looking ahead to the negotiations that might follow the blockade, he offered a huge carrot intended to "make it as easy as possible for Khrushchev to back down." If asked, he said pointedly, he would have guaranteed Khrushchev that "there was no intention to invade Cuba," nor would the United States support an invasion. But, he added, the Soviet arms buildup had created "the most dangerous situation since the end of the war [World War II]." He then read his September 4 and 13 public statements to reinforce his warning.

Gromyko, "the Sphinx," did not react.

Restrict nuclear testing was the final and least contentious topic. The meeting ended about 7:15 with Kennedy agreeing to meet Khrushchev when he came to the United States for the UN General Assembly meeting in November. Gromyko thought it went well.

The president left angry, telling Robert Lovett, Rusk, and Thompson, whom he met immediately afterward, that Gromyko had "told more bare-faced lies than I have ever heard in so short a time. . . . I had the low-level pictures in the center drawer of my desk and it was an enormous temptation to show them to him."

4

BEYOND BEING angry, the president was anxious to bring the decision-making process to closure while covering his political flanks. He had sent McCone to brief Eisenhower, he had invited Dean Acheson to join the ExComm debate, and before seeing Gromyko, had politely listened to the former secretary of state's uncompromising insistence that the missiles had to be attacked without warning.

His next outside confidant was Robert Lovett, for whom he

had an especially high regard. During the Korean War, Lovett had served with distinction as President Truman's secretary of defense, and in 1956 had joined Eisenhower's Board of Consultants on Foreign Intelligence Activities. Joseph Kennedy, the president's father, who had served with Lovett, urged his son to offer him the cabinet post of his choice. Lovett had declined for reasons of health, but had recommended McNamara for Defense, Rusk for State, and Dillon for Treasury. He was the ultimate outside insider.

In Kennedy's view Lovett was the wisest of the "Wise Men," and at this critical moment his opinion was important to the president. Come to Washington "at once," he had urged Lovett in a morning phone call, and by the time the former secretary of defense was huddled in the Oval Office with Rusk, Thompson, and Kennedy, he had been fully briefed by the CIA, Bundy, and the staff of the JCS.

To the president's relief (but probably not to his surprise), Lovett supported the blockade as the first step. Among its "great advantages," he said, was a demonstration of national will without bloodshed. "We would look ridiculous as the most powerful military nation in the world if we grabbed a sledgehammer in order to kill a fly," he recalled thinking.

After dinner, at about 9:15, the president called several ExComm members back to the White House. Meeting in a room on the second floor to avoid attracting reporters' attention, he pushed for a consensus around the blockade. A few hours earlier, the State Department's acting legal adviser, Leonard Meeker, had suggested a name change to "defensive quarantine," a clever tweak to elude the legal implications of "blockade." But to everyone's surprise (and Kennedy's annoyance), Bundy made an about-face and argued that any action against Cuba, even a blockade, would give Khrushchev an excuse to move against West Berlin. He declined to recommend any overt action.

But the president had settled on the blockade (now aka "quarantine"), and he asked Sorensen to begin drafting his announcement. He also discussed its timing, and gave the go-ahead for detailed planning. As midnight approached, the meeting ended, and as the others headed for White House exits, the president walked to the

Oval Office to record for posterity—and no doubt for the memoirs he intended to write—the meeting's details.

5

DURING THE past forty-eight hours Kennedy had not only changed his mind about how to react to Khrushchev's deception, he had changed his attitude. On the first day of the crisis he had followed the recommendations of his advisers to bomb the missiles and, if necessary, invade Cuba. But, as he considered Stevenson's warnings, reinforced by Thompson and Ball, he had become increasingly assertive about refusing to attack the missiles and issuing a declaration of war.

Switching on the tape recorder, he dictated a list of those with whom he had just met. With his future memoirs obviously in mind, he began by linking several with their official titles: "Secretary McNamara, Deputy Secretary Gilpatric, General Taylor, Attorney General, George Ball, Alexis Johnson, Ed Martin, McGeorge Bundy, Ted Sorensen." (Rusk and Thompson were having dinner with Gromyko.)

"During the course of the day," he recorded, "opinions had obviously switched from the advantages of a first strike on the missile sites and on Cuban aviation to a blockade." While this was not entirely true, it was true enough to provide the president with sufficient support for his switch.

After summarizing his afternoon meeting with Acheson, he provided historical documentation in support of his position by noting that Lovett "was not convinced that any [military] action was desirable." A strike on the missiles would be "very destructive to our alliances." Lovett had also argued that if the Soviets seized Berlin, "we would be blamed for it."

The president then explained Bundy's position: He "continued to argue against any action on the grounds that there would be, inevitably, a Soviet reprisal against Berlin and that this would divide our alliance and that we would bear that responsibility. He felt we would be better off to merely take note of the existence of these missiles, and to wait until the crunch comes in Berlin, and not play what he thought might be the Soviet game.

"Everyone else felt that for us to fail to respond would throw into question our willingness to respond over Berlin, [and] would divide our allies and our country.

"The consensus was that we should go ahead with the blockade beginning on Sunday night. Originally, we should begin by blockading Soviets against the shipment of additional offensive capacity, [and] that we could tighten the blockade as the situation requires. I was most anxious that we not have to announce a state of war existing, because it would obviously be bad to have the word go out that we were having a war rather than that it was a limited blockade for a limited purpose.

"It was determined that I should go ahead with my [campaign] speeches so that we don't take the cover off this, and come back Saturday night [October 20]."

With that, the president shut off the tape recorder.

29

The Chief Confronts the Chiefs

When we balance off that our problem is not merely Cuba
but it is also Berlin, and when we recognize the importance of
Berlin to Europe, and recognize the importance of our allies
to us, that's what has made this thing be a dilemma for three
days.
—PRESIDENT KENNEDY TO THE JOINT CHIEFS,
OCTOBER 19

Friday, October 19, was an exasperating day for the Joint Chiefs. As
their 9:00 a.m. meeting got under way, General Taylor announced
that in less than an hour the president would see them before he left
to campaign in Ohio and Illinois. In the meantime he described the
discussion at the previous night's ExComm meeting. They did not
like what they heard. "The tendency [in ExComm] is more and more
toward political actions plus a blockade," Taylor explained, adding
that this also seemed to be the president's preference.

1

THE CHIEFS were to develop plans for both a total blockade and a
selective (offensive weapons only) blockade; the latter, Taylor noted,
was the State Department's preference. They were also to consider
"the necessity for a declaration of war."

"It would be a disaster to try that!" General LeMay barked.

Taylor didn't disagree but, having served in the White House
as the president's special military adviser for eighteen months prior

to assuming the chairmanship of the JCS, he understood that in a discussion with John Kennedy, reason was more effective than wrath. Faced with a choice between a full military assault and "the new alternative of political action plus blockade," he proposed that they recommend three steps, with explanations: "(1) surprise attack on comprehensive targets, (2) reconnaissance surveillance, and (3) complete blockade."

The discussion that followed coalesced around six points based on Taylor's initial three:

1. Notify Great Britain's prime minister, Harold Macmillan, and West Germany's chancellor, Konrad Adenauer, two hours before commencing air strikes on Soviet missiles.
2. The strikes should be comprehensive and initiated without any warning to either the Cubans or the Soviets.
3. Launch reconnaissance surveillance preceding and following the attacks.
4. Establish a complete blockade.
5. Invade Cuba. This point was followed by a question mark and the explanation that Generals Wheeler and LeMay, as well as Admiral Anderson, supported an invasion, while General Taylor "[said] only be prepared to do so." (There is no mention of marine corps commandant General Shoup's position.)
6. Realize that the recommended actions will cause "a strain upon NATO and problems about Berlin."

Before departing, Defense Intelligence Agency representatives presented an update on the Cuban order of battle. The Soviet aircraft count totaled thirty-five to thirty-nine MiG-21s and twenty-one IL-28 nuclear-capable bombers, seventeen of which were still in their shipping crates. There were seven identified ballistic missile sites. Four of them contained SS-4 MRBMs with ranges estimated at 1,100 nautical miles, and three were being prepared for the 2,200-nautical-mile SS-5 IRBMs. There were twenty-two SAM sites, of which nine were believed to be operational. "In just a few weeks," the briefer noted, "they can have a couple of air defense nets with real capability."

Their briefing over, the Chiefs headed for their cars and 1600 Pennsylvania Avenue.

2

THE RECORD of the meeting between the JCS and the president reveals how differently they each analyzed the challenge. Assumptions—stated and unstated, recognized and unrecognized— are the invisible navigators of decision making, and the meeting's recordings offer a unique insight into the assumptions that guided the Chiefs' recommendations, and the very different assumptions that led the president to his decisions.

General Taylor's introduction could not have been more diplomatic. Explaining that the JCS were unified about the need to actively eliminate the missiles, he listed three necessary steps: The first was a surprise attack against the known missile sites, followed by continued surveillance, and third, a blockade to prevent reinforcements from entering Cuba. He conceded that there were "political requirements . . . to offset the obvious political disabilities of this course of action," and urged the president to "hear the other Chiefs' comments . . . [on] the military plan, or how they would see the blockade plan."

But before any of the Chiefs could speak, the president interrupted: "Let me just say a little, first, about what the problem is, from my point of view." Returning to a question he had asked during the initial ExComm meeting, he proposed that "we ought to think of why the Russians did this." For them it's "a quite desirable situation." If we allow their missiles to remain they have offended our prestige, and are in a position to pressure us. On the other hand, if we attack the missiles or invade Cuba "it gives them a clear line to take Berlin." That "leaves me only one alternative," he explained, after analyzing the results of a Soviet seizure of Berlin, "which is to fire nuclear weapons—which is a hell of an alternative."

To complicate the situation further, Kennedy continued, our blockade of Cuba will give Khrushchev an excuse to blockade Berlin, which will infuriate our allies. We will be blamed for jeopardizing the city because we overreacted. "So, I don't think we've got any satisfactory alternatives," he admitted. "When we balance off that our problem is not merely Cuba but it is also Berlin, and when we recognize the importance of Berlin to Europe, and recognize the importance of our allies to us, that's what has made this thing be a dilemma for three days. Otherwise, our answer would be quite easy [presumably, attack the missiles]."

Ignoring General LeMay's attempt to interrupt, Kennedy conceded that "we've got to do something" because doing nothing will not make the Berlin problem go away. But what?

"We recognize all these things, Mr. President," General Taylor responded, laying out the basic assumption that shaped the Chiefs' recommendations. Cuba and Berlin are paired, but in the Chiefs' view Cuba is the test of U.S. resolve. "If we don't respond here in Cuba," Taylor claimed, "we think the credibility of our response in Berlin is endangered."

LeMay, dismissing the president's analysis, blurted, "We don't have any choice except direct military action." The blockade will provide the Soviets with time to hide their missiles, and it will even encourage them to move against Berlin.

They will not make any reprisal, he responded when the president asked how Khrushchev would react to an attack on Cuba. We just have to be clear that "if they make a move we're going to fight."

And then he famously said: "This blockade and political action, I see leading into war. I don't see any other solution for it. It will lead right into war. This is almost as bad as the appeasement at Munich" (which, it was well known, had been supported by the president's father, Joseph Kennedy, when he was American ambassador to Great Britain).

It is a loss to history that there is no photograph of John Kennedy's face at that moment. But one can imagine his jaw tightening, his temples pulsing, and his eyes fixed firmly on the air force chief of staff.

After a brief pause, Admiral Anderson moved the conversation along. The Chiefs had recommended the right course from both a military and political point of view, he said. As long as Castro was supported by the Soviet Union, a military assault was the only solution to the Cuban problem. It was, he suggested, the same dilemma we had faced in Korea, "only on a grander scale."

But if the decision was to blockade, it was easier to organize a complete blockade, as a partial one involved boarding and searching ships. On the other hand, a complete blockade would lead to confrontations with Soviet-bloc ships. Either way, he agreed with LeMay: The blockade "will escalate . . . to other military action at greater disadvantage" to us.

Army chief of staff Wheeler made a similar point, but pinned it on "protecting the people of the United States against a possible strike." It was not possible to "be absolutely sure [that all the missiles were destroyed] until and unless we actually occupy the island," he insisted, and went on to offer a lengthy analysis of why Khrushchev would not respond, why the missiles threatened U.S. leadership in Latin America, and why the missiles provided the Soviets with significant additional firepower. "From a military point of view," he concluded, "I feel that the lowest risk course of action is the full gamut of military action by us. That's it, sir."

"Thank you, General," Kennedy responded.

Marine corps commandant Shoup then presented a convoluted argument in support of Wheeler's "full gamut" that was promptly followed by another (oft-quoted) intervention by Gen. LeMay. Reminding the president that he had made several strong public statements warning the Soviets against sending offensive weapons of any type to Cuba, he said: "I think that a blockade and political talk would be considered by a lot of our friends and neutrals as being a pretty weak response to this. And I'm sure a lot of our own citizens would feel that way, too. In other words," LeMay said, "you're in a pretty bad fix at the present time."

"What did you say?" the president asked deliberately.

"You're in a pretty bad fix," LeMay repeated.

"You're in there with me," Kennedy shot back. And to be certain that LeMay got his point, Kennedy added, *"Personally!"*

It is germane, and perhaps even an understatement at this moment, to repeat Ted Sorensen's observation after the Bay of Pigs: "In addition, of course, the President did not have confidence in the Joint Chiefs of Staff."

3

UNDERSTANDABLY THE Chiefs' primary objective was to be in the best position to fight a war, while the president's goal was to select the strategy that was least likely to start a war. The Chiefs assumed that a prompt military response (attack and/or invasion) would coerce the Soviets, but the president thought otherwise: "They can't let us . . . take out their missiles, kill a lot of Russians and not do anything."

Both assumptions were plausible, and perhaps the Chiefs were correct that the Soviets would not have responded militarily. Khrushchev did not want a war, and he was trying not to stumble into one. But despite his aversion to a conflict, he was driven by obligations and pressures that could force him to respond violently to an invasion of Cuba. His decision would depend on too many variables to be anticipated.

The president's more cautious assumption reflected the advice he had first received from Adlai Stevenson and that Ambassador Llewellyn Thompson had validated: Make it as easy as possible for Khrushchev to back down.

During the remainder of the meeting the Chiefs and the president discussed and debated a variety of topics that focused on the consequences of a blockade. There was the need for surveillance, and therefore the likelihood of air warfare over Cuba. There was Guantánamo's vulnerability, requiring the reinforcement of its garrison and the evacuation of dependents. It could even "become a sort of Cuban Quemoy, where they shell us on odd days . . . ," General Taylor speculated.

Then there was the possibility that the missiles could fall under Castro's control: "Castro would be quite a different fellow to own missiles than Khrushchev," Taylor remarked (implying a certain level of confidence in Khrushchev's rationality). "I don't think that's the case now, and perhaps Khrushchev would never willingly do so. But there's always the risk of their falling into Cuban hands."

By this point the president realized that he was confronting a solid wall of military assumptions, and he attempted to breach it with logic and history. "The problem," he explained—for what must have seemed to him the umpteenth time—"is not really some war against Cuba. But the problem is part of this worldwide struggle where we face the Communists, particularly, as I say, over Berlin. And with the loss of Berlin, the effect of that and the responsibility we would bear. As I say, I think the Egyptian and the Hungary thing [the Suez crisis and the USSR invasion of Hungary, both in the fall of 1956] are the obvious parallels that I'm concerned about."

He was also concerned about the possibility of nuclear war, he told the Chiefs. The missiles in Cuba might add to the danger, but they didn't create it. The Soviet Union's ICBMs, bombers, and submarines can kill eighty to one hundred million Americans. "You're talking about the destruction of a country," he said. Taking everything into account, "the logical argument is that we don't really have to invade Cuba. . . . [It's] just one of the difficulties that we live with in life, like we live with the Soviet Union and China."

That was an analogy the Chiefs couldn't accept, and they continued to press their case. They repeated their concerns about the missiles, about Guantánamo's vulnerability, about the blockade's inadequacy, and the advantages of a direct attack. Clear that continuing to debate was counterproductive, the president shifted to asking detailed questions that acknowledged his respect for their expertise:

"What can we do about Guantanamo if we do this air strike and they retaliate on Guantanamo?"

"If we go ahead with this air strike, either on the missiles or on the missiles and the planes . . . When could that be ready?"

"They've got two of them [MRBM sites] ready, [are we] running out of time?"

"Why is it [the first attack] Tuesday instead of Sunday, General? What's the argument for that?"

"How effective is an air strike of this kind generally against a missile base?"

His questions answered, and the time to depart for his campaign appearances at hand, the president tried to conclude the meeting with a restatement of his bottom line: "I appreciate your views. As I said, I'm sure we all understand how rather unsatisfactory our alternatives are. The argument for the blockade was that what we want to do is to avoid, if we can, nuclear war by escalation or imbalance. The Soviets increase; we use [force]; they blockade Berlin. They blockade for military purposes. Then we take an initial action. . . . We've got to have some degree of control. Those people [Gromyko and Dobrynin] last night were so [far] away from reality that there's no telling what the response would be."

But comments from Taylor and Shoup forced another restatement. The additional firepower that the missiles in Cuba added to the Soviet arsenal didn't add "particularly to our danger," the president repeated. "The real danger is [any] use of nuclear weapons," especially on urban targets. The major argument for forcing the removal of the missiles from Cuba "is the political effect [they will have] on United States [prestige]." An invasion may be the most thorough solution, but "a lot of people [will] . . . move away from us. . . . So that we've got a real problem in maintaining the alliance."

"Am I clear," General Wheeler asked, "that you are addressing yourself as to whether anything at all should be done?"

"That's right," Kennedy responded.

"But that if military action is to be taken," Wheeler pressed, "you agree with us."

"Yeah," Kennedy responded, sounding more like a parent exhausted from a debate with his teenagers than a president discussing strategy with his military commanders.

"These brass hats have one great advantage in their favor," he later grumbled to his aide Dave Powers: "If we listen to them and do what they want us to do, none of us will be alive later to tell them that they were wrong."

4

THE CHIEFS' arguments had been more effective than they imagined. Despite the president's firmly stated opposition to beginning with any of their attack scenarios, he left the meeting less confident about the blockade. He had admitted that every alternative was "unsatisfactory," and had listened for almost two hours to his five senior military commanders explaining why the blockade was the most unsatisfactory option of all.

It seemed prudent, as he prepared to leave for his campaign tour, to take a small step back, and he directed Bundy to allow ExComm to continue debating the air-attack option. But he also told Bobby and Sorensen to "pull the group together." With his advisers divided, he was not going to initiate actions that could lead to a nuclear war.

When a consensus was reached—and it was clear that he meant a consensus supporting the blockade—he directed his brother to call him back to Washington.

30

"Pull the Group Together"

It would be better for our children and grandchildren
if we decided to face the Soviet threat, stand up to it, and
eliminate it now.
—ROBERT F. KENNEDY, OCTOBER 19, 1962

The agreement to blockade, confirmed on Saturday, was fought out on Friday afternoon after the president departed on his campaign tour. By following his instructions to Bobby, and the discussions in ExComm, it is possible to see how Jack Kennedy controlled and deployed his (often hotheaded) brother to support his policies. Adhering to instructions to "pull the group together," Robert Kennedy, joined by McNamara (who was always attuned to the president's preferences), spent the afternoon and early evening debating and cajoling Bundy, Acheson, Dillon, McCone, Nitze, and Taylor, who all favored an air assault. Only with the proviso that air strikes would follow the blockade if the missiles were not promptly removed did they agree to support the president's strategy.

1

WITH JACK Kennedy gone, ExComm moved its venue to the State Department, compelling historians to rely on minutes composed by State's deputy legal adviser, Leonard Meeker. Sufficiently detailed to make it clear that the differences within the room were profound, those minutes indicate that Bundy—who changed his mind again— led the air strike advocates, and that McNamara—who had also shifted sides—argued for the blockade and negotiations.

The first order of business focused on the legitimacy of a blockade, and whether it was necessary to invoke a declaration of war. It was not, State's lawyers concluded, and added that the blockade was a legal defensive action under the UN Charter if the twenty members of the OAS voted to approve it.

That worried Robert Kennedy. What if the OAS refused to endorse the blockade? A rejection would put the president in an untenable position. Assistant Secretary for American Affairs Edwin Martin did his best to calm the attorney general with assurances that a majority of fourteen votes were certain, and within twenty-four hours might be increased to as many as nineteen. The administration's Alliance for Progress, and no doubt the president's refusal to send U.S. troops to support the Bay of Pigs invaders, had burnished Washington's standing with Latin America's governments.

None of this impressed Dean Acheson. It was essential, he insisted, to destroy the missiles without warning. Meeker captured the former secretary of state's imperious reasoning, and it is interesting to compare it with how the president analyzed the situation.

Acheson interpreted the missiles as a direct challenge—"a test of wills"—that the United States could not avoid, "and the sooner we got to a showdown the better." In addition, the missiles were "in the hands of a madman [Castro] whose actions would be perfectly irresponsible; the usual restraints operating on the Soviets would not apply."

He agreed with State's lawyers that self-defense was adequate justification for any U.S. action, but "he could not go along" with any "requirement of approval by the OAS." This was a confrontation with the USSR, and the United States had no need to ask for OAS support. Dillon, McCone, Bundy, and Taylor agreed.

As instructed, Bobby objected. He said ("with a grin," Meeker noted) that he had discussed the options with his brother that morning. The first—to do nothing—was "unthinkable." The second was an air strike, and the third a blockade. "It would be very, very difficult indeed for the President," he explained to the air strike advocates, to support their proposal. "A sneak attack was not in our traditions," and it would not serve us well "in whatever world there would be afterward."

Making the president's point, he said that he "favored action" and a clear message to the Soviets that the missiles would not be tolerated. But the action should leave room for Khrushchev to "pull back."

Meeker also made note of a discussion that occurred at an unspecified time "during the afternoon." It began when McNamara reaffirmed that "the US would have to pay a price to get the Soviet missiles out of Cuba." Surrendering the Jupiter missile bases in Turkey and Italy was the minimum, and he believed there would be more.

If the Soviets established a substantial military position in the Western Hemisphere they would bring the United States "directly and immediately under the gun," making everything forever different. "The possibility of nuclear conflict breaking out" followed logically, and this unhinged Bobby. As he had at the second ExComm meeting, he again lost his equanimity. He had suggested then that it was better to have it out with the Soviets immediately, possibly by "sink[ing] the *Maine* again" and invading Cuba.

Today he went off-script again, saying, "It would be better for our children and grandchildren if we decided to face the Soviet threat, stand up to it, and eliminate it now. The circumstances for doing so at some future time were bound to be more unfavorable, the risks would be greater, the chances of success less good."

As the debate narrowed, Dean Rusk took charge. The decision was the president's, he said, and our responsibility was to present him with "fully staffed-out alternatives." The ExComm were advisers, and to clarify their advice he suggested that they form two teams: one to make the case for the blockade and the other for air strikes. The deputy undersecretary for political affairs, Alexis Johnson, would lead the blockade team, and Bundy would manage the air strike advocates. The cabinet officers (Rusk, McNamara, and Robert Kennedy) would not participate.

2

As the blockade and air strike groups prepared their arguments, the JCS reassembled at the Pentagon in a somber mood. They were being sidelined, and they didn't like it. "Somebody's got to keep them from doing the goddamn thing piecemeal . . . do the son of a bitch and do it right, and quit friggin' around," General Shoup had groused after their meeting with the president, and LeMay and Wheeler had wholeheartedly agreed.

The purpose of their gathering this afternoon was to hear Chairman Taylor's briefing on the ExComm meeting. How that briefing differed in emphasis from Meeker's minutes is particularly interesting.

Robert Kennedy had initially taken a position that supported the Chiefs, Taylor reported, no doubt referring to the AG's outburst about the need to confront the Soviets now. He had proposed attacking Cuba without warning, Taylor said, and "then go to the OAS." But State had objected, arguing that OAS support required an approach to its membership before initiating any action. Bobby then revised his view, according to Taylor, who repeated his comment that "if we make a surprise attack, we will be accused of another Pearl Harbor."

That raised a question for the Chiefs: Would they be willing to accept a twenty-four-hour delay (before an attack) in order to inform NATO allies? LeMay, Anderson, and Taylor agreed that it could be done.

3

AT 4:00 p.m. the secretaries returned to ExComm, and the groups reassembled to present their positions. The blockade group went first, and the discussion of their position lasted for two hours. There is no record of exactly how the air strike advocates critiqued the blockade plans, but we can be confident of their two major criticisms: One was the inability of a blockade to do anything about the missiles in Cuba. General Taylor stated the other critique earlier in the afternoon: "A decision now to impose a blockade was a decision to abandon the possibility of an air strike."

Eliminating the air strike option may have been the strongest argument against the blockade, but "in the course of the [late-] afternoon discussion," Meeker noted, "the military representatives, especially Secretary McNamara, came to expressing the view that an air strike could be made some time after the blockade was instituted in the event the blockade did not produce results as to the missile bases in Cuba."

The "military representatives" had to have included General Taylor, who (like Bundy and McNamara earlier) now executed a U-turn.

It was the opening Bobby was hoping for, and he "took particular note of this shift," Meeker recorded, making "clear that the firmly favored blockade [would be] the first step."

In effect ExComm had reached a consensus—albeit grudgingly— that amounted to a turning point. As the meeting wound down, Adlai Stevenson arrived. He supported the blockade, but he insisted that it was also important to develop a plan for negotiations to settle "wider problems." He mentioned as an example the demilitarization of Cuba (the elimination of Soviet military bases), to be monitored by UN observers (another Stevenson plan the president adopted without attribution).

The meeting concluded about seven o'clock with an agreement that the president would be asked to return to Washington on Sunday morning.

31

"I Trust That You Will Support Me"

October 20, Saturday

General Maxwell Taylor said he did not share Secretary
McNamara's fear that if we used nuclear weapons in Cuba,
nuclear weapons would be used against us.
—MINUTES OF OCTOBER 20 EXCOMM MEETING

On Saturday, October 20, ExComm formally agreed on the plan that
would govern how the crisis played out. It was a contentious compromise that yielded to John Kennedy's determination to have his
advisers in agreement, and on record. He did not intend to allow a
repetition of the disavowals that had followed the Bay of Pigs.

1

AT THEIR 10:00 a.m. meeting the Chiefs were surprised by what
they heard. Twenty-four hours earlier, the JCS minutes record General Taylor saying that the president had rejected any military action
other than a blockade. But now "the President might want to hit
them [the missiles in Cuba] as early as tomorrow morning." For that
they were not prepared. The meeting notes record their support of
Taylor's intention to send Kennedy a memo recommending "against a
hasty attack." Tuesday, October 23, was a more propitious date, then
to "include all offensive weapons and supporting defenses."

A briefing followed with bad news: A missile complex with eight
missiles and four launchers at San Cristóbal was operational, and two
more sites in the Sagua la Grande area would be operational within a
week. Equally troubling was the news that there were sixteen opera-

tional SAM sites, which markedly increased the danger to reconnaissance aircraft. However, the notes record: "There is no evidence
of nuclear warheads in Cuba." (In fact all the nuclear warheads had
been delivered.)

The next challenge was to evaluate the efficacy of a blockade versus a surprise attack, and for that the Chiefs emulated ExComm by
dividing into two groups. But even considering the idea of a blockade infuriated Admiral Anderson, who complained aloud to McNamara that it was closing the barn door after the horse had escaped. A
blockade was not only useless: It was dangerous. The missiles were
operational and could be launched during a blockade. And a blockade
could bring a confrontation with the Soviet Union rather than with
Cuba. During a blockade Guantánamo could be attacked, as could
U.S. shipping in the Florida Strait. It was a bad idea, and Anderson
wanted no part of it.

Gen. Lucius Clay Jr., deputy director for operations, joined the
meeting after Taylor left to report something very different (and more
accurate) from what Taylor had described. He said that ExComm
was considering two courses: "(1) Limited blockade followed by an
air strike three days later and (2) limited blockade followed by negotiations." In summary, he said, "We will have to go through political
shenanigans, followed by blockade and then air strike." UN ambassador Adlai Stevenson "is strong for blockade less POL [petroleum,
oil, lubricants]," Clay noted.

At 12:30 General Taylor reported that in a few hours the president (who had cut short his campaigning in Chicago) will convene a
White House meeting. In the meantime, McNamara wants an "in-
between plan": five days of blockade followed by a strike. Taylor, still
promoting an air strike, added that he "will tell the President that we
have every reasonable chance of hitting all those missiles. If we wait,
they'll have time to hide them."

2

AFTER READING Sorensen's draft of a "blockade route" speech,
Bobby concluded that everything Jack wanted was in place. He called
his brother to warn him that delay could only unravel what he "had
pulled together."

Feigning a bad cold, the president aborted his campaign tour in Chicago and arrived at the White House at 1:30 p.m.

ExComm's "blockade confirmation" meeting began an hour later. The continuing concern for secrecy dictated avoiding the press corps, whose suspicions had been raised by the flimsy "bad cold" excuse. The Oval Room on the second floor of the White House was a secure venue, invisible to prying eyes, but one that foreclosed the possibility of a verbatim tape recording of the conversation.

It was assumed at the beginning of the meeting that the air strike option would not be the administration's first move. The president (working through Bobby) had been explicit that he would start with a blockade, and the air strike advocates had grudgingly conceded the point. But their skepticism persisted, and their repeated doubts led the president to waver, and to acknowledge that he might have to accept their logic if the blockade failed to produce the desired result.

Agreeing that time was not on his side, Kennedy remarked (while discussing follow-up air strikes) that "we might wish, looking back, that we had done earlier what we are now preparing to do."

After a thorough intelligence briefing on the current order of battle in Cuba, McNamara presented the case for the "blockade route." Its purposes, he said, were to prevent Soviet reinforcements, and to compel them to negotiate the removal of their missiles. To achieve that, he admitted, we would probably have to offer to decommission the Jupiter missile bases in Turkey and Italy and "possibly agree to limit our use of Guantanamo to a specified limited time."

Offering up Guantánamo as part of a negotiation was extremely controversial, as became obvious when Stevenson made a similar proposal. But Bromley Smith, the National Security Council's executive secretary, who composed the minutes, did not indicate any reaction to McNamara's suggestion. And, in a postcrisis interview, McNamara denied that he had ever made such a Stevensonian proposal.

The minute notes do not provide any indication of the discussion that followed the defense secretary's presentation, but there was quite a bit, for the next entry has the president sounding like an air strike advocate.

He [Kennedy] "point[ed] out," Smith wrote, "that additional Soviet missiles would become operational during the blockade," and asked General Taylor "how many missiles we could destroy by air action on Monday?" As he had told the Chiefs earlier, Taylor recommended delaying air strikes until Tuesday, and recommended attacking SAM sites and air bases in addition to the missiles.

Smith's minutes also indicate something extraordinary that historians have overlooked. Either in his presentation or during the discussion with General Taylor that followed, McNamara had warned against a proposal *to use nuclear weapons* against Soviet and/or Cuban targets. Exactly what he said was not recorded, but the minutes state that Taylor "said he did not share Secretary McNamara's fear that if we used nuclear weapons in Cuba, nuclear weapons would be used against us."

Had the Chiefs proposed that the missile sites be attacked with nuclear weapons? That is what Taylor's statement suggests, but the destruction in 1975 of the original JCS minutes means we can never be certain.

3

THE EXCHANGE between the president and General Taylor prompted the blockade advocates to assure the president that their proposal was still the best option. Rusk said the blockade would limit the Soviet missiles to those presently there. Ball thought that photo reconnaissance might reveal that there were no nuclear warheads in Cuba, and the blockade would prevent any from getting in. Taylor countered that they could be flown in, to which McNamara responded that we would shoot down any aircraft transporting nuclear weapons. He also "parenthetically" informed his colleagues that there were 6,000 to 8,000 Soviets in Cuba, a gross underestimate that fell an incredible 34,000 short of the actual number.

Continuing to worry aloud about the wisdom of his decision, the president wondered if the "free world" would see the blockade as a sufficiently robust response, and, Smith wrote, "he is particularly concerned" about how the Latin American countries would view it.

With his brother seemingly backtracking, Bobby felt free to express his aggression. "Now is the last chance we will have to destroy Castro and the Soviet missiles," he declared. Not so, replied Sorensen, who seldom argued with either Kennedy. But he had thought deeply about the advantages of the blockade while composing the "blockade route" speech and supported this approach so strongly that he had even declined to write a speech justifying an invasion. He was not about to remain silent and let the initiative he believed in—and the one he thought the president believed in—eliminated: "Mr. Sorensen said he did not agree with the Attorney General or with General Taylor that this was our last chance," Smith recorded. "He said a missile buildup would end if, as everyone seemed to agree, the Russians would not use force to penetrate the United States blockade."

4

THE MEETING had turned into a debate for the president's support, and General Taylor pushed hard. As Bundy began to present the air strike group's conclusions, Taylor took over. Predictably, he made the case that we could now eliminate both the missiles and the IL-28 bombers that reconnaissance indicated were lined up like sitting ducks on Cuban airbases.

Perhaps unpredictably, but surely unexpectedly to Taylor, Kennedy "stated flatly that the Soviet planes in Cuba did not concern him particularly." We could live with Soviet bombers, which, in his view, "did not affect the balance of power." The missiles were an entirely different matter.

McNamara (contradicting Taylor) claimed that there was little chance of destroying more than two-thirds of the missiles and their launchers. It was a remarkable moment, as the secretary of defense and the chairman of the Joint Chiefs of Staff debated this issue. The general concentrated on the problem at hand, while his boss focused on the consequences.

As Taylor "argued that a blockade would not . . . end the Cuban missile threat . . . and, if we waited, the use of military force would be much more costly," McNamara explained the details of the Chiefs' plans to the president.

The air strike would marshal eight hundred sorties, which surely would kill several thousand Russians. It would not only "lead inevitably to an invasion," but would produce "a very major response" from the Kremlin. "In such an event, the United States would lose control of the situation which could escalate to general war."

It was an effective argument that refocused the president on the blockade. He agreed with McNamara that a strike would produce a Soviet response, "such as blockading Berlin." But he also admitted that the blockade could result in the same reaction. The advantage of a blockade, however, was that within a day or two it would become clear whether the Soviets were continuing to work on their missiles or standing down. "Thus," he reasoned, "we would be in a better position to know what move to make next."

In short, the blockade appeared to be the best option for preventing an uncontrolled escalation to war.

The discussion continued to review both sides of the debate with Stevenson firmly adding his opposition to a surprise air strike. After asserting that the blockade would limit Soviet retaliation and reduce the chance of any uncontrolled escalation, he made a proposal that the president and the other ExComm members would use in the aftermath of the crisis to smear his reputation. "He urged," Smith recorded, "that we offer the Russians a settlement involving the withdrawal of our missiles from Turkey and our evacuation of Guantanamo base."

Offering up Guantánamo—which McNamara earlier had proposed, to no reaction from his ExComm colleagues—now elicited a "sharp rejection." That would suggest that we were "frightened into abandoning our position," the president said. He could support "discussing the withdrawal of our missiles from Turkey and Greece [sic]", the minutes record, but "we should only make such a proposal in the future."

5

SINCE THE second ExComm meeting, Kennedy had said several times that offering to dismantle the Jupiters could be the key to trading the Soviet missiles out of Cuba. But thinking further about the political consequences had hardened his negotiating position. Not nearly so much as his brother's, however. As a way of conveying "our firm intentions," Bobby now suggested that "we might tell the Russians that we were turning over nuclear weapons and missiles to the West Germans" (a suggestion that surely would have gotten Khrushchev's—not to mention de Gaulle's—attention).

Shortly after Bobby's bizarre proposal, the president ended the debate with a Solomonic declaration: The blockade should be instituted as quickly as possible, but so should all necessary actions "to put us in a position to undertake an air strike on the missiles and missile sites by Monday or Tuesday." Preparations for an invasion of Cuba were also authorized.

Then, leaning toward caution, he recommended informing the Turks and Italians that "they should not fire the strategic missiles they have even if attacked and, on second thought, their warheads should be dismantled."

Despite the clear distinction the president had made between the threat the missiles posed, and the insignificance of the Soviet aircraft, General Taylor persisted that any strike on Cuba include the MiGs and IL-28 bombers. Ball urged that the blockade restrict petroleum products to which Rusk replied that it was important to maintain the distinction between our objective of eliminating the Soviet missiles and, "not, at this time," attempting to overthrow Castro.

The secretary of state also mentioned that under international law a blockade was an act of war, and therefore he recommended (as Leonard Meeker had first suggested days ago) "the use of the word 'quarantine.'"

"Parenthetically," the minutes note, Kennedy then asked Rusk to reconsider our ban against providing France with assistance to their nuclear weapons program. Under the circumstances, it did not make sense to antagonize de Gaulle.

The president's final summation included a charge to Ambassador Stevenson: He was to make it clear to his UN colleagues that the Soviets had introduced their missiles in a "subterranean" manner, and he was *not* to mention that the administration might consider the removal of the missiles in Turkey and Italy.

With respect to dealing with the Turks and the Italians, he spoke especially to Paul Nitze, assistant secretary of defense for international affairs. He was to study the problems that would arise with the Turks, and with NATO, if the Jupiters had to be removed. They needed to be assured, he said, that removing the Jupiters was not a "retreat"; they would be replaced with Polaris submarines, a more effective deterrent.

"The President concluded the meeting," the minutes read, "by stating that we should be ready to meet criticism of our deployment of missiles abroad but we should not initiate negotiations with a base withdrawal proposal."

6

At 6:15 p.m. the Chiefs reassembled to hear from Taylor. "This was not one of our better days," they were told. The president had settled on the blockade. The decisive votes, Taylor reported, had been cast by Rusk, McNamara, and Stevenson. OAS support for the blockade would be solicited before the president's TV speech, which was to be scheduled for either Sunday or Monday.

The blockade would prohibit offensive weapons, but POL would probably be proscribed later in the week. In addition, preparations should be made to initiate air strikes against the Soviet missiles (1) without warning on Monday or Tuesday, or (2) after a twenty-four-hour notice. "The rationale," Taylor explained, "is that we don't want a Pearl Harbor on the American record, and we want to protect unprepared allies against retaliation" (presumably Soviet retaliation against Berlin or Turkey).

In conclusion Taylor passed on the president's very direct message: "I know that you and your colleagues are unhappy with the decision, but I trust that you will support me." Taylor confirmed that the Chiefs, although opposed to the decision, "would back him completely."

"I never thought I'd live to see the day when I would want to go to war," General Wheeler groused.

32

"Nuclear War That Week
Certainly Was Not Excluded from His Mind"

This world really is impossible to manage so long as we have
nuclear weapons. . . . [It] is really a terrible way to have to
live in this world.
—PRESIDENT KENNEDY TO DAVID ORMSBY-GORE

Sunday, October 21, was an interregnum (of sorts). It began with
Mass at Saint Stephen's, with Jacqueline, but quickly transitioned
back to the crisis. Last-minute confirmations, editorial changes to
his address, further deliberations with senior military commanders,
and a reassuring get-together with his friend, Britain's ambassador to
the United States, David Ormsby-Gore, filled the remainder of the
president's day.

Guiding everyone on board had been a delicate balancing act.
The factions in ExComm, the shifting views within his inner circle
(Bobby, McNamara, Bundy, Sorensen), the Chiefs' preference for
invading Cuba, and Kennedy's doubts were sorted out and integrated
into a strategic plan.

1

THE PROCESS of bringing the Chiefs on board had strained an already
difficult relationship. The military had been preparing for a confrontation with the Soviet Union since 1947, and the Chiefs viewed
Khrushchev's missile deployment as an opportunity to wrench Cuba
back from the Communist camp. America's military advantages were
overwhelming: conventional superiority in the Caribbean and a significant global nuclear weapons lead. The president's concern about

Berlin's vulnerability seemed overwrought to the Chiefs, and they worried whether he was really determined to see his plan through. They would follow his orders, but they would also strictly adhere to their own procedures, about which the president was not fully briefed.

The Chiefs met twice on Sunday, October 21, at 1:00 and 5:15 p.m. At their first meeting they learned that Gen. Walter C. Sweeney Jr., commander in chief of Tactical Air Command, General Taylor, McNamara, Bobby, and McCone, had met with the president an hour earlier. Sweeney said that "he needed an additional 150 planes to get the missiles and 500 planes for the whole job." But he agreed with Taylor and McNamara that, at best, only 90 percent of "the known missiles" would be destroyed.

Concerned that additional missiles could be hidden, Taylor recommended "that the air strike be conducted immediately, suggesting tomorrow morning, and that it be without warning." Curiously, the president then contradicted his earlier arguments against an invasion. If there is to be an air assault, "we will do the whole job," he said, and ordered that the attack be ready to launch on Monday morning. Was he pandering to the Chiefs, or just keeping all his options open?

There was "complete agreement," McCone's notes record, "that military action must include an invasion and occupation of Cuba."

The blockade was the next order of business. Admiral Anderson, who had attended the meeting, confirmed that the president was set to speak tomorrow night and that State (Dean Rusk) did not want the blockade to go into effect until the OAS had time to react. Anderson had agreed that the blockade could take effect twenty-four hours after the president spoke.

The next notation reveals the Chiefs' swelling anger in response to the president's attempts to manage their actions. President Kennedy had asked Assistant Secretary of Defense Nitze if he had informed the Chiefs—as earlier requested—that they issue clear orders to the Jupiter missile crews in Turkey and Italy not to fire their missiles without his explicit authorization, even after a Soviet nuclear or nonnuclear attack.

When Nitze's memo detailing that order was brought into the JCS meeting, the Chiefs rejected it: "JCS reply is JCSM-800-62, opposing any further steps," the meeting notes recorded. Special instructions were unnecessary, they insisted; the standing order [JCSM-800-62] was sufficient. It was an act of calculated insubordination, the first of several defiant responses to efforts by the White House to manage the military's actions.

2

AT 2:30 the president gathered the National Security Council (the now-expanded ExComm) in the Oval Room of the Executive Mansion to review last-minute details. Sorensen's third draft of the president's speech was the first order of business, and it set off a debate between those arguing for tougher language, and Ambassador Stevenson, who defended Sorensen's conciliatory wording.

The specific issues debated included whether to stress Soviet responsibility for the installation of the missiles, or Castro's irresponsible complicity. Always able to see the other side, Kennedy remarked that we had sent similar missiles to Turkey and Italy. How different was that?

"Our missiles were deployed to NATO countries only after those countries were threatened by deployed Soviet missiles," the meeting minutes record Rusk's response. But Secretary Dillon, a member of the Eisenhower administration during the deployment, offered a less calculated version. We sent them to Europe, he said, "because we had so many of them we did not know where to put them."

The president settled several other matters during the next hour. Taking account of Latin American sensibilities, he declared that "we were not taking action under the Monroe Doctrine."

The blockade would be labeled a "quarantine" to differentiate it as much as possible from the Berlin blockade.

Then, in response to a suggestion from Secretary Rusk that he disliked, the president proposed a strategy that seemed at odds with his general approach. He felt, the minutes of the meeting read, "that a better tactic was for us initially to frighten the United Nations representatives with the prospect of all kinds of actions and then, when a resolution calling for the withdrawal of missiles from Cuba, Turkey, and Italy was proposed, we could consider supporting such a resolution."

During the remainder of the meeting the president authorized a series of tough decisions that put the final touches on the planning process. Charges against the Soviet Union would be submitted to the UN, but only after the OAS had acted. The full responsibility for the missiles in Cuba should be pinned "directly on Khrushchev."

Assistant Secretary of Defense Nitze should "study the problem of withdrawing United States missiles from Turkey and Italy." The ban on nuclear assistance to France was to be dropped. The time between a decision to invade Cuba and the landing of the first troops should be compressed. And, distancing himself from Stevenson, whose conciliatory advice had created hostility among most ExComm members, Kennedy declared that there would be no call for a summit meeting as Ambassador Stevenson proposed.

"We would accept nothing less than the ending of the missile capability now in Cuba, no reinforcement of that capability, and no further construction of missile sites," a declaration that roused McNamara to comment that, "we would have to invade Cuba" to achieve that result.

Responding to the president's query about the blockade, Admiral Anderson said that he supported delaying its enforcement for twenty-four hours after the speech to give the Kremlin the opportunity to issue instructions to their captains. If any Soviet or Cuban planes or ships threatened hostile action, they would be destroyed, "thereby creating a new situation."

Looking ahead, he estimated that it would take the Soviet navy at least ten days to send surface ships to the area, and "Soviet submarines [which, unknown to the U.S. Navy, were already close to the blockade line] could not get to the area in less than ten to fourteen days." However, if a Soviet submarine was discovered heading for Havana, "he would ask higher authority for permission to attack it."

Asked if he wanted all ships, including those of our allies, stopped, the president answered that he preferred stopping all shipping "in the expectation that allied ships would soon become discouraged and drop out of the Cuban trade."

It was a cavalier response that bore no relation to how he would manage the blockade once it went into effect.

3

BEFORE MEETING with General Sweeney and the others, the president had telephoned his old friend David Ormsby-Gore, and asked him "to come unseen" to the White House. An arms-control expert, Ormsby-Gore and Jack Kennedy had developed a lasting friendship when they met in the late 1930s. The president was eager to review his decisions with someone he trusted and whose judgment he respected.

"When I came into the room I had a pretty good idea of what was already happening," Ormsby-Gore recalled, revealing (the interesting fact) that he "had had various indications of it from the CIA."

After disclosing all that he knew about the Soviet missiles, the president enumerated the options he had considered and asked which one Ormsby-Gore would choose. "I thought that bombing—an immediate strike would not be understood in the rest of the world and that some form of blockade was probably the right answer."

The president then asked if he had "fully examined the wisdom of passing up this chance" of overthrowing Castro, who "might not make the same mistake again." The question was, in part at least, what Ormsby-Gore called Kennedy's "devil's advocate act," but it was as likely also an expression of indecision about forgoing this opportunity to depose Castro.

In his follow-up report to Prime Minister Harold Macmillan on Monday, Ormsby-Gore noted that he told Kennedy that an invasion "would be most unwise." Displaying a keener understanding of the situation in Cuba than any member of the administration, he warned that U.S. invaders could not "expect any widespread popular support . . . and history indicated that an invasion without internal popular support usually led to endless trouble."

He noted too that Kennedy confessed to "admiring the Soviet strategy." If the United States reacted violently it would give Khrushchev the perfect excuse to move against Berlin. If, on the other hand, he accepted the missiles, Latin Americans and other allies would conclude that he was not determined to "resist the encroachments of Communism and would hedge their bets accordingly."

Berlin was a powder keg, since any attempt by the Soviets "to put the squeeze on us in Berlin," the president worried, would require the United States to threaten "the use of nuclear weapons." It was clear to

Ormsby-Gore that "nuclear war that week certainly was not excluded from his mind."

The conversation—which went on through dinner—also produced an important modification to the blockade. Discussing where the Soviet ships should be intercepted, Ormsby-Gore "argued rather strongly" that the blockade line should be as close as possible to Cuba to give the Soviets maximum time to consider the consequences of challenging it. That seemed right to Kennedy, and he called McNamara. The navy had fixed the blockade line eight hundred nautical miles from Cuba to assure that Cuban planes could not attack its ships, the secretary of defense explained. "The President was very unimpressed by this argument," Ormsby-Gore recalled, and ordered the decision reviewed.

Much to Admiral Anderson's chagrin, the blockade line was moved three hundred nautical miles closer to Cuba.

4

A DEBRIEFING of the afternoon's ExComm meeting appears to have been the sole agenda for the Chiefs' 5:15 meeting. After remarks about what was in the president's speech, and what would be eliminated or changed, Anderson reported that the blockade would be called a quarantine, and that the Chiefs and the services were to make all necessary preparations to compress the lead time for executing OPLAN 316 (bomb and invade Cuba) "from 7 to 5 days."

The meeting concluded with General Taylor's sarcastic remark: "The Pearl Harbor complex has affected the good people at the White House. . . . There will be no air strike, but it is in the offing."

5

THE STATE Department had gone into a frenzied round-the-clock schedule on Saturday morning to prepare the world for the president's Monday night speech. The text, and a personal letter from the president to Khrushchev, was sent to the U.S. Embassy in Moscow with instructions that they be delivered an hour before the president spoke. Similar documents were prepared for Ambassador Dobrynin in Washington.

Individual letters from the president were sent to Britain's Prime Minister Macmillan, France's President Charles de Gaulle, India's Prime Minister Jawaharlal Nehru, West Germany's Chancellor Konrad Adenauer, Canada's Prime Minister John Diefenbaker, Italy's Prime Minister Amintore Fanfani, and Willy Brandt, the mayor of West Berlin.

Dean Acheson (accompanied by CIA senior analyst Sherman Kent) was sent as the president's special emissary to brief de Gaulle and Adenauer. Chester L. Cooper, a senior CIA officer, carried the U2 photographs to London to brief Macmillan and his senior Cabinet ministers.

The U.S. ambassadors in twenty-one Latin American countries were each given a letter from the president, a Security Council resolution draft, a formal notice that the United States was calling for an OAS meeting on October 23, and the text of a proposed OAS resolution to pass on to their respective governments.

A separate letter from the president was sent to the heads of government in eighteen countries that were either allied with the United States or were represented on the UN Security Council.

Sixty other U.S. embassies in other parts of the world were sent instructions regarding how to represent the president's speech.

And, finally, a letter was sent to the president of the Security Council, a rotating position that, ironically, was then held by the Soviet ambassador to the UN, Valerian Zorin.

The letter called for an urgent meeting and enclosed a draft resolution.

33

"What's EDP?"

What is the distinction between these missiles and the
missiles which we sent to Turkey and Italy, which the Soviets
put up with?
—PRESIDENT KENNEDY, OCTOBER 22, 1962

Everyone was tense. The president's speech was scheduled for 7:00
p.m., and it was important that no detail be overlooked, including
appropriate political cover. Before attending any meetings, President
Kennedy called former presidents Eisenhower, Truman, and Hoover.
A succession of ExComm, NSC, and JCS meetings sought to cover
the remaining bases.

At 11:30 the president assembled an expanded ExComm—
officially established today as the Executive Committee of the
National Security Council. Most (though not all) of the necessary
decisions had been made, and this gathering was devoted to confirming the details, last-minute changes to the speech, discussions about
what to tell the press, and a lot of nervous "pregame" chatter. But there
were several notable exchanges that confirmed the president's intention to monitor carefully how the military executed his instructions.

1

THE IDEA of a missile trade was on the president's mind. "Maybe this
is just a political problem," he said, "but I think we ought to be looking forward to the day when [the missiles] are removed from Cuba,
Italy and Turkey."

The missiles in Turkey worried him most. They were vulnerable, a tempting reprisal target, and a potential tripwire into a nuclear exchange, a calamity he was determined to prevent. Had Nitze made it clear to the Chiefs that they were to inform the U.S. command in Turkey that their missiles were not to be fired without my specific instructions? the president asked.

"That's a question mark," Nitze confessed. He had not received an answer from the Chiefs. But Deputy Secretary of Defense Roswell Gilpatric had, and reported that the Chiefs said "that those instructions are already out."

"Well, why don't we reinforce them," the president persisted, "because, as I say, we may be attacking Cubans, and a reprisal may come. We don't want those nuclear warheads firing without our knowing about it. . . . Can we take care of that then, Paul? We need a new instruction out. . . . [Do] they object to sending a new one out?"

"They object to sending it out because it, to their view, compromises their standing instructions . . . ," Nitze responded, adding that "they did come back with another point, and that is: NATO strategic contact requires the immediate execution of EDP in such events."

More military jargon, which Kennedy hated. "What's EDP?" an annoyed president asked.

"The European Defense Plan, *which is nuclear war—*"

"Now, that's why we want to get onto that," the president repeated raising his voice. "They don't know in Greece and Turkey—ah, Turkey and Italy . . . there is a chance there will be a spot reprisal. And what we've got to do is make sure these fellows do know, so that they don't fire them off and put the United States under attack. I don't think we ought to accept the Chiefs' word on that one, Paul."

Making another attempt to avoid an unpleasant confrontation with the Chiefs, Nitze replied: "Surely, they [the U.S. command in Turkey] are indoctrinated not to fire. This is what Secretary McNamara and I went over, looked into, and they really are—"

The president knew exactly how he wanted this part of the operation handled, and he had heard enough from Nitze: "Well, let's do it again, Paul," he said with a finality that elicited Nitze's concession: "I've got your point and we're going to get that." (The recorded nervous laughter reflected the tension the exchange created.)

———

Panic struck about fifteen minutes later. A note passed to Kennedy reported that the Soviets had scheduled an announcement in two hours. Jumping to the worst conclusion, the president told his startled advisers: "They're going to announce it."

Do you want to "get on the air quicker?" Bundy asked.

"I wouldn't," George Ball responded.

"I think you ought to announce that I'm going on the air at 7:00," Kennedy said, and for at least ten more minutes the president, his brother, Rusk, Bundy, and Sorensen engaged in a worried discussion about the consequences of the Soviets preempting the president's speech with an announcement that everything they had sent to Cuba was strictly for the country's defense.

As 2:00 approached tension rose. But Foreign Minister Gromyko, who had been visiting the United States, gave a polite farewell.

The first crisis was a false alarm.

2

WITH THE blockade announcement looming, the Chiefs met several times. Their first meeting, at 9:00 a.m., was devoted to a briefing on the latest missile order of battle. Gen. Joseph Carroll, the Defense Intelligence Agency's [DIA] director, had bad news: Four of the six [thus-far identified] mobile MRBM sites were operational, and the two remaining would be ready within three to five days. Two fixed IRBM sites were under surveillance, and the estimate was that one would be "available for emergencies" by November 15 and fully operational by December 1. Two others would be ready for emergencies by December 1 and fully operational two weeks later.

Reassembling at 1:30, the Chiefs considered last-minute preparations for the confrontation that the president's speech was expected to provoke. Taylor announced that SAC would transition to 1/8 airborne alert, meaning that one-eighth of the fleet would remain aloft fully armed, 24/7. B-47s and CONAD (Continental North American Defense) interceptors would be dispersed to civilian and other bases across the country, complicating any attempts to target them.

McNamara next announced a direct order in response to the Chiefs' rejection of Nitze's "Jupiter" memo. "The President wants a message sent to USCINCEUR [U.S. commander in chief Europe]," McNamara told the Chiefs in unambiguous language, "saying in effect, make sure the Jupiter warheads in Turkey and Italy are not released if missiles come under attack, and if they are in danger of being taken by our angry allies, destroy them."

In less than an hour General Taylor transmitted the message to Gen. Lauris Norstad. It read: "Make certain that the Jupiters in Turkey and Italy will not be fired without specific authorization from the President. In the event of an attack, either nuclear or non-nuclear . . . U.S. custodians are to destroy or make inoperable the weapons if any attempt is made to fire them." The order, Norstad was told, was not to be revealed to the Turks or the Italians.

The next item considered the consequences of a missile attack. The news that several missiles were operational raised the obvious question, which McNamara, at the president's behest, put to the Chiefs: How should the United States respond if the Cubans launched one of those missiles, "authorized or not"?

The answer shifted the focus to the Soviet Union. Nitze pointed out that we wouldn't necessarily know if the missile came from Cuba. "It could come from a [Soviet] submarine," McNamara confirmed. There was general agreement that the onus for any missile firing had to be pinned on the Soviet Union.

Still thinking about the message to control the Jupiters that he had just relayed to the Chiefs, McNamara said that the Soviets should be warned that they would be held responsible for any missile launch, and "the US would fire missiles in retaliation. What we want is for the Soviets to send out a message like the one we just sent out to USCINCEUR."

Interestingly, Admiral Anderson, who was becoming more irritable with each passing day, disagreed. His concern, he said, was that a threat of nuclear retaliation was likely to create strong "adverse allied reactions." His JCS colleagues, the notes indicate, also believed that we should not announce "exactly what our retaliation would be."

3

THE NATIONAL Security Council (the now-expanded ExComm) reassembled at 3:00 p.m. for its final prespeech gathering. Offering disquisitions on why the Soviet missiles in Cuba were unacceptable, why the blockade was chosen, why "everyone should sing one song," and how he had analyzed the situation from the start, President Kennedy dominated the discussion. Much of what he said was a personal review of his thoughts over the past seven days, how he expected his advisers to respond to criticisms, and what remained to be carefully considered, such as how to react to a U2 shoot-down.

He was mentally preparing himself for the transition from the secret decision-making phase of the crisis into the public one. The recording of the meeting reveals how he understood what he had done, why he had done it, and what he worried about happening after his speech.

His first point was a command: It was essential that everyone wholly endorse the chosen strategy, which "represented a reasonable consensus." He had spoken with former presidents Eisenhower, Truman, and Hoover earlier, and they all supported the policy.

It was also important to have a unified response to the charge that the missiles in Cuba did not create a serious new threat, he said. The United States had lived with the possibility of a Soviet missile attack for years, and the Europeans faced even greater danger. But, having publicly warned the Kremlin in press conferences on September 4 and 13 that deploying offensive weapons systems in Cuba was unacceptable, it was incumbent that he honor his commitments.

Furthermore, if the United States failed to resist this secret Soviet deployment, "we would convey to the Russians an impression that we would never act, no matter what they did anywhere." That would have a devastating effect on our position in Latin America and elsewhere. And, if the Soviets acted in Berlin in response to our actions in Cuba, it was important to note that Foreign Minister Gromyko had indicated the previous Thursday that they intended to move against Berlin for reasons unrelated to Cuba.

———

"Now it may end up with our having to invade Cuba," the president conceded, but "we've done the best thing, at least as far as we can tell in advance." It was not possible not to have reacted: "I don't think there was anybody ever who didn't think we shouldn't respond" (anybody he had consulted, that is).

He had explained to all, he said (the Joint Chiefs were at this meeting), why he had chosen the blockade, even though, "as I've said from the beginning, the idea of a quick strike was very tempting, and I really didn't give up on that until yesterday morning. . . . After talking to General Sweeney . . . it looked like we would have all the difficulties of Pearl Harbor and not have finished the job. The job can only be finished by an invasion."

If an invasion appeared necessary at the end of the week, the president was confident that the forces required would be ready. But conceding that waiting a week would make the military's job more difficult, he said to the Chiefs: "We followed the course we have because . . . we are involved all around the world and not just in Cuba. I think the shock to the alliance might have been nearly fatal [had we decided to invade]. Particularly as it would have excused very drastic action by Khrushchev."

Nevertheless, there remained the major problem of justifying the American reaction. Anticipating allied objections, Kennedy put the central question as much to himself as to his advisers: "Inasmuch as the Soviet missiles are already pointed at the U.S., and U.S. missiles are [pointed] at the U.S.S.R. . . . *What is the distinction between these missiles and the missiles which we sent to Turkey and Italy, which the Soviets put up with?*"

State had prepared a secret briefing paper on that issue, and the president decreed that it be reviewed for declassification promptly and ready for distribution by that evening. "This is going to be one of the matters that are going to be most troublesome for our ambassadors," he warned. "We ought to get it clear in the American press and others as to why we object to something that the Russians [accepted]."

Kennedy then launched into his own explanation of why the Jupiter deployment was different. "The Soviet move was undertaken secretly, accompanied by false Soviet statements in public and private. . . . Our bases abroad are by published agreement to help local people maintain their independence against a threat from abroad. Soviet history is exactly the opposite."

And what will happen in Latin America if we fail to react? "Offensive missiles in Cuba have a very different psychological and political effect in this hemisphere than missiles in the U.S.S.R. pointed to us," the president continued. "Had we done nothing, Communism and Castroism are going to be spread through the hemisphere as governments frightened by this new evidence of power have toppled."

Then, perhaps recalling Khrushchev's anger over Berlin during the Vienna conference, he speculated that "if we accepted this one . . . [Khrushchev] would have tried more. In this sense this is a probing action preceding [a renewed confrontation over] Berlin, to see whether we accept it or not."

Another question that had to be answered was why we had not acted earlier. Senator Keating had been insisting in speeches for weeks that the Soviets were stationing missiles in Cuba. Why had the administration been so slow to react?

"The whole foreign policy of the United States since 1947 has been to develop and maintain alliances in this hemisphere as well as around the world," the president explained. Acting before we had photographic evidence would have reinforced Castro's waning prestige in Latin America, to our disadvantage. Since there was no precedent for a Soviet deployment beyond its territory, and no evidence of such until October 16, "we might have borne responsibility for the loss of Berlin, without having any justification for our action." "I wouldn't be too categoric that we had no information," McCone interjected. "There were some 15, I think, various refugee reports that circulated around that were indicative that something was going on."

"Mr. President," Bobby said respectfully, leaping to his brother's defense: "Of course we get the refugees' reports, which frequently prove inaccurate."

There were other specific unanswered questions still troubling the president. First was a decision about how to react "when" a U2 is shot down, "which we have to anticipate maybe in the next few days," he said. And, second, how do we respond if work continues on the missile sites, "which we assume it will"? He directed his advisers to begin providing the answers the next day.

One answer he was determined to keep under wraps was the possibility of invading Cuba. Now that the blockade was the settled policy, he forbade any mention of an invasion. "I don't think we ought to discuss [that we considered an air attack or invasion] under any conditions. We may simply have to do it. In any case, we don't want to look like we were considering it . . . just scratch that from all our statements and conversations, and not ever indicate that that was a course of action open to us. I can't say that strongly enough . . . it will become a propaganda matter, that this was a matter seriously considered by the [U.S.] government.

"Anybody else have any thoughts about this?"

After the meeting, the president welcomed the visiting prime minister of Uganda. He then met his cabinet, where he repeated what he had decided and why, and again gave instructions on how his decisions were to be explained. He then met with the leaders of Congress, which turned out to be his most difficult meeting of the week. When he appeared on television at 7:00 p.m., it was a wonder that he did not appear exhausted.

4

THE CHIEFS returned to the Pentagon and at 4:30 p.m. began considering last-minute preparations. The deputy CNO for plans and policy, Vice Adm. Ulysses Grant Sharp Jr., brought the news that no overt steps that suggest arrangements for an invasion were to be taken. "Thus requisitioning ships is out." Air force vice chief of staff General McKee announced that the president's order also prohibited the planned call-up of C-119s (Flying Boxcars) and interceptors. "If we can't lick the Cubans with what we already have," General Taylor quipped, "we are in terrible shape."

("Terrible shape" would have been an accurate assessment had the invasion gone forward. It bears repetition here that the CIA estimated Soviet troop strength at approximately 11,000, unaware that 42,000 Soviet troops had been secretly transported to Cuba along with dozens of tactical nuclear weapons.)

PART SEVEN

October 22 (Monday)–October 26 (Friday): Gambling with Armageddon—Kennedy, Khrushchev, and Castro

You convinced yourself, that Khrushchev will never go to war . . . so you scare us [expecting] us to retreat. True, we will not declare war, but we will not withdraw either, if you push it on us. We will respond to your war in kind. . . .
If [Kennedy] starts a war then he would probably become the last president of the United States of America.
—NIKITA KHRUSHCHEV TO JOHN MCCLOY

34

"We May Have the War in the Next Twenty-Four Hours"

October 22, Monday Evening

Any hostile move anywhere in the world against the safety
and freedom of peoples to whom we are committed, including
in particular the brave people of West Berlin, will be met by
whatever action is needed.
—PRESIDENT KENNEDY, OCTOBER 22, 1962

It was the speech heard around the world, as its author knew it would
be. It was the speech that might begin a Cuban missile war or prepare
a diplomatic path to peace. It was the most consequential speech Ted
Sorensen had ever drafted, perhaps that anyone would ever write.
It had to convince America's citizens and the citizens of America's
NATO allies, as well as the members of the UN General Assembly,
that the Soviet missiles in Cuba were illegitimate—different somehow from similar missiles that the United States had stationed in
Turkey and Italy; that the blockade ("quarantine") was an appropriate
response to the Soviet Union's secret installations; that the forced
removal of the Soviet missiles enhanced the security of the Western
Hemisphere; that a diplomatic solution was both possible and desirable; and, finally, if necessary, that the United States would be justified using force to eliminate the offending weapons.

It was President Kennedy's opening move in his gamble with
Armageddon. Every idea, every phrase, every word was considered
and reconsidered by Sorensen, Bobby, McNamara, Bundy, other
ExComm members, and the president himself. There would be
(almost) no histrionics or rhetorical flourishes. The focus was on evidence of Soviet duplicity, and rational arguments in support of the
blockade. The goal was to persuade both Americans and the global

audience that the Soviet Union was guilty as charged, and to convince Khrushchev that a diplomatic resolution was his best alternative. Its lawyerly, academic tone suggested that everything had been carefully considered, and that the president was in firm control.

1

PREPARATIONS FOR the broadcast were hectic but thorough. Dealing with the enemy was only half the challenge; friends, too, needed to be coaxed into supporting roles. Former presidents, allied heads of state, and congressional leaders could be recalcitrant, especially if surprised, so private briefings were carefully scheduled. The president had called his three living predecessors. "The General," whom McCone had kept up-to-date from the start, had set aside partisanship and declared on a Sunday TV news show that "the President's immediate handling of foreign affairs was not a legitimate topic."

Getting the Senate and House on board was especially important, and Kennedy had the Pentagon launch a scouting expedition to round up the campaigning and vacationing congressional leaders. It was an efficient operation. Most were easily tracked down in their home states and flown in military aircraft to Washington. But in some cases it was particularly complicated: Hale Boggs, the House Democratic whip from Louisiana, was fishing in the Gulf of Mexico when he was alerted to return to DC by a note in a plastic bottle dropped from an air force plane.

By late afternoon the operation was completed, and at 5:30 p.m. twenty congressional leaders, Democrats and Republicans, filed into the Cabinet Room. All knew that a crisis was imminent, but none were clear about the details. They were stunned when told, and their reactions provided "the only sour note of the day."

The briefing began with a summary from CIA director McCone. By August 29, he reported, numerous defensive SAM emplacements had been detected in Cuba, but there was no indication of offensive weapons. Within weeks, however, refugee reports raised concerns, but bad weather canceled the reconnaissance flights scheduled for September 17 and 22. Not until October 14, he explained, was there "unmistakable proof of the beginning of the installation of offensive missile sites."

After a thorough review of the missiles and associated equipment the Soviets had delivered to Cuba, the DCI concluded that "the latest evidence suggests that 4 of the MRBM sites containing 16 launchers are in full operational readiness." The meeting (which Kennedy secretly recorded) lasted an hour, and it quickly descended into a greater challenge than his Friday meeting with the Joint Chiefs. He had expected the Chiefs to disagree with his strategy. But he was their boss, and he was prepared to debate with them. Today, however, he was unprepared for what Sorensen later called the gathering's "captious and inconsistent" responses.

But the aggressive questions—especially from senior Democrats, Senators Richard Russell, the chairman of the Armed Services Committee, and William Fulbright, the chairman of the Foreign Relations Committee—were a boon to the historical record. They exposed how intense the expectation of war with the Soviet Union had become; they prodded Kennedy to explain why the vulnerability of West Berlin had guided his response to the missile challenge; and they produced the revelation that within seven days President Kennedy expected to approve invasion plans *that he had ordered prepared a year earlier.*

"We are presented with a very, very difficult problem because of Berlin," the president emphasized. "Whatever we do in regard to Cuba, it gives [Khrushchev] the chance to do the same with regard to Berlin." Therefore the blockade would only prohibit offensive weapons "in order not to give Khrushchev the justification for imposing a complete blockade on Berlin."

It was also important to recognize that if we invaded Cuba, he emphasized, "there's a chance that these weapons will be fired at the United States;" a consideration that Senator Russell was too worked up to acknowledge.

The blockade was inadequate, Russell lectured the president. The Soviets had been warned, very clearly, against stationing offensive weapons in Cuba, but had ignored the warnings. "We're either a first-class power or we're not." Giving Khrushchev time to reconsider would give him time "to get better prepared." The United States was fully justified, Russell insisted, in carrying out its announced foreign policy, and "we should assemble as speedily as possible an adequate force and clean out that situation."

The chairman of the Senate Armed Services Committee continued: "The time is going to come, Mr. President, when we're going to have to take this step in Berlin and Korea and Washington, D.C., and Winder, Georgia [Russell's hometown], for the nuclear war. . . . I think that the more that we temporize, the more surely he [Khrushchev] is to convince himself that we are afraid to make any real movement and to really fight."

It was the same critique that General LeMay and his colleagues had made on Friday. McNamara's assurances today that the blockade would be aggressive, and that preparations were under way for an invasion, had no more effect on Russell's opinion of the blockade's inadequacy than Kennedy's had had on the Chiefs. The Soviets had been warned, and that was enough, Russell reasserted. Delaying an invasion would result only in "los[ing] a great many more men than we would right now."

Agitated by the senator's assault, the president explained, in a strained voice, that a force of ninety thousand troops had to be assembled to invade Cuba, and that could not be done overnight. But the process was under way, and "I think," Kennedy said, "it may very well come to that [an invasion] before the end of the week."

Everything "was well prepared for an invasion," McNamara confirmed. However, he explained, the ninety thousand troops were only the invading party. The total air, sea, and ground forces would be almost three times that number: 250,000. The invasion could begin in seven days.

He then revealed that plans to invade Cuba were well developed. *"The President ordered us [the Department of Defense] to prepare an invasion of Cuba months ago. . . . I believe it was November of last year. . . .* We've developed a series of alternative plans . . . [and] *reviewed them with the President over the past 10 months on 5 different occasions"* (suggesting that Khrushchev's and Castro's fears were not without merit).

With a nod to Senator Russell ("I understand your point"), the president added "that we are going to move, with maximum speed, all of our forces to be in a position to invade Cuba within the 7-day period." But it was important to understand that we were taking a chance, if we invaded Cuba, that those missiles "which are ready to fire, won't be fired."

"It's one hell of a gamble," Kennedy added, but "we are prepared to take it."

He also warned that the Soviet Union might respond to his speech announcing the blockade by seizing "Berlin in the morning, which they could do within a couple of hours. *Our war plan at that point has been to fire our nuclear weapons at them.*

"So, we may have the war in the next 24 hours."

Incredibly (to Kennedy), Russell was unmoved: "We've got to take a chance somewhere, sometime, if we're going to retain our position as a great world power," he said, a remark he buttressed several minutes later with the declaration that "a war" was "coming someday. . . . Will it ever be under more auspicious circumstances?"

Senator Fulbright's critique was more nuanced than Russell's. He was trying to avoid a war with the Soviet Union, not start one. An invasion was "just between us and Cuba," he argued. A blockade, on the other hand, "is the worst of the alternatives, because if you're confronted with a Russian ship, you are actually confronting Russia."

It was an important point that had been thoroughly debated by ExComm on October 18. But the blockade had carried the day when it became clear (especially to the president) that any preinvasion bombing campaign—perhaps as many as two thousand sorties—was likely to kill thousands of the Russians deployed at the missile sites.

"But that's quite different," Fulbright responded, when McNamara repeated that point. The sites we would be bombing were Cuban, not Russian. Attacking a Russian ship, however, would be an act of war against Russia. "It is not an act of war against Russia to attack Cuba," Fulbright insisted.

The senator's cavalier approach to killing Russians made no sense to the president, and he replied with obvious impatience. "I think it would be foolish," he told Fulbright, "to expect that the Russians would not regard [killing thousands of their troops] as a far more direct thrust than they're going to regard on the ships. And I think that the inevitable end result will be the seizure of Berlin. . . . If we are talking about nuclear war, the escalation ought to be at least with some degree of control."

Keeping control of events was Kennedy's primary objective, but he was aware that it was not possible to manage everything. "I don't know where Khrushchev wants to take us," he admitted. If he seizes Berlin, "We [would] be taking action there and also in Cuba." Then, speaking directly to Fulbright again, he concluded—citing Ambassadors Thompson and Bohlen—that the course he had chosen was based on the "best advice we could get."

"I better go and make this speech," he said a few minutes later, and left the room as angry as Sorensen had ever seen him. "If they want this job, they can have it—it's no great joy to me," he fumed—probably the most exaggerated inaccuracy he ever uttered.

2

TED SORENSEN had drafted the speech several days earlier, but by 7:00 p.m. on Monday night it was the product of many minds, most especially John Kennedy's. He "made dozens of changes, large and small," Sorensen remembered. He specifically vetoed a proposal to include photographs of several missile sites (in retrospect an error). He thought they would not be clear to the average viewer, and worried that "the presence of pictures might contribute to panic." That latter concern also led to the removal of references to the megatonnage of the Soviet missiles compared with the atomic bomb that had obliterated Hiroshima. "Striking" also replaced "wiping out" cities in the United States. But it was impossible to dull the sharp edges of his message, and these decisions did little to alter its reception.

The president spoke for seventeen minutes and forty-three seconds, but what most listeners heard can be summarized in ten words: *Nuclear war with the Soviet Union was a real possibility.*

"Good evening my fellow citizens," the president began in his strong Boston accent. "This government, as promised, has maintained the closest surveillance of the Soviet military buildup on the island of

Cuba. Within the past week, unmistakable evidence has established the fact that a series of offensive missile sites is now in preparation on that imprisoned island."

As a victim of Communist subversion, "imprisoned" Cuba was a pawn of Soviet policy, not an independent actor; its government's role was irrelevant as far as the United States was concerned. This was not the "Caribbean Crisis" (as the Soviets called it), but a U.S.–Soviet global showdown: "The purpose of these bases can be none other than to provide a nuclear strike capability against the Western Hemisphere."

The remainder of the speech was divided into five parts. The first explained the damage the missiles were capable of inflicting on U.S., Canadian, and Latin American cities: "Each of these missiles, in short, is capable of striking Washington, D.C., the Panama Canal, Cape Canaveral, Mexico City, or any other city in the southeastern part of the United States, in Central America, or in the Caribbean area. Additional sites not yet completed appear to be designed for intermediate-range ballistic missiles—capable of traveling more than twice as far—and thus capable of striking most of the major cities in the Western Hemisphere, ranging as far north as Hudson Bay, Canada, and as far south as Lima, Peru."

The Soviet Union's duplicity was next. Quoting Kremlin assurances that only defensive weapons had been sent to Cuba, the president branded Khrushchev and his minions liars: "The Soviet Government publicly stated on September 11 that 'the armaments and military equipment sent to Cuba are designed exclusively for defensive purposes'. . . . [and that, quoting Foreign Minister Gromyko] 'the Soviet Government would never become involved in rendering such [offensive-weapons] assistance.' That statement was false." (The president added "false" to Sorensen's draft after each Soviet quotation.)

The third part of the speech summarized the dangerous situation the missiles created, and stated—in words the president inserted—what should properly be acknowledged as the "Kennedy Doctrine": "Nuclear weapons are so destructive and ballistic missiles are so swift, that any substantially increased possibility of their use or any sudden change in their deployment may well be regarded as a definite threat to peace."

That threat, "in an area well known to have a special and historical relationship to the United States and the nations of the Western Hemisphere, in violation of Soviet assurances, and in defiance of American and hemispheric policy . . . is a deliberately provocative and unjustified change in the status quo which cannot be accepted by this country."

The missiles had to be withdrawn, or they would be eliminated: "Our unswerving objective, therefore, must be to prevent the use of these missiles against this or any other country, and to secure their withdrawal or elimination from the Western Hemisphere."

And, to validate his actions in the light of historical experience (which he had described in his 1940 book, *Why England Slept*): "The 1930's taught us a clear lesson: aggressive conduct, if allowed to go unchecked, ultimately leads to war."

The heart of the speech, the U.S. response—the blockade—was next.

Outlining what he had authorized in seven points, the president used the most combative language of the evening as he revealed what would be either the first ill-advised step toward nuclear war, or an astute evasion of a holocaust: "We will not prematurely or unnecessarily risk the costs of worldwide nuclear war in which even the fruits of victory would be ashes in our mouth—but neither will we shrink from that risk at any time it must be faced.

"Acting, therefore, in the defense of our own security and of the entire Western Hemisphere . . . I have directed that the following *initial* steps be taken immediately:

"*First:* a strict quarantine on all offensive military equipment under shipment to Cuba."

Thinking again about Berlin, he had added that the "quarantine" would not deny "the necessities of life as the Soviets attempted to do in their Berlin blockade of 1948."

He further "directed the continued and increased close surveillance of Cuba and its military buildup . . . [and] directed the Armed Forces to prepare for any eventualities," including a nuclear war that sounded more like Eisenhower's massive retaliation than his own more calibrated flexible response: "It shall be the policy of this Nation to regard any nuclear missile launched from Cuba against any nation in the Western Hemisphere as an attack by the Soviet Union on the United States, requiring a full retaliatory response upon the Soviet Union."

Additional preparations included "reinforce[ing] our base at Guantanamo [and] evacuat[ing] today the dependents of our personnel there; calling tonight for an immediate meeting of . . . the Organization of American States . . . to invoke articles 6 and 8 of the Rio Treaty in support of all necessary action; . . . asking tonight that an emergency meeting of the [United Nations] Security Council be convoked . . . to take action against this latest Soviet threat to world peace. Our resolution will call for the prompt dismantling and withdrawal of all offensive weapons in Cuba, under the supervision of U.N. observers, before the quarantine can be lifted."

The president's "final and seventh point" was an appeal to Khrushchev "to halt and eliminate this clandestine, reckless, and provocative threat to world peace and to stable relations between our two nations." Having eliminated a proposal for a summit meeting from Sorensen's draft, he instead urged Khrushchev "to join in an [unspecified] historic effort to end the perilous arms race and to transform the history of man."

Handing off the responsibility for war or peace, the president declared that Khrushchev "has an opportunity now to move the world back from the abyss of destruction—by returning to his government's own words that it had no need to station missiles outside its own territory, and withdrawing these weapons from Cuba—by refraining from any action which will widen or deepen the present crisis—and then by participating in a search for peaceful and permanent solutions.

"This Nation is prepared to present its case against the Soviet threat to peace, and our own proposals for a peaceful world, at any time and in any forum—in the OAS, in the United Nations, or in any other meeting that could be useful—without limiting our freedom of action.

"We have no wish to war with the Soviet Union. . . . [but] Any hostile move anywhere in the world against the safety and freedom of peoples to whom we are committed—including in particular the brave people of West Berlin—will be met by whatever action is needed."

The fifth and final segment of the speech was directed "to the captive people of Cuba, to whom this speech is being directly carried by special radio facilities."

Arrangements for those "special radio facilities" is one of the untold sidebars to the Cuban missile crisis, and is worth describing for what it reveals about the administration's persistent belief that the Cuban population could be induced to overthrow Castro.

The task was handed to Donald Wilson, the deputy director of the United States Information Agency (USIA), who was substituting for its ailing director, Edward R. Murrow. After identifying nine commercial radio stations in the United States with signals strong enough to reach Cuba, Wilson had the Bell Telephone (later ATT) representative (who was permanently stationed at the White House) surreptitiously link the Voice of America (VOA) Spanish-language broadcast into those stations. He also secretly established direct lines to the phones of each of the station owners and/or managers.

An hour before the president spoke, press secretary Pierre Salinger called each of them. Reading from a prepared script, he asked "in the interest of national security" to allow the White House to take over their stations at 7:00 p.m. to broadcast the president's speech, and to rebroadcast it to Cuba during nighttime hours throughout the crisis.

All agreed.

Recalling the president's editorial changes, Sorensen later wrote that "Kennedy struck from the speech any hint that the removal of Castro was his true aim"—a statement that the language does not support. The section referenced by Sorensen reads more like a call to revolution. "I speak to you as a friend," the president began his Cuban section: ". . . I have watched and the American people have watched with deep sorrow how your nationalist revolution was betrayed—and how your fatherland fell under foreign domination. Now your leaders are no longer Cuban leaders inspired by Cuban ideals. They are puppets and agents of an international conspiracy which has turned Cuba against your friends and neighbors in the Americas—and turned it into the first Latin American country to become a target for nuclear war—the first Latin American country to have these weapons on its soil. . . .

"Many times in the past, the Cuban people have risen to throw out tyrants who destroyed their liberty. And I have no doubt that most Cubans today look forward to the time when they will be truly free—free from foreign domination, free to choose their own leaders, free to select their own system, free to own their own land, free to speak and write and worship without fear or degradation. And then shall Cuba be welcomed back to the society of free nations and to the associations of this hemisphere."

The speech ended with the ominous warning that "no one can foresee precisely what course it will take or what costs or casualties will be incurred," and an apparently irresistible peroration: "Our goal is not the victory of might, but the vindication of right—not peace at the expense of freedom, but both peace and freedom, here in this hemisphere, and, we hope, around the world. God willing, that goal will be achieved.

"Thank you and good night."

3

JOHN KENNEDY's gamble with Armageddon had begun. The week of secret preparations in Washington—phase one of the administration's Cuban missile crisis—was over. He had chosen the blockade option, and his speech had metaphorically dealt the cards that he and his Soviet counterpart would play.

Whether either one held a winning hand was not immediately clear, but both would raise the stakes.

35

"Kennedy Sleeps with a Wooden Knife"

October 22, Monday Night, Moscow

If the United States insists on war, we will all meet in hell.
—KHRUSHCHEV TO WILLIAM E. KNOX,
OCTOBER 24, 1962

Until hours before the president's address, the denizens of the Kremlin believed that everything was proceeding as planned. Forty-two thousand troops had survived the difficult six-thousand-mile voyage accompanied by an impressive arsenal of planes, SAMs, and tactical nuclear weapons. Twenty-four MRBMs and their warheads had been unloaded and deployed to their assigned areas around the island. Sixteen IRBMs and their warheads were hidden in ships that were only a few sailing days from Mariel, their intended Cuban port. The reports from the general in charge of the operation, Issa Pliyev, were encouraging.

Khrushchev could hardly contain his exhilaration over the advantages he anticipated from his daring initiative. Speaking to his Presidium colleagues on October 16, he boasted about his imminent foreign policy coup. He was about to even the "balance of fear" with the Americans by establishing a missile base just ninety miles from Florida, and he was confident that President Kennedy would be too scared to do anything about it.

"Kennedy sleeps with a wooden knife," he quipped.

"Why a *wooden* one?" Mikoyan asked.

"When a person goes bear hunting for the first time, he takes a wooden knife with him, so that cleaning his trousers will be easier."

In less than a week every Presidium member would be carrying a figurative "wooden knife."

1

THE FIRST hint that something was amiss arrived in Moscow late on October 22. It was a report that within hours President Kennedy was scheduled to deliver a speech about Cuba. Fearing the worst—that the missiles would be attacked—Khrushchev called the Presidium to an emergency meeting to anticipate what Kennedy would say, and to consider their options. The most widely shared expectation was that the president would announce an imminent invasion, exactly what the missile deployment had been designed to prevent.

"From the very beginning of the crisis," Georgy Korniyenko, the deputy minister of foreign affairs, recalled, "Soviet government officials experienced a sense of fear that increased with every hour that went by." Vladimir Semichastny, the KGB chief, "was in such a situation that I could see anything happening now . . . it became frightening." "The prospect of an exchange of nuclear attacks with the United States," Leonid Brezhnev admitted, "threw me (as, probably, it did Khrushchev) as if into ice cold water."

As Khrushchev discussed the possible scenarios, he lapsed into panic. "We were not going to unleash a war. . . . We just wanted to intimidate them, to deter the anti-Cuban forces," he feebly protested to his equally unhinged colleagues. "We didn't deploy everything we wanted to and we didn't publish the [defense] treaty [with Cuba as Che Guevara had urged]." Perhaps that was a mistake, but this result "was tragic," he confessed. They had come so close to success, but now, suddenly and unexpectedly, they were facing the worst possible disaster. "They can attack us . . . [and] this may end in a big war."

Whatever was going to happen would follow from what Kennedy was about to announce. "There is a possibility they will begin with actions against Cuba," Khrushchev speculated, in which case a proclamation that it was the Soviet Union's obligation to defend its ally might lead them to reconsider.

That was both doubtful and dangerous.

Another possibility was to announce that "all of the equipment belonged to the Cubans and the Cubans would announce that they will respond"—not with ballistic missiles, Khrushchev quickly reassured his overwrought colleagues. The Cubans could reveal that they had the capability to "use the tactical ones."

Such a ploy invited too many unpredictable risks.

There was also the possibility, a long shot to be sure, that Kennedy "might declare a blockade . . . and then do nothing," while insisting the missiles be removed. Since almost all present assumed that the United States intended to invade Cuba, that possibility was promptly set aside. Orders to General Pliyev, the commander in Cuba, stipulating just how to respond to the expected attack were quickly drafted—and almost as quickly redrafted.

The first set of orders reflected the unadulterated fear shared by all. Pliyev was to put his forces "on alert," but was forbidden to use any of the nuclear weapons under his command (reversing the authority that Khrushchev had given him orally in July, when they discussed how he would defend his forces against an American invasion).

On reconsideration, however, such an order seemed pusillanimous. Why had tactical nuclear weapons been deployed with the troops if not to defeat an "imperialist" invasion? The Cuban and Soviet troops would be outnumbered and outgunned. Those weapons—the nuclear-armed Lunas and FKR cruise missiles—were their only chance; they had to be used. So new orders were written that rescinded the restrictions on the use of tactical nuclear weapons and, in so doing, accepted the possibility of precipitating a nuclear war.

The one note of caution was to withhold permission to fire the R-12 MRBMs. That was forbidden without specific orders from Moscow. If an exchange of tactical nuclear weapons erupted, perhaps the nuclear war could be limited to Cuba.

2

IN THEORY the difference between tactical and strategic weapons is clear. Tactical weapons are for use against localized targets, designed to achieve finite results, such as destroying buildings, troops, ships, or tanks. Strategic weapons are far more powerful, designed to wreak massive damage, such as the destruction of a large industrial area or an entire city. Cannons and tanks are tactical weapons; bombers and medium- and intermediate-range and intercontinental missiles are strategic weapons.

But in many ways not generally acknowledged, a tactical nuclear weapon can have a strategic impact. The Lunas shipped to Cuba each had two-kiloton warheads and a range of about twenty-five miles. The FKR cruise missiles had twelve- to twenty-kiloton warheads (equivalent to the Hiroshima and Nagasaki bombs), with enough range and explosive force to decimate U.S. aircraft carriers and other ships participating in an invasion.

A Luna exploded in the air above a beachhead would destroy everything within a half mile, and cause additional radiation injuries and damage beyond. As the historians Aleksandr Fursenko and Timothy Naftali vividly describe the power of these weapons in *One Hell of a Gamble:* "Had Lunas been available to Field Marshal Erwin Rommel, who defended the Normandy coast of France from an Allied invasion in [June] 1944, the Nazis would probably have been able to obliterate all five D-Day beachheads with no more than ten of these weapons."

General Pliyev had at his disposal nuclear warheads for twelve Lunas and twenty-four FKR cruise missiles. If he fired any of them, a conventional invasion would become a nuclear war. The order to use them was ready, but the minister of defense, Marshal Rodion Malinovsky, acting cautiously, argued that if the Americans somehow intercepted it, they would have an excuse to use their own nuclear weapons. Better to wait a few hours to see what Kennedy intended to do.

3

A COURIER from the U.S. Embassy delivered a copy of the president's speech (and an accompanying letter from Kennedy to Khrushchev) to the Kremlin an hour before the president's address. It was 1:00 a.m. in Moscow. Drained with worry, Khrushchev and his colleagues read the text with relief. The news was good; the United States was not going to invade Cuba.

As their mood changed, so did their strategy.

Khrushchev reverted to his combative persona. He did not want a war, and he was now confident that Kennedy didn't either. He so much as said so in the letter that accompanied his speech.

Since the president could not be certain of his intentions, Khrushchev turned bellicose. He faced a new question. He no longer had to consider how much humiliation to bear to prevent a war; the question was now how high he could safely raise the nuclear meniscus to preserve Anadyr? Defense Minister Malinovsky provided support. "The speech on the radio is a pre-election stunt," he told the Presidium. "If an invasion of Cuba will be declared, this will be after another 24 hours has passed in order to get ready."

The Presidium turned first to the thirty Soviet ships transporting troops, munitions, and other supplies to Cuba. Forty hours of sailing time remained before the blockade went into effect, and so a triage was established. The *Aleksandrovsk*, with its cargo of nuclear warheads for the FKR cruise missiles and IRBMs, could beat the blockade if it steered a course to the nearest Cuban port. Four other ships—the *Almeteyevsk, Divnogorsk, Dubna,* and *Nikolayev*—transporting the IRBMs also had a good chance of reaching port safely, and so they too were ordered to proceed. The rest of the armada was instructed to return.

Additional orders raised the meniscus. The four nuclear-armed Foxtrot submarines were to proceed to the blockade line and remain there to protect the five ships racing to Cuban harbors. In addition, Soviet and Warsaw Pact commands were "to raise the military readiness of the military, navy and air forces." All leaves were suspended, as were the discharges of recruits serving in the Soviet strategic rocket forces, submarine commands, and antiaircraft units.

After settling responses to the military-related issues, the Presidium turned to formulating a political strategy. It would publicly protest the "lawlessness and unprecedented treachery" of the Americans by immediately bringing the matter to the UN Security Council. "The Charter of the UN was being trampled on," the meeting notes record, and the "peoples of all countries must raise their voices." There was also a cryptic notation in those notes suggesting that, from the first, Khrushchev and his colleagues intended to resolve the crisis through diplomacy: "All issues in dispute—by means of negotiations."

Khrushchev's final task of his long first crisis night was to respond to Kennedy's letter. Over the course of the next six days—the final day of the crisis being Sunday, October 28—the president and the Soviet leader exchanged ten letters.

Beyond the public pronouncements of the two governments, the debates at the United Nations, and the decision-making debates in the White House and Kremlin, the Kennedy-Khrushchev correspondence reveals how the men who were ultimately responsible for deciding how the crisis would end maneuvered to avoid "the final failure."

Arguably, the letters contributed to transforming the two leaders from erstwhile enemies into allies, each driven by fear of a dreadful mistake, each increasingly fearful of an unintentional catastrophe. "War can happen as a result of purely psychological circumstances," Khrushchev had warned his colleagues earlier. "When military emergencies are declared, one of the people who have access to nuclear weapons might lose his nerve, and he can pull all of us into the war. It won't be clear in the country where [the missile] falls whether it was accidental or intentional."

4

KENNEDY'S LETTER of October 22 was a synopsis of his speech, reworked to be more accommodating and to the point. He emphasized that while the missiles must be removed, a diplomatic solution was possible. "I have not assumed," the president wrote, "that you or any other sane man would, in this nuclear age, deliberately plunge the world into war which it is crystal clear no country could win and which could only result in catastrophic consequences to the whole world, including the aggressor."

But, "I must tell you that the United States is determined that this threat to the security of this hemisphere be removed," he repeated. "At our meeting in Vienna and subsequently, I expressed our readiness and desire to find, through peaceful negotiation, a solution to any and all problems that divide us."

On October 23 those problems had no obvious solution.

Kennedy's letter had begun with the polite salutation "Sir" and had signed off, "Sincerely, John F. Kennedy." Whether or not Khrushchev had taken note of that is unknown, but he was in no mood to reciprocate. "Mr. President," he began and concluded with his signature. In between was anger and bluster. Kennedy's speech was "a serious threat to peace," and a gross violation of the UN Charter.

The blockade was illegal, an "undisguised interference in the internal affairs of the Republic of Cuba, the Soviet Union and other states." The weapons being sent to Cuba are for defensive purposes only.

The "actions pursued by you," on the other hand, "may lead to catastrophic consequences for world peace."

36

"A Game Which We Don't Know the Ending Of"

October 23, Tuesday Morning

What we are doing is throwing down a card on the table
in a game which we don't know the ending of.
—PRESIDENT KENNEDY TO EXCOMM, OCTOBER 23

On Tuesday, October 23, all elements of the crisis came into play.
Ambassador Adlai Stevenson presented a resolution to the Security
Council condemning the Soviet deployment. Dean Rusk and Edwin
Martin appeared before the Organization of American States to
solicit its support. Adm. Robert Dennison, the commander in chief
of Atlantic forces (CINCLANT), ordered his ships to their quarantine stations. The army and marine corps prepared for an invasion.
Tactical air command units loaded nuclear weapons. An armed battalion was prepared to challenge any Soviet or East German attempt
to blockade West Berlin. And the Strategic Air Command advanced
to defense condition three [DEFCON 3], two short of nuclear war
[DEFCON 1].

Across the country Americans emptied supermarket shelves and
wondered if they would live to consume their purchases. "The reaction among students [at Columbia University]," Professor Richard
Neustadt noted, "was qualitatively different from anything I've ever
witnessed. . . . These kids were literally scared for their lives." In a
letter to a friend, Jonathan Schell, who, twenty years later, would
write *The Fate of the Earth*, the classic study of the consequences of
a nuclear war, wrote that there was much talk at Harvard "about the
possibilities of being blown up."

In Cuba, Fidel Castro began to rally his forces. "The nation has
woken up on a war footing, ready to repulse any attack," he dictated

for the front page of the newspaper *Revolución*. "We shouldn't worry about the Yankees," he told his colleagues. "They're the ones who should worry about us."

As the Soviet submarines approached the quarantine area, Presidium members began to have second thoughts about their deployment. They were certain to be detected, Anastas Mikoyan warned, and urged that they be recalled. His argument carried, but too late. The U.S. Navy's antisubmarine forces had spotted submarine B-59.

1

ASSEMBLING AT 9:00 a.m., the Chiefs first considered how best to monitor the Soviet-Cuban reaction to the president's speech. Low-level reconnaissance flights were the eyes of choice, and a call to McNamara, who was at the White House attending the morning ExComm meeting, explained that six flights were needed to photograph all the missile sites. The flights were approved by 11:00 a.m.

Looking ahead, the Chiefs again discussed the possibility of an S-75 Dvina SAM destroying a U2 over Cuba. They reached a curious consensus. If a U2 was shot down, one to two more U2 flights should be sent daily over Cuba "until another U-2 loss occurred. Then determine whether the projected attrition rate was acceptable. If so, continue the flights. If not, attack all surface-to-air missile sites and then resume U-2 flights."

Coincidentally, ExComm discussed the U2 question, but reached a stricter decision. It recommended that any offending SA-2 site be destroyed and, if additional incidents occurred, eliminate the entire SAM network.

At 11:25 General Taylor arrived with "a somewhat different guidance from the White House." The blockade was to go into effect the next day, Wednesday, October 24, at 9:00 a.m., he reported, an error that reflected the strain he and all the others were under. He had transposed Greenwich Mean Time to Eastern Standard Time rather than Eastern Daylight Time [EDT]. The blockade was scheduled to begin at 10:00 a.m. EDT.

2

THE PRESIDENT'S quarantine announcement had initiated a crisis in slow motion, intently watched by an anxious world. Before considering the U2 issue, ExComm spent almost an hour—after an intelligence briefing from DCI McCone—plotting public relations strategies. To maintain allied backing, public support was required, but hard questions were being asked. Editorials in the French, West German, and UK press suggested that the American reaction was irresponsible, out of proportion. "The President had no moral right, some [British] newspapers said, to endanger world peace for the sake of a few real or imaginary missiles in Cuba."

"The British [press] today are saying our action is too [unclear]," the president fumed. "The Manchester [Guardian] and all the lousy British press. They're not even with us today." Nor was Canada's prime minister, John Diefenbaker. In addition, the Scandinavian governments were skeptical.

In 1962 world opinion counted. The Cold War was still as much a contest for the hearts and minds of the uncommitted as it was a potential military struggle. Was the U.S. action justified? If Soviet ships challenged the blockade, would they be fired on? Would the Cuban air force intervene? Would a nuclear war begin with a skirmish at sea, as Senator Fulbright had warned?

There were thirty-eight and a half tense hours between the end of the president's speech and the onset of the blockade, and the administration devoted much of that time to justifying its actions. The endorsement of journalists appeared as important to the president as the approval of congressional leaders. "Will you see Scotty [Reston, the *New York Times* chief Washington correspondent]?", Kennedy asked McNamara. He had briefed 125 journalists, he said, but agreed that "we need more than that."

And there were more. George Ball reported speaking with Reston, columnist Stewart Alsop, Alfred Friendly of the *Washington Post*, and Walter Lippmann, by far the most influential columnist in the United States. Bundy suggested that someone contact *New York Times* editorial board member Arthur Krock. "Who wants to talk to [Hearst columnist] Bill [William S.] White?" the president asked.

The litany eventually included Philip Graham, the publisher of the *Washington Post*, Benjamin McKelway, the editor of the *Washington Star*, and Hanson Baldwin, the independent-minded *New York Times* military affairs reporter.

3

THE PRESIDENT had not yet considered the details of the blockade. He had been briefed by Admiral Anderson on the navy's standard operating procedures for enforcing a blockade, but he had not made it clear to the admiral that the blockade was a political message: Khrushchev's missiles had to go, but a deal was possible. Did that call for different procedures? If so, what were they?

For the time being the Pentagon's plans would prevail. As soon as the OAS acted, McNamara advised the president to issue the quarantine proclamation effective at dawn on Wednesday, October 24. The navy wanted to intercept the *Kimovsk*, a ship with hatches large enough to accept missiles; a delay would allow it to outrun the blockade.

"Wouldn't you guess anything that has a missile on it would be turned around last night?" the president asked, reasoning (correctly) that Khrushchev would not want a Soviet missile to fall into American hands. "We just have to assume," he repeated, "that any Russian ship, in view of our statement, that has offensive weapons will be turned around now."

There was no evidence of that, McNamara countered, and continued to press his case. "I think that it is extremely important to try to pick a ship that has offensive weapons on it. It would be . . . an unfortunate incident if we . . . disable[d] [a ship] and found it didn't have offensive weapons on it. That would be a poor way to start."

It was a gamble. "What we are doing," Kennedy reminded his advisers, "is throwing down a card on the table in a game which we don't know the ending of."

One ending was likely to begin with an invasion. Preparations by the navy, marines, and air force were well under way, McNamara explained, but "the most important single action we need to take, and the one with the longest lead time, is the chartering of merchant vessels, cargo vessels in particular." About 134 ships were needed, and almost 100 would have to be requisitioned, 60–70 percent of them from East Coast ports, "a tremendous dislocation of shipping."

That dislocation troubled DCI McCone, a former business executive. McNamara's plan was going to have an adverse effect on many industries, he warned. The lumber industry in the Northwest, for example, depended on the availability of American-flag ships. "What you do by preempting these ships is . . . [to] turn the entire East Coast lumber business over to Canada," McCone persisted until the president, obviously annoyed by his DCI's focus on business interests, put an end to the discussion.

The Chiefs' request for additional low-level photography was discussed next, but it too became a public relations issue. The military wanted those photographs for its attack profiles. But they were also useful, McNamara suggested, to convince the skeptics in Europe and elsewhere that the missiles really existed. "The question of evidence is becoming of great importance in the international debate," Bundy added. "We've had a number of calls, both from Mr. Stevenson and from Mr. [John] McCloy, emphasizing the importance of proof at the UN."

"There is a question about whether these things really exist?" the president asked, sounding incredulous.

"Oh, Mr. President," Bundy responded, "we have an immediate question as to what to say about what we now know." The photographs had been shown to journalists and to friends, but they had not been published or viewed in the UN Security Council. This was being corrected, he said, but to make the American case more convincing, Stevenson believed that the locations of the missile sites should be revealed.

The president hesitated—until McCone reminded him of the hostile editorials in the British and French press, and the statement by Mexico's president López Mateos that, "if the evidence was conclusive, the attitude of Mexico toward Castro and Cuba would change."

Invading Cuba was still a possibility, and the president was fully engaged with its preparations. "The question is," he reminded his advisers, "whether we are doing all the things that we would have to do [for an invasion]?" Were the 82nd and 101st Airborne Divisions ready?

They were. In addition, he was told, marines were moving from the West Coast, and an armored division from Fort Hood in Texas was also moving into position. It was not necessary to call up the reserves, McNamara explained, but the tours of all navy and marine corps personnel were being extended.

President Kennedy then turned to a topic he knew intimately— airfields in Florida. He had wintered for decades at the Kennedy compound at 1095 N. Ocean Blvd, in Palm Beach, and had flown in and out of its nearby airports. He knew (better than General Taylor) that "West Palm Beach is a pretty good [air]field and it was a good base in the [Second World] war, and it isn't used much now." Was the air force aware of this? Were the planes at Florida air bases dispersed? Or were they lined up as easy targets for a reprisal strafing run?

General Taylor's assurances aside, the president wanted a reconnaissance plane to photograph the airfields. "You see," he told Taylor, "these people don't know that we're maybe going to hit a SAM site tomorrow and their reprisal would be to strafe on our fields."

4

THE UNITED NATIONS was about to become the global stage on which the public phase of the crisis would be played out, a high priority for President Kennedy. He had recruited John McCloy, a Republican and acknowledged tough negotiator, to return from Europe and act as Stevenson's deputy under the pretense of bipartisanship. In fact he was the ambassador's "minder," detailed to ensure that Adlai forcefully promoted the president's positions.

Public relations was critical, Stevenson and McCloy argued. It was necessary to present irrefutable evidence that Soviet offensive missiles were in Cuba. Saying that we had proof was not enough. Many delegates—even from friendly countries—were skeptical. Hard evidence was needed to convince them that the United States was being truthful. Photographs of the missile installations, Stevenson insisted, and a map that identified their locations, were the minimal requirements for countering Soviet denials.

It was another of Stevenson's intuitive diplomatic initiatives—an unprecedented revelation of intelligence sources—that proved brilliantly effective when executed.

"I'll do two things," CIA director McCone conceded. "I'll have [Arthur] Lundahl [the head of the CIA's National Photographic Intelligence Center] come up there to work with you. Then I'll be prepared to get this other stuff [today's low-level photography] up to you just as quick as available."

When the conversation ended, McCone remarked to George Ball, "If it's this hard to start a blockade around Cuba, how the hell did we ever start World War II?" (We didn't. Germany and Japan did that.)

5

SHORTLY AFTER 11:00 a.m., when the ExComm meeting ended, the president retired to the mansion, where he met with his personal assistant, Priscilla Wear, dubbed "Fiddle" by the Secret Service. By 11:35 he was back in the Oval Office, ready to switch from crisis mode to the routine of accepting the credentials of the new ambassador from Jamaica.

He then edited a State Department letter to the president of Ghana, Kwame Nkrumah, who had become increasingly hostile to the United States. "It does seem to me regrettable," he dictated, "in view of my persistent support of the concept of national independence and sovereignty in Africa . . . as well as my long interest in Ghana, that Ghana finds itself unable to support on so few occasions the positions taken by the United States at the United Nations."

Nkrumah would soon have the opportunity to reconsider his nation's policies.

A series of phone calls followed. There was a discussion with Gilpatric about a proposal for a governors' conference on civil defense. ("We really ought to get some civil defense arrangements in those communities which are within the range of these things," the president acknowledged.) Another call discussed a *Life* magazine article on the crisis that his press secretary, Pierre Salinger, was helping to arrange. And a call to Gen. Lucius Clay, who had served as the head of the military government in the U.S. occupation zone of Germany.

President Kennedy began his conversation with the retired general by reading him the text of Khrushchev's response to his speech, which he had just received. It accused the United States of violating the Charter of the United Nations and international norms regarding freedom of navigation, and conducting aggression against Cuba and the Soviet Union. It insisted that regardless of classification, the armaments in Cuba were strictly defensive, "to secure the Cuban Republic from the attack of an aggressor." And it concluded with the hope that the United States would renounce the actions that "could lead to catastrophic consequences for peace throughout the world."

There was no hint of reprisals in Khrushchev's letter, but Kennedy surmised that "we can anticipate difficulties in Berlin as well as other places." He hoped that Clay might come to Washington later in the week. "It seems to me," Kennedy reiterated, "[that] Berlin is a key problem, as it has been from the beginning in this whole matter."

Turning from the potential threat to Berlin to the more immediate prospect of a dangerous incident at sea, Kennedy was back on the phone to Gilpatric. He had heard a report, he said, "that the Russian ships were not going to stop and that we were going to have to sink them in order to stop them." Had the navy been issued instructions about what it could and could not do if its blockade was challenged? "We'd want two or three things," he said, which, tellingly, had more to do with politics and public relations than with military procedures.

"First," he told the deputy secretary of defense, "I'd think we'd want to have some control over cameras aboard these boats so that we don't have a lot of people shooting a lot of pictures, which, in the press, might be embarrassing to us." He wanted all sailors to turn in their cameras. "Secondly . . . where they [the navy] ought to fire [at the Soviet ship], or whether they ought to go through three or four steps such as asking them to stop. If they don't stop, asking them to have their crew come above deck so that they don't [get injured]. And three, so that we have this record made."

Nor did the president forget his earlier order to send a reconnaissance aircraft over Florida. "You're getting that one for me," he asked Gilpatric, "aren't you, of those Florida bases?" And, "Have you taken a look at West Palm Beach?"

As the president worked the telephone, the first good news of

the day arrived. The response of the OAS, which had been anticipated for a week, was better than expected. The U.S. resolution had
received unanimous support.

Rusk had been persuasive, and every Latin American government
had backed the American resolution to force the Soviet missiles out
of Cuba.

37

"The Mobs Turned Up in London Instead of Havana"

October 23, Tuesday Evening

The mobs [of protesters] that we stimulate[d] turned up
in London instead of Havana. Two thousand people stormed
the American Embassy.
—DEAN RUSK, REPORT ON INTERNATIONAL REACTION
TO JFK SPEECH. OCTOBER 23

As scheduled, ExComm assembled at 6:00 p.m. The first item on
the agenda was the proclamation authorizing the quarantine. Read-
ing the first sentence brought Kennedy up short. It referred to the
"Sino-Soviet powers" establishing "an offensive military capability in
Cuba." Why were the Chinese in this proclamation? he asked Rusk:
"Is that necessary, and why?"

That was the language used in the OAS resolution, and in the
resolution submitted to the UN Security Council, Rusk explained,
leaving the president convinced that there was nothing, absolutely
nothing, that he did not have to review. The witlessness of involving
China was not going to be received well in Asia, he muttered.

1

AFTER THE rest of the proclamation was reviewed, the question of
how to implement the blockade was debated: "Can we search a vessel
which was proceeding toward Cuba, was hailed, requested to stop,
did not do so, but turned around and proceeded to reverse direction away from Cuba?" McNamara asked. Both he and the president
agreed: "Not right now."

That issue appeared settled until, once again, Bobby's zeal got the better of him. Wouldn't it be "a hell of an advantage," he said, to capture a ship with missiles and examine it? Why not establish a zone and pick up any ship within that zone? We could say: "You don't know whether, when they turn around, whether they're going to try to come into Cuba in a different fashion." But on second thought, he conceded, perhaps it shouldn't be done during the first forty-eight hours.

Though not opposed to capturing a ship transporting missiles, the president repeated his earlier conviction that Khrushchev was not about to use such a vessel "to have the test case. They're going to turn that thing around."

Weirdly, however, enthusiasm for the attorney general's idea caught on. Even McNamara, who moments earlier had declared "I don't believe we should undertake such an operation," reversed course: "This ought to be our primary objective, early after the effective date of the blockade, to grab a vessel obviously loaded with offensive weapons."

Only Rusk had the presence of mind to object: "From the Soviet point of view, they're going to be as sensitive as a boil," he said. "The question is whether they think we're really trying to capture, and seize, and analyze, and examine their missiles and their warheads and things." The purpose of the quarantine, he emphasized, was "to keep them [missiles] out of Cuba." Then, just as he was about to add something, the president interrupted.

2

KENNEDY'S CONFIDENCE that the blockade would lead to a peaceful diplomatic settlement had waned. What the Soviets intended to do, he said, would become clear the next day. If they challenged the blockade, "We'll have to shoot at them," but he didn't know what they are going to do. "So I think we're going to have all our troubles tomorrow morning. Let's get on with this thing [the proclamation] now."

Before moving on, however, the historian in John Kennedy turned back to 1948–49, and his analysis was pessimistic: "They're [the Soviets] actually faced with the same problem we were faced with in the Berlin blockade," he analogized. Truman had the option of challenging Stalin's blockade by sending an armed convoy up the autobahn toward West Berlin. There was the belief afterward, he added, that the Soviets wouldn't have attacked that convoy. "Now, that's about what they're going to do next. We've given them as clear notice as they gave us. Even in '47 and '48, when we had an atomic monopoly, we didn't push it, [but it] looks like they're going to.

"What are the other policy questions?" he snapped.

The first day of the quarantine posed two requirements, McNamara responded. The first was to establish the quarantine line far enough from Cuba to avoid being attacked by the Cuban air force, and the second was to find, stop, and search a ship carrying offensive weapons "and get the evidence."

The *Kimovsk* was the target of choice, and it seemed to Douglas Dillon that a consensus was building to send the navy beyond the blockade line to seize it. "Picking up Soviet ships anywhere, just on the prima facie supposition that they're heading toward Cuba"—he cautioned—"well, it'll get us into difficulties," he wisely (for the first time) counseled.

A convoluted discussion about exactly what the proclamation should and should not say proceeded from Dillon's warning, until Ambassador Thompson urged its prompt publication to give Khrushchev as much time as possible to understand "that there is an alternative to going ahead with forcing this thing, which makes us fire on them . . . then retaliation in Berlin."

His second suggestion was "to put the ball in [Khrushchev's] court" by immediately answering his letter.

"I have received your letter of October 23rd," the State Department's draft reply read. "I think you will recognize that the step which started the current chain of events was the action of your government in secretly furnishing offensive weapons to Cuba." The issue will be discussed in the Security Council, and "I hope that you will issue immediately the necessary instructions to your ships to observe the terms of the quarantine, established by the order of the Organization of American States this afternoon. . . . We have no desire to seize or fire upon your vessels."

The draft—with the last sentence inserted by the president—was wired to the U.S. Embassy in Moscow within the hour, with instructions to deliver it promptly to Khrushchev.

3

WITH THE proclamation and the response to Khrushchev out of the way, Rusk reported the global reaction to the president's speech. It was not what Kennedy had expected.

"The mobs [of protesters] that we stimulate[d] turned up in London instead of Havana," the secretary of state reported. "Bertrand Russell's [British peace movement] people stormed the [American] embassy there. We haven't had any reports of any disorder happening in Cuba," he commented with regret, and McCone added that a nationwide strike was being organized in Chile.

Bad news, but Kennedy was too worried about the dangers at sea he was going to confront tomorrow to focus on riots abroad today. What was the navy going to do in the morning, he asked, "when these eight [Soviet] vessels continue to sail on?"

There was a tacitly shared assumption among ExComm members and the JCS that every Soviet ship would be subject to inspection, and that any ship refusing to cooperate would be forced, one way or another, to yield. General Taylor's response to the president's question—"Shoot the rudders off of them"—was therefore not out of line. But it was a wake-up call that served an unintended purpose. It stirred McNamara to warn: "Max. . . . We want to be very careful," and he went on to initiate a discussion of tactics that redefined how the blockade would be conducted.

It made no sense to fire on a Soviet ship carrying wheat or medicine to Cuba, the defense secretary said, and suggested not stopping any ship until one was found that appeared to be carrying offensive weapons. Given the limited intelligence currently available, he believed it was better to wait until early morning before issuing precise instructions to the navy.

Like the president, McNamara was becoming increasingly pessimistic that the blockade would lead to a peaceful resolution. Assuming that Khrushchev would instruct his ship captains not to "stop under any circumstances," he worried that the navy would fire on a ship carrying baby food and "We shoot three nurses," Bundy interjected.

"That's what could happen," the president agreed, and repeated what was fast becoming a shared fatalism: "They're going to keep going." Without mentioning Fulbright's warning that the blockade was the riskiest option, he spelled out a scenario that tracked the senator's concern: The navy would disable the uncooperative vessel, and then its boarding party would be fired on with machine guns. "They may have 5 or 6 or 700 people aboard there with guns." Things could get so bad that "you may have to sink it rather than just take it," he concluded.

And then the president's self-deprecating sense of humor, which he often deployed to mask his deepest anxieties, surfaced: "I'll tell you," he said, "for those who considered the blockade course to be the easy way, I told them not to do it," which set off a round of boisterous laughter.

But the president remained serious, He again raised the machine-gun scenario and returned to his earlier concern "that nobody on our boats have cameras"—an order already issued, McNamara assured him.

As the conversation progressed, cautious suggestions replaced the uncompromising confidence expressed during earlier meetings. If a Soviet ship was disabled but refused to accept a boarding party, Kennedy now thought that "at the beginning it would be better . . . not to try to board it."

"Well, Mr. Secretary," the president said to McNamara after a discussion about how a Soviet submarine in the area could influence the navy's tactics, "I think I'd like to make sure that you have reviewed these instructions that go out to the navy, having in mind this conversation that we've just had."

"I will do so again tonight, Mr. President," he replied.

4

THE FINAL segment of the meeting reinforced the president's fear that a failure to end the crisis peacefully would produce horrific results. The assistant secretary of defense for civil defense, Steuart Pittman, summarized how prepared (more accurately, how unprepared) the nation was for a nuclear strike. He reported that ninety-two million people, mostly in fifty-eight cities with populations over one hundred thousand, were within range of the MRBMs, and sufficient shelters (with limited protection) were available in urban areas for forty million.

Having become increasingly pessimistic about the quarantine, the president explained that "the most likely problem we're going to have in the next ten days is if we decide to invade Cuba. They may fire these weapons." Could the vulnerable cities be evacuated before an invasion?

"If we knew that there would be no nuclear response," Pittman explained, evacuating the cities "might make some sense." But urban shelters were the only protection against fallout; there was no defense against radiation in rural areas.

"What is it that we ought to do with the population of the affected areas, in case some bombs go off?" a frustrated president asked.

"I got the conclusion," John McCone wrote in his summary of this exchange, "that not very much could or would be done."

"In reality," the historian Alice George explained in *Awaiting Armageddon*, "plans to save the president and other officials were inadequate, and strategies to protect the public were even worse. Unwilling to finance an elaborate civil defense program, the government had stocked virtually no public shelters with food and survival supplies.

If war came, most Americans would be on their own."

38

"You Would Have Been Impeached"

October 23, Tuesday Night

There isn't any choice. . . . You would have been impeached.
—ROBERT KENNEDY TO HIS BROTHER

When the meeting adjourned, the president and his brother remained in the Cabinet Room and drifted into a (recorded) discussion that revealed the depth of their shared fatalism. What they did not know—what they could not know—was how thoroughly their anxieties were shared by their counterparts in the Kremlin.

General Taylor's parting remark that everything "on land" was under control, but "at sea I'm not quite sure," did little to buoy their spirits.

"Looks like hell—looks real mean," Jack conceded. "But, on the other hand, there is no other choice. If they get this mean on this one, it's just a question of where they go about it next."

Bobby agreed. "There isn't any choice. . . . You would have been impeached."

"That's what I think," Jack acknowledged. "I would have been impeached. I think they would have moved to impeach."

It was far more likely that inaction would have resulted in a one-term presidency, but rationalizing decisions taken under stress is understandable. The president's next decision was to communicate that stress, and his sense of urgency, to Moscow by sending his brother to talk with the Soviet ambassador.

1

IT WAS after 1:00 a.m. when Anatoly Dobrynin greeted Bobby at the Soviet Embassy's front door. They had met confidentially before, and Dobrynin found his conversations with the AG difficult. Robert Kennedy, he noted in his memoir, was socially awkward, lacked a sense of humor, and "was impulsive and excitable," characteristics on full display as they talked alone in the ambassador's third-floor sitting room. "He was in a state of agitation," Dobrynin recalled, "and what he said was markedly repetitious."

Bobby was angry. Khrushchev had betrayed the president's trust, he told Dobrynin. His brother had "staked his political career" on Moscow's word that only defensive weapons were being sent to Cuba. It was "deliberate deceit which had also compromised the confidential channel." Gromyko, too, had lied to the president. The Soviet Union had violated whatever trust had been established with the administration, and the results could lead to universal disaster.

As he left, Bobby asked what the Soviet ship captains had been ordered to do when they reached the quarantine line. "I replied," Dobrynin noted in his report to Moscow, "that I knew about strict instructions issued earlier: Shipmasters were not to bow to any unlawful demands for a search on the high seas. . . . Robert Kennedy wondered how it all would end, for the Americans were set on stopping our ships by force."

"But that would be an act of war," Dobrynin responded, but Bobby just "shook his head and left," the ambassador reported.

"I conveyed all of Robert Kennedy's harsh statements to Moscow word by word, including those that were not at all flattering to Khrushchev and Gromyko," he recorded in his memoir. It was important to convey "the genuine state of agitation in the President's inner circle."

Apparently the report did exactly that. When Gromyko read Dobrynin's cable he ordered that it not be circulated. He would discuss it confidentially with Khrushchev. Afterward he either kept it with his personal papers or destroyed it, as Dobrynin was never able to locate it in any archive.

Bobby's conversation—perhaps performance is more accurate—clarified for Khrushchev that his options were limited to withdrawal or war.

39

"We Are Trying to Convey a Political Message . . . Not Start a War"

October 23–24, Tuesday Night and Wednesday Morning

There will be no firing of any kind at that Soviet ship without
my personal authority.
—SECRETARY OF DEFENSE MCNAMARA TO
CNO ADM. GEORGE ANDERSON

During the five most dangerous days so far in world history, John
Kennedy dealt with two intertwined challenges. Internationally, he
dueled with Khrushchev, who shared both the president's determination not to back down and his hope that the crisis could be ended
without bloodshed. Domestically, the president contended with the
Joint Chiefs, who believed that he was missing the perfect opportunity to dispose of Castro. They would not disobey his orders, but neither would they monitor their standard operating procedures (SOP)
to conform to the spirit of his strategy. There was a clear disconnect
between the Pentagon and the White House that, in retrospect, was
among the most perilous aspects of the Cuban missile crisis.

1

ADM. GEORGE Whelon Anderson Jr. was a "by the book" officer with
a low opinion of his civilian supervisors. An ardent anti-Communist,
he loathed Castro and judged Khrushchev's secret deployment of
missiles to Cuba an existential threat. He was a leading voice for
bombing the offending weapons, invading the island, and jettisoning
its Communist government. "We should use this particular crisis to
solve the Cuban problem," he told his JCS colleagues.

He considered the quarantine a lame response by a president

who had ducked military intervention at the Bay of Pigs, and seemed intent on repeating his timidity. Surprise air strikes followed by an invasion, Anderson had declared at the Joint Chiefs' first Cuban missile crisis meeting, was "the only way to eliminate the Communist regime from Cuba."

Nor was the CNO happy with the secretary of defense. "Tension between the two had started almost as soon as McNamara took office," according to the historian David Coleman. "Anderson quickly became resentful of McNamara's so-called whiz-kids meddling in navy affairs," and had not been shy about confronting the secretary about the intrusions.

At a JCS meeting Anderson angrily told McNamara: "We are being inundated with demands from your office on matters that are basically the responsibility of the Chief of Naval Operations. . . . These requests are being imposed by one of your staff officers who cannot even pass a U.S. naval security clearance."

It appeared to Anderson, as it did to most of the navy's top brass, that the secretary and his deputies were determined to diminish its missions. Soon after being sworn in, McNamara canceled production of a navy aircraft (F6D Missileer), questioned the merits of nuclear power for submarines and ships, promoted the conveyance of military cargo by air rather than sea, and placed several hundred of the navy's vessels under the control of the U.S. Strike Command. He also insisted that the navy adopt the TFX, the replacement for the air force's F-105. It was "one more way," a military historian observed, "to marginalize Navy requirements."

McNamara, on the other hand, found Anderson arrogant, resistant to rational cost-saving efforts, and generally difficult to work with. Their differences over the TFX, and other disputes, "had even spilled out into press reports." It was a delicate relationship, very hard to maintain under the best of circumstances; no surprise that it came apart during the tension-filled days of the Cuban missile crisis.

The precipitating issue was civilian control over military operations.

To Anderson's way of thinking, there was a bright red line between civilian control over the military, and civilian interference in military operations. He respected the former; it was within the purview of the president, and his designated representatives, to order the

military to carry out a particular task. It was the president's preroga-
tive to review and critique the military's plans for carrying out a task.

But once plans had been approved, and an operation initiated,
civilian interference was unacceptable. He could not abide "amateurs"
telling professionals how to carry out their responsibilities. During the quarantine, he explained in his reminiscences, "We did not
want . . . any intrusion by McNamara or anybody else in the direct
operations of any ship or squadron or anything of the sort." The navy
was in charge, and the navy knew how to manage a blockade; it did
not need coaching.

But coaching—in the form of very specific instructions—was
exactly what the president was determined to impart to any military
commander in a position to ignite a war. At the last ExComm meeting, Kennedy had made it clear to McNamara that he was responsible
for providing Admiral Anderson and his deputies with specific operating instructions.

"I will do so again tonight, Mr. President," McNamara had
replied.

2

THE SURPRISE discovery of two Soviet submarines near the quarantine line led to the first "coaching" crisis. Deeming them a serious
threat, Admiral Anderson immediately alerted his fleet commanders: "I cannot emphasize too strongly how smart we must be to keep
our heavy ships, particularly our carriers, from being hit by surprise
attack from Soviet submarines."

From that point in the crisis through to its conclusion, the
navy's operational nerve centers, Flag Plot (FP) and the more closely
guarded Intelligence Plot (IP), were hives of activity engaged in following the progress of the anti-submarine warfare (ASW) units that
were working to force the Soviet submarines to the surface.

On Monday night, October 22, soon after President Kennedy
completed his address to the nation, McNamara left the White House
for the Pentagon. Accompanied by several members of his staff, the
secretary of the navy, and Admiral Anderson, he arrived at IP for an
update on Soviet submarine and shipping activity. While McNamara
and his staff were informed about the location, speed, and direction

of the Soviet merchant ships headed toward the quarantine line, the submarine activity, considered particularly sensitive by the navy, was imparted only to the Secretary of Defense. The designated submarine intelligence briefer knelt next to McNamara's chair and, using a folding plotting board as a prop, described the situation.

About six hours later (3:00 a.m., Tuesday morning, October 23) McNamara and several assistants returned to Intelligence Plot. Although the secretary had retired to his Pentagon office, where he spent every night during the public phase of the crisis, he had clearly not gone to sleep. He and his staff had reviewed his IP briefings and concluded that something had been overlooked. He was back in search of answers.

An eyewitness recalled the secretary doing a rapid survey of the displays, and then pulling up a chair in front of the large plotting board that showed the quarantine area and the positions of the navy's ships patrolling it.

He seemed particularly concerned with the status of the Soviet Komar (NATO designation) guided-missile boats. Each had two missile-launching tubes that fired a radar-guided Styx missile with a range of fifteen miles. The weapon had a lethal history. In 1956, during the Suez Crisis, an Egyptian Komar missile boat had sunk the Israeli destroyer *Elath* with a single Styx.

Where were the Komars? McNamara asked. After being assured by the duty officer that they were being closely watched, and had not moved from their berths at Mariel and Banes, he departed.

There is no information detailing what he did after leaving IP, but it is clear that he did not get very much sleep before his 9:45 a.m. briefing in FP. He was tense, and the atmosphere in the room was strained. No one knew how the Soviets were going to react to the blockade scheduled to go into effect at 10:00 a.m. the next day, Wednesday, October 24. After being briefed on the locations and progress of the Soviet ships, the status of the submarine search, and the navy's plans for low-level photo reconnaissance flights over Cuba that day, McNamara headed for the White House.

Throughout the day intelligence sources reported intercepting numerous coded high-priority messages from Moscow to its ships bound for Cuba. What these coded messages said could not be deciphered, but it was assumed that they contained instructions to the captains about how to react to U.S. interference when they reached the blockade line. President Kennedy was kept informed.

3

BY THE start of the 6:00 p.m. ExComm meeting (Tuesday evening, October 23), the president's heightened sense of caution, and his discussions with McNamara, had convinced him that the navy needed coaching. "We couldn't get enough details of how the navy was going to carry out this operation," Deputy Secretary of Defense Roswell Gilpatric recalled. "We [McNamara and his staff] were just being assured that . . . the navy would take care of everything," an attitude that did not instill presidential confidence.

"The greatest danger of war as we saw it then," Paul Nitze remembered, "was that we would sink a Russian ship trying to run the blockade. If that happened, it would seem highly doubtful that Khrushchev would hold still without further action."

After signing "the blockade proclamation" (as CIA director John McCone referred to Presidential Proclamation 3504), the president "instructed McNamara to review all details of instructions to the Fleet Commanders regarding procedures to be followed in the blockade."

4

SOON AFTER the ExComm meeting concluded, at 7:30, McNamara called a press conference to discuss the quarantine. To his surprise, reporters kept asking for copies of the U2 photos of the Soviet missiles in Cuba. Intelligence officials were opposed to revealing aerial photography, the secretary responded. But those photos had just been broadcast in Britain by BBC television, the reporters said. Surprised, McNamara confessed that he knew nothing about their release. "[I] felt like an ass out there," he angrily remarked when it was over.

Tired and irritated, he returned with Gilpatric to the Pentagon, and to Flag Plot, to carry out the president's instructions.

It was 8:45 p.m. Tuesday evening, October 23.

In 1962 FP was a secluded room in which every detail of the quarantine was being tracked—although not always with precision, according to Gilpatric. Guarded by marines and furnished with large maps and charts covering all the world's oceans, seas, and water passageways, it reflected the navy's global role. Entering FP for the first time was like stepping into a chamber inhabited by members of a secret order whose proconsul was the chief of Naval Operations [CNO].

5

THERE ARE several versions of what transpired when McNamara and Gilpatric entered FP that night, and each is *in*correct about one or another aspect of the event. The journalist Elie Abel wrote the first draft, which has been repeated for five decades in numerous histories. Abel's most egregious error relates to its timing. He dated the event on Wednesday, October 24, but it occurred on October 23, the night before the blockade went into effect. He also located it in the wrong place: It did not occur in Flag Plot.

In addition to Abel's account, there is Admiral Anderson's retelling, which (not surprisingly) denies that he lost his temper. The most thorough investigation of the event appears in an article by retired navy captain William H. J. Manthorpe Jr., but it is based entirely on internal navy sources, including the CNO's logs. And, finally, there are very detailed statements by McNamara and Gilpatric, which, from both internal and external evidence, appear to be the most accurate rendering.

After entering Flag Plot the secretary quickly surveyed the charts that covered the Caribbean area, noting the locations of the ships that loosely formed the quarantine line. Noticing a ship's marker far removed from the others, he asked the officer on duty—Admiral Anderson was not present at the time—to explain why it was away from the quarantine area. His ambiguous answer annoyed the secretary, who then began to aggressively question him about what would occur on the quarantine line if the captain of a Soviet ship refused to cooperate.

The questions included "what one of our commanders would do if a Soviet ship approached, didn't respond to our signals, didn't stop, or fired when boarded, didn't cooperate—a whole series of possibilities." McNamara "got no answers at all," probably because the unnerved duty officer did not know how to respond.

President Kennedy with his closest confidant: his brother, Robert (left). RFK formally handled domestic issues as the attorney general, but was informally deeply involved in U.S.-Soviet and U.S.-Cuban relations.

On April 17, 1961, a force of 1,400 anti-Castro Cubans trained and led by the CIA landed at the Bay of Pigs. The invaders were quickly defeated by Castro's forces.

(Above) President Kennedy's June 4, 1961, meeting with Khrushchev in Vienna was a diplomatic failure. Khrushchev denounced the American Jupiter missiles in Turkey and threatened the survival of West Berlin.

During the Cuban missile crisis, the Joint Chiefs of Staff with President Kennedy (center) unanimously favored bombing and invading Cuba.

On October 14, 1962, a U2, like the one to the left, flew over Cuba and photographed the construction of medium-range Soviet missile installations. Thus began the Cuban missile crisis.

President Kennedy announced the "quarantine" of Cuba in a public television address on the evening of October 22, 1962.

Adlai Stevenson (at left) warned the president, on the first day of the crisis, that the military solution he favored was likely to begin a war. Kennedy soon came to agree with the diplomatic strategy recommended by his UN ambassador.

(Below) On October 25, in reaction to Soviet denials that their missiles were in Cuba, Ambassador Stevenson dramatically presented photographic evidence to the UN General Assembly, and to millions of American television viewers, that the Soviets were lying.

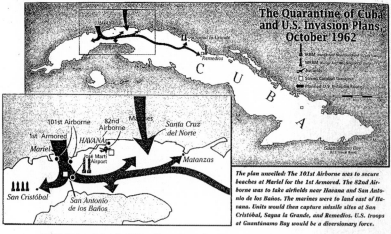

The Quarantine of Cuba and U.S. Invasion Plans, October 1962

The plan unveiled: The 101st Airborne was to secure beaches at Mariel for the 1st Armored. The 82nd Airborne was to take airfields near Havana and San Antonio de los Baños. The marines were to land east of Havana. Units would then capture missile sites at San Cristóbal, Sagua la Grande, and Remedios. U.S. troops at Guantánamo Bay would be a diversionary force.

Graphic by James Lebbad for Military History Quarterly, reprinted by permission. From Dino A. Brugioni, "The Invasion of Cuba." MHQ 4, no. 2 (Winter 1992).

(Top) The Joint Chiefs recommended several days of bombing followed by a massive invasion that was certain to kill many of the 42,000 Soviet troops on the island.

(Center) A map from Cuba's "October Crisis" Museum showing the flight path of Maj. Rudolph Anderson's U2 that a Soviet surface-to-air missile shot down (area circled at lower right) on October 27.

(Right) Entrance to the bunker in the Hotel Nacional in Havana that was later turned into the Crisis museum.

On October 18 Kennedy met with Foreign Minister Andrei Gromyko (center) and Ambassador Anatoly Dobrynin. Gromyko assured Kennedy that the Soviet Union had sent only defensive weapons to Cuba.

The American Jupiter missiles in Turkey shown here were partly responsible for initiating the crisis and secretly partly responsible for its peaceful solution.

A meeting of the Executive Committee of the National Security Council (ExComm). Every member, with the exception of Adlai Stevenson, at one time urged bombing and or invasion.

White House counsel and close adviser to the president Ted Sorensen wrote Kennedy's October 22 "quarantine speech."

Chairman of the Joint Chiefs of Staff Gen. Maxwell Taylor favored bombing and invasion, as did his colleagues. Secretary of Defense Robert McNamara alternated between supporting a military attack and diplomacy.

Crew #1 Wave Makers

John Bordne   Richard Marshal   SSgt Voorhes   Eugene Boozer   Captain Bassett   James Day   William O'Hara   Michael Schaubach
Mech #2   Mech #5   Mech #1   Launch Officer   Mech 5   Mech #4   Mech #3
                                                                   (Not assigned to a crew)

Capt. William Bassett (fourth from right) and his missile crew on Okinawa were allegedly ordered to fire missiles at Soviet and Chinese targets. Bassett, like Soviet Navy officer Vasily Arkhipov, may have prevented a nuclear war by remaining calm and analyzing the situation as a mistake.

LAUNCH SITE 3
CRISTOBAL, CUBA
OCTOBER 1962

NUCLEAR WARHEAD BUNKER U/C

LAUNCH AREA

PERMANENT BLDGS

TRENCH

A Soviet missile launch site on October 27, the last and most dangerous day of the crisis. Several of the Soviet missile sites were operational.

The crisis safely behind them, President Kennedy, Secretary of State Dean Rusk (center), and Secretary of Defense Robert McNamara relax happily in the White House.

Herblock got it right.

Khrushchev sent Anastas Mikoyan to patch up relations with Castro. This photograph makes it clear that it was not an easy assignment.

McNamara and Gilpatric left FP and headed for Admiral Anderson's office. "We went into his room, and he had a phalanx of fifteen or twenty, at least, navy brass all lined up around him," Gilpatric recalled. "We were the two civilians. Almost certainly, the duty officer had called and briefed the CNO about McNamara's questions and Anderson was very high in color and obviously very, very angry about the whole, what he regarded [as an] intrusion." McNamara repeated his questions: What was the navy planning to do when the first Soviet vessel approached the quarantine line?

It would be stopped, Anderson replied.

How would it be stopped? And in what language would the Soviet vessel be hailed?

Not unreasonable questions under the circumstances. Perhaps because Anderson did not know the answer, and felt humiliated in front of his lieutenants, he responded belligerently: "How the hell do I know? I presume we will hail it in English."

And what, McNamara wanted to know, would the navy do if the Soviet ship did not stop?

First a shot would be fired across its bow, and if it continued, then its rudder would be taken out, the CNO responded angrily. "You've imposed a quarantine," he told the secretary, "and our job is to stop the vessels from passing the line."

"Let me tell you something," McNamara firmly replied. "There will be no firing of any kind at that Soviet ship without my personal authority, and I'm not going to give you permission until I discuss it with the president. We are trying to convey a political message, we're not trying to start a war."

"And then Anderson just sort of exploded," Gilpatric recalls. "And I don't know whether he said Goddamnit, but he used some very strong expletive to the effect that 'This is none of your goddamn business. This is what we're here to do. We know how to do this. We're doing this ever since the days of John Paul Jones, and if you will just go back to your quarters, Mr. Secretary, we'll take care of this.'"

"During this tirade," Gilpatric could see "the color rising in McNamara's neck and face. It wasn't clear at first whether he was going to reply in kind, or just leave, which is what he did. There was little point engaging in a shouting match with Anderson in front of a collection of Admirals and Captains."

Furious, the "two civilians" returned to McNamara's office. "That's the end of Anderson," McNamara told Gilpatric. "He won't be reappointed, and we've got to find a replacement for him. As far as I'm concerned, he's lost my confidence."

In the meantime, back in Anderson's office, a discussion commenced about the confrontation. With McNamara out of the room, the emotional energy subsided and rational bureaucratic behavior took over. Damage control was required.

Within thirty minutes an officer from the CNO's office appeared in McNamara's quarters and requested a detailed list of the questions the secretary wanted answered. "From that point on," Gilpatric remembered, "they were submitting, asking approvals." Navy briefings that updated McNamara about activities on the quarantine line were now offered almost every three hours.

McNamara had "really accomplished what he wanted." The navy would follow the president's coaching.

6

THE COMMANDER of the Strategic Air Command (SAC) was as independent minded as his navy counterpart, and in a better position to avoid coaching. The navy's blockade, and its critical role in support of an invasion, commanded Kennedy's attention, but he had not inquired about SAC's operations.

Since 1948, when Gen. Curtis LeMay assumed its command, SAC had been hyped as the nation's ultimate deterrent, and had managed to operate more independently than the other services. "It was a fiefdom, not easily challenged," according to historian Fred Kaplan. Promoted to vice chief of staff of the air force in 1957, LeMay continued to protect SAC's independence despite his skeptical view of his successor, Gen. Thomas Power. "A brutal easily angered man who struck Air Staff officers outside SAC as dim witted and insensitive to the dilemmas that the [nuclear] bomb raised," his rigid demands for discipline and fealty led LeMay (among others) to suspect that he was mentally "not stable" and a "sadist."

"Why are you so concerned with saving their lives?" he famously responded at a Rand Corporation briefing on counterforce [avoiding cities] nuclear-targeting strategy. "The whole idea is to kill the bastards," and added: "Look. At the end of the war, if there are two Americans and one Russian, we win." (To which the briefer responded: "Well, you'd better make sure that they're a man and a woman.")

On October 24 General Power was determined that SAC would be ready to "kill the bastards."

The Standard Operating Procedures (SOP) that guided U.S. military commands was clear. In nonthreatening conditions DEFCON 5 set the readiness status of U.S. forces throughout the world. Cold War tensions often moved the alert status to DEFCON 4. Following the president's "quarantine" speech, a higher alert, DEFCON 3, was authorized by the JCS, with the approval of the secretary of defense and the president.

However, on Wednesday, October 24, at 10:00 a.m., as the quarantine commenced, General Power advanced SAC's forces to DEFCON 2, one condition short of nuclear war, the first and only time that level of nuclear alert has been instituted. He broadcast his order to his command "in the clear," assuring that Soviet monitors would intercept the message. "The immediate effect of this escalation," the military historian Blaine Pardoe noted, "was that the USSR's Air Defense Command brought its level of alert to the same level as that of the United States."

"What [General Power] did," Kennedy's national security adviser McGeorge Bundy told ABC news anchor Peter Jennings in 1992, "was to engage in a process of alert . . . designed as a powerful signal to Moscow. I didn't know about that at the time, and don't believe that that kind of use of strategic forces for diplomatic signaling should happen without presidential approval. So that was very much of a loose end."

General Power was "freelancing," Jennings concluded.

Secretary of Defense McNamara was as uninformed as Bundy. Asked directly, in a 1986 interview, whether the move to DEFCON 2 was authorized, he responded with a wager based on an assumption. "I suppose it's conceivable [that it was not authorized]," he admitted, "but SAC was an extraordinarily well-disciplined force and I believe that we had procedures in effect for the declaration of alerts. I would be willing to bet 10 to 1 that SAC didn't declare an alert that was not properly authorized." Which is to say that he, the secretary of defense, did not recall authorizing DEFCON 2.

Actually, McNamara would have won his bet, but it would have been a hollow victory: Power's order to DEFCON 2 was authorized, but through a process that assured that neither the national security adviser, the secretary of defense, nor the president would realize what was happening.

It was authorization cloaked in obfuscation, and McNamara's answer hinted at that possibility. "To the extent that the procedures allowed them to move to a higher alert status without permission from higher authority," he continued, "they may have done so."

On October 22, as the president prepared to address the nation, the move toward DEFCON 2 began within the JCS. General LeMay sent a memorandum to General Taylor with two proposals. The first: "(a) Direct SAC to initiate 1/8 airborne alert beginning at noon local time today . . . [and] (b) Direct SAC to generate its force toward a maximum readiness posture, also at noon today. The strategic air forces will be in maximum readiness by noon tomorrow, the force generation should not be apparent until after the President's speech tonight."

As chairman of the JCS, Taylor authorized LeMay's first suggestion with a penciled "OK," and wrote "A-hour to be blockade hour," next to the second recommendation. Officially, from the JCS point of view, SAC was thus authorized "to generate its force toward a maximum readiness posture," with the commencement of the blockade.

At 8:06 p.m. EDT, the JCS "directed [Power] to initiate generation of SAC forces effective 241400Z [October 24, 10:00 a.m. EDT]," a cable noted. Stating clearly that this order was limited to SAC. The message read: "A-Hour worldwide has not, repeat, not, been established."

The transmittal notice (the distribution form) indicated that the White House was not on the list of original recipients. Someone penciled the White House in, but it is not clear whether that was done before or after the notice was initially distributed.

No orders were disobeyed, and no procedures were violated, but at the same time no effort was made by the Joint Chiefs to be certain that their civilian leaders understood that the phrase "maximum readiness posture" authorized General Power to proceed to DEFCON 2.

It was authorized "freelancing," and definitely a "loose end."

40

"A Russian Submarine—
Almost Anything but That"

His [JFK's] hand went up to his face and covered his mouth.
He opened and closed his fist. His face seemed drawn, his
eyes pained, almost gray. . . . "Isn't there some way we can
avoid having our first exchange with a Russian submarine—
almost anything but that?"
—RFK OBSERVING JFK, OCTOBER 24

If there was going to be a war it would begin within the hour. As
Soviet ships steamed toward the quarantine line, U.S. anti-submarine
warfare (ASW) units reported at least two Russian submarines in
their vicinity. They were being tracked and harassed with the intention of forcing them to surface.

There was no indication that Khrushchev intended to accept the
blockade. On Saturday it had appeared to be a cautious response to
the missiles, but today it was beginning to look like a miscalculation.

Over the course of the morning, the president made several critical decisions governing how the navy would operate. But as the summary minutes of the JCS meeting indicate, the navy was not under
his control.

1

THE CHIEFS gathered at 9:00 a.m., an hour before the quarantine
went into effect. General Taylor reported that the president wanted
to be clear about procedures related to a Soviet ship that refused to
be boarded: "Will the Navy fight its way on board?" Kennedy asked.
The (abridged) meeting notes offer no clues about Admiral Ander-

son's response. The previous night's angry clash with McNamara was still smoldering.

If a confrontation was somehow avoided at sea, it was not likely that one could be evaded on land if Khrushchev blockaded Berlin. As Taylor explained to his colleagues, the president had ordered that an armed battalion be prepared to advance up the Berlin autobahn within two hours of any attempt to isolate West Berlin.

Following Kennedy's instructions, McNamara suggested that the aircraft now crowded onto Florida airfields be dispersed. But the Chiefs demurred, sending the secretary a memo that said: "The tactical advantages of having units positioned forward far offset the risks of loss in a surprise attack."

"Are you going to announce a quarantine line and pick up ships as they cross it?" Taylor asked Anderson. The president had the impression that such a line existed, and he wanted to know exactly where it was. But the navy had no intention of restricting its ships to a line. Interceptions would be initiated as the navy saw fit after taking account of threats from Cuban aircraft and Soviet submarines. "We will pick them all up, and not announce a line," Anderson responded.

Anderson then reminded his colleagues that both Kennedy and McNamara believed that the Chiefs were preparing forces for an invasion "seven days from yesterday, but we have never sent the messages out." The notes record: "JCS agree that the message should now be sent."

2

ExComm convened as the quarantine commenced. It was 10:00 a.m. McCone's intelligence report was not reassuring: the Soviet Union was bringing its "military forces into a complete state of readiness." The forces of the Warsaw Pact were likewise in a heightened state. The missile sites in Cuba were rapidly moving toward completion, as were buildings that appeared to be nuclear storage facilities. There were twenty-two Soviet vessels headed for Cuba, and in the past twenty-four hours they had received considerable undecipherable message traffic. Soviet submarines were heading toward the quarantine line.

The submarines caught the president's attention, but a myriad of details distracted him: the disposition of aircraft at bases in Florida, a State Department estimate of Soviet intentions, complex communications problems in South America, preparations for the alert force that would bomb any SAM site that attacked a U2, the positions of two Soviet ships, the *Gagarin* and the *Kimovsk,* that appeared to be transporting missiles. "There is a submarine very close to each of them," McNamara warned. "It's a very dangerous situation."

An intercept—and its unknown consequences—appeared imminent.

And, at that very moment, as if the transcript of the ExComm meeting were a Hollywood movie script, CIA director McCone interrupted: "Mr. President, I have a note just handed to me. . . . It says that we've just received information through ONI [Office of Naval Intelligence] that all six Soviet ships currently identified in Cuban waters—and I don't know what that means—have either stopped, or reversed course."

Did "in Cuban waters" mean inbound or outbound?

McCone didn't know. McNamara thought outbound.

"Why don't we find out whether they're talking about the ships leaving Cuba or the ones coming in?" the president cut in. It was an order not a question. McCone scurried from the room.

"If this submarine should sink our destroyer, then what is our proposed reply?" the president asked. No one answered.

General Taylor avoided the issue by suggesting that the navy's ASW forces would prevent such a disaster. In addition to the aircraft carrier *Essex,* with its ASW helicopters, "we have a signaling arrangement with that submarine to surface, which has been communicated" to the Soviets.

Alexis Johnson confirmed that he had notified Moscow of the standard signaling plan, only to be corrected by McNamara: "No. This is a new procedure I asked them to set up yesterday, Alex," and he launched into an explanation of his "new procedure" with the enthusiasm of a teenage science student describing his prizewinning experiment.

"We have depth charges that have such a small charge that they can be dropped and they can actually hit the submarine, without damaging the submarine," McNamara boasted. They were warning depth charges. When the ASW forces detect an unidentified submarine "we will ask it to come to the surface for inspection by . . . using a depth charge of this type . . . it is the depth charge that is the warning notice and the instruction to surface."

It was an uninformed, dangerous fantasy, totally disconnected from the reality of how submarine commanders operated. The president recognized its perils. "His [JFK's] hand went up to his face and covered his mouth," Robert Kennedy recalled the moment: "He opened and closed his fist. His face seemed drawn, his eyes pained, almost gray. . . . 'Isn't there some way we can avoid having our first exchange with a Russian submarine—almost anything but that?'"

The president then returned to his earlier question: "If he doesn't surface or if he takes some action—takes some action to assist the merchant ship, are we just going to attack him anyway?" Then, taking a step back from the precipice toward which McNamara was heading, he said: "I think we ought to wait on that today. We don't want to have the first thing we attack as a Soviet submarine."

The plan, McNamara explained, was to send ASW helicopters with their weapons that can "damage the submarine" to harass it and move it out of the area "by the pressure of potential destruction," and then intercept the ship. "But this is only a plan and there are many, many uncertainties."

One of those uncertainties surfaced when Robert Kennedy asked if a Russian speaker would be on the destroyer. "We've asked about that, Bobby. I don't have any answers," was McNamara's unexpected reply. Bundy added that the navy was making those arrangements, while the president probably wondered why the secretary of defense was unaware of them. "May we get this matter of procedure to the quickest possible point?" he barked. "You can get a Russian-speaking person on every one of these ships?"

"Yes, Mr. President," McNamara responded.

"That is being done," Bundy confirmed.

Another worrisome uncertainty was the possible sinking of the *Gagarin* or the *Kimovsk*. If that happened, Khrushchev would blockade West Berlin. "Then we would be faced with ordering in air . . . which is probably going to be shot down. . . . What do we do then?"

Paul Nitze had the answer. Start a war!

"We try to shoot down their planes," he explained matter-of-factly, "and keep the air corridor open up to the point where it looks as though this is militarily no use." If the Soviets were determined, NATO would have to decide whether to escalate by attacking Soviet SAM sites and air bases. "Or whether we want to go into phase two, then regroup, and produce more force before we go further."

Before the president could respond to Nitze's World War III scenario, McCone returned with good news. "These ships are all westbound, all inbound for Cuba," he reported. They had either stopped or reversed course, which immediately suggested to Kennedy that Khrushchev was not just "picking out the ones that might have these weapons on [them]."

3

THE UNEXPECTED realization that Armageddon was not minutes away shifted the president's thoughts from preparing for war to preventing one. He now wanted the navy to pause at the very moment that its ships were ready to act on his earlier order to intercept all Soviet ships steaming toward Cuba. "If this report is accurate," he addressed McNamara with another order framed as a question, "then we're not going to do anything about [any] ships close in to Cuba. . . . We're not planning to grab any of those, are we?"

"We should call [Admiral] George Anderson," Ted Sorensen urged, and Rusk added: "We better be sure the navy knows that they're not supposed to pursue these ships."

Exactly what the navy knew about the president's new instructions remained unclear until Taylor spoke with Anderson. Three ships were turning back, and it appeared that others were preparing to follow. Anderson was directing scouting aircraft into the area for a closer look.

"We want to give that specific ship [*Kimovsk*] a chance to turn around," the president ordered. "You don't want to have word going out from Moscow: 'Turn around,' and suddenly we sink a ship." The *Essex* was to be contacted and told "to wait an hour and see whether that ship continues on its [return] course. . . ." Time was of the essence. "We have to move quickly," Kennedy warned, "because they're going to intercept between 10:30 and 11:00."

The president's orders were faithfully transmitted, and for the time being, the threat of a confrontation at sea was averted. But the missiles remained in Cuba, and other Soviet ships were approaching the quarantine line. They would confront twenty-five destroyers, two cruisers, the ASW aircraft carrier *Essex,* and roaming P2V patrol aircraft.

4

As THE president and his advisers monitored what they feared could be the start of a war at sea, Soviet ambassador Dobrynin and his staff were equally anxious. "As if it were yesterday," he wrote in his 1995 memoir, "I can recall the enormous tension that gripped us at the embassy as we all watched the sequences on American television showing a Soviet tanker as it drew closer and closer to the imaginary line." The announcer's voice was "choked with emotion" as he counted down the miles. "Four, three, two, finally one mile was left . . . the ship crossed the line without the destroyers opening fire."

A sigh of relief echoed through the room, but as Dobrynin noted, he did not know whether or not the remaining ships would challenge the blockade. "We, in the embassy," he remarked, "were again not informed of this by Moscow."

The lack of instructions, or any helpful communications throughout the crisis, Vasily Kuznetsov, the deputy foreign minister, later explained to Dobrynin, was due to "the sense of total bewilderment that enveloped Khrushchev and his colleagues after their plot had taken such an unexpected turn."

5

IT WAS late afternoon when the president had his next crisis meeting. Accompanied by Rusk, McNamara, McCone, and Lovett, he confronted the congressional leaders who had taken him to task on Monday. But Senators Russell and Fulbright, his most vocal critics, now offered their full support. The delegation received an up-to-date assessment of Khrushchev's behavior, and a clear explanation of the political purposes behind the president's blockade strategy.

Rusk believed that the quarantine had surprised and confused

Khrushchev. It appeared that the Soviet leader's plan was "to come to the UN in late November, prepared to lay on a real crisis over Berlin in direct talks with the president. He wanted to have all this [the missiles] in his pocket when he had that talk," the secretary explained. Both he and Ambassador Thompson believed (correctly) that Khrushchev had not made any contingency plans, and he was now scrambling to formulate his response.

McNamara described two categories of Soviet ships. Those with sensitive cargoes appeared to be returning to their home ports, while others were continuing toward Cuba. Their intentions were unknown.

A "test case either to have us sink it [a ship], or disable it and have a fight about it," was a possibility, the president warned his audience. But it was also possible that Khrushchev would order the ships not transporting offensive weapons to accept the quarantine. "When we know that . . . we'll have some indication of where we're going," he reasoned. Given the positions of the ships, Khrushchev's intentions would be clear within twenty-four hours.

In response to a question from Senator Fulbright about interdicting Soviet aircraft, the president explained that his blockade strategy was related to Berlin: "We thought the first thing we ought to do is do the ships," he said, "because the only way you can stop a plane is to shoot it down. And with our problem in Berlin, at least at the first stage, we ought to just rely on the ships."

Was it true, Senator Hickenlooper asked, that the administration would allow a ship reported to be delivering five thousand rifles to reach Cuba?

The question allowed Kennedy to explain the blockade strategy's fine-tuning. It was important to "emphasize offensive weapons" for the OAS, the UN, and our allies. The first confrontation with the Soviets should involve offensive weapons "*for political reasons. If they once accept quarantine, we're not going to let the rifles go through, but we wanted to put the whole emphasis on this missile thing, because this puts us in a much stronger position around the world."

6

THE PRESIDENT'S next meeting was a strategy session in the Oval Office with Bundy, Lovett, McCone, and McNamara. Concerned that pressure was building from the military, Lovett led off with an analysis of the crisis that emphasized caution. The primary benefit of the blockade, he counseled, was that it would quickly reveal Khrushchev's intentions. He was "off balance" now, and would probably remain so for a few more days. No decision should be taken until Khrushchev's intentions were known.

Cuba, Lovett continued, had to be regarded "as an extension of Berlin," and Khrushchev's missile deployment was, "at least in part," aimed at Berlin. An invasion or air strike at this point would be a mistake. "There's no such thing as a small military action," the former secretary of defense declared. "The moment we start anything in this field, we have to be prepared to do everything."

"I saw Cuba as our hostage," McNamara added in support of Lovett's call for prudence. "I think it's just as much our hostage as Berlin is a Soviet hostage. I think if we can remain cool and calm here, we've really got the screws on."

But the screws can unwind, Kennedy reminded his advisers. "It is a fact that if they put the screws on Berlin in the way that Gromyko said they were going to, then we are bound to invade Cuba."

"Yes. Exactly," McNamara replied, jettisoning his "cool and calm."

Another problem "we've got to be thinking about" suddenly occurred to the president. Our blockade could be successful while work on the missiles continues. We're now faced with thirty missiles, but by November it could be fifty or sixty. "Under what conditions would the Russians fire them? They might be more reluctant to fire them if they've already grabbed Berlin than they would be if we suddenly go in there [invade Cuba] . . . that's what we've got to make a judgment on."

It was an important issue, but inexplicably Kennedy dropped it and began to read aloud a proposal he had received from UN secretary general U Thant:

"I have been asked by the permanent representatives of a large number of member countries of the UN to address an urgent appeal to you in the present critical situation.

"These representatives feel in the interests of international peace and security that all concerned should refrain from any action which may aggravate the situation and bring with it the risk of war.

"In their view it is important that time should be given to enable the parties to get together to resolve the situation the present crisis presented and normalize the situation in the Caribbean.

"This involves on the one hand the voluntary suspension of all armed shipments to Cuba and also the voluntary suspension of the quarantine measures involving the searching of ships bound for Cuba.

"I believe the voluntary suspension for a period of two or three weeks will greatly ease the situation and give time to the parties to get together to resolve the situation the present crisis presented and normalize the situation in the Caribbean."

The president had discussed this initiative with Stevenson, and had agreed with his ambassador's view that it was advantageous to respond promptly. But there would be no agreement without an iron-clad guarantee that UN inspectors could assure that work on the missiles had halted.

7

BEFORE CALLING Britain's prime minister Macmillan—as he would every evening of the crisis—the president visited the White House Situation Room to check on the quarantine line. His pessimism had not abated. Explaining to Macmillan that he did not know what the Soviet ships would do when they reached the blockade, he quipped: "We'll be wiser by tomorrow night, but maybe not happier." Khrushchev (he *in*correctly believed) did not seem to be frightened.

Tracking Lovett's analysis, he told Macmillan that once the blockade was fully established he would have to decide whether to invade Cuba ("taking our chances") or whether to "use Cuba as a sort of hostage in the matter of Berlin."

An unspoken standoff existed, and it was not necessarily tilted in America's favor. "If he takes Berlin," Kennedy said, "then we will take Cuba. If we take Cuba now, we have the problem, of course, of these missiles being fired, or a general missile firing, and we certainly will have the problem of Berlin being seized." In either case the invasion force would be ready in days.

There was also the "second stage of this problem," he explained. It was possible that Khrushchev would accept the quarantine, but order work on the missiles to continue. "Do we then tell them that if they don't get the missiles out, that we're going to invade Cuba?" he asked. That could lead to "general nuclear war" and the loss of Berlin. "Or do we just let the nuclear work go on, figuring he won't ever dare fire them, and when he tries to grab Berlin, we then go into Cuba."

Well put, the prime minister replied, and promised to send the president his thoughts.

U Thant's proposal was "rather tiresome," Macmillan volunteered. It looked sensible but was in fact "very bad." A pause and a summit were not good solutions, but it was possible that a summit could "do a deal." The president was skeptical. "I don't know quite what we will discuss at the meeting, because he'll be back with his same old position on Berlin, probably offer to dismantle the missiles if we'll neutralize Berlin."

But, Kennedy mused aloud, it was also possible to rethink the Soviet missiles as a way to guarantee the security of West Berlin. "We can keep on the quarantine, the buildup of missiles will continue, and then we would threaten to take action in Cuba if they go into Berlin." It was an interesting thought that neither he nor Macmillan pursued.

8

IT HAD been a long day, but Khrushchev was about to make it longer—and more daunting. At about nine-thirty that evening his response to President Kennedy's letter arrived at the White House. Angry and rambling, it charged that the United States was violating international law, behaving arbitrarily, abandoning reason, and "threatening that unless we subordinate ourselves to your demands, you will use force." If our positions were reversed, he said, Kennedy would react as he was reacting. "I do not doubt that if someone had attempted to dictate conditions of this sort to you, the USA, you would have rejected such an attempt."

Khrushchev was also contemptuous of the motives that instigated the blockade: "hatred for the Cuban people and its Government, [and] considerations of the election campaign in the USA." He would not consider bending to "the folly of degenerate imperialism." His ships would obey "generally recognized norms" of international navigation law. "If the American side violates these rules," he warned, "we will then be forced for our part to take the measures which we deem necessary and adequate in order to protect our rights. For this we have all that is necessary."

It was signed: "Respectfully yours, N. Khrushchev."

After studying the letter with several advisers, the president called George Ball. There was no option, the undersecretary said, "but to go ahead and test this thing out, in the morning." The Soviet tanker *Bucharest* would be the guinea pig.

Ball also mentioned that Stevenson was "kicking like a steer," alarmed by the president's intention to reject U Thant's proposal. It would appear that the United States was not interested in negotiating a settlement, Stevenson warned.

As Kennedy so often did, he dismissed Adlai's advice but went on to absorb it as his own. It was clear from the reply to U Thant that Stevenson's concerns initiated a presidential recalculation. In a call back to Ball, Kennedy suggested that U Thant redraft his message so as to allow Khrushchev to stop his ships "without looking like they [the Soviets] completely crawled down."

At 2:00 a.m. Stevenson was called and instructed to pass the following idea to the secretary general: "Hope that Khrushchev will hold his ships out of interception area for limited time in order to permit discussions of modalities of agreement."

The United Nations, and the U.S. ambassador to the UN, were moving onto center stage, while another ambassador, Averell Harriman, offered useful advice. "Khrushchev is sending us desperate signals to get us to help take him off the hook," Harriman said. "He is sending messages exactly as he did to Eisenhower directly after the U2 affair.

"Eisenhower ignored these messages to his cost. We must not repeat Eisenhower's mistake."

41

"Events Have Gone Too Far"

October 25, Thursday

If the work [on the missiles] continues, we either have to do
this air business [attack the missiles], or we have to put POL
on . . . otherwise the work's going on and we're not really
doing anything about it.
—PRESIDENT KENNEDY TO EXCOMM, OCTOBER 25

Thursday, October 25, offered a pause. The most dangerous moment
had passed without incident; the blockade had not been challenged.
Yet there was no resolution in sight. More than a dozen Soviet vessels
continued toward the quarantine line, work on the missiles continued, and Khrushchev warned that he would respond with force if the
United States interfered with his ships.

Was there a way to enforce the blockade while avoiding a major
incident? What type of ship—dry cargo or tanker—should be targeted? When should the first Soviet ship be boarded? What considerations should be given to Secretary General Thant's efforts to
mediate? How should the Pentagon spin the quarantine's success?
Was an invasion or bombing campaign becoming more likely?

1

THE DAY did not begin as the president had hoped. Having asked
Macmillan for his advice, Kennedy awoke to a reply suggesting that
he rethink his strategy. "After much reflection," the prime minister
wrote, "I think that events have gone too far." The blockade was an
overreaction. It was time to "try to attain your objectives by other

means." Perhaps, he suggested, a negotiated solution with UN inspection teams monitoring the missile sites. The U.S. military buildup could continue, Macmillan added, "for any emergency," and perhaps to help persuade Castro to cooperate. But for now a military solution was a gamble too far.

The prime minister's note reflected British opinion, which made his critique more alarming. Peace demonstrations were ubiquitous throughout the United Kingdom, and editorial commentary was overwhelmingly critical. A cartoon in the *Evening Standard* showed President Eisenhower holding Prime Minister Anthony Eden's coattails as he stepped toward a ledge labeled "Suez"; the adjoining panel pictured Macmillan merely watching as Kennedy stepped onto the Cuban brink.

2

WHEN THE president turned to the *Washington Post* he may have been pleased. In his nationally syndicated column, "Today and Tomorrow," Walter Lippmann suggested a trade for peace. The United States should offer to remove its Jupiter missiles from Turkey in exchange for the Soviet Union withdrawing its missiles from Cuba. "The two bases could be dismantled without altering the world balance of power," he wrote.

It is possible, of course, that such an obvious idea had occurred to Lippmann. But there is internal evidence that it was an administration plant, approved by the president: "In my opinion we must be most careful in working out any horse trade of this type," Lippmann wrote, tracking the president's concerns, "to be sure it does not set a pattern for handling future Russian incursions in other parts of the world."

Ambassador Stevenson had proposed such a trade on the first day of the crisis and thereafter, but he was now in New York defending America's actions at the UN. George Ball, on the other hand, was in Washington meeting with Lippmann almost daily, as he had acknowledged at the previous day's ExComm meeting. The president had repeatedly said that he expected a trade to be part of any settlement, and it is possible that he had authorized Ball to suggest the proposal. Coming from a journalist, it could not be pinned on the administration, and floating the idea publicly might open a path to resolving the crisis. As it happened, newspapers in Britain seized on the idea, and Austrian foreign minister Bruno Kreisky, speaking in Vienna, endorsed Lippmann's trade proposal.

As did Khrushchev. There no longer seems to be any doubt that Lippmann's column—which Khrushchev followed—led the Soviet leader to offer to remove his missiles from Cuba in exchange for the removal of the Jupiter missiles from their base in Turkey. Anastas Mikoyan told Castro as much shortly after the crisis ended.

3

THE CHIEFS had their own solution, and they did not share the president's satisfaction that "the Soviets apparently have accepted our quarantine." Five tankers and five cargo ships turned around, and the tanker *Bucharest* had identified itself when asked, McNamara reported at their 9:00 a.m. meeting. "I suggest," he continued, that "we establish the boarding precedent by boarding, say, a British ship and, immediately thereafter, board a Soviet ship, preferably one carrying offensive weapons." Did the Chiefs agree?

Their response is not recorded, but a brief exchange about establishing an air blockade (which McNamara rejected) suggests that they were eager to ramp up the pressure.

About an hour later, after McNamara and Taylor left to attend the 10:00 a.m. ExComm meeting, Admiral Anderson received instructions that the *Bucharest* was to be followed but not harassed, and the *Grozny* was to be stopped and boarded.

At 10:40 General LeMay received authorization to commence the low-level reconnaissance flights the Chiefs had requested. And, should air attacks be authorized, the target criteria included—in addition to the MRBM and IRBM missiles—IL-28s, MiGs, Komars, SAMs, and targets of opportunity. Absent the invasion, it was everything the JCS recommended.

At noon General Taylor returned from the ExComm meeting reporting (in a sarcastic vein that was becoming habitual): "Last week they were talking like the blockade would bring down Castro. Now Rusk is saying that the blockade is only to keep out offensive weapons and if we do that we have accomplished the mission."

4

McNAMARA AND Taylor had arrived at the White House in time for McCone's intelligence briefing. It offered a mixed message. U Thant was working to "find machinery for easing tension," and fourteen of the twenty-two Soviet ships in transit to Cuba had reversed course. But work on the missile sites was continuing, Soviet and bloc forces were on "a high level of alert," Castro's police were rounding up dissidents, and "Havana was preparing for an invasion."

An invasion was still on the president's mind, as his questions to McCone suggest. How would American troops be received? What was the state of Cuban morale? Were Cubans even aware of the Soviet missiles? Was there a means of determining "their knowledge of the missile sites now, their reaction to it, and their support of the regime?"

McNamara's confidence in the blockade had waned, and he was now eager to promote the Chiefs' latest attack scenario. After a brief discussion about authorizing the navy to board the Soviet tanker *Grozny*, he urged the president to approve low-level surveillance sorties. The flights would not only provide valuable intelligence, he explained: "They will [also] establish a pattern of operation consistent with an attack, and cannot be differentiated from an attack, and therefore reduces the warning of an attack, and may make it possible to attack with lesser forces because we reduced the warning."

Abandoning concerns about Soviet casualties that he had voiced earlier, he urged preparations for a bombing campaign. The low-level photography could be analyzed within hours, he said, and if, as he suspected, it showed all the missile sites eight hours from launch, "then we have very little risk of going in [attacking] within that eight-hour period" and taking them all out.

It would not be difficult. "If we have been going in with low-level surveillance for a day or two, and that's the pattern of our operation, we send in the same number of ships [planes], but now they're armed instead of unarmed."

In addition, he reported, the Soviets had ordered the Cubans "not to attack." The perfect excuse for an invasion would be a UN vote against the United States, he added. If the Security Council vetoed the U.S. proposal to send UN inspectors to Cuba, "this might set up the circumstances in which we can go in and take those missiles out."

But President Kennedy was thinking about more immediate consequences, and he turned to the blockade. What were the political repercussions of boarding, or not boarding, a Soviet ship that day? The discussions at the UN were coming to a head. U Thant had appealed to both sides to stand down. Was it wise to take an action that could cause an incident, such as forcing an inspection of the *Bucharest*?

"That's really the question," he said. "What is the political effect of our letting that [ship] pass? Are we better off to make this issue come to a head today, or is there some advantage in putting it off 'til tomorrow?"

The *Bucharest* had been hailed, had replied that it was carrying petroleum, and was being tracked by a destroyer. "Now they've [the *Bucharest*] already wired back [to Moscow] that they were accosted by a destroyer and they were left at sea," the president continued. "What impression will they [Khrushchev and his advisers] get over there that we let this one go?" Would this suggest that Kennedy was not serious about the quarantine? That he was not tough enough?

The question prompted a long, disorganized discussion. Did it make sense to board a tanker when POL had been specifically left off the contraband list? Would Khrushchev get the wrong message if the *Bucharest* was not boarded? Would a boarding attempt lead to an embarrassing incident? In what direction was the UN leaning? Was the *Grozny*, which could not be boarded for another twenty-four hours, a better choice?

The president refined the discussion: "The problem is that we've got to face up to the fact that we're going to have to grab a Russian ship," he declared, "and [Khrushchev] says he's not going to permit it. Now, the question is whether it's better to have that happen today or tomorrow?"

What was Khrushchev planning? And what was happening at the UN? "Unless more time is going to make it more likely that we're going to get something out of either the UN or Khrushchev," the president reasoned, "then I suppose you have to grasp the nettle."

Bundy was optimistic. We might "get the kind of thing we're asking U Thant for [Soviet agreement to stay away from the quarantine line]. It's not likely, but it's conceivable," he said. And, probably because Kennedy was leaning toward the same conclusion (or hope), he acquiesced: "All right . . . in that case we might as well wait."

As the discussion meandered from the need to add missile fuel to the contraband list, to the criteria for boarding tankers, to the information the Pentagon should release about the blockade, to whether the *Grozny* was carrying something more suspicious than petroleum, McNamara turned belligerent. The navy should go after the *Grozny* even if it turned around, he proposed: "I would seriously . . . apply the idea that you had, Bobby, that we go out there and, if it turns around, board it anyhow."

Rusk objected: "If it's under orders to turn around and it has radioed Moscow that it has turned around and it's still boarded," he said, "that's bad." Bad enough, Bundy thought, to steer the conversation to another subject. "Why don't we turn to the UN for a while, Mr. President, and then come back to this question?"

5

THE DEBATE at the United Nations was one of Kennedy's central concerns, and he was eager to turn to it. Even though the secretary general's proposals did not confront the central problem—the removal of the Soviet missiles—he didn't want to appear unsympathetic to U Thant's initiatives. The UN proceedings were being televised and were receiving worldwide attention.

"Would it be possible for us to say," Kennedy asked, that "the quarantine can be lifted only if the UN can substitute effective guarantees against the introduction of this material during this period?" He did not think that was likely, but said it "doesn't make us look quite as negative." ("I'd rather stick the cat on his back," he added.)

No one objected, but almost everyone had something to say about the importance of continuing the blockade, with McNamara particularly determined that it be maintained: "I never have thought we'd get them [the missiles] out of Cuba without the application of substantial [economic or military] force."

After numerous awkward proposals, the clarity of the final draft of the letter to U Thant suggests that it was completed by Sorensen: "I deeply appreciate the spirit which prompted your message of yesterday," it read. "As we made clear in the Security Council, the existing threat was created by the secret introduction of offensive weapons into Cuba, and the answer lies in the removal of such weapons." Ambassador Stevenson, it went on to assure the secretary general, could discuss arrangements that would hopefully lead to "a peaceful solution."

6

WITH THE response to U Thant off the table, Rusk enthusiastically announced an initiative that he considered potentially helpful: The Brazilians had proposed declaring Latin America a nuclear-free zone. To his surprise, however, he was alone in thinking it "a very interesting possibility." No ExComm member endorsed it, and Kennedy was not interested. "Okay. What else have we got?" the president said, cutting off Rusk's warning that "this could create an enormous pressure in the [UN General] Assembly and around the world."

The "what else" was the latest Khrushchev letter, which Bundy described as "about our immorality, and that the quarantine's no good, and the OAS is no good, and their people will follow the norms of combat." After it was read aloud, Ambassador Thompson concluded that Khrushchev intended to compel "forcible action," a troubling assessment from the person everyone relied on to interpret Khrushchev's communications.

The president's reply was measured. Parrying the chairman's anger with a calm restatement of facts, it reviewed events since August, emphasizing his September warning that the United States "would regard any shipment of offensive weapons as presenting the gravest issues." Having ignored that warning, and lied about its actions, the Soviet government was responsible for the present crisis. In closing, the president regretted the "deterioration in our relations," and hoped that Khrushchev would move to restore comity.

The exchange of letters brought the conversation back to the quarantine, and another convoluted conversation about whether to stop and board the *Bucharest*.

The timing to board the *Bucharest*, however, depended on what was happening in the United Nations. With a critical UN debate imminent, Kennedy decided that "this is not the appropriate time to blow up a ship. . . . Let's think a little more about it."

7

THE THINKING began immediately after the meeting disbanded. The *Bucharest* problem was resolved with a Pentagon announcement that it had been "intercepted" and allowed to continue. U Thant adjusted his original proposal to a call for the Soviet Union to avoid the blockade, and to the United States to refrain from confronting Soviet ships.

Shortly after 4:00 p.m., with the Security Council gathered in tense anticipation, Stevenson dramatically revealed photographs of the missile sites during a heated exchange with Soviet UN ambassador Valerian Zorin. When ExComm convened an hour later, the president was absent. He was glued to his television in the Oval Office monitoring (and quietly admiring) Stevenson's aggressive performance.

The topic du jour—what ship to board, or not to board?—had a new contender, McNamara announced. It was a Lebanese dry-cargo [that is, not a tanker] ship, the *Marucla*. If it didn't turn back, it was a prime candidate.

Another candidate was an East German passenger ship, the *Völkerfreundschaft* (*Peoples' Friendship*), suspected of transporting 1,500 industrial workers including 550 Czech technicians, plus twenty-five East German students. Was it wise to stop a passenger ship? "How do you tell a missile technician from an agricultural technician?" Sorensen asked. McNamara also demurred, warning that forcibly boarding a ship crammed with passengers was fraught with danger.

The president, who now had joined the meeting, was frustrated. He was beginning to feel hostage to "this U Thant thing," which called for disengagement on the high seas without any mention of removing the Soviet missiles. Some action was necessary "to prove sooner or later that the blockade works," he said. It was important to demonstrate that he was not backing off. Was the *Grozny* within reach?

It was still about one thousand miles from Cuba, McNamara reported, but "we can send a ship out tonight to meet it tomorrow." It would be about seven or eight hundred miles from Cuba when it was intercepted.

At about this time Bobby entered the room and proposed a very different strategy: Simply announce that the quarantine has been effective. Explain that we let the *Bucharest* through because we had not yet prohibited petroleum, oil, and lubricants [POL]. In a day or two McNamara could announce that we were adding POL to the list, which would indicate that we were tightening the blockade. Our low-level surveillance demonstrated that we were not backing off. We would thus have avoided a clash with the Soviets at sea. "Ultimately," he admitted, we might decide that it is "better to have knocked out their missile base, as the first step."

Bobby's suggestion intrigued his brother, who reviewed it aloud, and circled back to wondering how Khrushchev was going to respond to U Thant's proposal. He was not likely to accept the idea of "his ships being suspended," the president thought, which would probably lead to our adding POL as contraband, and reconsidering attacking the missiles.

For reasons best explained by a specialist in groupthink theory, the idea of stopping and boarding the *Völkerfreundschaft* continued to be promoted until the president ended further discussion. "Given the U Thant thing that's going to be published to the world, where it looks like a chance of easing this," he firmly told his advisers, "it's probably a mistake [to stop] the East German [passenger] ship." If it doesn't cooperate, he said, we might have to shoot its rudder off, and it could catch fire. "We don't want to sink that ship tomorrow. So, I think we can let that one go." Nevertheless, he added, some type of strong action would be necessary to demonstrate our resolve. "Otherwise the work's going on and we're not really doing anything about it."

8

WHEN THE meeting ended, President Kennedy returned to the Oval Office to phone Prime Minister Macmillan. Reviewing the day's events, he mentioned Khrushchev's angry letter and the navy's cautious (so far) handling of the quarantine. He would take no aggressive action before the Soviet government responded to U Thant's proposal. "I don't want to have a fight with a Russian ship tomorrow morning, and a search of it at a time when it appears that U Thant has got the Russians to agree not to continue," he reassured the anxious prime minister.

In turn, Macmillan complimented the president on his response to U Thant. It was "extremely ingenious and very firm. Because you are saying that the real point is how to get rid of these weapons."

That was the nub of the crisis, and the president explained that any clash at sea would be avoided if Khrushchev signed on to U Thant's initiative. Either way, however, he was going to insist that work on the missile sites be discontinued. If not, "we must tighten the blockade and possibly take other action."

For that, the Chiefs were ready.

42

"Trade Them Out or Take Them Out"

October 26, Friday

We're going to have to pay a price in order to get those missiles out without fighting to get them out.
—PRESIDENT KENNEDY TO EXCOMM, OCTOBER 26

Friday, October 26, was the fourth full day of the confrontation—and only day 3 of the blockade—but it seemed a lot longer to the president and his advisers. Time was not on their side. The quarantine had yet to elicit a compromise from Khrushchev, and work on the missiles continued unabated. Once they were operational, bombing or invading the island held out the possibility that, by accident or design, one or more would be launched against the United States.

Even the early-morning boarding of the *Marucla,* "carefully and personally selected by the President," had not moved the chairman. In his memoir of the crisis, Robert Kennedy recalled a shared foreboding that "a military confrontation between the two great military powers was inevitable. . . . Our combination of limited force and diplomatic efforts had been unsuccessful."

Could the slide toward war be averted?

After his meeting with Khrushchev in Vienna, Kennedy was convinced that he could not "deal with the Soviet leader as an equal until he had shown strength." He had been tough during the Berlin crisis. But Khrushchev did not appear to understand that, barring an agreement, his missiles would be destroyed.

Sending a clear message to Moscow was the president's top priority.

1

THE CHIEFS met twice on the twenty-sixth. At their 9:00 a.m. meeting General Taylor reported that ExComm would authorize round-the-clock reconnaissance to learn whether the Soviets were working on their missiles at night. "The SecDef is anxious to act on grabbing a Russian ship," he noted, but Secretary Rusk preferred to avoid that. Admiral Anderson announced that the next day the navy would board the *Grozny*—suspected of carrying missile fuel—but as of its last sighting, it was dead in the water.

Concluding the meeting, the Chiefs agreed that OPLAN 314 (bombing only) should be abandoned in order to "concentrate on OPLAN 316 [bombing and invasion]." The operation would begin with a massive seven-day bombing campaign, followed by an invasion by two hundred thousand troops.

At 2:00 p.m. the Chiefs' preference for military action seemed close to being realized. ExComm was endorsing an attack, Taylor reported, although not the preferred plan. "The White House's present concept is to carry out a limited attack upon six missile sites and the IL-28s, the objective being the lowest level of force at the lowest possible price."

Once again, that was not what the secret taping system recorded. Taylor was referring to the views of several ExComm members who had met at the State Department after the morning meeting. It was not the "White House's [that is, the president's]" concept.

2

THE SENSE of foreboding that Robert Kennedy described in his memoir was not evenly distributed. The shared optimism earlier in the week had drained faster from the secretary of defense than from the secretary of state. McNamara had come to despair of a peaceful solution. Rusk, who was seriously engaged with Secretary General Thant's diplomatic efforts, remained hopeful. The tension between the two became palpable.

It was important, Rusk argued, not to do anything that could be interpreted as undermining Thant's efforts to broker an end to the crisis. To have "a real shot at the U Thant talks," Rusk urged the president to delay twenty-four hours before adding any POL to the prohibited list.

"I don't believe . . . there are alternative [political] courses [to invasion]," McNamara countered, and launched into a forceful argument for day-and-night surveillance. "Mr. President," Rusk objected, "I wonder really again on the nighttime reconnaissance, whether we ought to start that tonight, until we've had a crack at the U Thant discussions." The need to use flares, he feared, could be interpreted as anticipating, or even being associated with, a bombing attack.

"Why don't we wait on this surveillance until we get the political talks," President Kennedy said, backing Rusk, and moved the discussion to what those talks needed to achieve. "No further arms shipments; no continued buildup; and a defanging of the sites that are already there," Rusk proposed. Everyone agreed that "defanging the sites" was the highest priority.

"Even if the quarantine's 100 percent effective it isn't any good because the missile sites go on being constructed. So [the quarantine's] only a first step," Kennedy added. Then, again with Solomonic ambiguity, he combined McNamara's preference for military action with Rusk's resolve to give U Thant's diplomacy a chance: "Obviously we can't expect them [the Soviets] to remove [the missiles] at this point without a long negotiation," he conceded, and simultaneously admitted that he did not expect negotiations to succeed: "Of course you won't get them out unless you take them out."

But the consequences of "taking them out" remained unappealing, and he was not ready to side with McNamara. "Obviously," he said when Rusk once again urged consideration of the Brazilian idea for a Latin American nuclear-free zone: "We're going to have to pay a price in order to get those missiles out without fighting to get them out."

In addition to suggesting a nuclear-free zone, the Brazilian government had offered to serve as a conduit to Castro. Both proposals were long shots, but aware that it would be a political error to reject the Brazilian offer, Kennedy snapped: "So let's get this message out . . . Mr. Secretary. It won't get any place. But let's send it . . . because the time's running out for us. . . . We can't screw around for two weeks and wait for them [the Soviets] to finish these [missiles]."

"Governor"—he turned to Stevenson, who had traveled from

New York to attend this meeting—"do you want to talk a little and give us your thoughts?"

3

THE FORMER governor of Illinois, Adlai Stevenson, had burnished his image during the previous day's UN debate. He had surpassed all expectations for toughness by interrogating his Soviet counterpart, Valerian Zorin, with a ferocity that surprised many, most especially the president. Televised internationally, he had thrown the Soviet ambassador on the defensive with prosecutorial zeal: "Do you, Ambassador Zorin," he had demanded, "admit that the Soviet Union has stationed medium- and intermediate-range missiles in Cuba. Yes or no? Don't wait for the translation! Yes or no?"

He was prepared to "wait until hell freezes over," he declared, as Zorin fumbled and dissembled. Then he revealed to the delegates—and to the international TV audience—photographs of the missile sites that proved that the Soviet Union had been lying.

It was a stunning performance that swept away lingering doubts. "Mr. President"—Rusk interjected, possibly remembering that Stevenson had been the first to call for the public display of the missile photography—"I think we all greatly appreciate the job that Adlai Stevenson did in the Security Council last night. He put Zorin in the position where Zorin made himself ridiculous."

As ambassador to the UN, Stevenson was the president's point man for U Thant's mediation efforts. He had encouraged and promoted the secretary general's initiatives and was now in a position to encourage Kennedy to support them. His timing could not have been better.

"Well, sir," Stevenson said with a renewed sense of confidence, "I think it's well for you all to bear in mind that the concept of [U Thant's] proposal is a *standstill*." That meant no initiatives by anyone for two or three weeks while a settlement was negotiated. It was not possible, he explained with grammarian precision, to insist on "[making] the weapons inoperable." That's "a reversal of something that has already taken place." But we could, and should, insist that the missiles "be *kept* inoperable."

To the president's question, "Would the work on the sites be ceased?" he answered: "Of course," and explained that three things would occur immediately. "There would be no more construction, no more quarantine, no more arms shipments." During the negotiations that followed over the next two or three weeks, the objective would be the withdrawal of the missiles and the dismantling of the missile sites.

We might even push for Cuba's agreement to a Latin American nuclear-free zone, Stevenson added, and "defanging Cuba for subversion and penetration. I'm not sure how we could do that, or whether we could do that, or should do that."

Of course, he warned, there would be a price, and then laid out the two elements that would form both the secret and the public basis of the settlement. As he had suggested to the president on October 16, and as Kennedy had repeated during several ExComm meetings, the Jupiter missiles in Turkey and Italy might have to be removed, a trade that most of the ExComm members (but not the president) rejected.

It would likely be necessary, he said, also to offer a "guarantee of the territorial integrity of Cuba. Indeed, that's what they've said these weapons were for. The territorial integrity of Cuba," Stevenson repeated, anticipating the no-invasion pledge that became the public basis of the final settlement. (Once again, he was more far-seeing than his ExComm colleagues.)

He wanted to repeat, he concluded, that U Thant's proposal was a *standstill*. Once agreed to, all construction and shipping, as well as the quarantine, would stop.

End the quarantine? "I don't agree with that, Mr. President," McCone interrupted. "I feel very strongly about it. . . . That [missile] threat must be removed before we can drop the quarantine." Then, banging the table, he concluded: "We must say that the quarantine goes on until we are satisfied that these are inoperable."

The DCI was not merely challenging Stevenson; he was taking issue with a public diplomatic initiative closely watched around the world. Undermining the secretary general's efforts to peacefully end the crisis was not smart politics, and the president said as much.

Unlike McCone's, Kennedy's expectations for the quarantine had evolved. Begun as an action designed to force Khrushchev to compromise, after three days it remained a symbol of the president's commitment to remove the missiles, but it was no longer the instrument that was likely to force their extraction. "The quarantine itself won't remove the weapons," he told McCone. "So, we've only got two ways of removing the weapons. One is to negotiate them out . . . the other is to go in and take them out." Squeezing them out with the blockade was not going to work.

As always, the details mattered, and in the time remaining the president moved the discussion to examining U Thant's proposal. The first two days, Stevenson explained, were set aside for negotiating the details of the "standstill." Did Thant expect the blockade to be terminated during this period?

"If we lift the quarantine, and the quarantine is substituted for by a UN group [of observers]," President Kennedy worried, "you're never going to get the quarantine back in again." The pressure had to be maintained. "Why should the Soviets take these things out? I don't see why they should," he carped. "The Soviets aren't going to take them out."

The president's comments encouraged supporters of the quarantine to insist that it must remain at least until a satisfactory inspection system was in place, and such a system was problematic. "The Soviets will find it far easier to remove these weapons . . . than they would to accept inspections," Ambassador Thompson warned. "We can't expect a bunch of Burmese [U Thant was Burmese] to go down there [as inspectors] and take the security of the United States in its hands," John McCloy said to general agreement. "I think we've got to insist upon having our own people down there."

President Kennedy had backed himself into both corners of the debate. On the one hand, he had stated that he saw no sure path to the peaceful removal of the missiles; on the other, he wanted to keep that peaceful path open.

"As I understand the Governor's proposal," he repeated, "what he's suggesting is that we give this thing the time to try to negotiate them out of there. Now maybe we're not going to be able to negotiate them out of there. But otherwise I don't see how we're going to get them out of there unless we go in and get them out," an option that most of the ExComm (with the exception of Stevenson) accepted. After more back-and-forth, to which President Kennedy listened patiently, his frustration boiled over. As he saw it, his

ExComm advisers were not facing reality, and they were not being helpful.

"At least Governor Stevenson has this proposal," he said, but "nobody [that is, none of you] is very much interested in [it]." The point "is that the blockade is not going to accomplish the job either." Alternatives, not just criticisms, were needed if Stevenson's plan was not going to work. Continuing "the blockade . . . isn't going to accomplish it, except it's going to bring the conflagration closer, which may or may not be desirable."

Dillon interrupted, but the president was not finished. Almost scolding, he urged his advisers to *think*. "We have to be thinking" about what else could be done [short of bombing and invasion] if negotiations failed. "What other devices are we going to use to get them out of there?" Focusing on just maintaining the "blockade" [as everyone was now referring to the quarantine] was not the answer.

The next question was whether it was useful to announce that we had photographic evidence that work was continuing on the missile sites. If announced today, he thought they would be in a better position tomorrow to decide "if we're going to go with [expanding the blockade to include] POL, or if we're going to decide to go the other route, the force route."

At the mention of "the force route," General Taylor offered a list of options to demonstrate "mounting activity," including night photography of Havana. Rusk again objected. "Mr. President, I do think it would be important to explore the political thing, to be sure that the Soviets have turned down these three conditions [no more construction, no more quarantine, no more arms shipments] before we put on the night photography."

"That's fair enough," Kennedy responded, backing Rusk again, and went on to discuss arrangements for having the White House announce that work was continuing on the missile sites.

4

THE MEETING had frustrated the president. It had ended where it began: with no idea of how to force the missiles out of Cuba, short of war. The so-called force route promised unpredictable consequences, a "conflagration," he had said. His support of Rusk and Stevenson—as against McNamara and McCone—indicated the direction in which he wanted to go. But with the work on the missile sites accelerating, he told Ambassador Ormsby-Gore after the meeting ended, something would have to be done soon.

Sometime before 1:00 p.m. McCone returned to the Oval Office with an intelligence update. Based on yesterday's low-level photo reconnaissance flights, he reported the possible discovery of Soviet tactical missile launchers [NATO designation, FROG] and further progress on the MRBM sites. The FROGs were capable of firing both conventional and nuclear warheads, but McCone ignored the implications of their nuclear capability and focused on the ballistic missiles. "They could start [assembling] at dark and have [MRBMs] pointing at us the following morning." If the "political route" didn't ensure that those missiles were immediately immobilized, he was not inclined to support it.

Kennedy too missed the significance of the FROGs. "If we invade," he told McCone, "by the time we get to these sites after a very bloody fight . . . they [the ballistic missiles] will be pointing at us. So, it still comes down to a question of whether they're going to fire the missiles."

"That's correct," McCone agreed, adding that "invading is going to be a much more serious undertaking than most people realize." There was a lot of "very evil stuff" on the island. . . . They'll give an invading force a pretty bad time." His recommendation was to move quickly to an "air strike."

5

JOHN KENNEDY was not a serious poker player, but the calculations he was making today were analogous to the strategies that skilled players make in a high-stakes game. Without invading Cuba, he was trying to force Khrushchev to fold while believing that the chairman had no intention of quitting.

"The Soviets aren't going to take them out," he had told ExComm. Yet he continued to up the ante in the hope that something short of war could induce the Soviet leader to remove his missiles.

The quarantine had failed, he concluded, and he did not believe that U Thant and Stevenson held cards that would induce Khrushchev to fold; but their diplomatic efforts were his last hope. "There's no action, other than diplomatic, that we can take, which does not immediately get rid of these," he had told McCone.

The president's focus on diplomacy might explain the "*Coolangatta* incident," a breach of the quarantine line that is not mentioned in any Cuban missile crisis literature, with the exception of the volume that transcribed the October 26 ExComm meetings, *The Presidential Recordings of John F. Kennedy: The Great Crises,* edited by Philip Zelikow and Ernest May. Its importance should not be overlooked.

The *Coolangatta* was a Swedish dry-cargo ship bound for Cuba under Soviet charter. Having uploaded at Leningrad on October 9, it refused to heed a U.S. destroyer's order to stop when it reached the quarantine line on the afternoon of October 26. Rather than immediately force the issue, the destroyer's captain requested further instructions. "The matter was bumped up to Washington," Zelikow and May report. Given the careful monitoring that McNamara had imposed on the navy, it is inconceivable that he was not informed, and it is equally unlikely that he did not consult the president.

The destroyer was ordered to allow the *Coolangatta* to proceed. The obvious conclusion is that President Kennedy was not going to take any action that might subvert U Thant's opportunity to play his diplomatic hand. It was the first of several decisions he would make over the next thirty-six hours that revealed his determination to avoid any incident that could lead to bloodshed and a confrontation with Soviet forces.

6

THE PRESIDENT returned to his West Wing office at 4:15 p.m. still pessimistic. After his daily swim and lunch, he had spent several hours in the mansion keeping abreast of negotiations at the UN, and activities on the quarantine line. It was probably between 2:00 and 4:00 p.m. when he ordered the navy to allow the *Coolangatta* to pass unopposed.

Glimmers of good news began to appear. Rusk called at 4:35 p.m. to report that U Thant's diplomacy "may move faster than we had expected." Discussions that morning with Stevenson's deputy, Charles Yost (and no doubt with a Soviet representative), suggested that a no-invasion pledge might "be a quid pro quo for getting the missiles out." Information from "the Canadians" appeared to confirm this, Rusk noted. "I think we'd have to do that [no-invasion pledge]," the president replied, (adding, perhaps for the historical record), "because we weren't going to invade them anyway."

An hour later he called Stevenson, who had returned to New York with John McCloy. A telegram from the State Department had provided them with detailed guidance. They were to insist that U Thant "at least attempt to achieve" agreement on (1) no delivery of offensive arms, (2) a halt to work on the missiles and the IL-28s, and (3) all nuclear-strike capability "being kept inoperable [the language that Stevenson had advocated during the ExComm meeting]." If these conditions were met, an arrangement for inspections would follow.

U Thant did not expect the Soviets and Cubans to accede to these demands, but he was optimistic nevertheless. Relying on an October 8 speech to the General Assembly by Cuba's president, Osvaldo Dorticós, U Thant was betting that a no-invasion pledge could be the key to a diplomatic solution. "Were the U.S. able to give us proof, by word and deed, that it would not carry out aggression against our country," Dorticós had proclaimed, "then, we declare solemnly before you here and now, our weapons would be unnecessary and our army redundant."

Stevenson too was optimistic. "I think this looks rather hopeful on the whole," he told the president.

"What we would ideally like to get," Kennedy responded, "is their [the Soviets'] agreement within the next day or so that they'll take these things out and we [and the OAS] would agree to guarantee . . . the integrity of Cuba."

It was the most agreeable possible solution.

43

"Time Is Very Urgent"

I have reason to believe that the USG sees real possibilities
and supposes that the representatives of the two governments
in New York [at the UN] could work this matter out with
U Thant and with each other. My impression is, however,
that time is very urgent.

—DEAN RUSK

Forty years later, in February 2002, Secretary of Defense Donald
Rumsfeld famously answered a question with an utterance surprisingly relevant to the next forty-eight hours of the missile crisis: "There
are known knowns; . . . things we know we know . . . There are
known unknowns; things we [know we] do not know. But there are
also unknown unknowns—the ones we don't know we don't know."
Tellingly, he neglected to mention the most important "known"—the
one that led the George W. Bush administration astray, namely, the
things that *we know, but don't know are false.*

On Friday afternoon and Saturday, October 26 and 27, such
"false knowns" *im*probably helped to guide decisions in Washington and Moscow to a peaceful resolution of the crisis. It was a lucky
assemblage of erroneous information.

1

KENNEDY KNEW that he didn't want war, and also that he would not
accept Soviet missiles in Cuba. What he did not know was whether
Khrushchev was willing to trade his missiles out of Cuba, or if he
would keep them there to confront a U.S. invasion. His "false known"

was his conviction that Khrushchev intended to attack Berlin if the United States invaded Cuba.

Khrushchev knew that he didn't want war, and that he was willing to negotiate his missiles out of Cuba. But he would trade only if he believed that an invasion was imminent. Whether it was or not, was his known unknown. His "false known" was his (now-shattered) belief that Kennedy would accept his missile deployment.

First among the several influential "false knowns" promulgated in the next thirty-six hours was a compromise solution fostered by a Soviet spy and an American correspondent.

Col. Aleksandr Feklisov, the KGB station chief in the Soviet Embassy, was accredited as a journalist and assigned the pseudonym Aleksandr Fomin. Intelligent and experienced (he had directed the Soviet penetration of the Manhattan Project during World War II), he was increasingly worried that the country he worked for, and the country he was living in, were jostling each other toward unintended disaster. Certain that neither Kennedy nor Khrushchev wanted a war, he was perplexed by the seeming lack of diplomatic initiatives. Was a negotiated solution possible? Was an invasion imminent? What was the administration thinking? How could he find answers to these critical questions?

His best source was an American he knew with "ties to the Kennedy clan." About twelve months earlier, soon after arriving in Washington, he had contacted John Scali, ABC's diplomatic correspondent. Scali covered the State Department, traveled with the secretary of state, and moderated *Questions and Answers*, a news program that interviewed politicians, cabinet members, and congressmen. They had met at least eight times, and Scali was aware of Fomin's real position: He had checked him out with the FBI.

On October 22 Scali's anger at the Soviet buildup in Cuba led him to invite Fomin to breakfast for a scolding. He "launched into accusations of Khrushchev's aggressive politics," Fomin recalled, "saying that . . . he [Khrushchev] threatened the US with missile launches from Cuba." Listening that night to Kennedy's speech, Fomin concluded that his ABC contact was as well connected as he had suspected: He appeared to have had advance knowledge of what Kennedy was going to say. That "nervous conversation" on Monday (October 22) convinced Fomin on Friday (October 26) that Scali could be helpful.

"Considering that the situation was reaching a critical point," Fomin wrote four decades later, he "invited Scali for lunch [at 2:00 p.m. at the Occidental Restaurant], hoping to get some useful information." As he recounted their meeting—which Scali remembered quite differently—Scali warned him that the military was pressing to invade Cuba and the members of ExComm "were inclined to accept" their recommendation. After debating the results of an invasion, Fomin suggested that it would precipitate retaliation against West Berlin, an action, he later admitted, that "no one authorized me to suggest. It was more like an outburst of my consciousness."

The conversation ended, in Fomin's telling, with the shared hope that Kennedy and Khrushchev "wouldn't allow bloodshed. . . . I went to report my conversation to Moscow and Scali went to the White House."

2

SCALI ACTUALLY returned to his correspondent's desk in the State Department, tense with excitement. Fomin had made a remarkable proposal that Scali summarized in a short memorandum that he passed to his friend, Roger Hilsman, the State Department's director of intelligence and research. The KGB station chief, he wrote, had urged him to "check immediately with your high State Department sources" to see if the crisis could be resolved along the following lines: (1) The Soviet Union would remove its missiles from Cuba; (2) UN inspectors would monitor the process; (3) the Soviet Union would pledge never to reintroduce them; (4) the United States would publicly pledge not to invade Cuba.

Fomin had added that Valerian Zorin "would be interested" if Ambassador Stevenson promoted this proposal at the United Nations. He then gave Scali two phone numbers. One was his direct line that bypassed the embassy switchboard, and the second was his home telephone to call "anytime day or night" if he was not in his office.

The next few hours were a whirlwind of activity. Immediately after broadcasting his *Evening News Report*, Scali was chauffeured in an official car to the State Department to meet with Rusk. The secretary was animated. He had discussed the memo with McNamara and Kennedy. The Soviets occasionally tested the American government's reaction to proposals through unofficial sources, he said, and Fomin's proposal seemed consistent with other hints of compromise.

Authorizing Scali to reply to Fomin, Rusk wrote a brief message on a yellow legal pad. "I have reason to believe that the USG sees real possibilities and supposes that the representatives of the two governments in New York [at the UN] could work this matter out with U Thant and with each other. My impression is, however, that time is very urgent."

At 7:35 p.m. Scali met Fomin in the Statler Hilton Hotel's Coffee Shop. After repeating Rusk's message from memory, he was nonplussed to hear Fomin suggest a quid pro quo: inspections of American bases in Florida and the Caribbean, where invasion forces were massing. This was something new that was sure to complicate the original proposal, he said, and he believed the president would reject it.

The conversation—including Fomin's inspection proposal—was quickly reported to Rusk, who, Scali recalled, said: "You have served your country well, John."

3

THE SCALI-FOMIN conversations are an intriguing historical conundrum. While both participants agree that they met twice on October 26, they disagree about who said what to whom. Contradicting Scali's account, a quarter century later Fomin claimed that no proposal was discussed during their 2:00 p.m. lunch at the Occidental Restaurant. But around four o'clock he reported receiving "a frantic call from Scali," who insisted that they meet promptly.

Within ten minutes, according to Fomin, they were sitting together in the café of the Statler Hilton. Scali reported that he was instructed by the "highest authority" to pass along a proposal to resolve the crisis peacefully. The Soviet Union would dismantle and evacuate its missiles from Cuba under UN inspection. The United

States would end the blockade. President Kennedy would publicly declare that the United States would not invade Cuba.

Fomin said that he took careful notes, read them back to check their accuracy, and asked for clarification regarding "highest authority." Scali said that the offer was from President Kennedy. After some further discussion, during which Scali warned that the military was urging the president to invade, Fomin rushed back to the embassy. About three hours later he forwarded his report to KGB headquarters in Moscow, after Soviet ambassador Anatoly Dobrynin refused to send it to the Foreign Ministry. Such negotiations were not authorized, the ambassador explained.

4

WHOM TO believe? And to whom did it matter? Scali's account is more credible for several reasons. First, it was confirmed in 1967 by Roger Hilsman, to whom Scali had given his summary of Fomin's 2:00 p.m. proposal. It is inconceivable that Hilsman would have published a patently false description of the events he and others, including Dean Rusk, had witnessed and abetted.

Second, Scali's narrative has a compelling logic as it moves from Fomin's proposal at the Occidental Restaurant (which both principals agree was initiated by Fomin), to the second meeting at the Statler's café (which both agree occurred, but at different times). If Fomin had not suggested the peace proposal at lunch, what could have led Secretary of State Dean Rusk to recruit a journalist to propose a solution to a KGB colonel he did not know?

But does it matter whether the proposal was initiated by Fomin or Scali? It apparently mattered to Feklisov [Fomin]. He presented his version of his meetings with Scali at the 1989 Moscow history review meeting of American and Soviet veterans of the Cuban missile crisis. It may also have mattered to Feklisov's former KGB colleagues, who wanted history to record that the initial proposal for the withdrawal of Soviet missiles from Cuba be laid at the doorstep of 1600 Pennsylvania Avenue.

Feklisov's effort to ensure that it was a White House initiative further undercuts the credibility of his account. In his telling, Scali confirmed that the highest authority is "John Fitzgerald Kennedy—

the president of the United States." That is not what Rusk had authorized, nor was that something that Scali, an experienced and sophisticated reporter, would ever have said without authorization.

Finally, there are compelling hints that Fomin was freelancing on October 26, which he did not want to admit. His proposal to Scali so accurately reflected U Thant's ideas that he had to have been briefed about them, probably by his KGB colleagues in the Soviet Union's UN delegation. Two of his statements are particularly revealing. The first was his suggestion that Soviet UN ambassador Valerian Zorin "would be interested" if Ambassador Stevenson promoted this proposal at the United Nations.

What could have given Fomin this idea had it not come from the Soviet delegation?

His approach to Scali appears to have been a personal decision to reinforce the negotiations at the UN, or a suggestion from Zorin, or someone associated with him, that he do so.

Second, Fomin's suggestion that the UN should inspect American bases in Florida and the Caribbean was a notion that U Thant had conceived that afternoon to encourage the Soviets to accept the Kennedy administration's conditions. As the historians Philip Zelikow and Ernest May noted: "U Thant thought the Russians would want to have some face-saving reciprocal right of inspection, perhaps of Cuban refugee camps in the United States." By the time Fomin and Scali met at 7:35 p.m. in the Statler Hilton coffee shop, Fomin was informed about that caveat.

Surprisingly—and tellingly—the recordings of President Kennedy's phone conversations with Stevenson at 5:00 p.m., and with Prime Minister Macmillan at 6:30 p.m., confirm that Kennedy was not opposed to authorizing some quid pro quo inspections. It seemed a small price to pay for a quick and peaceful resolution.

The pieces of the puzzle fit Scali's account far better than they fit Feklisov's. Not in doubt, however, is that ExComm and the president accepted Scali's report as a genuine proposal from the Soviet government. It was not. As the historians Aleksandr Fursenko and Timothy Naftali conclude after reviewing Feklisov's cables and other relevant KGB documents: "The story of the Scali-Feklisov back channel remains significant as a prime example of how governments can misinterpret each other, especially in the grip of a crisis."

PART EIGHT

October 27 (Saturday)–October 28 (Sunday):
The Jupiter Missile Crisis

It is "insane that two men, sitting on opposite sides
of the world, should be able to decide to bring an end to
civilization."

—PRESIDENT KENNEDY

44

"Let Us Take Measures to Untie That Knot"

October 26, Friday Evening

At this stage any movement by you may produce a result
in Berlin which would be very bad for us all. That's
the danger now.
—PRIME MINISTER MACMILLAN TO JFK

Missiles in Cuba were not the only international crisis the president confronted. Six days earlier, on October 20, Chinese forces invaded India, claiming that it had encroached on Chinese territory. They had penetrated deep within India's Northeast Frontier and Kashmir, and had proposed a cease-fire in place, rejected by India but supported by Khrushchev.

1

AT ABOUT 6 p.m., Friday evening, the president, McNamara, Bundy, and several others met for about twenty-five minutes with India's ambassador Braj Kumar Nehru. The meeting's purpose was to figure out how the United States could support India. But the Soviet missiles were on the president's mind, and several of his questions and comments offer further insights into how he was analyzing Khrushchev's thinking, and China's strategy.

As during the first days of the Cuban crisis, Kennedy's initial instinct was to understand "their reason for doing this. . . . What is it they're getting out of this?" No obvious answer was forthcoming, but one of his conclusions was that the overlapping crises are "going to bring China and Russia back very close together." Strategic considerations were controlling. They were closer when they were both under pressure, and they drifted apart when the pressure relaxed, Kennedy told Nehru. "But right now they're together [Khrushchev's support of China's cease-fire offer] because the Chinese are involved in a war and the Russians *are involved nearly in a war.*"

Speaking as an "anti-Communist now to an anti-Communist," Kennedy urged Nehru not to "let Khrushchev sit this one out urging peace and holding up your [military] arms and pacifying that way the Chinese . . . and at the same time maintaining his influence as a real friend of India, which he isn't." He wanted Khrushchev "called out," he said.

Additional pressure from the crisis in southern Asia, the president thought, might make Khrushchev more flexible in the Caribbean.

2

AMBASSADOR NEHRU was barely out of his office when Kennedy placed his daily call to Prime Minister Macmillan. Those conversations continued to be a revealing summary of his thoughts, and that evening he divulged that within two days he might have to authorize a military action against Cuba if the Soviets continued to ready their missile sites.

He began by describing U Thant's mediation efforts at the UN, but told Macmillan that in the next forty-eight hours he was going "to be faced with a problem of what to do about this buildup."

He was aware of the Soviet offer to remove their missiles in exchange for a pledge not to invade Cuba, but so far it was "a couple of hints, not enough to go on yet." He also mentioned the Soviet request for quid pro quo inspections, which he did not consider a serious problem. "I don't think we have got anything going [in the areas they want to check] that would be difficult to inspect, but this is all part of the political proposals which are now being looked at."

He expected this element of the negotiations to be clearer the following day.

Macmillan, who had become deeply worried over the course of the week that a war was in the making, was determined to prevent that from happening. To make it easier for Khrushchev to remove his missiles, the prime minister volunteered to dismantle the Thor missiles that the Eisenhower administration had deployed to England in

1958–59. Surprised by the idea, Kennedy said he would "put that into the machinery," but he didn't want "too many dismantlings." On the other hand, "it may be advantageous," he admitted.

Their conversation turned to Berlin, the consideration that had modulated the president's entire strategy. It was important, Macmillan emphasized (as he had several times since their first crisis communication), that the United States avoid any military action. "At this stage any movement by you [against Cuba] may produce a result in Berlin which would be very bad for us all. That's the danger now."

The president agreed. "That is really why we have not done more than we have done, up till now." On the other hand, he told his friend (as they often referred to each other), if we don't do anything about the continued construction of the missile sites, "then I would suppose that it would have quite an effect on Berlin anyway."

That was possible, Macmillan admitted, and said he would think about the issues and forward his suggestions. Kennedy in turn promised to "not take any further action until I have talked to you."

3

PRESIDENT KENNEDY had made meticulous efforts to maintain control over events. He had managed to keep the press from learning about the discovery of the Soviet missiles until his October 22 speech. He had micromanaged (from Admiral Anderson's point of view) how the navy was to act in support of the quarantine. He had recalled John McCloy from Germany to ensure that Adlai Stevenson negotiated as he wished him to. He had dispatched his brother to warn Dobrynin that he would not tolerate the continued presence of the Soviet missiles. Ultrasensitive to the media's influence, he had insisted that the White House control how the crisis was explained to the press: News reports could influence Soviet behavior.

This afternoon, however, Lincoln White, the State Department's press officer, had stated that the administration was preparing for "further action" if the crisis was not soon resolved. Discussing administration plans without White House clearance was prohibited, and so before retiring Kennedy called White and angrily chewed him out. His irate criticisms reveal how worried he was that any hint of U.S. action could cause Khrushchev to act hastily.

"Christ, we're meeting every morning on this to control the escalation!" he shouted at White. "The fact that you refer back to my
speech, that then gives them a lead headline saying, 'The United
States Is Planning Further Action.' . . . Now we got to get this under
control, Linc, cause it's too important. . . . Nothing dealing with the
Cuban crisis of any importance is to go out until it goes through
[Press Secretary Pierre] Salinger and comes to me. . . . The problem is when you say further action's going to be taken, then they all
say: 'What action?' And it moves this escalation up a couple of days,
when we're not ready for it. . . . So, therefore you have to be goddamn
careful!"

That was the nub of the president's strategy: "Be goddamn
careful!"

4

HOURS EARLIER a letter addressed to President Kennedy was delivered to the U.S. Embassy in Moscow. Khrushchev had spent an anxious afternoon dictating his fears about the escalating danger, but his
initial intention to propose a solution had itself escalated. The result
was an emotional exegesis (2,765 words) explaining his reasons for
deploying the missiles, his desire for peace, his critique of the U.S.
blockade, and his suggestion for a resolution.

To facilitate translation, the embassy staff divided the letter into
sections. As each segment was completed it was forwarded to the
State Department. Arriving in no particular order between 6:00 and
9:00 p.m., the letter parts were delivered to the White House. The
contents were so disordered, so personal, and so unofficial sounding that the ExComm members who pored over them—tired and
irritable—were baffled.

Had Khrushchev lost his senses? Was he drunk when he wrote
it? What exactly was he proposing? Their skeptical reaction missed
the letter's importance. It was a cri de coeur, a passionate appeal for
a peaceful solution embedded in an obsessive attempt to justify why
he had sent missiles to Cuba, why a war had to be avoided, and how
determined he was to meet the American challenge if the blockade
was intended "as the first step towards the unleashing of war."

"Everyone needs peace: both capitalists . . . and communists," he declared, and went on to warn that while elections were transient, the "logic of wars" was that they could not be stopped. "I have participated in two wars and I know that war ends when it has rolled through cities and villages, everywhere sowing death and destruction." Threatening war against the Soviet Union makes no sense, he warned, as "you would receive in reply that which you send."

He then assured the president "that your conclusions regarding offensive weapons in Cuba are groundless." Those weapons were for defense only, he insisted, and offered a disquisition on the definition of defense and offense: "Let us take, for example, a simple cannon. What kind of means is this: offensive or defensive? A cannon is a defensive means if it is set up to defend boundaries or a fortified area. But if one concentrates artillery, and adds to it the necessary number of troops, then the same cannons do become an offensive means, because they prepare and clear the way for infantry to attack. The same happens with missile nuclear weapons as well, with any type of this weapon."

He did not expect to persuade the president of his position, he admitted, but asked if Kennedy seriously thought "that Cuba can attack the United States and that even we together with Cuba can attack you from the territory of Cuba?" He did not believe that such thoughts were possible, adding that "I say precisely attack, and not destroy, since barbarians, people who have lost their sense, destroy."

The substantial remainder of the letter explained that it was the Soviet Union's position that ideological differences should be resolved by peaceful competition rather than military means, that the Soviet ships still proceeding to Cuba carried only peaceful cargoes, that the quarantine was illegal, that the Soviet missile deployment was a response to the Bay of Pigs invasion, that armaments "bring only disasters," and finally that it was necessary now for both of them to "show statesmanlike wisdom."

He then proposed a solution: "We, for our part, will declare that our ships, bound for Cuba, will not carry any kind of armaments. You would declare that the United States will not invade Cuba with its forces and will not support any sort of forces which might intend to carry out an invasion of Cuba. Then the necessity for the presence of our military specialists in Cuba would disappear."

Was the last sentence a signal that he was ready to remove the missiles? And was the memorable flourish with which he concluded his letter a hint?

"If, however, you have not lost your self-control and sensibly conceive what this [war] might lead to, then, Mr. President, we and you ought not now to pull on the ends of the rope in which you have tied the knots of war, because the more the two of us pull, the tighter this knot will be tied. And a moment may come when that knot will be tied so tight that even he who tied will not have the strength to untie it, and then it will be necessary to cut that knot. And what that would mean is not for me to explain to you, because you yourself understand perfectly of what terrible forces our countries dispose. Consequently, if there is no intention to tighten that knot and thereby to doom the world to the catastrophe of thermonuclear war, then let us not only relax the forces pulling on the ends of the rope, let us take measures to untie that knot. We are ready for this."

Exactly what Khrushchev was willing to do to "untie that knot" was the "known unknown."

45

"Liquidate the Bases in Turkey and We Win"

October 27, Saturday, Moscow

> It never occurred to anyone that publicizing the Turkish
> aspect of the deal would create additional difficulties for the
> White House.
> —OLEG TROYANOVSKY

Crises call for judgment. Judgment drives decisions, and decisions shape history. On October 27, in Washington, Moscow, and Havana, Kennedy, Khrushchev, and Castro made decisions that determined whether the Cold War remained cool or became an inferno. Their contrasting judgments made it a close call.

1

KHRUSHCHEV AWOKE in his Kremlin office on Saturday morning with a renewed sense of confidence. The fact that his missiles had not been bombed, and that no military intervention had occurred, convinced him that Kennedy did not intend to escalate the conflict, at least not in the immediate future. Ignoring the numerous intelligence reports to the contrary, he set about formulating a new strategy. The conciliatory letter he had written the previous night, he decided, was premature.

And so was his positive attitude that morning. Unbeknownst to him, Defense Minister Malinovsky had received a coded cable at 9:00 a.m. from the Soviet commander in Cuba, Gen. Issa Pliyev, reporting that he expected an air strike "in the night between October 26 and 27 or at dawn on October 27." In response he intended to "employ all available means of air defense."

Malinovsky supported Pliyev's intent, and cabled his approval at 11 a.m. He wanted the Americans to pay a heavy price if they attacked Soviet installations, but it was up to Khrushchev and the Presidium to make the final decision about how Pliyev should react.

When the Presidium gathered, Khrushchev first supported Malinovsky, but then launched into a lecture about why a war with the United States was not going to happen. Few, if any, agreed with his analysis, but they held their counsel. The United States could attack us, Khrushchev admitted, but "I think they won't venture to do this." The blockade was declared five days ago, yet there had been no attack. Why? Because we stood firm. "The measures which we have undertaken were right," he insisted.

There was still time to negotiate, and he had a new idea for resolving the crisis favorably: "We must not be obstinate," he said. First, it would be useful "to give some satisfaction to the Americans and acknowledge that we have R-12s [MRBMs] there." And second, there was an opportunity for victory: "If we could achieve additionally the liquidation of the bases in Turkey, we would win," he said, to the surprise of his colleagues.

While the Jupiters in Turkey had inspired his missile deployment, their removal had never been discussed in the Presidium. But the American journalist Walter Lippmann had suggested such a trade in his October 25 syndicated column. And, among others, Robert Kennedy's "friend," the military intelligence [GRU] officer Georgi Bolshakov, reported that the administration was open to such an exchange.

Convinced that he had hit on the perfect resolution, Khrushchev summoned a stenographer and, with the Presidium still in session, dictated his revised terms. He was pleased, he began, to read Kennedy's October 25 letter to U Thant pledging not to harass Soviet ships outside the quarantine zone: "This reasonable step on your part persuades me that you are showing solicitude for the preservation of peace."

Soviet missiles had been sent to Cuba to prevent an invasion. The president's willingness to pledge that the United States would neither invade nor support an invasion of Cuba removed the need for their presence. The Soviet Union, he wrote, would "state this commitment [to withdraw its missiles] in the United Nations."

He had said all that, more or less, in his last night's letter. He now added the bombshell: In exchange for the withdrawal of Soviet missiles, "your representatives will make a statement to the effect that the United States, on its part, bearing in mind the anxiety and concern of the Soviet state, will evacuate its analogous weapons from Turkey."

Despite his professed confidence that an invasion was not imminent, it is clear that he understood—and that the vast majority of the Presidium believed—that a peaceful resolution to the crisis was time sensitive. To avoid the delays associated with official communications channels—and for no other reason—Khrushchev decided to broadcast the text over Radio Moscow.

"It never occurred to anyone that publicizing the Turkish aspect of the deal would create additional difficulties for the White House," Khrushchev's foreign policy assistant recalled.

"In periods of crisis," the Soviet historian A. K. Kislov perceptively noted, "it is not the intentions of each side that are important, but the way that such intentions are interpreted."

"To Any Rational Man It Will
Look Like a Very Fair Trade"

October 27, Saturday, Washington

I think you're going to have it very difficult to explain why we are
going to take hostile military action in Cuba . . . when he's saying,
"If you'll get yours out of Turkey, we'll get ours out of Cuba."
—PRESIDENT KENNEDY TO EXCOMM, OCTOBER 27, 1962

Saturday, October 27, dawned a warm Indian-summer day in
Washington, D.C. It was a good omen. Following Scali's report,
Khrushchev's last letter, and U Thant's mediation efforts at the UN,
everything pointed to the possibility of a compromise. But soon after
the 10:00 a.m. ExComm meeting began, the first in a cascade of
ominous events began the most dangerous twenty-four hours of the
crisis, perhaps some of the most dangerous hours in world history.

Advisers in the White House, the Joint Chiefs in the Pentagon,
Fidel Castro in Havana, hard-liners in the Kremlin, Soviet submariners in the quarantine area, and a rogue American officer in the
missile fields of Okinawa came close to initiating a military confrontation that could have led to a nuclear holocaust. Robert McNamara
recalled thinking that he might not live to see another Saturday night.

Determined to avoid any action that might force Khrushchev to
abandon a political settlement, President Kennedy became increasingly isolated. The decisions he took that day, against all advice, literally prevented a nuclear war.

1

THE EXCOMM meeting began with a mixed report from DCI
McCone. Work on the missile installations was proceeding rapidly;

several more were now operational, and Cuba's air defense capabilities had increased. On the other hand, the Cuban military had been ordered to avoid hostilities unless fired upon, and the country's diplomats were encouraging the UN negotiations, provided there was "proof" that the United States would not attack.

McNamara reported that the Soviet freighter *Grozny* was approaching the quarantine line. He was confident that it was not transporting prohibited material, but he recommended that "we ought to stop it anyhow, and use force if necessary."

Was he determined to avoid another *Coolangatta* incident? Or did he believe that a show of force would hasten a diplomatic resolution? Before those questions were answered, Ted Sorensen interrupted with an Associated Press report: "Premier Khrushchev told President Kennedy yesterday he would withdraw offensive weapons from Cuba if the United States withdrew its rockets from Turkey."

"He didn't!" Bundy exclaimed.

Sorensen agreed.

Check on that report, Rusk told an aide.

ExComm was thrown into disorder. Was this an additional demand? Was the report a reference to a new letter? Whatever it was, the public knew as much about it as the president. By broadcasting his proposal over Radio Moscow, Khrushchev had informed the world that the Soviet Union offered a simple trade that would eliminate the possibility of war.

"Well, this is unsettling now," the president commented, "because he's got us in a pretty good spot here. Because most people would regard this as not an unreasonable proposal."

"But what 'most people,' Mr. President?" Bundy asked. Though brazen, Bundy's question reflected ExComm's collective attitude. A public Turkey-Cuba missile trade was unacceptable. The president alone appeared to recall that most had acknowledged the likelihood of this very deal at several earlier meetings. "I think you're going to have it very difficult to explain why we are going to take hostile military action in Cuba . . . when he's saying, 'If you'll get yours out of Turkey, we'll get ours out of Cuba,'" Kennedy said—convincing no one.

For the remainder of the meeting everyone resisted the president's view that Khrushchev had them "in an insupportable position." They argued that the Jupiters had no relation to the Soviet missiles in Cuba; that Khrushchev's offer in the letter he sent to Kennedy last night (the withdrawal of his missiles in exchange for a pledge not to invade Cuba) should take precedence over his latest proposal; that the two proposals were a clever "dual-track" strategy designed to confuse and divide; that Khrushchev's real objective was to eliminate our base in Turkey; and, as George Ball explained: "If we talked to the Turks, they would bring it up in NATO. This thing would be all over western Europe, and our position [would] be undermined."

Sorensen, Bundy, and Gilpatric began drafting responses to Khrushchev's announcement, and, within the hour, the White House released a statement that hewed closer to ExComm's consensus than it did to the president's preference. "Several inconsistent and conflicting proposals have been made by the U.S.S.R. within the last 24 hours, including the one just made public by Moscow," it began.

Explaining that the missiles in Cuba threatened the Western Hemisphere only, it insisted they be rendered inoperable before negotiations proceeded. "As to proposals concerning the security of nations outside this hemisphere," it concluded, "the United States and its allies have long taken the lead in seeking properly inspected arms limitation, on both sides. These efforts can continue as soon as the present Soviet-created threat is ended."

2

AT THIS point the recording system shut down, but other meeting notes document that, like everyone else, Robert Kennedy disagreed with his brother. As Bobby made the case for rejecting a trade, Jack again reminded him, and the others, that Berlin was the central consideration. The United States would have a hard time—even to its allies—justifying an attack on Cuba if it led to the loss of Berlin.

The easiest way out of the dilemma, President Kennedy suggested, was to persuade Turkey to accept the trade. It was important, therefore, to warn the Turks that the Jupiter missiles made them a prime target for Soviet retaliation should the United States move against Cuba.

At noon the president left for another meeting, having failed to convince anyone that "to any man at the United Nations, or any other rational man, it will look like a very fair trade."

If a diplomatic solution was still possible, he would have to pursue Khrushchev's offer privately.

47

"Attacking Sunday or Monday"

The President has been seized with the idea of trading
Turkish for Cuban missiles; he seems to be the only one
in favor of it. The President has a feeling that time is
running out.
—GEN. MAXWELL TAYLOR TO JCS

The longest JCS meeting, and the most intense of the crisis, began
at 1:30 and lasted until 8:00 p.m. It was six and a half hours of continuous crises, each one of which could have precipitated a military
confrontation.

1

MCNAMARA WAS present during the first hour and asked that two
plans be quickly developed. The first was to move a Polaris submarine off the Turkish coast "before we hit Cuba," with a clear warning
"to the Russians" before they had a chance to attack Turkey. The submarine would assure that NATO had sixteen invulnerable missiles
that could retaliate against Soviet targets. The second plan was to
assume "we hit the missiles in Cuba" and the Soviets then destroyed
the Jupiters in Turkey: "I think this is a very real possibility," McNamara said.

He then turned to General LeMay, who had suggested that the
JCS compose a "simple paper" based on current intelligence, recommending execution of "full-scale OPLAN 312 followed by OPLAN
316 (bomb and invade)." McNamara wanted to know "exactly" what
was meant by the phrase: "early and timely execution of OPLAN 312."

"Attacking Sunday [tomorrow] or Monday," LeMay answered. It was obvious to Taylor that LeMay's answer was unacceptable. Would the secretary agree to a recommendation to attack "after a reasonable period of time" if work on the missiles continued? he asked.

McNamara agreed, adding that it was not necessary "to say how long. But I would not accept a recommendation for attack 'now.'"

2

AT 1:41 p.m. the predicament that Khrushchev's letter had caused was magnified by a second crisis. General LeMay was informed that a U2 that had taken off from Alaska to collect air samples from Soviet nuclear tests near the North Pole had strayed over USSR territory. MiG-21s had tried to intercept it, and U.S. fighters based in Alaska (armed with air-to-air nuclear missiles as DEFCON 2 required) had taken off to protect it. "I must tell Rusk at once," McNamara said, and left the room to telephone the secretary of state.

No more than twenty-two minutes later, at 2:03, a senior officer entered the room with the news that a U2 on a mission over Cuba was thirty to forty minutes overdue. The discussion that followed is not available, but the seriousness of the issue is apparent. McNamara and Taylor left for the White House.

The JCS returned immediately to redrafting the "simple paper" General LeMay and Adm. Claude Ricketts (Vice CNO) promoted: initiating OPLAN 312 on Sunday, or Monday morning at the latest, barring positive proof that the Soviets had begun to dismantle their missile sites. Generals Wheeler and Shoup concurred, but added the proviso that OPLAN 316 (invasion) be executed as well. The draft was forwarded to the White House.

At 6:00 p.m. the Chiefs learned from communications intercepts that the overdue U2 had been destroyed, and that the Cubans had recovered the wreckage of the aircraft and the pilot's body. In addition, several of the low-level reconnaissance flights had received hostile fire, indicating that McCone's intelligence was wrong about Cuba's military having been ordered to avoid hostilities.

A half hour later General Taylor was back at the Pentagon debriefing the Chiefs about the most recent ExComm meeting. After reading President Kennedy's reply to Khrushchev's latest message, he said the "President has been seized with the idea of trading Turkish for Cuban missiles; he seems to be the only one in favor of it. The President has a feeling that time is running out."

Taylor reported that when ExComm was told about the destruction of Major Rudolph Anderson's U2, the decision was taken to discontinue reconnaissance that night, but to definitely continue the next day, "so as to get a better background for attack on Cuba."

The next exchange provides a historical surprise. Numerous histories of the Cuban missile crisis report that the Joint Chiefs pressured President Kennedy to attack the SAM site that had fired the missile that destroyed Major Anderson's U2. But the meeting notes contradict that claim. It is clear that General Taylor was alone in recommending retaliation against the SAM site. The other Chiefs were focused on attacking Cuba within forty-eight hours, and they did not want to do anything that would alert Castro to an imminent invasion.

"Should we take out a SAM site?" General Taylor asked.

"No," General LeMay replied. "We would open ourselves to retaliation. We have little to gain and a lot to lose."

"I feel the same way," General Wheeler said. "Khrushchev may loose one of his missiles on us."

Taylor disagreed: "Gentlemen, you all recommended retaliation if a U2 was downed. If this was wise on the 23rd, it should be just as wise on the 27th." The meeting notes continue with a parenthetical comment: "(Note: This is not an accurate recollection of the JCS position on 23 Oct.)"

"Intelligence this morning showed concrete pads," Wheeler reminded Taylor. "I'm afraid they have nuclear weapons there."

After some further discussion, the notes record that the JCS scrubbed the next day's U2 mission: "If an attack is to be made on Monday, there is no need for further reconnaissance."

48

"We're Going to Have to Take Our Weapons Out of Turkey"

October 27, Saturday Afternoon, Washington

We all know how quickly everybody's courage goes when
the blood starts to flow, and that's what is going to happen to
NATO. When they . . . grab Berlin, everybody's going to say:
Well, that [missile swap] was a pretty good proposition.
—PRESIDENT KENNEDY TO EXCOMM, OCTOBER 27

Events were overtaking decisions, exactly what President Kennedy
most feared. Yesterday's expectations of compromise had become
today's presumptions of war. Khrushchev's Radio Moscow broadcast had set the diplomatic agenda. Hypersensitive to public reaction,
the president began the 4:00 p.m. ExComm meeting determined to
counter the Soviet offer. In the process, he had to repeatedly explain
to his advisers why he could not summarily reject Khrushchev's
proposal.

1

THE STATE Department's draft reply to Khrushchev's letter(s)
reflected the ExComm consensus: The missiles in Turkey were unrelated to the missiles in Cuba. That was inadequate, the president
insisted. His response had to be "more forthcoming," and he proceeded to conduct a lesson on the subtleties of language. It was necessary, he added to the letter: "to first address the crisis in Cuba . . .
when we get action there, I shall certainly be ready to discuss the
matters you mentioned in your public message."

"You see," he explained, "that's more forthcoming because we're
not [rejecting his public message]. . . . None of this might be suc-

cessful," he admitted. But offering to discuss Khrushchev's proposal, after work halted on the missile sites, "is our only defense against the appeal of his trade."

Why his advisers did not recognize the trade's "appeal" baffled him.

He then parsed their disagreement. *He* was willing to negotiate the issues related to Turkey while "there's a sort of standstill in Cuba." *They* would not discuss the issues related to Turkey until the Cuba crisis was settled.

But consider this, he said: The Soviets are "not going to settle the Cuban question until they get some compensation on Cuba. [Therefore] the best position now . . . is to say we're glad to discuss this matter [Turkey] . . . and all the rest, once we get a positive indication that they have ceased their work [on their missile sites]."

The crisis was not a private U.S.–Soviet struggle, as ExComm seemed to believe. It was a public confrontation playing out on a global stage—at the UN and in the world's media—and world opinion had to be considered. If we did not reject Khrushchev's missile swap proposal outright, he emphasized, we were "in a much stronger world position because most people [would] think his offer [was] rather reasonable." If we rejected his offer outright, he reemphasized, "he [was] going to have [world] public opinion with him."

2

AS THE crisis evolved, the UN had never been absent from the U.S.–Soviet dialogue. In fact, it had never *been* a bilateral dialogue. Not only had Castro been communicating with Khrushchev, but Khrushchev, Kennedy, and Castro had been in frequent contact with U Thant. The secretary general's involvement was not unlike that of the moderator in an atomic reactor: the medium that slows the action of the neutrons and keeps the pile from going critical.

With the crisis threatening to go critical, Kennedy turned again to U Thant's moderating influence. He wanted him contacted immediately, and asked to "get any assurances from the Soviet Union that work [on the missile sites] has ceased. . . . We ought to get that, it seems to me, before the end of the afternoon. . . . He ought to call Zorin in before we discuss these other matters."

He then outlined the message he wanted sent to the secretary general. It insisted that work on the Soviet missiles in Cuba had to cease, and then he would be willing to discuss the Jupiter missiles and all related issues. But even more significant, he urged U Thant—actually deputized him—to become a major participant in the negotiations. "I, therefore, request," his message concluded, "with the utmost urgency that you seek such assurances from the Soviet Union in order that negotiations can go forward."

His dictation completed, he looked around the room, and asked in a firm voice: "I think that's the best position for us. Does anybody object to that?"

"No, it's fine," someone replied.

But within seconds one of the most telling exchanges of the crisis erupted. It was a frank debate that revealed how differently from his advisers John Kennedy analyzed Khrushchev's challenge.

Alexis Johnson worried aloud "that it [the president's message] really injects Turkey as a quid pro quo," prompting Bundy to add what was on everyone's mind: There were two audiences, the national security adviser told the president. If we appeared anxious to accept Khrushchev's trade we would be "in real trouble" with NATO. "I think that we'll all join in doing this if it is the [your] decision," he said. "But I think we should tell you that that's the universal assessment of everyone in the government that's connected with these alliance problems."

The ambassadors to NATO and Turkey had confirmed this assessment, he added. Both Thomas Finletter (NATO) and Raymond Hare (Turkey) agreed that we would "face a radical decline in the effectiveness [of the alliance]" if we appeared to be trading Turkey's defense for removal of the missiles from Cuba.

It was a strong argument—on its surface—but President Kennedy dug deeper. Like it or not, Khrushchev's trade proposal was both appealing and public. "Now, if we reject it out of hand, and then have to take military action against Cuba, then we'll also face a decline [in the alliance]," he rejoined. He was open to trying "to word it so that we don't harm anyone in NATO." But there had to be "a cessation of work. . . . If they [the Soviets] won't agree to that . . . then we retain the initiative. That's my response."

Having made his position clear, he left the room to take a call from Gen. Lauris Norstad.

3

DURING HIS absence several drafts were created, although none of them acknowledged the president's willingness to discuss Khrushchev's swap offer. But that didn't seem to matter—at least to the drafters—since "the justification for this message," Bundy explained to President Kennedy when he returned, "is that we expect it to be turned down, and expect to be acting [against Cuba] tomorrow or the next day. That's what it's for, and it's not good unless that's what happens."

And it was *arranged* to happen—in a way likely to ignite a war between the Warsaw Pact and NATO. "The military plan is very clear," McNamara explained. "A limited strike is out. . . . The military plan now is basically invasion."

Before initiating the assault, however, it was important to "minimize the Soviet response against NATO," and to have in mind "how we are going to respond to a Soviet response against NATO." Rendering the Jupiter missiles in Turkey inoperable, replacing them with Polaris submarines, and informing the Soviet Union of these changes had the best chance of avoiding "an immediate Soviet military response [against Turkey]," the secretary of defense claimed.

General Norstad, Kennedy reported, recommended calling a NATO Council meeting the following morning to consider the Jupiter trade proposal. The president liked the idea: It forced the Europeans to share responsibility for the decisions he would make in the next twenty-four to forty-eight hours. "The advantage of the meeting," he explained, "is that, if we reject it [Khrushchev's Cuba-Turkey proposal], they participate in it. And, if we accept it, they participate in it."

To the objection that the council was likely to refuse the proposal flatly, and thereby "tie our hands," the president responded that "they haven't had the alternatives presented to them. They'll say: 'Well God! We don't want to trade them [Jupiters] off.' They don't realize that in two or three days we may have a military strike which would bring perhaps the seizure of Berlin or a strike on Turkey. And then they'll say: 'My God! We should have taken it.'"

What concerned him, he repeated, was a "cheap turndown" without a clear understanding of the decision's implications: the possible loss of Berlin resulting from "an invasion of Cuba because we wouldn't take the missiles out of Turkey."

The more he thought about going to war to preserve obsolete missiles, the more irresponsible it appeared.

"We all know how quickly everybody's courage goes when the blood starts to flow," he warned his advisers, "and that's what is going to happen to NATO. When they [Soviets] start these things and they grab Berlin, everybody's going to say: 'Well, that [the missile swap] was a pretty good proposition.'" So NATO participation was absolutely necessary. "Otherwise we'll find no matter, if we take no action or if we take action, they're all going to be saying we should have done the reverse."

4

"THE QUESTION is whether we can get the Turks to do it," the president declared. McNamara believed their security concerns would lead them to cooperate. Taylor thought that pressuring them would create serious trouble with NATO. Thompson worried that a missile trade would leave Soviet planes and technicians in Cuba, which "would surely be unacceptable." Nitze was certain that only NATO could force the Turks to exchange Polaris submarines for the Jupiter missiles. And President Kennedy said he was "just thinking about what we're going to have to do in a day or so—500 sorties . . . and [then] possibly an invasion—all because we wouldn't take missiles out of Turkey."

The thought of attacking Cuba because of ExComm's intransigence irritated him. There were only two good options, he said. The first was to approach the Turks immediately with the plan to replace the Jupiter missiles with Polaris submarines. If they refused, the second option was to urge NATO to pressure them to accept the swap as a matter of alliance security.

"I just tell you," he repeated, "I think we're better off to get those missiles out of Turkey and out of Cuba [through negotiations] because . . . getting them out of Turkey and out of Cuba [militarily] is going to be very, very difficult and very bloody, in one place or another."

"Another" place was Berlin, and all the bravado about bombing and invading Cuba within a day or two was making him reconsider the invasion option. There had to be a diplomatic solution. "I'd rather go the total blockade route [adding POL]," he told ExComm; it's "a lesser step than the military action."

It was a clear message.

Sorensen got it first. The president was set against unleashing the military if there were alternatives. "I wonder, Mr. President," he said, suggesting an idea that Robert Kennedy later claimed as his own and dubbed the "Trollope ploy." Why not respond privately to the proposal Khrushchev made in last night's letter? "There's always a chance that he will still accept that," Sorensen added.

Rusk concurred, and read a draft that Adlai Stevenson had composed with the same idea in mind: "I have read your letter of October 26 with great care and find in it an indication of a willingness on your part to seek a prompt solution of the problem," it began and went on to insist that work on the missiles cease, and that discussions at the UN continue. "I therefore most earnestly urge you to join us in a rapid settlement of the Cuban crisis as your letter of October 26 suggests is possible," it concluded, "so that we can then go on to an early solution of other serious problems which I am convinced are not insoluble."

It was a good letter, but the president thought it should more forcefully emphasize that work on the missiles had to cease, and the discussion that ensued left him pessimistic. "We're not going to get these weapons out of Cuba . . . by negotiation [alone]," he fretted. "We're going to have to take our weapons out of Turkey." And, turning to Ambassador Thompson, he asked: "He's not going to take them out of Cuba, [is he]?"

5

THE DIALOGUE that followed between the president and Ambassador Thompson played a critical role in moving the Sorensen-Stevenson idea forward, and it deserves attention. It reveals the president's conviction that Khrushchev was determined to force the Jupiter missiles out of Turkey, and his willingness to listen to a contrary view.

"I don't agree, Mr. President," Thompson replied. "I think there's still a chance that we can get this line going."

"That he'll back down?" Kennedy sounded surprised.

"Well," Thompson said, "because he's already got this other proposal which he put forward [to remove the missiles for a promise not to invade Cuba]."

"But now this other public one, it seems to me, has become their public position. Isn't it?" Kennedy responded.

"This is maybe just pressure on us to accept . . . this non-invasion of Cuba," Thompson said.

"The important thing for Khrushchev," McCone added, supporting Thompson, "is to be able to say: 'I saved Cuba. I stopped an invasion.'"

The president seemed swayed, if not quite convinced, and proposed that his letter urge "a rapid settlement of the Cuban crisis as your letter starts to suggest." However, before discussing the other issues, he added, the missiles must be rendered inoperable. "I mean I want to just come back to that," he said. "Otherwise time ticks away on us."

Whether or not this was going to work, he then surmised, "depends on whether we believe that we can get a deal on just the Cuban [trade], or whether we have to agree to his position of tying [Cuba to Turkey]. Tommy doesn't think we do. I think," he said, stating how he would react if he was in Khrushchev's place, "that having made it public, how can he take these missiles out of Cuba if we just do nothing about Turkey?"

"His position," Thompson responded, "even in this public statement, is this is all started by our threat to Cuba. Now he's [able to say that he] removed that threat."

"He must be a little shaken up," Robert Kennedy guessed (correctly), "or he wouldn't have sent the message to you in the first place. . . . It's certainly conceivable that you could get him back to that [settling for the president's no-invasion pledge]. I don't think we should abandon it."

"Well," President Kennedy conceded, "I think that Adlai's letter [referencing Khrushchev's October 26th letter] is all right then."

6

THE PRESIDENT tried to shift the conversation. "Now, the other two questions that we have to decide are, one, about the NATO meeting and the timing. And the second is, what we are going to do about the Turks."

But even he could not redirect the attention of his advisers who were drafting a letter responding to Khrushchev's Friday-night proposal. The Sorensen-Stevenson idea of shifting the focus back to Khrushchev's original offer—his missiles out of Cuba in exchange for the president's pledge not to invade—had engaged everyone. The expectation was to send a White House response to U Thant, who would make it public.

"Why is U Thant going to publish this?" the president asked.

"To force out the [private] Khrushchev letter [received on Friday night] to which this is a response," George Ball replied.

"This is U Thant['s idea]?" the president asked.

No, Alexis Johnson explained. "This was Stevenson's proposal. Stevenson's proposal is that we release this letter . . . in order to get this back on the Cuba track, and the focus away from his [Khrushchev's] letter of this morning about Turkey."

It was a brilliant response to the Soviet broadcast, and it would play a major role in moving a diplomatic solution forward.

"There's going to be a hell of a fight about that [publicly pledging not to invade Cuba]," the president said. "I don't mind taking it on if we're going to get somewhere," but unless he could be confident that Khrushchev would pull out his missiles in exchange for a noninvasion pledge, it made no sense to make that offer public.

The drafting continued, and eventually everyone reached agreement on the final wording. But there are a few especially interesting exchanges along the way as the president continued his lesson in the use of diplomatic language.

"Here we go. Will everyone listen?" Kennedy said, bringing all side discussions to a halt.

"I have read your letter of October 26th with great care," Rusk read from the draft, "and find in it the indication of a willingness on your part to seek a calm solution to the problem. . . ."

Not right, the president said, and dictated an alternative. "I read your letter with great care and welcome your statement of your *desire*, because we don't really find 'willingness,'" he said.

Nor did he think that the word "welcome" in a later sentence— "I note and welcome indications in your second letter"—made sense, since he certainly did *not* "welcome" the introduction of the Turkey-Cuba swap idea.

The editing continued, line by line, perhaps for twenty minutes, until Robert Kennedy took up the Sorensen-Stevenson recommendation, and argued that the letter be trimmed down to accepting Khrushchev's Friday-night offer. "I think we just say: He made an offer. We accept the offer. And it's silly bringing up NATO at this time."

Whether it was Ambassador Thompson or his brother arguing for this strategy, President Kennedy couldn't be convinced that such an easy solution was likely. He didn't believe that Khrushchev could accept a solution that left the Jupiter missiles in Turkey. "He's not going to now [retract his public proposal]," he said. "Tommy isn't so sure. But anyway, we can try this thing. But he's going to come back, I'm certain."

7

"Now THE next question"—the president practically shouted to get everyone's attention—"is the Turkish one and NATO." The choice was either a direct arrangement with Turkey based on McNamara's proposal to substitute Polaris submarines for the Jupiter missiles, or getting NATO to apply pressure. We need "to explain to the Turks what's going to happen to them," he said, "if they end up slowing things down."

Once again the problem was time, and once again McNamara had a confrontational solution. The president should simply inform Turkey's prime minister about the problem and his proposed solution, and say, "I'm prepared to do it tonight. And I need an answer from you within six hours, or eight hours." And then he added, "Let me tell you about my conversation with [Giulio] Andreotti because it bears on this."

"Who's Andreotti?" Kennedy asked.

"The defense minister of Italy. I talked to him just two weeks ago about these Jupiters in Italy, and the Italians would be happy to get rid of them. We can swap them for Polaris submarines with both the Turks and Italians, and this will put some additional pressure on Turkey."

"That may be the way we ought to do it," the president replied halfheartedly, still wondering about how removing the Jupiter missiles would be received by NATO. "Do we want to go through NATO to do that, or do we want to do it bilaterally?"

McNamara favored a simultaneous approach and, practically in the same breath, raised two new questions: "We had [antiaircraft] fire on the surveillance [planes today]," and the *Grozny* is approaching the quarantine area. Should our surveillance continue, and should the *Grozny* be stopped and boarded? We would look "too weak," McNamara thought, if the flights were canceled and the ship was allowed to pass without being inspected.

"The main thing is to assure effective reconnaissance," General Taylor insisted. Boarding or not boarding a ship was a secondary consideration.

"Do the reconnaissance tomorrow," President Kennedy decided. "If we get fired on, then we meet here and we decide whether to do a much more general [air strike]. . . . Now let's get on with the Turkish thing."

"The Turkish thing" continued to pose problems. Almost everyone, including the president, expected the Turks to be uncooperative, and no one was confident that the NATO council would pressure them into compliance. "Well, those missiles kind of make us a hostage," McCone noted, and Rusk added that Turkey's position was: "The missiles are here. And as long as they're here, you're here."

Taking all this in, President Kennedy began to calculate how to make the best of a risky political situation. "If the Turks say no to us, it would be much better if NATO was also saying no . . . [otherwise] when the trouble comes, [they will say] that we should have asked them, and they would have told us to get them out."

The discussion about how to proceed continued for several minutes, with Bobby urging that the president allow time to negotiate with the Turks. "What is the rush about this, other than the fact of when we have to make the [air] strike [against Cuba]?" he interjected.

8

SUDDENLY EVERYTHING changed. The destruction of the U2 that the Chiefs had learned about first was passed to McNamara, who announced the report.

"Well now, this is much of an escalation by them, isn't it?" the president said, and raised the questions he always asked first. Why did Khrushchev do this? What does it mean? "How do we explain the effect of this Khrushchev message of last night and their decision [to shoot down a U2]?" Was it possible to continue high altitude reconnaissance? "How can we send a U2 fellow over there tomorrow unless we take out all the SAM sites?" he wondered.

"We should retaliate against the SAM site, and announce that if any other planes are fired on we will come back," General Taylor declared. "It's what we agreed to do two days ago." Bundy, Rusk, Dillon, Nitze, and Gilpatric agreed.

"We ought to go in at dawn and take out that SAM site," McNamara added, "and we ought to be prepared to take out more SAM sites."

49

"An Act of Legitimate Defense"

It goes without saying that in the event of an invasion
we would have had nuclear war.
—FIDEL CASTRO

On Friday night, as the president and his advisers retired contem-
plating Khrushchev's letter, Fidel Castro prepared for an invasion.
He had ordered his antiaircraft crews to fire on American planes,
alerted his military to resist any attack, briefed General Pliyev about
his intentions, and awakened Soviet ambassador Alekseyev at two in
the morning. Moscow had to be warned about the impending assault.

1

HE HAD analyzed the situation, Fidel told Alekseyev. A large number of American forces were assembling, and negotiations had not
produced a solution. Brazil's president, João Goulart, had warned
him that the United States would bomb the missiles if they were not
removed. "In twenty-four to seventy-two hours the Americans would
take some action against Cuba," he said, and he began to dictate a
letter to Khrushchev.

Whether it was the late hour preceded by nights with little sleep,
the stress, the sausages and beer he was nervously consuming, or
genuine uncertainty about what he wanted to suggest, Castro had a
difficult time explaining to Alekseyev (who was prepared to translate
the message into Russian) what he wanted to say. "I'd write it and
dictate it, and then I'd revise it again," Castro remembered. "You

have to understand that on the night of the twenty-sixth we saw no possible solution."

As Fidel dictated, edited, and discarded draft after draft, Alekseyev became increasingly confused. "I could not understand what he meant by his complicated phrases," he recalled. Was he suggesting that "we should be first to launch a nuclear strike on the enemy?" he asked Fidel.

"I don't want to say that directly," Castro replied, "but under certain circumstances, we must not wait to experience the perfidy of the imperialists, letting them initiate the first strike and deciding that Cuba should be wiped off the face of the earth."

History was the source of Castro's writer's block. Recalling Stalin's failure to heed warnings that Hitler was planning to attack the Soviet Union, he feared that Khrushchev could make the same mistake. "It goes without saying," he reflected, thinking of the tactical nuclear weapons that the Soviet forces were sure to use, "that in the event of an invasion we would have had nuclear war."

In that situation, he finally wrote: "If . . . the imperialists invade Cuba with the goal of occupying it the danger that that aggressive policy poses for humanity is so great that following that event the Soviet Union must never allow the circumstances in which the imperialists could launch the first nuclear strike against it."

It was his personal opinion, he continued, "if they [the United States] actually carry out the brutal act of invading Cuba . . . that would be the moment to eliminate such danger forever through an act of legitimate defense, however harsh and terrible the solution would be."

2

Castro's letter baffled Alekseyev, worried Khrushchev, and led to debates about its recommendations and intent. Had he urged Khrushchev to initiate a Soviet preemptive strike? Khrushchev thought so. "Fidel Castro openly advised us to use nuclear weapons," he told the Presidium in December, arguing—according to his biographer William Taubman—that Castro "forced him to yield too soon."

Given the ample evidence that Khrushchev had decided to

remove his missiles before Castro's letter arrived at the Kremlin, the charge was disingenuous. Nevertheless, it is a mistake to conclude that Castro did not influence Khrushchev's decision, or at least its timing.

As Fidel struggled to find the right language, Alekseyev began to wonder if the invasion would begin before he decided what he wanted to say. "That went on for about three hours," Alekseyev remembered, and "since the letter still wasn't ready and since its main idea was that in twenty-four or seventy-two hours an invasion or bombing could begin, I quickly wrote a little telegram to Moscow."

He was with Fidel, who was composing a letter warning about an invasion, he reported. "I wrote 'an attack,'" he confessed. "But really of course I should have written either 'invasion' or 'bombing,' which is what Fidel said. And that telegram naturally arrived considerably earlier than Fidel's letter."

It was a fortuitous mistake.

"Aside from other factors, your telegram also played a role in our being forced to accept Kennedy's conditions," Khrushchev later told his ambassador. "The conditions were such that we didn't plan to go to war, and war would have meant the death, above all, of the Cuban revolution, for which we had done all this. . . . And if before your telegram, we had been sure that nothing would happen, that we had to be firm with the Americans, well, if now you think that the Americans might attack and we're not planning to use nuclear weapons, that would mean the death of the Cuban revolution."

"So we made this decision [to remove our missiles from Cuba], literally a day later."

50

"There Is Very Little Time to Resolve This Issue"

We can't very well invade Cuba, with all this toil and blood
it's going to be, when we could have gotten them [the Soviet
missiles] out by making a deal on the same missiles in Turkey.
If that's part of the record, then I don't see how we'll have a
very good war.
—PRESIDENT KENNEDY TO EXCOMM, OCTOBER 27

President Kennedy left the Cabinet Room at 6:30 p.m. convinced of
several things: Khrushchev's swap proposal was a reasonable offer.
The Turks would resist surrendering their Jupiter missiles. The
NATO Council would not pressure them to exchange Polaris submarines for the Jupiter missiles. Forcing the exchange would damage
U.S. credibility with NATO. Not forcing the exchange would lead to
an invasion of Cuba. An invasion of Cuba would prompt the Soviets
to attack the Jupiters and seize West Berlin.

It was a nightmare scenario—and unnecessary. There had to be
a way to pull back from this slippery slope to war.

1

THE PRESIDENT returned to the ExComm meeting about seven-
twenty, having approved his draft reply to Khrushchev. To reinforce
the letter's demand for a prompt settlement, he directed his brother
to contact Dobrynin. It had to be made clear to Khrushchev, through
all available avenues, that his missiles would be destroyed if they were
not removed.

Bobby called the Soviet ambassador, and they agreed to meet within the hour at the AG's Justice Department office.

Always polite, President Kennedy restarted the ExComm meeting with an apology: "I'm sorry. I didn't mean to keep you," he said to his advisers, and asked about the state of their discussion.

There is "a very substantial difference between us," Bundy reported, and surrendered the floor to Ambassador Thompson.

"We clearly have a choice here," Thompson explained. "Either we go on the line that we've decided to attack Cuba and therefore are set to prepare the ground for that. Or we try to get Khrushchev back on a peaceful solution, in which case we shouldn't give any indication that we're going to accept anything on Turkey because the Turkish proposal is, I should think, clearly unacceptable."

Thompson's conclusion was based on a questionable interpretation: In addition to swapping missiles, Khrushchev had included "plane for plane and technician for technician," he argued. That would eliminate NATO's role in Turkey, and "leave the Russians installed in Cuba," an unacceptable result. "We ought to keep the heat on him and get him back on the line which he obviously was on the night before."

The president agreed, up to a point. "We ought to try to . . . get him back. That's what our letter's doing. That's what we're going to do by one means or another." But he still thought "we ought to have a discussion with NATO about these Turkish missiles."

The conversation during the president's absence had revealed other complications. Vice President Johnson, who had been unusually assertive in the debate, explained: "We have two alternatives. Secretary McNamara suggests that we draft a message to the Turks and to the NATO people, saying that we will give you Polaris for the Jupiters in Turkey. And then we're going to hit Cuba."

Alternatively, he added, "Ball takes the position that . . . if you're going to give up the Jupiters, you ought to get him to take care of Cuba."

"Well, there's a third view," the president responded, "which is that you take him back to his [Friday-night letter]."

"Ambassador Thompson has another idea," Douglas Dillon said approvingly. "Instead of the ultimatum . . . it would probably be more effective and make more of an impression on him if we did do what we said we were going to do before, and just go in and knock out this one SAM site."

"That would be the best way of impressing him," Bundy agreed.

At first the president ignored the suggestion and then, perhaps as a diversion, questioned whether the offending SAM site could be accurately identified.

But he was focused on the missile trade, and to bring the conversation back to it he asked if Khrushchev's radio message had said "if we took out the missiles in Turkey, he'd take out the missiles in Cuba?" If that's accurate, the president stated again, Khrushchev had painted them into a corner. "We can't very well invade Cuba, with all this toll and blood it's going to be, when we could have gotten them [the Soviet missiles] out by making a deal on the same missiles in Turkey. If that's part of the record, then I don't see how we'll have a very good war."

"It [Khrushchev's proposal] doesn't mean just missiles," the vice president said, returning to Thompson's view. One trade would lead to another, he predicted, and "then your whole foreign policy is gone."

But "how else are we going to get those missiles out of there then?" an exasperated president repeated. And sensing that the discussion was again drifting toward narrowing his options, he ended the meeting. "I think we've got two or three different proposals here. Can we meet at nine and everybody get a bite to eat?"

It was 7:45 p.m.

2

As THE meeting disbanded, the president asked Rusk, McNamara, Bundy, Ball, Gilpatric, Thompson, Sorensen, and his brother to join him in the Oval Office to consider what Bobby should say to Dobrynin. All agreed that he should warn the ambassador that the missiles would be attacked if Khrushchev failed to promptly accept the "noninvasion pledge" exchange he had proposed the night before.

Dean Rusk then made a proposal that may have enabled Khrushchev's decision to remove his missiles. It was a variant of one of the four options Ambassador Hare had proposed in his cable from Ankara: a "strictly secret" missile trade with the Soviets. While the president believed that it was politically unwise to agree publicly to exchanging missiles in Turkey for Soviet missiles in Cuba, Bobby could say that the Jupiters in Turkey would be removed within months, provided this pledge was kept secret.

Secrecy was also the overriding domestic consideration. As Bundy later wrote: "Concerned as we all were by the cost of a public bargain struck under pressure at the apparent expense of the Turks, and aware [that] . . . even this unilateral private assurance might appear to betray an ally, we agreed without hesitation that no one not in the room was to be informed of this additional message." And, in fact, no one else was told—including Vice President Johnson, who continued to believe, in his later dealings with the North Vietnamese, that not compromising was a fundamental lesson of the Cuban missile crisis.

3

BEFORE BOBBY left for his rendezvous with Dobrynin, the president's reply to Khrushchev was wired to Moscow. "Dear Mr. Chairman," it began. "I have read your letter of October 26 with great care and welcomed the statement of your desire to seek a prompt solution to the problem. The first thing that needs to be done, however, is for work to cease on offensive missile bases in Cuba and for all weapons systems in Cuba capable of offensive use to be rendered inoperable, under effective United Nations arrangements."

It continued with assurances that Ambassador Stevenson was authorized to work out the details with his Soviet counterpart and U Thant for "an arrangement for a permanent solution to the Cuban problem along the lines suggested in your letter of October 26." And, to avoid any ambiguity, the letter described "the key elements of your proposals—which seem generally acceptable as I understand them." They included removing from Cuba "these weapons systems" under UN supervision, and never reintroducing them. In exchange the United States would discontinue the quarantine and provide "assurances against an invasion of Cuba."

Rather than ignore Khrushchev's proposal for a Turkey-Cuba missile swap, as so many members of ExComm recommended, the letter finessed the idea by stating forthrightly that settling the Cuban issue first "would enable us to work toward a more general arrangement regarding 'other armaments,' as proposed in your second letter which you made public." As the historian Sheldon Stern has noted, there was no "Trollope ploy," but rather "a calculated blend of Khrushchev's October 26 and 27 proposals."

Finally, the letter continued with the president's assurance that he was "very much interested in reducing tensions and halting the arms race," that the missile sites in Cuba had to be promptly rendered inoperable, and that linking the missiles in Turkey to those in Cuba "would surely lead to an intensification of the Cuban crisis and a grave risk to the peace of the world." For this reason, he concluded: "I hope we can quickly agree along the lines outlined in this letter and in your letter of October 26."

4

DOBRYNIN ARRIVED at the Justice Department before the attorney general, keenly aware that events were approaching a critical juncture. Neither wasted time with niceties; Bobby got right to the point. The meeting lasted about thirty minutes, and Dobrynin hurried to his embassy to cable a detailed summary to Moscow. It was replete with Robert Kennedy quotations.

"I want to lay out the current alarming situation the way the president sees it," Dobrynin echoed Kennedy. "Because of the plane that was shot down, there is now strong pressure on the president to give an order to respond with fire if fired upon when American reconnaissance planes are flying over Cuba."

The flights had to continue, he said, as they were the only means by which work on the missile bases could be monitored. "The USA government is determined to get rid of those bases—up to, in the extreme case, of bombing them," and he described the dire consequences that were likely to follow: "Soviet specialists might suffer, [and] the Soviet government [would] undoubtedly respond with the same against us, somewhere in Europe. A real war [would] begin, in which millions of Americans and Russians [would] die."

This was not something the president wanted, but the time for a peaceful resolution was running out. "Here R. Kennedy mentioned as if in passing," Dobrynin wrote parenthetically, "that there are many unreasonable heads among the generals, and not only among the generals, who are 'itching for a fight.'"

The situation was terribly dangerous, Robert Kennedy had emphasized, Dobrynin reported, but he noted that the president believed that Khrushchev had proposed an acceptable solution in his letter of October 26.

"The most important thing for us, R. Kennedy stressed, is to get as soon as possible the agreement of the Soviet government to halt further work on the construction of the missile bases in Cuba and take measures under international control that would make it impossible to use these weapons." As soon as that was done the United States government would lift the quarantine and give "assurances that there will not be any invasion of Cuba." He added, Dobrynin said, that "the US government is certain of this."

Dobrynin then asked the critical question: What about Turkey?

"If that is the only obstacle to achieving the regulation I mentioned earlier," Kennedy responded, "then the president doesn't see any unsurmountable difficulties in resolving this issue." While he could not remove the Jupiter missiles without seriously damaging NATO, and his leadership of the alliance, R. Kennedy said that "President Kennedy is ready to come to agree on that question with N.S. Khrushchev, too. I think that in order to withdraw these bases from Turkey . . . we need 4–5 months."

R. Kennedy then warned that his comments about Turkey were extremely confidential; "besides him and his brother, only 2–3 people know about it in Washington." (The actual number was nine).

"The president also asked N.S. Khrushchev to give him an answer if possible within the next day [Sunday] . . . The current serious situation, unfortunately, is such that there is very little time to resolve this whole issue. Unfortunately, events are developing too quickly. The request for a reply tomorrow," stressed R. Kennedy, "is just that—a request, and not an ultimatum. The president hopes that the head of the Soviet government will understand him correctly."

The ambassador then noted that Kennedy mentioned Scali's conversation with "an Embassy adviser," another indication that the administration believed that Moscow had authorized Fomin's initiative.

"I should say that during our meeting," Dobrynin wrote in conclusion, "R. Kennedy was very upset; in any case, I've never seen him like this before. True, about twice he tried to return to the topic of 'deception' (that he talked about so persistently during our previous meeting), but he did so in passing and without any edge to it. He didn't even try to get into fights on various subjects, as he usually does, and only persistently returned to one topic: time is of the essence and we shouldn't miss the chance."

It was an extraordinary presentation, a jumble of sticks and carrots. The latter included the promises that Cuba would not be invaded, and that the Jupiters would be removed from Turkey. The former was a plea for cooperation coupled with a warning that the missiles in Cuba would be bombed, and that was likely to lead to a war that neither leader could control. A nuclear holocaust could be the price of recalcitrance.

The arsenals that both countries had relied on to provide them with security and influence were on the verge of assuring their destruction.

5

EARLIER ON October 27—several hours before the Soviet submarine B-59 prepared to fire a nuclear torpedo at U.S. Navy warships—it has been reported that one of those arsenals came close to precipitating a holocaust, and no one in Washington or Moscow was aware of the event.

General Power's order to raise SAC's Defense Condition (DEF-CON) to level 2 had not only put its bombers one step from nuclear war but also had ramped up the readiness of the U.S. missile complexes surrounding the Soviet Union and China. In October 2015 an article by Aaron Tovish in the *Bulletin of the Atomic Scientists* (*BAS*) recounted that one of those commands, the 873rd Tactical Missile Squadron on Okinawa, was mistakenly ordered to fire its thirty-two cruise missiles—each capped with a 1.1-megaton warhead—at their preset targets in the Soviet Union and China.

The article's source was John Bordne, a member of the launch crew, whose revelations were first published by Masakatsu Ota, a senior reporter for Japan's Kydo News agency. Ota had interviewed Bordne in Washington DC. Two months after Tovish's further investigations appeared in the *BAS*, the military newspaper, *Stars and Stripes,* challenged the veracity of Bordne's account with dissenting statements by other members of the 873rd.

The alleged incident began October 28 while the missileers were playing cards about four hours into their midnight shift [3:00 p.m. October 27 in Washington]. The normal coded message traffic—which always began with a weather report—arrived on schedule. But Bordne reports that the scrambled codes matched a preexisting alert code that required the launch officer, Air Force Capt. William Bassett, to open his top-secret pouch. If the codes in the pouch matched the third part of the transmitted code, he was to open a pouch that contained targeting instructions and launch keys.

To everyone's shock the codes matched. Bassett's orders were to launch the four missiles under his command.

"They called me out [of the power room] when they were opening up the black pouches with the launch codes in them," a second crewmember wrote in an email to Dr. Masakatsu Ota. "We all were saying that something was wrong since we would never have been opening those pouches unless we were at Def-Con 1," he recounted. "Our captain was the Senior Officer on duty for all of the sites, so the other launch officers called him and wanted to know what he thought. He told them not to launch the missiles."[*]

Unflappable and prudent—very much like Capt. Vasily Arkhipov, the Soviet Navy officer aboard submarine B-59 who dissuaded Captain Savitsky from launching a nuclear torpedo—Captain Bassett was calm and analytical. "We have not received the upgrade to DEFCON 1," Bordne recalled him saying, "so we need to proceed with caution." He told the launch officers in the adjoining three complexes to hold their countdowns until he received confirmation.

The information in his top-secret pouch revealed that three of the four missiles were assigned to targets in China. When another

[*] For further details, see note on p. 548.

launch officer reported that two of his missiles were similarly targeted, Bassett became convinced that the order to fire was an error. Attacking China made no sense, and he requested a confirmation from the Missile Operations Center [MOC].

When MOC confirmed the launch order, Bassett was faced with another difficult decision. A junior launch officer, a lieutenant whose missiles were targeted for the Soviet Union, announced that he was going to fire them. Captain Bassett, he said, did not have the authority to override a confirmed order from a major.

Nuclear war hung in the balance, and according to Bordne, he ordered the launch officer closest to the lieutenant (who was thirty yards away through an underground tunnel) "to send two airmen over with weapons and shoot the [lieutenant] if he tries to launch without [either] verbal authorization from the 'senior officer in the field' [Bassett] or the upgrade to DEFCON 1 by Missile Operations Center."

Checking again with MOC, Bassett demanded that the major who had transmitted the coded messages either confirm that the defense condition had been raised to 1, or issue a launch-stand-down order. Bordne could only hear Bassett's end of the phone conversation, but it was clear that the major withdrew the launch order.

Instructions to stand down the missiles were received over the same frequency as the original "weather report" alert.

"It is my opinion," the other member of Bassett's launch crew wrote to Ota, "our captain with his level head stopped a potential catastrophe. The buck stopped with him. He was the best officer I ever knew."

Fantasy or fact? For now it is an important historical conundrum that will remain in limbo until a series of Freedom of Information Act requests are investigated and made public. In the meantime, however, it is of sufficient concern to be noted. And, if Bordne's story is confirmed, it was among the luckiest chance events in world history that Capt. William Bassett, "with his level head," was the senior officer on duty in the missile fields of Okinawa on October 27–28, 1962.

51

"You Got Us into This, Now You Get Us Out"

October 28, Sunday, Moscow

Now we found ourselves face to face with the danger of
war and of nuclear catastrophe, with the possible result
of destroying the human race.
—NIKITA KHRUSHCHEV TO PRESIDIUM

At 2:00 a.m. Sunday, October 28, clocks retreated in the United
States. With the end of Daylight Saving Time Moscow was now
eight hours (rather than seven) ahead of Washington. That extra
hour would prove helpful to Khrushchev as the plans and expectations he had presented to the Presidium yesterday rapidly unraveled.

After broadcasting his "bombshell" letter on Saturday afternoon
(Moscow time), Khrushchev was confident that he had the right strategy. President Kennedy was willing to offer a no-invasion pledge, and
there were numerous reasons—among them intelligence reports that
Polaris submarines would soon be stationed near Turkey—to believe
that he would accept the missile-trade proposal. As the president and
his advisers struggled with the alarming events of "Black Saturday,"
Khrushchev received a series of communications on Sunday—several
about those same events—that led him to share the anxieties wafting
through the White House.

1

ALEKSEYEV'S MESSAGE arrived first. His warning that Fidel was certain that the United States would "attack" Cuba within twenty-four
to seventy-two hours was worrisome. But Khrushchev had hardly

processed this alert when he was assaulted by a cascade of equally unnerving events.

The Ministry of Defense reported that an American U2 had entered Soviet airspace over Chukotka, the easternmost peninsula of the Soviet Union. Was it a scouting mission preparing for an attack? On Chukotka? There was nothing there to attack. MiGs had been launched in pursuit, but the U2 had escaped Soviet territory. It wasn't clear what to conclude, but it was unsettling just the same.

Later that evening, he was shocked to learn about a far more serious U2 incident. A Soviet surface-to-air battery had fired several missiles at a U2 flying over Cuba. The aircraft had been destroyed, and the pilot had been killed. How did that happen? He had not authorized such a thing. Had his Cuban command gone rogue? Without authority his troops had drawn the first blood.

When Malinovsky explained that the Dvina crew had not been able to contact Gen. Pliyev and "had decided to be guided," as William Taubman wrote, "by Fidel Castro's instructions to his troops," Khrushchev exploded: "Whose army is our general in? The Soviet or Cuban army? If he's in the Soviet army then why does he follow someone else's order?"

"Deep down," Khrushchev later told his son, it was the U2's destruction that made him realize he would have to remove his missiles.

Next came Castro's letter, which dispelled any doubt Khrushchev may still have harbored. It arrived at the Kremlin shortly before 1:00 a.m. (Sunday), and within minutes Oleg Troyanovsky, Khrushchev's foreign policy aide (a graduate of Swarthmore College), called his home and read him the letter. As the chairman listened, he could hardly believe what he heard. He asked Troyanovsky to repeat several sentences. Could it be that Castro was proposing a nuclear first strike? "Fidel totally failed to understand our purpose," he later wrote. The missiles were sent "to keep the United States from attacking Cuba," not to start a war. The crisis was beginning to spin out of control. It had to be ended.

2

ELEVEN HOURS later, noon on Sunday, Khrushchev gathered the Presidium at Novo-Ogaryovo, the Soviet leader's spacious dacha in an exclusive Moscow suburb. The atmosphere was "highly electric," Troyanovsky recalled. As usual, Khrushchev dominated the conversation. Only Gromyko and Mikoyan commented. Seated around a large table, the others remained silent, "as if to say to Khrushchev, 'You got us into this, now you get us out.'"

Harried but blustering, Khrushchev cited Lenin's actions during World War I to explain (and justify) his exit strategy. In March 1918 Lenin had agreed to surrender Russian territory for peace with Germany. The treaty of Brest-Litovsk had been a retreat, but it had saved Bolshevism. "Our interests dictated that decision—we had to save Soviet power. Now we found ourselves face to face with the danger of war and of nuclear catastrophe, with the possible result of destroying the human race," Khrushchev said. "To save the world," it was necessary to follow Lenin's example.

He had called them together, he concluded, "to consult and debate whether you are in agreement with this kind of decision."

Whereas Lenin had yielded Russian territory to save Bolshevism, Khrushchev was merely proposing to forgo eliminating the Jupiter missiles in Turkey to "save the world." If the Presidium agreed to remove its missiles from Cuba, Kennedy would end the quarantine and pledge neither to invade, nor to abet an invasion of, Cuba. That was a good arrangement, especially since a further delay held out the possibility of an American attack. The decision was easy.

However, if an invasion did occur, how were Soviet troops in Cuba to respond? Surrender was unthinkable, and an ignominious defeat was unacceptable. General Pliyev had tactical nuclear weapons at his disposal, and while they were not specifically mentioned, the Presidium agreed that "if the attack is provoked, it is ordered to repel it with a responsive blow."

A discussion of Khrushchev's proposal was barely under way when Troyanovsky was summoned to the phone. The call was from the Foreign Ministry. Ambassador Dobrynin's cable detailing his conversation with Robert Kennedy had arrived. Troyanovsky took notes and hurried back to the meeting.

There was both good and worrying news in what he read aloud. The president didn't "see any insurmountable difficulties" with respect to removing the missiles from Turkey. But the military was pressing him hard to act. "Time was running out," the president's "agitated" brother had emphasized: "We mustn't miss our chance." The president wanted ("requested," Bobby had said) an answer on Sunday.

"It goes without saying," Troyanovsky recalled, "that the contents of the dispatch increased the nervousness in the hall by some degrees." First Deputy Foreign Minister Vasily Kuznetzov was more evocative: "Khrushchev shit [in] his pants."

3

THERE WAS no doubt about the need to act promptly. Khrushchev called for a stenographer. "I have received your [President Kennedy's] message of October 27," he dictated. The Soviet government had issued "a new order to dismantle the arms which you described as offensive, and to crate and return them to the Soviet Union."

To be certain that the secret arrangement Robert Kennedy had proposed to Dobrynin was part of the settlement, he wrote a second, confidential letter to Kennedy. Ambassador Dobrynin was told to deliver it. "In my letter to you of October 28, which was designed for publication, I did not touch on [the removal of the Jupiters]. . . . But all of the offers . . . were given on account of your having agreed to the Turkish issue raised in my letter of October 27."

He had his "victory," and to be sure that it was not undercut by another unauthorized action by his forces in Cuba—or by an impetuous general in the Pentagon—his first letter to Kennedy was rushed to Radio Moscow. At 5:00 p.m. Moscow time, Sunday, October 28 (9:00 a.m. in Washington), the news from Radio Moscow produced a sigh of relief around the world.

But not in the Pentagon.

52

"I Thought It Was My Last Meal"

October 27, Saturday Night, Washington

The essence of ultimate decision remains impenetrable to
the observer—often, indeed, to the decider himself.
—PRESIDENT KENNEDY

I'd rather my children be red than dead.
—PRESIDENT KENNEDY

Bobby returned to the White House in a dark mood, convinced that
his conversation with Dobrynin had flopped. It was about 8:40 p.m.
when he entered the residence living room, next to the presidential
bedroom. He greeted his brother and Dave Powers, the president's
pal, who, as he often did, was keeping him company. As he grimly
described his meeting, Powers continued to eat the dinner that had
been prepared by the White House staff.

"God, Dave," President Kennedy interrupted, "the way you're
eating up all that chicken and drinking up all my wine, anybody
would think it was your last meal."

"The way Bobby's been talking, I thought it was my last meal,"
Powers responded.

It was an amusing exchange, which Mimi Alford quoted in her
memoir, *Once Upon a Secret,* the story of her affair with John Kennedy. She had slipped into the bedroom before Bobby appeared "so
he wouldn't see me."

She had arrived at the White House from Wheaton College a
few hours earlier. Powers had called her dorm last night: "Come to
Washington," he said. "Mrs. Kennedy is going to Glen Ora. I'll send
a car."

What does the president's sordid affair with a nineteen-year-old college intern, whom he had seduced on his wife's bed in June, have to do with his handling of the Cuban missile crisis in October?

Mimi Alford may have been the most discerning witness of the president's mood on that fateful night.

She had "played the Waiting Game" while the president was attending the evening ExComm meeting. When he finally arrived, "his mind was clearly elsewhere," she recalled. "His expression was grave. Normally, he would have put his presidential duties behind him, had a drink, and done his best to light up the room. . . . But not on this night. . . . At one point, after leaving the room to take another urgent phone call, he came back shaking his head and said to me, 'I'd rather my children be red than dead.'"

He had made up his mind that any action that could lead to a war had to be avoided, and any initiative that could avoid a war had to be considered. Well after the last ExComm meeting, close to 11:00 p.m., Rusk had suggested a ploy that appealed to the president.

Should his letter to Khrushchev and Bobby's warning to Dobrynin not lead to a compromise, the president would authorize Rusk to call Andrew Cordier, the dean of the School of International Affairs at Columbia University. Cordier, who had worked closely with U Thant, was to suggest to the secretary general that he make a public appeal to Kennedy and Khrushchev that they accept a Turkey-Cuba missile swap.

Convinced that "war was likely if things continued on their present course," the president would comply.

Kennedy returned to the family quarters tense and exhausted. The Cuban Missile Crisis taxed the poise of even the "Great Compartmentalizer," as Alford labeled the president when, years later, she struggled to understand his behavior: "Although our get-togethers were always quite sexually charged, it wasn't to be on this occasion. . . . I was asleep by the time he came upstairs again."

Too stressed to sleep, Kennedy relaxed with Powers by watching *Roman Holiday*—a 1953 romantic film starring Gregory Peck as a middle-aged journalist and Audrey Hepburn, a young runaway princess, enjoying a brief, improbable affair in Rome.

On Sunday morning Alford awoke early to return to Wheaton. The president was sitting on (another) bed and working the phones. "I waved goodbye just before 8 A.M.," she recalled. "Thus, he was alone that Sunday morning, October 28, when word came that there would be an important announcement from Moscow at 9 A.M."

53

"We Have Ordered Our Officers to Stop Building Bases"

October 28, Sunday Morning, Washington

The great enemy of the truth is very often not the lie—
deliberate, contrived, and dishonest—but the myth—
persistent, persuasive, and unrealistic.
—PRESIDENT KENNEDY, YALE COMMENCEMENT ADDRESS,
JUNE 11, 1962

It ended with a whimper: "I express my satisfaction and thank you for the sense of proportion you have displayed and for realization of the responsibility which now devolves on you for the preservation of the peace of the world," Khrushchev's letter announced over Radio Moscow.

"It is for this reason that we instructed our officers . . . to take appropriate measures to discontinue construction of the aforementioned facilities, to dismantle them, and to return them to the Soviet Union. . . . We are prepared to reach agreement to enable United Nations Representatives to verify the dismantling of these means."

1

THE DANGER of a Cuban missile *war* caused by a miscalculation, or a misunderstanding between Kennedy and Khrushchev, was over. The danger of war caused by a panicked commander of a Soviet submarine, or a rogue American officer ordering missiles launched from Okinawa against Chinese and Soviet targets, was over. The danger of war initiated by another U2 destroyed over Cuba, or any one of a dozen other events beyond the control of the White House or the Kremlin that in the last six days had almost started a war, was over.

And the danger of ExComm members and the Joint Chiefs pressuring the president into bombing or invading Cuba was also over—although General LeMay did his best to start a war anyway.

"The Soviets may make a charade of withdrawal and keep weapons in Cuba," LeMay fumed when he heard the news of Khrushchev's capitulation. "Monday will be the last time to attack the missiles before they become fully operational," he warned. "I want to see the President later today and I hope all of you will come with me."

2

GENERAL LeMAY'S angry reaction to Khrushchev's message was the only opinion he ever shared with Fidel Castro, albeit for different reasons. Khrushchev had failed Cuba, Castro raged. He had agreed to withdraw his missiles in exchange for an empty no-invasion pledge. He had even failed to force the Jupiter missiles out of Turkey (as far as Castro or anyone else not privy to the secret agreement knew). Worse, he had not consulted his ally before announcing the missile withdrawal. He had treated Cuba like a pawn.

Consumed with resentment, Castro refused to cooperate. If the United States wanted UN inspectors to verify that the missiles were dismantled and shipped, it would have to agree to five conditions: cessation of all commercial and economic pressure against Cuba; an end to all "subversive activities" carried out against the Castro regime from the United States and other "accomplice territories"; cessation of "pirate attacks" on Cuba; an end to U.S. aircraft and ships "violating" Cuban airspace and naval space uninvited; evacuation of the U.S. Naval Base at Guantánamo.

Cuba was a proud and independent nation, and neither Khrushchev, Kennedy, nor U Thant could tell its government who could enter the island.

3

THE *IMMEDIATE* danger of war had passed, but the crisis lingered. Khrushchev's haste in agreeing to retrieve his missiles saddled him with two entwined crises that extended the quarantine—and the negotiations to end it—until November 20.

Khrushchev referred to the missiles he was removing from Cuba as "the weapons which you describe as offensive." Kennedy demanded that the IL-28 bombers—also offensive weapons—depart with the missiles. Dated and out of production, the IL-28s nevertheless could deliver nuclear bombs, and the Joint Chiefs argued that the aircraft depart with the missiles. Castro rejected the demand, and Khrushchev—caught in the middle—sent emissaries to the United States and Cuba for three weeks of tedious, humiliating negotiations.

As the missile crisis with the United States cooled down, a new "Soviet Cuban Missile Crisis" heated up.

PART NINE

Lies and Legacies

By drawing both the great powers as close to nuclear war as they dared, the Cuban Missile Crisis became the watershed in understanding how far they could go. For the next thirty years, these became the rules and the limits of the nuclear game.

—ANATOLY DOBRYNIN, SOVIET AMBASSADOR
TO THE UNITED STATES

Every man, woman and child lives under a nuclear sword of Damocles hanging by the slenderest of threads, capable of being cut at any moment by accident or miscalculation or by madness.

—JOHN F. KENNEDY, SEPTEMBER 25, 1961,
TO THE UN GENERAL ASSEMBLY

54

"Most of Them Did Not Like Adlai"

Stevenson was strong during the U.N. debate, but inside the
White House the hard-liners thought he was soft.
"IN TIME OF CRISIS," *Saturday Evening Post*, DEC. 8, 1962

The Bay of Pigs had been a "perfect failure," an embarrassment that
dogged the president's every subsequent foreign policy initiative. It
had convinced Khrushchev that Kennedy was naive and easily bul-
lied, the Republicans that he was inexperienced and politically vulnerable, and his NATO allies that he was irresolute.

But now, eighteen months later, he had achieved a "perfect triumph," and the spinning began. The view from 1600 Pennsylvania
Avenue was that neither Abraham Lincoln nor Teddy Roosevelt
could have done it better. In the days, weeks, and months that followed, the administration set about ensuring that the American public agreed with their assessment.

The president had exposed Khrushchev's duplicity, faced down
the Kremlin's nuclear threats, and forced the Soviet Union to withdraw its nuclear-armed missiles from Cuba. He had demonstrated
wisdom, resolve, and courage. Whatever foreign policy stumbles he
had made during his first twenty months were eclipsed by his actions
during his twenty-first.

1

WITH THE crisis over, John Kennedy abandoned his best instincts.
Informing his three living predecessors—Herbert Hoover, Harry
Truman, and Dwight Eisenhower—how the crisis had been resolved,

he assured each that there had been no missile trade. "We couldn't get into that [Turkey] deal," he informed Eisenhower. Khrushchev had gone back "to their more reasonable [Friday] position," he told Hoover, and "we rejected" the Jupiter trade, he lied to Truman.

While prohibiting gloating, the president encouraged ExComm alumni and their aides to speak with friendly reporters. Among the friendliest were Stewart Alsop, and one of the president's closest friends, Charles Bartlett (who in 1952 had introduced him to a beautiful socialite, Jacqueline Bouvier).

About six weeks after that happy Sunday morning when Khrushchev conceded, the *Saturday Evening Post* published the results of Alsop's and Bartlett's investigations. "In Time of Crisis" was an insider's account of "the drama and struggle out of which emerged a turning point in the Cold War." Launching the heroic narrative of the world's closest encounter with nuclear war, the article anointed Secretary of State Dean Rusk's alleged remark "at the climactic moment of the crisis" as marking "a great moment in American history: We're eyeball to eyeball, and I think the other fellow just blinked."

The authors offered three additional interpretations: John Kennedy had been a perfect leader who "never lost his nerve." He had demonstrated the courage to take necessary risks, the grit to see them through, and the wisdom not to cross the line to rash decisions. The man who had overseen the "fiasco" of April 1961 had mutated into a strategic genius: "The Bay of Pigs thing was badly planned and never really thought out," an adviser averred. "This was different. We knew the facts, knew each other and we thought it through, right to the end."

The article's second nod went to those who had "thought it through," the ExComm advisers. They confessed in interviews that their ranks had divided between hawks and doves, that "Robert Kennedy was the leading dove," but "a rolling consensus had developed, and except for Adlai we had all ended up as dawks or hoves."

And there was the article's third, most politically charged, point. "Adlai wanted a Munich. He wanted to trade U.S. bases for Cuban bases," the editors emblazoned across the top of the page in large type. And, to be certain that readers who had admired Stevenson's televised UN confrontation with his Soviet counterpart, Valerian Zorin, understood that Adlai lacked Kennedy grit, the caption on his photo read: "Stevenson was strong during the U.N. debate, but inside the White House the hard-liners thought he was soft."

"Soft"? Actually worse: He had been *right*. He had rejected the advice of the hawks, insisted from the start that a peaceful resolution was possible, and had composed an alternative to invasion that the president's best instincts had compelled him to follow.

Neither John nor Robert Kennedy, nor the ExComm Cold Warriors, could bring themselves to admit that Stevenson's insistence on a diplomatic solution had been more sensible—and more effective— than the military solutions each and every one of them had at one time or another supported.

He had committed an unpardonable error of judgment: He had rejected a military response from the outset. As a premature dove he was not worthy of respect.

2

THE PUBLICATION of "In Time of Crisis" was a major event and an example of how history can be distorted by those who control its first draft. It established the American narrative of the crisis, burnished the president's image, and validated crisis management—as allegedly practiced by ExComm—as an effective strategy for the nuclear age. It also demolished—as it was intended to do—any remaining political ambitions that Stevenson might have harbored.

John Kennedy was the article's impresario.

Bartlett was not merely Jack Kennedy's close friend; he was a confidant to whom the president turned when he needed emotional support or a trusted diplomatic gofer. Recalling his dinners at the White House during the final week of the crisis, Bartlett thought "the pressure of this period made [Kennedy] desire more to have friends around . . . for a little bit of relief from the pressure."

No doubt. But what Bartlett failed to reveal in his oral history interview for the John F. Kennedy Presidential Library was that on October 23 he had been sent by Robert Kennedy, at the president's behest, to deliver a message to Georgi Bolshakov, the GRU operative in the Soviet Embassy, who—recall—had served for more than a year as the Kennedy brothers' back channel to the Kremlin.

The president had proof that there were missiles in Cuba, that they must be removed, and that he preferred diplomacy to war, he was to tell Bolshakov: "I gave Charlie Bartlett a picture of the missiles [to show Bolshakov]," Robert Kennedy remembered.

Bartlett's dinner conversations with the president were about more than "relief from the pressure."

In November 1962 no journalist knew more about the administration's secret diplomacy than Bartlett, and he was determined to write about the episode in a way that burnished his friend's reputation: "I was over there [at the White House] for dinner, Monday or Tuesday night [after the final Sunday] and I said to the President that I was going to do this thing.

"My role, I've decided," Kennedy said, "will be not to talk to writers. . . . I would just be putting credit on myself." But with that conversation Bartlett obtained both a green light and access to all members of ExComm.

And they were willing to talk. "But when we did run into this story about Adlai Stevenson having proposed to give up the Guantanamo Naval Base, plus the missiles in Turkey, plus the missiles in Italy, having proposed this at an ExComm meeting, why, I was fascinated by it," Bartlett recalled.

"And we checked it out very quickly. . . . We first heard of it from somebody who was not in the meeting [Michael Forrestal], who had learned it from somebody who was [Bundy]. We checked it, and it checked out very quickly. There were sixteen people. . . . Most of them did not like Adlai Stevenson, and most of them were very happy to verify it." (One of "them" who did not like Stevenson was John F. Kennedy and, according to the historian Gregg Herken, "the president had penciled in the 'Munich' line when he annotated a typescript of the draft article.")

Continuing his fabricated story, Bartlett said that while dining with the president a few days later, "that this was one piece of information that we had picked up. . . . And he had that sort of wary look, you know, but he said, 'Did you hear about that?' I said, 'Yes, we got it.' He said, 'Are you going to put it in the article?'

"I said, 'Yes.' He sort of shook his head. That was the only real comment that he made. My own guess, knowing him well, would be that he was not too displeased that this had turned up."

Indeed! Is it possible that McGeorge Bundy would have told this story about Stevenson to his aide, Michael Forrestal, without John Kennedy's approval? And would Forrestal have told Bartlett, had he not been cleared to do so?

"I don't think at that point that he [JFK] or I had any idea that this thing would be linked to him," Bartlett recalled in an interview, "or that it would be a gesture of rebuff to Adlai."

Did he really say that?

"It Ain't Necessarily So. . . ."

Reflections on History's Alternatives

It ain't necessarily so
The things that you're liable
To read in the Bible
It ain't necessarily so. . . .
—*Porgy and Bess*

War had been possible—even likely—not because President Kennedy or Chairman Khrushchev saw any advantage in war, but because they had limited control over events, a realization they both came to, albeit almost too late. "Indeed, the Russian retreat came only just in time," Prime Minister Harold Macmillan believed. "We had to act very quickly," Khrushchev told the president of Czechoslovakia on October 30: "*This time we really were on the verge of war.*"

The crisis itself—independent of the leaders in Washington and Moscow—sowed the seeds of conflict, as military crises invariably do. "I think that you and I, with our heavy responsibilities for the maintenance of peace were aware that developments were approaching a point where events could have become unmanageable," President Kennedy replied to Khrushchev's October 28 message.

"Crisis managers cannot manage everything," McGeorge Bundy told me in 1988 after a "spacebridge" discussion with Soviet students on the Cuban missile crisis. "And that's where luck comes in," adding a tap on my shoulder for emphasis.

Accidents and miscalculations are as intrinsic to international relations, he implied, as they are to the rest of life, and nations have been devastated as a result. But the legacy of Hiroshima is that an accident or miscalculation involving nuclear weapons can "destroy civilization" (as Stimson told Truman), or even eradicate our species. Humanity's survival depends on the willingness of nuclear-armed leaders to prioritize long-term consequences over short-term advantages. *That*, history makes clear, is the "slenderest of threads" from which to hang a "nuclear sword of Damocles."

The decision to "quarantine" (rather than invade) Cuba prevented a repetition of the origins of World War I—a war nobody wanted but that nobody knew how to stop. Yet in the final analysis, luck ("dumb luck," Dean Acheson insisted) was also necessary to shield diplomacy from the multiple accidents and miscalculations that almost created a war.

In this sense the crisis was the ultimate reality check: Nuclear threats could lead to conflicts regardless of intentions. "We were not going to unleash a war," Khrushchev fretted as he awaited the details of Kennedy's "quarantine" speech. "We just wanted to intimidate them, to deter the anti-Cuban forces."

As the political scientist Scott Sagan determined in *The Limits of Safety*: "Neither . . . view [that of the hawks nor that of the doves] adequately considers the possibility that an *accidental nuclear war* could have occurred during the crisis."

1

WE KNOW how the Cuban missile crisis started and ended; which is to say that we know history as it happened. But what about the alternative history, the counterfactual history (as historians call it) that the Joint Chiefs and most ExComm members sought to create? Having followed the ExComm discussions and the Chiefs' recommendations, we know that bombing and invading Cuba were their preferred options, and that those options remained possibilities until the moment that Khrushchev announced he would withdraw his missiles.

In other words, what became the *alternative history* of the crisis— invading Cuba—was the one that would have unfolded if President Kennedy had not insisted on the blockade, and if Khrushchev had not accepted Kennedy's public pledge never to invade Cuba, along with his secret commitment to remove the Jupiter missiles from Turkey.

Let those who believe that history is immutable—that events had to happen the way they did—consider this: If the United States *had* invaded Cuba, and if we had lived to write about it, what would be the reaction to a revisionist history arguing that the invasion had *not* been necessary, and that a blockade could have led to a peaceful resolution?

Derision! Monday-morning-quarterbacking critics would charge: How can anyone imagine that the president, the Joint Chiefs, and the majority of ExComm were wrong? What happened had to happen if the United States was to survive the diabolical Soviet scheme, as Douglas Dillon argued in his October 17 memo to President Kennedy: "The survival of our nation demands the prompt elimination of the offensive weapons now in Cuba. . . . The blockade course [should be rejected] insofar as it is designed to lead to negotiations."

But Adlai Stevenson urged negotiations on the first day of the crisis, and President Kennedy chose to reject the militant advice advocated by the Joint Chiefs and the ExComm's majority. The president's singular decision to blockade rather than invade Cuba was the counterfactual that he forced into historical fact.

The most important takeaway from our close study of decision making in the White House is that there were, there are, and there always will be alternatives.

2

No DECISION by Presidents Truman, Eisenhower, and Kennedy, or by Chairman Khrushchev, was inevitable. That was as true about the decision to atomic-bomb Hiroshima as it was about Eisenhower's decision to publicly promote massive retaliation, and Khrushchev's to secretly deploy missiles to Cuba. History happened the way it did *not* because it had to happen that way, but because individuals in positions of authority chose particular options.

If Roosevelt had lived, would he have used atomic bombs as Truman did? If the Democrats' 1952 candidate for president, Adlai Stevenson, had won the election, would he have promoted nuclear weapons as President Eisenhower did? If Richard Nixon had been president in October 1962 would he have opted not to invade Cuba?

It's impossible to answer counterfactuals with certainty, but considering them is essential to understanding the full implications of actual decisions.

3

"OUR LEADERSHIP in the war and in the development of this weapon"—Secretary of War Henry Stimson told President Truman on April 25, 1945—"has placed a certain moral responsibility upon us which we cannot shirk without very serious responsibility for any disaster to civilization which it would further."

Whether the United States government lived up to its "moral responsibility" in the first seventeen years of the nuclear age has been long debated. Some argue that John Kennedy's decision not to invade Cuba was an exception to an irresponsible historical record.

But recall that the president chose to risk a war with the Soviet Union even though neither he nor his secretary of defense believed that Khrushchev's missiles altered the balance of nuclear power or seriously endangered the United States.

"What is the strategic impact on the position of the United States of MRBMs in Cuba?" McGeorge Bundy asked during the second ExComm meeting. "How gravely does this change the strategic balance?"

"I asked the Chiefs that this afternoon," the secretary of defense answered. "And they said: 'Substantially.' My own personal view is: *Not at all.*"

"You may say," the president added, that "it doesn't make any difference if you get blown up by an ICBM flying from the Soviet Union or one that was 90 miles away."

Two days later, at the October 18 ExComm meeting, McNamara declared the strategic value of the Soviet missiles irrelevant, "because it is not a military problem that we're facing. *It's a political problem.* It's a problem of holding the alliance together. It's a problem of properly conditioning Khrushchev for our future moves . . . and the problem of dealing with our domestic public [the president's reelection?], all requires action that, in my opinion, the shift in military balance does not require."

4

THE REAL lesson of the Cuban missile crisis—the lesson that is consistently resisted because it marginalizes the value of nuclear weapons—is that nuclear armaments create the perils they are deployed to prevent, but are of little use in resolving them.

Avoiding a nuclear war depends on the judgment of the national leaders who control nuclear arsenals, which is to say that it is contingent on the world's dwindling reservoir of good luck.

"This world really is impossible to manage so long as we have nuclear weapons," President Kennedy confided to his British friend, David Ormsby-Gore, the day before his blockade speech: "[It] is really a terrible way to have to live in this world."

Naturally, the common people don't want war; neither in Russia nor in England nor in America, nor for that matter in Germany. That is understood. But, after all, it is the *leaders* of the country who determine the policy and it is always a simple matter to drag the people along, whether it is a democracy or a fascist dictatorship or a Parliament or a Communist dictatorship. . . . voice or no voice, the people can always be brought to the bidding of the leaders. That is easy. All you have to do is to tell them they are being attacked, and denounce the pacifists for lack of patriotism and exposing the country to danger. It works the same way in any country.

—GERMAN REICHSMARSCHALL HERMAN GOERING, 1945

Notes

JFKLOHP	John F. Kennedy Library Oral History Project
JMATE	CIA Plan for overthrowing Castro [aka Bay of Pigs]
JMH	*Journal of Military History*
JSS	*Journal of Strategic Studies*
LOC	Library of Congress, Washington DC
MOC	Missile Operations Center
MRBM	Medium Range Ballistic Missile
NA	National Archives
NACP	National Archives, College Park, MD
NATO	North Atlantic Treaty Organization
NPIHP	Nuclear Proliferation International History Project, Woodrow Wilson International Center for Scholars
NRDC	National Resources Defense Council
NSAGW	National Security Archive, George Washington University, Washington, DC
NSAM	National Security Action Memorandum
NSC	National Security Council
NYPL	New York Public Library
NYT	*New York Times*
OAS	Organization of American States
OPLAN	Operational Plan
PREM	Prime Minister's Office Records [UK National Archives]
POF	President's Office Files
POL	Petroleum, Oil, and Lubricants
RFK	Robert F. Kennedy
RG	Record Group
SA-2	Surface to Air [Soviet anti-aircraft missile]
SAC	Strategic Air Command
SECDEF	Secretary of Defense
SNIE	Special National Intelligence Estimate
UK	United Kingdom National Archives
UN	United Nations
UPI	United Press International
USAF	United States Air Force
USCINCEUR	United States Commander in Chief Europe
USIA	United States Information Agency
USGPO	U.S. Government Printing Office
USNWR	*U.S. News and World Report*
WP	*Washington Post*
WWCIS	Woodrow Wilson Center for International Scholars
WWCDA	Woodrow Wilson Center Digital Archive
YLSAP	Yale Law School Avalon Project

Epigraph

vii   **"Man has mounted science"**: Letter to Charles Francis Adams Jr., London, 11 Apr. 1862. In J. C. Levenson, E. Samuels, C. Vandersee, and V. Hopkins Winner, eds., *The Letters of Henry Adams: 1858–1868* (1982), vol. 1, 290.

Prologue

xiii *Some Like It Hot*: Directed and produced by Billy Wilder, starring Marilyn Monroe, Tony Curtis, and Jack Lemmon (1959).

xiv **Friends at El Toro**: Aleksandr Fursenko and Timothy Naftali, *One Hell of a Gamble: Khrushchev, Castro, and Kennedy, 1958–1964* (Norton, 1997), 244.

xiv **Valery Yarynich**: David E. Hoffman, *The Dead Hand: The Untold Story of the Cold War Arms Race and Its Dangerous Legacy* (Doubleday, 2009), 145–47.

xv **"I cannot forget"**: Ibid., 18.

xv **They were the last survivors**: The Pentagon opposed the film and refused to cooperate. I saw *On the Beach* in the spring of 1959 sometime during the last months of my senior year at Dartmouth College and can testify to its powerful emotional impact on the audience, young and old alike.

Chapter 1: A Reflection on Luck in History

4 **"plain dumb luck"**: "Dean Acheson's Version of Robert Kennedy's Version of the Cuban Missile Crisis: Homage to Plain Dumb Luck," *Esquire*, February 1969, 76–77; Robert F. Kennedy, *Thirteen Days: A Memoir of the Cuban Missile Crisis* (Norton, 1969). R. N. Lebow and B. Pelopidas, "Facing Nuclear War. Luck, Learning and the Cuban Missile Crisis," in C. Reus-Smit et. al. (eds.), *Oxford Handbook of History and International Relations*.

Chapter 2: World War III Was About to Begin

5 **"In foreign affairs"**: "Dean Acheson's Version," 76–77.

5 **how the Cuban missile crisis was resolved**: "While the missile crisis was well-managed, under very trying circumstances, the escape from it without a major war, even a nuclear war, seems nothing short of miraculous. In the end we lucked out." Unpublished article by Robert S. McNamara and James G. Blight, "The Miracle of October: Lessons from the Cuban Missile Crisis," 3, http://the-puzzle-palace.com/files/OctMiracle.pdf.

5 **"These actions may only be the beginning"**: President John F. Kennedy, "Quarantine Speech," Oct. 22, 1962. [JFK Quarantine Speech.]

6 **the U.S. Navy deployed an armada**: Chief of Naval Operations, Report on the Naval Quarantine of Cuba, Operational Archives Branch, Post 46 Command File, Box 10, 7–9. Naval Historical Center, Washington, DC.

6 **Without the president's knowledge**: See chap. 39 for a detailed analysis of the DEFCON 2 decision.

6 **In Europe SAC**: National Security Action Memorandum [NSAM] 199, authorizing the loading of nuclear weapons. John F. Kennedy Library [JFKL], Presidential Papers, National Security, Digital Identifier: file JFKNSF-339-006-p0001.

6 **On the island of Okinawa**: Aaron Tovish, "The Okinawa Missiles of October," *Bulletin of the Atomic Scientists* (Oct. 25, 2015): https://thebulletin.org/2015/10/the-okinawa-missiles-of-october/. See also chap. 50.

7 **an attack is "almost imminent"**: Fidel Castro to Nikita Khrushchev, night of Oct. 26–27, 1962: https://nsarchive2.gwu.edu/nsa/cuba_mis_cri/621026%20Castro%20Letter%20to%20Khrushchev.pdf See also "Castro-Khrushchev, 10/26–27/62," in James G. Blight, Bruce J. Allyn, and David A. Welch, *Cuba on the Brink: Castro, the Missile Crisis, and the Soviet Collapse* (Pantheon, 1993), 509–10.

7 **"to repulse the enemy"**: Gen. Anatoly I. Gribkov and Gen. William Y. Smith, *Operation Anadyr: U.S. and Soviet Generals Recount the Cuban Missile Crisis* (Edition q, 1994), 7 and 181, for Russian text of the order.

7 **If "the imperialists invade Cuba"**: Castro to Khrushchev, Oct. 26–27, 1962, *CWIHB*, 17/18, "Global Cuban Missile Crisis at 50" [GCMC50], doc. 2, 327.

7 **Embracing Armageddon**: Castro's influence on Khrushchev's decision to bring the crisis to an end seldom receives the attention it deserves.

8 **"outright banditry"**: Letter from Chairman Khrushchev to President Kennedy, 10/24/62, *FRUS, vol.* 11, *1961–1963*, doc. 61, 185–87.

8 **"Consequently, if there is no intention"**: Telegram from the embassy in the Soviet Union to the Department of State, 10/26/62, *FRUS, vol.* 11, *1961–1963*, doc. 84, 236–40.

9 **"A very McNamara attitude"**: McGeorge Bundy interview in the documentary film *The Missiles of October: What the World Didn't Know* (1992).

9 **Having recently read Barbara Tuchman's history**: Barbara Tuchman, *The Guns of August: The Outbreak of World War I* (Macmillan, 1962); Timothy Naftali, ed., *The Presidential Recordings: John F. Kennedy, The Great Crises*, vol. 1 (Norton, 2001), 457.

9 **"200 million people"**: Pierre Salinger, quoted in the documentary film *The Missiles of October: What the World Didn't Know* (1992).

9 **He is infuriated**: Sheldon Stern, *The Cuban Missile Crisis in American Memory: Myths Versus Reality* (Stanford University Press, 2012), offers the most thorough analysis of the counsel the president received from his advisers.

10 **"You would have been impeached"**: Kennedy, *Thirteen Days*, 45.

10 **"One of the ironic things"**: President Kennedy interview with Norman Cousins, "Norman Cousins Letter to Monsignor Igino Cardinale," May 13, 1963, Norman Cousins Papers, UCLA, Box 1221, Folder: Msg Ignacio Cardinale, Archbishop Dell' Agua; Allen Pietrobon to author. See also N. Cousins, "The Improbable Triumvirate: Khrushchev, Kennedy, and Pope John, *Saturday Review*, Oct. 30, 1971, 24–35.

10 **"squeeze the Soviets"**: McNamara and Blight, "The Miracle of October," 3.

Chapter 3: "We Will Die, But We Will Sink Them All"

11 **"Each of you has in your hands"**: Quoted in Peter A. Huchthausen, *October Fury* (Wiley, 2002), 53.

11 **"The immediate cause"**: C. Wright Mills, *The Causes of World War III* (Simon & Schuster, 1958), 90.

12 **the Foxtrots are the fallback**: Ryurik A. Ketov, "The Cuban Missile Crisis as Seen Through a Periscope," *Journal of Strategic Studies [JSS]* 28, no. 2 (Apr. 2005): 218.

12 **"While it is one thing to move ships openly"**: Ibid., 219. (Emphasis added.)

12 **Ketov's revelation**: Although the (Cuban) cat was out of the bag for the submarines' officers, they nevertheless received "top-secret envelopes, which they could open only after leaving Kola Bay," the afteraction report stated. Undated report (circa December 1962), prepared by USSR Northern Fleet Headquarters, about the participation of submarines B-4, B-36, B-59, and B-130 of the Sixty-Ninth Submarine Brigade of the Northern Fleet in operation "Anadyr" during the period Oct.–Dec. 1962, translated by Svetlana Savranskaya for the National Security Archive [NSA], George Washington University [GWU].

12 **"Operation Anadyr"**: V. I. Yesin, "The Participation of the Strategic Rocket Forces in the operation 'Anadyr,'"in V. I. Yesin, ed., *Strategicheskaya Operatsiya "Anadyr": Kak Eto Bylo* (MOOVVIK, 1999): 65.

13 **forces in the Sargasso Sea**: The Sargasso Sea is a region in the middle of the North Atlantic Ocean. (It is the only sea on Earth that has no coastline.)

13 **At 0400 hours**: Ketov and the other commanders repeatedly confirmed in interviews and writings that communications with Moscow were very difficult, and, during the most critical periods of the crisis, next to impossible.

13 **"We went in blindly"**: Ketov, "The Cuban Missile Crisis as Seen Through a Periscope,": 218. The ultimate intention was to establish a major naval base in Cuba. See "Report from General Zakharov and Admiral Fokin to the Defense Council and Premier Khrushchev on Initial Plans for Soviet Navy Activities in Support of Operation Anadyr, 18 September 1962," and "Report from General Zakharov and Admiral Fokin to the Presidium, Central Committee, Communist Party of the Soviet Union on the Progress of Operation Anadyr, 25 September 1962." NSA Briefing Book No. 75, "The Submarines of October."

13 **"All of our outboard hatches"**: Svetlana Savranskaya, interviews with Captains Shumkov and Dubivko, in "New Sources on the Role of Soviet Submarines in the Cuban Missile Crisis," *JSS* 28 (Apr. 2005), 233–59.

13 **On October 24**: Vice Adm. Vasily Arkhipov, Presentation at the Conference on the Cuban Missile Crisis, October 14, 1997, Moscow, Kirov Naval Academy, National Naval Academy, Baku Web site. Provided to the author by Svetlana Savranskaya, NSA.

14 **picking one's way through a Foxtrot submarine**: A Foxtrot submarine, B-39, now a tourist attraction, can be visited at the Maritime Museum of San Diego, California. Its interior is freshly painted and it is well ventilated, but passing through it, as I did, it is easy to imagine the difficulties associated with one hundred men crowding into that confined, overheated space for an extended period.

15 **When a *nuclear* weapon is on board**: Savranskaya, "New Sources on the Role of Soviet Submarines," 239.

15 **"get over it or shut up"**: Quoted in "Crew Organization of B-39" chart, B-39 exhibit, Maritime Museum of San Diego.

16 **Yet for days it has been impossible**: Capt. Anatoly Andreyev's diary, quoted in Nikolai Cherkashin, *Povsednevnaya Zhizn' Rossiiskikh Podvodnikov* [Daily Life of Russian Submariners] (Moscow: Molodaya Gvardiya Publishing House, 2000), 111, quoted in Savranskaya, "New Sources on the Role of Soviet Submarines," 241.

16 **"14 surface units"**: "Recollections of Vadim Orlov (B-59): 'We Will Sink Them All, but We Will Not Disgrace Our Navy,'" in Alexander Mozgovoi, "The Cuban Samba of the Quartet of Foxtrots: Soviet Submarines in the Caribbean Crisis of 1962," *Military Parade, Moscow,* 2002. See also "IV. Chronology of Submarine Contact During the Cuban Missile Crisis, Oct. 1, 1962–Nov. 14, 1962," prepared by Jeremy Robinson-Leon and William Burr, part of "The Submarines of October," Electronic Briefing Book No. 75, NSA.

16 **Thirty minutes later, at 5:29**: Joseph Bouchard, *Command in Crisis: Four Case Studies* (Columbia University Press, 1992), is an excellent examination of naval operations during the crisis.

16   **"sitting in a metal barrel"**: "Orlov," in Mozgovoi, "The Cuban Samba of the
     Quartet of Foxtrots." Encasing the grenades in toilet paper tubes was intended
     to assure that the grenades didn't explode before they reached the submarine.

17   **rashes and ulcers**: Huchthausen, *October Fury*, 98.

17   **"just been freed from Auschwitz"**: Dubivko, quoted in Huchthausen, *October
     Fury*, 61.

17   **"dropping like dominoes"**: Orlov, quoted in Savranskaya, "New Sources on
     Soviet Submarines," 246.

17   **"Up to 14 cases a day"**: Andreyev Diary [Daily Life of Russian Submariners],
     111; Savranskaya, "New Sources on the Role of Soviet Submarines," 241;
     Dubivko, "In the Depths of the Sargasso Sea," *On the Edge of the Nuclear Preci-
     pice* (Moscow: Gregory Page, 1988), 318-23.

17   **Three days earlier**: President Kennedy's chosen advisers had no official status
     until October 23 when they were officially designated the Executive Commit-
     tee of the National Security Council (ExComm), but for clarity I have referred
     to them as ExComm throughout.

17   **"Quarantine Forces will drop"**: See Secretary of Defense McNamara's expla-
     nation in chapter 40. See also Peter T. Haydon, "Canadian Involvement in
     the Cuban Missile Crisis Reconsidered," *Northern Mariner* 17, no. 2 (April
     2007): 45.

18   **The Soviet government officially rejected it**: Haydon writes: "One is left to
     draw the conclusion that the Soviet political leaders were knowingly playing a
     dangerous game and that US and Canadian ASW forces attempted to identify
     the various Soviet submarines using legally-established procedures in a situa-
     tion where those submarines could have been deemed 'hostile.'" Ibid., 46. See
     also Huchthausen, *October Fury*, 151–54.

18   **"The responsibility"**: Savranskaya, "New Sources on the Role of Soviet Sub-
     marines," 242, and Ketov interview, "Soviet Subs."

18   **"Of course, once one had"**: Ketov, "The Cuban Missile Crisis as Seen Through
     a Periscope," *JSS* (Apr. 2005), 225.

19   **"in the world above"**: Ibid. and Ketov interview, "Soviet Subs": "By mid Oct.
     the situation had become very tense. Each sub had a radio-intercept team to
     intercept messages between the US and British forces, and it was getting to be
     quite alarming. It was obvious there was trouble brewing, not just in our vicin-
     ity but in Cuba proper."

19   **"Moscow was totally jammed"**: Ketov and Dubivko interviews, "Soviet Subs."

19   **The persistence of the explosions**: Shumkov and Dubivko, who were close
     friends, referred to Savitsky as "the Sweater" and to Ketov as "the Cautious."
     Huchthausen, *October Fury*, 53.

19   **"Maybe the war has already started"**: Savranskaya, "New Sources on the
     Role of Soviet Submarines," *JSS* (April 2005), 245–46. I wrote that Savitsky
     "directed" that the nuclear torpedo be readied because Svetlana Savranskaya
     told me that she did not think an "order" had been given. Emphasis added.

20   **Superman swooping out of the sky**: Rational explanations of how nuclear war
     was prevented are misleading. Of course "cool heads [and] professionalism"
     were partly responsible, but "*some amount of luck*" prevented a nuclear exchange.
     "The Submarines of October: U.S. and Soviet Naval Encounters During the
     Cuban Missile Crisis," NSA Electronic Briefing Book No. 75, William Burr

and Thomas S. Blanton, editors, October 31, 2002. https://nsarchive2.gwu.edu
/NSAEBB/NSAEBB75/index.html#9.

20 **The four captains had made a pact**: Ketov, "Soviet Subs" interview; Aleksei F.
Dubivko, "In the Depths of the Sargasso Sea," *On the Edge of the Nuclear Preci-pice*, 318–23.

20 **"If they slap you"**: Savranskaya interview with Captain Shumkov in Savran-skaya, "New Sources on the Role of Soviet Submarines," 240.

20 **"The commander's nerves"**: Andreyev Diary, in Cherkashin, *Povsednevnaya Zhizn' Rossiiskikh Podvodnikov'* [Daily Life of Russian Submariners], 111.

Chapter 4: Capt. Vasily Alexandrovich Arkhipov

22 **"Mere chance"**: Ketov, "Periscope," 227.

22 **Handsome, married**: Interview with Olga Arkhipova, *The Man Who Saved the World*, PBS documentary (2012).

23 **The atmosphere of the academy**: Arkhipov's biography, City of Baku and Kirov Caspian Higher Naval School Web sites. Translated by Evgeniya Khilji.

24 **"That was the first time"**: P. L. Ølgaard, "Accidents in Nuclear Ships," Risø National Laboratory, NKS-RAK-2(96)TR-C3, Dec. 1996; T. Nilson, I. Kudrik, and A. Nikitin, "The Russian Northern Fleet: Sources of Radiation Contamination," Bellona Foundation, Feb. 1996; M. Bivens, "Horror of Soviet Nuclear Sub's '61 Tragedy Told," *Los Angeles Times*, Jan. 3, 1994. See also Daniel Lowet, "K-19 Nuclear Submarine 1961 Incident," Stanford University, PH241, Mar. 18, 2017. Arkhipov, along with everyone else aboard K-19, received dan-gerous doses of radiation contamination from the radioactive steam that spread through the ventilation system.

25 **Savitsky "had spent all day"**: Ketov, "The Cuban Missile Crisis as Seen Through a Periscope," *JSS* 28 (Apr. 2005), 227.

25 **a bitter exchange**: The angry exchange ended with McNamara telling Ander-son: "You are not going to fire a single shot at a tanker [or anything else] with-out my express permission. Is that clear?" See chap. 39.

26 **"*Mere chance*," Ketov continues**: Ketov, "The Cuban Missile Crisis as Seen Through a Periscope," *JSS* 28 (Apr. 2005): 227. (Emphasis added.)

26 **"The destroyers maneuvered"**: Undated report, circa Dec. 1962, prepared by the USSR Northern Fleet Headquarters, about the participation of subma-rines B-4, B-36, B-59, and B-130 of the Sixty-Ninth Submarine Brigade of the Northern Fleet in operation "Anadyr" during the period Oct.–Dec. 1962, translated by Svetlana Savranskaya, NSA.

26 **"But we did not fire"**: Savranskaya, "New Sources on the Role of Soviet Subma-rines," 246.

27 **"past and along the boat"**: Arkhipov, Presentation at the Conference on the Cuban Missile Crisis, Oct. 14, 1997; Also Svetlana Savranskaya's notes on "Nuclear Close Calls," which she provided to me.

27 **Orlov "emphasized the crucial role"**: Savranskaya, "New Sources on the Role of Soviet Submarines," 246. Savranskaya reports that the story of a near-use of a nuclear torpedo by a Soviet submarine commander remains controversial in Russia. Orlov's report is from Mozgovoi, *The Cuban Samba of the Foxtrot Quartet.*

27 **And, as confirmation**: Savranskaya, "New Sources on the Role of Soviet Sub-

marines," 246 and 254, n 37; *Sobesednik: Obscherossiiskaya Yezhednevnaya Gazeta [Interlocutor: Russian Daily Newspaper]* 10, 17–23 Mar. 2004, Moscow.

27 **"He'd seen with his own eyes"**: Arkhipova, *The Man Who Saved the World*, PBS documentary (2012).

28 **He saved not only himself**: In 2003 he was posthumously awarded the Italian National Premium Rotondi Angels of Our Time award for courage and self-control in times of emergency.

28 **The extraordinary (and surely disconcerting) conclusion**: Scott D. Sagan, *The Limits of Safety: Organizations, Accidents, and Nuclear Weapons* (Princeton, 1993), 55. "Neither [the hawkish nor dovish] view," Sagan writes, "adequately considers the possibility that an *accidental nuclear war* could have occurred during the [Cuban missile] crisis."

Chapter 5: The Long Cuban Missile Crisis, 1945–1962

29 **"For every action"**: Newton's Third Law of Motion accurately reflects the Soviet response to U.S. nuclear weapons policies.

29 **"Every action produces"**: "Khrushchev's Secret Speech on the Berlin Crisis, August 1961" *(CWIHP)* https://www.mtholyoke.edu/acad/intrel/khrush.htm.

29 **"the final failure"**: John F. Kennedy, quoted by Sheldon Stern, *Averting "The Final Failure": John F. Kennedy and the Secret Cuban Missile Crisis Meetings* (Stanford University Press Nuclear Age Series, 2003): xxxi.

29 **It was "insane"**: Michael Dobbs, *One Minute to Midnight: Kennedy, Khrushchev, and Castro on the Brink of Nuclear War* (Alfred A. Knopf, 2008), 229.

30 **Would they make war obsolete**: Three of the many books that cover this issue: Fred Kaplan, *The Wizards of Armageddon* (Stanford University Press Nuclear Age Series, 1991), Gregg Herken, *The Winning Weapon: The Atomic Bomb in the Cold War, 1945–1950* (Princeton, 1988), and *Counsels of War* (Oxford University Press, 1987).

30 **Into this opportunity gap**: The best example is Herman Kahn, *On Thermonuclear War* (Princeton, 1960): passim. Two excellent studies of the "defense intellectuals" are Kaplan, *The Wizards of Armageddon*, and Herken, *Counsels of War.*

30 **Theories of nuclear weapons**: Henry Kissinger, *Nuclear Weapons and American Foreign Policy* (Council on Foreign Relations, 1957); Bernard Brodie, *The Absolute Weapon* (Harcourt, Brace, 1946); Kahn, *On Thermonuclear War*; Thomas Schelling, *The Strategy of Conflict* (Harvard U. Press, 1960).

30 **As Cold War historian Melvyn Leffler determined**: Melvyn Leffler, *A Preponderance of Power: National Security, the Truman Administration, and the Cold War* (SUP, 1992), 356–57; Melvyn Leffler, *For the Soul of Mankind: The United States, the Soviet Union, and the Cold War* (Hill and Wang, 2007) discusses the role of nuclear weapons in the superpower relationship in detail.

31 **In the familiar American telling**: The best "thirteen days history" of the crisis is Dobbs, *One Minute to Midnight*. It is a deeply researched corrective to *Thirteen Days*, which was completed by Theodore Sorensen after RFK's assassination. RFK intended his memoir to support his 1968 campaign for president. Sorensen eliminated the missile trade. See also Graham Allison and Philip Zelikow, *Essence of Decision: Explaining the Cuban Missile Crisis* (Addison-Wesley, 1999). Allison's influential early study (Oxford University Press, 1971) was the first to analyze the crisis by applying theories to the Kennedy adminis-

tration's decision making. An early influential "thirteen days history" was Elie Abel's *The Missile Crisis* (Lippincott, 1966).

31 **the Camelot legend**: Sheldon Stern published three books that detail the daily ExComm debates: *The Cuban Missile Crisis in American Memory: Myths Versus Reality* (2012); *The Week the World Stood Still: Inside the Secret Cuban Missile Crisis* (2005); *Averting "The Final Failure": John F. Kennedy and the Secret Cuban Missile Crisis Meetings* (2003). See also Ernest May and Philip Zelikow, *The Kennedy Tapes: Inside the White House During the Cuban Missile Crisis*. Under the auspices of the University of Virginia's Miller Center, Philip Zelikow and Ernest May (with Timothy Naftali et al.) corrected transcription errors in *The Kennedy Tapes* and published the revised transcripts, *The Presidential Recordings: John F. Kennedy*, vols. 1–3, *The Great Crises* (Norton, 2001). Vols. 2 and 3 were essential resources for this book.

31 **In their pathbreaking history**: Fursenko and Naftali, *One Hell of a Gamble: Khrushchev, Castro & Kennedy, 1958–1964* (Norton, 1997), x.

31 **Seemingly an impetuous choice**: Leffler, *For the Soul of Mankind*, 11–157 passim.

31 **"we would have a balance"**: Sergei Khrushchev, ed., *Memoirs of Nikita Khrushchev*, vol. 3, *Statesman, 1953–1964* (Pennsylvania State University, 2007). James Hershberg, "The Cuban Missile Crisis," in Leffler and Westad, *The Cambridge History of the Cold War*, vol. 2, *Crisis and Détente* (Cambridge University Press, 2010), 73, concludes that Khrushchev's assessment of U.S. caution in the face of a possible nuclear strike was confirmed years later by President Kennedy's secretary of defense, Robert McNamara, who said that JFK chose the blockade option as a precaution against the possibility of even a lone nuclear warhead being fired from Cuba at an American city. McNamara, "The Military Role of Nuclear Weapons: Perceptions and Misperceptions," *Foreign Affairs*, vol. 62, Fall 1983: 59–80.

32 **"crisis management"**: See especially Stewart Alsop and Charles Bartlett, "In Time of Crisis," *Saturday Evening Post*, Dec. 8, 1962, 15–20.

32 **Finally, recordings**: The first recordings were declassified in the early 1980s. Stern, *Averting "The Final Failure,"* xiii–xv. Several months before the crisis, President Kennedy ordered recording systems installed in the Oval Office and the Cabinet Room where ExComm met to discuss how to respond to the situation in Cuba. See also Michael Beschloss, *The Crisis Years: Kennedy and Khrushchev, 1960–1963* (Edward Burlingame Books/HarperCollins, 1991), 346–47.

32 **"a fly on the wall"**: Stern, *Averting "The Final Failure,"* xix.

33 **But within two days**: Barton J. Bernstein, "Reconsidering the Missile Crisis: Dealing with the Problems of the American Jupiters in Turkey," in *The Cuban Missile Crisis Revisited*, edited by James A. Nathan (St. Martin's Press, 1992), 104: "But in the most fundamental way, President John F. Kennedy was dominant: the key decisionmaker."

33 **42,000 Soviets**: For the size of Soviet troops deployed to Cuba, and CIA's substantial underestimation, see Raymond L, Garthoff, *Reflections on the Cuban Missile Crisis* (Brookings Institution, 1987), 21; Bruce J. Allyn, James G. Blight, and David A. Welch, "Essence of Revision: Moscow, Havana, and the Cuban Missile Crisis," *International Security* 14, no. 3 (Winter 1989–1990): 151–52; and Dobbs, *One Minute to Midnight*, 28.

33 **"An attack would very likely result"**: Stevenson to JFK, Memorandum summarizing conversation with the president on Oct. 16, dated Oct. 17, 1962, in *The*

Cuban Missile Crisis 1962 (Revised edition, 1998), National Security Archive Documents Reader, edited by Laurence Chang and Peter Kornbluh, 129. Carolyn Lipka performed initial research for this book in the Adlai Stevenson Papers located in the Harvey Mudd Library, Princeton University.

33 **"a peaceful solution"**: Ibid.

34 **"Our problem"**: See chap. 29.

34 **"The world in its present state"**: Secretary of War Henry L. Stimson, "Memorandum discussed with the President, April 25, 1945." Martin J. Sherwin, *A World Destroyed: Hiroshima and Its Legacies* (Stanford U. Press, 2003), app. I: 291–92.

34 **"might well put us"**: Harry S. Truman, *Year of Decisions* (New American Library, 1955), 104.

34 **"It was ever present"**: James F. Byrnes, *The Decision to Use the Atomic Bomb*, documentary narrated by Chet Huntley (NBC, 1965).

34 **atomic monopoly**: David Holloway, *Stalin and the Bomb* (Yale University Press, 1994), 134–49.

35 **the unease Truman and Byrnes shared**: Sherwin, *A World Destroyed*, 138. See also Leon V. Sigal, *Fighting to a Finish: The Politics of War Termination in the United States and Japan, 1945* (Cornell University Press, 1988), 221.

35 **Eisenhower's assumption**: Robert J. McMahon, "US National Security Policy from Eisenhower to Kennedy," 293–97, and David Holloway, "Nuclear Weapons and the Escalation of the Cold War, 1945–1962," in Leffler and Westad, eds., *The Cambridge History of the Cold War*, vol. 1, *Origins* (Cambridge University Press, 2010), 385. See also Richard Immerman, "Foreign Policy in the 1950s," in Robert D. Schulzinger, ed., *A Companion to American Foreign Relations* (Blackwell Publishing Ltd., 2003).

35 **Significant attention**: Fursenko and Naftali, *One Hell of a Gamble*, 336–38.

35 **In the past 3 years**: American Rhetoric, Online Speech Bank, John F. Kennedy, Fort Worth Chamber of Commerce, Nov. 22, 1963, https://americanrhetoric.com/speeches/jfkfortworthcocommerce.htm.

35 **"I think that now"**: Provided to author by David Holloway, who references "Zapiska N. S. Khrushcheva v Prezidium TsK KPSS o dal'neishem sokrashchenii Vooruzhennykh Sil SSSR," in Ivkin and Sukhina, eds., *Zadacha osoboi gosudarstvennoi vazhnosti*, 875–80. See also Khrushchev's memorandum to CC CPSU Presidium, Dec. 8, 1959, Woodrow Wilson Center Digital Archive, doc. 117083.

36 **Castro's revolution was secured**: However, Khrushchev could not take credit for the removal of the missiles. He was sworn to secrecy.

36 **The "Caribbean Crisis"**: Khrushchev ignored the Soviet surface-to-air missile that downed a USAF U2 over Cuba on Oct. 27, 1962, killed the pilot, Maj. Rudolph Anderson, and almost led to an air attack on the SA-2 sites in Cuba.

37 **Other ironies associated**: For a balanced evaluation of the Cordier ploy, see Philip Nash, *The Other Missiles of October: Eisenhower, Kennedy, and the Jupiters, 1957–1963*, 144–45 and chap. 6: "A Very Tidy Job: Taking Them Out, 1962–1963." Also Graham Allison and Philip Zelikow, *Essence of Decision: Explaining the Cuban Missile Crisis*, 2nd ed. (Longman, 1999), 447–66. Terry Sullivan, "Confronting the Kennedy Tapes: The May-Zelikow Transcripts and the Stern Assessments," *Presidential Studies Quarterly* 30, no. 3 (2000): 594–97; Philip D. Zelikow and Ernest R. May, "'Source Material: Controversy: The Kennedy

Tapes': Past and Future," *Presidential Studies Quarterly* 30, no. 4 (2000): 791–96; Sheldon M. Stern, "Response to Zelikow and May," *Presidential Studies Quarterly* 30, no. 4 (2000): 797–99. Mark White questions Rusk's version of the Cordier initiative. He suggests that Rusk was misremembering that on Oct. 24–25 he had discussed U.N. monitoring both Turkish and Cuban missile sites. See Mark J. White, *The Cuban Missile Crisis* (Macmillan, 1996), 202-203. Zelikow and May, *The Presidential Recordings, JFK*, vol. 3, Oct. 27, 1962: 485, n. 42. My own interpretation is that it was Rusk's Oct. 24–25 conversation with Cordier that led him to suggest to the president that Cordier ask U Thant to propose a missile swap.

37   **"the result of our adventurism"**: Sergo Mikoyan, *The Soviet Cuban Missile Crisis: Castro, Mikoyan, Kennedy, Khrushchev, and the Missiles of November* (Stanford University Press, 2012), edited and translated by Svetlana Savranskaya, NSA.

38   **those very missiles**: Philip Nash, *The Other Missiles of October.* See esp. p. 6 and chaps. 1 and 2. For the most thorough studies of the Jupiter missiles in Italy, Leopoldo Nuti, *La sfida nucleare: La politica estera italiana e le armi atomiche, 1945–1991* (Il Mulino, 2007); see also Nuti's "Missiles or Socialists? The Italian Policy of the Kennedy Administration," in Douglas Brinkley and Richard Griffiths, eds., *Kennedy and Europe* (Louisiana State University Press, 1999), and "Dall'operazione *Deep Rock* all'operazione *Pot Pie*: Una storia documentata dei missili SM 78 Jupiter in Italia," in *Storia delle Relazioni Internazionali*, 11/12, no.1 (1996/1997) and vol. 2 (1996/1997), 95–138 and 105–49, and "Italy's Nuclear Choices," *UNISCI Discussion Papers* 25 (Jan. 2011).

38   **Secretary of State Dean Rusk's energetic effort**: The Alliance for Progress failed for many reasons, including limited support to anti-Communist governments. Stephen Rabe, "Alliance for Progress," *Oxford Research Encyclopedias, Latin American History* (Oxford University Press Online.)

39   **Among the many ironies**: Dobbs, *One Minute to Midnight,* provides numerous examples of dangerous U.S., Soviet, and Cuban activities beyond the control of those nations' leaders that could have led to a military conflict: 144, 213, 234, 287, 301.

39   **"one out of three and even"**: Theodore Sorensen, *Kennedy* (Harper & Row, 1965), 705.

39   **a rogue U.S. officer in Okinawa's missile fields**: Aaron Tovish, "The Okinawa Missiles of October," *Bulletin of the Atomic Scientists* (Oct. 25, 2015): 22–25. See chap. 50.

39   **"seriously considered"**: Fursenko and Naftali, *One Hell of a Gamble,* ix.

39   **"In the supercharged atmosphere"**: Hershberg, "The Cuban Missile Crisis," 65.

40   **"I call upon Chairman Khrushchev"**: JFK Quarantine Speech. See chap. 34.

40   **That risk led each nation's**: Ira Chernus, *Apocalypse Management: Eisenhower and the Discourse of National Insecurity* (Stanford University Press, 2008), 183–96.

40   **"we would be forced to consider"**: John L. Gaddis, *Strategies of Containment* (Oxford University Press, 1982), 147. Also McGeorge Bundy, *Danger and Survival: Choices About the Bomb in the First Fifty Years* (Random House, 1988), 251. (Emphasis added by Bundy). Eisenhower to Dulles, Sept. 8, 1953, *FRUS*, vol. 2, *1952–1954*, 460. Chernus, *Apocalypse Management*, cites numerous other Eisenhower apocalyptic suggestions, 183–96.

43   "The glitter of nuclear weapons": An interview with Freeman Dyson in the documentary film "The Day After Trinity: J. Robert Oppenheimer and the Atomic Bomb" (Jon Else, 1981).

Chapter 6: "This Is the Greatest Thing in History"

44   "When a 'bomb'": Memo of conversation between Roosevelt and Prime Minister Winston Churchill at Hyde Park, New York, September 18, 1944. President's Map Room papers, Naval Aide's file, box 172, General folder, FDRL, Hyde Park, NY (Emphasis added).

44   "If we, as a professedly Christian nation": John Foster Dulles, Harry S. Truman Papers, President's Secretary's Files, Box 167, File National Security Council—Atomic File, 1945–1952, HSTL. Also available at: Press Release, 10 August 1945, Dulles Papers, Box 26, "Re Atomic Weapons," Seeley Mudd Library, Princeton University.

45   Everyone knew someone: Almost 400,000 women served the armed forces— a number that exceeded total male troop strength in 1939.

45   America lost many young men: John W. Chambers, ed. *The Oxford Companion to American Military History* (OUP, 1999), 849.

46   "As long as we can outproduce": Melvyn Leffler, *A Preponderance of Power: National Security, the Truman Administration, and the Cold War* (SUP, 1992), 17.

47   "Our leadership in the war": Stimson Diary, April 25, 1945, and Manhattan Engineering District Records, Harrison-Bundy Files, folder 60, National Archives [Emphasis added.]; Sherwin, *A World Destroyed*, App. I, 291.

47   "at least as much concerned": Truman, *Year of Decisions*, 87.

47   "If the problem of the proper use": Stimson memo, April 25, 1945.

47   The primary question: Sherwin, *A World Destroyed*, 194–95.

47   "went right down to the bottom": Stimson Diary, March 6, 1945. See also Barton J. Bernstein, "Truman and the A-Bomb: Targeting Noncombatants, Using the Bomb, and His Defending the 'Decision,'" *Journal of Military History* (July 1998): 547–69.

47   He knew that his close adviser: Kai Bird, *The Chairman: John J. McCloy & the Making of the American Establishment* (Simon & Schuster, 1992): 245–47.

48   Yet he never suggested: However, Stimson was responsible for eliminating Kyoto from the atomic bomb target list. Otis Cary, "The Sparing of Kyoto: Mr. Stimson's 'Pet City,'" *Japan Quarterly*, no. 22 (Oct.–Dec. 1975): 337–47. See also Alex Wellerstein, "The Kyoto Misconception," *Restricted Data: The Nuclear Secrecy Blog:* http://blog.nuclearsecrecy.com/2014/08/08/kyoto-misconception.

48   "like the needle of an old Victrola": Elting E. Morison, *Turmoil and Tradition* (Houghton Mifflin, 1960): 167–68.

48   As early as December 1944: Stimson Diary, December 31, 1944; Sherwin, *A World Destroyed*, 5.

48   this unique peculiarity: Stimson Diary, summary entry April 6–11, 1945; Sherwin, *A World Destroyed*, 140.

49   tangled wave of problems: Stimson Diary, May 15, 1945. For a more complete discussion of Stimson's thinking about the military use of the atomic bomb, see Sherwin, *A World Destroyed*, 193–202.

49   The test of the [plutonium] bomb: On the postponement of the Potsdam Conference to coincide with the atomic bomb test, see Richard G. Hewlett and Oscar E. Anderson, Jr., *The New World, 1939–1946: A History of the United*

States Atomic Energy Commission, vol. I. (Pennsylvania State University Press, 1962): 352. Sherwin, *A World Destroyed*, 186–87, and Gar Alperovitz, *Atomic Diplomacy: Hiroshima and Potsdam* (Simon & Schuster, 1965): 65. Alperovitz makes the case for a "strategy of delayed showdown."

49   **the heady conclusion:** Truman, *Year of Decisions*, 87.

50   **"quid pro quo from the Soviet Union":** Stimson Diary, December 31, 1944; Sherwin, *A World Destroyed*, 134.

50   **"some way of persuading Russia to play ball":** Stimson Diary, May 16, 1945. See also Sherwin, *A World Destroyed*, 165–92.

50   **"The bomb as a merely probable weapon":** Henry L. Stimson and McGeorge Bundy, *On Active Service in Peace and War* (Harper & Brothers, 1947), 637. Emphasis added.

51   **To make his point even clearer:** Sherwin, *A World Destroyed*, 223–24.

51   **"tremendously pepped up":** Stimson Diary, July 21, 1945.

51   **"Now I know what happened":** *FRUS: The Conference of Berlin, 1945*, vol. I, 225; Winston S. Churchill, *The Second World War*, vol. 6, *Triumph and Tragedy* (Houghton Mifflin, 1953): 640.

52   **"the news from US":** Stimson Diary, July 23, 1945.

52   **"He was apparently relying greatly":** Ibid., July 22, 1945.

52   **"a hard time with reparations":** Byrnes's attitude disturbed Davies. He wrote: "Byrnes's attitude that the atomic bomb assured ultimate success in negotiations disturbed me more than his description of its success amazed me. I told him the threat wouldn't work, and might do irreparable harm." Joseph E. Davies Diaries, July 28, 1945, Joseph E. Davies Papers, Library of Congress [LOC].

52   **a royal straight flush:** Stimson Diary, May 14, 1945.

52   **"the Great Equalizer":** Ibid., July 23, 24, 1945; Stimson and Bundy, *On Active Service*, 638.

52   **"get along without them":** Stimson Diary, July 23, 1945.

53   **But he was quick to add:** Ibid., July 23, 24, 1945.

53   **"the Secretary [Byrnes] was still hoping":** Clemson University Libraries, Special Collections, Clemson, SC; Mss. 243, Walter J. Brown Papers, box 10, folder 12, Byrnes, James F.: Potsdam, Minutes, July–Aug. 1945, Walter Brown Diaries, July 10–Aug. 3, 1945. See Brown's entry for July 24, 1945, "W.B.'s Book," July 24, 1945, James F. Byrnes papers, folder 602; see also Byrnes, *Speaking Frankly*, 208; Truman, *Year of Decisions*, 444; Thomas G. Paterson, "Potsdam, the Atomic Bomb, and the Cold War: A Discussion with James F. Byrnes," *Pacific Historical Review* (May 1972): 225–30.

54   **The American public applauded:** As president, Truman had to approve the decision, but he was not directly involved in the decision-making process. General Groves, the Army Officer in Charge of the Manhattan Project, summed up Truman's role as akin to "a little boy on a toboggan." Fletcher Knebel and Charles W. Bailey, "The Fight Over the Atom Bomb," *Look* magazine, August 13, 1963, 20; Leslie R. Groves, *Now It Can Be Told* (Harper, 1962).

54   **"saved a million American lives":** Stimson, "The Decision to Use the Atomic Bomb," *Harper's* magazine, February 1947, first asserted the million number. https://www.atomicheritage.org/key-documents/stimson-bomb See also Barton Bernstein, "Reconsidering Truman's Claim of 'Half a Million American Lives' Saved by the Atomic Bomb: The Construction and Deconstruction of a Myth," *Journal of Strategic Studies* 22, no. 1 (Mar. 1999): 54–95, and B. Bernstein,

"The Atomic Bombings Reconsidered," *Foreign Affairs,* vol. 74, no. 1 (Jan./Feb. 1995): 135–52. A Gallup poll conducted in late August found that 85 percent of those questioned approved of the use of the bomb against Japanese cities. "The Quarter's Polls," *Public Opinion Quarterly* 9, no. 3 (Autumn 1945): 385; and John E. Mueller, *War, Presidents and Public Opinion* (John Wiley, 1973), 172–73.

54 **"the greatest thing in history":** Truman, *Year of Decisions,* 465.

Chapter 7: "The Secret of the Atomic Bomb Might Be Hard to Keep"

55 **little progress at Potsdam:** Gar Alperovitz, *Atomic Diplomacy, Hiroshima and Potsdam,* argues that the American negotiators resisted resolving any of the major issues with the Soviets on the assumption that the United States would have more leverage after the atomic bomb had been demonstrated. David Holloway, *Stalin and the Bomb,* 130–33. Herbert Feis, *The Atomic Bomb and the End of World War Two* (Princeton University Press, 1966); Tony Judt, *Postwar: A History of Europe Since 1945* (Penguin Books, 2005); Michael S. Nieberg, *Potsdam: The End of World War II and the Remaking of Europe* (Basic Books, 2015).

55 **His atomic energy advisory committee:** Stimson organized the Interim Committee to provide a forum for discussions of the postwar role of the atomic bomb. But at the May 31 meeting the question of how the bomb should be used during the war arose. The consensus was that "we could not give the Japanese any warning; that we could not concentrate on a civilian area; but that we should seek to make a profound psychological impression on as many of the inhabitants as possible. At the suggestion of Dr. Conant" [James B. Conant, a chemist, president of Harvard, and chairman of the National Defense Research Committee] the Secretary agreed that the most desirable target would be a vital war plant employing a large number of workers and closely surrounded by workers' houses." Manhattan Engineer District Records, Harrison-Bundy Files, folder # 100, National Archives; Sherwin, *A World Destroyed,* app. L, 302.

55 **"we have a new weapon":** Holloway, *Stalin and the Bomb,* 117–18.

56 **a highly placed British citizen:** Christopher Andrew and Oleg Gordievsky, *KGB: The Inside Story* (HarperCollins, 1990), 293. The five infamous British spies were John Cairncross, Anthony Blunt, Guy Burgess, Donald Maclean, and Kim Philby.

56 **By the summer of 1945:** David Holloway, "Barbarossa and the Bomb: Two Cases of Soviet Intelligence in World War II," in *Secret Intelligence in the European States System, 1918–1989,* edited by Jonathan Haslam and Karina Urbach (Stanford University Press, 2013), 55–59; *Citizen Kurchatov: Stalin's Bomb Maker,* a documentary film (Oregon PBS, 1999), Martin J. Sherwin and Brian Kaufman co-executive producers.

56 **"I hope you make good use of it":** Truman, *Year of Decisions,* 458. It appears that Truman fabricated Stalin's response to provide added support for the bombings of Hiroshima and Nagasaki.

56 **"Thank you":** Holloway, *Stalin and the Bomb,* 116–18. Anthony Eden, the British foreign secretary, who was close and intently watching the conversation, wrote that Stalin merely nodded his head and said, "Thank you." A. Eden, *The Reckoning* (Houghton Mifflin, 1965), 635.

56 **Before leaving for Potsdam:** David Holloway lecture, June 11, 2016, Nuclear History Boot Camp, Allumiere, Italy.

57 **"Let them. We'll have to have a talk"**: Igor Kurchatov was the director of the Soviet atomic bomb project, which was a relatively insignificant effort until after Hiroshima was bombed. See: Georgiĭ Konstantinovich Zhukov, *The Memoirs of Marshal Zhukov* (Delacorte Press, 1971), 675.

57 **the success of the Alamogordo test**: Holloway, *Stalin and the Bomb*, 117–18.

57 **"tenacity and steadfastness"**: David Holloway, "Nuclear Weapons and the escalation of the Cold War, 1945–1962," *Cambridge History of the Cold War*, vol. 1, 179.

57 **like a "thunderbolt"**: Vladislav Zubok, *A Failed Empire: The Soviet Union in the Cold War from Stalin to Gorbachev* (University of North Carolina Press, 2007), 27.

57 **The fact that he should have expected it**: David Holloway, "Racing Toward Armageddon? Soviet Views of Strategic Nuclear War, 1955–1972," in *The Age of Hiroshima*, ed. by M. Gordin and G. J. Ikenberry (Princeton University Press, 2019), chapter 5. Holloway makes the case that Stalin probably did not know that a Japanese city would be atomic bombed.

57 **"on an essentially defeated enemy"**: J. Robert Oppenheimer, "The International Control of Atomic Energy," Bulletin of the Atomic Scientists (June 1, 1946). See also J. Robert Oppenheimer, Speech to the American Philosophical Society, Nov. 2, 1945, American Philosophical Library Scientists Collection and James A. Hijiya, "The 'Gita' of J. Robert Oppenheimer," *Proceedings of the American Philosophical Society*, vol. 144, no. 2 (June, 2000), 123–67.

57 **"a gauntlet thrown down by Truman"**: Holloway, "Racing," chap. 5 in Gordin and Ikenberry, *The Age of Hiroshima*. See also Sergey Radchenko and Campbell Craig, *The Atomic Bomb and the Origins of the Cold War* (Yale University Press, 2008).

58 **"Unconditional surrender"**: Sherwin, *A World Destroyed*, 235. The USA intercepted this message. For an excellent collection of primary sources see NSA, Electronic Briefing Book No. 162, ed. by William Burr, https://nsarchive2.gwu.edu/NSAEBB/NSAEBB162/index.htm

58 **Signing a new set of orders**: Tsuyoshi Hasegawa, *Racing the Enemy: Stalin, Truman, and the Surrender of Japan* (Harvard University Press, 2005), 195–96.

58 **"On the surface the conversation"**: Kennan telegram to the Department of State, 8 August 1945, A. Harriman papers, Kai Bird collection. See also Harriman papers, Box 181, LOC and David Holloway, *Stalin and the Bomb*, 128–29.

59 **Stalin may have found it difficult**: For works on WWII atomic espionage see: Robert Chadwell Williams, *Klaus Fuchs: Atom Spy* (Harvard University Press, (1987); Joseph Albright and Marcia Kunstel, *Bombshell: The Secret Story of America's Unknown Atomic Spy Conspiracy* (Times Books, 1997); and John Earl Haynes, Harvey Klehr, and Alexander Vassiliev, *Spies: The Rise and Fall of the KGB in America* (Yale University Press, 2009).

59 **"Japan will surrender"**: Robert Messer, *The End of an Alliance: James F. Byrnes, Roosevelt, Truman, and the Origins of the Cold War* (University of North Carolina Press, 1981), 105.

60 **"Hiroshima was not as immediately threatening"**: Holloway, *Stalin and the Bomb*, 129.

60 **"a New Fact in the world's power politics"**: Ibid.

60 **"Before the atom bomb was used"**: Gar Alperovitz and Kai Bird, "The Centrality of the Bomb," *Foreign Policy*, No. 94 (Spring, 1994), 3.

60   **"my legs practically gave way"**: Andrei Sakharov, *Memoirs,* translated by Richard Lourie (Alfred A. Knopf, 1990), 92.

60   **"They are killing the Japanese"**: Holloway, "Racing Toward Armageddon?" in *Age of Hiroshima,* edited by Michael D. Gordin and John Ikenberry (Princeton University Press, 2020), chap. 5.

60   **designated Problem No. 1**: Ibid.

61   **"The balance has been destroyed"**: Andrew and Gordievsky, *KGB: The Inside Story,* 376. Cited by Thomas Cochran, Robert Norris, and Oleg Bukharin, *Making the Russian Bomb from Stalin to Yeltsin* (Westview Press, 1995), chap. 1.

61   **He soon put Lavrenty Beria**: David Holloway, "Nuclear Weapons and the Escalation of the Cold War," *Cambridge History of the Cold War,* vol. 1, 377.

61   **"Washington's blackmail"**: Radchenko, "The Soviet Union and the Arms Race," manuscript, 1. See also Craig and Radchenko, *The Atomic Bomb and the Origins of the Cold War,* esp. chap. 4, "Responding to Hiroshima and Nagasaki."

61   **"Take measures to organize acquisition"**: Holloway, *Stalin and the Bomb,* 129.

61   **At about the same time**: Ibid.

61   **Stalin was kept apprised**: Ibid., 129–30.

62   **But Stalin also wanted to occupy Hokkaido**: Boris N. Slavinsky, "The Soviet Occupation of the Kurile Islands and the Plans for the Capture of Northern Hokkaido," *Japan Forum* (Apr. 1993): 97–98, referenced in Holloway, *Stalin and the Bomb,* 124. Marshal Zhukov and Molotov had opposed the occupation arguing that the Allies would see it as a violation of the Yalta Agreements, but Stalin ignored their concerns, 131, 168. Hasegawa, *Racing the Enemy,* 115–16.

62   **angered by Truman's rejection**: Ibid.

62   **"To avoid the creation of conflicts"**: Holloway, *Stalin and the Bomb,* 131.

62   **Stalin may have taken this action**: Between August 1945 and the spring of 1947 Stalin's Sovietization of Central European countries was "very subtle"—"a gesture to the West"—because he still hoped for economic aid. Quoted from a lecture at the Woodrow Wilson Center for International Scholars, Washington DC, by Csaba Békés, Nov. 19, 2015.

Chapter 8: "Our Momentary Superiority"

64   **"The question then is how long we can afford"**: Secretary of War Henry L. Stimson, "Memorandum for the President: Proposed Action for Control of Atomic Bombs," September 11, 1945. Stimson Diaries, Yale University Sterling Library.

64   **a debate over the bomb's expected impact**: Alice Kimball Smith, *A Peril and a Hope: The Scientists' Movement in America* (University of Chicago Press, 1965) discusses the debate throughout. See also Gregg Herken, *Brotherhood of the Bomb: The Tangled Lives and Loyalties of J. Robert Oppenheimer, Ernest Lawrence, and Edward Teller* (Henry Holt, 2002), 159-228; Bird and Sherwin, *American Prometheus,* 323–50.

64   **Harry Truman was fatefully dropped**: Sherwin, *A World Destroyed.* See esp. chapter 6, "The New President," 143–164.

64   **Convinced that dropping atomic bombs**: Messer, *The End of an Alliance;* David Robertson, *Sly and Able: A Political Biography of James F. Byrnes* (Norton, 1994); Alperovitz, *Atomic Diplomacy;* and Alperovitz, *The Decision to Use the Atomic Bomb* (Knopf, 1995). Alperovitz was the first historian to identify the central

role that Byrnes played during the early months of the Truman administration.

65 **"the most influential Southern member"**: Robertson, *Sly and Able*, 126.

66 **From the beginning of his tenure**: Ibid.

66 **"the bomb in his pocket"**: Stimson Diary, August 12, to Sept. 3, 1945. [Summary entry.]

66 **"In handing you today my memorandum"**: Stimson memo to Truman, Sept. 11, 1945; Stimson summary of his conversation with Truman, diary entry Sept. 12, 1945.

66 **"I believe that this long process of change"**: Stimson Diary, "Memorandum on the Effects of Atomic Bomb," Sept. 12, 1945.

67 **Echoing President Roosevelt's primary postwar goal**: H. W. Brands, *Traitor to His Class: The Privileged Life and Radical Presidency of Franklin Delano Roosevelt* (Anchor Books, 2009); Michael Dobbs, *Six Months in 1945: FDR, Stalin, Churchill, and Truman from World War to Cold War* (Vintage, 2013); and Robert Dallek, *Franklin D. Roosevelt: A Political Life* (Viking, 2017).

67 **"an all-out effort"**: On August 20, 1945, Stalin established a Committee on the Atomic Bomb. David Holloway, "Nuclear Weapons and the Escalation of the Cold War, 1945–1962," *Cambridge History of the Cold War*, vol. 1, 377.

68 **"Whether Russia gets control"**: Stimson's presentation of the short and long estimates of when the USSR might develop its own atomic arsenal reflected the debate between the Manhattan Project's leading scientists and Gen. Leslie Groves. The scientists predicted that the Soviet Union was capable of producing atomic weapons in three to five years. General Groves predicted twenty years. The Soviet Union tested its first atomic bomb on August 29, 1949.

68 **"The Soviets would be more apt"**: Stimson was ahead of his time. He had recommended the sort of arms-control initiative that the United States and Soviet Union would not realize until the Strategic Arms Limitation Talks (SALT I) were completed twenty-seven years later. Negotiations for SALT I, which began in Nov. 1969, produced the first U.S.–Soviet treaty to place a limit on nuclear weapons in May 1972.

68 **"Our leadership in the war"**: Stimson memo for Truman, Apr. 25, 1945, MED Records, Harrison-Bundy Files, folder 60, NA; Sherwin, *A World Destroyed*, App. I, 291.

68 **"he was in full accord"**: Stimson diary, Sept. 12, 1945.

68 **Truman was being solicitous**: Stimson suffered a heart attack in Nov. 1945. He died on Oct. 20, 1950. Truman, *Year of Decisions*, 524–25.

69 **he reiterated his two main points**: Stimson Diary, Sept. 21, 1945.

69 **There was little support**: Byrnes, who was at the London foreign ministers' meeting, did not attend, but it is clear that he opposed Stimson's suggestions. See Walter Millis, ed. (with E. S. Duffield), *The Forrestal Diaries* (Viking Press, 1951), and John Morton Blum, ed., *The Price of Vision: The Diary of Henry A. Wallace, 1942–1946* (Houghton Mifflin, 1974).

69 **The bomb had not yet altered**: Bernard Brodie, ed., *The Absolute Weapon: Atomic Power and World Order* (Yale Institute of International Studies, Preliminary Draft for Restricted Distribution, 1946). General Eisenhower's marked copy of the Brodie manuscript, esp. p. 5 of introduction by F. Dunn, and pp. 23 ("I've always lived by this doctrine."), 32, 38, 62. https://www.osti.gov/opennet/servlets/purl/16380564-wvLB09/16380564.pdf.

70   The intellectual leader of the atomic-arms-for-security: Nicholas Thompson, *The Hawk and the Dove: Paul Nitze, George Kennan and the History of the Cold War* (Henry Holt, 2009).

70   **Developed over six weeks:** Richard G. Hewlett and Oscar E. Anderson, Jr., *The New World, 1939/1946*, vol. 1, *A History of the United States Atomic Energy Commission* (Pennsylvania State University Press, 1962), 536–40. Kai Bird and Martin J. Sherwin, *American Prometheus: The Triumph and Tragedy of J. Robert Oppenheimer* (Alfred A. Knopf, 2005), 339–49.

71   **As Oppenheimer and Acheson predicted:** Bird and Sherwin, *American Prometheus*, 339–49.

71   **Was the appropriate response:** Bird and Sherwin, *American Prometheus*, 339–47.

71   **"a quantum leap":** Lewis Strauss, a commissioner on Atomic Energy Commission. Eric Schlosser, *Command and Control: Nuclear Weapons, the Damascus Accident, and the Illusion of Safety* (Penguin, 2013), 123. See also Richard Rhodes, *Dark Sun: The Making of the Hydrogen Bomb* (Simon & Schuster, 1995), 378.

71   **"its use carries much further":** The General Advisory Committee Report of Oct. 30, 1949, United States Atomic Energy Commission, Washington, D.C., Historical Doc. 349.

71   **approved the hydrogen bomb initiative:** Oppenheimer was the chairman of the GAC, and his opposition to the hydrogen bomb was a major reason for his security hearing. Bird and Sherwin, *American Prometheus*, 546.

71   **"*if only for bargaining purposes*":** Arnold Offner, *Another Such Victory: President Truman and the Cold War, 1945–1953* (Stanford University Press, 2002), 363. (Emphasis added.)

71   **"nothing more than a major contractor":** Ibid.

72   **Nitze's document argued:** Ernest R. May, *American Cold War Strategy: Interpreting NSC 68* (Bedford/St. Martin's, 1993) and Melvyn Leffler, "The Emergence of an American Grand Strategy, 1945–1952," in *The Cambridge History of the Cold War*, vol. 1, *Origins*, edited by Melvyn Leffler and Odd Arne Westad (Cambridge University Press, 2010): 67-89.

72   **"utilize[d] promptly and effectively":** R. Norris and H. Kristensen, "Global Nuclear Weapons Inventories, 1945–2010," *Bulletin of the Atomic Scientists* (July 2010): 77–83.

72   **In the event of war:** David Rosenberg, "The Origins of Overkill: Nuclear Weapons and American Strategy, 1945–1960," *International Security* (Spring 1983): 15–17, and his revised "The Origins of Overkill," in Norman Graebner, ed., *The National Security: Its Theory and Practice, 1945–1960* (Oxford, 1986), 123-95.

72   **"the entire stockpile of atomic bombs":** Tom Engelhardt, *The End of Victory Culture: Cold War America and the Disillusioning of a Generation* (University of Massachusetts Press, 2007), 155. Kaplan, *The Wizard of Armageddon*, 4. See also, Marco Borghi, "Political Authority or Atomic Celebrity? The Influence of J. Robert Oppenheimer on American Nuclear Policy after the Second World War," NPIHP Working Paper #14 (August 2019).

72   **"I fear that the atomic bomb":** George F. Kennan, "Memorandum: The International Control of Atomic Energy," quoted in Bird and Sherwin, *American Prometheus*, 425–26. For domestic consequences of nuclear weapons see: Paul Boyer, *By the Bomb's Early Light: American Thought and Culture at the Dawn of the Atomic Age* (New York: Pantheon, 1985); Spencer R. Weart, *Nuclear Fear: A*

History of Images (Cambridge: Harvard University Press, 1988); Robert Jay Lifton and Greg Mitchell, *Hiroshima in America: Fifty Years of Denial* (New York: Putnam's Sons, 1955); Gerard J. DeGroot, *The Bomb: A Life* (London: Pimlico, 2005); Allan M. Winkler, *Life under a Cloud: American Anxiety about the Atom* (New York: OUP, 1993); Margot A. Henriksen, *Dr. Strangelove's America: Society and Culture in the Atomic Age* (Berkeley: University of California Press, 1997).

72   He had hinted at "atomic diplomacy": Truman, *Years of Trial and Hope*, 93.

72   In 1948, during the Berlin Blockade: They were not modified for nuclear weapons (a "hollow threat"). William Burr, NSA, letter to the *New York Review of Books*, April 18, 2019.

72   And during the Korean War: Roger Dingman, "Atomic Diplomacy During the Korean War," *International Security*, vol. 13, no. 3 (Winter 1988–89): 50–91.

72   Asked at a press conference: Sean L. Malloy, "A 'Paper Tiger'? Nuclear Weapons, Atomic Diplomacy, and the Korean War," *New England Journal of History*, 60 (Fall 2003–Spring 2004), 227–52.

73   "I don't think we ought": David E. Lilienthal, *The Journals of David E. Lilienthal*, vol. 2: *The Atomic Energy Years, 1945–1950* (Harper & Row, 1964), 391.

73   "It is a terrible weapon": John Woolley and Gerhard Peters, "The American Presidency Project," https://www.presidency.ucsb.edu/node/230485 See also Offner, *Another Such Victory*, an incisive critical assessment of Truman's impact on U.S. foreign policy.

73   nuclear weapons against Chinese targets: H. W. Brands, *The General vs. the President: MacArthur and Truman at the Brink of Nuclear War* (Penguin Random House, 2016).

73   "being hurried forward": Truman's language closely tracks the memorandum that Stimson read to him on April 25, 1945. "The world in its present state of moral advancement compared with its technical development would be eventually at the mercy of such a weapon. In other words, modern civilization might be completely destroyed." Stimson Diary, Apr. 25, 1945; Sherwin, *A World Destroyed*, App. I, 291.

Chapter 9: "We Face a Battle to Extinction"

76   "Russia is definitely out": Quoted in Stephen E. Ambrose, *Eisenhower: Soldier and President* (Simon & Schuster, 1990), 233.

76   to end corruption: Eisenhower won more than 55 percent of the popular vote. The Electoral College was 442 for Eisenhower to 89 for Stevenson. The importance of Eisenhower's anticorruption theme cannot be overemphasized. See John A. Farrell, *Richard Nixon: The Life* (Doubleday, 2017), 182–83.

77   "Ph.D. from Dean Acheson's": Dwight Eisenhower, Campaign speech, National Radio-TV address, Denver, Colorado, June 26, 1952. Richard Nixon, campaign speech, Indianapolis, Indiana, Oct. 30, 1952 . https://spartacuseducational.com/USAacheson.htm Researched by Kevin Woelfel.

77   "It was not until Eisenhower's presidency": Andrew P. N. Erdmann, "'War No Longer Has Any Logic Whatever': Dwight D. Eisenhower and the Thermonuclear Revolution," in *Cold War Statesmen Confront the Bomb: Nuclear Diplomacy Since 1945*, edited by J. L. Gaddis et al. (Oxford University Press, 1999), 88.

77   "the class the stars fell on": Fifty-nine members of the class of 1915 were promoted to the rank of general.

77   "At West Point and during his career": Matthew Holland, *Eisenhower Between*

the Wars: The Making of a General and Statesman (Praeger, 2001), 61. Evan Thomas uses Eisenhower's poker skills to interpret his nuclear weapons policies as a brilliant bluff. See his *Ike's Bluff: President Eisenhower's Secret Battle to Save the World* (Little, Brown, 2012). For the most recent thorough biography of Eisenhower's presidency, see William I. Hitchcock, *The Age of Eisenhower: America and the World in the 1950s* (Simon & Schuster, 2018).

78 **whether Ike was present or not**: Lack of engagement at Columbia University appears to have had a precedent in World War II. Field Marshal Alan Brooke, chief of the Imperial General Staff, complained in his diary (Nov. 24, 1944) that Eisenhower was "by himself with his Lady chauffeur [most likely Kay Summersby] in the golf links at Reims—entirely detached from the war." Quoted in Stanley B. Hirshson, *General Patton: A Soldier's Life* (HarperCollins, 2002), 558.

78 **In place of the hapless Harry Truman**: Richard Nixon came closest during the summer of 1974 with 24 percent. https://en.wikipedia.org/wiki/United _States_presidential_approval_rating.

78 **Eisenhower's World War II experience**: D. D. Eisenhower, *Crusade in Europe* (Doubleday, 1948), 519–21. Philip Nash provides an excellent analysis of "Eisenhower, Nuclear Weapons, and Arms Control," in *A Companion to Dwight D. Eisenhower*, edited by Chester J. Pach (Wiley, 2017), chap. 17.

79 **"on the basis of my belief"**: *Newsweek*, Nov. 11, 1963, 107; Dwight D. Eisenhower, *The White House Years: Mandate for Change: 1953–1956: A Personal Account* (Doubleday, 1963), 312–13.

79 **"I was against it"**: A few months after the atomic bombings of Hiroshima and Nagasaki, Eisenhower commented during a social occasion, "how he had hoped that the war might have ended without our having to use the atomic bomb." This previously unknown confirmation of DDE's view from the diary of Robert P. Meiklejohn, an assistant to Ambassador W. Averell Harriman, was published for the first time by the National Security Archive, George Washington University, Washington, DC, on August 4, 2015, https://nsarchive2.gwu.edu /nukevault/ebb525-The-Atomic-Bomb-and-the-End-of-World-War-II/. Barton J. Bernstein offers a skeptical analysis of Eisenhower's early opposition to Hiroshima, "Ike and Hiroshima: Did He Oppose It?" *Journal of Strategic Studies* 10: 377–89.

79 **Eisenhower bet on a "silver bullet"**: Herbert York, *The Advisers: Oppenheimer, Teller and the Superbomb* (Stanford University Press, 1989); Rhodes, *Dark Sun*.

79 **His administration's "New Look"**: "The Strategy of Massive Retaliation," *Speech of Sec. of State JFD before the Council on Foreign Relations, January 12, 1954*. http://msthorarinson.weebly.com/uploads/4/1/4/5/41452777/dulles_addr ess.pdf.

79 **With that gamble**: For essays that investigate how nuclear weapons influenced presidential decisions, see: John Gaddis et al., *Cold War Statesmen Confront the Bomb*. Also available at Oxford Scholarship Online: https://www.oxford scholarship.com/view/10.1093/0198294689.001.0001/acprof-9780198294689; also Thomas, *Ike's Bluff*.

80 **On March 31, at a special meeting**: *FRUS*, vol. 15, *1952–1954*, part 1, doc. 427.

80 **"complete agreement"**: Ibid., Eisenhower's Atoms for Peace initiative was likewise an attempt to moderate the nuclear taboo. See "'Atoms for Peace' Was Actually a Threat to Peace," NSA Briefing Book 678, ed. William Burr.

80 **"Every gun that is made"**: DDE speech to American Society of Newspaper Editors, Apr. 16, 1953,. https://archive.org/details/dde_1953_0416.

80 **"the President inquired"**: *FRUS*, vol. 15, *1952–1954*, part 1, doc. 500. Omar Bradley, chairman of the Joint Chiefs of Staff, did not agree with Eisenhower's inclination to increase reliance on nuclear weapons. (Emphasis added.)

81 **The key to success**: For an inciteful summary see Philip Nash, "Eisenhower, Nuclear Weapons, and Arms Control," in *A Companion to Dwight D. Eisenhower*, edited by Pach, chap. 17.

81 **"a strong military posture"**: NSC 162/2 is readily accessed: https://fas.org/irp/offdocs/nsc-hst/nsc-162-2.pdf.

81 **a radical shift**: Marc Trachtenberg, *History and Strategy* (Princeton, 1991), 161. Trachtenberg emphasizes the continuity.

81 **"Eisenhower personally intervened"**: McGeorge Bundy, *Danger and Survival: Choices About the Bomb in the First Fifty Years* (Random House, 1988), 247. (Emphases added.)

81 **The military's strategic mission**: Against strong air force objections the navy acquired a significant strategic nuclear role in 1960 when the USS *George Washington* (SSBN-598) successfully test-fired two Polaris A-1 missiles with a range of twelve hundred miles. http://www.navy.mil/navydata/cno/n87/history/chrono.html

81 **"put all our resources"**: Quoted in Ira Chernus, *Apocalypse Management: Eisenhower and the Discourse of National Insecurity* (Stanford University Press, 2008), 187.

82 **"our main reliance"**: Ibid.

82 **"will consider nuclear weapons"**: NSC 162/2.

82 **as an equal**: Vladislav Zubok and Hope Harrison, "The Nuclear Education of Nikita Khrushchev," in Gaddis et al., *Cold War Statesmen Confront the Bomb*, 141–70.

82 **"nuclear brinkmanship"**: Fursenko and Naftali, *Khrushchev's Cold War: The Inside Story of an American Adversary* (Norton, 2006), 41.

82 **"Our enemies probably feared us"**: *Khrushchev Remembers*, vol. 1, 247; Holloway, *Stalin and the Bomb*, 343.

83 **"approved by him"**: Robert Bowie and Richard Immerman, *Waging Peace: How Eisenhower Forged an Enduring Cold War Strategy* (Oxford, 1998), 198–201. See also Geoffrey Perret, *Eisenhower* (Random House, 1999), 459.

83 **"would rely in the future"**: Richard Nixon, "President Calls Nixon: 'Not Displeased' at Talk," *New York Times*, Mar. 14, 1954, 45.

83 **safe and solvent**: "One of the best kept secrets of the past sixty years has been the high cost of producing and maintaining nuclear weapons, somewhere between $5 and $6 trillion, which represents one-fourth to one-third of overall defense spending." M. Goodman, "The Great Cost and Myth of U.S. Defense Spending," Counterpunch.org (Aug. 30, 2019); S. Schwartz, *Atomic Audit*.

84 **Dulles's "Massive Retaliation" speech**: Sergei Khrushchev, ed., *The Memoirs of Nikita Khrushchev*, vol. 3, *Statesman, 1953–1964*, translated by George Shriver (Pennsylvania State University Press, 2007), 31.

84 **"In the months following"**: Zubok, *Failed Empire*, 86. See also Khrushchev, *Khrushchev Remembers*, 100–101.

84 **"pretty much rejected détente"**: Melvyn Leffler, "In Time of Austerity," paper

presented to the Aspen Strategy Group, July 2014; Leffler, *For the Soul of Mankind*, chap. 2, esp. 122–38.

84   **"There is no evidence"**: As Soviet premier in 1953, Georgy Malenkov oversaw the first signs of the Soviet "peace offensive," in which a series of overtures to the West indicated the beginning of a change in Party policies.

84   **Such an initiative was a distraction**: Leffler, *For the Soul of Mankind*, 84–150.

84   **"The risk of Soviet aggression"**: NSC 162/2.

84   **"damnable philosophy"**: Ambrose, *Eisenhower*, 233. Dulles shared Eisenhower's revulsion for communism, but he was far more vocal and petulant about it. See Ira Chernus, *General Eisenhower: Ideology and Discourse* (Michigan State University Press, 2002).

85   **"a war of light against darkness"**: Ambrose, *Eisenhower*, 233.

85   **"a moral program"**: Chernus, *General Eisenhower*, 186.

85   **"our duty to future generations"**: Eisenhower to Dulles, September 8, 1953. Gaddis, *Strategies of Containment: A Critical Appraisal of American National Security Policy during the Cold War* rev. ed (OUP, 2005), 147; Bundy, *Danger and Survival*, 251.

85   **"rather be atomized than communized"**: Chernus, *General Eisenhower*, 186.

85   **a colossal expansion**: James Carroll, *House of War: The Pentagon and the Disastrous Rise of American Power* (Houghton Mifflin, 2006), 235–36.

85   **an "insane accumulation"**: James Carroll, *Boston Globe*, Opinion, "Nukes Have Momentum of Their Own," Aug. 13, 2012.

Chapter 10: "An Extraordinary Departure"

86   **"What made Khrushchev remarkable"**: L. Thompson speech to the Industrial College of the Armed Forces, "Vital Interests and Objectives of the United States" (1965), paraphrased in Jenny and Sherry Thompson, *The Kremlinologist: Llewellyn E. Thompson, America's Man in Cold War Moscow* (Johns Hopkins University Press, 2018), 150.

87   **Speaking at a secret session**: The Party congress included about fifteen hundred Communist leaders from fifty-six countries around the world, and its twentieth meeting opened in Moscow on February 14, 1956. For internal reactions to Khrushchev's speech see Miriam Dobson, "The Post-Stalin Era: De-Stalinization, Daily Life, and Dissent," *Kritika: Explorations in Russian and Eurasian History* 12 (Fall 2011): 905–24.

87   **"It was the bravest and most reckless"**: William Taubman, *Khrushchev: The Man and His Era* (Norton, 2003), 274 and chap. 11.

87   **"What made Khrushchev remarkable"**: S. and J. Thompson, *The Kremlinologist*, 150.

87   **"a global superpower"**: Rósa Magnúsdóttir, "'Be Careful in America, Premier Khrushchev!': Soviet Perceptions of Peaceful Coexistence with the United States in 1959," *Cahiers du Monde russe* 47, no. 1/2 (Jan.–June, 2006): 111. See also Mark B. Smith, "Peaceful Coexistence at All Costs: Cold War Exchanges Between Britain and the Soviet Union in 1956," *Cold War History* 12 (Aug. 2012): 537–58.

88   **No initiative**: The only comparable initiative was Anwar Sadat's decision to make peace with Israel.

88   **Passed to the CIA by Israeli intelligence**: Saki Dockrill, *Eisenhower's New-Look National Security Policy, 1953–61* (Palgrave Macmillan, 1996), 159. In April

1956, the Polish-Israeli journalist Viktor Grajewski gave the representative of the Shin Bet [Israel's internal security service] in Warsaw a copy of Khrushchev's "Secret Speech," which he secured from a friend who worked with the secretary general of the Polish Communist Party. https://history.state.gov/milestones/1953-1960/khrushchev-20th-congress.

88 **"If you don't like us"**: "We will bury you!" (Russian: «Мы вас похороним!» romanized: *"My vas pokhoronim!"*), *New York Times*, 11/19/1956, 1. The phrase was originally translated into English by Khrushchev's personal interpreter, Viktor Sukhodrev. In an article in the *New York Times* in 2018 the translator Mark Polizzotti suggested that the phrase was mistranslated at the time and should properly have been translated "We will outlast you," which gives an entirely different sense to Khrushchev's statement.

89 **"The Texan Who Conquered Russia"**: *Time,* May 19, 1958.

89 **existed on two levels**: There are more books on the Cold War than there is room here to list. But several that are particularly relevant that have not been cited yet are: Odd Arne Westad, *The Global Cold War* (Cambridge, 2005); John Lewis Gaddis, *The Cold War: A New History* (Penguin Press, 2005); Paul Erickson et al., *How Reason Almost Lost Its Mind: The Strange Career of Cold War Rationality* (University of Chicago Press, 2013); and Toshihiro Higuchi, *Political Fallout: Nuclear Weapons Testing and the Making of a Global Environmental Crisis* (SUP, 2020).

89 **"General war is unthinkable"**: DDE to Frank Altschul, 10/25/57, Ann Whitman Files, DDE Diaries Series, box 27, quoted in Chernus, *Apocalypse Management*, 186.

90 **"another expression"**: Geoffrey Perret, *Eisenhower* (Random House, 1999), 460–62.

90 **"Korean proportions"**: Ibid., 461.

90 **If war breaks out**: Kaplan, *The Wizards of Armageddon*, 196, and Fred Kaplan, *The Bomb: Presidents, Generals and the Secret History of Nuclear War* (Simon & Schuster, 2020): 12.

90 **"only place in the world"**: Lee Jae-Bong, "U.S. Deployment of Nuclear Weapons in 1950s South Korea & North Korea's Nuclear Development: Toward Denuclearization of the Korean Peninsula," *Asia-Pacific Journal* 7, issue 8, no. 3 (Feb. 17, 2009): article ID 3053. The Honest John [MGR-1] could not reach the Soviet Union. It was a free-flight (unguided) rocket with a range of only 12–15 miles.

91 **Composed of military representatives**: Ibid. Swedish and Swiss inspectors were stationed in the North Korean regions of Shinuju, Chongjin, Hungnam, Manpo, and Shinanju, while Polish and Czechoslovakian inspectors resided at Inchon, Taegu, Pusan, Kangrung, and Kunsan, South Korea.

91 **The JCS proposed three options**: Ibid. The charge was that the North had acquired several hundred upgraded jet aircraft. The United States similarly supplied upgraded aircraft to the ROK. Bruce Cummings, *Korea's Place in the Sun: A Modern History* (Norton, 1997), 478. See also David Stone MacDonald, *U.S. Korean Relations from Liberation to Self-Reliance: The Twenty Year Record: An Interpretive Summary of the Archives of the U.S. Department of State for the Period 1945–1965* (Westview Press, 1992), 23, 78–79.

91 **It was the only time**: "The First Nukes on the Korean Peninsula," National Security Archive, Washington, DC, Briefing Book #690, edited by William

Burr. The release contains twenty-five documents detailing the debate over the deployment of tactical nuclear weapons to South Korea. A NSA summary states that "John Foster Dulles worried 'These Great Monsters' would be 'disastrous' for U.S. political position."

91 **"the kinds of nuclear-capable weapons"**: Ibid. Memorandum from the Assistant Secretary of Defense for International Security Affairs (Gray) to the Secretary of Defense (Wilson), Washington, Dec. 6, 1956.

91 **In April, for example**: *FRUS*, vol. 23, *1955–1957, Korea*, part 2, Memorandum of Discussion at the 318th Meeting of the National Security Council, Washington, Apr. 4, 1957, doc. 212. "Reluctantly, however, [Dulles] had been forced to conclude that he could not go all the way desired by the military, because he believed that if we introduced the two disputed items (280 mm guns and 762 mm rockets), the political disadvantages of such a course of action would be greater, in his mind, than the military advantages."

92 **"permanently stationed a squadron"**: Cummings, *Korea's Place in the Sun*, 479; Peter Hayes, *Pacific Powderkeg: American Nuclear Dilemmas in Korea* (Lexington Books, 1991), 35.

92 **The president's orders**: Lee Jae-Bong, "U.S. Deployment of Nuclear Weapons in 1950s," 2. Nuclear weapons remained in South Korea until they were removed in 1991.

Chapter 11: "There Is Not Communists . . . but Cubanists"

93 **"didn't even invite me"**: Castro to delegates of the 1992 Cuban missile crisis conference in Havana. Quoted in Blight, Allyn, and Welch, *Cuba on the Brink: Castro, the Missile Crisis, and the Soviet Collapse* (Pantheon, 1993), 178.

93 **"The thing we should never do"**: Walter Lippmann quoted in Sergo Mikoyan, *The Soviet Cuban Missile Crisis*, edited by Svetlana Savranskaya (Stanford University Press, 2012), 170.

93 **"on a mission of friendship"**: Jules Dubois, "Castro Arrives to Begin 10 Day Speaking Tour," *Chicago Daily Tribune*, Apr. 15, 1959, 1.

93 **"This man has made news"**: "Editors Under Fire," ibid., Apr. 16, 1959, 10.

94 **"Smiles, lots of smiles"**: The PR agent was Bernard Rellin. He urged Castro and his entourage to shave their beards, but Castro (who had better public relations instincts than Rellin) refused. *New York Times*, Apr. 18, 2019, D2; Carlos Franqui, *Family Portrait with Fidel: A Memoir*, translated by Alfred MacAdam (Random House, 1984), 31.

94 **The greetings concluded**: E. W. Kenworthy, "Castro Due in Capital Today," *New York Times*, Apr. 15, 1959, 1.

95 **an instant media star**: Despite the fact that his visit was "unofficial," the U.S. government arranged for significant security. Jules Dubois, "Castro Arrives," *Chicago Tribune*, Apr. 16, 1959, 1; "Crowd Hails Castro," *New York Times*, Apr. 16, 1. See also "Castro Defies Threats," "Cuban Prime Minister Fidel Castro, defying threats against his life, today went on a handshaking, autograph-signing stroll through the streets of Washington," *Los Angeles Times*, Apr. 16, 1959, 3.

95 **He saw no reason**: William Stringer, "Castro Faces Quiz," *Christian Science Monitor*, Apr. 17, 1959, 1.

95 **"That's not true"**: Jules Dubois, "Castro Tells Hope for U.S., Cuban Amity," *Chicago Tribune*, Apr. 17, 1959, 1.

95   **paid to protest:** Edward Folliard, *Washington Post and Times-Herald,* Apr. 18, 1959, A1.

95   **Augusta National Golf Club:** Trumbell Higgins, *The Perfect Failure: Kennedy, Eisenhower and the CIA at the Bay of Pigs* (Norton, 1989), 44.

95   **denying Castro a visa:** William LeoGrande and Peter Kornbluh, *Back Channel to Cuba: The Hidden History of Negotiations Between Washington and Havana* (University of North Carolina Press, 2014), 16.

95   **Castro neither forgot:** Thomas G. Paterson. *Contesting Castro, The United States and the Triumph of the Cuban Revolution* (Oxford University Press, 1994).

96   **a progressive revolutionary:** Anthony DePalma, *The Man Who Invented Fidel: Castro, Cuba, and Herbert L. Matthews of* The New York Times (Public Affairs, 2006).

96   **the political provenance of Castro's policies:** Carlos Franqui, "Fidel Castro's Trip to the United States," http://www.historyofcuba.com/history/franqui3 .htm.

96   **The public trials and executions:** William Stringer, "Castro Faces Quiz," *Christian Science Monitor,* Apr. 17, 1959, 1.

96   **"Revolution first, elections later":** Thomas C. Wright, *Latin America in the Era of the Cuban Revolution* (Praeger, 2001).

96   **news accounts from its encampments:** *New York Times* reporter Herbert Matthews did most of the reporting on Castro. https://archive.nytimes.com/www .nytimes.com/ref/world/americas/CASTRO_ARCHIVE.html?ref=world special2.

96   **if he could feed his people:** William Stringer, "Castro Faces Quiz," *Christian Science Monitor,* Apr. 17, 1959, 1.

96   **"If we are happy":** "Castro Defies Threats," *Los Angeles Times,* Apr. 17, 1959, 1.

97   **a historic three-hour conversation:** E. W. Kenworthy, "Castro Due in Capital Today," *New York Times,* Apr. 15, 1959, 1.

97   **"Rough draft of a summary":** Jeffrey J. Safford, "The Nixon-Castro Meeting of 19 April 1959," *Diplomatic History* (Fall 1980): 425–31.

102   **Why had Nixon quoted:** Nixon, *Six Crises* (Doubleday, 1962), 351–52; Nixon, *The Memoirs of Richard Nixon* (Simon & Schuster, 1978), 201–3.

102   **"He [Castro] seems to be sincere":** Nixon apparently feared that Americans would conclude that Castro had hoodwinked him.

102   **No one in Moscow believed:** Khrushchev, *Khrushchev Remembers,* 489–90.

102   **"When I visited in April":** The reforms he outlined in his speech ("History Will Absolve Me") at his 1953 trial after leading a failed attack on the Moncada Barracks on July 26, 1953. Castro later called his revolution the July 26th movement.

103   **"a very fine young man":** "TV Ratings 1959–1960," http://www.classictvhits .com/tvratings/1959.htm; James Maguire, *Impresario: The Life and Times of Ed Sullivan* (Billboard Books, 2006).

103   **"didn't even invite me":** Blight, Allyn, and Welch, *Cuba on the Brink,* 178.

103   **"American economic pressures":** Ibid., 178–79.

103   **guided by two commitments:** Franqui, *Family Portrait with Fidel,* 37, 72, 142, 164, 229, 246.

104   **"acquitted himself":** Robert C. Albright, "Castro Is Quizzed by Senators," *Washington Post and Times-Herald,* Apr. 18, 1959, A8 and 10.

104   **"a most interesting individual":** Higgins, *The Perfect Failure,* 45.

104 **"10,000 Hear Castro at Harvard"**: In New York, Castro attracted "crowds larger than any foreign leader in its history." *New York Times*, Apr. 18, 2019, D2.

105 **"The Situation in the Caribbean"**: Board of National Estimates, "The Situation in the Caribbean through 1959," SNIE 80-59, June 30, 1959.

105 **"our information shows"**: U.S. Senate, 86th Congress, 1st Session, Judiciary Subcommittee Hearings on "Communist Threat to the US Through Caribbean," part 3, Nov. 5, 1959, Testimony of Gen. C. P. Cabell, 162–63. "On the other hand," he stated, "they are delighted with the nature of his government."

105 **"The Americans had cut off"**: Khrushchev, *Khrushchev Remembers*, 490.

105 **"Castro's scenario at this time"**: Philip W. Bonsal, *Cuba, Castro, and the United States* (University of Pittsburgh Press, 1971), 67.

105 **"unpardonable steps"**: Interview with Alexander Alekseyev, Soviet ambassador to Cuba, April 7, 1986. WGBH, Open Vault interviews from the TV series, *War and Peace in the Nuclear Age*. http://openvault.wgbh.org/catalog/V _E6DE72DD9B5A4DCBAB83543D67949E77.

106 **"an oil delivery to Cuba"**: Khrushchev, *Khrushchev Remembers*, 490.

106 **Tankers were in short supply**: Bruna Bagnato, *Prove di Ostpolitik: Politica ed economia nella strategia italiana verso l'Unione Sovietica, 1958–1963 [Ostpolitik trials: Politics and economics in the Italian strategy towards the Soviet Union, 1958-1963]*, (Leo Olschki Editore, 2003), chap. 5. "La questione delle petroliere" [The issue of oil tankers] 408–22. References provided by Leopoldo Nuti.

106 **"The thing we should never do"**: Walter Lippmann, "Today and Tomorrow," *Washington Post*, July 23, 1959.

Chapter 12: "General Disarmament Is the Most Important"

107 **"It turned out that everything"**: Khrushchev, *Memoirs*, vol. 3, *Statesman*, 98. Justin Zawistowski's research contributed to this chapter.

107 **The question of general**: *Public Papers of the President of the United States, Dwight D. Eisenhower, 1959: Containing the public messages, speeches, and statements of the president, January 1 to December 31, 1959* (Office of the Federal Register, 1950), 242.

107 **had prompted the invitation**: Bryce Harlow, Memorandum, 3/26/59 (DDC 1978, doc 118C, 2; Thompson telegram to DOS, 3/4/59, in *FRUS*, vol. 8, *1958–1960*, doc. 197, 410–11.

107 **Worried about escalating tensions**: Peter Carlson, *K Blows Top: A Cold War Comic Interlude Starring Nikita Khrushchev, America's Most Unlikely Tourist* (Public Affairs, 2009). "The trip was hilarious but the humor was darkened by the shadow of the atomic bomb," Carlson wrote in his Prologue.

108 **"ace in the hole"**: Bryce Harlow, Memo for the record, Mar. 26, 1959, Harlow papers, DDEL.

108 **In a March 4 telegram**: L. Thompson to DOS, Mar. 4, 1959, *FRUS*, vol. 8, *1958–1960, Berlin Crisis*, doc. 197.

108 **"I must confess"**: See the CIA transcript of the Nixon-Khrushchev debate on July 24, 1959, at the American National Exhibition in Moscow: https://www .cia.gov/library/readingroom/docs/1959-07-24.pdf.

108 **"It was all so unexpected"**: Sergei Khrushchev, ed., *Memoirs of Nikita Khrushchev*, vol. 3. *Statesman, 1953–1964* (Pennsylvania State University Press, 2007), 93.

108 "How proud we were": Ibid., 98.

108 "So we descended": Ibid., 102.

109 "some kind of strange creatures": Ibid., 103.

109 "more like a funeral procession": Quoted in Jay P. Whitefield, "Early Cold War Summits: Eisenhower, Nixon, Kennedy, and Khrushchev, 1959 and 1961" (MA thesis, Texas Tech University, 2007), chap. 3, n. 97; Dan Adams Schmidt, "Khrushchev Sees Sights from Car and Helicopter," *New York Times*, Sept. 16, 1959, A1.

109 "from the moon": Rada Khrushcheva interview, *The Missiles of October: What the World Didn't Know* (ABC documentary, 1992).

109 "We will bury you": https://www.cia.gov/library/readingroom/docs/CIA-RDP 73B00296R000200040087-1.pdf.

109 Eisenhower's invitation: "We Will Bury You," *Time*, Nov. 26, 1956. See also Eisenhower's invitation of Khrushchev to the United States: *FRUS*, vol. 10, *1958–1960*, part 1, *Eastern Europe Region, Soviet Union, Cyprus* (USGPO, 2010), doc. 87.

109 "Our relations then": Khrushchev, *Memoirs*, vol. 3, *Statesman*, 92–93.

110 "A Soviet Union [and leader] that interacted": J. and S. Thompson, *The Kremlinologist*, 150.

110 a polite, serious start: Fursenko and Naftali, *Khrushchev's Cold War*, 229–39.

111 the Soviet Union's reality check: Khrushchev, *Memoirs*, vol. 3, *Statesman*, 100.

111 "our country's most powerful opponent": Ibid., 93.

111 harvested by "slave labor": Ibid.

111 "To the day of his death": Ibid., 100–101.

111 "wring your necks": Strobe Talbott, *Khrushchev Remembers*, 392; quoted in Melvyn P. Leffler, *For the Soul of Mankind: The United States, the Soviet Union, and the Cold War* (Hill and Wang, 2007), 88.

111 Any apparent insult: Khrushchev's first trip to a Western country took place in 1956, when he visited Britain: Mark B. Smith, "Peaceful coexistence at all costs: Cold War exchanges between Britain and the Soviet Union in 1956," *Cold War History* 12 (Aug. 2012): 537–58.

112 Khrushchev's experiences: Khrushchev, ed. *Memoirs* vol. 3, *Statesman*, 103–7.

112 He had welcomed Western influence: William Taubman, *Khrushchev: The Man and His Era* (Norton, 2003), 399.

112 "rearming Germany": Philip Nash, *The Other Missiles of October*, 6–33; Gates Brown, *Eisenhower's Nuclear Calculus in Europe: The Politics of IRBM Deployment in NATO Nations* (McFarland Publishers, 2018).

112 "This we have also rejected": Department of State telegram no. 1773, Mar. 9, 1959, from Thompson to Secretary of State, CF 762.00 /3-959, RG 59, National Archives, College Park, MD. Also doc. 922 in William Burr, ed., *The Berlin Crisis, 1958–1962,* (NSA). Taubman, *Khrushchev*, 399. Jenny and Sherry Thompson, *The Kremlinologist: Llewellyn E. Thompson, America's Man in Cold War Moscow* (Johns Hopkins University Press, 2018), 173–74.

112 "What do Eisenhower and Dulles want?": Taubman, *Khrushchev*, 401.

112 now that John Foster Dulles had died: Dulles resigned as secretary of state on April 15, 1959, and died of cancer on May 24, 1959.

113 "I really like [Eisenhower]": Taubman, *Khrushchev*, 403.

113 "We were somewhat concerned": Khrushchev, *Memoirs*, vol. 3, *Statesman*, 94.

113   **Was the invitation:** In the Soviet Union these were separate entities and individuals, unlike the arrangement in the United States, where the president is
both head of state and head of government.

113   **"Ordinary people abroad":** Khrushchev, *Memoirs*, vol. 3, *Statesman*, 95.

113   **should they include a scientist:** On his earlier trip to Britain, Khrushchev had
included the Soviet physicist Igor Kurchatov, who "had made a big impression."
But Kurchatov was ill, so Khrushchev included the writer Mikhail Sholokhov,
"so we could establish contacts with writers in the United States." Ibid.

113   **"our demands were exaggerated":** Ibid.

114   **"What exactly was this Camp David?":** In 1967 Leonid Brezhnev, who succeeded Khrushchev in 1964, authorized Georgi Arbatov to form the Institute
for USA and Canada Studies [ISKAN]. Arbatov oversaw the creation of a large
group of knowledgeable specialists in North American studies, including Kon-
stantin Pleshakov, Sergei Tikhanov, and Vladislav Zubok.

114   **"That's how uninformed we were":** Khrushchev, *Memoirs*, vol. 3, *Statesman*, 98.

114   **a slim majority of the public:** Ranging from 51 percent in 1956 down to 46 percent (with 37 percent against) in 1959.

115   **Soviet determination to expand:** Jacob Liss, *Khrushchev-Eisenhower Visits: The
Truth About Coexistence with Russia* (Alfred Printing Co., 1959), 4. *New York
Times Magazine*, Sept. 6, 1959, 4–5, 44–45; *USNWR*, Aug. 10, 1959, 108, and
Aug. 31, 1959, 104; *Wall Street Journal*, Aug. 14, 1959, 6; *National Review*, Aug.
22, 1959, 1, 2.

115   **"just another Hitler":** *USNWR*, Aug. 10, 1959, 108, and Aug 31, 1959, 104.

115   **"figurative river of blood":** William Buckley, *National Review*, Aug 22, 1959,
1–2.

115   **"The dumb resignation":** Liss, *Khrushchev-Eisenhower Visits*, 4; *New York
Times Magazine*, Sept. 6, 1959, 5, 44–45; *Wall Street Journal*, Aug. 14, 1959, 6.

115   **draped its church's facade:** Gary John Tocchet, "September Thaw: Khrushchev's Visit to America, 1959," PhD diss., Stanford University, Dissertations
& Theses: Full Text database. (Publication No. AAT 9535677), 97; *New York
Times*, Sept. 6, 1959, 20, and Sept. 17, 1959, 22; *Los Angeles Times*, Sept. 12, 1959,
4; Sept. 15, 1959, 7; Sept. 17, 1959, 8; and Sept. 18, 1959, 10.

116   **a mass prayer rally:** The ICCC invited representatives from Eastern European
countries to participate and expected at least 2,500 individuals to turn out.
When the prayer rally began, officials were disappointed that only 600 people
had showed up for the event. *New York Times*, Aug. 4, 1959, 1, 6; Aug. 5, 1959, 5;
Aug. 13, 1959, 11, and Sept. 15, 1959, 12.

116   **meager immediate results:** Fifteen senators, various American Jewish organizations, and numerous rabbis requested the State Department and the Soviet
Embassy that they be allowed to hold a conference with Khrushchev. In the end
the Soviets invited some high-level American Jews to the Soviet Embassy for
a quick reception, but they did not make any special considerations for a formal meeting. *New York Times*, Sept. 7, 1959, 1; Sept. 13, 1959, 3, 5; and Aug. 31,
1959, 4; Sept. 4, 1959, Richard Pederson (Ambassador Lodge's staff) and John
McSweeney (Office of Soviet Affairs, Department of State), Subject: Khrushchev Visit (to include issue of American Jewish Organizations), Department of
State, ICF, Doc.# 033.6111/9-459, 2; Sept. 9, 1959, Murphy, Menshikov, et al.,
Subject: The Khrushchev Visit, Department of State, ICF, Doc.# 033.6111/9-
959. It was an initiative that planted the seeds harvested fifteen years later by

the Jackson-Vanik Amendment which restricted trade with the Soviet Union as long as it restricted emigration and other human rights.

116 **the chorus of contempt**: *New York Times*, Aug. 20, 1959, 1; Aug. 21, 1959, 1, 3; Aug. 26, 1959, 3, 5; Aug. 27, 1959, 1; Aug. 28, 1959, 4; Sept. 1, 1959, 8; Sept. 4, 1949, 3; Sept. 17, 1959, 34; and Sept. 21, 1959, 1; *US News & World Report*, Aug. 31, 1959, front page; Sept. 7, 1959, 67–69.

116 **the reaction of organized labor**: *New York Times*, Aug. 20, 1959, 1; Aug. 21, 1959, 1, 3; Aug. 26, 1959, 3, 5; Aug. 27, 1959, 1; Aug. 28, 1959, 4; Sept. 1, 1959, 8; Sept. 4, 1949, 3; Sept. 17, 1959, 34; and Sept. 21, 1959, 1; *US News & World Report*, Aug. 31, 1959, front page; Sept. 7, 1959, 67–69.

117 **The escalating nuclear arms race**: Natural Resources Defense Council (NRDC), Archive of Nuclear Data, Table of Global Nuclear Weapons Stockpiles, 1945–2002.

117 **"makes strong men weak"**: Phyllis Mooney to James Hagerty, Sept. 21, 1959, James C. Hagerty Papers, DDEL.

118 **On the soundstage**: Taubman, *Khrushchev*, 431. He was said to have been offended by the sight of Shirley MacLaine in bloomers.

118 **"go and see Disneyland"**: Ibid.

118 **"talk [the] Mayor out of this speech"**: "Khrushchev Scolds L.A. Mayor," *Los Angeles Times*, Sept. 19, 1959.

119 **"our own selfish interests"**: Quoted in Roswell Garst obituary, *New York Times* Nov. 7, 1977, 38.

119 **This "summit entre-nous"**: The Eisenhower Presidential Library has posted documents describing some details of the Camp David meeting, including the members of the USA and USSR delegations: See also *FRUS*, vol. 10, *1958–1960: Eastern Europe Region, Soviet Union, Cyprus*, part 1, docs. 129–34.

119 **Eisenhower even admitted**: *FRUS*, vol. 9, *1958–1960. Berlin Crisis, 1959–1960; Germany; Austria*, "Memorandum of Conversation Between President Eisenhower and the President's Special Assistant for National Security Affairs (Gray)," Doc. 19.

119 **"[broken] the ice"**: Khrushchev, *Last Testament*, 415.

120 **a "more reasonable fashion"**: Memorandum of Conference with the President, Nov. 13, 1959, Eisenhower, McCone, Lord Plowden et al., Eisenhower Papers, AWF, DDE, Diaries, Box 45, Staff Notes, 2.

120 **"If only the President"**: Taubman, *Khrushchev*, 449. But the summit in Paris collapsed after the Soviets shot down the U2 piloted by Gary Powers on May 1, 1960, 455-68.

120 **"This was his finest hour"**: A report by State Department personnel traveling with Khrushchev noted that there was "every reason to suppose our productive capacity, high standard of living, popular solidarity, etc., did make an impression on him." "Briefing Memorandum for the Cabinet Meeting," attached to Memorandum, Nov. 5, 1959, from Kohler to Herter, Box 19, 1959, C. A. Herter Papers, DDEL.

120 **"It was the first time"**: Rósa Magnúsdôttir, "'Be Careful in America, Premier Khrushchev!': Soviet Perceptions of Peaceful Coexistence with the United States in 1959," *Cahiers du Monde russe* 47, no. 1/2 (Jan.–June, 2006), 110.

121 **"He felt some pressure"**: Interview with Alexei Adzhubei and Rada Khrushcheva by Sherry Jones, "Cuban Missile Crisis: What the World Didn't Know," produced by Sherry Jones for Peter Jennings Reporting, *ABC News* (Wash-

ington Media Associates, 1992). Transcript made available by the National
Security Archive: https://nsarchive2.gwu.edu/NSAEBB/NSAEBB400/docs
/Interview%20with%20Adzhubei%20&%20Rada.pdf.

Chapter 13: "We Cannot Let the Present Government There Go On"

122   "It would be desirable": Minutes of Special Group Meeting [from Thomas A.
      Parrott], 29 Dec. 1960, quoted from Livingston Merchant's notes of his Dec.
      28, 1960, meeting with Eisenhower, in Pfeiffer, *CIA Official History of the Bay
      of Pigs Operation,* vol. 3, 187. All references to Pfeiffer's CIA histories are to
      the original CIA typescript volumes found online: https://www.cia.gov/library
      /readingroom/collection/bay-pigs-release.

122   it took 136 more years: In 1937 Franklin Delano Roosevelt became the first
      president inaugurated on January 20.

122   "do almost anything": Eisenhower was clearly irked by Kennedy's youth.
      "Young whippersnapper" was another oft-used term of opprobrium.

123   "the repudiation of everything": Geoffrey Perret, *Eisenhower* (Random House,
      1999), 597–98; Timothy Naftali, Chautauqua lecture reported by Grant Engle,
      Chautauquan Daily (Aug. 21, 2012), online.

123   Dealing with Castro: Peter Wyden, *Bay of Pigs* (Simon & Schuster, 1979), 30.

123   Eisenhower demanded progress: As early as August 1960 the CIA had begun
      to enlist the Mafia to assassinate Castro, Jack B. Pfeiffer, *CIA Official History
      of the Bay of Pigs Invasion,* vol. 2, *Participation in the Conduct of Foreign Policy,*
      166–67. Plans to assassinate troublesome leaders had become a regular part of
      the Eisenhower administration's regime-change programs. An assassination
      option was part of the Árbenz coup, and Patrice Lumumba, the first demo-
      cratically elected prime minister of the Congo, was assassinated on Jan. 17, 1961
      (three days before Kennedy's inauguration) in a plot organized by the CIA and
      the Belgian government using Congolese accomplices. For Eisenhower's pro-
      motion of JMATE, see Wyden, *Bay of Pigs,* 68: "I want to make sure the damn
      thing works," DDE to Bissell and Dulles. On Aug. 16, 1960, CIA operatives
      launched the first assassination attempt against Castro, with poisoned cigars
      Castro and Eisenhower," http://www.fsmitha.com/h2/ch24t-cuba2.htm.

123   He indicated to Dulles: Wyden, *Bay of Pigs* (for "expedited"), 69. *CIA Official
      History of the Bay of Pigs Operation,* vol. 3, *Evolution of CIA's Anti-Castro Poli-
      cies, 1959–January 1961,* 186, 189; Jim Rasenberger, *The Brilliant Disaster: JFK,
      Castro, and America's Doomed Invasion of Cuba's Bay of Pigs* (Simon & Schuster,
      2011).

123   "it would be desirable": Minutes of Special Group Meeting [from Thomas A.
      Parrott], 29 Dec. 1960, quoted from Livingston Merchant's notes of his Dec.
      28, 1960, meeting with Eisenhower, in Pfeiffer, *CIA Official History of the Bay of
      Pigs Operation,* 187.

123   "He [Eisenhower] was inclined": Memo of Conference with the President, 29
      Dec 60, from A. J. Goodpaster, 6 Jan 61. (DDEL, DDE Clean-Up Files, Box
      51—Cuba). Quoted in Pfeiffer, *CIA Official History of the Bay of Pigs Operation,*
      vol. 3, 187 (Emphases added.)

124   "This calculated action": Dwight D. Eisenhower: "Statement by the President
      on Terminating Diplomatic Relations with Cuba," Jan. 3, 1961. Online by Ger-
      hard Peters and John T. Woolley, *The American Presidency Project.* http://www
      .presidency.ucsb.edu/ws/?pid=12048.

124　**The last legal barrier:** Lawrence Freedman, *Kennedy's Wars: Berlin, Cuba, Laos, and Vietnam* (Oxford University Press, 2000), 123–38, is an excellent analysis of the planning for the Bay of Pigs invasion.

124　**the importuning of his closest constituency:** Robert Griffith, "Dwight D. Eisenhower and the Corporate Commonwealth," *American Historical Review* 87, no. 1 (Feb. 1982): 87–122.

124　**"Get off of dead center":** Pfeiffer, *CIA Official History of the Bay of Pigs Operation,* vol. 3, 182.

124　**Organized by Henry Holland:** The Cuban Democratic Revolutionary Front (Frente Revolucionario Democrático [FRD]) was composed of five major anti-Castro groups.

124　**a proactive agenda:** The "Special Group" was also known as the 5412 committee because all covert operations were operated under authority of National Security Council Directive NSC 5412/2.

124　**blow up a ship in Cuba's Levisa Bay:** Levisa Bay is in Holguín Province.

124　**"designed to help":** Pfeiffer, *CIA Official History of the Bay of Pigs Invasion,* vol. 3, 183.

125　**"not [to] authorize any action":** Ibid. See also p. 197 for the "increasing frequency" of the Special Group's meetings.

125　**"no definite schedule":** Ibid., 190. (Emphasis added.)

125　**to the right of Richard Nixon:** Philip Nash, "Bear *Any* Burden? John F. Kennedy and Nuclear Weapons," in *Cold War Statesmen Confront the Bomb: Nuclear Diplomacy Since 1945* (Oxford University Press, 1999), edited by J. L. Gaddis et al., chap. 6. Nash suggests that Kennedy simultaneously campaigned to Nixon's right *and* left.

125　**"eight jet minutes from the coast":** Papers of John F. Kennedy, Pre-Presidential Papers. Senate Files, Series 12, Speeches and the Press. Box 913, Folder: "Jacksonville, Florida, 18 October 1960," JFKL.

125　**"If you can't stand up":** Quoted in Elie Abel, *The Missile Crisis* (Bantam, 1966), 2.

125　**"fighters for freedom":** That debate was held on October 21, 1960. The "fighters for freedom" press release was composed by Richard Goodwin without consultation with Kennedy. See Wyden, *The Bay of Pigs,* 66–67.

126　**"Kennedy probably did":** On July 23, 1960, Allen Dulles had visited Kennedy at his summer retreat in Hyannis Port on Cape Cod. Their conversation had lasted more than two hours and included "general" information about the CIA's anti-Castro guerrilla program, which had not yet evolved into a plan to invade the island. Wyden, *The Bay of Pigs,* 67, fn. There is a discrepancy regarding when Dulles and Bissell briefed Kennedy: Pfeiffer records Nov. 11 on 273; Wyden reports Nov. 27 on 68.

126　**what Kennedy thought at that moment:** Shortly before the Bay of Pigs, in the Oval Office, Kennedy told Richard Goodwin, the author of the press release suggesting the unleashing of Cuban freedom fighters: "We're about to put your Cuba policy into action." Wyden, *Bay of Pigs,* 66 fn.

126　**"units of Cuban refugees":** Eisenhower, *Waging Peace,* 613–14.

126　**"doubts that Kennedy felt":** *Newsday,* Sept. 10, 1965, 50–51.

126　**"On meeting his successor":** Max Frankel, *High Noon in the Cold War: Kennedy, Khrushchev, and the Cuban Missile Crisis* (Presidio Press, 2005), 68.

127　**"Eisenhower, with Kennedy on his left":** Wyden, *Bay of Pigs,* 87–88 fn.

(Emphasis added.); Jim Rasenberger, *The Brilliant Disaster*; James G. Blight and Peter Kornbluth, *Politics of Illusion: The Bay of Pigs Invasion Reexamined* (Lynne Rienner, 1998); Howard Jones, *The Bay of Pigs* (Oxford University Press, 2008).

127 **"the present government"**: Wilton B. Pearsons, "Discussion between DDE, JFK et al.," 1/19/61 memo in Post-Presidential Papers, box 2, DDEL. Also quoted in Mark J. White, *The Cuban Missile Crisis* (Macmillan, 1996), 22.

127 **"It was the policy of this government"**: Wyden, *Bay of Pigs*, 87–88 fn.

127 **the "meaning of 'is'"**: President Bill Clinton's famous (infamous?) explanation to the grand jury on why he was not lying when he said he had not had sex with Monica Lewinsky: "It depends on what the meaning of the word 'is' is. If the—if he—if 'is' means is and never has been, that is not—that is one thing. If it means there is none, that was a completely true statement. . . ." Timothy Noah, "Bill Clinton and the Meaning of 'Is,'" *Slate*, Sept. 13, 1998.

127 **"The definition of a military plan"**: Pfeiffer, *CIA Official History of the Bay of Pigs Invasion*, vol. 3, 201.

127 **"conveniently ignored"**: Ibid., 201–3. (Emphasis added.)

127 **"apparently banned as a topic"**: Ibid., 203 fn. Included among this group, in addition to Eisenhower himself, were James H. Douglas Jr. (Department of Defense), Thomas Mann (Department of State), Gen. David Shoup (Marine Corps), Thomas S. Gates Jr. (Department of Defense), and Livingston Merchant (Department of State).

128 **The new administration's claims**: Lucien S. Vandenbroucke, "The 'Confessions' of Allen Dulles: New Evidence on the Bay of Pigs," *Diplomatic History* 8, no. 4 (Fall 1984): 365–75.

128 **"our hand should not show"**: William I. Hitchcock, *The Age of Eisenhower: America and the World in the 1950s* (Simon & Schuster, 2018), 455.

128 **the "plausible deniability" caveat**: The CIA's postinvasion analysis of the Bay of Pigs termed the operation a "perfect failure." Higgins, *The Perfect Failure*.

128 **During his Senate career**: Papers of John F. Kennedy. PrePresidential Papers. Senate Files. Series 09. Legislation. Box 784, Folder: "Algeria Speech".

128 **American corporations owned**: Frankel, *High Noon in the Cold War*, 67–68.

129 **It was a mini–Marshall Plan**: Edward M. Kennedy, *True Compass: A Memoir* (Twelve, 2009), 177.

129 **JMATE had to be covert**: JMATE and Operation Zapata were synonymous.

129 **"any reluctance or hesitation"**: Wyden, *Bay of Pigs*, 88 fn.

129 **forbidden to discuss**: JMATE was the code name for the Bay of Pigs operation.

129 **being asked to "advise"**: Wyden, *Bay of Pigs*, 88.

129 **"If this kind of an operation"**: Ibid., 90.

130 **"the chance of uprisings"**: Ibid. To prepare for the rebellion, arms for thirty thousand rebels were part of the buildup.

130 **"Dick, remember"**: Ibid., 92.

Chapter 14: "Eisenhower Is Going to Escape"

132 **He had kept his good opinion**: On Saturday, February 10, 1962, twenty-one months after his capture, Francis Gary Powers was exchanged (along with an American student, Frederic Pryor) in a spy swap for Soviet KGB colonel Vilyam Fisher (aka Rudolf Ivanovich Abel) at the now-famous Glienicke Bridge.

132 **He believed Kennedy**: Taubman, *Khrushchev*, 484–85. But Taubman also cites

Khrushchev telling Ambassador Thompson that he preferred Nixon because he knew how to deal with him.

132 **Khrushchev's letter of congratulations**: The other was from Charles de Gaulle.

133 **"to solve such a pressing problem"**: "Message from Chairman Khrushchev to President-elect Kennedy," *American Foreign Policy: Current Documents, 1960*, 476.

133 **two leading Soviet experts**: The other was Llewellyn E. "Tommy" Thompson Jr., who served as American ambassador to the USSR from 1957 to 1962. Bohlen was his predecessor.

133 **"I am most appreciative"**: Ibid., 476.

133 **It was an early sign**: Theodore Sorensen, *Kennedy* (HarperCollins, 1965), 231, and Sorensen, *Counselor: A Life at the Edge of History* (HarperPerennial, 2009), passim.

134 **"a campaign to subvert"**: Sorensen, *Kennedy*, 228.

135 **"in disarray"**: Ibid.

135 **"Other nations were uncertain"**: Ibid., 229.

135 **The country was rudderless**: Ibid.

135 **"He'd often discuss"**: Jill Cowan and Priscilla Wear, recorded interview by William J. vanden Heuvel, March 16, 1965: 11, John F. Kennedy Library Oral History Program.

135 **During most of American history**: William Appleman Williams, *The Contours of American History* (World Pub. Co., 1961); Walter LaFeber, *The New Empire: An Interpretation of American Expansion, 1860–1898* (Cornell U. Press, 1963).

136 **To counter Soviet initiatives**: Kaplan, *The Wizards of Armageddon*, 144–54.

136 **"the effect of any such exchange"**: Gen. Robert Cutler, "Massive Exchange of Nuclear Weapons," Mar. 16, 1958, *FRUS*, vol. 3, *1958–1960*, doc. 11, cited in Peter Shinkle, *Ike's Mystery Man: The Secret Lives of Robert Cutler* (Steerforth Press, 2018), 266–67.

137 **Flexible response would replace**: The literature on the flexible response strategy of the Kennedy administration is too voluminous to list. Samples include Freedman, *Kennedy's Wars*, 92–111; Francis Gavin, "The Myth of Flexible Response: United States Strategy in Europe during the 1960s," *International History Review*, vol. 23 (Dec. 2001): 847–75; Nash, "Bear Any Burden?"; Jane E. Stromseth and Denis Healey, *The Origins of Flexible Response: NATO's Debate over Strategy in the 1960s* (Palgrave Macmillan, 1988).

137 **His strategy for escaping**: Kennedy was profoundly influenced by Gen. Maxwell Taylor's critique of Eisenhower's nuclear weapons policy, *The Uncertain Trumpet* (Harper, 1960).

137 **Only seven years**: The fighting officially ended on July 27, 1953, with the signing of an armistice.

137 **Only five years since 1955**: Vojtech Mastny, "The Warsaw Pact as History," in *Cardboard Castle?: An Inside History of the Warsaw Pact* edited by V. Mastny, Malcom Byrne, and Magdalena Klotzback (Central European University Press, 2005), 1–74.

138 **"a message beyond"**: James R. Killian Jr., *Sputnik, Scientists, and Eisenhower: A Memoir of the First Special Assistant to the President for Science and Technology* (MIT Press, 1977), 2.

138 **"Ask not what your country"**: Douglas Brinkley, *American Moonshot: John F. Kennedy and the Great Space Race* (HarperCollins, 2019).

138　**France was on the brink**: For Konrad Adenauer's nuclear intentions, see Andreas Lutsch, "Nuclear Illusions and Protectorate Reality: A Reappraisal of West German Nuclear Security Policy, 1956–1963," and "The Persistent Legacy: Germany's Place in the Nuclear Order," papers available at the Proliferation International History Project, Woodrow Wilson Center for International Scholars.

138　**Just two weeks before Kennedy's inauguration**: The speech led a subcommittee of the Senate Judiciary Committee to hold a special hearing (on June 16, 1961) on an "Analysis of the Khrushchev Speech of January 6, 1961." In his hyperbolic testimony the conservative economist and military strategist Stefan Possony stated: "I want to express my firm conviction that the parallels between Khrushchev and Hitler are becoming very clear indeed."

138　**His "undue capitulation"**: Arthur Schlesinger Jr. to Marietta Tree, Jan. 1, 1961, *The Letters of Arthur Schlesinger, Jr.*, edited by Andrew Schlesinger and Stephen Schlesinger (Random House, 2013), 239–40.

139　**"It may be"**: Adm. Stansfield Turner, *Burn Before Reading* (Hyperion, 2005), 91.

139　**No member of the administration**: David Talbot, *The Devil's Chessboard: Allen Dulles, the CIA, and the Rise of America's Secret Government* (HarperPerennial, 2015).

139　**By the time he was recruited**: Ibid.

140　**Whatever it takes**: Douglas Waller, *Wild Bill Donovan* (Free Press, 2011); Anthony Cave Brown, *Wild Bill Donovan: The Last Hero* (Times Books, 1982).

140　**He was in contact with the plotters**: Talbot, *The Devil's Chessboard*, 94. For the "ratline" see Michael Phayer, *Pius XII, the Holocaust and the Cold War* (Indiana University Press, 2007).

140　**the 1947 National Security Act**: The act also created the National Security Council, an independent air force (severed from army control), and the Joint Chiefs of Staff. It was amended in 1949 to create the Department of Defense.

141　**had nationalized the assets**: CIA's official history written in March 1954 by Donald Wilber: "Clandestine Service History: Overthrow of Premier Mossadeq of Iran, November 1952–August 1953," and James Risen, "The CIA in Iran," *New York Times*, https://archive.nytimes.com/www.nytimes.com/library/world/mideast/041600iran-cia-index.html?_r=1.

141　**"But in the privacy of the Oval Office"**: Stephen Ambrose, *Eisenhower: Soldier and President* (Simon & Schuster, 1990), 333.

141　**Mossadeq was arrested**: Stephen Kinzer, *All the Shah's Men: An American Coup and the Roots of Middle East Terror* (Wiley, 2003).

141　**While at Sullivan & Cromwell**: Richard Immerman, *The CIA in Guatemala: The Foreign Policy of Intervention* (University of Texas Press, 1982), offers good background analysis of the Guatemalan coup of 1954.

142　**To the agency's distress**: Immerman, *The CIA in Guatemala;* Nicholas Cullather, *Operation PBSuccess: The United States and Guatemala, 1952–1954* (CIA History, 1994), https://www.cia.gov/library/readingroom/docs/DOC_0000134974.pdf; Piero Gleijeses, *Shattered Hope: The Guatemalan Revolution and the United States, 1944–1954* (Princeton University Press, 1991).

142　**could be cajoled**: Pfeiffer, *CIA History of the Bay of Pigs Invasion*, vol. 3, 72. Pfeiffer's interpretations generally defend the CIA, but his history nevertheless provides valuable documentation that cannot be ignored. See National Security

Archive analysis by Peter Kornbluh: https://nsarchive2.gwu.edu/NSAEBB/NS
AEBB355/index.htm.

142 "A Castro victory": Ibid., 16. For the evolution of U.S. foreign policy in Cuba,
see Stephen G. Rabe, "Eisenhower and Latin America: Arms and Dictators,"
Peace and Change (Apr. 1985): 55–57.

142 "Communists and other extreme radicals": Dwight D. Eisenhower, *The White
House Years: Waging Peace, 1956–1961* (Doubleday, 1965), 521, 524.

142 "because they originated": Ibid.

142 Allen Dulles, he should have known: Talbot, *The Devil's Chessboard*, 13.

143 A search was launched: Pfeiffer, *CIA History*, vol. 3, 7.

143 "a practical way": "Memo for Chief, PP Staff from Alfred T. Cox, 25 Aug. 1958,
sub: US Course of Action in Cuba." Pfeiffer, *CIA Official History of the Bay of
Pigs Operation*, vol. 3, 8.

143 "including direct intervention": Ibid., 16.

143 Castro entered Havana: Paris was liberated on Aug. 25, 1944.

143 "the idol of the masses": Pfeiffer, *CIA Official History of the Bay of Pigs Operation*, vol. 3, 19.

143 Castro was determined: In response to stringent U.S. sugar quotas, the Cuban
government implemented Law 851 on July 6, 1960, which nationalized all major
U.S. corporate assets across the island.

143 They had successfully: Stephen G. Rabe, *Eisenhower and Latin America: The
Foreign Policy of Anti-Communism* (University of North Carolina Press, 1988).
Rabe makes the case that Eisenhower was a "virulent anti-communist" who
lacked a sophisticated understanding of Latin American problems.

144 It called for creating: "A Program of Covert Action Against the Castro
Regime," dated 16 March 1960. "Approved by the President at a meeting in the
White House on 17 Mar. 1960." Pfeiffer, *CIA Official History of the Bay of Pigs
Operation*, vol. 3, app. B, 302.

144 "Because the policy makers": Ibid.

144 "acting out of control": Wyden, *The Bay of Pigs*, 7.

144 "The President told Mr. Dulles": Pfeiffer, *CIA Official History of the Bay of Pigs
Operation*, vol. 3, 72–73. (Emphasis added.) Gen. Andrew J. Goodpaster was
staff secretary and defense liaison officer to President Eisenhower (1954–1961).
See also ibid., 25.

144 "You may recall that not so very long after": Pfeiffer, *CIA Official History of the
Bay of Pigs Operation*, vol. 3, 79.

144 "On 29 November 1960": Ibid., 165–66.

145 "the President [Eisenhower] made it clear": Ibid., 166–67.

Chapter 15: "AES Wholly Disapproves of the Project"

146 "And I say to you now": Lucien S. Vandenbroucke, *Perilous Options: Special
Operations as an Instrument of U.S. Foreign Policy* (Oxford University Press,
1993), 36.

146 Adlai Stevenson often awoke: On April 30, 1961, Eastern Airlines began its
regular shuttle service.

146 Representing his country: Michael R. Beschloss, *The Crisis Years: Kennedy and
Khrushchev, 1960–1963* (HarperCollins, 1991), 463–69, provides an excellent
description of the difficult JFK-AES relationship.

146   **"I don't think he'd be"**: Barbara Mary Ward Jackson, Oral History interview
      by Walter and Elsbeth Rostow, JFKL, 6. "All I can tell you is that Adali [*sic*]
      said, "Look, my difficulty is that I don't think he'd be a good president. I do not
      feel that he's the right man for the job; I think he's too young; I don't think he
      fully understands the dimensions of the foreign dilemmas that are coming up;
      and I cannot in conscience throw my support to someone whom I do not really
      think is up to it." He said, "I admire him; I think he's a fine young man; I don't
      see him as a president. I can't in conscience suddenly say, because I want to be
      Secretary of State, 'Okay, I have changed my mind.'

      "Then he went on to talk about his own prospects. He said no, he didn't. . . .
      He wasn't sure; he would not refuse a draft, the usual thing. But then he went
      on to say that he felt pretty certain that he could beat Nixon and that he wasn't
      going to exclude himself on the grounds that he couldn't."

147   **"Look, I have the votes"**: Mark White, *Against the President: The Impact of Dis-
      sent in the White House* (Ivan R. Dee, 2007), 177.

147   **snag the nomination**: On May 22, 1960, Schlesinger recorded in his diary:
      "JFK called re his conversation with AES [Adlai Stevenson] in Libertyville
      Saturday morning. He believed AES's 'real reason' for not coming out in sup-
      port of Kennedy was that 'if he said nothing, there might still be a possibil-
      ity that he would emerge out of the scramble as the candidate,'" Arthur M.
      Schlesinger Jr., Journal, box 311, NYPL.

147   **"We want Stevenson"**: John Bartlow Martin, *Adlai Stevenson and the World*
      (Doubleday, 1977), 527.

147   **They judged his caution**: Mark J. White, *The Cuban Missile Crisis* (Macmillan
      Press Ltd, 1996), 181. In a 1960 report Hoover accused Stevenson of being a
      member of a NYC gay group.

147   **"He never quite accomplishes"**: The Kennedys were not alone in their view of
      Stevenson's irresolution. Schlesinger's diary records that on Monday, July 11,
      Teddy White switched to JFK after concluding that AES was afflicted with
      "hopeless indecisiveness," P. 6 of what appear to be manuscript (NYPL, Arthur
      Schlesinger Jr. Papers); White, *Cuban Missile Crisis*, 180.

147   **"Jack can't bear"**: Carl S. Anthony, *First Ladies*, vol. 2, 59; RFK quoted in
      White, *Cuban Missile Crisis*, 181.

148   **might not be up to the task**: On Dec. 1, 1960, Schlesinger recorded Kennedy's
      view of the importance of the UN position: "I understand that Adlai doesn't
      want to do the UN job. Why is that? . . . "The UN is different now. I think this
      job has great possibilities" (also published in Schlesinger, *Journals*, 96).

148   **We "were hysterical"**: Quote in David Robarge, *John McCone as Director of
      Central Intelligence, 1961–1965* (Center for the Study of Intelligence), 83, See
      theblackvault, McCone.

148   **"Had the invasion succeeded"**: Sorensen Oral History Interview #2 by Carl
      Kaysen, 19.

148   **"What I really mean"**: Richard M. Bissell Jr., *Reflections of a Cold Warrior: From
      Yalta to the Bay of Pigs* (Yale University Press, 1996), 159, quoted in David Tal-
      bot, *Brothers: The Hidden History of the Kennedy Years* (Free Press, 2007), 43.

148   **"our hand should not show"**: Hitchcock, *The Age of Eisenhower*, 455.

149   **"this damned invasion"**: "We agreed that the critical point—and the weak part
      of the case for action—lay in the theory of an immediate local response to a
      landing." Schlesinger, *Journal* (Mar. 28, 1961), 114.

149 "Mr. President, I know you're doubtful": Sorensen Oral History Interview #2 with Carl Kaysen, JFKL, 24. See also Jones, *The Bay of Pigs*, 71.

149 the shift of the landing site: Pfeiffer, *CIA Official History of the Bay of Pigs Operation*, vol. 1, *Air Operations, March 1960–April 1961*, 176–77.

149 The message was duly delivered: Bissell sent Tracy Barnes to NYC to get the necessary agreement. Schlesinger, *Journal*, NYPL, Box 311, 140. The Cuban Revolutionary Council was formed, with CIA assistance, three weeks before the invasion to "coordinate and direct" the activities of another group known as the Cuban Democratic Revolutionary Front, which planned to establish an anti-Castro government immediately after the invasion had some success. (Emphasis added.)

150 "Castro doesn't need agents here": W. Joseph Campbell, *Getting It Wrong: Debunking the Greatest Myths in American Journalism* (University of California Press, 2017), 94.

150 mostly a collection of newspaper clippings: The entire file is available at the web site "Government Attic," at http://www.governmentattic.org/4docs/FBI-FileOverthrowCastro_1960-1965.pdf.

150 "I was in Guatemala": *Executive Sessions of the Senate Foreign Relations Committee (Historical Series)*, vol. 13, part 1, *Eighty-Seventh Congress, 1st Session, 1961* (USGPO, 1984), 333.

151 know "absolutely nothing about": Peter Kornbluh, "Cuba Libre," *The Nation*, Apr. 2015, 62.

151 knew almost everything: Ernesto "Che" Guevara made the error of believing that the revelations of the training camps indicated that John Kennedy was opposed to any such operation. James G. Hershberg, "Chatting with Che," edited by James G. Hershberg and Christian F. Ostermann, *Woodrow Wilson Center Cold War International History Project Bulletin: The Global Cuban Missile Crisis at 50* 17/18 (Fall 2012): 158. https://www.wilsoncenter.org/publication/bulletin-no-1718-fall-2012.

151 If disbanded, the anti-Castro brigade: Sorensen, Oral History Interview #2, Apr. 16, 1964, 17.

151 "the best possible plan": McGeorge Bundy, "Memorandum of Discussion on Cuba, March 11, 1961"; National Security Action Memorandum No. 31, *FRUS*, vol. 10, *1961–1963* (1997), *Cuba*, doc. 60.

152 "we would have undone": Wyden, *Bay of Pigs*, 122–23; *Executive Sessions of the Senate Foreign Relations Committee (Historical Series)*, vol. 13, part 1, *Eighty-Seventh Congress, 1st Session, 1961* (USGPO, 1984), 3–4.

153 "[He] objects to the fact": Schlesinger, *A Thousand Days*, 271.

153 Preinvasion action: Three days earlier, on April 12, 1962, the Soviet Union had launched "a second sputnik," sending the cosmonaut Yuri Gagarin and his space capsule, Vostok 1, into a round-the-earth orbit.

153 "a group of Cuban pilots": "Exile Chief Sees Start of Cuban Military Fall," *Los Angeles Times*, Apr. 16, 1961, 5.

153 After flying close enough: "Bombs Dropped on Cuban Strategic Centers," *Christian Science Monitor*, Apr. 15, 1961, 3.

153 "Three Cuba Air Bases Bombed": *Los Angeles Times*, Apr. 16, 1961, 1.

153 "Castro Pilots Revolt": *Chicago Daily Tribune*, Apr. 16, 1961, 1.

153 "A heroic blow": *Christian Science Monitor*, Apr. 15, 1961, 3.

153 The planes "were Castro's own": Schlesinger, *A Thousand Days*, 271.

153   **"I have emphasized before"**: UPI Audio Archives, "Bay of Pigs Invasion." http://www.upi.com/Archives/Audio/Events-of-1961/Bay-of-Pigs-Invasion.

154   **The Cubans had located**: Pfeiffer, *Official CIA History of the Bay of Pigs Invasion*, vol. 1, *Air Operations*, 174–212.

154   **"shocked by his appearance"**: White, *Against the President*, 201.

155   **second wave of air strikes**: On 22 Apr. 1961, after the failure of the U.S.-backed invasion of Cuba at the Bay of Pigs, Kennedy privately told Eisenhower that he had minimized U.S. military backing for the invasion because he feared Soviet retaliation against Berlin. Eisenhower then answered, as he recorded in his diary at the time: "Mr. President, that is exactly the opposite of what would really happen. The Soviets follow their own plans, and if they see us show any weakness that is when they press us the hardest. The second they see us show strength and do something on our own, that is when they are very cagey" (from Eisenhower's notes of the meeting in his Post-Presidential Papers, Box 11, at the Dwight D. Eisenhower Library, which are also reproduced in the *FRUS* Microfiche Supplement on Cuba, 1961–1963). The conversation is described in Richard Reeves, *President Kennedy: Profile of Power (*Simon & Schuster, 1993), 102–3.

155   **"hate US intervention"**: Philip Agee, *Inside the Company: CIA Diary* (Penguin Books, 1978), 167, quoted from Agee's diary, Apr. 18, 1961.

155   **"We were already mobilized"**: Blight, Allyn, and Welch, *Cuba on the Brink*, 110.

155   **Surprise overwhelmed**: Castro's "forces displayed a greater will to fight than we had expected," Allen Dulles and Richard Bissell explained to the Senate Foreign Relations Committee, *Executive Sessions of the Senate Foreign Relations Committee (Historical Series)*, vol. 13, part 1, *Eighty-Seventh Congress, 1st Session, May 2, 1961* (USGPO, 1984), 412.

155   **the 2506's chances of success**: During the battle at the Bay of Pigs, the CIA officers fired at, and destroyed, several CIA aircraft. The B-26s provided by the CIA were painted to match those in the Cuban air force. "We couldn't tell them from the Castro planes," the CIA's invasion leader, Grayston Lynch, recalled. "We ended up shooting at two or three of them. We hit some of them there because when they came at us . . . it was a silhouette, that was all you could see." NSA, "Top Secret CIA 'Official History' of the Bay of Pigs: Revelations." https://nsarchive2.gwu.edu/NSAEBB/NSAEBB355/index.htm.

155   **the president's warnings to the contrary**: John F. Kennedy, quoted by William Bundy in James Srodes, *Allen Dulles: Master of Spies* (Regnery, 1999), 526.

156   **"straight into Havana"**: Higgins, *The Perfect Failure*, 128.

155   **The entire operation**: Thomas Lowe Hughes, interview with author, Jan. 27, 2010. See also Walt Rostow's observation in Srodes, *Allen Dulles*, 532: "In retrospect I have concluded that there was this belief in the CIA and the Pentagon that once they got the invasion started, Kennedy would have to involve the U.S. armed forces. It was absolute nonsense and Kennedy had made it clear beforehand; the fact that he was strong enough to hold the line and to take the blame on himself later explains the operation."

156   **"Only 135 of them"**: Jones, *The Bay of Pigs*, 71. See also Che Guevara's analysis of the crisis: https://digitalarchive.wilsoncenter.org/document/115179.

156   **"Our feeling of trust"**: Gen. Gerhard Wessel quoted in Beschloss, *The Crisis Years*, 241.

156   "Jack had been on the phone": Amanda Smith, ed., *Hostage to Fortune: The Let-
      ters of Joseph P. Kennedy* (Viking, 2000), 697–98.

156   "anguished and fatigued": http://www.nytimes.com/2011/05/24/science/
      space/24space.html.

156   "The largest contribution": Srodes, *Allen Dulles*, 532, quoted from interview
      with Walt Rostow.

157   "People like leaders": President Kennedy also discussed the Bay of Pigs with
      "General Eisenhower, Mr. Nixon [Richard M. Nixon], Mr. Hoover [Herbert
      C. Hoover], General MacArthur [Douglas A. MacArthur], Mr. Truman
      [Harry S. Truman], and other national leaders," according to Ted Sorensen.
      Sorensen Oral History Interview #2, JFKL, 26. Kennedy's poll numbers went
      up to about 90 percent, according to Evan Thomas. https://www.youtube
      .com/watch?v=Y3xh7Z_349Y.

157   "You always assume": Quoted in Edward Kennedy, *True Compass*, 176.

157   "Allen Dulles was a frivolous man": Stansfield Turner, *Burn Before Reading:* 92.

157   "I doubt my Presidency": White, *Against the President*, 201.

157   "I think that after the Bay of Pigs": Sorensen, Oral History Interview #2, 22.
      "On at least two different occasions," Sorensen recalled, Kennedy said "that had
      it not been for the Bay of Pigs, we would have been deeply involved in a war in
      Southeast Asia."

158   It appears that there was only one thing: Thomas Hughes recalled JFK's anger
      at Chester Bowles, who also had opposed the Bay of Pigs and said so after.
      Interview with author, Jan. 27, 2010.

158   "Of one thing we may be sure": Adlai Stevenson, "Some Lessons from Cuba"
      (Apr. 23, 1961), A. Stevenson papers, Seeley G. Mudd Library, Princeton
      University.

Chapter 16: "Cuba Might Become a Sino-Soviet Bloc Missile Base"

160   "If people are not ready": *Executive Sessions of the Senate Foreign Relations Com-
      mittee [ESSFRC] (Historical Series)*, vol. 13, part 1, *Eighty-Seventh Congress,
      First Session, May 2, 1961* (USGPO, 1984), 393.

160   "If they [the USSR] should ever build": Ibid., 420.

160   "I just see nothing": Ibid., 354.

160   "The reluctance": Ibid., 314–16, 318–19, 327.

161   "to understand how": Ibid., iii.

161   historians of the Cuban missile crisis: An exception is Philip Nash, *The Other
      Missiles of October*, 95.

161   "a Sino-Soviet missile base": *ESSFRC*, vol. 13, 1, 349.

161   "It is most unfortunate": Ibid., 338.

161   his ex post facto rationalization: No evidence to support Rusk's claim has been
      located.

162   It was necessary "to relate": By 1961 relations between China and the USSR had
      deteriorated to the point where the concept of a Sino-Soviet Bloc was an anach-
      ronism. But the Sino-Soviet Bloc as a useful political reference remained a staple
      for the secretary of state. The ideological underpinning of his testimony—
      which tracked the rhetoric of his predecessor, John Foster Dulles—anticipated
      his many defenses of American intervention in Vietnam. (Emphasis added.)

162   "Do you really believe": *ESSFRC*, vol. 13, 1, 349.

162   "an additional security threat": In June 1959, as Eisenhower considered the

deployment of medium-range missiles to Europe, he worried about how provocative they would be and made the analogy of the Soviets putting similar missiles in Cuba or Mexico. But he went ahead nevertheless. Nash, *The Other Missiles of October*, 63. (Emphasis added.)

162   **"This is somewhat speculative":** *ESSFRC*, vol. 13, 1, 349.

163   **"There was not objective evidence":** Ibid., 360.

163   **"any 6-year-old kid":** Ibid., 413, 426. Capehart made the "Boy Scout" and the "6-year-old kid" remarks at separate points in the hearing.

163   **the "operation was a Cuban one":** Ibid., 412. The unexpected resistance of Castro's forces was also part of Bissell's explanation.

164   **"If they should ever build":** Ibid., 420.

164   **"No, sir":** Ibid., 436.

164   **"not know whether":** Ibid., 449.

164   **But the testimony:** Ibid. Special National Intelligence Estimate [SNIE 85-3-62], Sept. 19, 1962, "The Military Buildup in Cuba," predicted that Khrushchev would not deliver missiles to Cuba. https://history.state.gov/historical documents/frus1961-63v10/d433.

164   **"We came out of World War II":** *ESSFRC*, vol. 13, 1, 452.

164   **"It is not lost":** Ibid., 454.

165   **a peripheral player:** Ibid., 572–73.

165   **"in my appearances":** Ibid., 580.

Chapter 17: "It Will Be a Cold Winter"

167   **"They controlled":** Sorensen Oral History with Carl Kaysen, JFKL, 29.

167   **He had not had the courage:** During Khrushchev's 1959 visit to the United States, Eisenhower admitted at their Camp David meeting that West Germany was "abnormal." See chap. 12.

167   **An independent East German state:** Initially between the American, British, and French zones of occupation.

168   **John Kennedy may have been raised:** Robert Dallek, *An Unfinished Life: John F. Kennedy, 1917–1963* (Little, Brown, 2003).

168   **"great compartmentalizer":** Robert McCrum review of *Once Upon a Secret: My Affair with President John F. Kennedy and Its Aftermath*, by Mimi Alford (Random House, 2012), Feb. 10, 2012, *The Guardian* (online).

168   **He refused to allow:** Ibid. and Seymour M. Hersh, *The Dark Side of Camelot* (Little, Brown, 1997).

168   **"a story of lifelong suffering":** Dallek, *An Unfinished Life*. Insights into JFK's health and personality can be found throughout, but Dallek has brought them together in "The Medical Ordeals of JFK," *Atlantic*, Dec. 2002. The details that follow about Kennedy's health issues are all from Dallek's article as read online, unless otherwise referenced. https://www.theatlantic.com/magazine/archive/2002/12/the-medical-ordeals-of-jfk/305572/.

169   **Despite his maladies:** Michael O'Brien, *John F. Kennedy: A Biography* (St. Martin's, 2005), 81.

169   **"Jack feigned being well":** Dallek, "The Medical Ordeals of JFK," *Atlantic*, Dec. 2002.

169   **"his fatalism and his pragmatism":** Edward J. Renehan Jr., *The Kennedys at War, 1937–1945* (Doubleday, 2002), 318.

169   **"That young American":** At the time Pamela was married to Winston

Churchill's son, Randolph. For JFK's medical condition see: Lee R. Mandel, MD, MPH, "Endocrine and Autoimmune Aspects of the Health History of John F. Kennedy," *Annals of Internal Medicine.* https://annals.org/aim/full article/744707/endocrine-autoimmune-aspects-health-history-john-f-kennedy. The article indicates that JFK had Autoimmune Polyendocrine Syndrome type 2, passim.

170   **"The record of these two and a half years"**: Dallek, "The Medical Ordeals of JFK," *Atlantic* (Dec. 2002).

170   **"President Kennedy was the first president"**: Averell Harriman, Oral History, Kai Bird collection.

170   **"They controlled"**: Sorensen, Oral History #2, JFKL, 29.

171   **Kennedy had responded**: Kennedy to Khrushchev, Feb. 22, 1961, delivered to Khrushchev by Ambassador Llewellyn Thompson on Mar. 9, 1961; "Crisis over Berlin: American Policy Concerning the Soviet Threats to Berlin, Nov. 1958–Dec. 1962," part 5, Bureau of Public Affairs, DOS, Research Project # 614-E, Feb. 1970, 40. https://www.cia.gov/library/readingroom/docs/1970-02-01b.pdf.

171   **"is *not* for the purpose"**: Ibid. (Emphasis added.)

171   **"It's a new, young president"**: Soviet ambassador Anatoly Dobrynin interviewed by Sherry Jones, 1992, "Interviews with Soviet veterans of the Cuban Missile Crisis," NSA, https://nsarchive2.gwu.edu/NSAEBB/NSAEBB400/.

171   **a country of six million people**: Nash, *The Other Missiles of October*, 98–102.

171   **The first was his anger**: Ibid.

172   **more direct with Kennedy**: For Khrushchev's understanding of the differences he shared with Eisenhower on Berlin: Khrushchev, *Memoirs*, vol. 3, *Statesman*, 174.

172   **"liquidation of a dangerous"**: DOS, "Crisis over Berlin," 40, https://www.cia.gov/library/readingroom/docs/1970-02-01b.pdf.

172   **The conclusion of a peace treaty**: Khrushchev to Kennedy, May 12, 1961, quoted in ibid., 40 n 1.

172   **cling to the status quo**: Carolyn Eisenberg, *Drawing the Line: The American Decision to Divide Germany, 1944–1949* (Cambridge University Press, 1996).

172   **Any alternative acceptable**: See Bundy to JFK, 6/10/61, subject: Berlin, *FRUS, 1961–1963*, vol. 14, *Berlin Crisis, 1961–1962*, doc. 38. Walter Lippmann offered an alternative that Kennedy found interesting but problematic.

172   **"to preside over the isolation"**: DOS, "Crisis over Berlin," 42–43, https://www.cia.gov/library/readingroom/docs/1970-02-01b.pdf.

173   **"It will be a cold winter"**: Ibid., 46 n1. Memorandum of conversation between the president and Khrushchev, June 4, 1961.

173   **"beat the hell out of me"**: James Reston, *New York Times*, June 5, 1961. See also Frederick Kempe, *Berlin 1961: Kennedy, Khrushchev, and the Most Dangerous Place on Earth* (Putnam, 2011), 209–68.

173   **"he could never negotiate"**: Tom Wicker, *JFK and LBJ: The Influence of Personality upon Politics* (Penguin Books, 1970), 208. Wicker reports in his footnote that Reston gave him a full account of his conversation with Kennedy. He also cites Reston, *The Artillery of the Press* (Harper & Row, 1967), 28, and *Sketches in the Sand* (Alfred A. Knopf, 1967), 472–73; Reston, *Deadline: A Memoir* (Random House, 1991), 287–99.

174   **"when he shook hands"**: Jill Cowan and Priscilla Wear, recorded interview by William J. vanden Heuvel, Mar. 16, 1965, JFKL Oral History Program: 15.

174   Two consequential results: Nash, *The Other Missiles of October,* 98–102.

174   precipitating a war: Sorensen Oral History #2, 35, JFKL.

175   "The prospects": Ibid., 51.

175   "[Khrushchev's] aide-memoire": Ibid., 30–32.

175   "worse than a waste of time": Kempe, *Berlin 1961,* 281.

175   "McNamara was the best advocate": Sorensen., Oral History Interview #2, 33, JFKL.

175   "an investment of men": Ibid., 31.

176   "If East Germany goes": W. W. Rostow, *The Diffusion of Power: An Essay in Recent History,* 231, quoted in Kempe, *Berlin 1961,* 293; "Khrushchev Is Losing." Rostow, recorded interview by Richard Neustadt, Apr. 11, 1964: 60-61, John F. Kennedy Library Oral History Program. See also Michael O'Brien, *John F. Kennedy: A Biography* (St, Martin's, 2005), 555.

176   "an island of freedom": For Kennedy's July 25, 1961, speech, see Office of the Federal Register, ed., *John F. Kennedy, Containing the public messages, speeches and statements of the president: January 20 to December 31, 1961* (USGPO, 1962), 908; (Public Papers of the Presidents), 533–40; "Radio and Television Report to the American People on the Berlin Crisis," July 25, 1961.

177   "the worst spurt of intimidation": Khrushchev's secret speech on the Berlin crisis, August 4, 1961, ". . . so far the worst spurt of intimidation was in the Kennedy speech [on 25 July 1961]. . . . Kennedy spoke [to frighten us] and then got scared himself," 141. (*CWIHPB*) https://www.mtholyoke.edu/acad/intrel/khrush.htm.

177   He did not tell the delegates: Hope Harrison, *Driving the Soviets Up the Wall: Soviet–East German Relations, 1953–1961* (Princeton, 2003), 195, 201.

177   "the Soviets held their breaths": Taubman, *Khrushchev,* 506.

177   "There wouldn't be any need": O'Brien, *John F. Kennedy: A Biography,* 556.

178   a propaganda bonanza: Ibid., according to Donald Wilson, the deputy director of the United States Information Agency.

178   Eight months later: Taubman, *Khrushchev,* 502–3.

178   an audacious, irresponsible action: Andrei Sakharov, *Memoirs,* translated by Richard Lourie (Alfred A. Knopf, 1990), 219–22.

178   It sent a warning: Taubman, *Khrushchev,* 537–41.

179   "The president bears the burden": Kennedy interview two months after the Cuban missile crisis, *Washington Post,* December 18, 1962. Quoted in Graham Allison and Philip Zelikow, *Essence of Decision: Explaining the Cuban Missile Crisis,* rev. ed., (Longman, 1999), 355.

181   "My thinking went like this.": Khrushchev, *Khrushchev Remembers,* 494. Taubman, *Khrushchev,* 535.

181   In the spring of 1962 Soviet: Anatoly Dobrynin, *In Confidence* (Times Books, 1995), 63. (Emphasis added.) "Khrushchev believed he had a chance to shift the status quo in his favor through Berlin. Soviet leaders therefore exerted pressure on the Kennedy administration, a mistaken strategy that only promoted international tension and the arms race."

Chapter 18: "What If We Put Our Nuclear Missiles in Cuba?"

182   "I believe [Khrushchev's] decision": Fidel Castro, interviewed by Maria Shriver, Sept. 26, 1992. I obtained a Spanish language copy of the interview in 2015 during a research trip to Cuba. According to Cuban intelligence, the

"primary purpose [of the missile deployment to Cuba] was to challenge American nuclear supremacy, not to deter an American invasion of Cuba." Domingo Amuchástegui, "Cuban Intelligence and the October Crisis," *Intelligence and National Security* 13, no. 3: 109. https://doi.org/10.1080/02684529808432495

182   **"no big reaction":** Quoted in ibid., 196; Taubman, *Khrushchev,* 553, attributes the quotation to Khrushchev.

182   **a lightweight:** Khrushchev's secret speech on the Berlin crisis, Aug. 4, 1961. (CWIHP) https://www.mtholyoke.edu/acad/intrel/khrush.htm.

182   **a fallback plan:** Dobrynin, *In Confidence,* 79.

182   **"When some idea":** Taubman, *Khrushchev,* 541.

182   **No incident more clearly reveals:** *New York Times* reporter Harrison Salisbury, who knew Khrushchev well, ended his review of *Khrushchev Remembers* (*New York Times Book Review,* Jan. 3, 1971): "I thought, on balance he was good for his country and good for the world. He made hair-raising mistakes. But he didn't mind admitting his blunders. He had the eternal curiosity of a child. And, at heart, it was difficult to believe that he was not sincere in his desire to make a better world."

183   **Mao Zedong continued to challenge him:** Mao's challenge was a critical factor behind Khrushchev's missile deployment to Cuba according to Odd Arne Westad, *The Global Cold War: Third World Interventions and the Making of Our Times* (Cambridge University Press, 2007), 170–80.

183   **the German Democratic Republic:** Communist East Germany.

183   **real security for Castro:** Khrushchev, *Khrushchev Remembers,* 493.

184   **"the USA has completed":** March 17, 1962, Intelligence Report on Plan to Attack Cuba, Woodrow Wilson Center, Digital Archive. CWIHP. https://digitalarchive.wilsoncenter.org/document/114514. The report alleged offensive forces arriving from Guatemala and Panama, followed by support units out of Guantanamo Bay. It notes that Cuban intelligence also supported the claim, which may not have been true. According to a Cuban intelligence officer during the crisis: "Cuban intelligence concluded that no aggression was imminent." However, Castro rejected this assessment according to Domingo Amuchástegui, "Cuban Intelligence and the October Crisis," *Intelligence and National Security* 13, no. 3, 96. Brought to my attention by Philip Zelikow.

184   **an "answer [to] the American threat":** Khrushchev, *Khrushchev Remembers,* 511.

184   **just as important, Philip Zelikow argues:** For a thorough analysis of the debate about the extent of West Berlin's influence on Khrushchev's decision to deploy ballistic missiles to Cuba, see Philip Zelikow, "'Documentary Evidence' and Llewellyn Thompson's Berlin/Cuba Assessment of Soviet Motives in the October 1962 Missile Crisis," *H-Diplo Commentary* (Dec. 10, 2018), http://tiny.cc/CR2. See also Allison and Zelikow, *Essence of Decision,* which proposes four hypotheses that may have motivated Khrushchev's decision: (1) the defense of Castro's government, (2) Cold War politics, (3) the opportunity to adjust the nuclear balance, and (4) expelling the U.S. and its allies from West Berlin. "We find a good deal of evidence," they conclude, "to support the Berlin hypothesis." 105. The evidence is discussed on pages 99–109. See also Marc Trachtenberg, "La crise de Cuba à la lumière de l'ouverture des archives americaines,"in Maurice Vaisse (ed.) *L'Europe et la crise de Cuba* (Paris: Colin, 1993), 25–33.

184   **They were a "cure-all":** Taubman, *Khrushchev,* chap. 19, "The Cuban Cure-all: 1962," 529–77. Philip Nash, *The Other Missiles of October*—a comprehensive and

careful study of the Eisenhower administration's decision to deploy U.S. Jupiter missiles to Turkey, see introduction.

184   **"Then I became convinced"**: Taubman, *Khrushchev*, 347; Holloway, *Stalin and the Bomb:* "There appears now to have been a dual—even a schizophrenic—attitude to nuclear war in the Soviet leadership: a recognition of its destructive consequences for the Soviet Union as well as the West, and an official position that nuclear war would mean the end of capitalism," 339–40.

184   **"Any fool can start a war"**: Khrushchev, *Khrushchev Remembers*, 546. "It was no secret that Khrushchev stood in awe of nuclear weapons," according to Fursenko and Naftali, *One Hell of a Gamble*, 178.

185   **What else were the doctrines**: Francis J. Gavin, *Nuclear Statecraft: History and Strategy in America's Atomic Age* (Cornell University Press, 2012), 65–67.

185   **Over Premier Nikolai Bulganin's signature**: As premier (1955–1958) Bulganin was second in command to Khrushchev who was the first secretary of the Communist Part of the Soviet Union from 1953–1964 and chairman of the Council of Ministers (aka premier) from 1958–1964.

185   **The French and Israeli governments**: Francis Fukuyama, *Soviet Threats to Intervene in the Middle East, 1956–1973* (Rand, June 1980, N-1577-FF), 6.

185   **like Chaucer's rooster**: *Chanticleer and the Fox.* adapted from Geoffrey Chaucer's *Canterbury Tales* (HarperCollins).

185   **"What does Anthony [Eden]"**: Quoted by Evan Thomas, *New York Times Book Review*, Oct. 16, 2016, 17; Alex von Tunzelmann, *Blood and Sand: Suez, Hungary, and Eisenhower's Campaign for Peace* (HarperCollins, 2016).

185   **such a brazen challenge**: Ambrose, *Eisenhower: Soldier and President*, 431.

186   **as furious as Hitler**: Donald Neff, *Warriors at Suez* (Simon & Schuster, 1981), 403.

186   **"If the Soviets attack"**: Keith Kyle, *Suez: Britain's End of Empire in the Middle East* (Weidenfeld, 1991), 458.

186   **"irrational acts"**: John Lewis Gaddis, *We Now Know* (Clarendon, 1998), 240. What—other than his rabid anti-Communism and his stereotypical image of Russians—prompted Dulles to believe that Khrushchev was a drunkard is unknown.

186   **Suddenly Khrushchev's nuclear**: This brought to mind what President Nixon told his White House chief of staff, H. R. "Bob" Haldeman in 1969: "I call it the Madman Theory, Bob. I want the North Vietnamese to believe I've reached the point where I might do anything to stop the war. We'll just slip the word to them that, 'for God's sake, you know Nixon is obsessed about communism. We can't restrain him when he's angry—and he has his hand on the nuclear button and Ho Chi Minh himself will be in Paris in two days begging for peace." H. R. Haldeman, *The Ends of Power* (Times Books, 1978), 122.

186   **Sputnik, the first human-made**: Matthew Brzezinski, *Red Moon Rising: Sputnik and the Hidden Rivalries That Ignited the Space Age* (Times Books, 2007).

186   **"Sputnik seemed to herald"**: David Halberstam, *The Fifties* (Fawcett, 1993), 625.

186   **Perhaps to "rub it in"**: Memorandum of Conference with President Eisenhower After Sputnik, Oct. 8, 1957, DDEL, NA identifier: 186623.

187   **his Sputnik moment**: Photographs from the USA's Corona satellite (which had replaced U2 overflights of the USSR) indicated that the USSR had only 4 ICBMs.

187   On October 21, 1961: Kempe, *Berlin 1961*, 444–47.

187   "In short," he reported: Roswell L. Gilpatric, Oct. 21, 1961, The Homestead
      Resort, NSA, Nuclear Vault, 3, 7, Department of Defense, OPA NO 1173-61.
      See also Daniel Ellsberg, *The Doomsday Machine*, (Bloomsbury, 2017), 173.

187   "the Pentagon wants": Denis Aldokhin, Карибский кризис: как мир был на
      волоске от ядерной войны. Cuba Crisis: "How the World Was Within the
      Balance of a Nuclear War"]. This document was marked by hand: "Reported
      to comrade N. S. Khrushchev personally on June 29, 1960, by A. Shelepin"
      (Shelepin in Central Committee, June 29, 1960, file no. 84, 124, vol. 12, pp.
      237–38, Archive of Russian Foreign Intelligence Service), translated by Angela
      Greenfield, https://42.tut.by/566293.

187   new surface-to-air missile: NATO designation SA-2 Guideline.

187   illegal U2 overflights: By 1961 the U2 overflights of the USSR had been
      replaced by the Corona, the first generation of spy satellites.

188   The missiles in Turkey: Nash, *The Other Missiles of October*, 29.

188   "It really bothered him": Interview with Sergei Khrushchev in *The Missiles of
      October: What the World Didn't Know* (documentary film, 1992).

188   In a January 1962 interview: "Alexei Adzhubei's Account to the Central Com-
      mittee of the Communist Party of the Soviet Union of His Visit to Wash-
      ington," Mar. 12, 1962, History and Public Policy Program Digital Archive,
      Archive of the President of the Russian Federation (APRF), Moscow, Special
      declassification, April 2002; translated by Adam Mayle (NSA), http://digital
      archive.wilsoncenter.org/document/115124. See also *CWIHPB, The Global
      Cuban Missile Crisis at 50*, 316–23.

188   "Saving Cuba for Socialism": Khrushchev, *Khrushchev Remembers*, 546.

188   The turning point for his decision: Igor Belov, Карибский кризис [Caribbean
      crisis], translated by Angela Greenfield, http://www.encyclopaedia-russia.ru
      /article.php?id=228, See also "Cuban Missile Crisis," http://www.russianspace
      web.com/cuban_missile_crisis.html.

189   France's president, Charles de Gaulle: Frédéric Bozo, "France, 'Gaullism,' and
      the Cold War," in *The Cambridge History of the Cold War*, edited by Melvyn P.
      Leffler and Odd Arne Westad, vol. 2, 158–78; Sebastian Reyn, "The Clash:
      Kennedy and de Gaulle's Rejection of the Atlantic Partnership, 1962–1963,"
      Atlantis Lost: The American Experience with De Gaulle, 1958–1969, 141–94; and
      Samuel F. Wells, "Nuclear Weapons and European Security During the Cold
      War," *Diplomatic History* 16, no. 2 (1992): 278–86.

189   "rais[ing] questions about": The summary continues: He doubts that Presi-
      dent Eisenhower would direct "stategic bombardment of the Soviet Union if
      the Soviet attack in Europe was not a clear-cut all-out attack." He empha-
      sizes the importance of flexibility in U.S. nuclear strategy and of developing
      a strategic concept that is "more credible" than massive retaliation and takes
      into account the availability of low-yield tactical nuclear weapons. (Memcon,
      4/7/58 [00099]), Digital National Security Archive collection: Nuclear History
      1, 1955–1968, "Chronology: U.S. Nuclear History: Nuclear Arms and Politics
      in the Missile Age, 1955–1968."

189   "Spending on the IRBM": Hitchcock, *The Age of Eisenhower*, 387.

189   "Our potential enemy": Honoré M. Catudal, *Soviet Nuclear Strategy from Stalin
      to Gorbachev* (Humanities Press International, 1989), 46. Research by Kevin
      Woelfel.

189 **The R-5 had a range**: Neil Sheehan, *A Fiery Peace in a Cold War* (Random House, 2009), 218. Research by Kevin Woelfel.

189 **"a missile of about 1500"**: Ibid., 2.

190 **"establish two IRBM"**: Memo for USAF Chief of Staff, Operational deployment of the Intermediate Range Ballistic Missile, Mar. 1, 1956. http://ns archive.chadwyck.com.mutex.gmu.edu/nsa/documents/NH/00556/all.pdf. Research by Kevin Woelfel.

190 **"to present a unified front"**: Report by the Joint Intelligence Committee to the JCS on Soviet Reaction to U.S. Deployment of Intermediate Range Ballistic Missiles," Mar. 12, 1958. Digital National Security Archives collection [DNSA]: collection Cuban Missile Crisis https://search-proquest-com.mutex.gmu.edu /dnsa/docview/1679066075.

190 **"We needed to discuss"**: Khrushchev, *Khrushchev Remembers*, 547.

191 **a Soviet version of brinkmanship**: Hershberg, "The Cuban Missile Crisis," 70.

191 **"only one or two nuclear bombs"**: Martin J. Sherwin, "One Step from Nuclear War: The Cuban Missile Crisis at 50: In Search of a Historical Perspective," in *Prologue: The Journal of the National Archives* 44, no. 3 (2012) : 12; *Memoirs of Nikita Khrushchev*, vol. 3, *Statesman, 1953-1964*, 326.

191 **"They [Americans] surrounded us"**: Khrushchev, *Memoirs*, vol. 3, *Statesman*.

191 **"Let the enemy believe"**: Aleksandr Fursenko and Timothy Naftali, *Khrushchev's Cold War: The Inside Story of an American Adversary* (Norton, 2006), 5–6. For Khrushchev's concern that a mistake could lead to war, see I. Drogovoz, *Raketnye Voiska SSSR*, AST (Kharvest, 2005). See also http://www.russian spaceweb.com/cuban_missile_crisis.html.

192 **"Every idiot can start a war"**: Fursenko and Naftali, *One Hell of a Gamble*, 182.

192 **"The deployment of the missiles"**: Fyodr Burlatsky, *Literaturnaya Gazeta*, "Karibskii krizos i ego ypoki" ["The Cuban Crisis and Its lessons."], Nov. 11, 1987, translated by Anastasia Poliakova, Dec. 2015. Burlatsky was a Central Committee of the Communist Party adviser and a Khrushchev speechwriter.

Chapter 19: "Without Our Help Cuba Will Be Destroyed"

193 **Kennedy "would not set off a thermonuclear war"**: Fursenko and Naftali, *One Hell of a Gamble*, 182.

193 **They had neither warned**: Nash, *The Other Missiles of October*, 124.

193 **"no place to hide a chicken"**: Maj. Gen. A. A. Dementiev to Nikita Sergeyovich, quoted in Sergo Mikoyan, edited by Svetlana Savranskaya, *The Soviet Cuban Missile Crisis: Castro, Mikoyan, Kennedy, Khrushchev, and the Missiles of November* (Stanford University Press, 2012), 103–4.

193 **"totally inexperienced"**: See У края ядерной бездны (из истории Карибского Кризиса 1962 г. Факты. Свидетельства. Оценки . . .), редактор А.И. Грибков, Москва, «Грэгори-Пейдж», 1998. [*At the Edge of the Nuclear Abyss: Facts, Eyewitness Accounts, and Analyses from the History of the 1962 Caribbean Crisis]*, A. I. Gribkov, ed. (Moscow, Gregory-Page, 1998). Translated by Hans Fenstermacher.] Sergei Khrushchev confirmed that his father told him that the missiles would be disguised as palm trees. S. Khrushchev interview in the documentary film *The Missiles of October: What the World Didn't Know*.

194 **Kennedy is "intelligent"**: Fursenko and Naftali, *One Hell of a Gamble*, 182.

194 **"an offensive policy"**: Fursenko and Naftali, *Khrushchev's Cold War*, 435.

194 **"Some soft-hearted advocates"**: Donald Zagoria, *The Sino-Soviet Conflict,* 203. See also Fukuyama, "Soviet Threats to Intervene in the Middle East," 22.

194 **influential Maoists**: Che Guevara for example.

195 **several Presidium meetings**: Aleksandr A. Fursenko, ed., *Archivii Kremlya: Prezidium TsK KPSS, 1954–1964, Tom. 1, Chernovie protocolniye zapisi zasedanii; Stenogrammi* [Archives of the Kremlin: Presidium of the Central Committee of the Communist Party of the Soviet Union, 1954–1964, vol. 1, Notes of State Meetings; Stenographic Accounts], translated by Angela Greenfield (Moscow, Rosspen, 2003).

195 **the problem that irked him most**: The construction of the Berlin Wall in August 1961—which had come as a complete surprise to both West and East Berliners—emboldened Khrushchev's confidence that he could pull off another surprise.

195 **"Solving the Berlin problem"**: Fursenko and Naftali, *One Hell of a Gamble,* 176. See also Fursenko and Naftali, *Khrushchev's Cold War,* 436–64.

195 **After discussing the deployment**: Interview with Alexandr Alekseyev [Soviet ambassador to Cuba] from *War and Peace in the Nuclear Age,* WGBH, Open Vault. http://openvault.wgbh.org/catalog/V_E6DE72DD9B5A4DCBAB83543 D67949E77.

195 **"Without our help Cuba"**: May 21, 1962, "Central Committee of the Communist Party of the Soviet Union Presidium Protocol 32," Woodrow Wilson Center, Digital Archive, CWIHP.

195 **"We have to defend Cuba"**: Anastas Mikoyan, *Tak Bylo* [As It Was] (Moscow, Vagrius, 1994), 606; Fursenko and Naftali, *Khrushchev's Cold War,* 435; *Anadyr,* 14 [translated by Angela Greenfield]. This appears to contradict Alekseyev's recollections. According to Alekseyev, Mikoyan supported the missile deployment. See Alekseyev interview, *War and Peace in the Nuclear Age,* WGBH, Open Vault.

196 **"That was how [I] understood"**: Hershberg, "The Cuban Missile Crisis," 70; Timothy Naftali, "The Malin Notes: Glimpses Inside the Kremlin During the Cuban Missile Crisis," in *CWIHPB* 17/18 (Fall 2012): 337.

196 **"offered not to speed up"**: Ibid.

196 **Alone in his office**: Alekseyev interview, *War and Peace in the Nuclear Age,* WGBH, Open Vault.

196 **reported to be enthusiastic**: G. Kornienko, *Kholodnaya Voina, Svidetelstvo ego Uchastnika [Cold War: Testimony of Participants]* (OLMA-PRESS, 2001). http://www.russianspaceweb.com/sources.html#kornienko, located and translated by Karl Cherepanya.

197 **as the historian Philip Brenner has argued**: Philip Brenner, "Cuba's Perspective on the Missile Crisis," in *The Cuban Missile Crisis Revisited,* edited by James A. Nathan (St. Martin's Press, 1992), 187–217.

197 **But Khrushchev was adamant**: Fursenko and Naftali, *One Hell of a Gamble,* 196–97.

197 **We "simply used the same means"**: Nash, *The Other Missiles of October,* 121–25.

197 **Even more galling**: Khrushchev, *Memoirs,* 336, and Malin notes. Having first claimed that Gary Powers's U2 was a weather reconnaissance aircraft that had drifted off course, and then embarrassed by having been caught in a lie when it was revealed that Powers had survived the destruction of his aircraft, Eisen-

hower claimed that the United States had the right to do what it had to do to learn about the Soviet nuclear arsenal.

197 **"I don't doubt"**: Maria Shriver, interview with Fidel Castro, Havana, Sep. 26, 1992, 17.

198 **"The main feature"**: General Alexei S. Butski, Стратегическая операция «Анадырь»: как это было, 3-е издание, редактор В.И. Есин, (Москва, МООВВИК, 2004), 76–82. [V. I. Yesin, ed. *Strategic Operation "Anadyr": How It Really Was*, 3rd ed. (MOOVVIK, 2004).] trans. by Hans Fenstermacher.

198 **"Now we can swat your ass"**: Aleksandr Fursenko and Timothy Naftali, *Khrushchev's Cold War: The Inside Story of an American Adversary* (Norton, 2006), 457. Khrushchev met Udall in September, 1962.

199 **"authorized to use"**: Kenneth Michael Absher, *Mindsets and Missiles: A First-hand Account of the Cuban Missile Crisis* (Booklife, 2012), 34. Ambiguity surrounds Pliyev's authority to use nuclear weapons. In September the Ministry of Defense drafted orders to Pliyev confirming Khrushchev's July oral authority. But Minister of Defense Malinovsky never signed or sent them to Pliyev. In *One Minute to Midnight*, Dobbs states that Malinovsky "prepared a decree authorizing Soviet troops on Cuba" (33) but that Khrushchev rejected this cessation of nuclear control. Fursenko and Naftali concur in *One Hell of a Gamble*, citing Khrushchev's statement that "the missiles have one purpose—to scare [the Americans], to restrain them so that they have appreciated this business" (182). Khrushchev did not want to lose control over the decision to use nuclear weapons. The document was to sit unsigned in the files until events in Cuba warranted a change."

199 **If deterrence failed**: Defense Minister Malinovsky withdrew Khrushchev's prior authorization on Oct. 22, but the possibility of unauthorized use in response to an attack cannot be ignored, according to General Gribkov. Gen. Anatoli I. Gribkov and Gen. William Y. Smith, *Operation Anadyr: U.S. and Soviet Generals Recount the Cuban Missile Crisis* (Edition Q, 1994), 61–76.

199 **People who could have anticipated**: Anatoly Gribkov, "The Development and Implementation of Operation 'Anadyr,'" in *Strategic Operation 'Anadyr'*, 34, translated by Karl Cherepanya.

199 **Thirty-six R-12s**: Fursenko and Naftali, *One Hell of a Gamble*, 188, and Taubman, *Khrushchev*, 457.

199 **twice the range**: The Americans calculated the range of the R-14 as 2,300 miles. The Soviets calculated its range at 2,800 miles. https://en.wikipedia.org /wiki/R-14_Chusovaya.

199 **every state except Washington**: Alaska became a state on Jan. 3, 1959. Hawaii became a state on Aug. 21, 1959.

199 **Unwilling to risk**: Taubman, *Khrushchev*, 565.

200 **In addition to the thirty-six**: Michael Dobbs, *One Minute to Midnight: Kennedy, Khrushchev, and Castro on the Brink of Nuclear War* (Alfred A. Knopf, 2008), 26–28.

200 **11,000 Soviet troops on the island**: For the size of Soviet troops deployed to Cuba, and CIA's substantial underestimation, see: Raymond L, Garthoff, *Reflections on the Cuban Missile Crisis* (Brookings Institution, 1987), 21; Bruce J. Allyn, James G. Blight, and David A. Welch, "Essence of Revision: Moscow, Havana, and the Cuban Missile Crisis," *International Security* 14, no. 3 (Winter 1989–1990): 151–52; and Dobbs, *One Minute to Midnight*, 28.

200 **this historic initiative:** "The Submarines of October: U.S. and Soviet Naval Encounters During the Cuban Missile Crisis," in *NSA Electronic Briefing Book No. 75*, edited by William Burr and Thomas S. Blanton. See esp. "Initial Plans for Soviet Navy Activities in Support of Operation Anadyr, 18 Sept. 1962, from Admirals M. Zakharov and V. Fokin to Defense Council and N. S. Khrushchev."

201 **The antiaircraft missile systems:** Ibid., "The Soviet Task Force in Cuba," translated by Karl Cherepanya. See Russian Ministry of Defense URL: "The Association of CMC Veterans, a list of Soviet military units that took part in Operation 'Anadyr.'" http://www.gsvsk.ru/content/21/read64.html.

201 **"brought to full military readiness":** V. I. Yesin, ["The Participation of the Strategic Rocket Forces in the Operation 'Anadyr,'"], 65–74. General Yesin further states that Colonel I. S. Sidorov's rockets were ready to be fired within 2.5 hours, 71 [trans. by Angela Greenfield].

201 **"the *lowest risk* course of action":** Naftali and Zelikow, *The Presidential Recordings of John F. Kennedy, The Greatest Crises*, vol. 2, September–October 21, 1962 (Norton, 2001), Oct. 19, 1962, meeting with the president, 586. (Emphasis added.)

Chapter 20: "They're There"

204 **"After all":** *FRUS, 1961–1963*, vol. XI, *Cuban Missile Crisis and Aftermath* doc. 21, "Off the Record Meeting on Cuba," Oct. 16, 1962.

204 **"They're there":** Bundy, *Danger and Survival*, 395.

205 **"deceiving the American people":** James Reston, "On Cuba and Pearl Harbor—the American Nightmare," *New York Times*, Oct. 12, 1962. For other investigations of the source of Keating's information, see Thomas Patterson, "The Historian as Detective: Senator Keating, His Mysterious Sources and Missiles in Cuba," *Diplomatic History* 11 (Winter 1987): 67-70. Max Holland appears to have solved the mystery; see his "A Luce Connection: Senator Keating, William Pawley, and the Cuban Missile Crisis," *Journal of Cold War Studies* 1, no. 3 (Fall 1999): 139–67. See also Holland, "The 'Photo Gap' That Delayed Discovery of the Missiles," *Politics and Intelligence*, CIA, https://www.cia.gov /library/center-for-the-study-of-intelligence/csi-publications/csi-studies/stud ies/vol49no4/Photo_Gap_2.htm. Another interesting article is Daniel Gorman Jr., "Candid Ken and the Cuban Crisis: Senator Kenneth Keating, the Red Menace, and the Missile Crisis of 1962," *Proceedings of the National Conference on Undergraduate Research (NCUR), 2014*.

205 **"There is no evidence":** Presidential Press Conference, Sept. 13, 1962, quoted in Bundy, *Danger and Survival*, 393.

205 **"The major danger":** Cited in Alan Brinkley, *John F. Kennedy* (Times Books), 113.

205 **"if at any time":** Ibid.

205 **"In light of his public commitments":** Bundy, *Danger and Survival*, 393–94.

206 **"there is no present evidence":** Bundy, *Danger and Survival*, 395.

206 **He had been telling the president:** Absher, *Mindsets and Missiles*, 36–37. On Sept. 8, 1962, a U2 from Taiwan was shot down over the Chinese mainland. This gave Bundy and Rusk pause about sending U2 flights over Cuba.

207 **The CIA's failure:** The Soviet MRBMs [SS-3 "Shysters"] were located in East Germany 2.5 km northwest of Jüterbog, near Neuheim. On August 11, 1960,

the CIA wrote a secret "Current Support Brief" titled "Possible Shyster Missile Base in East Germany." See Office of Research and Reports, CIA/RR CB-60-41. https://www.cia.gov/library/readingroom/docs/DOC_0001264256.pdf.

207 **"Everything that has been delivered":** Bundy, *Danger and Survival*, 395.

207 **"a doctor's appointment":** *Bottom Line Health* 27, no. 5 (May 2013): 1–2.

207 **"It was . . . [s]hocking":** Robert Lovett, Oral History interview #4, Nov. 19, 1964, 48, JFKL.

208 **"good for nothing":** For the 1992 Havana Conference, see James G. Blight, Bruce G. Allyn, and David A. Welch, "Legacy of the Brink: Unfinished Business of the Havana Conference," in *Cuba on the Brink* (Pantheon, 1993), 371–400. For Gribkov's revelation of the potential uses of nuclear weapons if the United States were to invade, see James G. Blight and Janet M. Lang, *Dark Beyond Darkness: The Cuban Missile Crisis as History, Warning, and Catalyst* (Rowman & Littlefield, 2017), 60–71; Gribkov and Smith, *Operation Anadyr*, 61–76.

208 **And the director of the CIA:** Hershberg, "The Cuban Missile Crisis," 71.

208 **Many historians of the CIA:** Higgins, *The Perfect Failure*; Tim Weiner, *Legacy of Ashes: The History of the CIA* (Anchor, 2008); David Shamus McCarthy, *Selling the CIA: Public Relations and the Culture of Secrecy* (University Press of Kansas, 2018).

209 **One reason seems clear:** For more on the life and career of Allen Dulles, see Immerman, *The CIA in Guatemala*; Stephen Kinzer, *The Brothers: John Foster Dulles, Allen Dulles, and Their Secret World War* (Times Books, 2013); and David Talbot, *The Devil's Chessboard: Allen Dulles, the CIA, and the Rise of America's Secret Government* (HarperCollins, 2015).

209 **To save weight:** *Historic Wings*, "The Photos That Nearly Started World War III," posted Oct. 14, 2012. http://fly.historicwings.com/2012/10/the-photos-that-nearly-started-world-war-iii/.

209 **He had flown across:** David M. Barrett and Max Holland, *Blind over Cuba: The Photo Gap and the Missile Crisis* (Texas A&M University Press, 2012). An excellent analysis of the politics behind the Cuban missile crisis intelligence failures.

210 **He would learn:** *FRUS*, vol. 11, *1961–1963, The Cuban Missile Crisis*, Editorial Note, doc. 16; Michael Dobbs, "Into Thin Air," *Washington Post*, Oct. 26, 2003, W14. http://area51specialprojects.com/heyser.html.

211 **Oleg Penkovsky:** Penkovsky was a disillusioned Soviet military intelligence [GRU] colonel who provided the British and Americans valuable technical information about the Soviet missile program. He was arrested soon after President Kennedy announced the blockade of Cuba and was later executed. For an exaggerated view of his impact see: Jerold Schecter and Peter Deriabin, *The Spy Who Saved the World: How a Soviet Colonel Changed the Course of the Cold War* (Scribner, 1992).

211 **Bundy was called at home:** Bundy, *Danger and Survival*, 395. *FRUS*, vol. 11, *The Cuban Missile Crisis, 1961–1963*, doc. 16.

211 **"He can't do that to me":** Stern, *Averting "The Final Failure*," 31.

212 **"Oh shit! Shit! Shit!":** Ibid.

212 **Another Soviet specialist:** As he prepared to depart for Paris, Bohlen wrote a memo to Rusk (Oct. 17) that tracked Stevenson's advice: "No one can guarantee that this can be achieved by diplomatic action—but it seems to me essential that this channel should be tested out before military action is employed. If our

decision is firm (and it must be) I can see no danger in communicating with Khrushchev privately worded in such a way that he realizes that we mean business. [. . .] This I consider an essential first step no matter what military course we determine on if the reply is unsatisfactory." "Recommendations by Bohlen for Handling the Missile Crisis—Handwritten and Typed Copy," DNSA, Top Secret Memorandum, Oct. 17, 1962, 5; Cuban Missile Crisis, CC0645.

213 **"how much bad advice":** John Kenneth Galbraith, *Name-Dropping: From FDR On* (Houghton Mifflin, 1999), 105.

213 **He was more skeptical:** Sorensen Oral History interview #2 by Carl Kaysen, Apr. 6, 1964, 22, JFKL Oral History Program.

Chapter 21: "Actions Were Begun on October 3 to Prepare for Military Action Against Cuba"

215 **"I have great respect":** Pierre Salinger, "Kennedy and Cuba: The Pressure to Invade was Fierce," *International Herald Tribune,* Feb. 6, 1989.

215 **"centers of unusual activity":** Capt. Sanders A. Laubenthal, "The Missiles in Cuba, 1962: The Role of SAC Intelligence," *SAC Intelligence Quarterly Project Warrior Study* (544th Strategic Intelligence Wing, May 1984). U2s carried two cameras. The second camera correlated ground track positioning. 2–6. Dan Martins, "The Cuban Missile Crisis and the Joint Chiefs: Military Operations to Meet Political Ends," *Naval War College Review,* vol. 71, no. 4, article 7: 94.

216 **"without precipitating":** Walter S. Poole, *History of the Joint Chiefs of Staff: The Joint Chiefs of Staff and National Policy, 1961–1964, Vol. VIII* (Office of the Chairman of the Joint Chiefs of Staff, 2011), 159.

216 **After the humiliation:** James G. Hershberg, "Before 'The Missiles of October': Did Kennedy Plan a Military Strike Against Cuba?" in *The Cuban Missile Crisis Revisited,* edited by James A. Nathan (St. Martin's Press, 1992), 237–80.

216 **"Solicitations were being made":** Anderson, *The Reminiscences of Admiral George W. Anderson Jr., U.S. Navy (Retired),* vol. 2 (U.S. Naval Institute, Jan. 1981). This is a collection of oral history interviews. https://www.usni.org/press/oral -histories/anderson-george; also: https://www.usni.org/sites/default/files/2018 -05/Anderson%2C%20George%20W.%20—%20Vol.%20II%20Index_1.pdf.

216 **refused to reappoint Lemnitzer:** Lemnitzer was denied reappointment as JCS chairman. Talbot, *Brothers.* The Northwoods plan was presented by the JCS to McNamara on Mar. 13, 1962.

217 **"as dumb as a post":** Nash to author, July 2, 2019.

217 **"And we call ourselves":** Dean Rusk, *As I Saw It* (Norton, 1990), 246–47.

217 **"absolutely reprehensible":** https://spartacus-educational.com/JFKlemnit zer.htm.

217 **Beyond Cuba, the memo:** The memo from the JCS was sent to McNamara on March 13, 1962. The NSA has made the memo available: https://nsarchive2. gwu.edu//news/20010430/northwoods.pdf.

217 **"pointed unmistakably":** "The Naval Quarantine of Cuba, 1962," Chief of Naval Operations, Report on the Naval Quarantine of Cuba, Operational Archives Branch, Post 46 Command File, Box 10, Washington, DC. Provided to author by Robert Petrusak, Dec. 2007. It appears to have been withdrawn from circulation and replaced by a modified document with a similar title. See also "The Naval Quarantine of Cuba, 1962," *Naval History and Heritage Command.*

https://www.history.navy.mil/research/library/online-reading-room/title-list
-alphabetically/n/the-naval-quarantine-of-cuba.html.

218   **On September 17:** Ibid.

218   **They included evidence:** *FRUS*, vol. 11, *The CMC, 1961–1963*, doc. 4.

218   **"Accordingly," the report continued:** "Naval Quarantine of Cuba, 1962."(Emphasis added.)

218   **It is possible:** Ibid. See also, *FRUS*, vol. 11, *The Cuban Missile Crisis, 1961–1963*, doc. 17, editorial note. See also James G. Hershberg, "Before 'The Missiles of October'," *DH* 14 (Spring 1990): 163–98.

219   **"Although the[ir] general appraisal":** "The Naval Quarantine of Cuba, 1962."

219   **"advance planning":** Ibid., "Advance Preparatory Action: 1–21 October."

219   **The Chiefs' initial discussion:** The original minutes are not available. The record of the Joint Chiefs of Staff meetings is based on "Notes Taken from Transcripts of Meetings of the Joint Chiefs of Staff, Oct.–Nov. 1962 Dealing with the Cuban Missile Crisis." This document carries the notation: "[Handwritten notes were made in 1976 and typed in 1993.]" I was informed that the original transcripts were destroyed in 1976 after these notes were transcribed. NSA, GWU, "The Cuban Missile Crisis, 1962: The 40th Anniversary."

219   **"wants no military action":** Ibid.

220   **"We should bring this problem":** Ibid.

220   **"an all-out effort":** Ibid., Tuesday, 16 Oct. 3.

220   **"Castro can threaten":** Ibid. Air force chief of staff Gen. Curtis LeMay was in Europe and returned on Oct. 18; Warren Kozack, *LeMay: The Life and Wars of General Curtis LeMay* (Regnery, 2009), 347–48.

220   **"to pose a nuclear threat":** "Notes Taken from Transcripts of Meetings of the JCS, Oct.–Nov., 1962," Oct. 16, 1962 at 1000: 3. (Emphasis added.)

221   **"the only way to eliminate":** CNO Anderson, Ibid.

221   **"The recommended sequence":** Ibid., 4.

Chapter 22: "Bomb the Missiles; Invade Cuba"

222   **"I think we ought to, beginning right now":** Oct. 16, 1962 11:50 ExComm meeting: 422. For the transcripts of the secretly recorded ExComm meetings, see the University of Virginia's Miller Center transcripts, *The Presidential Recordings: John F. Kennedy, The Great Crises*, vol. 2 (Sept.–Oct. 21, 1962), edited by Timothy Naftali and Philip Zelikow, et. al., (Norton, 2001), and vol. 3 (Oct. 22–28, 1962), edited by Philip Zelikow and Ernest May, et. al. (Norton, 2001). Also see the books by the John F. Kennedy Presidential Library's emeritus historian of the Cuban missile crisis, Sheldon M. Stern: *Averting "The Final Failure": John F. Kennedy and the Secret Cuban Missile Crisis Meetings* (Stanford University Press, 2003) and *The Cuban Missile Crisis in American Memory: Myths versus Reality* (Stanford University Press, 2012).

222   **But at 7:55 he departed:** Also in attendance were France's ambassador to the United States, Hervé Alphand, and Mrs. Thomas Byrandon.

223   **At 11:50 a.m.:** For an excellent introduction and overview of the ExComm tapes see "Preface: The JFK Cuban Missile Crisis Tapes," in Stern: *Averting "The Final Failure":* xiii–xxx.

223   **the Tandberg tape-recording system:** Bouck told only two people of the system—his immediate superior, James J. Rowley, chief of the Secret Service,

and a subordinate who helped him monitor the equipment. It was Bouck's understanding that only two others knew of the system while JFK was alive—Bobby Kennedy and Evelyn Lincoln, the president's longtime personal secretary. Hersh, *The Dark Side of Camelot*, 6–7. Recording systems were installed in the Cabinet Room, the Oval Office, and the president's second-floor living quarters.

223 **"Once they [the missiles]"**: Quoted in Ronald Steel, "End Game," review of Robert Kennedy, *Thirteen Days*, in the *New York Review of Books*, Mar. 13, 1969. see also Richard Ned Lebow, "The Traditional and Revisionist Interpretations Reevaluated: Why Was Cuba a Crisis?" in *The Cuban Missile Crisis Revisited*, edited by James A. Nathan (St. Martin's Press, 1992), 165.

223 **Nevertheless the president left**: Mark J. White, "Belligerent Beginnings: JFK on the Opening Day," *The Cuban Missile Crisis* (Macmillan Press Ltd, 1996), chap. 5. White's writings on the Cuban missile crisis are perceptive.

224 **"How do you know"**: Interview with photointerpreter Dino Brugioni, "Master of the Surveillance Image." http://www.pbs.org/wgbh/nova/spiesfly/brugioni .html.

224 **"It's inconceivable"**: Dobbs, *One Minute to Midnight*, 59–60. Both nuclear bombs and warheads were stored in old barracks and nondescript shacks.

224 **"Cuba might become"**: See Rusk testimony in chap. 16.

225 **"General Eisenhower"**: On several occasions during the crisis JFK sent DCI John McCone to brief Eisenhower.

228 **"Khrushchev may feel"**: Fursenko and Naftali, *Khrushchev's Cold War*, 434–36.

228 **"the importance of Cuba"**: For an excellent analysis of the role that nuclear weapons played with respect to Germany during the critical first seventeen years of the Cold War, see Marc Trachtenberg, *A Constructed Peace: The Making of the European Settlement, 1945–1963* (Princeton University Press, 1999).

229 **to take drastic action**: For the influence of the East German government on Khrushchev's Berlin policies, see Hope M. Harrison, "Ulbricht and the Concrete 'Rose': New Archival Evidence on the Dynamics of Soviet–East German Relations and the Berlin Crisis, 1958–1961" (CWIHP Working Paper No. 5) and Vladislav M. Zubok, "Khrushchev and the Berlin Crisis: 1958–1962" (CWIHP Working Paper No. 6). Also Harrison, *Driving the Soviets Up the Wall*.

229 **On September 30, 1949**: Eisenberg, *Drawing the Line*.

229 **spin out of control**: Kempe, *Berlin 1961*.

Chapter 23: "I'll Tell My Big Brother on You"

236 **"We would be prepared to immediately"**: Naftali and Zelikow, *The Presidential Recordings, JFK*, vol. 2, Oct. 16, 1962: 437. (Emphasis added.)

236 **The Special Group**: Kennedy and Cuba: Operation Mongoose. NSA Briefing Book 687, ed., John Prados and Arturo Jiminez-Bacardi.

237 **"as soon as I became"**: Anderson, *The Reminiscences of Admiral George W. Anderson Jr., U.S. Navy (Retired)*, vol. 2 (U.S. Naval Institute, 1983), 540.

237 **"If the President says it's okay"**: Thomas Powers, *The Man Who Kept the Secrets: Richard Helms and the CIA* (Alfred A. Knopf, 1979), 136.

237 **three martinis at every lunch**: Ibid., 137. Harvey's primary assignment at this time was with Operation Mongoose. For an overview of his career see David C. Martin, "The CIA's 'Loaded Gun,'" *Washington Post, Outlook*, Sunday, October 10, 1976, C1.

237 **The meeting began**: As an undercover agent fighting communism, Lansdale was ubiquitous moving from fighting the Hukbalahap (Huks) in the Philippines after World War II, to Cuba and then to Vietnam. Max Boot, *The Road Not Taken: Edward Lansdale and the American Tragedy in Vietnam* (Liveright, 2018).

237 **"very difficult to deal with"**: Evan Thomas, *Washington Monthly*, December 1995.

238 **Henceforth he would meet daily**: Richard Helms memorandum of Mongoose Meeting, October 16, 1962, *FRUS*, vol. 11, *1961–1963*, doc. 19. The sabotage paper was written by Walter Elder and is referenced in Helms's memo as Central Intelligence Agency, Cuban Files, Job 80-B1676R, Box 17, Secret; Eyes Only. For another memorandum of the record of this meeting, drafted by Parrott, see ibid. Also reproduced in *CIA Documents on the Cuban Missile Crisis, 1962*, Mary S. McAuliffe, ed., 153–54. See the Yale Avalon Project. https://avalon.law.yale.edu /subject_menus/msc_cubamenu.asp.

238 **At 4:30 General Taylor**: The group of advisers assembled at the president's request had no official title during its first week of deliberations. On Oct. 22 it was designated the Executive Committee of the National Security Council, generally referred to as ExComm. The group of advisers and other members of the NSC had its first meeting as ExComm on Oct. 23. For continuity I have referred to Kennedy's advisers as ExComm from start of the crisis.

238 **Taylor announced the welcome news**: "Notes Taken from Transcripts of Meetings of the JCS, Oct.–Nov., 1962, 1000 meeting, Oct. 16: 4-5.

239 **the general view of the "conferees"**: Ibid., 4.

239 **The "JCS agreed"**: Ibid., 5. (Emphasis added.)

239 **move Polaris subs**: In 1960 Holy Loch, Scotland, became the U.S. Navy's forward submarine base.

Chapter 24: "Negotiation and Sanity, Always"

241 **"But the means adopted"**: Laurence Chang and Peter Kornbluh, *The Cuban Missile Crisis 1962 (Revised)*, National Security Archives Documents Reader (New Press, 1998), 130.

241 **Stevenson attended the luncheon**: Naftali and Zelikow, *The Presidential Recordings, JFK*, vol. 2, Oct. 16, 1962: 428.

241 **"Let's not go into an air strike"**: Ibid.

242 **"To start or risk starting"**: Stevenson to JFK, Oct. 17, 1962, *FRUS*, vol. 11, *The Cuban Missile Crisis and Aftermath, 1961–1963*, doc. 25; Chang and Kornbluh, *The Cuban Missile Crisis 1962 (Revised)*, 129.

242 **"But the means adopted"**: Ibid. (Stevenson's emphasis).

242 **109 UN ambassadors**: In 1962 the United Nations had 110 member states.

243 **And if we struck them**: Eisenhower made the same point while reconsidering his administration's rash decision to deploy intermediate-range ballistic missiles to NATO countries. Nash, *The Other Missiles of October*, 63, 73–75. (Stevenson's emphasis).

243 **Stevenson's suggestions of October 16 and 17**: This was not the first time Stevenson influenced a Kennedy foreign policy shift. See Stephen Buono, "This Grim Game," *Diplomatic History* 43, no. 5 (Nov. 2019): 855.

244 **advocated "a Munich"**: Stewart Alsop and Charles Bartlett, "In Time of Crisis," *Saturday Evening Post*, Dec. 8, 1962, 15–21. While serving as the prime

minister of Britain (1937–41) Chamberlain sought to prevent war by following a policy toward Adolf Hitler's Germany known as "appeasement." In 1938 he signed the Munich Agreement that ceded part of Czechoslovakia to the Nazis in exchange for Hitler's promise that he would seek no further territories.

244 **to confess grudgingly:** Sorensen, *Kennedy*, 696.

244 **"annoyed" the president:** Ibid., 695. See also White, *The Cuban Missile Crisis*, 173.

245 **"determine the future course":** Dillon to JFK, Oct. 17, 1962, in Chang and Kornbluh, *The Cuban Missile Crisis, 1962*, 126–28.

245 **"a battle to extinction":** Quoted in Stephen E. Ambrose, *Eisenhower: Soldier and President* (Simon & Schuster, 1990), 233.

246 **"crazier than hell":** George W. Ball, *The Past Has Another Pattern: Memoirs* (Norton, 1983), 366.

Chapter 25: "Last Month I Should Have Said That We Don't Care"

247 **"We certainly have been wrong":** Naftali and Zelikow, *The Presidential Recordings, John F. Kennedy*, vol. 2, Oct. 16, 1962: 440.

248 **Even the limited option:** A sortie designates the combat mission of an individual aircraft, starting when the aircraft takes off and ending on its return.

249 **He was clearly tired:** According to Dallek in *An Unfinished Life*, 471–73, Kennedy depended on an array of medications to function. There were antispasmodics to control his colitis, antibiotics to deal with a periodic urinary-tract problem, and hydrocortisone and testosterone along with salt tablets to control his Addison's disease and boost his energy. See Lee R. Mandel, M.D. "Endocrine and Autoimmune Aspects of the Health History of John F. Kennedy," *Annals of Internal Medicine* (Sept. 1, 2009), passim. https://annals.org /aim/fullarticle/744707/endocrine-autoimmune-aspects-health-history-john-f -kennedy.

249 **"He's initiated the danger":** Naftali and Zelikow, *The Presidential Recordings, John F. Kennedy*, vol. 2, Oct. 16, 1962, 439.

250 **"the Communist buildup in Cuba":** See Bundy, *Danger and Survival*, 411–12.

254 **"Yeah, but that was during":** In response to Kennedy's "senior moment," Philip Nash reminds readers of the scene in *Dr. Strangelove* in which President Muffley asks General Turgidson how General Ripper was able to launch SAC bombers against the Soviet Union: Muffley: "Plan R.?" Turgidson: "That's right, sir. Plan R. . . . You approved it, sir. You must remember." *The Other Missiles of October*, 118–19.

254 **through an intermediary (James Donovan):** The same James Donovan featured in Steven Spielberg's 2015 movie *Bridge of Spies*. Victor S. Navasky, *Kennedy Justice* (Atheneum, 1971), 327–29.

Chapter 26: "Possible Courses of Action and Unanswered Questions"

258 **"The main objective of taking Cuba away":** John McCone, DCI, "Memorandum for the File," October 17, 1962. *FRUS, 1961-1963*, vol. XI, *Cuban Missile Crisis and Aftermath*, doc. 23.

258 **It had been discussed:** On January 25, 1960, President Eisenhower, frustrated that the OAS would not support the removal of Castro from power, proposed a U.S. blockade of the island. See Ambrose, *Eisenhower: Soldier and President*, 499.

259   **"It would be a pure disaster"**: "Notes Taken From Transcripts of Meetings of the JCS, Oct.-Nov. 1962," Oct. 19, 0900 meeting: 10. LeMay is identified as CSAF (chief of staff of the air force).

259   **"which is this gamble which he's shown for years"**: Naftali and Zelikow, *The Presidential Recordings, John F. Kennedy*, vol. 2, Oct. 18, 1962, 544.

260   **"Pearl Harbor indictment"**: Ibid. McCone appears to be the first to equate a surprise attack on Cuba with Pearl Harbor.

260   **"after political preparations"**: It was not an accurate representation of the meeting, as the transcripts make clear, but it was McNamara's takeaway.

260   **"The JCS felt they should go"**: JCSM-794-62, 7. "Notes Taken from Transcripts of Meetings of the JCS," Oct.-Nov., 1962, 7. The most limited strike prepared by the JCS joint staff was "Missile and Nuclear Storage Sites only." Naftali and Zelikow, *The Presidential Recordings, John F. Kennedy*, vol. 2, Oct. 18, 1962: 513.

260   **"If we want to go to a blockade"**: "Notes Taken from Transcripts of Meetings of the JCS," Oct.-Nov. 1962, 7.

262   **"the Soviets will react"**: John McCone, Memorandum for the File, Oct. 17, 1962, CIA, DCI/McCone Files, Job 80-B01285A, Yale Law School, Avalon Cuban Missile Crisis collection, doc. 23. http://avalon.law.yale.edu/20th_century/msc_cuba023.asp.

262   **Then, Ted Sorensen recalls**: Sorensen recounts this exchange in the documentary film *The Missiles of October: What the World Didn't Know*.

262   **Countering Acheson**: Charles Bohlen, *Witness to History, 1929–1969* (Norton, 1969), 491–92.

262   **"world opinion would go along"**: McCone, Memorandum for the File, Oct. 17, 1962, YLSAP, doc. 23.

263   **"Summary of Agreed Facts"**: Chang and Kornbluh, *The Cuban Missile Crisis, 1962*, (rev. ed.), doc. 18: 124–25. (The correct date of the document is Oct. 18, not Oct. 17.) See Naftali and Zelikow, *The Presidential Recordings, JFK*, vol. 2, Oct. 18, 1962: 514.

263   **"political actions, pressure"**: S.J. Res. 230 (87th): Joint resolution expressing the determination of the United States with respect to the situation in Cuba, passed October 3, 1962. The resolution essentially reaffirms the Monroe Doctrine.

263   **authority of the Rio Pact**: The Rio Pact is a Latin American and United States security agreement positing the principle that an attack against one is considered an attack against all. It is authorized by Article 51 of the United Nations Charter.

264   **At 9:30 this morning**: May and Zelikow, *The Kennedy Tapes: Inside the White House During the Cuban Missile Crisis* (Belknap Press, 1997), 118; Naftali and Zelikow, *The Presidential Recordings, JFK*, vol. 2, 469.

264   **Nor did he have time**: After conferring with McCone, and dispatching him to brief President Eisenhower at his farm in Gettysburg, Pennsylvania, he met with the foreign minister of the German Federal Republic, Gerhard Schröder, and discussed West Berlin (without any mention of Cuba). He again lunched with the Libyan crown prince before flying to Connecticut to campaign for Abraham Ribicoff, his secretary of health, education, and welfare, who had resigned in July to run for the Senate.

265   **"served the purpose of airing"**: McCone, Memorandum for the File, Oct. 17, 1962, YLSAP, doc. 23.

Chapter 27: "What Action Lessens the Chance of a Nuclear Exchange?"

266   I am persuaded: "Position of [Under Secretary of State] George W. Ball" in support of blockade option against Cuba, ca. October 18, 1962. Chang and Kornbluh, *The Cuban Missile Crisis, 1962* (Revised edition), 131–32.

266   **"During the course of the day"**: Naftali and Zelikow, *Presidential Recordings, JFK, The Great Crises*, vol. 2, Oct. 18, 1962, 576.

266   "obviously switched": Sorensen, *Kennedy*, 691, and Roger Hilsman, *To Move a Nation* (Dell, 1967), 204. Both record this shift. Noted by Elizabeth Cohn, "President Kennedy's Decision to Impose a Blockade in the Cuban Missile Crisis: Building a Consensus in the ExComm After the Decision," in *The Cuban Missile Crisis Revisited*, edited by James A. Nathan (St. Martin's Press, 1992), chap. 7.

267   a "test of will": The "test of will" idea persisted through the following week. See George Herman's report quoting that phrase on Walter Cronkite's *CBS Special Report*, Oct. 24.

267   **"the days of the Castro regime will be numbered"**: "Position of [Under Secretary of State] George W. Ball," Chang and Kornbluh, *The Cuban Missile Crisis, 1962*, 131–32.

268   **Another memo from Sorensen**: Sorensen memo, Oct. 18, 1962, JFKL CMC collection: http://microsites.jfklibrary.org/cmc/oct18/doc2.html.

268   **"I now feel air strikes"**: "Notes taken from transcripts of Meetings of the Joint Chiefs of Staff, Oct.–Nov. 1962,". The notes are dated and arranged chronologically; 7.

269   **"minimum should be course E"**: Ibid., 8.

270   **Reviewing the U2 images**: May and Zelikow, *The Kennedy Tapes*, 122; Naftali and Zelikow, *The Presidential Recordings, JFK*, vol. 2, 516–17.

270   **References to *The Guns of August***: Fursenko and Naftali, *Khrushchev's Cold War*, 447.

271   **"an essential first step"**: May and Zelikow, *The Kennedy Tapes*, 130, 525.

272   *"because it is not a military problem"*: Ibid., 133.

272   "slightly demented": Ibid., 134.

272   "a god-damned Murder Incorporated": Alan Brinkley, *John F. Kennedy* (Times Books, 2012), 113.

273   **There was no certainty**: Nash, *The Other Missiles of October*, 127–32.

274   **Kennedy thought Eisenhower**: Timothy Naftali, "The Peacock and the Bald Eagle: The Remarkable Relationship Between JFK and Eisenhower." lecture presented at the Chautauqua Institution, Chautauqua, NY, 2012. https://www .youtube.com/watch?v=SLloV_w8YcM. A brief summary is available here: https://chqdaily.wordpress.com/2012/08/21/naftali-jfk-ike-put-presidency -above-bipartisanship-despite-frosty-relations/. Brought to my attention by David Schrack.

274   Admitting that he had altered: Ibid.

Chapter 28: "Flipping a Coin as to Whether You End Up with World War or Not"

277   **"You want to make it . . . as easy"**: Naftali and Zelikow, *Presidential Recordings, JFK*, vol. 2, Oct. 18, 1962, 534.

278   **Moreover, the CIA estimated**: Michael B. Petersen, *Legacy of Ashes, Trial by Fire: The Origins of the Defense Intelligence Agency and the Cuban Missile Crisis*

Crucible (DIA Historical Research Support Branch, 2011), 22. This information was revealed by the Soviet participants in the crisis thirty years later.

278 **Most of the analytical dialogue:** Jenny and Sherry Thompson, *The Kremlinologist: Llewellyn E. Thompson. America's Man in Cold War Moscow* (Johns Hopkins University Press, 2018), 298–333.

280 **Rusk urged:** President Kennedy issued an even stronger warning at a press conference on Sept. 13. https://www.jfklibrary.org/asset-viewer/archives/JFKWHA/1962/JFKWHA-126/JFKWHA-126.

281 **If there is a psychological lesson:** "Notes Taken From Transcripts of Meetings of the JCS," Oct. 18, 1962, 7–9.

282 **The meeting with Gromyko:** On Friday morning JFK told the JCS: "Even last night we [Soviet foreign minister Andrei Gromyko and I] talked about Cuba for a while, but Berlin—that's what Khrushchev's committed himself to personally. So, actually, it's a quite desirable situation from their point of view." Naftali and Zelikow, *Presidential Recordings, JFK*, vol. 2, Oct. 19, 1962, 581.

283 **"the most dangerous situation":** Ibid., Oct. 18, 1962, 573–74.

283 **Gromyko thought it went well:** See "Cable from Soviet Foreign Minister Gromyko on 18 Oct. 1962 Meeting with President Kennedy," Woodrow Wilson Center Digital Archive. https://digitalarchive.wilsoncenter.org/document/111911.

283 **"told more bare-faced lies":** Ibid., 574.

284 **wisest of the "Wise Men":** Walter Isaacson and Evan Thomas, *The Wise Men: Six Friends and the World They Made* (Simon & Schuster, 1986). They were George F. Kennan, Dean Acheson, Charles Bohlen, Robert Lovett, Averell Harriman, and John McCloy.

284 **"We would look ridiculous":** Robert A. Lovett, recorded interview #4 by Dorothy Fosdick, Nov. 19, 1964, John F. Kennedy Library Oral History Program, 49.

284 **suggested a name change:** Both Robert Kennedy and Dean Acheson on occasion claimed responsibility for the name change, but it appears certain that Meeker was its original author. Naftali and Zelikow, *The Presidential Recordings, JFK,* vol. 2, Oct. 18, 1962, 575. State's acting legal adviser, Leonard Meeker, had been brought into the deliberations to do a legal analysis of blockade options. Meeker suggested the term "defensive quarantine" instead of "blockade."

284 **As midnight approached:** Ibid., 577.

Chapter 29: The Chief Confronts the Chiefs

287 **"When we balance off that our problem":** Naftali and Zelikow, *The Presidential Recordings, JFK,* vol. 2, 582.

289 **The record of the meeting:** Ibid., 578–98.

291 **"In addition, of course":** Sorensen Oral History #2, interviewed by Carl Kaysen, JFKLOHP, 22.

292 **His decision would depend:** Theodore Voorhees, *The Silent Guns of Two Octobers: Kennedy and Khrushchev Play the Double Game* (University of Michigan Press, 2020), insists that war was unlikely and the threat of war has been exaggerated. He argues that the resolution of the confrontation in Berlin on October 27, 1961, between U.S. and Soviet tanks provided Kennedy and Khrushchev with a template for the resolution of the Cuban Missile Crisis. It is revealing, however, that the resolution of the October 1961 Berlin crisis was never mentioned in the ExComm meetings by the president, nor did anyone else refer to it. Also, the fact that neither Khrushchev nor Kennedy wanted a war does not

mean that circumstances could not force them into one, which was their shared fear.

292 **"become a sort of Cuban Quemoy"**: Taylor proposed this analogy referring to China's 1958 bombardment of Taiwan's islands of Quemoy and Matsu. Morton Halperin, "The 1958 Taiwan Straits Crisis: A Documented History" (Rand Corporation research memorandum series). https://www.rand.org/pubs/research_memoranda/RM4900.html.

294 **"Yeah," Kennedy responded**: Naftali and Zelikow, *The Presidential Recordings: John F. Kennedy, The Great Crises* vol. 2, *Sept.–Oct. 21, 1962.* http://web1.miller center.org/presidentialrecordings/jfk_2_pub/25_oct19.pdf. The online version of *The Presidential Recordings* is published by the University of Virginia's Miller Center. At the conclusion of the transcript of this meeting the editors write: "President Kennedy was now less sure that the blockade was the right answer. This might have been because of the weight of arguments he had heard from the Joint Chiefs. He had also talked again to Bundy, probably at the start of his day, before the meeting with the Joint Chiefs. Bundy had changed his mind during the night and had switched from supporting no action (because of concerns about Berlin) to supporting a surprise air strike."

294 **"These brass hats"**: Kenneth P. O'Donnell and David F. Powers, *Johnny, We Hardly Knew Ye* (Little, Brown, 1972), 368.

295 **"pull the group together"**: For the Kennedy "pull the group together" quote, see Naftali and Zelikow, *The Presidential Recordings, JFK*, vol. 2, Oct. 20, 1962: 599; Sorensen, *Kennedy*, 692. For JFK telling Bundy to keep air strike alive, see Kai Bird, *The Color of Truth: McGeorge Bundy and William Bundy, Brothers in Arms* (Simon & Schuster, 1998), 234–35.

Chapter 30: "Pull the Group Together"

296 **"It would be better for our children"**: Naftali and Zelikow, *Presidential Recordings, JFK*, vol. 2, Oct. 20, 1962, 600; *FRUS*, 1961–1963, vol. 11, 121.

296 **Adhering to instructions**: Bending to President Johnson's views, McNamara buried his doubts about the possibility of the United States winning the war in Vietnam. See H. R. McMaster, *Dereliction of Duty: Lyndon Johnson, Robert McNamara, the Joint Chiefs of Staff and the Lies That Led to Vietnam* (Harper-Collins, 1997).

296 **changed his mind again**: Bird, *The Color of Truth*, 234–35.

297 **It was not, State's lawyers**: Meeker Record of Meeting, *FRUS*, vol. 11, *1961–1963*, doc. 31.

298 **Surrendering the Jupiter missile bases**: Nash, *The Other Missiles of October*, 127–32.

298 **"sink[ing] the *Maine* again"**: Robert Kennedy made his "Maine remark on Oct. 16 at the 6:30 P.M. ExComm meeting. Naftali and Zelikow, *Presidential Recordings, JFK*, vol. 2, Oct. 16, 1962, 452.

298 **"It would be better"**: Naftali and Zeilikow, *Presidential Recordings, JFK*, vol. 2, Oct. 20, 1962, 600; *FRUS*, vol. 11, *1961–1963*, 121.

299 **"A decision now to impose"**: Ibid., 118.

Chapter 31: "I Trust That You Will Support Me"

301 **"Secretary McNamara's fear that if we used nuclear weapons in Cuba"**: Naftali and Zelikow, *Presidential Recordings, JFK*, vol. 2, Oct. 20, 1962, 605.

301   **a repetition of the disavowals:** After the Bay of Pigs "President Kennedy took the responsibility [for the disaster in part] to put an end to constant squabbling within the administration as to who took what position." Sorensen Oral History Interview #2, by Carl Kaysen, JFKLOHP, 26.

301   **"include all offensive weapons":** The source of Taylor's information is a mystery, and it is incorrect. The president was not in Washington on Friday night or Saturday morning, and had not spoken with Taylor. One explanation is that these minutes—abridged and retyped from the originals in 1975—incorrectly refer to the meeting on Saturday morning when they might be the record of a meeting later in the day.

302   **In fact all the nuclear warheads:** Dobbs, *One Minute to Midnight,* 58.

302   **deputy director for J-3:** The director for operations (DJ-3) assists the chairman in carrying out responsibilities as the principal military adviser to the president and secretary of defense.

302   **"will tell the President":** "Notes Taken From Transcripts of Meetings of the JCS," 12.

303   **"we might wish, looking back":** *FRUS, 1961–1963,* vol. 11, doc. 34.

303   **"possibly agree to limit our use of Guantanamo":** Naftali and Zelikow, *Presidential Recordings, JFK,* vol. 2, Oct. 20, 1962, 604.

303   **But Bromley Smith:** Ibid.

303   **And, in a postcrisis interview:** In his Oral History Interview with Arthur Schlesinger Jr. for the JFK Library (4/4/64) Robert McNamara described this ExComm meeting in detail (sections 15 and 16) but never mentioned that he had suggested eventually abandoning Guantánamo, which Naftali and Zelikow call "this Stevenson-like position." Naftali and Zelikow, *Presidential Recordings, JFK,* vol. 2, Oct. 20, 1962, n. 9, 604.

304   **He also "parenthetically":** See chap. 19.

304   **But he had thought deeply:** It began: "With a Heavy Heart . . .", "Secret JFK Speech Could Have Signaled Start of WWIII." The attack speech was probably drafted by McGeorge Bundy, who was the leader of the attack group; "My fellow Americans, with a heavy heart, and in necessary fulfillment of my oath of office, I have ordered—and the United States Air Force has now carried out—military operations with conventional weapons only, to remove a major nuclear weapons build-up from the soil of Cuba." Richard Solash, Radio Free Europe/Radio Liberty (Oct. 19, 2012). https://www.rferl.org/a/speech-that-wasnt-kennedy-prepared-speech-cuban-missile-crisis/24744628.html.

305   **"Mr. Sorensen said he did not agree":** *FRUS,* vol. 11, *1961–1963,* doc. 34, 130.

306   **"Thus," he reasoned:** Ibid., 133.

306   **"He urged," Smith recorded:** Ibid., 134.

306   **"from Turkey and Greece":** Ibid. He meant Italy.

306   **"we might tell the Russians":** Marc Trachtenberg, *History and Strategy* (Princeton University Press, 1991), 170. Trachtenberg argues that Khrushchev's demands that the West abandon West Berlin between 1958 and 1962 were motivated by his fears "that West Germany was well on the way to acquiring nuclear forces under her own control."

307   **"the use of the word 'quarantine'":** Meeker suggested the phrase "defensive quarantine" in a State Department meeting late in the evening of October 18. See Naftali and Zelikow, *Presidential Recordings, JFK,* vol. 2, Oct. 18, 1962, 575.

Chapter 32: "Nuclear War That Week Certainly Was Not Excluded from His Mind"

309 **"This world really is":** Lord Harlech (William David Ormsby-Gore), interview by Richard Neustadt, 3/12/1965, [section 11], JFKLOHP.

310 **At their first meeting:** The meeting was at noon in the White House Cabinet Room. In addition to the president, Taylor, and Sweeney, those present included McNamara, Robert Kennedy, and McCone. May and Zelikow, *The Kennedy Tapes*, 204–5.

310 **"that the air strike be conducted":** John McCone, Meeting Memorandum, Oct. 21, 1962, in McAuliffe, ed., *CIA Documents on the Cuban Missile Crisis*, 241.

310 **There was "complete agreement":** McAuliffe, ed., *CIA Documents*: 24; May and Zelikow, *The Kennedy Tapes*, note 3, 206.

310 **"JCS reply is JCSM-800-62":** "Notes Taken from Transcripts of Meetings of the JCS, Oct.–Nov., 1962," Sunday, Oct. 21, 1962. 1300, 14.

311 **At 2:30 the president:** Dillon and McCone were the primary advocates for tougher language. May and Zelikow, *The Kennedy Tapes*, 208–11.

311 **"because we had so many of them":** Ibid. See also Nash, *The Other Missiles of October*, "Trying to Dump Them on Our Allies," chap. 2.

311 **"that a better tactic":** It was an idea he would return to on Saturday night, Oct. 27, with the so-called Cordier ploy. See chap. 50.

312 **"he would ask higher authority":** May and Zelikow, *The Kennedy Tapes*, 212.

312 **"in the expectation":** Ibid.

313 **"When I came into the room":** Ormsby-Gore Oral History interview, JFKLOHP, March 12, 1965, 14.

313 **The question was, in part:** Ibid.

313 **"expect any widespread":** Ambassador David Ormsby-Gore to Prime Minister Harold Macmillan, Public Record Office [UKNA], Cuban Missile Crisis: Contacts Between John F. Kennedy . . . and Harold Macmillan, Collection: FO 598/29, F.O. 2636, Oct. 22, 1962: 11.

313 **"resist the encroachments":** Ibid.

314 **It was clear to Ormsby-Gore:** Ibid.

314 **"The Pearl Harbor complex":** "Notes Taken From Transcripts of Meetings of the JCS," Oct. 21, 1962, 14.

315 **Chester Cooper:** Cooper's decision to release the photographs to the British press turned the British from skeptics to supporters. For the details of why and how he released them see Chester L. Cooper, recorded interview by Joseph E. O'Connor, May 16, 1966, 23–32, JFKLOHP. https://www.jfklibrary.org/sites/default/files/archives/JFKOH/Cooper%2C%20Chester%20L/JFKOH-CLC-02/JFKOH-CLC-02-TR.pdf.

315 **The letter called for:** A summary of State Department activities records the creation and dissemination of fifteen separate letters from President Kennedy to various heads of state, and other documents distributed to 441 recipients. There were 95 oral briefings to foreign ambassadors in Washington by senior State Department officials, who also briefed the press. May and Zelikow, *The Kennedy Tapes*, 214–15.

Chapter 33: "What's EDP?"

316 "What is the distinction": Zelikow and May, *The Presidential Recordings, JFK,* vol. 3, Oct. 22, 1962, 47.

316 At 11:30 the president assembled: *FRUS,* vol. 11, *1961–1963,* doc. 42. National Security Action Memorandum 196: Establishment of an Executive Committee of the National Security Council.

316 "Maybe this is just": Zelikow and May, *The Presidential Recordings, JFK,* vol. 3, Oct. 22, 1962, 16.

317 "Well, let's do it again": Nitze "had a very strong emotional bias for military action," Roswell Gilpatric said in his Oral History Interview, #2, 5/27/1970, Dennis J. O'Brien, interviewer, JFKLOHP, 55.

318 Two others would be ready: "Notes Taken From Transcripts of Meetings of the JCS," Oct. 22, 1962, 0900 meeting, 15.

319 "The President wants a message": Ibid.

319 "Make certain that the Jupiters": Zelikow and May, *The Presidential Recordings, JFK,* vol. 3, Oct. 22, 1962, 35; May and Zelikow, *The Kennedy Tapes,* 223.

319 "the US would fire missiles": "Notes Taken From Transcripts of Meetings of the JCS," Oct. 22, 1962, 0900, meeting, ref. JCS 5866 to USCINCEUR, Camp Desloges, 15. This explains the line in the president's speech saying that any missile attack will be assumed to have come from the USSR.

320 The recording of the meeting: The first 10–15 minutes of the meeting were not recorded but are reported in the Minutes of the 507th Meeting of the National Security Council, Oct. 22, 1962, in *FRUS,* vol. 11, *1961–1963,* 152–53. See also Zelikow and May, *The Presidential Recordings, JFK,* vol. 3, Oct 22, 1962, 40–58; May and Zelikow, *The Kennedy Tapes,* 228.

321 "Now it may end up with": For JFK's aversion to those who might have thought reacting militarily (blockading is a military action), see Mark J. White, *The Cuban Missile Crisis* (Macmillan Ltd, 1996), 1–21.

321 "as I've said from the beginning": Zelikow and May, *The Presidential Recordings, John F. Kennedy: The Great Crises,* vol. 3, Oct. 22, 43.

321 "We followed the course": Ibid., 47.

321 "Inasmuch as the Soviet": Ibid. (Emphasis added.)

322 "if we accepted this one": Ibid., 48.

322 Since there was no precedent for a Soviet deployment: The President was wrong. On August 11, 1960, a CIA report noted that the Soviets secretly installed Shyster MRBMs in East Germany in late 1958 or 1959, but withdrew them a year later. It is a mystery why this information was not part of the analysis of the Soviet deployment to Cuba. See chap. 20. CIA, Current Support Brief, "Possible Shyster Missile Base in East Germany," Office of Research and Reports, (Aug. 11, 1960), CIA/RR CB-60-41. https://www.cia.gov/library/readingroom/docs/DOC_0001264256.pdf.

322 "I wouldn't be too categoric": Zelikow and May, *The Presidential Recordings, John F. Kennedy: The Great Crises,* vol. 3, 45.

323 his most difficult meeting: Ibid., 57–58.

325 "You convinced yourself": Khrushchev reported his remarks to John McCloy (sometime during the week of July 25, 1961) in his August 1961 secret speech on the Berlin Crisis. For excerpts from the speech (and Khrushchev's specific reference to McCloy), see: https://www.mtholyoke.edu/acad/intrel/khrush.htm.

Chapter 34: "We May Have the War in the Next 24 Hours"

326   Any hostile move anywhere: President Kennedy, "Quarantine" Speech, Oct. 22, 1962.

327   "the President's immediate handling": *New York Times*, Oct. 22, 1962, 1; cited in May and Zelikow, *The Kennedy Tapes*, 245. Calls to former presidents first reported in Sorensen, *Kennedy* (Harper & Row, 1965), 701.

327   fishing in the Gulf of Mexico: Sorensen, *Kennedy*, 702.

327   twenty congressional leaders: For a list of the congressional members present see May and Zelikow, *The Kennedy Tapes*, 246. They have the meeting beginning at 5:00 p.m., but the president's daily calendar notes that it was 5:30–6:30: http://web2.millercenter.org/jfk/dailydiaries/JFKL-POF-DailyDiary-1962 -10.pdf.

327   "the only sour note": Sorensen, *Kennedy*, 702.

327   numerous defensive SAM: Zelikow and May, *The Presidential Recordings, JFK*, vol. 2, Oct. 22, 1962, "Meeting with the Congressional Leadership on the Cuban Missile Crisis," 60. May and Zelikow, *The Kennedy Tapes*, "5 PM Cabinet Room" meeting, 247–48.

328   "the latest evidence": May and Zelikow, *The Kennedy Tapes*, 248.

328   "captious and inconsistent": Sorensen, *Kennedy*, 702.

328   They exposed how intense the expectation: May and Zelikow, *The Kennedy Tapes*. Regarding plans to invade Cuba, see esp. McNamara's comment, 263. See also James G. Hershberg, "Before 'The Missiles of October': Did Kennedy Plan a Military Strike Against Cuba?" *Diplomatic History* 14 (Apr. 1990): 163–68.

329   "The time is going to come": Zelikow and May, *The Presidential Recordings, JFK*, vol. 3, Oct. 22, 1962, 72; May and Zelikow, *The Kennedy Tapes*, 258–59.

329   "I think," Kennedy said: Ibid., 260–61.

329   *"The President ordered us"*: Hershberg, "Before the 'Missiles of October.'" *DH* (April 1990): 163–98. (Emphasis added.)

330   *"So, we may have the war"*: Zelikow and May,*The Presidential Recordings, JFK*, vol. 3, Oct. 22, 1962, 78; May and Zelikow, *The Kennedy Tapes*, 264. (Emphasis added.)

330   "a war" was "coming someday": Ibid., 58.

330   But the blockade had carried: For Fulbright's remark, see Zelikow and May, *The Presidential Recordings, JFK*, vol. 3, Oct. 22, 1962, 86; for the ExComm meeting, May and Zelikow, *The Kennedy Tapes*, 147–48, 195.

331   "I better go and make this speech": May and Zelikow, *The Kennedy Tapes*, 271–75; Sorensen, *Kennedy*, 702.

331   "Striking" also replaced: Sorensen, *Kennedy*, 698–701.

332   "Nuclear weapons are so destructive": Ibid., 699–700.

333   "in an area well known": Mindful of the need to secure the support of the OAS, it was an easy decision *not* to mention the Monroe Doctrine, generally regarded by Latin Americans as the declaration that underpins U.S. imperialism in the Western Hemisphere.

333   "The 1930's taught us": John F. Kennedy, *Why England Slept* (Wilfred Funk, 1940). Originally Kennedy's Harvard University senior thesis. It was expanded for publication with the editorial assistance of the *New York Times* reporter Arthur Krock.

333 "Acting, therefore, in the defense": Emphasis in the transcript of the speech. https://www.mtholyoke.edu/acad/intrel/kencuba.htm.

333 "It shall be the policy": Philip Nash, "Bear *Any* Burden? John F. Kennedy and Nuclear Weapons," in *Cold War Statesmen Confront the Bomb: Nuclear Diplomacy Since 1945*," edited by John Gaddis et al., 132.

334 Having eliminated a proposal: Sorensen, *Kennedy*, 699.

335 All agreed: Donald Wilson, Oct. 22, 1982, The JFK panel on the Cuban Missile Crisis was video-taped, JFKL. I have a copy of the tape.

335 a call to revolution: Sorensen, *Kennedy*, 700: "A direct appeal to the Cuban people was expanded considerably by one of Kennedy's top appointees in State. Arturo Morales Carrión, from Puerto Rico, who understood the nuances in Spanish of references to "fatherland," "nationalist revolution betrayed," and the day when Cubans "will be truly free."

Chapter 35: "Kennedy Sleeps with a Wooden Knife"

337 "If the United States insists on war": For a summary of Knox's memorandum of Khrushchev's remarks see Roger Hilsman to the secretary [Rusk], Oct. 26, 1962. https://nsarchive2.gwu.edu/nsa/cuba_mis_cri/dobbs/knox.pdf.

337 "When a person goes bear hunting": Khrushchev, "Central Committee of the Communist Party of the Soviet Union, Presidium Protocol No. 61," Oct. 25, 1962, Woodrow Wilson Center Digital Archive (WWCDA), doc. 115136.

338 "From the very beginning": G. M. Korniyenko, *Kholodnaya Voina: Kvidetelstvo ee ychastnika* [*Cold War: A Participant's Memoir*], 2nd ed., text translated by Anastasia Poliakova (OLMA Press, 2001), 104.

338 "was in such a situation": Ibid.

338 "as if into ice cold water": P. P. Petrik, *Diplomati Vspominaut: Mir glazami veteranov diplomaticheskoi slyzhbi* [*Diplomats Remember: The World Through the Eyes of Veterans of the Diplomatic Services*] (1997), 250. Text translated by Anastasia Poliakova.

338 "They can attack us": Malin notes of Presidium meetings, Oct. 22–23, 1962. https://www.wilsoncenter.org/sites/default/files/CWIHP_Bulletin_17-18_Cuban_Missile_Crisis_v2_s3_Soviet_Union.pdf; Fursenko and Naftali, *One Hell of a Gamble*, 241.

338 "all of the equipment belonged": The sense of panic is described in Fursenko and Naftali, *One Hell of a Gamble*, 240-43.

339 Pliyev was to put his forces "on alert": Gribkov and Smith, *Operation Anadyr: U.S. and Soviet Generals Recount the Cuban Missile Crisis*, 166. See also Absher, *Mindsets and Missiles*, 34.

339 So new orders were written: On September 8 the Defense Ministry drew up such an order, but the minister of defense, Marshal Malinovsky, did not sign it. Fursenko and Naftali, *One Hell of a Gamble*, 243.

340 "Had Lunas been available": Fursenko and Naftali, *One Hell of a Gamble*, 243.

340 Better to wait a few hours: Ibid.

340 He so much as said so: *FRUS, Kennedy-Khrushchev Exchanges, 1961–1963*, vol. VI, doc. 60, letter from President Kennedy to Chairman Khrushchev, Oct. 22, 1962.

341 "The speech on the radio": Malin notes, *CWIHPB: The Global Cuban Missile Crisis at 50*, 306.

341 Forty hours of sailing time: The blockade went into effect at 10:00 a.m. on

October 24, which was forty hours from the time that Kennedy's speech was delivered to the Kremlin.

341 **The rest of the armada**: Fursenko and Naftali, *One Hell of a Gamble*, 247–48.

341 **All leaves were suspended**: Ibid.

341 **"All issues in dispute"**: Ibid., 307.

341 **exchanged ten letters**: The ten letters exchanged between October 23–28, 1962 are in *The Department of State Bulletin*, vol. LXIX No. 1795, November 19, 1973. For the full JFK-Khrushchev correspondence during and after the crisis, see: https://www.jfklibrary.org/learn/about-jfk/life-of-john-f-kennedy /fast-facts-john-f-kennedy/kennedy-khrushchev-correspondence-during -cuban-missile-crisis.

342 **"War can happen as a result"**: *Prezidium TsK KPSS / Postanovleniia (1959–64)*, 852, quoted in Sergey Radchenko, *The Soviet Union and the Arms Race*, introduction, manuscript, 12. When he met Khrushchev at Vienna in June JFK had tried to discuss the danger of accidental war, but Khrushchev got angry and defensive. Radchenko, "The Cuban Missile Crisis: Assessment of New, and Old, Russian Sources," *International Relations* 26, no. 3 (Sept. 19, 2012): 327–43.

Chapter 36: "A Game Which We Don't Know the Ending Of"

344 **"What we are doing"**: Zelikow and May, *The Presidential Recordings, JFK*, vol. 3, Oct. 23, 113.

344 **An armed battalion**: Zelikow and May, *The Presidential Recordings, JFK*, vol. 3, Oct. 23, 173.

344 **"The reaction among students"**: Ibid., 102. For the American public's reactions, see Alice George, *Awaiting Armageddon: How Americans Faced the Cuban Missile Crisis* (University of North Carolina Press, 2003).

344 **In a letter to a friend, Jonathan Schell**: Jonathan Schell Papers, Harvard folder, Special Collections, the New York Public Library. See also: Martin J. Sherwin, editor, *Jonathan Schell: The Fate of the Earth, The Abolition, The Unconquerable World* (The Library of America, 2020).

344 **"The nation has woken up"**: Dobbs, *One Minute to Midnight*, 53–54.

345 **His argument carried**: Ibid. The commander of the Soviet navy, Adm. Sergei Gorshkov, supported Mikoyan.

345 **"until another U-2 loss occurred"**: "Notes Taken From Transcripts of Meetings of the JCS," 9:00 a.m., Oct. 23, 1962.

345 **It recommended that**: Zelikow and May. *The Presidential Recordings: John F. Kennedy: The Great Crises*, vol. 3, 114–16.

345 **"a somewhat different guidance"**: The time indicated in the minutes is incorrect. Taylor appears to have mistakenly calculated Greenwich Mean Time to Eastern Standard Time rather than Eastern Daylight Time. The blockade was scheduled to take effect at 10:00 a.m. EDT. The order was sent to CINCLANT as JCS 6958.

346 **"The President had no moral right"**: Abel, *The Missile Crisis*, 147.

346 **"The British [press] today"**: Zelikow and May, *Presidential Recordings: JFK*, vol. 3, Oct. 22–28, 113.

346 **the Scandinavian governments were skeptical**: Notes et Études Documentaires, L'Affaire de Cuba, Mar. 22, 1963, N 2.975, Ministère des Affaires Étrangères, Direction des Archives et de la Documentation, Paris, France. Translated by Susan Sherwin.

347 **"What we are doing"**: Zelikow and May, *The Presidential Recordings, JFK*, vol. 3, Oct. 23, 110–13.

348 **"What you do by preempting"**: Near the conclusion of the meeting Roswell Gilpatric reported that the impact on U.S. shipping was far less than originally anticipated: "There are only 18 American-flag ships now engaged in the coastal trade or any coastal trade on the Atlantic, and they're all specialized types of design, John, and they would not be the types we would take." Ibid., 168. http://webl.millercenter.org/presidentialrecordings/jfk_3_pub/09_oct23.pdf.

348 **"The question of evidence"**: Ibid., 119.

348 **"the attitude of Mexico"**: López Mateos was visiting Manila when the crisis broke. When his plane refueled in Honolulu it was met by Americans bearing evidence of the missile deployment. See ibid., 121 n. 12. Canada's Prime Minister Diefenbaker too initially refused to "modify [his government's] commercial policy toward Cuba." Kennedy never forgave Diefenbaker's skepticism.

348 **"The question is," he reminded**: Zelikow and May, *The Presidential Recordings, JFK*, vol. 3, Oct. 23, 123.

349 **the ambassador's "minder"**: Kennedy had called McCloy in Europe and asked him to return to Washington. Bird, *The Chairman*, 527–28. Abel, *The Missile Crisis*, 113–14; "Memo to Mr. McCloy—European Trip," Box 1, folder 10, John J. McCloy Papers, Amherst College.

350 **"I'll do two things"**: Ibid., 135. McCone also sent Ray Cline, the head of the CIA's Directorate of Intelligence.

350 **Shortly after 11:00 a.m.**: Zelikow and May, *Presidential Recordings*, vol. 3, Oct. 23, 1962, 140 n. 23: "At 11:23 the White House photographer for *Look* magazine [Stanley Tretick] telephoned for 'Fiddle,' the Secret Service nickname for Wear. He was referred to Evelyn Lincoln, who told Tretick that Wear was in with the president. Jill Cowan, another personal assistant was designated, 'Faddle.'"

350 **He then edited**: Ibid., 141–47.

350 **"It does seem to me regrettable"**: Ibid., 145.

350 **"We really ought to get"**: Ibid., 142.

351 **"cameras aboard these boats"**: *Dr. Strangelove* fans will make the analogy with Gen. Jack Ripper's order that the military police confiscate all radios on Burpelson Air Force Base.

351 **"Secondly"**: Dictabelt 32.3, Cassette J, John F. Kennedy Library, President's Office Files, Presidential Recordings Collection, cited in Zelikow and May, *Presidential Recordings, JFK*, vol. 3, Oct. 23, 149.

352 **unanimous support**: Initially Uruguay abstained as its ambassador awaited instructions, but later switched its vote to yes.

Chapter 37: "The Mobs Turned Up in London Instead of Havana"

353 **"The mobs [of protesters] that we stimulate[d]"**: Zelikow and May, *The Presidential Recordings, JFK*, vol. 3, Oct. 23, 163.

353 **As scheduled**: See Zelikow and May, *Presidential Recordings, JFK*, vol. 3, Oct. 23, 150, n. 34.

353 **"Is that necessary?"**: "Interdiction of the Delivery of Offensive Weapons to Cuba," Oct. 23, 1962, Digital Identifier, 62 JFKPOF-041-019-p0001, Folder Title, Proclamation 3504: Presidential Papers, President's Office Files, JFKL.

353 **The witlessness of involving China**: Dean Rusk's unchanging view of the Chi-

nese communist threat was formed during his tenure as Assistant Secretary of State for Far Eastern Affairs from 1950–52. See Chong-Do Hah, "Dean Rusk and Communist China," *The Centennial Review*, vol. 15, no. 2 (Spring 1971), 182-203.

355　**challenging Stalin's blockade:** President Kennedy ordered a battalion-size convoy prepared to do just that within two hours of any attempt to blockade West Berlin.

356　**The draft—with the last sentence:** The redrafted last sentence emphasized the concurrence of Latin America's nations and beseeched Khrushchev not to force a confrontation: "I hope that you will issue immediately the necessary instructions to your ships to observe the terms of the quarantine, the basis of which was established by the vote of the Organization of American States this afternoon, and which will go into effect at 1400 hours Greenwich time [10:00 a.m. EDT] October 24."

356　**Given the limited intelligence:** Zelikow and May, *The Presidential Recordings, JFK,* vol. 3, Oct. 23, 6:00–7:10 p.m., 164–166.

358　**"I got the conclusion":** McCone to File, "Executive Committee Meeting," Oct. 23, 1962. Ibid., note 47, 172.

358　**"plans to save the president":** George, *Awaiting Armageddon,* 2.

Chapter 38: "You Would Have Been Impeached"

359　**"There isn't any choice":** R. Kennedy, *Thirteen Days,* 45.

359　**"That's what I think":** Ibid.

360　**It was "deliberate deceit":** RFK probably meant JFK's private correspondence with Khrushchev, rather than RFK's contacts with GRU officer Georgi Bolshakov.

360　**Afterward he either kept it:** Dobrynin, *In Confidence,* 81–83.

Chapter 39: "We Are Trying to Convey a Political Message . . . Not Start a War"

361　**"There will be no firing of any kind":** Lawrence S. Kaplan, Ronald D. Landa, and Edward J. Drea, *The History of the Office of the Secretary of Defense: The McNamara Ascendancy, 1961–1965* (Historical Office, Secretary of Defense, 2006), 212.

361　**"this particular crisis":** *The Reminiscences of Admiral George W. Anderson Jr., U.S. Navy (Retired),* vol. 2 (U.S. Naval Institute, 1983), 544. https://www.usni.org /press/oral-histories/anderson-george

362　**Surprise air strikes:** Anderson quoted in "Notes Taken from Transcripts of Meetings of the Joint Chiefs of Staff, Oct.–Nov. 1962, http://nsarchive.gwu .edu/nsa/cuba_mis_cri/621000%20Notes%20Taken%20from%20Transcripts .pdf4.

362　**"Anderson quickly became":** David Coleman, *The Fourteenth Day: JFK and the Aftermath of the Cuban Missile Crisis* (Norton, 2012). See also David Coleman, "Robert McNamara's Feud with Admiral George Anderson," 2012, https:// jfk14thday.com/tape-mcnamara-anderson/. Anderson's recollections of the confrontation appear in vol. 2 of his oral history, 558–61. https://www.usni.org /press/oral-histories/anderson-george.

362　**"We are being inundated":** Anderson, *Reminiscences,* vol. 2, 496–97.

362　**the U.S. Strike Command:** STRICOM combined elements of Army and Air Force commands.

362	It was "one more way": Maj. Brian L. Reece, USAF, "Development of the TFX F-111 in the Department of Defense's Search for Multi-Mission, Joint-Service Aerial Platforms" (Air Force Academy, 1997), 58–59. www.dtic.mil/get-tr-doc /pdf?AD=ADA547500, accessed 2/8/2017.

362	"spilled out into press reports": Coleman, "Robert McNamara's Feud with Admiral George Anderson." http://jfk14thday.com/tape-mcnamara-anderson/.

363	"We did not want": Anderson, *Reminiscences,* vol. 2, 495.

364	The designated submarine: William H. J. Manthorpe Jr., "The Secretary and the CNO on 23–24 October 1962: Setting the Historical Record Straight," *Naval War College Review* 66, no. 1 (Winter 2013): 23.

364	After being assured: Ibid., 24; Dino A. Brugioni, *Eyeball to Eyeball: The Inside Story of the Cuban Missile Crisis* (Random House, 1990), 388.

364	McNamara headed for the White House: Manthorpe, "The Secretary and the CNO," 24.

365	"We couldn't get enough": Roswell L. Gilpatric, Oral History Interview #2, 5/27/1970, Dennis J. O'Brien, Interviewer, JFKLOHP, 59.

365	"The greatest danger of war": Abel, *The Missile Crisis,* 134.

365	the president "instructed McNamara": John McCone, Memorandum for the File, "Executive Committee Meeting on 23 October 1962, 6:00 p.m.," in McAuliffe, ed., *CIA Documents on the Cuban Missile Crisis, 1962,* 279.

365	"[I] felt like an ass": Brugioni, *Eyeball to Eyeball,* 189. See also Chester Cooper Interview #2, May 16, 1966 (24–29), JFKLOHP, in which he explains how and why he released the photographs to the British press.

365	8:45 p.m., October 23: In *The Missile Crisis,* Elie Abel reported the McNamara-Anderson confrontation as having occurred on Wednesday night, October 24, and other historians followed suit. But it was clearly established by Dobbs, *One Minute to Midnight,* 72, and Manthorpe, "The Secretary and the CNO," that the event occurred on the evening of Oct. 23, 1962.

365	In 1962 FP: "They'd run off a position at 1800 hours and operate on that for the next six or eight or twelve hours rather than constantly keep adjusting to moment by moment developments, it would seem." Gilpatric, Oral History Interview #2, 5/27/1970, JFKLOHP, 60. (Note that page 60 is out of order— follows page 50.)

366	repeated for five decades: For recent references to Abel, see Manthorpe, "The Secretary and the CNO," *Naval War College Review,* 21–40. See also Anderson, *Reminiscences,* vol. 2 (U.S. Naval Institute Oral Histories, 1983). Also George W. Anderson, Jr., interview by Joseph E. O'Connor, 25 Apr. 1967, JFKLOHP. Lawrence Korb, "George Whelan Anderson, Jr.," in *The Chiefs of Naval Operations,* edited by Robert William Love Jr. (Naval Institute Press, 1980).

366	very detailed statements by McNamara: Gilpatric, Oral History #2, 5/27/1970, JFKL, 60–61. See also Thomas R. Johnson, *American Cryptology during the Cold War, 1945–1989: Centralization Wins, 1960–1972, Book II* (National Security Agency: Center for Cryptological History, 1995), Top-Secret Umbra, excised copy, 329.

367	"You've imposed a quarantine": Kaplan, Landa, and Drea, *The History of the Office of the Secretary of Defense: The McNamara Ascendancy,* 212.

368	"That's the end of Anderson": Ibid.

368	"really accomplished": Gilpatric interview Oral History, 5/27/70, JFKL, 61.

368 **"It was a fiefdom"**: Kaplan, *The Wizards of Armageddon*, 245.

368 **"A brutal easily angered man"**: Ibid., 245–46, and Richard Rhodes, "The General and World War III," *The New Yorker* (19 June 1995), 56; Bruce Ashcroft, *We Wanted Wings: A History of the Aviation Cadet Program* (Randolph AFB Headquarters Air Education and Training Command, 2005); and Thomas M. Coffey, *Iron Eagle: The Turbulent Life of General Curtis LeMay* (Crown, 1986), 276–77.

368 **"Why are you so concerned"**: Kaplan, *The Wizards of Armageddon*, 246.

369 **"quarantine" speech**: "Executive Committee Meeting of the National Security Council on the Cuban Missile Crisis," 10:00–11:15, in Zelikow and May, *The Presidential Recordings, JFK*, vol. 3, Oct. 24, 183.

369 **"in the clear"**: *Special Annex to History*, 96th Strategic Aerospace Wing, Dyess Air Force Base, Abilene, Texas, 5. I am grateful to Dan Martins for making his research collection available.

369 **"The immediate effect"**: Blaine L. Pardoe, *Fires of October: The Planned US Invasion of Cuba during the Missile Crisis of 1962* (Fonthill, 2013), 169. DEFCON 2 also required that U.S. fighter aircraft be armed with Falcon air-to-air nuclear missiles, moving the firing of a nuclear weapon "out of the hands of generals into the fingertips of junior officers."

369 **"What [General Power] did"**: Bundy interview, *The Missiles of October: What the World Didn't Know* (1992).

369 **General Power was "freelancing"**: Ibid. Jennings's summary of Bundy's comments.

369 **"I suppose it's conceivable"**: Robert S. McNamara, Oral History Interview, part 3, July 24, 1986, Washington, D.C., for the Office of the Secretary of Defense. Interviewers were Alfred Goldberg, Lawrence Kaplan, and Maurice Matloff. https://robertmcnamara.org/wp-content/uploads/2018/05/Transcript-Oral-History-Interview-3-OSD-24-Jul-86p.pdf. A collection of McNamara oral history interviews can be found at https://robertmcnamara.org/speeches/interviews/. Dan Martins brought this interview and related documents to my attention.

370 **"To the extent"**: Ibid.

370 **with two proposals**: Curtis E. LeMay, "Memo LeMay to Maxwell," Oct. 22, 1962, Taylor File, Box 6, NSA, GWU; see also Dan Martins, "The Cuban Missile Crisis and the Joint Chiefs: Military Operations to Meet Political Ends," *Naval War College Review* 71, no. 4 (2018): article 7. http://digital-commons.usnwc.edu/nwc-review/vol71/iss4/7.

370 **penciled the White House in**: JCS Cable 6917 to CINCSAC, Oct. 23, 1962, Taylor File, Box 6, NSA, GWU. Zelikow and May state: "The enhanced generation of SAC forces was ordered, with McNamara's approval, in JCS 6917 to CINCSAC, 23 Oct. 1962." If McNamara had realized that this cable authorized DEFCON 2 he would certainly have informed the president and ExComm. There is no evidence that McNamara informed anyone.

Chapter 40: "A Russian Submarine—Almost Anything but That"

372 **"His [JFK's] hand went up"**: Kennedy, *Thirteen Days*, 47–48.

373 **"The tactical advantages"**: Notes Taken from Transcripts of the JCS, Oct.-Nov. 1962, 17.

373 **the navy had no intention**: "Cuba," Washington 2662 and Washington 2664, and both sent on 24 Oct. 1962, PRO, PREM 11/3690, 24020. Zelikow and May, *The Presidential Recordings, JFK*, vol. 3, Oct. 24, 183.

373 **"a complete state of readiness"**: Ibid., 185.

373 **twenty-two Soviet vessels**: Ibid., 191.

374 **"Mr. President, I have a note"**: Ibid.

376 **"These ships are all westbound"**: The *Poltava, Gagarin, Kimovsk, Dolmatova, Moscow Festival,* and the *Metallurg Kursk.*

377 **"the sense of total bewilderment"**: Quoted in Dobrynin, *In Confidence,* 83.

378 *"for political reasons"*: Zelikow and May, *The Presidential Recordings, JFK,* vol. 3, Oct. 24, 222. (Emphasis added.)

379 **"There's no such thing as a small military action"**: Ibid., 222.

379 **"I have been asked"**: Ibid., 224–25 n. 26. The full document is reprinted in David Larson, ed., *The "Cuban Crisis" of 1962: Selected Documents, Chronology, and Bibliography,* 2nd ed. (University Press of America, 1986), 134.

380 **Before calling Britain's**: Ibid., Oct. 24, 226–28 n. 29: The following is from "Record of telephone message between the Prime Minister and President Kennedy, 24.10.62," in PRO, PREM 11/3690, 24020. Zelikow and May report that they changed the punctuation of the original but not the text.

381 **"We can keep on the quarantine"**: Ibid.

382 **"If the American side"**: May and Zelikow, *The Kennedy Tapes,* 243, and Richard Reeves, *President Kennedy: Profile of Power* (Simon & Schuster, 1994), 404.

382 **"test this thing out"**: Zelikow and May, *The Presidential Recordings, JFK,* vol. 3, Oct. 24, 231 n. 31. Memorandum of Telephone Conversation between Ball and President Kennedy at 10:30 p.m., 24 Oct. 1962, in *FRUS,* vol. 11, *1961–1963,* 188–89.

382 **"Hope that Khrushchev"**: Zelikow and May, *The Presidential Recordings, JFK,* vol. 3, Oct. 24, 231 n. 32. See Memorandums for Telephone Conversations of President Kennedy and Ball (11:15 p.m.), Rusk and Ball (11:25 p.m.), Ball and Stevenson (11:45 p.m.), Ball and Bundy (12:30 a.m.), and the instruction, "Deptel 1084," in *FRUS,* vol. 11, *1961–1963,* 190–97, 199.

382 **"Khrushchev is sending us"**: Telegram from the Mission to the United Nations to the Department of State, Oct. 25, 1962, 8:40 p.m. UNMIS 18, For Harriman—State; Forrestal—White House. From Schlesinger. "Fol is text of memo I sent to Stevenson October 24: Memorandum to Governor Stevenson, October 24, 1962," Arthur Schlesinger Jr. Source: JFKL, National Security Files, Countries Series, Cuba, General. Confidential; Limited Distribution. For text of this memo, Oct. 24, see *American Foreign Policy, Current Documents, 1962,* 421–22.

Chapter 41: "Events Have Gone Too Far"

383 **"If the work"**: Zelikow and May, *The Presidential Recordings, JFK,* vol. 3, Oct. 25, 278.

383 **More than a dozen**: Letter, Khrushchev to Kennedy, Oct. 24, 1962, *FRUS,* vol. 11, *1961–1963, Cuban Missile Crisis and Aftermath,* doc. 61.

384 **A cartoon in the *Evening Standard***: Zelikow and May, eds., *The Presidential Recordings, JFK,* vol. 3, Oct. 25, 232–33.

384 **"The two bases"**: Walter Lippmann, "Today and Tomorrow," *Herald Tribune* and *Washington Post,* Oct. 25, 1962.

384 **"any horse trade of this type"**: Ibid.

385 **newspapers in Britain**: Thompson and Thompson, *The Kremlinologist*, 316.

385 **Anastas Mikoyan told Castro**: See Mikoyan's "memorandum of conversation with Cuban leaders," 5 Nov. 1962, NSAGW, Cuban Missile Crisis vault. "The Soviet Cuban Missile Crisis: Documents on Anastas Mikoyan's November 1962 Trip to Cuba," translated and introduced by Svetlana Savranskaya in *CWIHPB:The Global Cuban Missile Crisis at 50*, 331–48. Michael Dobbs, *One Minute to Midnight*, 387 n.199. See also Fursenko and Naftali, *One Hell of a Gamble*, 175. They add here that Khrushchev knew that the Kennedy administration planned to replace the Jupiters with U.S. Polaris submarines.

385 **Their response is not recorded**: Significant diplomatic efforts were made to block landing rights for Soviet aircraft to prevent them from reaching Cuba.

385 **"Last week they were talking"**: "Notes Taken From Transcripts of Meetings of the JCS."

386 **McCone's intelligence briefing**: Zelikow and May, eds., *The Presidential Recordings, JFK*, vol. 3, Oct. 25, 235.

386 **"their knowledge of the missile sites"**: McCone had sources, he said, but his responses are redacted.

388 **"I deeply appreciate"**: The letter was sent to Ambassador Stevenson at 2:00 p.m. Zelikow and May, *The Presidential Recordings, JFK*, vol. 3, Oct. 25, 262; see also 262 n. 14: State 12974, 25 Oct. 1962, National Security Files, JFKL.

389 **"Okay. What else have we got?"**: For a detailed account of Brazil's efforts to mediate see James G. Hershberg, "The United States, Brazil and the Cuban Missile Crisis, 1962," part 1, *Journal of Cold War Studies* 6, no. 2 (2004): 3–20, and part 2, 6, no. 3 (2004): 5–67.

390 **glued to his television**: Zelikow and May, eds., *The Presidential Recordings, JFK*, vol. 3, Oct. 25, 269.

Chapter 42: "Trade Them Out or Take Them Out"

393 **"We're going to have to pay"**: Zelikow and May, *The Presidential Recordings, JFK*, vol. 3, Oct. 26, 305.

393 **"a military confrontation"**: Robert F. Kennedy, *Thirteen Days*, 60, 61.

393 **"deal with the Soviet leader"**: Tom Wicker, *JFK and LBJ: The Influence of Personality upon Politics* (Penguin Books, 1970), 208. He reports in his footnote that Reston gave him a full account of his conversation with Kennedy. He also cites Reston, *The Artillery of the Press* (Harper & Row, 1967), 28, and *Sketches in the Sand*, 472–73; James Reston, *Deadline: A Memoir* (Times Books, 1992), 220.

394 **"concentrate on OPLAN 316"**: Zelikow and May, eds., *The Presidential Recordings, JFK*, vol. 3, Oct. 26, 286.

394 **To have "a real shot"**: Ibid., 294.

395 **"Of course you won't"**: It is worth considering, as Sanford Levinson suggested to me, that the president inherited his sense of caution from his father. See David Nasaw, *The Patriarch: The Remarkable Life and Turbulent Times of Joseph P. Kennedy* (Penguin Random House, 2012).

395 **"Obviously," he said**: Zelikow and May, *The Presidential Recordings, JFK*, vol. 3, Oct. 26, 305.

395 **a conduit to Castro**: Hershberg, "The United States, Brazil, and the Cuban Missile Crisis, 1962," part 1, 3–20, and part 2, 5–67. See also Zelikow and May, *The Presidential Recordings, JFK*, vol. 3, Oct. 26, 310 n. 18. "The message to

Brazil was sent at 2:00 that afternoon. After further discussion between the U.S. Embassy in Rio de Janeiro and Washington, the message was discussed with Brazil's foreign minister on the night of October 27. The Brazilian agreed to help, but the plan was overtaken by the events of October 28."

396   **"the job that Adlai Stevenson did"**: President Kennedy, watching the confrontation, had said, "Terrific. I never knew Adlai had it in him." Richard Reeves, *President Kennedy: Profile of Power* (Simon & Schuster, 1993), 406; Zelikow and May, *The Presidential Recordings, JFK*, vol. 3, Oct. 26, 297.

397   **"I don't agree with that"**: Zelikow and May, *The Presidential Recordings, JFK*, vol. 3, Oct. 26, 312.

400   **he told Ambassador Ormsby-Gore**: Zelikow and May, Ibid., 321. JFK spoke on the phone with Ormsby-Gore after the meeting ended.

400   **he reported the possible discovery**: Ibid., 327 n. 28. The FROG missile launchers were discovered on a low-level photo mission Oct. 25. See "Supplement 7 to Joint Evaluation of Soviet Missile Threat in Cuba," 27 Oct. 1962, in McAuliffe, ed., *CIA Documents*, 325.

401   **the "*Coolangatta* incident"**: Zelikow and May,*The Presidential Recordings, JFK*, vol. 3, Oct. 26. The volume misspells the ship as the "Coalangatta."

401   **Having uploaded at Leningrad**: "The Crisis USSR/Cuba, Information as of 0600, 27 Oct. 1962," Prepared for the Executive Committee of the National Security Council, CIA, II.-1.

401   **between 2:00 and 4:00 p.m.**: The lack of specific information about the *Coolangatta* incident is curious. The CIA report of the incident does not identify the destroyer, the time of the event, or anything about the communications between the Captain of the destroyer and higher authorities.

402   **Information from "the Canadians"**: Zelikow and May, *Presidential Recordings, JFK*, Oct. 26, 1962, 331–32.

402   **"being kept inoperable"**: *FRUS*, vol. 11, *1961–1963*, "Telegram from the Department of State to the Mission to the United Nations (Oct. 26, 1962, 5:16 p.m.)": 232–34.

402   **"Were the U.S. able"**: Department of State telegram from New York (Stevenson) to Secretary of State #1503 quoting U Thant message to Castro on Oct 26, 1962. U Thant files, UN Archives, NYC.

Chapter 43: "Time Is Very Urgent"

403   **"I have reason to believe"**: Roger Hilsman, *The Cuban Missile Crisis: The Struggle over Policy* (Praeger Publishers, 1996), 122.

403   **"There are known knowns"**: Donald Rumsfeld, Feb. 12, 2002. "Defense.gov News Transcript: DoD News Briefing—Secretary Rumsfeld and Gen. Myers, United States Department of Defense (defense.gov)."

403   **His "false known" was**: Taubman reports that Khrushchev told his son on Oct. 25 that attacking Berlin would be "stupid and wouldn't solve anything." *Khrushchev*, 567.

404   **"ties to the Kennedy clan"**: V. I. Yesin, ed., *Strategic Operation "Anadyr": How It Happened* (MOOVVIK, 1999), Aleksandr Feklisov, 290.

405   **"wouldn't allow bloodshed"**: Ibid., 291–92.

405   **"anytime day or night"**: Title of memorandum: "Expurgated Version of Events Which will be basis for ABC News Handling of Story," "Open Vault," WGBH, John Scali interview for *War and Peace in the Nuclear Age* (2/21/86).

406　He had discussed the memo: Ibid.

406　"I have reason to believe": Hilsman, *The Cuban Missile Crisis*, 122.

406　Contradicting Scali's account: Naftali and Fursenko, *One Hell of a Gamble*, 265.

406　"a frantic call from Scali": Aleksandr Feklisov, *Beyond the Ocean and on the Island. Notes of an Intelligence Officer* (DEM, 1994).

407　Such negotiations: Dobrynin, *In Confidence*, 94–95. Before Feklisov sent his report to the KGB through his own channels, he gave it to Ambassador Dobrynin, who studied it for about three hours before refusing to send it. Ambassador Dobrynin to the Soviet Foreign Ministry, "Meeting with Robert Kennedy," *CWIHP* Digital Archive. Source: Russian Foreign Ministry archives, translation from copy provided by NHK [Japan Broadcasting Corporation], in Richard Ned Lebow and Janice Gross Stein, *We All Lost the Cold War* (Princeton University Press, 1994), 523–26, with minor revisions. Cable reads: "In the course of the conversation, R. Kennedy noted that he knew about the conversation that television commentator Scali had yesterday with an Embassy adviser on possible ways to regulate the Cuban conflict [one-and-a-half lines whited out]."

407　confirmed in 1967: Roger Hilsman, *To Move a Nation: The Politics of Foreign Policy in the Administration of John F. Kennedy* (Doubleday, 1967), 217–22.

407　He presented his version: Alexandr Fursenko and Timothy Naftali, "Using KGB Documents: The Scali-Feklisov Channel in the Cuban Missile Crisis,"*CWIHPB* 5 (Spring 1995): 58–62.

408　"U Thant thought the Russians": Zelikow and May, *The Presidential Recordings, JFK*, vol. 3, Oct. 26, 333.

408　Surprisingly—and tellingly: Ibid., 334. See transcript of JFK-Stevenson telephone conversation and n. 34.

408　accepted Scali's report: Fursenko and Naftali, *One Hell of a Gamble*, 269–71.

408　"the Scali-Feklisov back channel": Fursenko and Naftali, "Using KGB Documents,"*CWIHPB* 5 (Spring 1995): 62.

409　It is "insane that two men": Dobbs, *One Minute to Midnight*, 229.

Chapter 44: "Let Us Take Measures to Untie That Knot"

410　"At this stage any movement": Zelikow and May, *The Presidential Recordings, JFK*, vol. 3, Oct. 26, 1962, 345.

410　deep within India's Northeast Frontier: Bertil Lintner, *China's India War: Collision Course on the Roof of the World* (Oxford, 2018); Bruce Riedel, *JFK's Forgotten Crisis: Tibet, the CIA, and Sino-Indian War* (Brookings, 2015).

411　Speaking as one "anti-Communist": Zelikow and May, *The Presidential Recordings, JFK*, vol. 3, Oct. 26, 342.

411　He expected this element: Ibid., 344–45.

411　To make it easier for Khrushchev: Beginning in 1959, sixty Thor missiles were deployed to the United Kingdom at four bases. They each carried a 1.44 megaton warhead and had a range of fifteen hundred miles. Stephen Twigge and Len Scott, "The Other Other Missiles of October: The Thor IRBMs and the Cuban Missile Crisis" *Electronic Journal of International History*, article 3, Institute of Historical Research, University of London, School of Advanced Study.

412　Ultrasensitive to the media's influence: Reporters seriously objected to the controls the Kennedy administration imposed on the press during the Cuban missile crisis. They were not only censured but their travel to certain areas in the United States was restricted. David R. Davis, "An Industry in Transition: Major Trends in American Daily Newspapers, 1945–1965," see chap. 8, "Kennedy and the Press, 1960–1963," dissertation (University of Alabama, 1997). See also M. Kern, P. Levering, and R. Levering, *The Kennedy Crisis: The Press, the Presidency, and Foreign Policy* (University of North Carolina Press, 1983).

413   "Christ, we're meeting": Zelikow and May, *The Presidential Recordings, JFK*, vol. 3, Oct. 26, 1962, 346–48.

413   an emotional exegesis: The letter was delivered to the U.S. Embassy at 4:43 p.m. Moscow time (9:43 a.m. in DC). Zelikow and May, *The Presidential Recordings, JFK*, vol. 3, Oct. 27, 370.

Chapter 45: "Liquidate the Bases in Turkey and We Win"

416   "It never occurred": Taubman, *Khrushchev*, 570.

417   "We must not be obstinate": Fursenko and Naftali, *One Hell of a Gamble*, 273–74.

417   open to such an exchange: Ibid., 249, 275. Taubman, *Khrushchev*, 570.

418   "In periods of crisis": A. K. Kislov, *Zhurmal Mirovaya a Ekonomika III*. (*Journal of World Economics*), Quotation located and translated by Anastasia Poliakova.

Chapter 46: "To Any Rational Man It Will Look Like a Very Fair Trade"

419   "I think you're going": Zelikow and May, *The Presidential Recordings, JFK*, vol. 3, Oct. 27, 364.

419   Advisers in the White House: For the near disaster on Okinawa, see chap. 50, sec. 5.

419   Robert McNamara recalled: Robert McNamara interview in the documentary film *The Fog of War* (2003).

420   provided there was "proof": McCone briefed the group before JFK turned on the taping system. His report was recovered from meeting notes. Zelikow and May, *The Presidential Recordings, JFK*, vol. 3, Oct. 27, 356–57.

420   "But what 'most people'": "The cumulative strain between President Kennedy and Bundy is unmistakable when listening to their pointed exchanges," historian Sheldon M. Stern concluded in *Averting "The Final Failure,"* 421.

421   "If we talked to the Turks": Zelikow and May, *The Presidential Recordings, JFK*, vol. 3, Oct. 27, 361 n. 5. Nitze said that U.S. ambassador to Turkey, Raymond Hare, was certain that the Turks would oppose a trade. But in a follow-up cable Hare suggested that the United States might pursue the missile trade on a "strictly secret basis with Soviets." Kennedy followed that idea, but Hare has not received the credit he deserves.

421   "These efforts can continue": Ibid., 385–86.

421   justifying an attack: Ibid., 386. John McCloy, at the UN with Stevenson, agreed that the trade made sense. See Bird, *The Chairman*, 529.

Chapter 47: "Attacking Sunday or Monday"

423   "The President has been seized": "Notes Taken from Transcripts of Meetings of the Joint Chiefs of Staff. Oct.–Nov. 1962," 23.

424   "to say how long": Zelikow and May, *The Presidential Recordings, JFK*, vol. 3, Oct. 27, 388. It is likely that McNamara phoned the president to discuss this recommendation.

424 "**I must tell Rusk at once**": As a result of navigation difficulties, the U2 had gone off course into Soviet airspace. Dobbs, *One Minute to Midnight*, 258–75.

424 **In addition, several of the low-level**: Joint Military Intelligence College, *Learning With Professionals: Selected Works from the Joint Military Intelligence College*, (JMIC, Washington DC), 176.

425 **Numerous histories**: Kennedy, *Thirteen Days*; James G. Blight and David A. Welch, *On the Brink: Americans and Soviets Reexamine the Cuban Missile Crisis* (Hill & Wang, 1989); Robert Smith Thompson, *The Missiles of October: The Declassified story of John F. Kennedy and the Cuban Missile Crisis* (Simon & Schuster, 1993); Fursenko and Naftali, *One Hell of a Gamble*; Allison and Zelikow, *Essence of Decision*; James G. Blight, Bruce J. Allyn, and David A. Welch, *Cuba on the Brink: Castro, the Missile Crisis, and the Soviet Collapse* (Pantheon Books, 1993); Stern, *Averting "The Final Failure"*; Dobbs, *One Minute to Midnight*; Barret and Holland, *Blind over Cuba*; and James G. Blight and Janet M. Lang, *The Armageddon Letters: Kennedy, Khrushchev, Castro in the Cuban Missile Crisis* (Rowman and Littlefield, 2012).

Chapter 48: "We're Going to Have to Take Our Weapons Out of Turkey"

426 "**We all know** ": Zelikow and May, *The Presidential Recordings, JFK*, vol. 3, Oct. 27, 421.

426 "**You see,**" **he explained**: Ibid., 392–93.

427 **the moderator in an atomic reactor**: A neutron moderator is water, graphite, or heavy water that ensures a *controlled* reaction by reducing the speed of fast neutrons.

428 **we would be "in real trouble"**: Zelikow and May, *The Presidential Recordings, JFK*, vol. 3, Oct. 27, 399.

429 **But that didn't seem to matter**: Ibid., 407. At the 2:00 p.m. rump session at the State Department, RFK argued against stopping the *Grozny* in order to be better prepared to attack Cuba on Monday or Tuesday. Ibid., 389.

429 "**minimize the Soviet response**": Ibid., 410.

429 "**they haven't had the alternatives**": Ibid., 417.

430 **resulting from "an invasion of Cuba"**: Ibid., 419.

430 "**We all know how quickly**": Ibid., 422.

431 "**I'd rather go the total**": Ibid., 423.

431 "**I wonder, Mr. President**": Kennedy, *Thirteen Days*, "I suggested, and was supported by Theodore Sorensen and others, that we ignore the latest Khrushchev letter and respond to his earlier letter's proposal . . . ," 79–80. The "Trollope ploy" is a term used to describe the purposeful interpretation of a proposal that suits the recipient. It is based on a story by the nineteenth century British novelist, Anthony Trollope, in which a woman deliberately misinterprets a romantic squeeze of her hand as a marriage proposal.

See also Stern, *Averting "The Final Failure,"* who convincingly explains that the idea of ignoring Khrushchev's Saturday letter and responding only to the Friday letter was exaggerated as a "Trollope Ploy," but was essentially "a myth," 330–37, 365–69, 379–83, 421; also Stern, *The Cuban Missile Crisis in American Memory: Myths vs. Reality* (Stanford University Press, 2012), 134–47. George Ball had mentioned this same idea ten or fifteen minutes earlier, but it had been ignored. "Now suppose that we give him [Khrushchev] a letter which is addressed to his letter of yesterday," Ball said, "and ask U Thant to release them both. . . . Then he releases correspondence which consists really of an offer from Khrushchev, and we come back and say . . . 'Thank you, yes.' And it doesn't mention Turkey." Zelikow and May, *The Presidential Recordings, JFK,* vol. 3, Oct. 27, 418.

431   **"I therefore most earnestly"**: Zelikow and May, *The Presidential Recordings, JFK,* vol. 3, Oct. 27, 423–24.

432   **"I don't agree"**: Thompson and Thompson, *The Kremlinologist: Llewellyn E. Thompson, America's Man in Cold War Moscow.* See especially 298–333.

432   **"a rapid settlement"**: Zelikow and May, eds., *The Presidential Recordings, JFK,* vol. 3, Oct. 27, 428.

433   **"I think that Adlai's letter"**: Ibid., 429.

434   **"I think we just say"**: Ibid., 436. See Sheldon Stern, "The Trollope Ploy Myth Lives On: Robert McNamara and the Cuban Missile Crisis," *History News Network,* Oct. 25, 2004, and "The Cuban Missile Crisis Myth You Probably Believe," *History News Network,* July 8, 2009.

435   **"The defense minister of Italy"**: Andreotti later served as Italy's prime minister (1972–1973, 1976–79, and 1989–92).

435   **"We can swap them"**: For the most thorough history of the Jupiter missiles in Italy, see Leopoldo Nuti, *La sfida nucleare. La politica estera italiana e le armi atomiche 1945–1991* [*The Nuclear Challenge: Italian Foreign Policy and Atomic Weapons*] (il Mulino, 2007).

435   **"Well, those missiles"**: McNamara pointed out that the United States had seventeen thousand troops stationed in Turkey and air squadrons armed with nuclear weapons. Zelikow and May, *The Presidential Recordings, JFK,* vol. 3, Oct. 27, 444.

435   **"If the Turks say no"**: Ibid.

436   **"We should retaliate"**: Taylor was recalling the ExComm contingency plan decided at its first meeting on Oct. 23.

Chapter 49: "An Act of Legitimate Defense"

437   **"It goes without saying"**: Taubman, *Khrushchev,* 570.

437   **A large number of American forces**: Fursenko and Naftali, *One Hell of a Gamble,* 272.

437   **"I'd write it and dictate it"**: Blight, Allyn, and Welch, *Cuba on the Brink,* 108–9.

438   **"I don't want to say"**: Fursenko and Naftali, *One Hell of a Gamble,* 272–73.

438   **"if they [the United States] actually"**: Ibid., 272.

438   **"Fidel Castro openly advised"**: Taubman, *Khrushchev,* 579, and Fursenko and Naftali, *One Hell of a* Gamble, 286.

438   **Given the ample evidence**: Fursenko and Naftali *One Hell of a Gamble,* 271–73, 306, and Taubman, *Khrushchev,* 573.

439   **"I wrote 'an attack,'"**: Sherry Jones interview with Aleksandr Alekseyev, "Interviews with Soviet veterans of the CMC," NSA, 16. https://nsarchive2 .gwu.edu/NSAEBB/NSAEBB400/docs/Interview%20with%20Alekseyev .pdf. The translation of the entire telegram that Alekseyev refers to [SPEC. No. 1666] reads: "In F. Castro's opinion, the *intervention* is almost inevitable and will occur in approximately 24–72 hours." *CWIHB: The Global Cuban Missile Crisis at 50 17/18,* doc. 2, 327.

439   **"Aside from other factors"**: In his interview, Alekseyev says that Khrushchev

made these remarks in Castro's presence. This is strong evidence that it was during Castro's visit to the Soviet Union in June 1963, 17.

Chapter 50: "There Is Very Little Time to Resolve This Issue"

440 **"We can't very well invade Cuba"**: Zelikow and May, *The Presidential Recordings, JFK*, vol. 3, Oct. 27, 481.

441 **Bobby called the Soviet**: Ibid., 477–88.

441 **"We ought to keep the heat"**: Zelikow and May make an important point about the interpretation of Khrushchev's message. They note that "since the message was broadcast, different U.S. officials were using unofficial translations of the message," prepared by assorted press agencies or wire services. The term *weapons* was also often translated as *means*. Thompson's version translated *analogous* as *similar*." Ibid., 481 n. 40.

442 **"best way of impressing him"**: General Taylor did not think it was possible to identify the SAM site that downed the U2.

442 **"non invasion pledge"**: Barton J. Bernstein, "Understanding Decisionmaking: U.S. Foreign Policy, and the Cuban Missile Crisis," *International Security* 25, no. 1 (Summer 2000): 161.

442 **"strictly secret" missile trade**: Zelikow and May, *The Presidential Recordings, JFK*, vol. 3, Oct. 27, 361–62 n. 5.

442 **While the president believed**: Analyzing a record of Presidium meetings, Timothy Naftali speculates that "the structure of the Malin notes for 28 October suggests that Khrushchev may have made this decision to end the crisis before knowing that late on 27 October (Washington time), the President's brother, Attorney General Robert F. Kennedy, had told the Soviet ambassador in Washington, Anatoly F. Dobrynin, that JFK was also prepared to order the removal of the Jupiter missiles from Turkey." *CWIHPB* 17/18, "The Malin Notes: Glimpses Inside the Kremlin during the Cuban Missile Crisis," 299–315.

443 **no one else was told**: Max Holland and Tara Marie Egan suggest that Bundy, McNamara, and Rusk kept the secret from Johnson in order to manipulate him on Vietnam. "What Did LBJ Know About the Cuban Missile Crisis? And When Did He Know It?" *Washington Decoded*, 19 Oct. 2007. See also Stern, *The Cuban Missile Crisis in American Memory*, 149.

444 **no "Trollope ploy"**: The "blend" included "the removal of the Soviet missiles from Cuba, an American noninvasion pledge (contingent on UN inspection), a willingness to talk later about NATO related issues *and* a secret commitment to withdraw the Jupiter missiles from Turkey." Stern, *Averting "The Final Failure,"* 422. See also, Stern, "The Trollope Ploy Myth Lives On: Robert McNamara and the Cuban Missile Crisis," (July 2009), History News Network (HNN), https://historynewsnetwork.org/article/97687.

444 **It was replete with**: On October 30, 1962, Robert Kennedy summarized the meeting in a memorandum to Dean Rusk. See James Hershberg, "Anatomy of a Controversy: Anatoly F. Dobrynin's Meeting with Robert F. Kennedy, Saturday, 27 October 1962," in *CWIHPB* 5 (Spring 1995). Dobrynin's account is not only more accurate but more relevant, as his was the account read in Moscow. See Cable, Ambassador Dobrynin to the Soviet Foreign Ministry, Meeting with Robert Kennedy, Oct. 27, 1962. digitalarchive.wilsoncenter.org.

446   **one of those commands:** Robert S. Norris, William M. Arkin, and William
       Burr reported in the *Bulletin of the Atomic Scientists*, vol. 55, no. 6 (Nov./Dec.
       1999): 26–35, that "Okinawa hosted 19 different types of nuclear weapons dur-
       ing the period 1954–1972." The 873rd Tactical Missile Squadron, under the
       498th Tactical Missile Group, had four launch sites each with two launch con-
       trol centers. Each site controlled four missiles for a total of 32 missiles.

447   **If the codes in the pouch:** Aaron Tovish, "The Okinawa missiles of October,"
       Bulletin of the Atomic Scientists, Opinion, Oct. 25, 2015. Masakatsu Ota, Senior
       Writer/Editorial Writer, Kyodo News Agency, broke this story on March 14,
       2015. I am grateful to Dr. Ota for sharing the transcript of his August 30, 2014,
       interview (in Washington DC) with John Bordne.

447   **"They called me out":** Crewmember email to Ota, Nov. 3, 2015. (Ota promised
       the writer anonymity, a pledge I am bound to honor. I am grateful to him for
       sharing this communication.) Strangely, however, when the crewmember was
       contacted by *Stars and Stripes* in December 2015 he retracted what he had writ-
       ten to Ota in March. I quote it here in full: "Dear Masa, You did not hurt my
       feelings, I swore an oath to the American government, that I would not dis-
       close anything that occurred during my stay on Okinawa. I feel that now I am
       able to agree with the other interviewees. When we got to the site our captain
       told me to go into the power room and keep checking everything because we
       did not want any mistakes tonight. I usually stayed in the power room for the
       shift anyway but this was the first time he told me too [*sic*]. So I missed out
       on a lot of the things that were going on in the Launch Control Center. *They
       called me out when they were opening up the black pouches with the launch codes in
       them* [emphasis added]. We all were saying that something was wrong since
       we never would have been opening those pouches unless we were at Def-Con
       1. Our captain was the Senior Officer on duty for all of the sites, so the other
       launch officers called him and wanted to know what he thought. He told them
       not to launch the missiles. It is my opinion that our captain with his level head
       stopped a potential catastrophe. The buck stopped with him. He was the best
       officer I ever knew. I hope this has helped you. Good luck with your article.
       Sincerely . . ."

447   **We all were saying that something:** T. J. Triton has challenged the incident
       in *Stars and Stripes*, Dec. 23, 2015. "Cold War missileers refute Okinawa near-
       launch." However, with the one exception noted above, none of Bordne's critics
       cited by Triton were members of his launch crew. Their criticisms appear to be
       based on their assumption that they would have heard about the incident if it
       had occurred.

448   **"It is my opinion":** Crewmember email to Ota, Nov. 3, 2015.

Chapter 51: "You Got Us into This, Now You Get Us Out"

449   **"Now we found ourselves":** Jonathan Colman, *Cuban Missile Crisis: Origins,
       Course and Aftermath* (Edinburgh University Press, 2016), 161.

449   **President Kennedy was willing:** Khrushchev, *Memoirs*, vol. 3, *Statesman*, 35.

450   **It wasn't clear what to conclude:** Taubman, *Khrushchev*, 571. It was also incred-
       ibly dangerous, as U.S. aircraft armed with nuclear missiles had been scrambled
       to protect the U2, which had strayed into Soviet territory due to a navigation
       error, Dobbs, *One Minute to Midnight*, chap. 11.

450 "Deep down": Taubman, *Khrushchev*, 272.

450 "Fidel totally failed": Ibid., 573.

451 Seated around a large table: Ibid., 574; Fursenko and Naftali, *One Hell of a Gamble*, 284.

451 "to consult and debate": Taubman, *Khrushchev*, 574.

451 "if the attack is provoked": Fursenko and Naftali, *One Hell of a Gamble*, 285.

452 "It goes without saying": Ibid.

452 First Deputy Foreign Minister: Vladislav Zubok and Konstantine Pleshakov, *Inside the Kremlin's Cold War*, 266-67. Stern, *Averting*, 332 n. 287.

Chapter 52: "I Thought It Was My Last Meal"

453 "The essence of ultimate": Quoted in Theodore C. Sorensen, *Decision-making in the White House: The Olive Branch or the Arrows* (Columbia University Press, 1964), xi.

453 "I'd rather my children": Mimi Alford, *Once Upon a Secret: My Affair with President John F. Kennedy and Its Aftermath* (Random House, 2012), 94.

453 "The way Bobby's been": Kenneth O'Donnell and David Powers, *Johnny, We Hardly Knew Ye* (Little, Brown, 1972), 394.

453 It was an amusing exchange: Alford, *Once Upon a Secret*, chaps. 4–8. Alford had not overheard the exchange but refers to O'Donnell and Powers, *Johnny, We Hardly Knew Ye*, 394.

453 "Come to Washington": Alford, *Once Upon a Secret*, 94.

454 "war was likely if things": James Blight quoted in "Rusk Tells a Kennedy Secret: Fallback Plan in Cuba Crisis," Eric Pace, *New York Times*, Aug. 28, 1987. Rusk confirmed his suggestion to JFK Presidential Library historian Sheldon Stern in an hour-long interview on February 10, 1984, in Washington, DC. (Stern to author.) See also Rusk's letter to James Blight, Feb. 25, 1987, explaining his suggestion to the president. "It was clear to me," Rusk wrote to Blight, "that President Kennedy would not let the Jupiters in Turkey become an obstacle to the removal of the missile sites in Cuba because the Jupiters were coming out in any event." Also Rusk's OpEd in the *NYTimes*, (Aug. 28, 1987). However, historians Philip Zelikow and Ernest May question its validity, based on research by Mark White. See Zelikow and May, editors, *The Presidential Recordings, JFK, The Great Crises*, vol. 3, Oct 27, 485 note 43. White, *The Cuban Missile Crisis*, 202–3. When Kennedy's assistant, Kenneth O'Donnell, asked him what he would do if he could not get a consensus in ExComm, he replied: "I'll make my own decision anyway. I'm the one who has the responsibility, so we'll do what I want to do." Quoted in Elizabeth Cohn, "President Kennedy's Decision to Impose a Blockade in the Cuban Missile Crisis," in *The Cuban Missile Crisis Revisited*, edited by James A. Nathan, 231. Cohn references O'Donnell and Powers, *Johnny, We Hardly Knew Ye*, 319–20. It is clear, she writes, that what he "wanted to do" was "end the crisis peacefully and quickly before he had to face another round of pressure to do what he did not want to do."

455 "I waved goodbye": Alford, *Once Upon a Secret*, 95.

Chapter 53: "We Have Ordered Our Officers to Stop Building Bases"

456 "The great enemy of the truth": Cited by Sheldon Stern, "Beyond the Smoke and Mirrors: The Real JFK White House Cuban Missile Crisis," in *The Cuban*

Missile Crisis: A Critical Appraisal, edited by Len Scott and R. Gerald Hughes (Routledge, 2015), 204.

456 **"It is for this reason"**: Message from Chairman Khrushchev to President Kennedy, announcement over Radio Moscow, *FRUS,* vol. 11, *1961–1963,* doc. 102.

456 **The danger of war**: Dobbs, *One Minute to Midnight,* see esp. chaps. 11, 25, and 26.

457 **"The Soviets may make"**: "Notes Taken From Transcripts of Meetings of the JCS," 0900 meeting, Oct. 28, 24. Admiral Anderson added that "the no-invasion pledge leaves Castro free to make trouble in Latin America." Bird, *The Color of Truth,* 240.

457 **agree to five conditions**: David G. Coleman, "Castro's Five Points," HistoryinPieces.com, https://historyinpieces.com/castro-five-points. See also Fursenko and Naftali, *One Hell of a Gamble,* 291.

458 **"the weapons which you describe"**: Khrushchev to Kennedy, *FRUS,* vol. 11, *1961–1963,* doc. 102.

458 **a new "Soviet Cuban Missile Crisis"**: Sergo Mikoyan and Svetlana Savranskaya, *The Soviet Cuban Missile Crisis: Castro, Mikoyan, Kennedy, Khrushchev, and the Missiles of November* (Stanford University Press, 2012); Coleman, *The Fourteenth Day.*

459 **"By drawing both"**: Dobrynin, *In Confidence,* 71.

459 **"Every man, woman and child"**: John F. Kennedy, Speeches, United Nations (1961019), JFKL.

Chapter 54: "Most of Them Did Not Like Adlai"

460 **"Stevenson was strong"**: Stewart Alsop and Charles Bartlett, "In Time of Crisis," *Saturday Evening Post,* Dec. 8, 1962, 15–21.

460 **It had convinced Khrushchev**: Taubman, *Khrushchev,* 490–97; Schlesinger, *A Thousand Days,* 272; Reeves, *President Kennedy,* 103; Shane J. Maddock, *Nuclear Apartheid: The Quest for American Atomic Supremacy from World War II to the Present* (University of North Carolina Press, 2010), 157, 159–60.

461 **"We couldn't get into"**: Stern, *Averting "The Final Failure,"* 388. For an overview of the consequences of presidential lying see Eric Alterman, *When Presidents Lie: A History of Official Deception and Its Consequences* (Viking, 2004).

461 **"the drama and struggle"**: *Saturday Evening Post,* Dec. 8, 1962, 13–20.

461 **"We're eyeball to eyeball"**: Michael Dobbs has made a convincing case that the moment Alsop and Bartlett described could not have occurred. *One Minute to Midnight,* 88.

461 **who "never lost his nerve"**: The remark is reported to have been made by "a member of the inner circle." Charles Bartlett made the same observation years later: "I must say that the President's coolness and temper were never more evident than they were that week [Oct. 22–28, 1962]." Charles Bartlett Interview #2 by Fred Holborn, Feb. 20, 1965 (sects. 124–25), JFKL Oral History Program.

461 **They confessed in interviews**: Stewart Alsop and Charles Bartlett, "In Time of Crisis," *Saturday Evening Post,* Dec. 8, 1962, 15–21.

461 **"Adlai wanted a Munich"**: The editor in chief of the *Saturday Evening Post* was Clay Drewry Blair Jr., no friend of Adlai Stevenson.

462 **He had rejected the advice**: Stevenson had suggested all the main points of the solution that Kennedy followed. The one suggestion JFK did not accept was returning Guantánamo Naval Base to Cuba.

462 **"the pressure of this period"**: Bartlett, Oral History, JFKL, sects. 131–33.

463 **"I gave Charlie Bartlett"**: Fursenko and Naftali, *One Hell of a Gamble*, 249–52.

463 **"My role, I've decided"**: Bartlett, Oral History, JFKL, sect. 128. (Emphasis added.)

463 **"[Michael Forrestal]"**: Michael Forrestal was the son of James Forrestal, the first Secretary of Defense, 1947–49.

463 **Gregg Herken**: *The Georgetown Set: Friends and Rivals in Cold War Washington* (Knopf, 2014), 278–79. Herken's source was Stewart Alsop's private papers.

464 **"'Yes'. He sort of shook his head"**: Bartlett Oral History, JFKL, sects. 129–30.

464 **"I don't think at that point"**: Ibid., sect. 130.

Chapter 55: It Ain't Necessarily So

465 **"It ain't necessarily so"**: *Porgy and Bess,* opera by George Gershwin, DuBose Heyward, and Ira Gershwin, 1935.

465 **"Indeed, the Russian retreat"**: Harold Macmillan, introduction to the original edition (1969) of RFK, *Thirteen Days*, 18.

465 *"This time we really"*: CWIHPB: *The Global Cuban Missile Crisis at 50,* "'We Were Truly on the Verge of War'—A Conversation with Nikita Khrushchev, 30 October 1962," 400–403. (Emphasis added.)

465 **"I think that you and I"**: *FRUS*, 11, *1961–1963,* doc. 104. "Telegram from the Department of State telegram to the Embassy in the Soviet Union for delivery to 'the highest available Soviet Official.'" Oct. 28, 1962, 5:03 p.m.

465 **"Crisis managers cannot"**: Conversation with McGeorge Bundy on Apr. 30, 1988, in Boston, MA, after his appearance on the third "Global Classroom," an international "spacebridge" organized by me and Tufts University's Nuclear Age History and Humanities Center in cooperation with Moscow State University, Mendeleev Institute of Chemical Technology (now Mendeleev University) and Dr. Yevgeny Velikov, vice president for mathematics and physics, Soviet Academy of Sciences.

465 **Accidents and miscalculations**: The classic example is the origins of World War I, as described in Barbara Tuchman, *The Guns of August,* which President Kennedy urged all his advisers to read. Timothy Naftali, *The Presidential Recordings: John F. Kennedy, The Great Crises,* vol. 1 (Norton, 2001), 457.

465 **can "destroy civilization"**: Henry Stimson memo to President Truman, Apr. 25, 1945, in Sherwin, *A World Destroyed,* app. 1, 291–92.

466 **the "slenderest of threads"**: President Kennedy speech to the UN General Assembly, Sept. 25, 1961.

466 **a war nobody wanted**: That is the theme of Tuchman's *The Guns of August.* "Human beings, like plans, prove fallible in the presence of those ingredients that are missing in maneuvers—danger, death, and live ammunition," 295.

466 **"dumb luck"**: Dean Acheson, "Dean Acheson's Version of Robert Kennedy's Version of the Cuban Missile Crisis Affairs: Homage to Plain Dumb Luck," *Esquire,* Feb. 1969, 76–77.

466 **necessary to shield diplomacy**: Capt. Joseph Bouchard, the author of a major study on naval operations during the missile crisis, suggests that the "biggest

danger" was not from "deliberate acts" but from "accidents." William Burr and Thomas Blanton, eds., "The Submarines of October: U.S. and Soviet Naval Encounters During the Cuban Missile Crisis," NSA Electronic Briefing Book No. 75 (Oct. 31, 2002), doc. 8.

466   "We were not going to unleash": Fursenko and Naftali, *One Hell of a Gamble*, 241.

466   "Neither . . . view": Scott D. Sagan, *The Limits of Safety: Organizations, Accidents, and Nuclear Weapons* (Princeton, 1993), 55. (Emphasis added.)

467   "The survival of our nation": Dillon to JFK, Oct. 17, 1962, in Chang and Kornbluh, *The Cuban Missile Crisis, 1962*, 126–28.

468   "Our leadership in the war": Stimson memorandum discussed with the president, April 25, 1945, Sherwin, *A World Destroyed*, app. I, 291–92.

468   Some argue that: David Alan Rosenberg, "The Origins of Overkill: Nuclear Weapons and American Strategy, 1945–1960," *International Security* 7, no. 4 (Spring 1983): 3–71; Scott D. Sagan, *The Limits of Safety: Organizations, Accidents, and Nuclear Weapons* (Princeton University Press, 1995); Stephen I. Schwartz, *Atomic Audit: The Costs and Consequences of U.S. Nuclear Weapons Since 1940* (Brookings Institution Press, 1998); Scott D. Sagan and Kenneth N. Waltz, *The Spread of Nuclear Weapons: An Enduring Debate*, 3rd ed. (Norton, 2012).

468   But recall that the president: Hersh, *The Dark Side of Camelot*, 341–71, makes the case that President Kennedy was generally reckless, and that his reaction to the Soviet missiles in Cuba was particularly irresponsible.

468   "I asked the Chiefs that this afternoon": ExComm meeting #2, 6:30 p.m., Oct. 16, 1962, 441.

468   "You may say": Ibid.

468   "because it is not a military": Ibid., 133. (Emphasis added.)

469   "The real lesson": Benoit Pelopidas, "We all lost the Cuban missle crisis" in L. Scott and R. Gerald Hughes, (eds.), *The Cuban Missile Crisis. A Critical Reappraisal*, Routledge, 2015, 167–182, 173–177; "A bet portrayed as a certainty. Reassessing the added deterrent value of nuclear weapons" in George P. Shultz and J.E. Goodby (eds.), *The War that Must Never be Fought, Dilemmas of Nuclear Deterrence*. Hoover Press, 2015, 5–55, 15–20; "The unbearable lightness of luck. Three sources of overconfidence in the controllability of nuclear crises" *European Journal of International Security* 2:2, July 2017, 240–262; "Power, luck and scholarly responsibility at the end of the world(s)", *International Theory*, forthcoming and R. N. Lebow and B. Pelopidas, "Facing Nuclear War. Luck, Learning and the Cuban Missile Crisis" in C. Reus-Smit et al. (eds), *Oxford Handbook of History and International Relations*, forthcoming.

469   "This world really is impossible": Oral History Interview, Lord Harlech (William David Ormsby-Gore), 3/12/1965, JFKLOHP, 11. Barton J. Bernstein, "The Week We Almost Went to War," *Bulletin of the Atomic Scientists* (Feb. 1976), wrote that the irony of the Cuban missile crisis was that "the Country might have to go to war to affirm the very credibility that is supposed to make war unnecessary," 20.

470   "Naturally, the common people": "April 18, 1945, to Dr. G. M. Gilbert, Prison Psychologist at the Nuremberg Trial of the Nazi War Criminals," in G. M. Gilbert, *Nuremberg Diary* (Da Capo Press, 1995), 279. Brought to my attention by Kevin Woelfel.

Bibliography

Archives/Libraries/Papers
Amherst College Library, Amherst, MA
    John J. McCloy Papers
Yale Law School, New Haven, CT
    Avalon Cuban Missile Crisis Collection (online)
Clemson University Libraries, Clemson, SC, Special Collections
    James F. Byrnes Papers
    Walter J. Brown Papers
Dwight D. Eisenhower Library, Abilene, KS
    Ann Whitman Files
    Bryce Harlow Papers
    C. A. Herter Papers
    Edward P. Lilly Papers
    Evan Aurand Papers
    James C. Hagerty Papers
    Lauris Norstad Papers
Franklin D. Roosevelt Library, Hyde Park, NY
    President's Map Room Papers
Harry S. Truman Library, Independence, MO
    President's Secretary's files, 1945–1953
    Official File, 1945–1953
    President's Personal File, 1945–1953
Harvey Mudd Library, Princeton University, Princeton, NJ
    Adlai Stevenson Papers
    John Foster Dulles Papers
John F. Kennedy Library, Boston, MA
    Oral History Program
    Presidential Papers, National Security Files
    Presidential Papers, White House Central Subject Files
Library of Congress, Washington, DC
    Joseph E. Davies Papers
    J. Robert Oppenheimer Papers
Ministère des Affaires Étrangères, Direction des Archives et dere la
    Documentation, Paris Fr.
National Archives and Records Agency II, College Park, MD
Natural Resources Defense Council, New York City, Archive of Nuclear Data

National Security Archive, George Washington University, Washington, DC
New York Public Library, New York City
    Arthur Schlesinger Jr. Papers
University of California at Santa Barbara, Santa Barbara, CA, American Presidency
    Project (online)
United Nations Archive, New York City
    U Thant Papers
U.S. President's Committee to Study the U.S. Military Assistance Program
    (Draper Committee)
White House Office, National Security Council Staff Papers
White House Office, Office of the Special Assistant for National Security Affairs
    (Robert Cutler, Dillon Anderson, and Gordon Gray)
White House Office, Office of the Special Assistant for Science and Technology
    (James P. Killian and George Kistiakowsky)
White House Office, Office of the Staff Secretary (Paul T. Carroll, Andrew J.
    Goodpaster, L. Arthur Minnich, and Christopher H. Russell)
Charles E. Young Research Library, University of California at Los Angeles, Los
    Angeles, CA
    Norman Cousins Papers
Woodrow Wilson International History Project, Digital Archive, Cuban Missile
    Crisis
    Eisenhower Administration Nuclear History

Documentaries

Else, Jon H., dir. *The Day After Trinity: J. Robert Oppenheimer and the Atomic Bomb.*
    1981.
Fitzpatrick, Eamon, line producer. *Secrets of the Dead.* Season 12, Episode 6, "The
    Man Who Saved the World." 2012.
Freed, Fred, and Len Giovannitti, dirs. *The Decision to Use the Atomic Bomb.* National
    Broadcasting Company, 1965.
Jones, Sherry, dir. *The Missiles of October: What the World Didn't Know.* American
    Broadcasting Company, 1992.
Kaufman, Brian, and Martin J. Sherwin. *Citizen Kurchatov: Stalin's Bomb Maker.*
    1999. Portland: Oregon PBS. 2003.
Morris, Errol, dir. *The Fog of War.* Culver City, CA: Sony Pictures Classics, 2003.

Dissertations/Theses

Davis, David R., "An Industry in Transition: Major Trends in American Daily News-
    papers, 1945–1965." PhD diss., University of Alabama, 1997.
Reece, Maj. Brian L., USAF. "Development of the TFX F-111 in the Department
    of Defense's Search for Multi-Mission, Joint-Service Aerial Platforms." PhD
    diss., Air Force Academy, Colorado Springs, 1997.
Whitefield, Jay P. "Early Cold War Summits: Eisenhower, Nixon, Kennedy, and
    Khrushchev, 1959 and 1961." MA thesis, Texas Tech University, 2007.

Periodicals

Allyn, Bruce J., James G. Blight, and David A. Welch. "Essence of Revision: Mos-
    cow, Havana, and the Cuban Missile Crisis." *International Security* 14, no. 3
    (Winter 1989–1990).

Alperovitz, Gar, and Kai Bird, "The Centrality of the Bomb." *Foreign Policy* 94 (Spring 1994).

Bernstein, Barton J. "Ike and Hiroshima: Did He Oppose It?" *Journal of Strategic Studies* 10, no. 3 (1987): 377–89.

———. "The Week We Almost Went to War." *Bulletin of the Atomic Scientists* 32 (February 1976): 13–21.

———. "The Cuban Missile Crisis: Trading the Jupiters in Turkey?" *Political Science Quarterly* 95 (Spring 1980): 97–125.

———. "Truman and the A-Bomb: Targeting Noncombatants, Using the Bomb, and His Defending the 'Decision.'" *Journal of Military History* (July 1998): 547–69.

———. "Reconsidering Truman's Claim of 'Half a Million American Lives' Saved by the Atomic Bomb: The Construction and Deconstruction of a Myth." *Journal of Strategic Studies* 22, no. 1 (March 1999): 54–95.

———. "The Atomic Bombings Reconsidered." *Foreign Affairs* (January/February 1995): 135–52.

———. "Considering John Lewis Gaddis's Kennan Biography: Questionable Interpretations and Unpursued Evidence." *European Journal of Social Sciences* no. 52-1 (2014): 255–75.

Buono, Stephen. "This Grim Game." *Diplomatic History* 43, no. 5 (Nov. 2019): 840–66.

Burr, William, and Thomas Blanton, eds. "The Submarines of October: U.S. and Soviet Naval Encounters During the Cuban Missile Crisis." *NSA Electronic Briefing Book* 75 (Oct. 31, 2002).

Dingman, Roger. "Atomic Diplomacy During the Korean War." *International Security* 13, no. 3 (Winter 1988–89): 50–91.

Dobson, Miriam. "The Post-Stalin Era: De-Stalinization, Daily Life, and Dissent." *Kritika: Explorations in Russian and Eurasian History* 12 (Fall 2011): 905–24.

Fursenko, Aleksandr, and Timothy Naftali. "Using KGB Documents: The Scali-Feklisov Channel in the Cuban Missile Crisis." *CWIHP Bulletin* 5 (Spring 1995): 58–62.

Gavin, Francis J. "The Myth of Flexible Response: United States Strategy in Europe During the 1960s." *International History Review,* (December 2001): 847–75.

Griffith, Robert. "Dwight D. Eisenhower and the Corporate Commonwealth." *American Historical Review* 87, no. 1 (February 1982).

Gorman, Daniel, Jr. "Candid Ken and the Cuban Crisis: Senator Kenneth Keating, the Red Menace, and the Missile Crisis of 1962." *Proceedings of the National Conference on Undergraduate Research 2014* (2014): 105–15.

Harrison, Hope M. "Ulbricht and the Concrete 'Rose': New Archival Evidence on the Dynamics of Soviet–East German Relations and the Berlin Crisis, 1958–1961." *CWIHPB* Working Paper Series, no. 5.

Hershberg, James G. "Before 'The Missiles of October': Did Kennedy Plan a Military Strike against Cuba?" *Diplomatic History* 14 (April 1990): 163–98.

———. "Chatting with Che." *The Global Cuban Missile Crisis at 50, CWIHPB* 17/18 (Fall 2012): 157-67.

———. "The United States, Brazil and the Cuban Missile Crisis, 1962," part 1. *Journal of Cold War Studies* 6, no. 2 (2004): 3–20.

———. "Anatomy of a Controversy: Anatoly F. Dobrynin's Meeting with Robert F. Kennedy, Saturday, 27 October 1962." *CWIHPB* 5 (Spring 1995): 75-80. See also comment by Richard Ned Lebow and Janice Gross Stein, *We All Lost the Cold War* (excerpt). Princeton University Press, 1995. 80.

Hijiya, James A. "The 'Gita' of J. Robert Oppenheimer." *Proceedings of the American Philosophical Society* 144, no. 2 (June 2000): 123–67.

Holland, Max. "A Luce Connection: Senator Keating, William Pawley, and the Cuban Missile Crisis." *Journal of Cold War Studies* 1, no. 3 (Fall 1999): 139–67.

———. "The 'Photo Gap' that Delayed Discovery of the Missiles." *Studies in Intelligence* 49, no. 4 (2005):

Ketov, Ryurik A. "The Cuban Missile Crisis as Seen Through a Periscope." *Journal of Strategic Studies* 28, no. 2 (April 2005): 217-231.

Khrushchev, N. S. "Zapiska N.S. Khrushcheva v Prezidium TsK KPSS o dal'neishem sokrashchenii Vooruzhennykh Sil SSSR." In Ivkin and Sukhina, eds., *Zadacha osoboi gosudarstvennoi vazhnosti*. ["Note by N.S. Khrushchev's Presidium Tsk Kpss about the further reduction of the Armed Forces of the USSR," in Ivkin and Sukhina, eds., *The Task of Special National Importance*].

Laubenthal, Capt. Sanders A., USAF. "The Missiles in Cuba, 1962: The Role of SAC Intelligence." *SAC Intelligence Quarterly Project Warrior Study* (May 1984).

Lee, Jae-Bong. "U.S. Deployment of Nuclear Weapons in 1950s South Korea & North Korea's Nuclear Development: Toward Denuclearization of the Korean Peninsula." *Asia-Pacific Journal* 7, no. 3 (February 17, 2009).

Magnúsdôttir, Rósa. "'Be Careful in America, Premier Khrushchev!': Soviet Perceptions of Peaceful Coexistence with the United States in 1959." *Cahiers du Monde russe* 47, no.1/2 (Jan.–June, 2006).

Malloy, Sean L. "A 'Paper Tiger?': Nuclear Weapons, Atomic Diplomacy, and the Korean War." *New England Journal of History* 60 (Fall 2003–Spring 2004): 227–52.

Mandel, Lee R., MD, MPH. "Endocrine and Autoimmune Aspects of the Health History of John F. Kennedy." *Annals of Internal Medicine* 151, no. 5 (Sept. 1, 2009): passim.

Manthorpe, William H. J., Jr. "The Secretary and CNO on 23–24 October 1962." *Naval War College Review* 66, no. 1 (Winter 2013): 21–40.

Martins, Dan. "The Cuban Missile Crisis and the Joint Chiefs: Military Operations to Meet Political Ends." *Naval War College Review* 71, no. 4 (2018).

McNamara, Robert. "The Military Role of Nuclear Weapons: Perceptions and Misperceptions." *Foreign Affairs* 62, no. 1 (Fall 1983): 59–80.

Mozgovoi, Alexander. "Kubinskaya Samba Kvarteta Foxtrotov" ["The Cuban Samba of the Quartet of Foxtrots"] Voennyi Parad [*Military Parade*]. Moscow: 2002. Translated by Svetlana Savranskaya. NSA, Washington, DC.

Naftali, Timothy. "The Malin Notes: Glimpses Inside the Kremlin During the Cuban Missile Crisis." *CWIHPB* 17/18 (Fall 2012).

Norris, R., and H. Kristensen. "Global Nuclear Weapons Inventories, 1945–2010." *Bulletin of the Atomic Scientists* 66, no. 4 (July 2010): 77–83.

Nuti, L. "Dall'operazione *Deep Rock* all'operazione *Pot Pie*: Una storia documentata dei missili SM 78 Jupiter in Italia." *Storia delle Relazioni Internazionali* 11/12, nos. 1–2 (1996/1997).

Otis, Cary. "The Sparing of Kyoto: Mr. Stimson's 'Pet City,'" *Japan Quarterly* (Oct.–Dec. 1975): 337–447.

Paterson, Thomas G. "Potsdam, The Atomic Bomb, and the Cold War: A Discussion with James F. Byrnes." *Pacific Historical Review* 41, no. 2 (May 1972): 225–30.

———. "The Historian as Detective: Senator Keating, His Mysterious Sources and Missiles in Cuba." *Diplomatic History* 11, no. 1 (Winter 1987): 67–71.

Pelopidas, Benoît, "The Unbearable Lightness of Luck." *European Journal of International Security*, 2:2 (July 2017): 240–262.

Rabe, Stephen G. "Eisenhower and Latin America: Arms and Dictators." *Peace and Change* 11 (April 1985): 49–61.

Radchenko, Sergey. "The Cuban Missile Crisis: Assessment of New, and Old, Russian Sources." *International Relations* 26, no. 3 (September 19, 2012): 327–43.

Rosenberg, David Alan. "The Origins of Overkill: Nuclear Weapons and American Strategy, 1945–1960." *International Security* 7, no. 4 (Spring 1983): 3–71.

Safford, Jeffrey J. "The Nixon-Castro Meeting of 19 April 1959." *Diplomatic History* 4, no. 4 (Fall 1980): 425–31.

Savranskaya, Svetlana. "New Sources on the Role of Soviet Submarines in the Cuban Missile Crisis." *Journal of Strategic Studies* 28 (April 2005): 233-59.

———. "The Soviet Cuban Missile Crisis: Documents on Anastas Mikoyan's November 1962 Trip to Cuba." *CWIHPB: The Global Cuban Missile Crisis at 50* 17/18 (Fall 2012) 331–48.

Sherwin, Martin J. "One Step from Nuclear War: The Cuban Missile Crisis at 50: In Search of a Historical Perspective." *Prologue: Journal of the National Archives* 44, no. 3 (2012), https://www.archives.gov/publications/prologue/2012/fall/cuban-missiles.html.

Slavinsky, Boris N. (translated by Ljubica Erickson) "The Soviet Occupation of the Kurile Islands and the Plans for the Capture of Northern Hokkaido." *Japan Forum* (April 1993): 95-114.

Smith, Mark B. "Peaceful Coexistence at All Costs: Cold War Exchanges Between Britain and the Soviet Union in 1956." *Cold War History* 12 (August 2012): 537–58.

Stern, Sheldon M. "Response to Zelikow and May." *Presidential Studies Quarterly* 30, no. 4 (2000): 797–99.

Sullivan, Terry. "Confronting the Kennedy Tapes: The May-Zelikow Transcripts and the Stern Assessments." *Presidential Studies Quarterly* 30, no. 3 (2000): 594–97.

Trachtenberg, Marc. "La crise de Cuba à la lumière de l'ouverture des archives americaines," in Maurice Vaisse (ed.) *L'Europe et la crise de Cuba* (Paris: Colin, 1993), 25–33.

Twigge, Stephen, and Len Scott. "The Other Other Missiles of October: The Thor IRBMs and the Cuban Missile Crisis." *Electronic Journal of International History* 3 (2000): 1–11.

Vandenbroucke, Lucien S. "The 'Confessions' of Allen Dulles: New Evidence on the Bay of Pigs." *Diplomatic History* 8, no. 4 (Fall 1984).

Wells, Samuel F. "Nuclear Weapons and European Security During the Cold War." *Diplomatic History* 16, no. 2 (1992): 278–86.

Zelikow, Philip D., and Ernest R. May. "'Source Material: Controversy: The Kennedy Tapes': Past and Future." *Presidential Studies Quarterly* 30, no. 4 (2000): 791–96.

Zubok, Vadislav M. "Khrushchev's Secret Speech on the Berlin Crisis, August 1961." *CWIHPB* 3 (1993).

Books

Abel, Elie. *The Missile Crisis.* Lippincott, 1966.

Absher, Kenneth Michael. *Mindsets and Missiles: A Firsthand Account of the Cuban Missile Crisis.* Booklife, 2012.

Acosta, Tomas Diez. *October 1962: The Missile Crisis as Seen from Cuba.* Pathfinder, 2002.

Agee, Philip. *Inside the Company: CIA Diary.* Penguin Books, 1975.

Albright, Joseph, and Marcia Kunstel. *Bombshell: The Secret Story of America's Unknown Atomic Spy Conspiracy.* Times Books, 1997.

Alford, Mimi. *Once Upon a Secret: My Affair with President John F. Kennedy and Its Aftermath.* Random House, 2012.

Allison, Graham, and Philip Zelikow. *Essence of Decision: Explaining the Cuban Missile Crisis.* 2nd ed. Pearson, 1999.

Alperovitz, Gar. *Atomic Diplomacy: Hiroshima and Potsdam.* Simon & Schuster, 1965.

———. *The Decision to Use the Atomic Bomb.* Alfred A. Knopf, 1995.

Alterman, Eric. *When Presidents Lie: A History of Official Deception and Its Consequences.* Viking, 2004.

Ambrose, Stephen E. *Eisenhower: Soldier and President.* Simon & Schuster, 1990.

Anderson, George. *The Reminiscences of Admiral George W. Anderson Jr., U.S. Navy (Retired).* Vol. 2. U.S. Naval Institute, 1983.

Andrew, Christopher, and Oleg Gordievsky. *KGB: The Inside Story of Its Foreign Operations from Lenin to Gorbachev.* HarperCollins, 1990.

Andreyev, Anatoly. Diary, in *Povsednevnaya Zhizn' Rossiiskikh Podvodnikov.* [Daily Life of Russian Submariners], ed. by Nikolai Cherkashin. Molodaya Gvardiya Publishing House, 2000.

Ashcroft, Bruce. *We Wanted Wings: A History of the Aviation Cadet Program.* Headquarters Air Education and Training Command, 2005.

Badash, Lawrence. *A Nuclear Winter's Tale: Science and Politics in the 1980s.* MIT Press, 2009.

Bagnato, Bruna. *Prove di Ostpolitik. Politica ed economia nella strategia italiana verso l'Unione Sovietica, 1958–1963.* Leo Olschki Editore, 2003.

Ball, George W. *The Past Has Another Pattern: Memoirs.* Norton, 1983.

Barrett, David M., and Max Holland. *Blind Over Cuba: The Photo Gap and the Missile Crisis.* Texas A&M University Press, 2012.

Beisner, Robert L. *A Life in the Cold War.* Oxford University Press, 2006.

Beschloss, Michael R. *The Crisis Years: Kennedy and Khrushchev 1960–1963.* HarperCollins, 1991.

Bird, Kai. *The Chairman: John J. McCloy and the Making of the American Establishment.* Simon & Schuster, 1992.

———. *The Color of Truth: McGeorge Bundy and William Bundy, Brothers in Arms.* Simon & Schuster, 1998.

Bird, Kai, and Martin J. Sherwin. *American Prometheus: The Triumph and Tragedy of J. Robert Oppenheimer.* Alfred A. Knopf, 2005.

Biswas, Shampa. *Nuclear Desire: Power and the Postcolonial Nuclear Order.* University of Minnesota Press, 2014.

Blight, James G., and David A. Welch. *On the Brink: Americans and Soviets Reexamine the Cuban Missile Crisis.* Noonday, 1990.

Blight, James G., and Janet M. Lang. *Dark Beyond Darkness: The Cuban Missile Crisis as History, Warning, and Catalyst.* Rowman & Littlefield, 2017.

———. *The Armageddon Letters: Kennedy, Khrushchev, Castro in the Cuban Missile Crisis.* Rowman and Littlefield, 2012.

Blight, James G., and Peter Kornbluh, eds. *Politics of Illusion: The Bay of Pigs Invasion Reexamined.* Lynne Rienner, 1998.

Blight, James G., Bruce J. Allyn, and David A. Welch. *Cuba on the Brink: Castro, the Missile Crisis, and the Soviet Collapse.* Pantheon, 1993.

Blum, John M., ed. *The Price of Vision: The Diary of Henry A. Wallace, 1942–1946.* Houghton Mifflin, 1974.

Bohlen, Charles. *Witness to History, 1929–1969.* Norton, 1969.

Bonsal, Philip W. *Cuba, Castro and the United States.* University of Pittsburgh Press, 1971.

Boot, Max. *The Road Not Taken: Edward Lansdale and the American Tragedy in Vietnam.* Liveright, 2018.

Bouchard, Joseph. *Command in Crisis: Four Case Studies.* Columbia University Press, 1992.

Bowie, Robert, and Richard H. Immerman. *Waging Peace: How Eisenhower Forged an Enduring Cold War Strategy.* Oxford University Press, 1998.

Boyer, Paul. *By the Bomb's Early Light: American Thought and Culture at the Dawn of the Atomic Age.* Pantheon, 1985.

Brands, H. W. *The Devil We Knew: Americans and the Cold War.* Oxford University Press, 1993.

———. *The General vs. the President: MacArthur and Truman at the Brink of Nuclear War.* Penguin Random House, 2016.

———. *Traitor to His Class: The Privileged Life and Radical Presidency of Franklin Delano Roosevelt.* Anchor Books, 2009.

Brinkley, Douglas. *American Moonshot: John F. Kennedy and the Great Space Race.* HarperCollins, 2019.

Brinkley, Douglas, and Richard Griffiths, eds. *Kennedy and Europe.* Louisiana State University Press, 1999.

Brodie, Bernard. *The Absolute Weapon.* Harcourt, Brace and Company, 1946.

Brown, Anthony Cave. *Wild Bill Donovan: The Last Hero.* Times Books, 1982.

Brown, Gates. *Eisenhower's Nuclear Calculus in Europe: The Politics of IRBM Deployment in NATO Nations.* McFarland Publishers, 2018.

Brown, Kate. *Plutopia: Nuclear Families, Atomic Cities, and the Great Soviet and American Plutonium Disasters.* Oxford University Press, 2013.

Brugioni, Dino A. *Eyeball to Eyeball: The Inside Story of the Cuban Missile Crisis.* Random House, 1990.

Brzezinski, Matthew. *Red Moon Rising: Sputnik and the Hidden Rivalries That Ignited the Space Age.* Times Books, 2007.

Bundy, McGeorge. *Danger and Survival: Choices About the Bomb in the First Fifty Years.* Random House, 1988.

Burr, William, ed. *The Berlin Crisis.* National Security Archive/Chadwyck-Healey, 1991.

Campbell, Craig, and Sergey Radchenko. *The Atomic Bomb and the Origins of the Cold War.* Yale University Press, 2008.

Campbell, W. Joseph. *Getting It Wrong: Debunking the Greatest Myths in American Journalism.* University of California Press, 2017.

Carlson, Peter. *K Blows Top: A Cold War Comic Interlude Starring Nikita Khrushchev, America's Most Unlikely Tourist.* Public Affairs, 2009.

Carroll, James. *House of War: The Pentagon and the Disastrous Rise of American Power.* Houghton Mifflin, 2006.

Castro, Fidel, and Ignacio Ramonet. *Fidel Castro: My Life: A Spoken Autobiography.* Scribner, 2008.

Catudal, Honoré M. *Soviet Nuclear Strategy from Stalin to Gorbachev.* Humanities Press International, 1989.

Chace, James. *Acheson: The Secretary of State Who Created the American World.* Simon & Schuster, 1998.

Chambers, John W., ed. *The Oxford Companion to American Military History.* Oxford University Press, 1999.

Chang, Laurence, and Peter Kornbluh, eds., *The Cuban Missile Crisis 1962.* A National Security Archives Documents Reader (Revised). New Press, 1998.

Cherkashin, Nikolai, ed. *Povsednevnaya Zhizn' Rossiiskikh Podvodnikov* [Daily Life of Russian Submariners]. Molodaya Gvardiya Publishing House, 2000.

Chernus, Ira. *Apocalypse Management: Eisenhower and the Discourse of National Insecurity.* Stanford University Press, 2008.

———. *Eisenhower's Atoms for Peace.* Texas A&M Press, 2002.

———. *General Eisenhower: Ideology and Discourse.* Michigan State University Press, 2002.

Churchill, Winston S. *The Second World War.* Vol. 6, *Triumph and Tragedy.* Houghton Mifflin, 1953.

Cochran, Thomas, Robert Norris, and Oleg Bukharin. *Making the Russian Bomb from Stalin to Yeltsin.* Westview Press, 1995.

Coffey, Thomas M. *Iron Eagle: The Turbulent Life of General Curtis LeMay.* Crown Publishers, Inc., 1986.

Cohen, Warren I. *Dean Rusk: The American Secretaries of State and Their Diplomacy—Vol. 19.* Cooper Square Publishers, 1980.

Coleman, David. *The Fourteenth Day: JFK and the Aftermath of the Cuban Missile Crisis.* Norton, 2013.

Colman, Jonathan. *Cuban Missile Crisis: Origins, Course and Aftermath.* Edinburgh University Press, 2016.

Cullather, Nicholas. *Operation PBSuccess: The United States and Guatemala, 1952–1954.* Central Intelligence Agency History, 1994.

Cummings, Bruce. *Korea's Place in the Sun: A Modern History.* Norton, 1997.

Dallek, Robert. *An Unfinished Life: John F. Kennedy, 1917–1963.* Penguin Books, 2001.

———. *Franklin D. Roosevelt: A Political Life.* Viking, 2017.

DeGroot, Gerard J. *The Bomb: A Life.* Pimlico, 2005.

DePalma, Anthony. *The Man Who Invented Fidel: Castro, Cuba and Herbert L. Mathews of* The New York Times. Public Affairs, 2006.

Deutschmann, David, and Deborah Schnookal, eds. *Fidel Castro Reader,* Ocean Press, 2007.

Dobbs, Michael. *One Minute to Midnight: Kennedy, Khrushchev, and Castro on the Brink of Nuclear War.* Vintage, 2008.

———. *Six Months in 1945: FDR, Stalin, Churchill, and Truman from World War to Cold War.* Vintage, 2013.

Dobrynin, Anatoly. *In Confidence: Moscow's Ambassador to America's Six Cold War Presidents.* Times Books, 1995.

Dockrill, Saki. *Eisenhower's New-Look National Security Policy, 1953–61.* Palgrave Macmillan, 1996.

Donovan, Robert J. *PT 109: John F. Kennedy in World War II.* McGraw-Hill, 1961.

Drogovoz, I. *Raketnve Volska, SSSR* [AST Missile Forces]. Kharvest, 2005.

Dubivko, Aleksei F. *On the Edge of the Nuclear Precipice.* Translated by Svetlana Savranskaya. Gregory Page, 1998.

Eden, Anthony. *The Reckoning*. Houghton Mifflin, 1965.

Eden, Lynn. *Whole World on Fire: Organizations, Knowledge, and Nuclear Weapons Devastation*. Cornell University Press, 2004.

Eisenberg, Carolyn. *Drawing the Line: The American Decision to Divide Germany, 1944–1949*. Cambridge University Press, 1996.

Eisenhower, Dwight D. *Crusade in Europe*. Doubleday, 1948.

———. *The White House Years: Mandate for Change: 1953–1956: A Personal Account*. Doubleday, 1963.

———. *The White House Years: Waging Peace, 1956–1961*. Doubleday, 1965.

Ellsberg, Daniel. *The Doomsday Machine*. Bloomsbury, 2017.

Engelhardt, Tom. *The End of Victory Culture: Cold War America and the Disillusioning of a Generation*. University of Massachusetts Press, 2007.

Erickson, Paul, Judy L. Klein, Lorraine Daston, Rebecca Lemov, Thomas Sturm, and Michael D. Gordin. *How Reason Almost Lost Its Mind: The Strange Career of Cold War Rationality*. University of Chicago Press, 2013.

Farrell, John A. *Richard Nixon: The Life*. Doubleday, 2017.

Feis, Herbert. *The Atomic Bomb and the End of World War Two*. Princeton University Press, 1966.

Feklisov, Aleksandr. *Beyond the Ocean and on the Island. Notes of an Intelligence Officer*. DEM, 1994.

———. *Strategic Operation "Anadyr": How it Happened*. MOOVVIK, 1999.

Flank, Lenny, ed. *At the Edge of the Abyss: A Declassified Documentary History of the Cuban Missile Crisis*. Red and Black Publishers, 2010.

Frankel, Max. *High Noon in the Cold War: Kennedy, Khrushchev and the Cuban Missile Crisis*. Presidio Press, 2005.

Franqui, Carlos. *Family Portrait with Fidel: A Memoir*. Translated by Alfred Mac-Adam. Random House, 1984.

Freedman, Lawrence. *Kennedy's Wars: Berlin, Cuba, Laos, and Vietnam*. Oxford University Press, 2000.

———. *The Evolution of Nuclear Strategy*. St. Martin's Press, 1981.

Friedberg, Aaron L. *In the Shadow of the Garrison State: America's Anti-Statism and Its Cold War Grand Strategy*. Princeton University Press, 2000.

Fukuyama, Francis. *Soviet Threats to Intervene in the Middle East, 1956–1973*. Rand, 1980.

Fursenko, Aleksandr, and Timothy Naftali. *Khrushchev's Cold War: The Inside Story of an American Adversary*. Norton, 2006.

———. *One Hell of a Gamble: Khrushchev, Castro, and Kennedy, 1958–1964*. Norton, 1997.

Gaddis, John Lewis. *Strategies of Containment: A Critical Appraisal of American National Security Policy During the Cold War*. Rev. and exp. ed. Oxford University Press, 2005.

———. *The Cold War: A New History*. Penguin Press, 2005.

———. *We Now Know*. Clarendon, 1998.

Gaddis, John L., Philip Gordon, Ernest May, and Jonathan Rosenberg, eds. *Cold War Statesmen Confront the Bomb: Nuclear Diplomacy Since 1945*. Oxford, 1999.

Galbraith, John Kenneth. *Name-Dropping: From FDR On*. Houghton Mifflin, 1999.

Garthoff, Raymond L. *Reflections on the Cuban Missile Crisis*. Brookings Institution, 1987.

Gavin, Francis J. *Nuclear Statecraft: History and Strategy in America's Atomic Age*. Cornell University Press, 2012.

George, Alice. *Awaiting Armageddon: How Americans Faced the Cuban Missile Crisis*. University of North Carolina Press, 2003.

Gilbert, G. M. *Nuremberg Diary*. Da Capo Press, 1995.

Gleijeses, Piero. *Shattered Hope: The Guatemalan Revolution and the United States, 1944–1954*. Princeton University Press, 1991.

Gordin, Michael, and G. J. Ikenberry. *The Age of Hiroshima*. Princeton University Press, 2019.

Graebner, Norman, ed. *The National Security: Its Theory and Practice, 1945–1960*. Oxford University Press, 1986.

Gribkov, A. I., ed., У края ядерной бездны *(из истории Карибского Кризиса 1962 г. Факты. Свидетельства. Оценки . . .)*, редактор А.И. Грибков, Москва, «Грэгори-Пейдж», 1998. [*At the Edge of the Nuclear Abyss: Facts, Eyewitness Accounts and Analyses from the History of the 1962 Caribbean Crisis.*] Moscow: Gregory-Page Publishers, 1998.

Gribkov, Anatoly I., and William Y. Smith. *Operation Anadyr: U.S. and Soviet Generals Recount the Cuban Missile Crisis*. Edition Q, 1994.

Groves, Leslie R. *Now It Can Be Told*. Harper, 1962.

Halberstam, David. *The Best and the Brightest*. Random House, 1969.

———. *The Fifties*. Fawcett, 1993.

Harrison, Hope. *Driving the Soviets Up the Wall: Soviet–East German Relations, 1953–1961*. Princeton University Press, 2003.

Hasegawa, Tsuyoshi. *Racing the Enemy: Stalin, Truman, and the Surrender of Japan*. Harvard University Press, 2005.

Haslam, Jonathan, and Karina Urbach. *Secret Intelligence in the European States System, 1918–1989*. Stanford University Press, 2013.

Hayes, Peter. *Pacific Powderkeg: American Nuclear Dilemmas in Korea*. Lexington Books, 1991.

Haynes, John Earl, Harvey Klehr, and Alexander Vassiliev. *Spies: The Rise and Fall of the KGB in America*. Yale University Press, 2009.

Henriksen, Margot A. *Dr. Strangelove's America: Society and Culture in the Atomic Age*. Berkeley: University of California Press, 1997.

Herken, Gregg. *Brotherhood of the Bomb: The Tangled Lives and Loyalties of J. Robert Oppenheimer, Ernest Lawrence, and Edward Teller*. Henry Holt, 2002.

———. *Counsels of War*. Oxford University Press, 1987.

———. *The Georgetown Set: Friends and Rivals in Cold War Washington*. Knopf, 2014.

———. *The Winning Weapon: The Atomic Bomb in the Cold War, 1945–1950*. Princeton University Press, 1988.

Hersh, Seymour M. *The Dark Side of Camelot*. Little, Brown, 1997.

Hewlett, Richard G., and Oscar E. Anderson Jr. *The New World, 1939–1946*. Vol. 1, *A History of the United States Atomic Energy Commission*. Pennsylvania State University Press, 1962.

Higgins, Trumbull. *The Perfect Failure: Kennedy, Eisenhower and the CIA at the Bay of Pigs*. Norton, 1989.

Higuchi, Toshihiro. *Political Fallout: Nuclear Weapons Testing and the Making of a Global Environmental Crisis*. Stanford University Press, 2020.

Hilsman, Roger. *The Cuban Missile Crisis: The Struggle over Policy*. Praeger Publishers, 1996.

———. *To Move a Nation: The Politics of Foreign Policy in the Administration of John F. Kennedy*. Doubleday, 1967.

Hirshson, Stanley B. *General Patton: A Soldier's Life*. HarperCollins, 2002.

Hitchcock, William I. *The Age of Eisenhower: America and the World in the 1950s*. Simon & Schuster, 2018.

Hoffman, David E. *The Dead Hand: The Untold Story of the Cold War Arms Race and Its Dangerous Legacy*. Doubleday, 2009.

Holland, Matthew. *Eisenhower Between the Wars: The Making of a General and Statesman*. Praeger, 2001.

Holloway, David. *Stalin and the Bomb*. Yale University Press, 1994.

Huchthausen, Peter A. *October Fury*. Wiley, 2002.

Immerman, Richard H. *The CIA in Guatemala: The Foreign Policy of Intervention*. University of Texas Press, 1982.

Isaacson, Walter, and Evan Thomas. *The Wise Men: Six Friends and the World They Made*, Simon & Schuster, 1986.

Johnson, Thomas R. *American Cryptology During the Cold War, 1945–1989: Book 2, Centralization Wins, 1960–1972*. National Security Agency/Center for Cryptological History, 1995.

Jones, Howard. *The Bay of Pigs*. Oxford University Press, 2008.

Jones, Matthew. *After Hiroshima: The United States, Race and Nuclear Weapons in Asia*. Cambridge University Press, 2010.

Judt, Tony. *Postwar: A History of Europe Since 1945*. Penguin Books, 2005.

Kahn, Herman. *On Thermonuclear War*. Princeton University Press, 1960.

Kaplan, Fred. *The Wizards of Armageddon*. Stanford University Press, 1983.

———. *The Bomb: Presidents, Generals, and the Secret History of Nuclear War*. Simon & Schuster, 2020.

Kaplan, Lawrence S., Ronald D. Landa, and Edward J. Drea. *History of the Office of the Secretary of Defense: The McNamara Ascendancy, 1961–1965*. Office of the Secretary of Defense, 2006.

Kempe, Frederick. *Berlin 1961: Kennedy, Khrushchev, and the Most Dangerous Place on Earth*. Putnam, 2011.

Kennan, George F. *The Nuclear Delusion: Soviet-American Relations in the Atomic Age*. Pantheon, 1976.

Kennedy, John F. *Why England Slept*. Wilfred Funk, 1940.

Kennedy, Robert F. *Thirteen Days: A Memoir of the Cuban Missile Crisis*. W. W. Norton & Company, 1969.

Kern, M., P. Levering, and R. Levering. *The Kennedy Crisis: The Press, the Presidency, and Foreign Policy*. University of North Carolina Press, 1983.

Khrushchev, Nikita S. *Khrushchev Remembers*. Translated by Strobe Talbott. Little, Brown, 1970.

Khrushchev, Sergei, ed. *The Memoirs of Nikita Krushchev*. Vol. 3, *1953–1964*. Translated by George Shriver. Pennsylvania State University Press, 2007.

Killian, James R., Jr. *Sputnik, Scientists, and Eisenhower: A Memoir of the First Special Assistant to the President for Science and Technology*. MIT Press, 1977.

Kinzer, Stephen. *All the Shah's Men: An American Coup and the Roots of Middle East Terror*. Wiley, 2003.

Kinzer, Stephen. *The Brothers: John Foster Dulles, Allen Dulles, and Their Secret World War.* Times Books, 2013.

Kislov, A. K. *Zhurmal Mirovaya a Ekonomika III.* Quotation located and translated by Anastasia Poliakova.

Kissinger, Henry. *Nuclear Weapons and American Foreign Policy.* Council on Foreign Relations, 1957.

Korniyenko, G. M. *Kholodnaya Voina: Kvidetelstvo ee ychastnika.* [Cold War: Testimony of Participants], 2nd ed. Translated by Anastasia Poliakova. Moscow, OLMA Press, 2001.

Kozack, Warren. *LeMay: The Life and Wars of General Curtis LeMay.* Regnery Pub., 2009.

Kyle, Keith. *Suez: Britain's End of Empire in the Middle East.* Weidenfeld, 1991.

LaFeber, Walter. *The New Empire: An Interpretation of American Expansion, 1860–1898.* Cornell University Press, 1963.

Larson, David, ed. *The "Cuban Crisis" of 1962: Selected Documents, Chronology, and Bibliography,* 2nd ed. University Press of America, 1986.

Lebow, Richard Ned, and Janice Gross Stein. *We All Lost the Cold War.* Princeton University Press, 1994.

Leffler, Melvyn. *For the Soul of Mankind: The United States, the Soviet Union and the Cold War.* Hill and Wang, 2007.

Leffler, Melvyn, and Odd Arne Westad, eds. *The Cambridge History of the Cold War.* Vol. 1, *Origins.* Cambridge University Press, 2010.

———. *The Cambridge History of the Cold War,* Vol. II, *Crises and Détente,* Cambridge University Press, 2010.

Leffler, Melvyn. *A Preponderance of Power: National Security, the Truman Administration, and the Cold War.* Stanford University Press, 1992.

LeoGrande, William, and Peter Kornbluh. *Back Channel to Cuba: The Hidden History of Negotiations Between Washington and Havana.* University of North Carolina Press, 2014.

Lifton, Robert Jay, and Greg Mitchell. *Hiroshima in America: Fifty Years of Denial.* G. P. Putnam's Sons, 1955.

Lilienthal, David E. *The Journals of David E. Lilienthal.* Vol. 2, *The Atomic Energy Years, 1945–1950.* Harper & Row, 1964.

Lincoln, Evelyn. *My Twelve Years with John F. Kennedy.* Bantam, 1965.

Lintner, Bertil. *China's India War: Collision Course on the Roof of the World.* Oxford University Press, 2018.

Liss, Jacob. *Khrushchev-Eisenhower Visits: The Truth About Coexistence with Russia.* Alfred Printing Co., 1959.

Love, Robert William, Jr. *The Chiefs of Naval Operations.* Naval Institute Press, 1980.

MacDonald, David Stone. *U.S.–Korean Relations from Liberation to Self-Reliance: The Twenty Year Record: An Interpretive Summary of the Archives of the U.S. Department of State for the Period 1945–1965.* Westview Press, 1992.

Maddock, Shane J. *Nuclear Apartheid: The Quest for American Atomic Supremacy from World War II to the Present.* University of North Carolina Press, 2010.

Maguire, James. *Impresario: The Life and Times of Ed Sullivan.* Billboard Books, 2006.

Martin, John Bartlow. *Adlai Stevenson and the World.* Doubleday, 1977.

Mastny, Vojtech, Malcolm Byrne, and Magdalena Klotzback, eds. *Cardboard Castle? An Inside History of the Warsaw Pact.* Central European University Press, 2005.

May, Ernest R. *American Cold War Strategy: Interpreting NSC 68.* Bedford/St. Martin's, 1993.

May, Ernest R., and Philip Zelikow, eds. *The Kennedy Tapes: Inside the White House during the Cuban Missile Crisis.* Belknap Press, 1997.

McAuliffe, Mary S., ed. *CIA Documents on the Cuban Missile Crisis, 1962.* History Staff, Central Intelligence Agency, 1992.

McCarthy, David Shamus. *Selling the CIA: Public Relations and the Culture of Secrecy.* University Press of Kansas, 2018.

McMaster, H. R. *Dereliction of Duty: Lyndon Johnson, Robert McNamara, The Joint Chiefs of Staff, and the Lies That Led to Vietnam.* HarperCollins, 1997.

Messer, Robert. *The End of an Alliance: James F. Byrnes, Roosevelt, Truman, and the Origins of the Cold War.* University of North Carolina Press, 1981.

Mikoyan, Anastas. *Tak Bylo* [As It Was]. Moscow, Vagrius, 1994.

Mikoyan, Sergo. *The Soviet Cuban Missile Crisis: Castro, Mikoyan, Kennedy, Khrushchev, and the Missiles of November.* Edited and translated by Svetlana Savranskaya. Stanford University Press, 2012.

Millis, Walter, ed., with E. S. Duffield.*The Forrestal Diaries.* Viking Press, 1951.

Mills, C. Wright. *The Causes of World War III.* Simon & Schuster, 1958.

Mueller, John E. *War, Presidents and Public Opinion.* University Press of America, 1985.

Munton, Don, and David A. Welch. *The Cuban Missile Crisis: A Concise History.* Oxford University Press, 2007.

Naftali, Timothy, and Philip Zelikow, eds. *The Presidential Recordings of John F. Kennedy: The Great Crises.* Vol. 2, *September–October 21, 1962.* W. W. Norton & Company, 2001.

Nasaw, David. *The Patriarch: The Remarkable Life and Turbulent Times of Joseph P. Kennedy.* Penguin Random House, 2012.

Nash, Philip. *The Other Missiles of October: Eisenhower, Kennedy, and the Jupiters, 1957–1963.* University of North Carolina Press, 1997.

Nathan, James A. *Anatomy of the Cuban Missile Crisis.* Greenwood Press, 2001.

———. *The Cuban Missile Crisis Revisited.* St. Martin's Press. 1992.

Navasky, Victor S. *Kennedy Justice.* Atheneum, 1971.

Neff, Donald. *Warriors at Suez.* Simon & Schuster, 1981.

Sheehan, Neil. *A Fiery Peace in a Cold War.* Random House, 2009.

Nieberg, Michael S. *Potsdam: The End of World War II and the Remaking of Europe.* Basic Books, 2015.

Nixon, Richard. *Six Crises.* Doubleday, 1962.

———. *The Memoirs of Richard Nixon.* Simon & Schuster, 1978.

Nuti, Leopoldo. *La sfida nucleare. La politica estera italiana e le armi atomiche 1945–1991* [The Nuclear Challenge: Italian Foreign Policy and Atomic Weapons]. Il Mulino, 2007.

O'Brien, Michael. *John F. Kennedy: A Biography.* St. Martin's, 2005.

O'Donnell, Kenneth P., and David F. Powers, *Johnny, We Hardly Knew Ye.* Little, Brown, 1972.

Offner, Arnold A., *Another Such Victory: President Truman and the Cold War, 1945–1953.* Stanford University Press, 2002.

———. *Hubert Humphrey: The Conscience of the Country.* Yale University Press, 2018.

Pach, Chester J., ed. *A Companion to Dwight D. Eisenhower.* Wiley, 2017.

Pardoe, Blaine L. *Fires of October: The Planned US Invasion of Cuba During the Missile Crisis of 1962*. Fonthill, 2013.

Paterson, Thomas G. *Contesting Castro: The United States and the Triumph of the Cuban Revolution*. Oxford University Press, 1994.

Perret, Geoffrey. *Eisenhower*. Random House, 1999.

Petersen, Michael B. *Legacy of Ashes, Trial by Fire: The Origins of the Defense Intelligence Agency and the Cuban Missile Crisis Crucible*. DIA Historical Research Support Branch, 2011.

Petrik, P. P. *Diplomati Vspominaut: Mir glazami veteranov diplomaticheskoi slyzhbi*. Translated by Anastasia Poliakova. 1997.

Pfeiffer, Jack B. *CIA History of the Bay of Pigs Operation*. Vol. 3, *Evolution of CIA's Anti-Castro Policies, 1959–January 1961*. CIA, 1979.

———. *CIA Official History of the Bay of Pigs Operation*. Vol. 2, *Participation in the Conduct of Foreign Policy*. CIA, 1979.

———. *CIA Official History of the Bay of Pigs Operation*. Vol. 1, *Air Operations, March 1960–April 1961*. CIA, 1979.

Polmar, Norman, and John D. Gresham. *DEFCON-2: Standing on the Brink of Nuclear War During the Cuban Missile Crisis*. John Wiley & Sons, 2006.

Poole, Walter S. *History of the Joint Chiefs of Staff: The Joint Chiefs of Staff and National Policy, 1961–1964, VIII*. Office of the Chairman of the Joint Chiefs of Staff, 2011.

Pope, Ronald R., ed. *Soviet Views on the Cuban Missile Crisis: Myth and Reality in Foreign Policy Analysis*. University Press of America, 1982.

Powers, Thomas. *The Man Who Kept the Secrets: Richard Helms and the CIA*. Alfred A. Knopf, 1979.

Rabe, Stephen G. *Eisenhower & Latin America: The Foreign Policy of Anti-Communism*. University of North Carolina Press, 1988.

Radchenko, Sergey, and Campbell Craig. *The Atomic Bomb and the Origins of the Cold War*. Yale University Press, 2008.

Rasenberger, Jim. *The Brilliant Disaster: JFK, Castro, and America's Doomed Invasion of Cuba's Bay of Pigs*. Scribner, 2001.

Reeves, Richard. *President Kennedy: Profile of Power*. Simon & Schuster, 1993.

Renehan, Edward J., Jr. *The Kennedys at War, 1937–1945*. Doubleday, 2002.

Reston, James. *Deadline: A Memoir*. Random House, 1991.

———. *Sketches in the Sand*. Alfred A. Knopf, 1967.

———. *The Artillery of the Press*. Harper & Row, 1967.

Reyn, Sebastian. *Atlantis Lost: The American Experience with de Gaulle, 1958–1969*. Amsterdam University Press, 2010.

Rhodes, Richard. *Dark Sun: The Making of the Hydrogen Bomb*. Simon & Schuster, 1995.

Riedel, Bruce. *JFK's Forgotten Crisis: Tibet, the CIA, and Sino-Indian War*. Brookings, 2015.

Robarge, David. *John McCone as Director of Central Intelligence, 1961–1965*. CIA, 2015.

Roberts, Priscilla, ed. *Cuban Missile Crisis: The Essential Reference Guide*. ABC-CLIO, 2012.

Robertson, David. *Sly and Able: A Political Biography of James F. Byrnes*. Norton, 1994.

Rostow, W. W. *The Diffusion of Power*. Macmillan, 1972.

Sagan, Scott D., and Kenneth N. Waltz. *The Spread of Nuclear Weapons: An Enduring Debate*, 3rd ed. Norton, 2012.

————. *The Limits of Safety: Organizations, Accidents, and Nuclear Weapons.* Princeton University Press, 1995.

Sakharov, Andrei. *Memoirs.* Translated by Richard Lourie. Alfred A. Knopf, 1990.

Schelling, Thomas. *The Strategy of Conflict.* Harvard University Press, 1960.

Schlesinger, Arthur M., Jr. *A Thousand Days: John F. Kennedy in the White House.* Fawcett Premier, 1971.

Schlesinger, Andrew, and Stephen Schlesinger, eds. *The Letters of Arthur Schlesinger, Jr.* Random House, 2013.

Schlosser, Eric. *Command and Control: Nuclear Weapons, the Damascus Accident, and the Illusion of Safety.* Penguin, 2013.

Schulzinger, Robert D., ed. *A Companion to American Foreign Relations.* Blackwell Publishing Ltd, 2003.

Schwartz, Stephen I. *Atomic Audit: The Costs and Consequences of U.S. Nuclear Weapons Since 1940.* Brookings Institution Press, 1998.

Scott, Len and R. Gerald Hughes, editors. *The Cuban Missile Crisis: A Critical Appraisal.* Routledge, 2015.

Sherry, Michael S. *The Rise of American Air Power: The Creation of Armageddon.* Yale University Press, 1982.

Sherwin, Martin J. *A World Destroyed: Hiroshima and Its Legacies.* Stanford University Press, 2003.

Shinkle, Peter. *Ike's Mystery Man: The Secret Lives of Robert Cutler.* Steerforth Press, 2018.

Sigal, Leon V. *Fighting to a Finish: The Politics of War Termination in the United States and Japan, 1945.* Cornell University Press, 1988.

Smith, Alice Kimball. *A Peril and a Hope: The Scientists' Movement in America.* University of Chicago Press, 1965.

Smith, Amanda, ed. *Hostage to Fortune: The Letters of Joseph P. Kennedy.* Viking, 2000.

Sorensen, Theodore C. *Counselor: A Life at the Edge of History.* HarperPerennial, 2008.

————. *Decision-making in the White House: The Olive Branch or the Arrows.* Columbia University Press, 1964.

————. *Kennedy.* Harper & Row, 1965.

Srodes, James. *Allen Dulles: Master of Spies.* Regnery, 1999.

Stern, Sheldon M. *Averting "the Final Failure": John F. Kennedy and the Secret Cuban Missile Crisis Meetings.* Stanford University Press, 2003.

————. *The Cuban Missile Crisis in American Memory: Myths Versus Reality.* Stanford University Press, 2012.

————. *The Week the World Stood Still: Inside the Secret Cuban Missile Crisis.* Stanford University Press, 2005.

Stimson, Henry L., and McGeorge Bundy. *On Active Service in Peace and War.* Harper & Brothers, 1947.

Stromseth, Jane E., and Denis Healey. *The Origins of Flexible Response: NATO's Debate Over Strategy in the 1960s.* Palgrave Macmillan, 1988.

Talbot, David. *Brothers: The Hidden History of the Kennedy Years.* Simon & Schuster, 2007.

————. *The Devil's Chessboard: Allen Dulles, the CIA, and the Rise of America's Secret Government.* HarperCollins, 2015.

Taubman, William. *Khrushchev: The Man and His Era.* Norton, 2003.

Taylor, Maxwell. *The Uncertain Trumpet.* Harper, 1960.

Thomas, Evan. *Ike's Bluff: President Eisenhower's Secret Battle to Save the World*. Little, Brown, 2012.

Thompson, Jenny, and Sherry Thompson. *The Kremlinologist: Llewellyn E. Thompson, America's Man in Cold War Moscow*. Johns Hopkins University Press, 2018.

Thompson, Robert Smith. *The Missiles of October: The Declassified Story of John F. Kennedy and the Cuban Missile Crisis*. Simon & Schuster, 1993.

Trachtenberg, Marc. *A Constructed Peace: The Making of the European Settlement, 1945–1963*. Princeton University Press, 1999.

———. *History and Strategy*. Princeton University Press, 1991.

Truman, Harry S. *Year of Decisions*. New American Library, 1955.

Tuchman, Barbara. *The Guns of August: The Outbreak of World War I*. Macmillan, 1962.

Tunzelmann, Alex von. *Blood and Sand: Suez, Hungary, and Eisenhower's Campaign for Peace*. HarperCollins, 2016.

Turner, Stansfield. *Burn Before Reading*. Hyperion, 2005.

Vandenbroucke, Lucien S. *Perilous Options: Special Operations as an Instrument of U.S. Foreign Policy*. Oxford University Press, 1993.

Voorhees, Theodore. *The Silent Guns of Two Octobers: Kennedy and Khrushchev Play the Double Game*. University of Michigan Press, 2020.

Waller, Douglas. *Wild Bill Donovan*. Free Press, 2011.

Weart, Spencer R. *Nuclear Fear: A History of Images*. Harvard University Press, 1988.

Weiner, Tim. *Legacy of Ashes: The History of the CIA*. Anchor, 2008.

Wells, Samuel F., Jr. *Fearing the Worst: How Korea Transformed the Cold War*. Columbia University Press, 2020.

Westad, Odd Arne. *The Global Cold War: Third World Interventions and the Making of Our Times*. Cambridge University Press, 2005.

White, Mark J. *Against the President: The Impact of Dissent in the White House*. Ivan R. Dee, 2007.

———. *The Cuban Missile Crisis*. Macmillan, 1996.

White, Mark J., ed. *The Kennedys and Cuba: The Declassified Documentary History*. Rev. ed. Ivan R. Dee, 2001.

Wicker, Tom. *JFK and LBJ: The Influence of Personality upon Politics*. Penguin Books, 1970.

Williams, Robert Chadwell. *Klaus Fuchs: Atom Spy*. Harvard University Press, 1987.

Williams, William Appleman. *The Contours of American History*. World Pub. Co., 1961.

Winkler, Allan M. *Life Under a Cloud: American Anxiety about the Atom*. Oxford University Press, 1993.

Wright, Thomas C. *Latin America in the Era of the Cuban Revolution*. Praeger, 2018.

Wyden, Peter. *The Bay of Pigs: The Untold Story*. Simon & Schuster, 1979.

Yesin, V. I., ed. *Strategic Operation "Anadyr": How It Really Was*. 3rd ed. Translated by Hans Fenstermacher. MOOVVIK, 2004.

York, Herbert. *The Advisers: Oppenheimer, Teller and the Superbomb*. Stanford University Press, 1989.

Zelikow, Philip, and Ernest May, eds. *The Great Crisis*. Vol. 3, *Oct. 22–29, 1962*. Norton, 2001. Online, University of Virginia, Miller Center [Assoc. eds., David Coleman, George Eliades, Francis Gavin, Max Holland, Erin Mahan, Timothy Naftali, David Shrek, and Patricia Dunn}.

Zhukov, Georgy Konstantinovich. *The Memoirs of Marshal Zhukov*. Delacorte Press, 1971.

Zubok, Vladislav. *A Failed Empire: The Soviet Union in the Cold War from Stalin to Gorbachev*. University of North Carolina Press, 2007.

Zubok, Vladislav, and Constantine Pleshakov. *Inside the Kremlin's Cold War: From Stalin to Khrushchev*. Harvard University Press, 1996.

Acknowledgments

Gambling with Armageddon has a history with a moral. I initially proposed to write a book on "The Military and the Cuban Missile Crisis," a subject I thought relevant, under-studied, and likely to reveal new insights. But after I signing my contract with Knopf I discovered that the military's role in the Cuban missile crisis was so entwined with their Commander-in-Chief's decisions—and Khrushchev's—that it was necessary to explore the background of U.S. and Soviet nuclear weapons policy that preceded the crisis. And so an entirely different book from the one I was contractually obligated to write emerged . . . about a decade late. To my mind, this story is more about the publishing house of Alfred A. Knopf than it is about me.

I doubt that many authors have been more fortunate in their publisher and editors than I have been. *Gambling with Armageddon* is the third book I've published with Knopf. The first, *A World Destroyed*, was a near completed manuscript when it was accepted, and so I began our association "on time." My second book, a biography of the physicist J. Robert Oppenheimer, was most certainly not on time. When my storied editor, Angus Cameron, proposed that I write a "definitive" biography of the father of the atomic bomb I hesitated. Something like that, I worried, could take almost a decade. No problem, he assured me.

Twenty five years later, Angus's idea became a book coauthored with my dear friend, Kai Bird, who, at my request, was written into my contract almost twenty years after my conversation with Angus. In all that time, no one at Knopf ever threatened to cancel our arrangement or recall my advance. The only question from Angus, and his wonderful successor, Bobbie Bristol, was an occasional telephone call: "Marty, are you still working on Oppenheimer? Yes? Then, we need to extend the contract." Finally, when Bobbie retired, Ann Close, my friend and editor of *Gambling*, took over and brought *American Prometheus: The Triumph and Tragedy of J. Robert Oppenheimer* into print in 2005.

The point of this history is to celebrate what I believe is the most serious and supportive publishing house in the United States. Knopf is an institution dedicated to literary quality; a publisher committed to its authors. I hope that it is not unique, but the experience of friends and colleagues suggests, sadly, that it might be. So thank you Angus Cameron, Bobbie Bristol and Ann Close, my editors. But also many thanks to the leaders of this special institution who established its culture: Alfred Knopf, Robert Gottlieb, Sonny Mehta, and now Reagan Arthur.

I also wish to thank the copy editor for *Gambling with Armageddon*, Susan Llewellyn, and the jacket designer, Jenny Carrow (and my talented son, Alex Sherwin, a graphic designer who contributed to that design). Todd Portnowitz, Ann Close's amazingly efficient assistant, facilitated my hunt for photographs and much more, and Abigail Endler, who handled publicity, also deserves a nod. It has been a privilege to work with all of you.

I also wish to thank my agent, Gail Ross, of the Ross Yoon Agency, for her great work on my behalf.

I have lived with the Cuban missile crisis my entire adult life. After participating on the edge of it in 1962, I began to teach it five years later as it was then conventionally understood in my earliest diplomatic history lecture courses and seminars at the University of California, Berkeley. But my views began to evolve about 1970 when I was introduced to the inimitable Barton Bernstein at a lecture he gave on his early studies of the Cuban missile crisis. Everyone teaching or writing about the subject is in his debt for his many probing articles on the subject. I cherish his tutalege and friendship that has spanned fifty years.

Between 1976 and 1995 I taught most summers in an interdisciplinary program at Dartmouth College with Donald Pease, an incomparable Professor of English whose imagination further expanded my view of the crisis. Simultaneously, at Princeton, I taught a nuclear history seminar with Hal Feiveson and Freeman Dyson that provided new insights. In 1981, as the Cardozo Visiting Professor at Yale, I conceived "America in the Nuclear Age," a lecture course I then taught for twenty-five years at Tufts University, and still teach at George Mason. More than anything else, it was that course that kept me thinking about the origins, consequences, and salience of the world's most dangerous confrontation.

During my first years at Tufts I taught a seminar on the nuclear issue at the Fletcher School for Law and Diplomacy that deepened my interest in the subject as a research topic. I recall papers by Tanya Gassel, who wrote on the Soviet view of the crisis, and Philip Nash, whose early work on the U.S. deployment of Jupiter missiles to Turkey evolved into his classic study, *The Other Missiles of October*, one of the finest monographs in Cold War history. James Hershberg, whose PhD I had the privilege of guiding, developed an early interest in the crisis and has written many of the field's most probing articles. Both Nash and Hershberg, valued friends, reviewed my manuscript at an early stage and corrected many errors. Phil generously reviewed it a second time after copy editing and made additional significant contributions. Another member of that memorable Fletcher seminar, Hans Fenstermacher, a talented linguist, translated many of my Russian documents. He could have translated documents in French, Spanish, German, and Portuguese if I had asked.

I moved to Washington DC as *American Prometheus* was completed. As I transitioned from my commute to Boston, I taught several graduate seminars on the Cuban missile crisis at George Washington University (thanks to its president, Stephen J. Trachtenberg), and then many more at George Mason University where I began teaching full time in 2006. Many of the GWU and Mason students (both graduates and undergraduates) wrote deeply researched, imaginative papers that continued to broaden my knowledge of the crisis and challenge my ideas. Some of their most notable contributions are referenced in my endnotes, but several students deserve a special call-out: Karl Cherepanya wrote about Operation Anadyr and located and translated many useful Soviet documents. Robert Petrusak did especially interesting research in the Navy's archives in Washington DC, and Justin Zawistowski discovered useful details about Khrushchev's visit to the United States. Kevin Woelfel wrote brilliantly on Eisenhower's Jupiter deployment, and Dan Martins wrote equally insightfully about the Joint Chiefs. Joel Christianson, who became a historian in the Office of the Secretary of Defense, guided me through a maze of declassified documents and photographs in the Pentagon's archives.

Four other people deserve special mention: Carolyn Lipka, Svetlana Chernovaya, Michael Dobbs, and Masakatsu Ota. At an early stage of my project, Carolyn, a high school junior at the time, did some amazingly thorough research for me in Princeton University's Seeley G. Mudd Manuscript Library. I was not surprised when she was accepted at Yale. Svetlana, a visiting fellow at the Woodrow Wilson Center, generously loaned me her rare Russian books on Operation Anadyr. When Michael Dobbs finished his pathbreaking history of the Cuban Missile Crisis, *One Minute to Midnight: Kennedy, Khrushchev and Castro on the Brink of Nuclear* War, he generously shared his voluminous collection of documents and interviews before sending them to the National Security Archive. And, Dr. Masakatsu Ota, senior writer for Kyodo News, kindly shared his research notes on the near accidental launch of missiles from Okinawa on October 28, 1962.

During the many years of researching and writing *Gambling with Armageddon*, George Mason University provided generous personal and financial support. Dean Jack Censer and Brian Platt, the chair of the History and Art History Department, helped me navigate the darkest period of my life. I am singularly grateful to them and to every member of my amazing department.

George Mason's History and Art History Department is a uniquely friendly and cooperative academic community. Even the department's staff was a cheering section for my work and I am indebted to them all: Sue Woods, department manager; Susie LeBlanc; Carrie Grabo; and Emily Gibson who, along with my impressive colleagues, has made teaching and researching at Mason one of the highlights of my long and varied career.

Another institution that provided significant support for my research and writing was the Woodrow Wilson Center for International Scholars. A fellowship at the WWC is a scholar's dream. It is one of the best places in the world to work and I doubt that *Gambling* would be in print now had I not had repeated opportunities to work there. I am beholden to Christian Ostermann, the director of the History and Public Policy Program, and to Rob Litwak, Senior Vice President, for their confidence, support and friendship. The assistance provided by the Center's Library team, Janet Spikes (Librarian) and her assistant Michelle Kamalich, was critical as was the daily warm welcome from my friend (actually everyone's friend) Lindsay Collins who manages the reception desk.

Readers will note that many of the citations in *Gambling* refer to Russian, Spanish, and French documents, perhaps implying that I possess an array of language skills. I don't. But what I did possess were research assistants who read and spoke Russian or Spanish; my book could not have been written without their help. Several were provided by the Woodrow Wilson Center during my fellowships: Yuri Borovsky, Ryan Eldredge, Mark Moll, Phillip Wilcox, and Andres Blancos. I also hired Julia Takhusheva, Yevgeniya Khilji and Angela Greenfield, who was especially helpful as both a translator of Russian and a researcher. Still others were students: Anastasia Poliakova and my friends Karl Cherepanya and Hans Fenstermacher mentioned earlier. And my dear wife, Susan (more about her later), who taught French before becoming a senior administrator at Harvard and the Aspen Institute, translated cables and reports about the Cuban missile crisis from France's ambassador in Havana. And, during a research trip to Havana, Estela Bravo provided me with accounts of the crisis in Cuba newspapers that were unavailable outside of the country.

Of course this book could not have been written without the assistance of archivists at the Harry S. Truman, Dwight D. Eisenhower, John F. Kennedy, and Lyndon Johnson Presidential Libraries and I am grateful to them all for their assistance. I also want to thank my friend, Susan Cooper, formally a senior archivist at the National Archives for her guidance.

A special note of gratitude goes to Sheldon Stern, my friend and the former historian at the JFKL, who was the first person to review the secret ExComm recordings. Sheldon wrote three important books and many articles about those recordings and they stand as indispensible guides to their interpretation and accuracy.

There are other insitutions equally important to scholars of the Cold War. The National Security Archive (NSA) at George Washington University is among America's most important guardians of our democracy. Skillfully using the Freedom of Information Act to open government records to public scrutiny, it has helped to assure that historical truth is revealed and democracy preserved. Its director, Thomas Blanton, and his staff are indefatigable in their pursuit of documents that reveal what really happened during the Cold War. The NSA's "Nuclear Vault" and its Cuban Missile Crisis collections were essential for my work. I am especially in the debt of William

Burr, NSA's nuclear specialist, Svetlana Savranskaya, its Soviet specialist, and Peter Kornbluh, its Latin American specialist, for their invaluable work, their support, and their friendship.

Similar kudos to the Woodrow Wilson Center's Nuclear Proliferation International History Project's digital archive. It too was indispensable for my research. All Cold War scholars owe Christian Ostermann and his staff a special note of gratitude for their dedication to making documents related to all aspects of nuclear history from governments around the world available for research.

Another institution that contributed to how I came to think about the Cuban missile crisis has the peculiar moniker, the Nuclear History Boot Camp. Supported by the Carnegie Corporation of New York, the NHBC has met annually at a former NATO base in the hills above Allumiere, Italy, every June for the past nine years (2020 excepted) to discuss global nuclear issues with young PhD students from around the world. The student's insights and the wisdom and knowledge of several of its core teaching staff—especially Leopold Nuti, David Holloway, and Giordana Pulcini—helped to shape *Gambling with Armageddon*.

The University of Virginia's Miller Center of Public Affairs was a crucial silent partner in composing *Gambling*. Permitting me to access the Center's transcription of the secret ExComm recordings on line expedited reading, analyzing and quoting their contents.

When I completed the first draft of *Gambling* I wondered if anyone would want to read what had so fascinated me. Susan assured me many would, but she is my wife, so I imposed all or part of my manuscript on friends and family. In addition to Philip Nash and James Hershberg, both mentioned earlier, Tom Leonard, Janet Lowenthal, Sanford Levinson, Marjorie Sherwin, Kai Bird, Dr. Martin Kleinman, and Mel Leffler were early readers. Their comments, criticisms and questions improved the manuscript and lowered my blood pressure. My former student and friend Ethan Pollock made important suggestions to the chapter on Khrushchev's visit to the United States, and Philip Zelikow sharpened my thinking about Khrushchev's decision to secretly insert medium and intermediate range missiles in Cuba. Finally, when the first draft of the manuscript was finished, Andrew Ross deftly helped me to review and complete errant endnotes.

Looking back to the beginning—to those crucial years as a graduate student in UCLA's history department—I recognize that no successful part of my career would have been possible without the support, confidence and tutalege of four amazing professors: Keith Berwick, Robert Dallek, Richard Rosecrance, and Stanley Wolpert taught me to think and write about history both critically and fairly. They were wonderful mentors and life-long friends.

Other friends have been important sustaining and encouraging my career and my commitments. Francine and Stephen Trachtenberg, Richard Rudders, Saul Singer and Steven Hirsch (aka Edward Bear), and Irene and Owen Fiss all go back to my days at either James Madison High School or Dartmouth

College. I met Arnold and Ellen Offner, Lawrence Friedman, Arno Mayer, Eric Foner, Peter Kuznick, and Robert J. Lifton later, but their friendships have been unfailing and intimately related to my scholarship.

It is common for historians to conclude their acknowledgements with fulsome praise for their spouses, for good reason, and I will not be an exception. Long research trips away from home, hours writing while oblivious to domestic and social obligations, boring recitations about the latest arcane document, all require a spouse's patience beyond "for better or worse." Possibly insulated from the worst by her own very successful career, Susan has been a steady partner in this enterprise providing love, support, literary criticism, French translation, and discipline. Without her encouragement and companionship *Gambling with Armageddon* probably could not have been completed, and it certainly would not have been as much fun.

Index

Illustration credits

p. 8
Top left: Associated Press
Top right: Photo by Stan Wayman/The LIFE Picture Collection via Getty Images
Bottom left: National Archives and Records Administration, U.S. Department of Agriculture
Bottom right: National Archives, Eisenhower Presidential Library, Abilene, Kansas

Insert 2
p. 1
Top: Cecil Stoughton. White House Photographs. John F. Kennedy Presidential Library and Museum, Boston
Bottom: MIGUEL VINAS/AFP via Getty Images
p. 2
Top: U. S. Department of State, John F. Kennedy Presidential Library and Museum, Boston.
Middle: John F. Kennedy Presidential Library and Museum, Boston.
Bottom: CIA
p. 3
Middle: Abbie Rowe. White House Photographs. John F. Kennedy Presidential Library and Museum, Boston
Bottom: Library of Congress, Prints and Photographs Division, LC-USZ62-128472
p. 4
Top: National Security Archive
Middle: Courtesy of the author
Bottom: Courtesy of the author
p. 5
Top: National Security Archive
Bottom: National Security Archive
p. 6
Top: Cecil Stoughton. White House Photographs. John F. Kennedy Presidential Library and Museum, Boston
Bottom left: Abbie Rowe. White House Photographs. John F. Kennedy Presidential Library and Museum, Boston
Bottom right: Office of the Secretary of Defense Historical Office
p. 7
Top: Courtesy of the author
Bottom: United States. Department of Defense. Department of Defense Cuban Missile Crisis Briefing Materials. John F. Kennedy Presidential Library and Museum, Boston
p. 8
Top: Cecil Stoughton. White House Photographs. John F. Kennedy Presidential Library and Museum, Boston
Middle right: National Security Archive
Bottom left: A 1962 Herblock Cartoon, © The Herb Block Foundation

A Note About the Author

Martin J. Sherwin is the author of *A World Destroyed: The Atomic Bomb and the Grand Alliance,* which won the Stuart L. Bernath Prize, as well as the American History Book Prize, and the coauthor, with Kai Bird, of *American Prometheus: The Triumph and Tragedy of J. Robert Oppenheimer,* which won the Pulitzer Prize for biography in 2006. He was the general editor of the Stanford University Press Nuclear Age Series from 1985 to 2015, and is currently the general editor of the Johns Hopkins University Press Nuclear History and Contemporary Affairs series. He and his wife live in Washington, DC, and in Colorado.

A Note on the Type

This book was set in a modern adaptation of a type designed by the first William Caslon (1692–1766). The Caslon face, an artistic, easily read type, has enjoyed more than two centuries of popularity in the English-speaking world. This version, with its even balance and honest letterforms, was designed by Carol Twombly for the Adobe Corporation and released in 1990.

Composition by North Market Street Graphics, Lancaster, Pennsylvania
Printed and bound by Berryville Graphics, Berryville, Virginia